TUTORIAL:
COMPUTER GRAPHICS HARDWARE
Image Generation and Display

HASSAN K. REGHBATI
UNIVERSITY OF BRITISH COLUMBIA

ANSON Y. C. LEE
SIMON FRASER UNIVERSITY

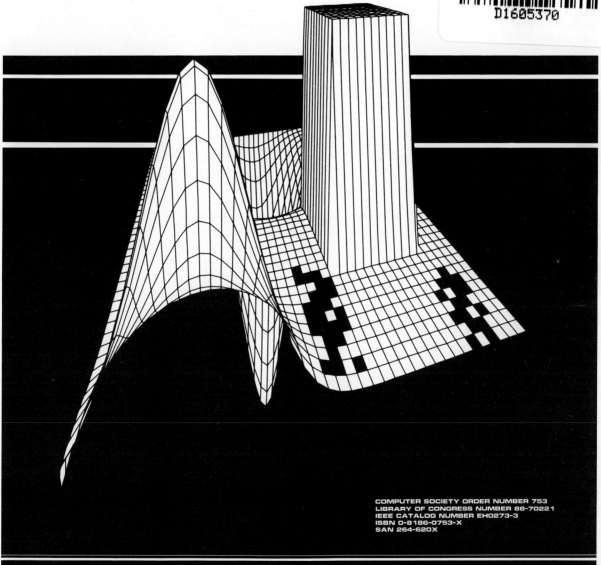

COMPUTER SOCIETY ORDER NUMBER 753
LIBRARY OF CONGRESS NUMBER 88-70221
IEEE CATALOG NUMBER EH0273-3
ISBN 0-8186-0753-X
SAN 264-620X

THE COMPUTER SOCIETY **IEEE** THE INSTITUTE OF ELECTRICAL AND ELECTRONICS ENGINEERS, INC.

COMPUTER SOCIETY PRESS

Published by

Computer Society Press
1730 Massachusetts Avenue, N.W.
Washington, D.C. 20036-1903

Cover designed by Jack I. Ballestero

Computer Society Order Number 753
Library of Congress Number 88-70221
IEEE Catalog Number EH0273-3
ISBN 0-8186-0753-X (Paper)
ISBN 0-8184-4753-1 (Microfiche)

Order from: Computer Society
Terminal Annex
Post Office Box 4699
Los Angeles, CA 90080

IEEE Service Center
445 Hoes Lane
P.O. Box 1331
Piscataway, NJ 08855-1331

Computer Society
13, Avenue de l'Aquilon
B-1200 Brussels
BELGIUM

 THE INSTITUTE OF ELECTRICAL AND ELECTRONICS ENGINEERS, INC.

IEEE

Preface

Since the early 1960's, when Ivan Sutherland demonstrated that a CRT display screen could be used as a tool for computer-generated graphics, graphics hardware has been a challenging area of research and development. New hardware architectures are continually being developed to cope with the ever increasing demands on computer graphics cost/performance. The bristling richness of this rapidly growing field unfolds in this text with 30 authoritative papers. The material of this text is organized into chapters based on major topic headings. Each major topic is introduced with additional material supplying background to the reprinted articles.

The opening chapter provides a comprehensive overview of the image generation and display hardware areas and provides the necessary background for the reader who might not be proficient in computer graphics hardware. The remaining six chapters review the state of the art of this exciting field. Chapter 2 is on graphics processors and special function units. Chapter 3 examines the design of frame buffers for raster systems. Smart image memories are discussed in Chapter 4. As the required degree of interactivity of graphics applications increases, speed is becoming an overriding design issue. The current state of the art in real-time scan-conversion hardware is the theme of Chapter 5. Chapter 6 discusses hardware for constructive solid geometry and ray tracing. Finally, in Chapter 7, architectures for image processing systems are discussed.

This book is designed for students, educators, and engineers involved in research, development, and application of various graphics systems. It is tutorial in nature and provides a state-of-the-art survey. It is expected that the tutorial will serve as a guide for beginners and as a major reference for computer graphics professionals. We hope that it will also promote more fruitful research efforts in the computer graphics hardware area.

The material in this book can be used for a graduate-level course in "image generation and display hardware." The book is also designed to be useful to computer scientists and electrical engineers who are interested in the computer graphics area. Background provided by university-level courses in "digital hardware," "computer architecture," and "computer graphics" is sufficient. Some knowledge of "VLSI systems" is useful but is not necessary.

This project has benefited immensely from the work of others. Their contribution is highly appreciated. The authors wish to express their thanks to Dr. Bill D. Carroll, C. G. Stockton, and Margaret Brown for their invaluable assistance during the preparation of the manuscript.

This book is dedicated by Hassan to Dr. Asghar Karimzadeh Reghbati and to Ms. Sakineh Eslami Nasab, and by Anson to his parents.

Table of Contents

Chapter 1: Introduction to Computer Graphics Systems

This book concerns itself with recent hardware developments and the impact these developments have on the discipline of computer-generated graphics. Here then, is a brief introduction to graphics system architectures.

Computer graphics had its start with X-Y plotters. The technology was soon extended to include calligraphic (line-drawing) CRT systems based on refresh-vector hardware and, at a later date, direct-view storage tubes followed by higher performance refresh-vector systems.

Meanwhile, a separate image processing technology had been following its own evolutionary path. Instead of dealing with lines and points randomly positioned anywhere on the display surface, image processing was based on a rectangular array of picture elements or *pixels*. Digital information defining the state of each pixel was stored in a random-access memory and was used to generate a television-type, raster-scan CRT display in monochrome or full color.

The division between vectorgraphic (also known as calligraphic) computer graphics and raster-scan image processing has now been bridged by the raster display technology. Low-cost memories have made it economically feasible to assemble high-resolution, fine-detail raster images that all but eliminate the objectionable stairstepping of vectorgraphic lines when displayed on earlier raster-CRT screens. The ability to fill areas with solid color (and shading) makes raster-CRT screens useful in certain applications. The result is *raster scan graphics*, which combines the full-color, pixel-by-pixel control potentials of image processing and the line-drawing capabilities of vectorgraphics in a single display system.

Unfortunately, the move from calligraphic to raster displays has brought new problems. For calligraphics, only the endpoint coordinates of lines needed to be stored, so memory requirements were held to a minimum. Refresh-vector writing speed made it possible to animate the display and to create interactive systems that allowed the operator to control the display in real-time through such input devices as lightpens, joysticks, and digitizer tablets. Again, however, only the endpoints needed to be recalculated with each refresh cycle, minimizing the need for high-speed computational capabilities.

However, in raster-scan graphics, each pixel must be computed explicitly. To generate a raster of image, millions of pixels must be computed. The proper value at each pixel is a function of the database (the simulated environment), the viewing position and orientation of the simulated

viewer, and the location(s) of the light source(s) in the simulated environment. A long-standing goal of researchers in computer graphics systems has been the development of real-time three-dimensional modeling systems. These systems, which produce a realistic image of a simulated three-dimensional environment, have a wide variety of potential uses, from flight simulators for pilot training to interactive computer-aided design (CAD) systems. The most sophisticated of these systems produce, in real-time, images of startling reality.

1.1: Functional Model of Computer Graphics Systems

A graphics system can be regarded as an implementation of a sequence of processes that transforms pictorial information into a perceptible form and presents it as an image on a graphics display device. Along the sequence a number of operations may be performed. This sequence of operations can be organized and abstracted into a functional model of a computer graphics system [CARL80, FOLE82].

The functional model consists of a sequence of logical processors (also known as the display pipeline) operating on the representations of the scene (see Figure 1.1). A logical processor in the functional model corresponds to one or more physical processors, and two logical processors in the model may share a physical processor. Similarly, representations may exist in one or more different memories. The elements in the model are as follows:

1. The application model (AM) contains a (hierarchical) description of the graphical and nongraphical properties of a scene in a format determined by the application program and/or the modeling software. The part of the AM used by the display file compiler (DFC) is the graphical data, and it consists of output primitives, attributes, transformations, and control information. The rest of the AM is nongraphical data and may contain information associated with part of an object or pointers relating certain parts of an object. The application model is independent of the graphics systems hardware. Usually, it is expressed as a data structure in the host.

2. The DFC is a logical processor that maps the application model to the structured display file (SDF). Usually, the DFC is implemented by the user. It compiles the AM by using system-provided functions to produce the various parts of the SDF. These system functions usually include add, modify, and

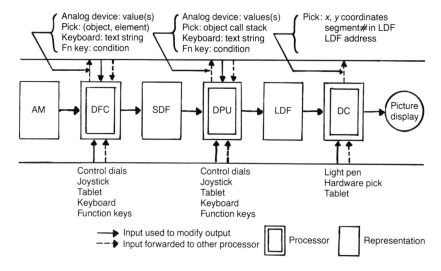

Analog device: value(s)
Pick: (object, element)
Keyboard: text string
Fn key: condition

Analog device: values(s)
Pick: object call stack
Keyboard: text string
Fn key: condition

Pick: *x, y* coordinates
segment# in LDF
LDF address

Control dials
Joystick
Tablet
Keyboard
Function keys

Control dials
Joystick
Tablet
Keyboard
Function keys

Light pen
Hardware pick
Tablet

→ Input used to modify output
--→ Input forwarded to other processor

Processor   Representation

Figure 1.1: Functional model of a computer graphics system.

delete for primitives, attributes, objects, and object calls in the SDF.

3. The SDF contains a (hierarchical) description of the graphical representation of the scene, usually in the world coordinate system. The SDF is graphical system dependent, although the general format of the SDF is often quite similar from one system to another. The SDF is analogous to a program structure consisting of procedures that may call other procedures. An SDF consists of objects that may reference, or call, other objects.

An object in the SDF is represented by output primitives, such as lines and text, object calls, attributes, such as font type and color, and transformations. *Modeling transformations*, also called *object construction transformations*, allow objects to be defined in a local coordinate system such that these objects can be combined into new objects. *Viewing transformations* define how an object or portion of an object is mapped to the display surface. In some systems, the SDF also contains general purpose instructions such as arithmetic, Boolean, and flow of control operations. Systems vary a great deal in their support for text primitives, addressing modes of primitives, and general purpose instructions.

4. The display processing unit (DPU) maps the structured display file (sometimes called the DPU program) to the linear display file. The DPU traverses the hierarchy in the SDF composing transformation matrices, applying these transformations to the graphical data, and clipping the data to the specified window or view volume.

5. The (segmented) linear display file (LDF) is a low-level special purpose data structure that contains graphical primitives and mode settings describing the objects produced after modeling and viewing. The

format of the LDF is highly dependent on the graphics system and the display device. For raster-scan graphics, the LDF commonly corresponds to the *bit-map* image of the scene and is buffered in a *frame buffer*.

6. The display controller (DC), or *video controller*, maps the linear display file to the image on the display device and refreshes the picture to maintain a flicker-free image on the display screen. It fetches the image representation from the LDF and produces signals to drive the display device.

7. The picture display screen displays a vector or raster image of the scene as described in the AM.

1.2: Graphics Systems Organization

One way to understand the scene-rendering sequence

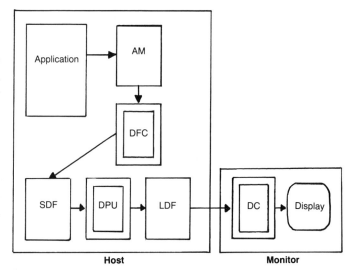

Host   **Monitor**

Figure 1.2: Host-screen graphics system.

2

concept is that successive representations contain a complete description of what is going to be displayed. Each representation differs only in the level of abstraction/detail of scene description and in the degree of machine dependence: Representations become successively more machine dependent (i.e., less abstract and finally result in a representation as a displayed image).

There is not, and may never be, a strict definition of the function and hardware that constitute a "graphics system." Too much depends on the relative importance of the graphics-generation process compared to the overall purposes served by the computer installation. However, some units along the processing sequence must be capable of performing the scene-rendering operations required by a particular system. In the early days, these operations had to be carried out by the mainframe (host) where the application model resides (see Figure 1.2). Later, system designers found that some of these operations could be removed from the host and set up as special-purpose logic. As they continued to study the scene-rendering sequence, they saw that more and more operations could be added to the special-purpose unit, and so the "wheel of reincarnation," as it was called by Myer and Sutherland [MYER68], rolled on. The wheel of reincarnation for graphics system design is analogous to the trend to offload hosts (mainframes/minicomputers) by distributing "intelligence" to I/O controllers, thereby making the controllers more capable and independent of the host. Graphics system architecture is a prime candidate for such functional specialization, primarily because the performance gains are so noticeable to the user and also because the tasks to be done are well defined and repetitive.

Depending on the amount of graphics generation responsibility offloaded from the host, a graphics system may take different forms of organization [ENGL86, MYER84].

1.2.1: Host-Driven Systems

At one extreme is the configuration illustrated by Figure 1.2. Nearly all of the graphics-generation functions must be performed, in this case by a host computer's hardware and software. The "graphics system" is reduced to a monitor. All the graphics-related data structures (AM, SDF, LDF) and image generation functions (functions performed by DFC, DPU) are incorporated into the host computer. With this organization, the generation of a raster image can impose a severe burden on a host computer's processor and memory resources. Therefore, only applications that require generation of simple imagery are suitable for this kind of configuration.

The graphics output of a process-control computer could be implemented in this form, for example, if the images are limited to relatively simple flow charts with alphanumeric notations indicating the state of process variables. However, although the application is simple, it is still impractical to have the host take care of all the graphic-generation jobs in a

multi-user environment. The answer has been to "offload" the host computer by transferring part or even all of the repetitive graphics functions to a separate graphics subsystem with its own processor hardware and graphics software.

1.2.2: Intelligent Terminals

One option is to add a graphics capability to the functions of a microprocessor-based intelligent CRT terminal, as illustrated in Figure 1.3. Now, the DPU, LDF, DC, and picture display are integrated to form a "graphics terminal." Usually, the DPU is implemented with a simple general purpose microprocessor that needs to work not only on image generation but also on communication with the host and on other housekeeping jobs. Thus, the resulting graphics terminal is usually limited to alphagraphic or, at most, vectorgraphic displays. However, this is more than adequate for a number of applications, such as the generation of business, process control, or educational graphics. Interaction with the system may be through the standard terminal keyboard or through such added accessories as lightpens and digitizer tablets. Modern hardware technologies permit more and more sophisticated graphics-generating functions be incorporated into a terminal. Consequently, a *workstation* type of intelligent terminal is capable of handling interactive high-quality 3D graphics [NICK84, SCHM84].

1.2.3: Graphics Controllers

Another approach is to concentrate display-generation functions into a "graphics controller," physically separated from the host computer and the CRT monitor (see Figure 1.4). The monitor may be, in fact, only one of several displays or recording devices controlled by the graphics subsystem. The host computer may also be only one of

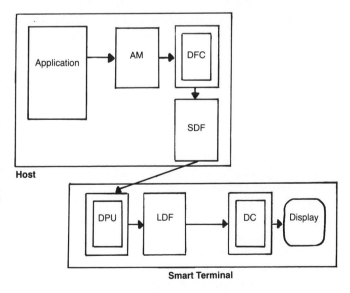

Figure 1.3: Intelligent terminal with graphics capabilities.

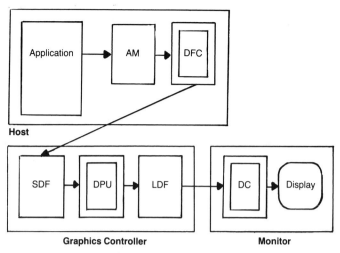

Figure 1.4: Programmable interface between host computer and monitor.

several data sources for the graphics controller. Display information may be supplied, for example, by mass storage devices or data communication links connected directly to the controller. In general, however, the host computer retains control over the graphics-generation process, including the operation of the graphics controller and its accessories.

1.2.4: Standalone Graphics Systems

In the standalone graphics system, shown in Figure 1.5, most of the system's computing capabilities and memory resources are dedicated to the graphics functions. A number of commercially available systems oriented to a specific application, such as flight simulation [SCHA81], image processing, or computer-aided design, fall in this category. The majority of high-performance raster graphics systems are also close to this extreme [IKED84, FUJI84].

Generally, standalone graphics systems with sufficient computing power to perform the extensive modeling and viewing functions are limited to a single specific application, such as a high performance CAD station, in which user interactivity is critical. Obviously, this type of graphics system is not cost effective for general usage.

1.3: Graphics System

The graphics system is not limited to a particular configuration, say the controller-monitor package that characterizes a number of commercially available systems. Instead, the system definition encompasses all of the functional resources, including those of the host computer, which contribute to the generation of a graphics image. Therefore, graphics system software could include program modules executed by the host computer, by the graphics controller, and by programmable hardware in the display monitor itself. The same would be true of accessories and peripherals that may be physically connected to the host computer,

graphics controller, or the monitor. As long as they contribute to the graphics-generation functions, they are considered a part of the graphics system.

1.4: VLSI Circuits and Graphics

Recent advances in VLSI technology create opportunities for designers to produce cost-effective special-purpose architectures. Computer graphics is one of the application areas that has benefited most from this situation. By using the custom VLSI design techniques introduced by Mead and Conway, a number of researchers in recent years have developed new hardware systems whose common goal is the high-speed implementation of algorithms essential to the production of high quality images by computer. Many such developments will be reported in later chapters. Some computer graphics applications considered infeasible are now not only possible but, in most cases, even preferable.

1.5: Article Overview

In the first paper, "VLSI Architectures for Computer Graphics," by Abram and Fuchs, a brief review of some major recent advances in graphics system hardware is given. A short discussion on the conceptual organization of a "generic" graphics system can also be found in this article.

In the second paper entitled "Staking Out the Graphics Display Pipeline," Myers gives an overview of eight different graphics systems and concentrates on how these systems offload the host computer by using special pipelined architectures.

England, in "A Graphics System Architecture for Interactive Application-Specific Display Functions," the third paper, categorizes graphics systems into three classes: special-purpose systems, limited-purpose systems, and gen-

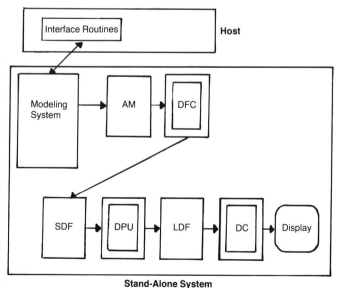

Figure 1.5: Standalone graphics system.

eral-purpose systems. The features and requirements of each class of graphics systems is addressed, and the required attributes to make a graphics system suitable for the various applications are discussed.

In the fourth paper, "High-Speed Techniques for a 3-D Color Graphics Terminal," Ikedo discusses the Seillac-7 desktop display terminal and investigates the architecture and peculiarities of the terminal. Ikedo also discusses concepts like graphics terminal architectures, host-terminal communication, and display file handling.

The last paper, "A 3-D Graphics Display System with Depth Buffer and Pipeline Processor" by Fujimoto, Christopher, and Iwata, concerns a high-performance graphics system for 3-D graphics. Through the descriptions of various rendering algorithms employed by the system, its architecture is explained. This system is able to generate smooth-shaded, anti-aliased images.

References

[CARL80] Carlbom, I.B., "System Architecture for High-Performance Vector Graphics," *PhD Thesis,* Dept. of Computer Science, Brown University, Providence, R.I., 1980.

[ENGL86] England, N., "A Graphics System Architecture for Interactive-Specific Display Functions," *IEEE Computer Graphics and Applications,* Vol. 6, No. 1, Jan. 1986, pp. 60–70.

[FOLE82] Foley, J.D. and A. Van Dam, Fundamentals of Interactive Computer Graphics, Addison-Wesley, New York, 1982.

[FUJI84] Fujimoto, A., C.G. Perrott, and K. Iwata, "A 3-D Graphics Display System with Depth Buffer and Pipeline Processor," *IEEE Computer Graphics and Applications,* Vol. 4, No. 6, June 1984, pp. 11–23.

[IKED84] Ikedo, T., "High-Speed Techniques for a 3-D Color Graphics Terminal," *IEEE Computer Graphics and Applications,* Vol. 4, No. 5, May 1984, pp. 46–58.

[MYER68] Myer, T.H. and I.E. Sutherland, "On the Design of Display Processors," *CACM,* Vol. 11, No. 6, June 1968, pp. 410–414.

[MYER84] Myers, W., "Staking Out the Graphics Display Pipeline," *IEEE Computer Graphics and Applications,* Vol. 1, No. 7, July 1984, pp. 60–65.

[NICK84] Nickel, R., "The IRIS Workstation," *IEEE Computer Graphics and Applications,* Vol. 4, No. 8, Aug. 1984, pp. 30–34.

[SCHA81] Schachter, B.J., "Computer Image Generation for Flight Simulation," *IEEE Computer Graphics and Applications,* Vol. 1, No. 10, Oct. 1981, pp. 22–68.

[SCHM84] Schmidt, D.G., "Color Graphics Display for an Engineering Workstation," *Hewlett-Packard Journal,* Vol. 35, No. 5, May 1984, pp. 12–15.

VLSI Architectures for Computer Graphics[1]

Gregory D. Abram
Henry Fuchs

Department of Computer Science
University of North Carolina at Chapel Hill, USA

Abstract

Both academic researchers and commercial concerns are increasingly interested in applying VLSI technologies to graphics systems:

● For researchers, graphics systems offer an attractive model for study of computer architectures in VLSI: these systems have a small well-defined set of operations and simple data and control structures, making these systems ripe for applying parallelism and modularization techniques; many of these systems, especially the interactive high-resolution color ones, have severe computation demands that are unfulfilled by solutions embodied in current systems.

● For commercial concerns, there is a rapidly increasing market for interactive graphics systems as personal workstations in which graphics displays replace text-only terminals.

In this paper, we cover: a) the conceptual organization of a "generic" graphics system and its realization in several state-of-the-art commercial products; b) the architecture of several recent VLSI chips and systems and their likely effect on the organization of future graphics systems; c) the architecture of several VLSI-based systems that are currently subjects of research. The design strategies used in these systems -- the structure of parallelism, intertwining of data and computation, the tradeoff between custom and off-the-shelf parts -- may provide insights into other applications as well.

1. INTRODUCTION

The design of graphics systems has been a challenging topic of study for several decades; the demands for ever-increasing performance have always pushed the available technology to its limits. The availability of off-the-shelf TTL circuitry in the early 1970's allowed custom designs of minicomputer-level complexity. The advent of large-scale RAMs allowed systems to store complete images and quickly and randomly address any pixel in them; this capability gave rise to the current boom in color raster systems. Inexpensive microprocessors allowed these frame buffer systems to perform many functions independently of the host computer.

The possibility of custom VLSI promises another level of power in affordable graphics systems. The increased plasticity of custom VLSI allows systems designed using this medium to take on radically different structures than seen heretofore. This paper explores some of these possible structures -- a few just recently announced, most yet to come.

We concentrate in this paper on interactive color raster systems aimed at laboratory or office use, mostly for 3D applications; a few related systems that focus on 2D applications are included [Gupta, Sproull, et. al., 1981]. Of course, most of the systems cited can be used for a wide variety of applications, not restricted to 3D. We have intentionally left out systems aimed at the expensive ($1M) flight simulator market, largely due to lack of available information in the public domain [Schachter, 1981], although a number of the systems covered in this paper may be used for flight simulator applications.

---

[1] This research was supported in part by the (USA) National Science Foundation under grant ECS-8300970 and by the Defense Advanced Research Projects Agency contract DAAG 29-83-K-0148.

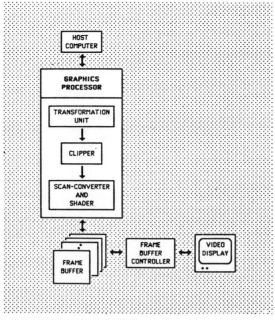

Figure 1: A Typical 3D Raster System Organization

The overall organization of many raster graphic display systems is quite similar (Fig. 1). The central feature is the frame buffer memory in which is stored the image currently being displayed -- and perhaps one or more additional images. To relieve the host computer from low-level tasks, one or more processors are attached to most frame buffers. The nature and organization of these processors is one of the major focuses of this paper. Its major tasks for 3D image generation are illustrated in Figure 2. An alternate organization is used for many general purpose workstations, in which the image usually shows one or more pages of mostly textual information (rather than an interactive 3D image). The major tasks involve generation and movement of 2D image data; the typical hardware organization for such systems is shown in Figure 3.

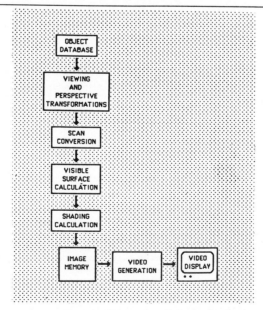

Figure 2: Functional Steps for 3D Image Synthesis

In studying many graphic system designs currently being developed, several distinct strategies become evident.

- Implementing innermost loops in hardware

One obviously reasonable strategy to consider is to transfer an often-executed inner loop from software to hardware [Atwood, 1984; T. Ikedo, 1984]. The details of these designs are discussed in section 2 . As some have noted, however, this strategy may not always succeed [Pike, 1984]. The new hardware inner loop solver may add so much more overhead as to swamp any gains it produces in solving the inner loop faster.

- Integrating a boardful of functions onto a single chip

Some systems have succeeded by restructuring an extant solution into VLSI components and thereby reducing a module that formerly needed one or more boards of parts to a few custom chips [Clark, 1982]. As will be seen below, however, it is not always obvious how to restructure the board-level function in such a way as to enable a VLSI-based solution.

- Alternative architectures

The restructuring for a VLSI-based solution can extend beyond the board to system level; with custom VLSI, it is appealing to attempt a radical restructuring of the problem in hopes of achieving a solution that's much more attractive in this new medium [Fuchs and Poulton, 1981; Fuchs, Poulton, et. al., 1982; Kedem and Ellis, 1984].

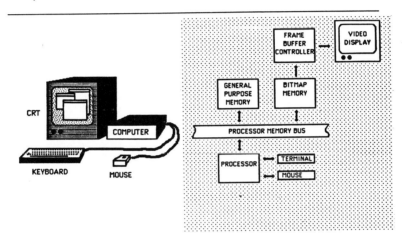

Figure 3: A Bitmap Display and Typical Hardware Organization

In this paper, we review several current and several proposed systems which take advantage of VLSI technology. Associated with each will be a figure noting the structure of such a system. It should be kept in mind that these architectural layouts are conceptual models only, reflecting our own understandings, and may bear only superficial resemblance to actual implementations.

2. HARDWARE FOR CRITICAL LOW-LEVEL FUNCTIONS

One characteristic of computer graphics systems is that a few low-level functions are used extremely frequently and, therefore, account for large portions of the total work done. Much work has been done to speed up the software algorithms used to perform these functions. Major advancements may be achieved by supporting these functions in hardware. Two such functions are the line drawing algorithm, which determines which pixels best approximate a line, and the "raster op", a complex function which allows logical functions between arbitrary rectangular regions of a bitmap display [Bechtolsheim and Baskett, 1980; Thacker and McCreight, 1979].

2.1 VLSI Support for Line Drawing

Although major strides have been made in the design of raster graphics systems, random-scan (also called vector or calligraphic) systems remain the technology of choice for line-drawing applications. This is for two reasons: image generation time and image quality. Raster systems must compute the set of pixels which best approximate lines and set them accordingly; random-scan systems use analog circuitry to drag the electron beam across the CRT screen from endpoint to endpoint. Since raster systems have only a relatively coarse grid of addressable pixels, images show distracting staircasing effects along edges (unless costly anti-aliasing algorithms are used); in contrast, lines on random-scan systems are smooth.

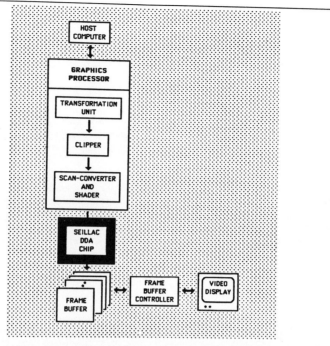

Figure 4: Organization of System Using SEILLAC DDA Chip

The SEILLAC-7, a new graphics system built by the Seillac Co., Ltd., utilizes a custom ECL DDA chip to achieve extremely high line drawing rates (Fig. 4). It is claimed to be about five times faster than previous raster systems that lack such special-purpose hardware (though other systems claim similar speeds, such as the Ramtek 2020) [Ikedo, 1984]. This chip, which achieves a speed of about 40 nanoseconds per pixel in the line, includes a function to modulate the pixel intensity to alleviate the staircasing effects. In doing so, the images generated are claimed to approach stroke-drawn systems both in image quality and in vector drawing speeds.

2.2 Bitmap Manipulations

A recent development in professional workstations has replaced the standard ASCII terminal with a high resolution black-and-white frame buffer system (a "bitmap" display). This approach, pioneered in the Xerox Alto system in the early 1970's [Thacker, McCreight, et. al., 1971], offers many advantages over standard ASCII terminals; for example, high quality graphics and arbitrary fonts can be used for document preparation.

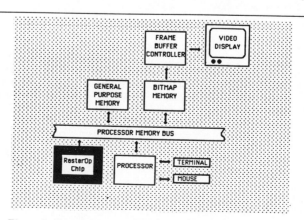

Figure 5: Bitmap System Organization Using RasterOp Chip

Bitmap displays require that the graphics system perform operations (Raster Ops) on bitmap memories efficiently (Fig. 5). Scrolling a bitmap window requires that the window be copied up one line; this must be done very quickly if the display is to be useful. Raster Ops typically allow logical operations on source and destination bitmaps; the copying process uses the function:

$$f(source, destination) = source$$

whereas the function:

$$f(font, destination) = \sim font$$

may be used to write reverse video characters.

The implementation of the RasterOp function, however, is tricky. First, source and destination areas may overlap; the algorithm must to careful to operate in an order which ensures that data will not be overwritten before it is used. For example, if the destination is to the *left* of the source, the operation must proceed from left to right across the source, whereas if the destination is to the *right* of the source, the pass must be in the opposite direction.

The problem is further complicated by the organization of the bitmap memory. Bitmap displays are often organized with 16 or 32 horizontally adjacent pixels in a single word. Since regions do not necessarily fall on word boundaries, corresponding pixels in source and destination words may fall at different bit positions within the words. In order to operate on the several pixels within each memory word in parallel, *two* source words must be available to be to aligned with the data within the destination data word. The logical operation is then applied to the aligned words, and the result written to the destination location. This must be repeated for each word which contains a destination pixel.

Silicon Compilers, Inc., in conjunction with Sun Microsystems, Inc., have implemented a chip to support the RasterOp function [Iannamico and Atwood, 1984]. This chip utilizes a two word FIFO to manage the source data words; the adjacent words are fed to a barrel shifter to align them with the destination data. Alternately, a pattern register is available for repetitive source data (for example, if a background pattern is to be written). The data words are fed to a simple ALU to compute the logical operation; a function decoder allows the host to choose among 8 possible functions of pattern, source, and destination pixel values. Finally, mask registers can be used to protect bits of the destination data words which lie outside the destination area.

A substantial amount of work remains for an external controller to do (either the host CPU or an external finite state machine). Unlike the Seillac DDA chip outlined above, the looping here must be handled by the controller. The chip has no memory-addressing capability; it must rely on the controller to spoon-feed it input data and to return the results to the destination memory locations. The chip does, however, provide functions which may be costly for conventional microprocessors, including in particular the arbitrary 32-bit shift necessary for data alignment.

3. INTEGRATED SYSTEM COMPONENTS

Whereas greater performance can be had by supporting critical functions in hardware, both performance and cost can be addressed by integrating large parts of the conventional graphics system. Some functions typically built out of large numbers of chips can, in fact, be implemented directly on a single (or a very few) VLSI ICs. This substantially decreases the chip count and can greatly improve the performance.

3.1 TI 4161 Memory Chip

Two related problems plague the frame buffer memory designers: 1) contention between image generation and scan-out for memory access, and 2) the high part count (and associated cost) of satisfactory designs (Fig. 6). For a 1024x1024x1 system refreshed at 60 Hz., a pixel (ie. one bit of the frame buffer memory) must be available for display every 16 nanoseconds (or less). This rate can be achieved by interleaving the pixel memory among several memory chips, which are read in parallel into a high speed shift register which then shifts pixels out at the desired rate. Assuming that the frame buffer is built using 64Kx1 RAM chips, 16 chips are required for a 1024x1024 bitplane, and scanout requires a memory cycle every 16x16 = 256 nanoseconds, leaving little for image generation (unless very high speed—and therefore expensive—memories are used). Using

Possible Memory Organizations		
memory chip size	desired access rate	data path width
256Kx1	64nsec.	4
64Kx1	256nsec.	16
16Kx4	1024nsec.	64

16Kx4 RAMs, we use the same number of chips and get 64 pixels in parallel, and we need a memory cycle every 1024 nanoseconds. Unfortunately, we now need four times as many memory chips and the data path is four times as wide. (Also, with these 4-bit wide chips, modifying a single bit is often awkward, necessitating a read-modify-write operation.)

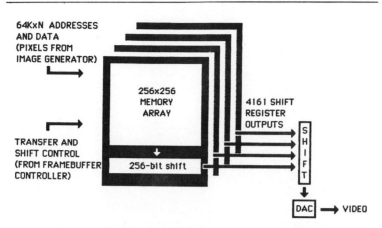

Figure 6: A Possible Frame Buffer Design Using TI 4161 RAMs

In other words, achieving the necessary data rates requires using small-capacity RAMs; whereas achieving low parts counts requires using large-capacity RAMs.

Texas Instruments has recently brought to market a special dynamic memory chip to help solve this problem [Pinkham, Novak, et. al., 1983]. Much like conventional 64K RAMs, the TI 4161 memory is organized as 256 rows of 256 columns. The difference is that a 256-bit 40 nanosecond shift register is included. A command causes an *entire row* to be transferred to the shift register; the chip then acts as two completely independent chips: the 256-bit shift register and a normal 64Kx1 DRAM. In this manner, the chip allows a low system parts count while not tying up memory for scan-out (one memory cycle accesses 256 pixels).

3.2 The Geometry Engine

Three-dimensional image generation requires that each coordinate in the scene be transformed from a object space coordinate system to an image space system and then clipped to the visible region. Because these functions are time-consuming (including multiplies and divides) and lie in the critical data path, this was one of the first image generation components to be implemented directly in hardware.

James Clark, of Stanford University and Silicon Graphics, Inc., has implemented a chip (the Geometry Engine) which, when organized in a twelve-stage pipeline, performs three-dimensional viewing transformations, a perspective transformation and clipping (Fig. 7) [Clark, 1982]. It achieves a rate of 65,000 coordinate points per second and (unlike most earlier systems) operates on floating point numbers. Because a relatively small number of identical ICs are used to implement this pipeline, the cost is low, The cost will be lower still when multiple copies of the present IC will fit onto a single die.

3.3 Graphics Display Controllers

Possibly the first specialized integrated circuits for video generation were single-chip video sync generators. Even with such chips, graphics display controllers typically require large amounts of logic, and hence are quite expensive to build out of off-the-shelf MSI and SSI components. Lately, however, two VLSI graphics display controllers have entered the market, each designed for a specific corner of the graphics market.

The NEC 7220 (second sourced as the Intel 82720) is designed to handle high-resolution (1024x1024) color raster graphics systems (such as the Vectrix VX384, a 670x480 system with 9 bits per pixel). The 7220 sits between the host processor (often an Intel micro) and the video memory (Fig. 8). Its video generation circuitry provides a great deal of flexibility, including provisions for zooming, panning, and windowing the image, plus the ability to use a light-pen input device. It also supports image generation by on-board line, arc, area fill and other graphic primitive display functions. Using the 7220, a complete high quality graphics system can be added to a microprocessor system at little more than the cost of the memories and the controller itself.

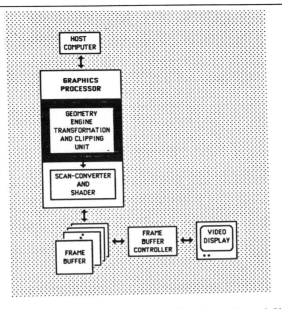

Figure 7: System with Geometry Engine for Transformation and Clipping

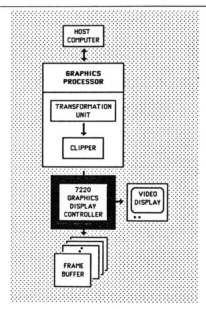

Figure 8: Graphics System Using 7220/82750 Graphics Display Controller

In contrast, the TI TMS9118 family of graphics display controllers are aimed at the low-cost world of video games, requiring only three chips to add graphics capability onto a standard microprocessor (Fig. 9) [Williamson and Rickert, 1983]. Although they allow only low resolution 256x192 images, they contain support for several specialized functions, including 32 so-called "sprites". A sprite is a small object defined by a rectangular grid of pixels whose position on the screen can be set by simply storing its location in a register, rather than actually copying its pixels from place to place in a (full-image) frame buffer. By using sprites for moving objects in the display, even extremely low-cost devices can support certain classes of very high quality interaction.

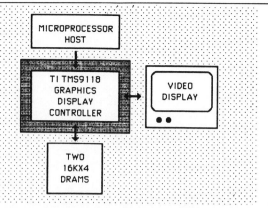

Figure 9: Low-cost System Using TI TMS9118 Graphics Display Controller

4. ALTERNATIVE ARCHITECTURES FOR VLSI

Several current research projects are investigating ways to restructure the traditional graphics architecture to take better advantage of VLSI technology; in particular, the capability of applying potentially many specialized processors to the problems of image generation. These alternative architectures divide into two classes: those that divide the problem in image space and those that divide the problem in object space. Image space strategies divide the *image plane* into independent subsets and associate a separate processor to each. Object space strategies instead divide the *object database* and assign a processor to each.

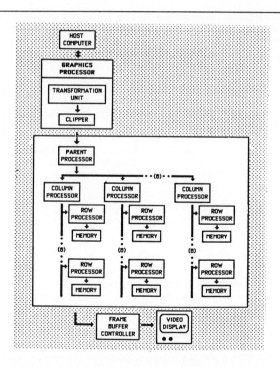

Figure 10: Clark and Hannah 8x8 Display Architecture

4.1 Image Space Strategies

A hard constraint on the performance of raster systems is the bandwidth into the frame buffer memories. However, we can increase the bandwidth to the memories by splitting the image memory into separate components (on the image generation side; the memory still should look contiguous to the scan-out hardware). By associating pixel generating power with each component, these separate components can be accessed in parallel, effectively multiplying the bandwidth to the memories by the number of separate components. In this section, we look at two such strategies. (For speeding up the restricted case of images composed solely of axis-oriented, filled rectangles, see [Whelan, 1982].)

4.1.1 Clark and Hannah

James Clark and Marc Hannah have proposed an image space segmentation approach which splits the image screen into segments the size of the RAM chips used (Fig. 10) [Clark and Hannah, 1980]. This organization is similar to an earlier system in [Fuchs and Johnson, 1979]. Both these systems distribute the image buffer in an interlaced fashion in X and Y among many small memories, each controlled by a small processor. For example, a 1024x1024 bit plane can be built out of 64 16K RAMs. These RAMs are interlaced so that for any 8x8 area of the bit plane, one bit comes from each of the these systems RAM chips. Thus, each memory contains every eighth pixel in every eighth row.

Clark and Hannah's system contains an intermediate layer of "column" processors between the main "parent" processor and the memory controlling "row" processors. Each of these processors then does a share of the image generation computation. To generate a line, the parent processor first determines the starting column, slope, line width and ending column of the line, and transfers this information to the column processors. The column processors then determine the part of the line intersecting the associated column of the image memory and transfers this to the row processors. Finally, the row processors actually write pixels into the image memory.

4.1.2 Pixel-Planes

We, together with colleagues A. Paeth and A. Bell at Xerox Palo Alto Research Center, have been working on an image-generating system, "Pixel-planes" that performs low level pixel operations within "smart" custom memory chips that make up the frame buffer (Fig. 11) [Fuchs and Poulton, 1981; Fuchs, Poulton, et. al., 1982]. The memory chips autonomously perform, 1) scan conversion (calculating the pixels that fall within a line-segment, convex polygon, or circle), 2) visibility calculations based on the depth ("Z") buffer algorithm, and 3) pixel painting (either "flat" or a limited Gouraud smooth shading).

Efficient implementation is possible because each of the above operations can be performed by variations of the same calculation at every pixel, $F(x,y)=Ax+By+C$ where x,y is the address of the pixel. This function can be efficiently realized on silicon by a complete binary tree with a pixel at each terminal node and a one-bit adder paired with a one-bit delay at each non-terminal node. This circuitry and the other needed processing circuitry (a one-bit ALU at each pixel) is sufficiently compact so that the area of the chips consist of half standard memory cells and half the processing circuitry described above.

Since both shading and depth can be formulated in similar equations, Pixel-Planes based systems can perform Gouraud-like smooth shading and Z-buffer visible surface computations. Two working prototypes have been built at UNC; the latest prototype's chips each contain 2K bits of memory distributed among 64 pixel processors, each with 32 bits of memory. Based on conservative speed estimates, (10 MHz clock), the system is expected to process 25,000 to 30,000 arbitrarily-sized polygons per second.

4.2 Object Space Subdivision Approaches

An alternative opportunity for parallel processing in image generation is to subdivide the *input data*, assigning separate hardware to each subdivision. Some of the earliest real-time flight simulation systems used this approach; unfortunately, at the time hardware had to be built out of a large number of simple parts, and was therefore extremely expensive and limited in scope [Schumacker, Brand, et. al., 1969]. Using VLSI technology, however, small, specialized processors can be built to perform the necessary operations. Several new designs have been proposed along these lines.

4.2.1 Gershon Kedem's CSG Machine

Gershon Kedem has proposed an architecture for the display of objects defined using Constructive Solid Geometry (CSG) (Fig. 12) [Kedem and Ellis, 1984]. CSG is a strategy for computer-aided design in which designs consist of several primitive shapes (spheres, cones, prisms etc.) which are combined using regularized set operations (UNION, INTERSECTION, ADDITION and SUBTRACTION). CSG structures are very naturally represented as binary trees in which leaf nodes correspond to primitives and internal nodes correspond to the operation which combines the objects described in the two subtrees.

Kedem's approach instantiates the CSG tree directly in hardware. A reconfigurable tree structure is built which consists of two types of nodes: Primitive Classifiers (PCs), for leaf nodes, and Combine Classifiers (CCs), for internal nodes. To compute a pixel value, the PCs compute (in parallel) the intersections of the ray rooted at the eye point and passing through the pixel center with their associated primitive objects. These intersections (actually line segments of the ray) filter up the tree. Each CC takes the line seg-

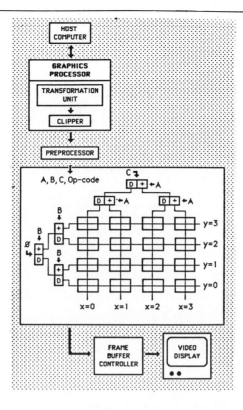

Figure 11: A Pixel-Planes System (4x4 resolution)

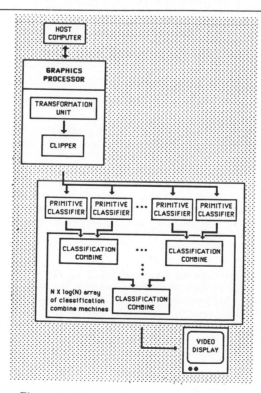

Figure 12: Kedem's CSG Machine Architecture

ments of its left and right subchild and applies its operator on them and passes the result up the tree. The final result, produced at the root of the tree, is then used to compute a pixel shade.

4.2.2 Cohen and Demetrescu Cohen and Demetrescu, in [Cohen and Demetrescu, 1980] have proposed a system that assigns a processor to each potentially visible polygon in the image space (i.e., already transformed world model polygon) (Fig. 13). These, processors are connected as a pipeline and are operated in synchrony with the video generation. For each pixel on the screen, a token is passed through the pipeline of polygon processors. This token carries the shade and depth of the closest point found for this pixel. This depth is the distance from the viewing position of the closest polygon encountered at this pixel; thus the shade is the best guess so far of the color seen at this pixel. Each processor in turn tests whether the pixel lies inside its polygon. If the point lies inside, the processor compares this depth with its polygon's depth at this point. If the polygon's depth is closer, its depth and color replace the token's data. For real-time image generation, tokens pass in raster-scan order and travel at video rates; that is, each processor must make each decision in one pixel time.

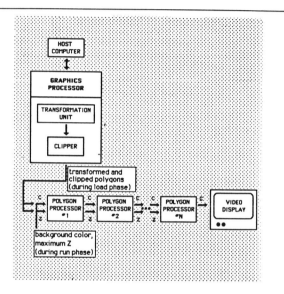

Figure 13: Cohen and Demetrescu's Pipelined Architecture

An elegant feature of this approach is that the pixels stream out of the end of the pipeline in raster-scan order and each value represents the color of the nearest polygon at that pixel; thus the data can be routed directly onto a video display screen.

Weinberg, in [Weinberg, 1981], proposes an elaboration on this design which addresses the problem of anti-aliasing by passing multiple depth-sorted tokens for each pixel along with subpixel masks. Each processor then determines the portion of the pixel covered by its polygon, and compares with the token's mask when the correct position in the depth order is found. If preceding polygons do not completely obscure it, it is added to the token chain. Subsequent tokens are then examined to see if the new polygon completely obscures them, deleting those that are. A filter section at the output uses this data to determine an output shade for each pixel.

This general approach features great modularity; it consists of identical processors hung together in a simple pipeline. It is easily expandable by simply adding more processor chips. The design costs are held down by the fact that only a single IC needs to be developed; manufacturing costs are held down by the simple structure. The only difficulties may be 1) implementing enough processors so that there is one for each and every polygon in the most complex scene in the intended application, and 2) making each processor sufficiently fast to complete all its calculations for a pixel in one pixel time.

5. SUMMARY AND CONCLUSIONS

As the reader is likely to gather from the above list of designs, we are currently witnessing a blossoming of creative designs for harnessing a new medium to solve an old problem. The good news in all this is that with all this attention, there is likely to be substantial progress; indeed, virtually with each passing month a new system with increased performance is introduced —usually found to contain some custom integrated circuitry. In the next few years, many of the designs described above will, no doubt, be developed, refined, and tested. The effective ones will be adopted, the others will be improved or abandoned. Further in the future, we may see designs that integrate even more of the display system functions -- perhaps including the display itself within the processing and image memory. We can then look forward to carrying around a display the size of a book, whose surface is a high-resolution display with built-in high-speed image generating capabilities -- thus approaching the predictions of visionaries' "dyna-books" [Kay, 1977] and eye-glass mounted "ultimate displays" [Sutherland, 1965].

References

Atwood, J. "Raster-Op Chip Overview", Silicon Compilers, Inc., Los Gatos, California (1984).

Bechtolsheim, A. and F. Baskett, "High-Performance Raster Graphics for Microcomputer Systems", *Computer Graphics (SIGGRAPH '80 Proceedings)*, Vol. 14, No. 3, (July 1980) 43-47.

Clark, J. and M. Hannah, "Distributed Processing in a High-Performance Smart Image Memory", *VLSI Design*, Vol. I, No. 3, 4th. Quarter, (1980).

Clark, J. "The Geometry Engine: A VLSI Geometry System for Graphics", *Computer Graphics (SIGGRAPH '82 Proceedings)*, Vol. 16, No. 3, (July 1982) 127-133.

Cohen, D. and S. Demetrescu, Presentation at SIGGRAPH '80 Panel on Trends on High Performance Graphic Systems, (1980).

Fuchs, H. and J. Poulton, "PIXEL-PLANES: A VLSI-Oriented Design for a Raster Graphics Engine", *VLSI Design*, Vol. II, No. 3, 3rd. Quarter, (1981).

Fuchs, H. and B. W. Johnson, "An Expandable Multiprocessor Architecture for Video Graphics", *Proceedings of 6th Annual (ACM-IEEE) Symposium on Computer Architecture*, (April 1979) 58-67.

Fuchs, H., J. Poulton, A. Paeth and A. Bell, "Developing Pixel-Planes, A Smart Memory-Based Raster Graphics System", *Proc. MIT Conference On Advanced Research in VLSI*, Artech House, Dedham, MA., (January 1982).

Gupta, S., R. Sproull, I. E. Sutherland, "A VLSI Architecture for Updating Raster-Scan Displays", *Computer Graphics (SIGGRAPH '81 Proceedings)*, Vol. 15, No. 3, (August 1981) 71-78.

Ikedo, T., "High-Speed Techniques for a 3-D Color Graphics Terminal", *IEEE Computer Graphics and Applications*, Vol. 4, No. 5 (1984).

Kay, A., "Microelectronics and the Personal Computer", *Scientific American*, Vol. 237 No. 3, (September, 1977).

Kedem, G. and J. Ellis, "Computer Structures for Curve-Solid Classification in Geometric Modelling", Technical Report TR137, Department of Computer Science, University of Rochester, (May, 1984).

Pike, R., Presentation at University of North Carolina at Chapel Hill, (1984).

Pinkham, R., M. Novak and K. Guttag, "Video RAM Excels At Fast Graphics", *Electronic Design*, (July 21, 1983) 161-172.

Schachter, B., "Computer Image Generation for Flight Simulation", *IEEE Computer Graphics and Applications*, Vol. 1, No. 4, (1981).

Schumacker, R. A., B. Brand, M. Gilland, W. Sharp, "Study for Applying Computer-generated Images to Visual Simulation", *U. S. Air Force Human Resources Lab. Tech. Rep.* AFHRL-TR-69-14, (September 1969).

Sutherland, I., "The Ultimate Display", *Proceedings of the IFIP Congress,* Vol. 2, 1965.

Thacker, C. P., E. M. McCreight, B. W. Lampson, R. F. Sproull, D. R. Boggs, "ALTO: A Personal Computer", Xerox Corp., (1979) in Siewiorek, D. P., C. G. Bell, and A. Newell, *Computer Structures: Principles and Examples,* McGraw-Hill, (1982) 549-572.

Weinberg, R., "Parallel Processing Image Synthesis and Anti-Aliasing", *Computer Graphics (SIGGRAPH '81 Proceedings),* Vol. 15, No. 3, (August 1981) 55-61.

Whelan, D., "A Rectangular Area Filling Display System Architecture", *Computer Graphics, (SIGGRAPH '82 Proceedings),* Vol. 17, No. 3, (July 1982) 147-153.

Williamson R. and P. Rickert, "Dedicated Processor Shrinks Graphics Systems to Three Chips", *Electronic Design,* (August 4, 1983) 143-148.

*Pipelined architecture dramatically off-loads the host computer.
Here's a quick look at how eight companies are applying
this technology to graphics display.*

SPECIAL FEATURE

Staking Out the Graphics
Display Pipeline

Ware Myers

Contributing Editor

In the beginning there was the mainframe. All the wondrous calculations necessary to generate and display an object had of necessity to be performed in it. Then a few people looked at this string of calculations and saw that some of them could be removed from the mainframe and set up as special-purpose logic to drive the display. As they continued to study the calculations, they saw that more and more of them could be added to the special-purpose unit. In time, that unit became the equivalent of a general-purpose computer. A few then saw that some of its calculations could be removed to a special-purpose unit, and so the "wheel of reincarnation," as it was called by Myer and Sutherland, rolled on.[1] Designers have been going around that wheel ever since.

Eventually, this stream of calculations was organized and abstracted and became a functional model of a computer graphics system. "The functional model consists of a pipeline of logical processors operating on representations of objects," said Foley and van Dam in their authoritative textbook.[2] "A logical processor in the functional model corresponds to one or more physical processors, and two logical processors in the model may share a physical processor. Similarly, representations may reside in one memory or in different memories."

The functional elements are classified as follows:

(1) The application model contains a description of the graphical and nongraphical properties of a (hierarchical) object in a format determined by the application program and/or modeling package.

(2) The display file compiler (a logical processor) maps the application model to the structured display file.

(3) The structured display file contains a (hierarchical) description of the graphical representation of the object, typically in world coordinates.

(4) The display processing unit maps the structured display file to the linear display file.

(5) The (segmented) linear display file contains graphical primitives and mode settings describing the object produced after modeling and viewing.

(6) The display controller maps the linear display file to the image on the display screen.

(7) The screen displays a vector or raster image.

One way to understand the pipeline concept is to realize that it transforms a model of some object into representations that become successively more machine-dependent and finally results in an image upon a particular screen. Along the way a number of operations may be performed: orthographic or two-dimensional modeling; three-dimensional modeling; solid modeling; translation or transformation of coordinates; clipping (to window or viewport limitations); dragging or rubberbanding; rotation; scaling; panning; zooming; representing depth by perspective or parallel techniques; hidden-line or surface removal; filling gray shades or color into surfaces; figuring shadows, reflections, highlights, or light transmission through a surface from scene lighting; scan conversion (vector to raster); and antialiasing. Some unit along the graphics display pipeline must be capable of executing the algorithms implemented in a particular system.

In the beginning, these algorithms had to be carried out by the mainframe; a little later, one of the processors along the wheel of reincarnation took over. The arrival of the minicomputer in the early 1970's reduced the cost of processing, and computer graphics began to spread. Later in the decade, the microprocessor speeded up this trend. Custom VLSI began to be applied to sections of the pipeline in the 1980's.

Consultant Carl Machover of Machover Associates Corporation lists 77 companies in a category he calls "interactive graphics displays," 91 in computer-aided design/drafting systems, and various numbers in related

Reprinted from *IEEE Computer Graphics and Applications*, Volume 4, Number 7, July 1984, pages 60-65. Copyright © 1984 by The Institute of Electrical and Electronics Engineers, Inc.

categories. Here, we are going to look at how eight companies—mostly new ones—have applied the latest technology to the graphics display pipeline.

Weitek Corporation

This Sunnyvale (California) company is in the business of supplying high-performance VLSI building blocks to compute-intensive applications, such as graphics and computer-aided design. In the past two years, Weitek has introduced 16-bit and 32-bit arithmetic-logic units and multipliers. Its 32-bit floating-point chip set, which is compatible with the IEEE 754 floating-point standard, is capable of up to 16 Mflops. It is developing a 64-bit multiplier and an ALU that will be able to handle both single- and double-precision formats. High-performance processors like these can perform many operations in the graphics pipeline.

Targeted more specifically at graphics opportunities are the Tiling Engine, WTE 6000, and the Solids Modeling Engine, WTE 7000. These units fit between display list processing and the frame buffer in a graphics pipeline. Application software, such as a solid modeling package, resides in main memory and runs on the host. The model database is transformed into a display list by a display list processor. The result, in world coordinates, is buffered in the display list memory. From here, the Solids Modeling Engine transforms the surface representation into a form suitable for display on a color raster device. The engine builds or modifies solid shaded models in real time. For example, it can generate a 6000-polygon model on a 1280×1024 raster display in less than 10 seconds.

The two major components of this engine are a high-speed transformation processor and the Tiling Engine. The transformation processor translates, rotates, and scales the image, tessellates bicubic patches into polygons, and prepares the results for tiling. It also performs light modeling and clipping calculations.

The Tiling Engine transforms polygons into high-resolution shaded images, using either Gouraud or Phong shading. Central to its performance is a z-buffer, which consists of an array of pixels, each described in 24 bits. These bits define the intensity and the depth (z value) of the polygon visible at each pixel. They can be allocated by the user to optimize the image for depth of field, broad spectrum of color, or shading refinement.

The Tiling Engine and the Solids Modeling Engine can be used as attached processors to Digital Equipment Corporation's families of Vax-11 and PDP-11 computers or to Apollo Computer's DN600 series of workstations, via high-speed, 16-bit parallel interfaces. As board sets, they may be interfaced to a Multibus.

Saber Technology Corporation

This two-year-old company announced a CAE/CAD workstation for original equipment manufacturers and system integrators at NCGA's Computer Graphics 84 in Anaheim, California, this May. Saberstation's application processor utilizes a 32-bit microprocessor, the NS32032. Operating at a 10-MHz clock rate, it executes its instruction set at 1.2 MIPS. It has a hardware floating-point coprocessor and demand-paged virtual memory.

The graphics processor employs a 32-bit, 20M-byte-per-second opcode/data bus structure. This structure permits an OEM to develop an application in software and later move it into VLSI, thus accelerating the performance of the software. The hardware accelerator can be operated by a graphic opcode.

The image processor does vector-to-raster conversion and bit alignment. The resulting pixel values are deposited in an exceptionally large image memory—1664×1248 pixels, or 2,076,672 pixels. Each pixel can be backed by two to eight image planes in the basic system or up to 24 image planes in an expanded system.

To display this large number of pixels requires a very fast video monitor. "Saber's new video monitor technology offers higher resolution and faster graphics than any other system now on the market," said Dennis Peck, president of the San Jose, California, company. The extremely high video rate produces a pixel every 5.5 nanoseconds. This performance is made possible by a new proprietary circuit technology for which Saber has filed a patent application. "For example, in the video amplifiers, the (circuit technology's) ability to slew over a 35-volt range in less than 2 ns gives the display a sharpness and degree of resolution that cannot be matched," Peck asserted.

The Saberstation display fits on a desktop, taking 18 inches of space. It is priced at less than $40,000 in single quantities with OEM discounts.

Sun Microsystems

The Sun workstations are in a different price range. A standard Sun-2/120 workstation, which includes a processor, one megabyte of memory, a bit-mapped graphics display, a keyboard, a mouse, an Ethernet interface, and all software, is priced at $16,900. A standard Sun-2/170 workstation, with 2M bytes of memory, has a price of $20,900. The processor is a 10-MHz MC68010 with 10M bytes of virtual address space per process. The demand-paged virtual memory feature lets each process use the complete addressing range of the 68010 while the system transparently moves user data between physical memory and secondary storage.

The memory management design supports up to 4M bytes of physical memory with no wait states, making all main memory as fast as cache memory. The processor also implements direct memory access for high-speed peripherals. An optional hardware floating-point processor supports IEEE standard formats for 32-bit single- and 64-bit double-precision operations.

The Sun-2 workstations include a custom VLSI chip called the Raster-op Controller. When invoked by the low-level window system and graphics software, the Raster-op Controller is inserted in the data path between the microprocessor and main memory. Here, it performs shifting, Boolean operations, and masking, using the source and destination data during a single read-modify-write memory cycle. The chip replaces what Sun calls "numerous MC68010 instructions that would be required to perform this task with software."

The multiwindow display manager is an example of an application that makes heavy use of these raster manipulations. To maintain the context of multiple parallel activities, as the user creates and modifies windows, the Raster-op Controller paints windows containing arbitrary alphanumeric text and/or graphics at arbitrary, possibly overlapping locations on the display.

To develop the Raster-op Controller, Sun made use of the services of Silicon Compilers, Inc., Los Gatos, California. (The relation of silicon compilation to custom VLSI is similar to that of a Fortran compiler to machine code.) Silicon Compilers is an offshoot of the Caltech Silicon Structures project. It has now brought silicon compilation to the stage where it has been used to help design several large-scale chips. The Raster-op Controller was designed by one engineer in five months. It is a MOS part, 182 × 151 mils, fabricated in three-micrometer design rules.

Lexidata Corporation

The Lex 90 family, introduced at Computer Graphics 84, is in about the same price range as the Sun workstations. Prices for the Lex 90/35 Model 2 range from $13,925 for the four-plane configuration to $22,925 for the "true color" system. The Lex 90/35 Model 3 is priced at $19,850 for the eight-plane configuration.

The principal hardware processor is based on the 2900 family bit-slice architecture. It features 12-MHz bipolar technology. It employs a 16-bit data path and 56-bit horizontal microcode. By processing multiple read/write and arithmetic instructions concurrently, the horizontal

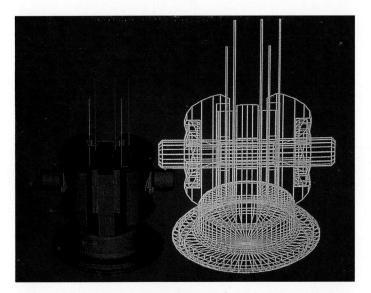

Figure 1. Lexidata's Lex 90/35 Model 2 graphics system features a function called "Simul Res" that allows simultaneous display of a 640 × 512 image (left) and a 1280 × 1024 overlay (right) on one screen. The transducer model was created using Matra Datavision software.

microcode greatly increases speed and efficiency. For example, it is capable of writing vectors at an average speed of 600 ns in any direction. It fills surfaces at 37.5 ns per pixel.

The Lex family provides on-board diagnostics by means of a 6801 microprocessor. After power-up, the diagnostics check registers, memory boards, and look-up tables. Another test performs an extensive diagnosis of the 2900 processor and random access memory; this test provides information on clipping, pan and zoom, blink, and monitor alignment.

An interesting feature of the Model 2 is its dual resolution. Both medium-resolution shaded images and high-resolution line drawings are software selectable. A special feature allows both a 640 × 512 × 8 image and a 1280 × 1024 × 4 overlay to be simultaneously displayed on one screen. See Figure 1.

An optional input/output processor is based on the MC68000. It provides four programmable RS-232 serial ports and an EEPROM in which to save baud rate, parity, and other local parameters during power-down.

Silicon Graphics, Inc.

The IRIS Graphics System is a combination of proprietary custom VLSI circuits, 32-bit microprocessors, and bit-slice microprocessors, as shown in the system block diagram in Figure 2. The system is priced at about $60,000 for a stand-alone workstation with a disk, or $37,500 for a terminal.

The most unusual feature of the IRIS system is the Geometry Engine, a custom VLSI chip developed and patented at Stanford University by James H. Clark, the founder, chairman, and chief technical officer of the Mountain View, California, company. The Geometry Engine chip contains seven principal elements: four function units, a clock generator, a microprogram counter with a pushdown subroutine stack, and a 40K-bit control store. Each of the four function units consists of two copies of a computing unit for a mantissa and characteristic. The control store contains the microcode.[3] The chip accepts points, vectors, polygons, characters, and curves in a user-defined coordinate system and transforms them to screen coordinates with arbitrary rotations, scaling, and other transformations.

The Geometry Engines are employed in a pipeline configuration in the IRIS system. The first four chips are called the matrix engine; the next four (or six in 3-D systems), the clipper engine; and the last two, the scaler engine. Each chip has a configuration register that is loaded when the system is powered on; this configuration code determines the particular functions the chip is to perform in the system. The system performs these functions at a rate in excess of 65,000 coordinates per second.

The matrix engine performs 2-D and 3-D transformations, including object rotations, translations, scaling, and perspective and orthographic projection. It performs a full floating-point transformation of incoming coordinates in 15 microseconds. It also generates cubic and rational cubic curves, producing new points in 10 microseconds.

IEEE CG&A

Each Geometry Engine in the clipping subsystem clips the objects to one of the boundary planes of the viewing window—left, right, top, bottom, and near or far, if they are needed. The objects it clips are outputs of the matrix engines in transformed coordinates.

The scaler engine converts the clipped objects to the coordinate system of the output device. This result is loaded into viewport registers, which hold up to 24-bit integer values, depending upon the needs of the output device. From the z-viewport registers, the output device can derive either perspective depth values or intensity depth-cue values. If it does not use z values, it may ignore these registers.

The geometry system performs its operations directly. It does not burden the workstation's central processor. "This use of proprietary VLSI helps the system outperform much more expensive minicomputer-based workstations," according to Clark. "It can, for example, handle geometric calculations faster than a Vax-780 (minicomputer). In graphics applications, the Geometry Engine offers 200 to 400 times the graphics performance of an advanced general-purpose processor such as the Motorola 68000. (The computation rate corresponds to more than six million floating-point operations per second.)"

The main processor (an MC68010) manages display lists, interprets graphics commands, handles engineering calculations, and performs other tasks required for a specific application. It also controls the geometry pipeline and the raster subsystem.

The raster subsystem generates lines, areas, and characters. It adds color or texture to images. It is controlled by a 4×4-bit American Micro Devices 2903 microprocessor.

This three-part system architecture—high-performance microprocessors and custom geometry chips—is balanced to provide sustained performance. There is "no perceived wait." The user works in what is essentially real time.

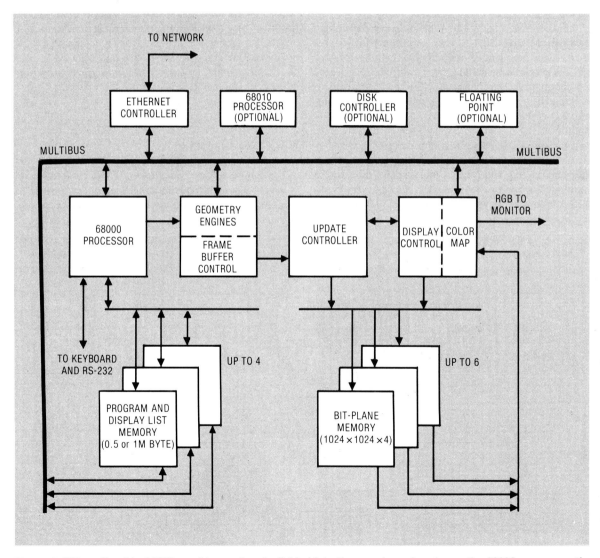

Figure 2. Silicon Graphics' IRIS graphics system is divided into three major subsystems: the 68000 processor, the Geometry Engines, and the raster display controller. The processor manages the display lists and controls the other two subsystems. The 68010 processor, disk controller, and floating-point coprocessor are optional.

22

Parallax Graphics, Inc.

This company was founded as recently as November 1982 by two electrical engineering students from Cornell University, who built on their thesis research. And only in November 1983 did their fledgling company acquire an experienced chief executive officer.

The company's first product was a high-speed color graphics controller targeted at the OEM and value-added reseller markets. These board-level controllers feature a proprietary bit-slice drawing processor with a drawing speed of 12 million pixels per second. The instruction set provides single-instruction polygon, box, circle, and vector drawing commands, and solid-fill, outline, stipple, cut-and-paste, and opaque/transparent modes. The price is in the vicinity of $5000.

At Computer Graphics 84, the company announced its 1000 series, which is capable of a drawing speed of 88 million pixels per second. This three-board set costs around $10,000 in quantity. Again, these controllers make use of "proprietary processor technology, developed by Parallax's design staff, to achieve near-real-time interactivity in Multibus and Q-bus systems."

"The two basic integration problems in new technology introductions have been solved," according to Michael Strozza, vice president of marketing, "(1) by using standard bus interfaces on an intelligent controller that is easy to program, and (2) by eliminating the need for expensive development systems by using a self-hosting board set coupled with standard microcomputers and color monitors."

Strozza thinks that Parallax can't be "matched at our price, resolution, and speed." He believes the new controller board sets will "force the graphics industry to rethink design and pricing strategies, moving everyone to VLSI solutions as we've done."

The company has published extensive specifications on what each set of controller boards does, but it provides no details about its proprietary technology.

Seillac Corporation

This Japanese manufacturer formally introduced its product line to the United States market at Computer Graphics 84. "Seillac's innovative products have propelled our company to a leadership position in the tough Japanese computer graphics industry," said David L. Peltz, vice president for sales and marketing. "Now, we're gearing up to take on the greatest market of them all, the American market."

The Carson (California) company's secret appears to lie in eight different custom VLSI chips developed by its engineers. The Seillac-7 minimizes the load on the host computer and the user's application program, Peltz noted, through advanced hardware architecture, pipeline-processing structure, high drawing speed, sophisticated buffer technology, and other innovations. It provides a resolution of 1400 × 1024, 60-Hz noninterlaced refresh, and a 120-MHz video bandwidth. Antialiasing hardware eliminates staircasing and generates "lines comparable to a random-stroke display." See p. 46 of the May 1984 issue of *IEEE Computer Graphics and Applications* for more information on the Seillac-7.

Megatek Corporation

This long-established computer graphics corporation is in the process of introducing its latest and most powerful graphics workstation, the Merlin 9200. This workstation,

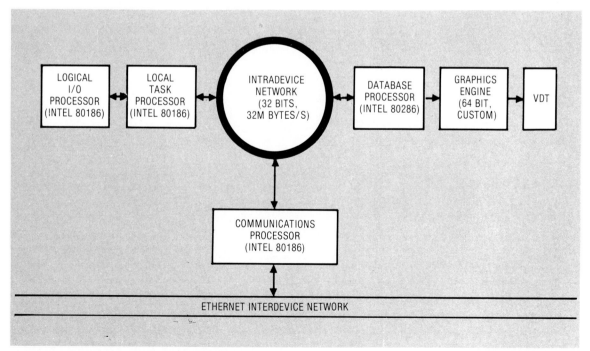

Figure 3. Merlin 9200 multiprocessor architecture.

as can be seen in Figure 3, has four processors along its pipeline: the local task processor, the database processor, the graphics engine, and the logical I/O processor. The processors are connected by a proprietary 32-bit bus.

The local task processor is based on the Intel 80186 16-bit microprocessor. It performs two types of functions: internal communications and local task execution. It handles communications to the host computer and among the various processors through RS-232 serial ports, Centronics-type parallel ports, floppy disks, and a Multibus. (An optional Ethernet interface, handled by a separate communications processor, allows local area networking.)

The local tasks can be implemented by users with Megatek's Local Task Language. Putting local tasks on the 80186 offloads them from the host computer, speeding up processing accordingly. Up to eight concurrent tasks can be run on the local task processor. These tasks may embrace the control of linkage to the host computer, the creation of menus, or the triggering of criteria-based actions.

The database processor is built on an Intel 80286 16-bit microprocessor. This unit views memory as a collection of segments of data and executable code. Each segment can be viewed as the physical embodiment of a software module—hardware organization follows software organization. Thus, the 80286 is well suited to carry out some of the sequence of software processes found along the graphics pipeline. Because the functions needed to support concurrency are in the chip hardware, tasks can be switched from one to another in only 21 microseconds, far faster than the several hundred milliseconds often taken to switch tasks by software means.

The database processor is associated with a 512K-byte local memory, expandable to 4.5M bytes. This memory contains a representation of three-dimensional coordinates together with object attributes, such as topological connections, texture, or depth. The object is maintained in a hierarchical data structure—lists or arrays. With so much local capability, objects can be created or modified locally without having to refer work to the host. Also, the view of the object can be changed locally.

The 64-bit graphics engine is custom designed. It takes data from the local database structure and converts it to vectors for stroke display or scan converts vector data to pixel locations for raster-scan output.

The logical I/O processor completes the pipeline and is, again, based on the Intel 80186 16-bit microprocessor.

A new feature included in the Merlin 9200 is the anti-aliasing hardware, which uses a technique Megatek calls "pixel phasing." While the actual raster resolution (and the corresponding frame-buffer size) is 768×576, the electron beam can be "micro-positioned" over a 3072×2304 grid in such a way that the jaggies can be smoothed out.

Now in "beta" site testing, the Merlin 9200 appears to approach real-time performance for objects of considerable complexity. On 3-D tasks, it is expected to be capable of processing 100,000 16-bit vectors in one second. The price ranges from $35,000 to $50,000, depending on the options selected. ■

References

1. T.H. Myer and I. E. Sutherland, "On the Design of Display Processors," *Comm. ACM*, Vol. 11, No. 6, June 1968; reprinted in *Tutorial: Computer Graphics*, J. C. Beatty and K. S. Booth, eds., IEEE Computer Society, Los Alamitos, Calif., 1982, pp. 131-135.

2. James D. Foley and Andries van Dam, *Fundamentals of Interactive Computer Graphics*, Addison-Wesley Publishing Co., Reading, Mass., 1982.

3. James H. Clark, "The Geometry Engine: A VLSI Geometry System for Graphics," *Computer Graphics* (Proc. Siggraph 82), Vol. 10, No. 3, July 1982, pp. 127-133.

Significant gains in interactivity can result when the graphics subsystem is tailored to a particular application.

A Graphics System Architecture for Interactive Application-Specific Display Functions

Nick England   Whitland Associates

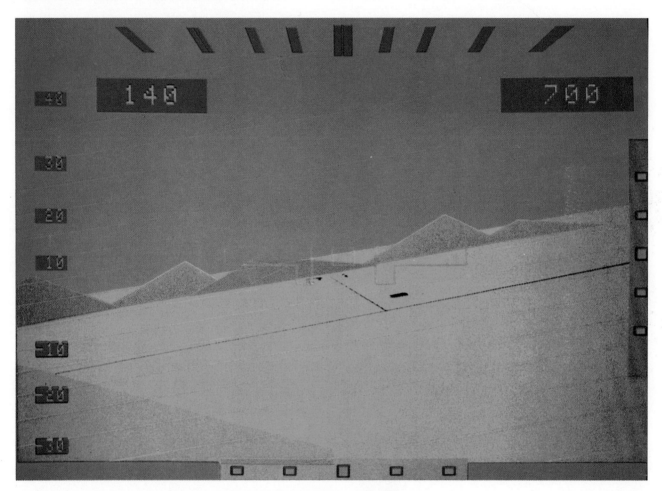

Interactive computer graphics display requirements have generally been met in one of two ways: by highly specialized systems designed for a particular application, or, more frequently, by devices with a limited set of display functions common to a wide range of applications. A third alternative, presented here, is to use a high-performance, general-purpose display architecture to provide both common and application-specific graphics functions. A sampling of a wide variety of display tasks, from seismic data display to solid modeling, shows that significant improvements in interactivity can be obtained by microprogramming such a machine.

Most interactive computer graphics tasks require that the overall computing load be split between an application processor and a graphics subsystem. The applications processor is a general-purpose machine—from an 8086 microprocessor in a workstation to a large mainframe—that sends commands to the graphics subsystem for image generation and manipulation. The latter generally consists of an optimized, specialized processor coupled to a raster display screen. This graphics processor also comes in a variety of guises, from a single-chip display controller to a large and power-hungry visual flight simulator.

Reprinted from *IEEE Computer Graphics and Applications*, Volume 6, Number 1, January 1986, pages 60-70. Copyright © 1986 by The Institute of Electrical and Electronics Engineers, Inc.

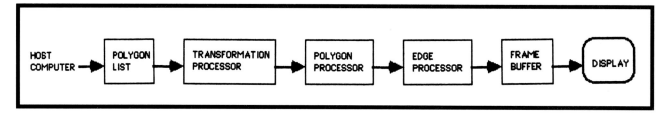

Figure 1. Typical CGI special-purpose architecture.

In many cases the designer of a graphics subsystem seeks to maximize market appeal by restricting the subsystem's operations to a small set of presumably application-independent functions. The purpose of this article is to illustrate the gains in interactivity that result when the functionality of the graphics subsystem can be tailored to the particular application at hand.

Graphics subsystem architectures

First, architectures for special-purpose processors, limited-purpose processors, and a general-purpose display processor are compared. Then, examples of customizing display functionality for specific applications are presented.

Special-purpose graphics processors. There can be no doubt that the highest levels of performance for a particular task can be achieved by a device designed specifically for that task. Performance is achieved by sacrificing flexibility. A Computer-Generated Imaging (CGI) system highly specialized for flight simulation (Figure 1) can severely restrain the types of graphics primitives that can be employed. Such a system might have hardware capable of dealing with only one data type: 3D polygons. Even though connections to a general-purpose application processor exist, all communications must take place though this narrow semantic bottleneck. A string of text can be displayed only by defining each character's polygonal outline and providing 3D coordinates for proper spacing. In this case the mighty real-time simulator system is appreciably less powerful— seen from the application's viewpoint—than a lowly alphanumeric CRT. To make a line drawing, the application must create a multitude of long, skinny polygons; to paint a digitized pattern, it must generate a host of pixel-sized polygons, each having the appropriate color.

A similar example of application specificity without flexibility can be found in the image processing world. There are many examples of architectures (Figure 2) that, though embedded with hardware for interactive image addition, subtraction, or convolution, still must rely on a host computer (or attached microprocessor) to generate the x,y address of every pixel of a graphic map overlay, for instance.

These difficulties are not faults within the special-purpose architectures; they simply reflect the fact that a decision was made to sacrifice flexibility for better performance in one narrow application area. Not so obvious is the fact that similar bottlenecks exist in display systems purporting to serve a more general purpose.

Limited-purpose graphics processors. This class of display system is by far the most numerous. Here, the types of display functions have been limited to a reasonably small set that can cover many applications. Some optimization has also been carried out within the hardware to provide a high level of performance for the modest set of functions. Typical functions are:

- line drawing
- character drawing
- polygon drawing (possibly with z-buffering)
- transformations

Such a display subsystem, be it chip, board, or terminal, is designed for broad usage in a wide variety of applications and satisfies many of them quite effectively.

A typical raster system architecture of this type is shown in Figure 3. A similar layout can be found in most modern high-performance 3D terminals, including Megatek Merlin, Ramtek 2020, Raster Technologies 1/380, Silicon Graphics Iris, Adage 6000, IBM 5080, and Lexidata Lex 90.

Note that the system contains multiple processing elements communicating in a fixed order. A general-purpose

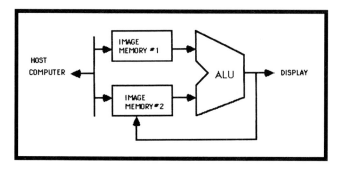

Figure 2. Typical image processor special-purpose architecture.

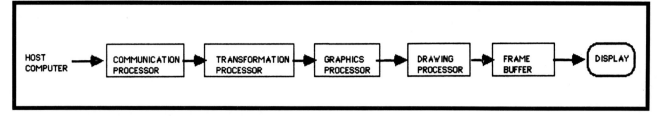

Figure 3. Typical limited-purpose architecture.

16/32-bit microprocessor handles communication to and from the application processor, including display list management. An integer or floating point transformation processor (bit-slice, custom VLSI, or Weitek VLSI) provides transformation of 3D data in a pipeline stage between the display list memory and the following graphics processor. On some units this transformation task can be collapsed into the graphics processor and there is no separate transformation processor.

A 16-bit bit-slice microprogrammed graphics processor receives the data and either performs an operation directly or sets up the drawing processor. The 16-bit graphics processor may have to decompose a polygon into triangles, or, more commonly, into horizontal scan segments that the drawing processor can handle. This processor also subdivides curves and circles into straight lines for the drawing processor.

The drawing processor itself is a high-speed (3-30 MIPS) gate array, MSI, or bit-slice device tightly coupled to the raster frame-buffer memory. This drawing processor is fast but simple. It might be capable of drawing only vectors and characters, but sometimes can handle points and triangles as well. In the last few years most of these systems have added a *z*-buffer memory, and the polygon drawing mechanism (graphics and drawing processors) has been modified to use this visible surface display technique.

Where, then, do bottlenecks exist in such a system? For many simple applications the architecture is well-balanced and there are no bottlenecks. For others, however, two areas cause problems.

The first is that all frame-buffer access must go through the drawing processor. For example, if the application requires that image data (an array of pixels of varying color) be displayed, a cumbersome process of loading the array to the display list and then having the graphics processor draw a series of one-pixel-long vectors of the desired colors may have to be carried out. In some systems the drawing processor cannot be read back from the frame-buffer memory; consequently, image manipulation is not possible.

The second potential bottleneck lies in the limited set of functions and data structures provided to the application program. For example, while all of the above systems provide that a vector list rather than individual vertex pairs can be used (Figure 4), few extend the notion to polygons. If an application deals with an $N \times M$ array of vertices forming a mesh of quadrilaterals, it would seem natural to pass just that $N \times M$ array rather than having to decompose the mesh into individual triangles of three vertices each and pass them one at a time to the graphics terminal.

This bottleneck might be eased by additional microcode for the bit-slice graphics processor, but this processor generally is saturated already. In addition, microcode for this processor is usually kept at a minimum because of limited microcode memory and the difficulty of code development. Perhaps more important, this bottleneck is related more to the conceptual design of the system than to the hardware implementation. Such limited-purpose processor systems were designed to do a few things well. They were optimized for tasks that were well-known and well-specified at the time of design. They perform in a balanced and economical manner when restricted to providing a basic set of display functions.

General-purpose graphics processors. The third category of display subsystem architecture is one that tries to give a moderately high level of performance in many different application areas. This is accomplished in much the same manner as a superminicomputer design serves many applications—by providing lots of memory, using a high performance general-purpose processor (with high memory-processor bandwidth), maintaining flexibility through modularity in hardware and software, and, finally, developing application-specific software. An example of such a graphics subsystem is shown in Figure 5. This is the architecture of a system originally developed by the author

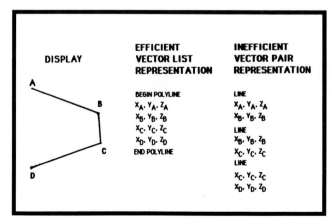

Figure 4. Data structures for line drawing.

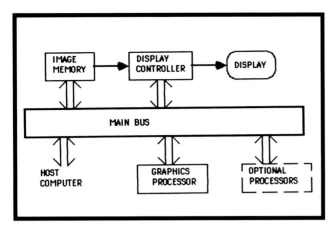

Figure 5. General-purpose architecture.

General-purpose 32-bit graphics processor. A straightforward implementation using eight 2903 bit-slice components (ALU plus 16 registers) was used. A 16-bit VLSI multiplier was added and a 64-bit-wide microcode word was chosen. All microprograms reside in RAM with $4K \times 64$ minimum and $64K \times 64$ maximum size (Figure 6). Communication between the processor and the rest of

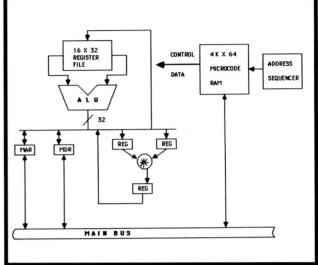

Figure 6. General-purpose graphics processor.

as a research tool and then expanded in commercial form as the Ikonas Raster Display System (now available as the Adage 3000).[1,2]

Key features of the system reflect the general-purpose nature of the design:

- single common bus structure
- modular architecture
- general-purpose 32-bit graphics processor
- large image memory
- flexible display controller

The benefits of these components of the system design are outlined below.

Single common bus structure. A 32-bit data, 24-bit address, 100 ns transfer, synchronous bus design was chosen. All control registers, image memory, lookup tables, and the like are mapped into the 24-bit address space. Image memory is arranged so that it is directly accessed as $2K \times 2K$ matrix—11 bits x address and 11 bits y address. Any bus master (graphics processor, host processor, etc.) connected to this bus has direct access to all system components. In other architectures an application program cannot set a lookup table value directly; it must issue a request to the communication processor which in turn might issue a request to a graphics processor to actually set the value.

Modular architecture. The bus was designed so that all physical card slots are identical. With a simple bus interface and a large address space, modules can be added at any time and in practically any configuration. A fast priority scheme was devised to allow multiple masters to reside on the bus and share control. During the system's development cycle a number of modules were developed in response to users' requests or by users themselves. Examples include:

- Winchester disk controller
- floating point processor
- image compression unit
- image transformation unit
- real-time color video input (frame grabber)

the system is through a simple memory address register (MAR) plus memory data register (MDR) scheme. With the 64-bit-wide microcode supplied over a separate bus and a 200-ns processor cycle, overlapped and parallel operations occur at a 5-20 MIPS instruction rate.

The 32-bit width was selected both for high-precision arithmetic operations and so that the processor could function as two 16-bit units with, for example, x pixel address calculation taking place in one half and y pixel address calculation taking place in the other. The memory address register was also designed to accommodate this split mode, with the lower 11 bits of each half word used for x and y pixel address as mentioned earlier.

All microcode is cross-assembled on a host computer and then downloaded to RAM within the graphics processor. Several C-subset compilers have been developed by users and subsequently marketed commercially. The availability of a higher level language coupled to a reasonably straightforward processor implementation has had a major impact on the amount of application-specific microcode development done so far. The remainder of this article focuses on these microcoded functions.

Large image memory. Many raster graphics subsystem implementations have an image memory exactly equal in size to the displayed screen resolution. Others, in order to accommodate dynamics, include a second memory of this size and toggle between the two. For visible-surface display a dedicated *z*-buffer holding an array of depth values can also be added. In the general-purpose architecture being described here, however, image memory was designed so that it was not dedicated to any specific function. Typical configurations include four times as much memory as can be displayed on the screen at one time—up to $2K \times 2K \times 24$ bits. Additional flexibility was provided by designing in multiple addressing modes. A $1024 \times 1024 \times 8$ memory board can also be addressed as $2048 \times 2048 \times 2$ or as $256K \times 32$, for example.

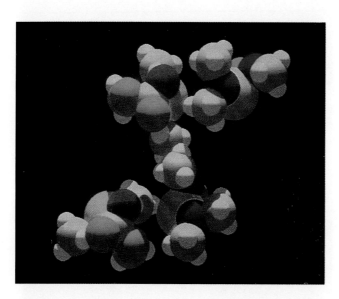

Figure 7. Interactive molecular model display. Intermetrics, Inc. SPHERE 3000 microcode package.

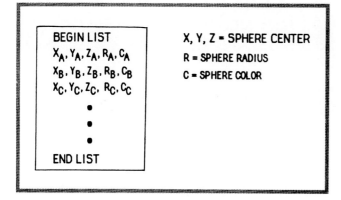

Figure 8. Data structure for molecular model.

Flexible display controller. The end result of any graphics device is an image on a display screen. It is often desirable to tailor the characteristics of the display device (as well as the graphics functions) to the particular application at hand. To accommodate this, the general-purpose system design incorporates a display controller set by software. The following video display characteristics are selectable according to need:

- number of bits per pixel
- pixel bit to lookup table input assignment
- number of pixels per scan line
- number of scan lines per frame
- number of frames per second
- miscellaneous—internal/external sync, video standard (RS170A, RS343, PAL)
- pixel pan, scroll, and zoom

Several examples of applications that use this flexibility to great advantage are included in the following sections.

Applications

The preceding section has focused on the rationale and design decisions made in developing a general-purpose graphics subsystem. This section will concentrate on actual applications and the adaptation of the system's functionality to the particular task at hand.

Basic functions. Almost all applications include the need for basic graphics functions—line drawing, character drawing, polygons, circles, transformations, and the like. A microcode library of these functions was developed for the general-purpose display system, yielding speeds roughly comparable to many contemporary systems but considerably slower than the newest systems with highly optimized hardware. For example, the vector drawing rate is two million pixels per second—about the same as a Raster Technologies 1/380 but one-fifth the speed of an IBM 5080. For the remainder of this discussion, the concentration will be on application-specific functions with adequate interactive performance assumed for these basic functions.

Molecular modeling. A research group at the University of North Carolina originally developed algorithms for the display of space-filling models of molecules.[3] This work was extended and commercialized by Intermetrics, Inc. A microcoded 2½D (flat objects in 3D space) shaded-disk drawing routine and a 3D shaded-sphere drawing routine are the principal features of this work (Figure 7).

Complex molecules can be manipulated at 5-15 updates per second depending on the display quality desired. Thus, performance is gained not just by microcoding a new type of primitive and its associated data structure (Figure 8) but also by trading off image quality for speed in a flexible manner.

Medical imaging. A library of the standard image-processing functions was developed by several users and by Dave Drewry, a member of the author's advanced development group at Adage, Inc. In addition to global area operations like addition and convolution, algorithms requiring local calculations such as adaptive histogram equalization,[4] median filtering, edge detection, and blob detection were developed.

IEEE CG&A

These local operations are difficult if not impossible on standard image-processing machines (and definitely impossible on a limited-purpose graphics machine) but are well-suited to the rapid random-pixel access afforded by the general-purpose processor coupled to a large image memory. The microcoded image-processing operations do not depend on a special-purpose hardware processor operating on entire frames at video rates as in a conventional image-processing system. Thus the general-purpose processor, while slower for simple operations on full images (1/2 second vs. 1/30 second) is faster for more complex operations on small areas.

In addition to these 2D imaging functions, Drewry has also developed routines including display of voxel data[5] and display of arbitrary slices from a 3D data set such as a series of CT slices. In this case the image memory is used to hold z (depth) values along with 2D image data received from the host and used to construct the display (Figure 9). This is a combination of techniques from two normally disparate disciplines—image processing and 3D graphics—made possible by the general-purpose nature of the system. Users at the University of North Carolina[6] and at the University of Texas Health Science Center in Dallas have developed microcoded routines allowing the 3D display of anatomical parts extracted from serial slices of 3D data (Figure 10).[7,8]

Extending this 3D idea even further, Fuchs' group at the University of North Carolina developed custom microcode to drive a vari-focal mirror device for true 3D display.[9] In this case the image memory is used to hold a description of the data and the system's outputs are used to drive the display's x deflection, y deflection, and intensity circuitry instead of the red, green, and blue intensities of a conventional display. Here, three of the advantages of the general-purpose design were called into play—processor, memory, and display controller.

Computer-aided design. For many applications within CAD the basic graphics functions discussed earlier (lines, text, polygons, transformations, etc.) are sufficient. In the area of solid modeling, however, customized display-system functions can have a significant impact on interactivity. Indeed, z-buffer visible surface display has become a standard because of its applicability to the solid modeling task.

Tim Van Hook (also at Adage, Inc.) has developed a number of application-specific microcode functions that increase speed in solid model display tasks dramatically.[10,11] Part of this work has involved supporting friendly data structures. Unlike other systems that require a complete list of vertices making up each polygon to be transferred from the application program to the graphics subsystem, Van Hook also supports mesh and object data structures. A mesh is simply an $M \times N$ array of vertices that are used to define a surface. An object structure consists of one list of all vertices in an object and another list with each polygon defined by a list of pointers to the appropriate vertices.

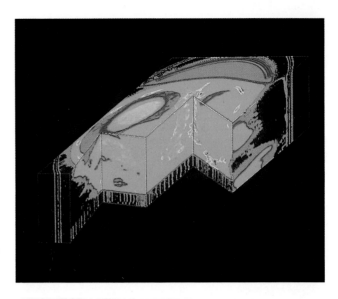

Figure 9. 3D volumetric medical data display. Courtesy Adage, Inc.

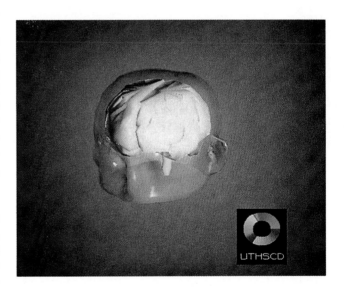

Figure 10. 3D surface medical data display. Courtesy University of Texas Health Science Center Dallas.

Two advantages are gained by this scheme. The first is one of simplicity—the formats match those typically used in an application program and the amount of data communication and computation is eased since no duplication of vertices is necessary. The second advantage is interactive manipulation. If a point in a mesh or object is picked and moved, all polygons that share that point are automatically altered (Figure 11). This cannot be done in a system that deals only with individual polygons.

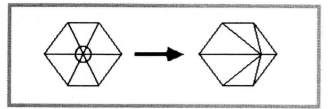

Figure 11. Moving one vertex affects all associated polygons.

This concept is also carried out in other modern display systems (notably Megatek's Merlin) and is extended by the strip and spoke data structures in Tektronix's 412X series.[12]

The second area in which Van Hook has developed display-specific solid model functions involves adding biparametric curved surfaces as display primitives. Since many modelers use B-spline, Bezier, and other patches described in this biparametric manner, it is highly efficient for the graphics device to recognize these as primitives. Van Hook's routines can use the mesh or object data structure for the definition of the control points of these curved surfaces (Figure 12). An adaptive subdivision algorithm is executed in the graphics processor to ensure good surface representation and then standard polygon rendering techniques are used for display.

actually require that normals (or shades) for every vertex be calculated by the application program and not within the graphics device where the task logically belongs. Van Hook has included transparency and antialiasing by using additional portions of image memory to hold information about density and partial pixel coverage, respectively.

Beyond surface descriptions, of course, are true solids as used in constructive solid geometry (CSG) modeling systems. Extending the work of Atherton,[13] Van Hook has microcoded an interactive CSG operator. Operations take place at screen resolution (for speed) and provide images suitable for interactive work. The first application of this local function has been in simulating machine tool operations (NC path verification).[14] Subtraction of a cutting tool from a solid part takes place at 8 to 10 updates per second. Two frames from a milling sequence are shown in Figure 13.

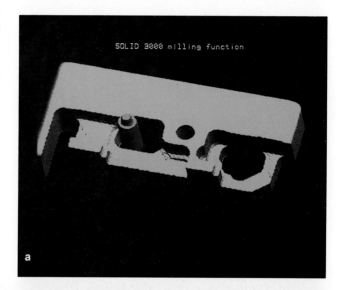

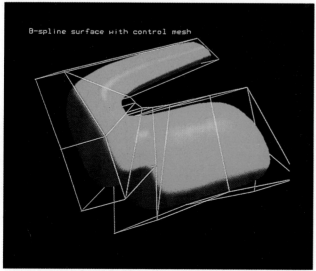

Figure 12. Bicubic B-spline surface with control mesh. Courtesy Adage, Inc.

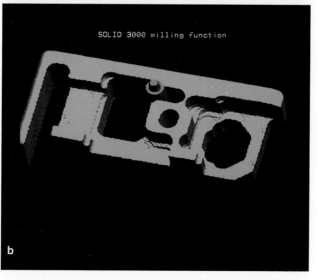

Figure 13. Successive stages in interactive CSG (milling) sequence. Courtesy Adage, Inc.

A final example of usefulness of a CAD-specific function is in an animation-playback technique developed by the author and Van Hook. The purpose is to provide the display of animated sequences (15 frames per second) of images that may take several seconds each to compute. The technique involves relying upon the large image memory and a simple hardware scan-line fill circuit. To prepare the animation, individual frames are rendered from polygonal (or other) descriptions. Each frame is scanned by a micro-coded routine that runs left to right, top to bottom, performing the logical exclusive-or (XOR) of each pixel value with the next. If the result is nonzero, then a change in color has taken place and a word containing the pixel location and XOR values is placed in a buffer (nonvisible portion of image memory). At the end of each frame a special code is inserted into the buffer and a list of frame locations within the buffer is updated. A typical display system has enough memory to buffer over 100 eight-bit images of moderate visual complexity (1000-2000 polygons). If longer sequences are desired, the buffer can be dumped to disk on a host computer.

Once the encoding of an animation sequence is accomplished in the manner described above, playback can begin. The graphics processor now reads the buffer and places the appropriate values into a visible portion of image memory. The on-screen image is formed by using a hardware-parity fill circuit to recreate shaded solid areas. The technique is similar to that used by Ackland and Weste in GUMBI.[15] This is an inexpensive (two SSI chips) and remarkably effective technique. Double buffering is used to create smooth sequences, and playback frame rate and selection of frames is easily provided.

This animation playback technique is useful in the simulation of the kinematics of mechanical parts, robot assembly movement, vehicle dynamics, deformation analysis, and ergonomic studies.

The ability of the general-purpose graphics processor to read the encoded buffer and write the appropriate pixel value rapidly (1-2 microseconds) is crucial to this technique, as is the concept of a large general-purpose image memory—used here to store encoded images. If long animation sequences are required, data can be loaded from the host computer disk at the same time that previously loaded data is being decoded. A transfer rate of about 250K bytes per second is required for typical images (a 15-to-1 reduction over unencoded images) and is achievable by most computers.

Seismic data display. Applications involving the display of seismic data for oil exploration and other such endeavors require specific display formats not easily handled by common graphics functions. The primary format used in seismic interpretation involves the display of wiggle traces (Figure 14). These traces are derived from amplitude, phase, velocity, and other characteristics of the reflected seismic signals acquired in the field and processed by large scientific computers. Almost all wiggle-trace display is now

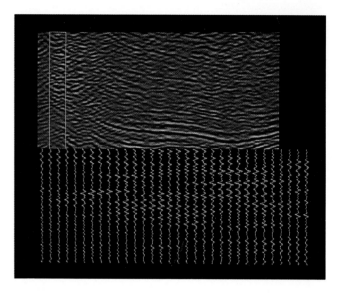

Figure 14. Wiggle-trace display of selected seismic data. Courtesy Adage, Inc.

done by electrostatic plotters, precluding any interactivity. Attempts at display on raster graphics devices have largely failed (except for special-purpose hardware such as that built by AMF Logic Sciences, Inc.) because of the processing time required to convert from the application's natural format of a string of values for each trace to the graphic device's natural format of vectors and polygons.

As part of a package of seismic data display functions developed by Drewry,[16] a fast wiggle-trace drawing algorithm was devised. With this highly application-specific microcoded routine, a wiggle-trace display can be updated in one-fourth of a second rather than the 15-20 seconds that might otherwise be required.

The performance improvement results not so much from any clever algorithm, but from simply performing the work (converting trace values to a raster graphics display) in the natural and proper place—the graphics processor.

Further techniques developed by Drewry in this package provide similar gains in interactivity for other display techniques common in the seismic interpretation industry. Most of these rely upon the manipulation of 2D or 3D data sets as images. Figure 15 shows an example of a common function called horizon flattening, in which data is shifted vertically in each column to flatten a particular seismic "horizon" or layer. Since the shift in each column may be a fraction of a pixel, interpolation is needed for accurate rendering. Again, the key to interactivity is a general-purpose processor with rapid access to pixel values.

Additional functions needed for seismic interpretation are applicable to other 2D and 3D imaging tasks such as medical imaging mentioned earlier. Figure 16 shows a seismic display with arbitrary sections combined in a 3D visible-surface view. This involves texture mapping the array of seismic data onto the appropriate geometric surface and the z-buffer visible-surface display of the resulting faces.

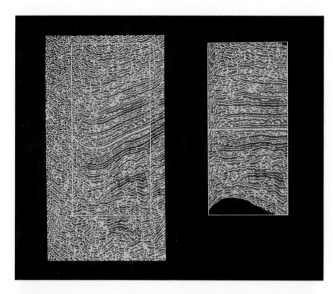

Figure 15. Horizon flattening of seismic section. Courtesy Adage, Inc.

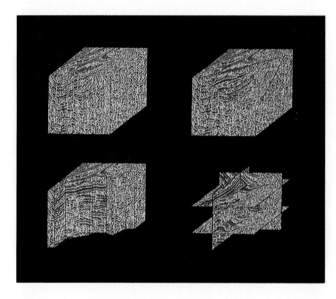

Figure 16. 3D volumetric seismic data display. Courtesy Adage, Inc.

Simulation. The general-purpose processor display system is fast enough for cockpit-instrumentation display in simulator systems. Some of the earliest microcode functions for the processor were developed by Steve Holzworth at Ikonas in response to NASA requirements. A display language, IDL2,[17] was devised to create programs that execute entirely within the microcoded graphics processor. It is important in simulation applications that host computer to graphics subsystem communication be kept at an absolute minimum. In a typical application, the host computer simply updates roll, pitch, and yaw angles, and all the rest of the computation is carried out in the graphics device.

Several hardware modules were developed to speed display generation in simulation applications. A fast transformation unit (280,000 points per second in perspective) and a fast polygon/symbol generator (20-30 million pixels per second) were designed as additional, separately microprogrammed units. In keeping with the modular design concept, these devices provide no functions that cannot be provided by the general-purpose processor, but they are able to off-load the tasks into specialized and optimized processors. Holzworth extended his previous work to include a fast polygon sort for visible-surface display and to take full advantage of the additional processor units. An example from the Research Triangle Institute of work done for NASA[19,20] is shown in Figure 17. The scene in this figure can be updated at 15 frames per second.

The value of the programmability of the transformation hardware developed for the simulation application was demonstrated by Whitton,[18] who wrote transformation-processor microcode for the evaluation of points on B-spline surfaces. Some additional work performed by the author's group at Adage includes the development of a floating-point transformation unit for evaluation of polynomials for curved-surface terrain and the development of fast display techniques for terrain defined by grids or quadtrees. Again, the value of using a general-purpose processor to perform application-specific functions was proven with better performance.

Application-specific functions for radar display were developed by John Lutz at the National Center for Atmospheric Research (NCAR). Radar data is gathered as intensity data at different distances along a radial from the radar site. To display this data on a raster screen, conversion must be made from polar to Cartesian coordinates and the pixels then written. Lutz microcoded this process to achieve interactive radar display without having to resort to special-purpose hardware that might otherwise be required. His work is being adapted by several others for the simulation of airborne radar displays. These displays typically operate at nonstandard display rates, 825 lines per frame, making use of the system's flexible display controller.

High-quality images. Two basic techniques are used for high-quality images—2D painting and 3D rendering. For 2D painting systems a number of users have microcoded brush, filter, and matting (image-blending) functions.[21-23] Here the graphics processor's high-speed random access to pixels throughout image memory (off-screen and on) plays a key roll. Some users also take advantage of the 2K × 2K image memory for production of very high-resolution images for film. For standard United States (525-line, 30-Hz) or European (625-line, 25-Hz) video, the flexible display controller provides gen-lock capability crucial to this application area.

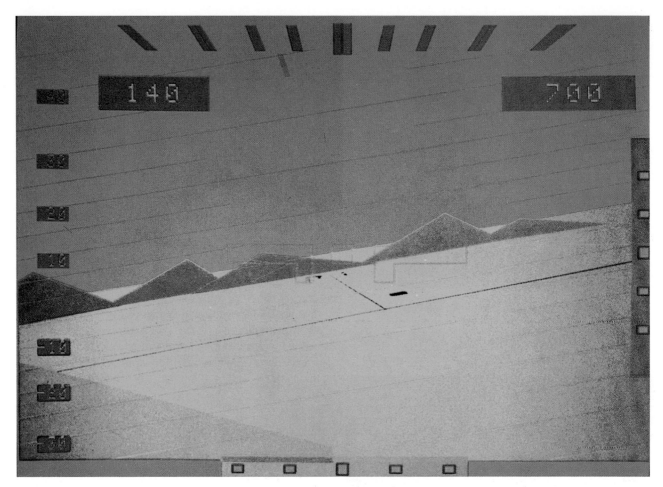

Figure 17. Real-time cockpit display. Courtesy Research Triangle Institute.

For 3D rendering a number of users have programmed polygonal or curved-surface display algorithms to speed up production work. In addition, Van Hook has developed a fast ray-tracing microcoded algorithm incorporating anti-aliasing, refraction, and reflection effects (Figure 18), and a stochastic surface ("fractal") generation routine. A special-purpose plug-in module for stochastic surface generation was constructed at the University of Toronto for near real-time operation.[24]

Summary

Experience with a graphics subsystem designed to be flexible and general purpose in nature has shown that the concept of application-specific graphics functions can lead to significant improvements in interactivity. A high-performance design can provide adequate performance in a wide range of tasks.

While higher interactivity can be gained from special-purpose processors designed for a limited set of tasks, it is important to recognize that any advantage these devices have can quickly be negated by the demands of particular applications. ■

Figure 18. Ray-traced rendering of PDA PATRAN data. Courtesy Adage, Inc.

Acknowledgments

My thanks to Ikonas cofounder Mary Whitton for her

January 1986

work and comments on this article, to Dave Drewry and Tim Van Hook for their innovative work, and to the employees and customers of Ikonas (and later Adage) who made it possible for this concept to be tested.

References

1. N. England, "A System for Interactive Modeling of Physical Curved Surface Objects," *Computer Graphics,* Vol. 12, No. 3, Aug. 1978, pp.336-340.

2. N. England, "Advanced Architectures for Graphics and Image Processing," *Proc. SPIE,* Vol. 301, Aug. 1981, pp.54-57.

3. M.E. Pique, "Fast 3D Display of Space-Filling Molecular Models," technical report 83-004, Dept. of Computer Science, University of North Carolina, Chapel Hill, N.C., 1983.

4. S.M. Pizer, J.B. Zimmerman, and E.V. Staab, "Adaptive Grey Level Assignment in CT Scan Display," *Journal of Computer Assisted Tomography,* Vol. 8, No. 2, Apr. 1984, pp.300-305.

5. G. Frieder, D. Gordon, and R.A. Reynolds, "Back-to-Front Display of Voxel-Based Objects," *IEEE Computer Graphics and Applications,* Vol. 5, No. 1, Jan. 1985, pp.52-60.

6. H. Fuchs, G.D. Abram, and E.D. Grant, "Near Real-Time Shaded Display of Rigid Objects," *Computer Graphics,* Vol. 17, No. 3, July 1983, pp.65-72.

7. G.B. Latamore, "Creating 3D Models for Medical Research," *Computer Graphics World,* Vol. 6, No. 5, May 1983, pp.31-38.

8. "Brain and Heart Analysis Using a Microcomputer," *Electronic Imaging,* Vol. 2, No. 6, June 1983, pp.26-32.

9. H. Fuchs, S.M. Pizer, L.C. Tsai, and S.H. Bloomberg, and E.R. Heinz, "Adding a True 3D Display to a Raster Graphics System," *IEEE Computer Graphics and Applications,* Vol. 2, No. 5, Sept. 1982, pp.73-78.

10. T. Van Hook, "Advanced Techniques for Solid Modeling," *Computer Graphics World,* Vol. 7, No. 11, Nov. 1984, pp.45-54.

11. Adage, Inc., *SOLID 3000 Programming Reference Manual,* Adage, Inc., Billerica, Mass., 1985.

12. Tektronix, Inc., *4110/4120 Series Command Reference Manual,* Tektronix, Inc., Beaverton, Ore., 1985.

13. P.R. Atherton, "A Scan-line Hidden Surface Removal Procedure for Constructive Solid Geometry," *Computer Graphics,* July 1983, Vol. 17, No. 3, pp.73-82.

14. T. Van Hook, "Real-Time Shaded NC Milling Display," in review, May 1985.

15. B. Ackland and N. Weste, "Real Time Animation Playback on a Frame Store Display System," *Computer Graphics,* Vol. 14, No. 3, July 1980, pp.182-188.

16. Adage, Inc., *SEISMIC 3000 Programming Reference Manual,* Adage, Inc. Billerica, Mass., 1984.

17. Adage, Inc., *IDL2 Programming Reference Manual,* Adage, Inc., Billerica, Mass., 1983.

18. M.C. Whitton, "Special Purpose Hardware for the Display of Free Form Surfaces," master's thesis, Dept. of Electrical and Computer Engineering, North Carolina State University, Raleigh, N.C., Dec. 1984.

19. R.J. Montoya, J.N. England, J.J. Hatfield, and S.A. Rajala, "An Advanced Programmable/Reconfigurable Color Graphics Display System for Crew Station Technology Research," paper no. 81-2314, AIAA/IEEE Digital Avionics Systems Conference, St. Louis, Mo., Nov. 1981.

20. R.J. Montoya, H.H. Lane, T.L. Turner, and J.J. Hatfield, "The Application of a Color Raster Scan Programmable Display Generator in the Generation of Multiple Cockpit Display Formats," paper no. 83-157, AIAA/IEEE Digital Avionics Systems Conference, Seattle, Wash., Oct. 1983, pp.83-157.

21. K.S. Booth, and S.A. MacKay, "Techniques for Frame Buffer Animation," *Proc. Graphics Interface '82,* Toronto, Ont., May 1982, pp.213-220.

22. T.F. Klimek and H.E. Towles, "The Computer Controlled Frame Buffer as a Production Tool," *SMPTE Video Pictures of the Future,* Feb. 1983, pp.126-135.

23. J. Paine, "The Making of Superman III—Pixel by Pixel," *IEEE Computer Graphics and Applications,* Vol. 3, No. 9, Sept. 1983, pp.7-10.

24. T.S. Piper, and A. Fournier, "A Hardware Stochastic Interpolator for Raster Displays," *Computer Graphics,* Vol. 18, No. 3, July 1984, pp.83-91.

Nick England is a computer graphics consultant with Whitland Associates in Raleigh, North Carolina. Until recently he was Vice President of Graphics Terminals for Adage, Inc., where he led a group developing high-performance interactive graphics and imaging hardware and software. He was a founder and President of Ikonas Graphics Systems from 1978 until its acquisition by Adage in 1982. His technical experience and interests include 3D graphics system architecture, real-time display techniques, image processing, and high-quality synthetic image generation.

England received degrees in electrical engineering from North Carolina State University in 1969 and 1974 and was with the Computer Graphics Laboratory there from 1972 until 1978. He is a member of IEEE and SIGGRAPH. England can be contacted at Whitland Associates, PO Box 10351, Raleigh, NC 27605.

Innovative concepts in hardware architecture and data structure enable graphics processing at a speed about five times that of conventional raster-scan devices.

Reprinted from *IEEE Computer Graphics and Applications,* Volume 4, Number 5, May 1984, pages 46-58. Copyright © 1984 by The Institute of Electrical and Electronics Engineers, Inc.

High-Speed Techniques
for
a 3-D Color Graphics Terminal

Tsuneo Ikedo

Seillac Co., Ltd.

Since the early 1960's, when Ivan Sutherland demonstrated with his Sketchpad programs that a CRT display screen could be a tool for the design of manufactured objects, the graphics display terminal has undergone remarkable development as a result of the rapid progress of LSI and monitor technology. Formerly functioning only as monitors, display terminals now have high-level local intelligence, as well as hardware and data structures, to enable complex functions and high-speed processing. Graphics display technology has evolved as well, from the random-stroke DVST display to the high-performance color raster-scan CRT. A trend toward the workstation with its own general-purpose processor has also become apparent.

The raster-scan terminal offers both a flicker-free display with a great number of colors and the ability to handle a large volume of data. The raster-scan terminal, however, presents numerous technical problems for high-speed display. These problems include polygon filling, color shading, surface generation, line smoothing, DDA (digital differential analyzer) speed, and the speed of writing into the frame buffer.

Techniques employed in the Seillac-7 Three-Dimensional Real-time Color Display Station were developed to solve these problems. The Seillac-7 achieves a processing speed approximately five times that of conventional raster-scan devices through several innovations:

- independently structured channel processor, display processor, I/O device controller, and pipeline coordinate transformation processor, according to function;
- hierarchically structured display files;
- local implementation of color-shading and line-smoothing operations;
- frame buffer structure designed for ultra-high-speed read/write operations.

High-speed displays

Raster-scan terminals have features unavailable in conventional random-stroke devices: They are flicker-free, can handle large volumes of data, and are capable of highly intelligent functions, such as polygon filling, color control, bit mapping, and the easy editing of hierarchically structured display files. But compared with terminals that simply monitor data from the host computer, intelligent terminals pose a major obstacle to high-speed processing.

One problem occurs in the interactive editing of images taken from hierarchically structured display files (using a tablet, dial controls, or other input device). This kind of processing is especially difficult to implement through random logic hardware techniques, so a general-purpose microcomputer (such as a display processor) is usually used. As a result, the processor's speed is the major determinant of system throughput for most display terminals. Other factors determining display speed include

- channel processing (the speed of data transmission and communication protocol processing between the host computer and the terminal);
- file management processing in the display processor;
- 2-D/3-D coordinate transformation (modeling and viewing, clipping, perspective projection, polygon filling);
- DDA operation;
- frame buffer read/write operations;
- video conversion.

The highest priority for design engineers is to maintain an equal speed among these functions during processing. The display terminal processes the functions—from data reception to image display—in a relatively sequential manner. So it is possible to modularize them into individual units and link them into a pipeline configuration for sequential processing. The system throughput will naturally be restricted by the pipeline section performing at the slowest speed.

Figure 1 shows the system architecture of a raster-scan display terminal similar to the Seillac-7. With the exception of the file buffer (frame buffer), high-density mounting of these units is achieved with six multilayered printed circuit boards. This diagram illustrates the largest possible configuration for a terminal device.

Display processing in the hardware is distributed according to function (channel management, file management, coordinate transformations, etc.) into the following 11 modules:

- channel processor;
- display processor;
- coordinate transformation processor (4×4 matrix multiplier, clipping circuit, perspective transformation circuit);

- curve generation processor (3-D polygon generator, display command analyzer);
- filling processor;
- 3-D vector generator (with brightness modulation line-smoothing circuit);
- color-shading processor;
- frame buffer and color matrix circuit;
- bit-map controller;
- color CRT monitor with 120-MHz video bandwidth, 60-Hz noninterlaced;
- input devices.

High-speed buses are used in both the display processor and in linking the hardware units for pipeline processing. For increased speed, the raster-scan display terminal shown in Figure 1 includes the following hardware:

- two 16-bit microcomputers,
- a 32-bit bit-slice processor,

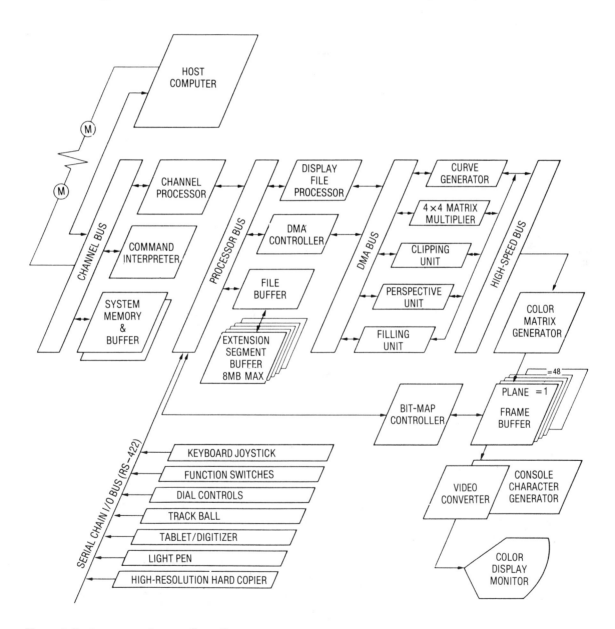

Figure 1. Raster-scan system configuration.

May 1984

- two 16-bit bit-slice processors,
- a bit-map processor,
- an 8-bit microcomputer,
- a 4×4 matrix multiplier,
- 50 Seillac custom LSI circuits.

Each of these components is part of the pipeline configuration and has a uniform processing speed to maintain a balanced processing flow.

As shown by the functional block diagram in Figure 2, Seillac-7's many functions are comparable to those of a workstation. They are processed at high speeds by the pipeline architecture.

Display processing modes

Several types of display modes support the terminal's various applications. The console mode enables Seillac-7 to function as a console terminal for character display. Two graphics modes common to display terminals are the retained mode, which permits local file storage and coordinate transformations, and the temporary mode for direct image display without file storage. To attain high-speed display, Seillac developed a new type of temporary mode for current modeling and viewing transformations. The menu function has a high-speed transmission route separate from the pipeline architecture and a separate frame buffer for rapid processing of character strings appearing in the menu as prompts for interactive operations.

With a separate mode for each graphics function, raster-scan displays can be as fast as random-stroke displays. The Seillac-7 employs four graphics modes: through, temporary, retained, and bit map. The internal processing of each mode is diagrammed in Figures 3 to 6.

Through mode. The through mode simply shows images without any coordinate transformations or clipping; therefore, image coordinates are defined within the screen volume (i.e., in screen coordinates). All output images and their attributes (excluding coordinate transformation data) remain active, with a writing speed approximately four times faster than otherwise. When the through mode is specified, graphic images are stored in the file buffer. Figure 3 shows the processing flow in the through mode.

Processing in the through mode is most effective for simple monitoring functions. This mode achieves the fastest system throughput.

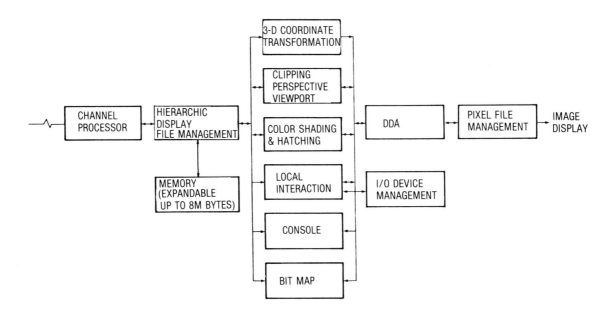

Figure 2. Functional diagram of the pipeline architecture.

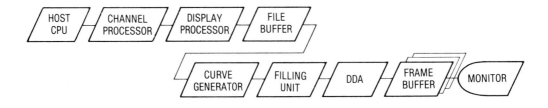

Figure 3. Processing in the through mode.

IEEE CG&A

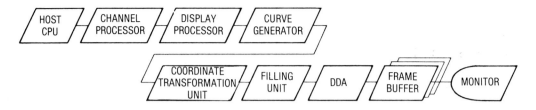

Figure 4. Processing in the temporary mode.

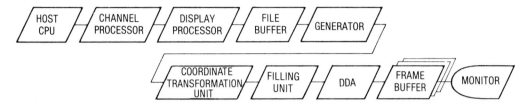

Figure 5. Processing in the retained mode.

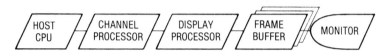

Figure 6. Processing in the bit map mode.

Temporary mode. The temporary mode performs the functions defined by the Siggraph Core system[1] for temporary segments. This mode displays information from the host computer without storing it at the terminal. Since the volume of data to be displayed does not depend upon the capacity of the file buffer, the temporary mode is suitable for the display of large-volume images that do not require any manipulation. Figure 4 shows the processing flow in the temporary mode.

Seillac-7's temporary mode is an expanded version of that described by the Core standard. Since its configuration enables locally specified coordinate transformations, primitives can be defined in the world coordinate system.

Retained mode. The retained mode performs the functions defined by the Core and the GKS[2] standards with respect to retained segments, storing display files and displaying images from these files. The retained mode is used for interactive operations such as coordinate transformations and the attribute control of segments. Figure 5 shows the processing flow in the retained mode, which provides the highest level flow of data processing for interactive operations.

Bit map mode. This mode is used for direct manipulation of pixel data. The data from the host computer are stored in the frame buffer directly by the display processor and are not processed by the file buffer, the function generator, the coordinate transformation unit, or the DDA. Data in the frame buffer can be read back directly. During operation in the bit map mode (as in the temporary mode), pixel data are not stored in the file buffer. As shown in Figure 6, the frame buffer interfaces directly with the display processor.

The block diagram in Figure 7 shows the data-processing relationship of the various modes. The ability to select a display mode for a specific application contributes to high-speed display capability.

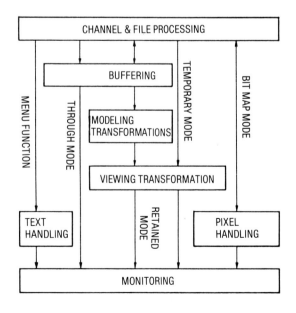

Figure 7. Data processing according to mode.

Hierarchical display file structures

For some applications, high-speed operations greatly depend on the structure of the display files as well as the hardware configuration.

Although the Core and GKS standards offer the concepts of segments and IDs (identifiers) for forming display files (commands) at the terminal, the local manipulation of hierarchically structured images (such as the simulation of a multijointed robot) cannot be performed using only the image units of segment and ID. Because the changes in the dynamic attributes of such images require calculation in the host computer, image display speed at the terminal would normally be very slow.

For this reason, the Seillac-7 incorporates a new concept for the structure of display files (Figure 8). This hierarchical display file structure is defined by four levels of image units and is capable of subroutine nesting of segments up to 18 levels (not shown in the diagram). Display effects can be enhanced by altering the dynamic attributes.

As shown in Figure 8, there are two kinds of display files: image files and viewing files. In the image file, management is performed for hierarchically structured images composed of output primitives, classes, segments, elements, and IDs. The image file also manages attributes, control data, and modeling transformation parameters (various coordinate transformation parameters, nesting data, etc.) required for assembling the image units in the world coordinate system.

In the viewing file, management is performed for data related to viewing transformations (from the world coordinate system to the normalized device coordinate system to the screen coordinate system).

Features of the image file. The features constituting the hierarchical data structure of the image file are primitives, IDs, elements, segments, and classes.

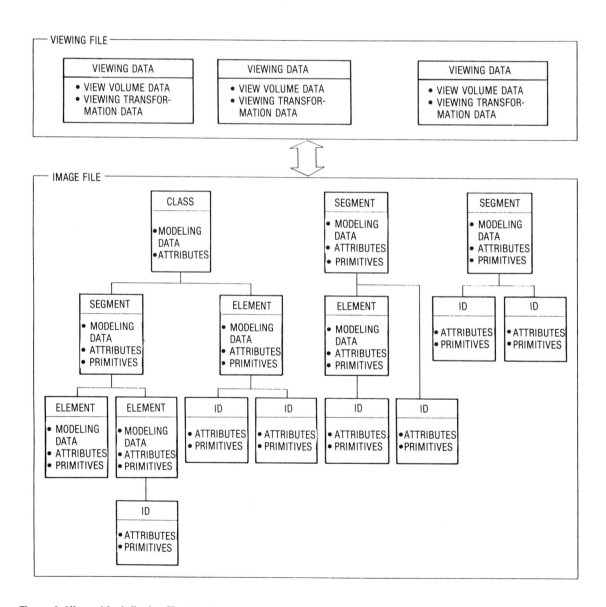

Figure 8. Hierarchical display file structure.

Primitives. A primitive is the lowest level image unit used to describe an image; the category includes output primitives and basic attributes. Primitives are defined by two- or three-dimensional parameters.

IDs. An ID is an identifier attached to an individual primitive or a group of primitives. When an ID is picked during interactive image manipulation, the Seillac-7 returns the number of the picked ID to the host computer. Thus, an application program can access the database, update data, or perform other data processing functions by means of the ID number. An ID has the attribute of highlighting.

Elements. An element is an image unit consisting of one or more IDs and/or primitives. An element is picked like an ID and is capable of both viewing transformations and modeling transformation/translation.

The translation of an element obeys a different algorithm from that of a segment. Defining an image as an element makes translation approximately 20 times faster than that of an image defined as a segment. This high-speed processing is appropriate in a CAD system for VLSI circuits, an application in which the layout can be obtained only by translations of large volumes of data in the database.

An element can be rotated with respect to any axis of the coordinate system of a segment that contains the element. An element has the attributes of highlighting and detectability.

Segments. A segment consists of one or more primitives, IDs, and/or elements and is capable of modeling transformations (scaling, rotation, and translation), segment nesting up to 18 levels, and viewing transformations. Scaling, rotation, and translation are performed in the sequence listed above. These modeling transformations of segments, together with those of classes and elements, can be used to increase the effectiveness of interactive image manipulation and various types of simulation.

Classes. A class consists of one or more segments, elements, IDs, and/or primitives. A class is capable of modeling transformations (rotation; translation for left and right matrix concatenations) and viewing transformations. The class modeling transformations are particularly useful when one or more segments constituting the class are to be rotated with respect to an arbitrary pivot in the world coordinate system. Classes have the attributes of highlighting, detectability, and visibility.

Features of the viewing file. Within a viewing file, the data for a maximum of 32 viewing transformations can be registered (Figure 9).

Viewing information consists of the definition of parameters for a window (2-D) or a view volume (3-D). Parameters are also defined for the mapping of a viewport in the normalized device coordinate space, as well as such viewing members as class, segment, element, etc., to which viewing transformations are applied.

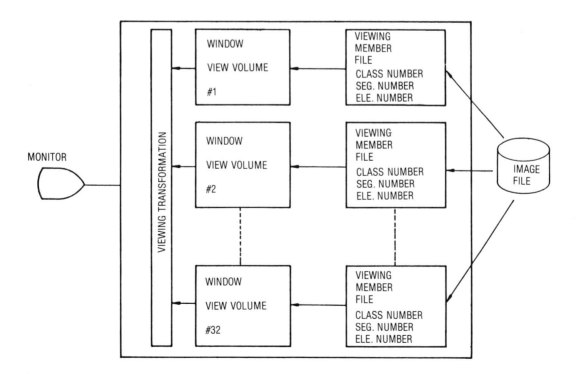

Figure 9. Structure of viewing file.

The role and limitations of the display processor

Most display processors employ either a 16-bit general-purpose microcomputer or a 32-bit bit-slice processor. Because of the relative ease of firmware design, a general-purpose computer is often used to provide the highly intelligent functions found in most raster-scan terminals (including the hierarchical structure of display files, coordinate transformations, filling, and parametric operations of quadratic functions).

Even if a 10-MHz microcomputer were employed, it would be difficult to achieve high-speed display when parameters are used to analyze the display commands, perform coordinate transformations, and generate vector data.

The Seillac-7's display processor is responsible only for file management and the processing of interactive operations. In contrast to the processing of coordinate transformations, the processing speeds of these two functions rely on either communication with the host computer or human interaction at the terminal. Thus, a microcomputer is fast enough for use as the display processor. Figure 10 shows a block diagram of the following file management functions:

- registration management (registration of files, addition and deletion of files);
- interaction management (search and detection of files, control and modification of dynamic attributes, I/O control);
- DMA management (processing of files).

Because the display processor handles only the functions shown in the diagram, its processing speed can be relatively moderate, and a general-purpose microcomputer can be used.

The pipeline architecture and command format

The execution of all modeling transformations, viewing transformations, and curve generation without the use of the display processor requires a systematically designed

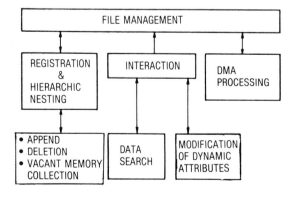

Figure 10. Block diagram of file management functions.

display command set suited to sequential pipeline processing.

To achieve the highest possible speed from file buffer to screen display, the display processor begins by analyzing commands. The pertinent command parameters are then converted to vector data for move/draw operations, and the vector data are stored in a file buffer. Next, the vector data are read by DMA processing, and only image transformations are applied.

Using hardware to perform the image transformations permits extremely high display speeds for simple operations like rewriting, zooming, and panning. This method is occasionally used in random-stroke displays.

Some of the literature (see Newman and Sproull,[3] for example) describes an architecture that focuses on the filling of vector data and the processing of coordinate transformations. This would be a simple problem if most output primitives in the display files were formed by polylines or polygons. However, as performance levels of display terminals rise, the data required for filling, color shading, and hierarchical modeling transformations (as well as the subroutine call procedures) grow increasingly complex and cannot all be readily converted to vector data at the input port of the pipeline. Consequently, the routing of data to their appropriate places in the pipeline and their assignment for processing become significant issues. An effective display command structure is the key to obtaining a uniform processing speed throughout the pipeline.

With the Seillac-7, the format of the data transmitted from the file buffer by DMA processing is practically identical to that sent from the host computer (in the case of integer representation). Both the analysis of commands and their conversion to vector data are accomplished during the course of the pipeline processing so that the vector data are generated in stages instead of in one concentrated operation. This pipeline processing is shown in Figure 11.

Figure 12 illustrates an example of the filling process for a three-dimensional surface that is part of a polyhedron. As shown in the diagram, the selective assignment of the processing of primitives and attributes to various parts of the pipeline results in the most efficient flow of data. A surface polygon (within a display file sent from the host computer) consists of a sequence of polygon vertices and matrix elements for normal vector generation.

The curve generator breaks down the polygon vertices into draw vectors. It uses the matrix parameters to generate matrix control commands, unit vectors, and a 4×4 matrix. The processing times for these operations are 0.7 μs per vector and 3 μs per matrix.

The matrix and vectors are concatenated by the matrix multiplier unit. Matrix calculation is then executed for the modeling and viewing transformation of the polygon. The filling unit receives both the sequence of vectors processed by the clipping/perspective unit, and the normal vector transmitted through the curve generator and the matrix multiplier. The filling unit executes filling of the surface by using the sequence of vectors as the data of the polygon vertices, based on the sign value of the normal vector. The total process, from matrix and vector generation until determination of the normal vector sign, is executed at 2.5 μs to 3 μs per vector. These speeds are more than 100 times faster than those achieved by the use of a microcomputer and over 20 times faster than those achieved by a bit-slice processor.

The pipeline facilitates effective processing by keeping to a minimum the variance in calculation times at each pipeline unit, according to the type of data being processed. This requires an architectural design that ensures an even distribution of processing to all units and an even flow of data.

The Seillac-7 is designed to minimize waiting intervals through the use of FIFO circuitry. Its curve generator contains a 4K-word cache memory, and the high-speed input to the matrix multiplier and filling unit are managed by 512-word and 64-word FIFO circuits, respectively. This design helps avoid temporary idle states during the DMA data transmission from the file buffer to the function generator. It also prevents a decline in throughput resulting from large time variances in calculation processing at the various pipeline units.

Because this pipeline architecture has been fixed by hardware, a problem can arise in the generation of a curve based on the parameters of a quadratic function: as the resolution of the curve is increased, more processing time is required.

Consider, for example, a circle with the current beam position as its center, to be drawn by providing the radius value. Because the optimum number of circle angles (resolution) is the minimum number required to smoothly draw the circle, this minimum value should be selected according to the radius value as expressed in screen coordinates. But especially in cases where the size of the circle is to be locally changed by zooming interactions within the matrix multiplier, the radius cannot be read in advance as a screen coordinate value during initial processing in the curve generator. Thus, it is most common to set the number of angles for the circle to its maximum value.

In the Seillac-7, a test value is passed through the pipeline for each segment, to determine the proper scaling value. The function generator references that value to generate a circle with the optimum number of angles.

As described in this section, the data stream constraints characteristic of the pipeline are contained in vector data obtained from the display files. The problem of selecting a

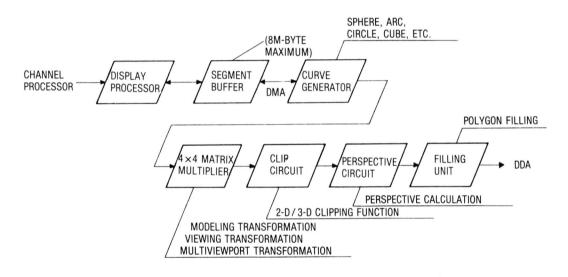

Figure 11. Pipeline processing diagram.

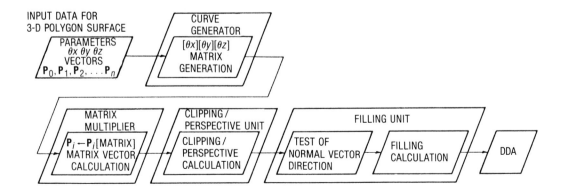

Figure 12. Filling process for a 3-D polygon surface.

method to process data (such as the above-mentioned quadratic function) without slowing down the pipeline speed has an immense influence on performance. This problem is one of the reasons why the speed values listed in the catalogs of many conventional display terminals differ so widely from the actual speeds.

High-speed DDA

After pipeline processing, vector data assume screen coordinate values and are then applied to the digital differential analyzer, where vector generation is performed.

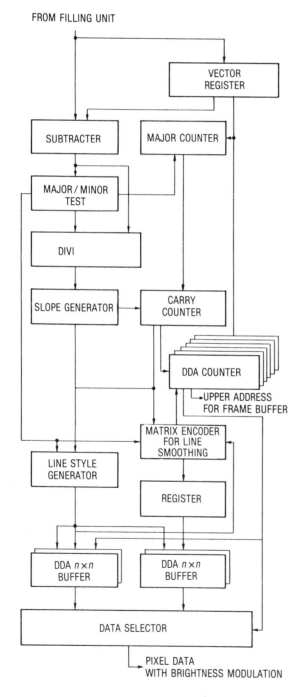

FROM FILLING UNIT

Figure 13. The DDA circuit.

Figure 13 illustrates the processing flow of the DDA circuits used in the Seillac-7.

The DDA, consisting of ECL LSI circuits, contains a line-smoothing (antialiasing) function. In a raster-scan display ''jaggies'' occur at slanting lines. Such lines can be displayed smoothly by means of a method that modulates the relative brightness values of multiple pixels. In the Seillac-7, brightness values are assigned by hardware in the DDA so that line quality approaches the level of random-stroke displays. One of the LSI circuits calculates the slope and data used for brightness modulation. The two additional LSIs constitute a dual DDA buffer system, for temporarily storing the basic and compensatory dots of the vector for which brightness modulation is to be performed, and a frame buffer interface.

The DDA performs calculations at the rate of eight nanoseconds in the brightness modulation section and 36 nanoseconds in the DDA counter section. So the brightness value for a given point is determined (within 36 ns) by applying three types of data to a matrix encoder: the slope data of the vector, the counter value that generates the overflow indication to be output from the fractional part of the DDA, and the previously generated compensatory data used for brightness modulation.

The data output from the DDA are first stored in a buffer that has a sequential $n \times n$ two-dimensional array structure. These data are then written into a frame buffer at a constant cycle. This presents a crucial problem: to transmit the data to the frame buffer at a rate faster than that of DDA operation, so that the DDA is not forced to wait.

As a solution, we installed a DDA buffer capable of high-speed write operations between the DDA circuit and frame buffer: when the incoming data overflow the DDA buffer capacity during a cycle, those data are written into the frame buffer. Although the DDA will not fall into wait states if the DDA buffer capacity is sufficiently large, the size of the buffer is restricted by both hardware cost and configuration.

High-speed writing circuitry

Because the data from the DDA buffer are simultaneously written into the frame buffer, the frame buffer is divided into n multiple blocks (Figure 14). Each block consists of n RAMs. With the DDA buffer's $n \times n$ configuration, n^2 output lines can be directly connected to each of the RAMs.

As shown in the diagram, the frame buffer is split up into a number of blocks corresponding to the number of y-axis buffers in the DDA buffer's two-dimensional array. But when the data from the frame buffer are to be output, they are read out serially as a sequence of data in the direction of the raster scanning.

If we consider that one block of the frame buffer consists of n RAMs, the values of the respective blocks are read out separately from the serial data of n raster lines. When these serial data are to be used as video signals, the serial data of only one raster line will be valid. Thus, if the speed of a video signal is t, the cycle time for reading from the frame buffer is nt. With an actual 60-Hz noninterlaced frame buffer (t is approximately 10 ns) with $1280 \times$ 1024-pixel resolution, n is approximately five ($nt = 50$ ns). The use of currently existing RAMs does not permit cycle times that approach access time, not even when static RAMs are used. The present solution is to design a circuit with separate routes for data output by the DDA buffer to the frame buffers. This is done according to the upper address of the DDA counter value.

The frame-buffer structure shown in Figure 15 permits both random writing and reading in the direction of raster

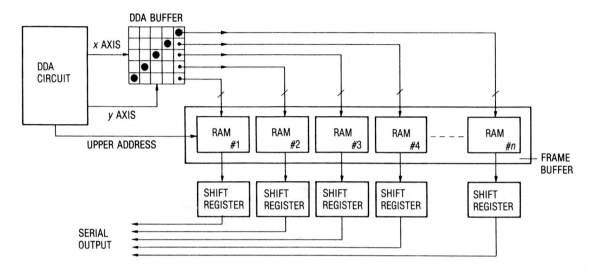

Figure 14. The DDA buffer interface.

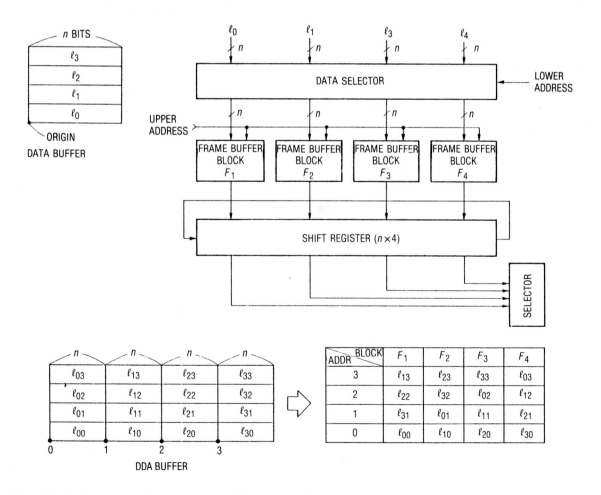

Figure 15. Block correspondence structure of the frame buffer.

scanning. As a result, writing operations are four times faster than conventional sequential writing methods.

The output data from the DDA are written sequentially into the DDA buffer, which consists of four layers (corresponding to the four raster lines of the screen) with n bits per layer. These vector data pass through the data selector and are allocated to specific blocks of the frame buffer. However, block allocation is determined by the coordinates of the origin of the DDA buffer—i.e., the upper address of the DDA counter value. The data at each level of the DDA buffer are then written into corresponding blocks 1 through 4, as shown in Figure 15.

This method of data allocation permits the data stored in all frame buffers to be read out collectively to the shift registers through the use of the same read address. The reading cycle of the frame buffers thus becomes $n \times 4$ and can be expanded fourfold.

The DDA buffer is the interface circuit for the frame buffer cycle time and the DDA speed. If the writing rates for these two speeds can be made to match, the DDA can perform calculation continuously with no wait intervals. To achieve this, the DDA buffer requires a dual structure.

The z-axis DDA and shading

For a three-dimensional DDA, the x and y axes correspond to the horizontal and vertical addresses of the screen. The z axis is used for either wireframe depth cueing or the shading of polygons where the distribution of brightness values changes linearly along the z axis.

High-speed processing becomes a problem for triple-axis DDAs where the length of the major axis determines the calculation time (as with x-y DDAs): display speed declines in proportion to the length of the z axis. This reduction in speed occurs even when the x-y segment on the screen consists of only a small number of dots.

For this reason, the longer of the x and y axes is compared with the length of the z axis. The z-axis DDA then adds the quotient $z/(x$ or y, whichever is longer) to either the integer or a fractional part of the DDA in accordance with the resulting value. The z-axis dot sequence is thus calculated.

By this method, the time required for DDA calculation is determined by the value of the major axis (x or y); therefore, the triple-axis DDA performs calculation at a speed equal to that of an x-y DDA.

Figure 16 shows the relationship between the z-axis DDA and color data. With a hardware configuration similar to that of the diagram, the DDA speed is 36 ns per pixel; the speed of writing pixel arrays into the frame buffer can also reach 36 ns per pixel.

The red, green, and blue video signals are generated by division processing of the respective matrices of the output data of the z-axis DDA, the RGB data, and the brightness modulation data.

Evaluation

Today's three-dimensional color graphics display devices face a diverse range of demands, from simple monitoring functions to complex functions requiring high-speed feedback processing—that is, functions that cannot be readily handled by conventional pipeline processing. To satisfy these demands without sacrificing overall system throughput, Seillac developed new methods for coordinate transformation, parametric curve generation, and manipulation of primitive attributes. Thus, the Seillac-7 has achieved one of the fastest overall execution speeds of today's raster terminals.

Many users have been disappointed with the slow speed of raster-scan displays, a result of both the frame buffer speed and the cycle time of the microprocessor. But cur-

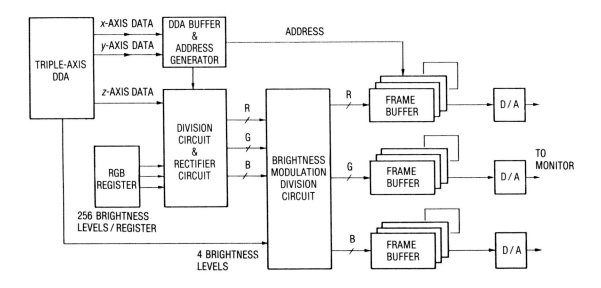

Figure 16. Relationship between z-axis data and color data.

rent LSI technology has speeded individual functions, such as filling, pixel writing, and coordinate transformations.

The Seillac-7's central focus on overall processing has introduced an innovative concept of data structure, with new coordinate transformation algorithms and hardware units.

During a trial manufacturing period, we recorded the Seillac-7's main characteristics, listed in Table 1. These values include the total I/O processing time of the pipeline interface.

Figure 17 shows a printed-circuit board mounted with the pipeline circuit used in the trial manufacture of the Seillac-7. On the frame-buffer PCB, shown in Figure 18, high-density mounting of eight frame buffers (2000 × 1024 pixels each) enables high-speed buffering at the DDA interface through the use of eight independently developed CMOS LSIs. Figure 19 shows the internal structure of the display terminal, configured in a compact desktop unit.

The future of display technology

The advantage of the raster-scan terminal is its capability of combined display of wireframes and solid polygons. Developing the technology to generate wireframes has

Figure 17. PCB for pipeline circuit.

Figure 18. PCB for frame buffer.

**Table 1.
Seillac-7 processing speeds.**

CHANNEL SPEED	UP TO 1M bps
SEGMENT REGISTRATION TIME	150 μs / SEGMENT
DMA TRANSMISSION TIME	0.7 - 0.9 μs / VECTOR
FUNCTION GENERATION UNIT— DECODING TIME (LINE, POLYLINE, POLYGON)	1.2 - 1.8 μs / VECTOR
4 × 4 MATRIX MULTIPLIER	APPROX. 15 μs
VECTOR · MATRIX MULTIPLIER [1]	2 - 4 μs (1.2 μs [2])
CLIPPING	3 - 4 μs (0.7μs [3])
THROUGH MODE	500,000 TYPICAL (2.5-mm) SHORT VECTORS / s
RETAINED MODE	200,000 TYPICAL (2.5-mm) SHORT VECTORS / s 25,000 TYPICAL (200-mm) LONG VECTORS / s
TEMPORARY MODE	SAME AS RETAINED MODE
RECTANGULAR FILLING	50,000 (8 × 8-PIXEL) RECTANGLES / s
DDA SPEED	36 ns / PIXEL
LINE-SMOOTHING CALCULATION	36ns / 2 PIXELS
VIDEO SIGNALS	8 ns / DOT

[1]CAN BE INCREASED 50% WITH FAST SCHOTTSKY ELEMENTS.
[2]MULTIPLIER PROCESSING TIME ONLY.
[3]CLIPPING CALCULATION TIME ONLY.

Figure 19. Seillac-7 desktop display terminal.

been fairly easy, since it could be based on the high-speed technology of the random-stroke display terminal. Furthermore, the Seillac-7's system architecture has so accelerated processing that any further increases in speed must depend on increases in the capacity of VLSI elements.

On the other hand, development of the technology for polygon filling and shading operations has just begun. Hardware architecture for ultra-high-speed, general-purpose shading, highlighting, and transparency operations is a field yet to be fully explored. A terminal capable of a wide range of diverse display effects may be achieved in the next five years or so through improvements in VLSI. For the time being, the distribution of functions among software and/or firmware and display hardware like that of the Seillac-7 is a partial solution. ■

Acknowledgments

I wish to thank Professor Tosiyasu Kunii of the University of Tokyo for his valuable suggestions.

References

1. "Status Report of the Graphics Standards Planning Committee of ACM/SIGGRAPH," *Computer Graphics,* Vol. 11, No. 3, Fall 1977.
2. "Graphical Kernel System (GKS)—Version 5.2," proposal of standard DIN 00 66 252, May 1979.
3. W. M. Newman and R. F. Sproull, *Principles of Interactive Computer Graphics,* 1st ed., McGraw-Hill, New York, 1973.

Tsuneo Ikedo is president of Seillac Co., Ltd., (Tokyo, Japan) and of Seillac Corporation (Carson, California). From 1971 to 1974, he worked in the development of communication control systems at Nippon Electric Co., Ltd. From 1974 to 1981, he was involved in the development of a computer graphics system, a CAD system for prefabrication, the world's first high-resolution digitizer, and a raster-scan color graphics display device and its data structure at Daini-Seikosha Co., Ltd., where he was the project leader of the Electric Division from 1978 to 1981.

His research interests include high-resolution display devices, hardware technology for solid modeling display, and CAD/CAM workstations.

Ikedo received an MS in electronic engineering from the Tokyo Metropolitan University.

Ikedo's address is 1-7-6 Onidaka, Ichikawa Chiba, Japan.

Capable of displaying 10,000 polygons per second, this interactive terminal produces smooth, color-shaded surfaces quickly for applications in science, engineering, training simulation, and animation.

A 3-D Graphics Display System with Depth Buffer and Pipeline Processor

Akira Fujimoto, Christopher G. Perrott, and Kansei Iwata

Graphica Computer Corporation

Lower costs and increased performance of semiconductor memory and microprocessors are driving a trend toward the use of realistic, three-dimensional, color-shaded displays. Raster technology, which has traditionally provided superior color shading, is now able to approach the speed of vector graphics displays. The use of a depth buffer allows hidden surface removal in parallel with update of the raster refresh buffer (see Newman and Sproull[1]).

The 16K dynamic RAM chip has been used in several frame buffer systems, and the advent of the 64K RAM has further reduced costs. Undoubtedly the 256K RAM will continue this trend. General-purpose microprocessors have been used to update the display, but even the current 16-bit machines are unable to provide data as fast as a frame buffer can accept it. Bit-slice microprocessors have been used successfully in graphics display processors, but the new generation of digital signal processor chips provides a more flexible and economical solution. These new devices also eliminate the processing-speed bottleneck by spreading the load across several processors arranged in a pipeline configuration.

This article describes the algorithms used for high-speed rendering of color-shaded, three-dimensional images on a raster display terminal under development by Graphica Computer Corporation. This terminal features

- a depth buffer for hidden surface removal,
- a processing speed of 10,000 polygons per second,
- smooth shading,
- antialiasing,
- subpixel addressability and subpixel detail,
- transparency,
- local segment memory,
- local viewing transformation,
- a nondestructive 3-D cursor,
- a cutting plane that works at any angle, and
- contouring.

An overview of the system

Polygon rendering. The main application of three-dimensional graphics terminals is the display of the visible surfaces of solid objects. Surfaces may be defined in terms of primitive shapes or surface patches, but for display purposes they can be represented as polygons (see Wördenweber[2]).

The Graphica system provides a Gouraud shading capability,[3] which causes the individual polygons to appear as a smooth surface. The advantage of using polygons is that all quantities required for pixel update can be computed with very fast incremental arithmetic. Vectors are treated as a special type of polygon.

The polygons are, in fact, divided into triangles before the actual rendering operation is performed. The triangles are then filled, or "painted," scan line by scan line. Each triangle edge is simultaneously generated and antialiased by means of a hardware digital differential analyzer (DDA), which incrementally calculates the position of the interior pixel on each scan line. Antialiasing the edges makes them jag-free by controlling the brightness of pixels adjacent to the edge.

Antialiasing provides an apparent resolution below the pixel level, an effect that is exploited to permit subpixel addressing of the display and the representation of subpixel-level details (see Crow[4]). The antialiasing hardware also provides two types of simulated transparency.

Reprinted from *IEEE Computer Graphics and Applications*, Volume 4, Number 5, May 1984, pages 11-23. Copyright © 1984 by The Institute of Electrical and Electronics Engineers, Inc.

As part of the polygon fill process, checking and updating of the depth buffer (or z-buffer) are performed by special-purpose hardware. The visibility test can be modified to require a surface to be both above the current contents of the depth buffer and below a cutting plane. In this way, "cutaway" pictures can be produced (see Atherton[5]).

When the display image has been generated, the depth buffer contains depth information for every visible opaque surface. This information is used to display a cursor, which moves in three dimensions and can intersect any of the visible opaque surfaces. The 3-D cursor is drawn in an auxiliary frame buffer, where it does not affect the main image. The depth information can also be used for other purposes, such as the generation of contour lines.

System organization. Display segments are defined by application software running in the host computer and transmitted to the terminal by an interface subroutine package using serial communication.

A 68000 microprocessor in the terminal can directly access the segment memory, frame buffer, depth buffer, auxiliary frame buffer, and look-up table (Figure 1). However, image generation is not performed by the 68000 but by the pipeline, in the following stages:

- segment memory,
- viewing transformation and lighting calculation,
- triangulator,
- initializer,
- incrementing hardware,
- update port, and
- video refresh hardware.

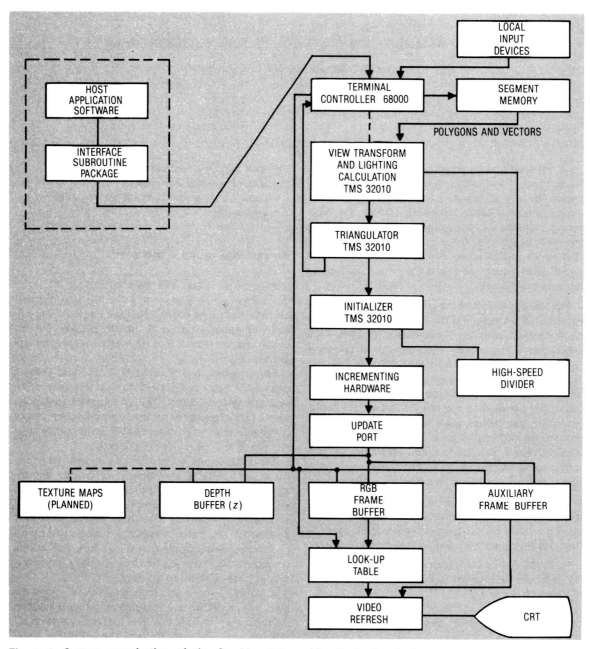

Figure 1. System organization of the Graphica 3-D graphics display terminal.

IEEE CG&A

Each of the specialized devices in the pipeline performs several times faster than the 68000, enabling the overall performance of the pipeline to be many times faster than that achieved with a single general-purpose microprocessor. (It is also considerably faster than a single bit-slice-based processor.)

Segment memory. The segment memory contains descriptions of objects, including polygons, vectors, rectangles, and circles. Only polygons can undergo the complete three-dimensional viewing transformation, but the other objects are supported because of their usefulness in two-dimensional graphics. In 3-D applications all shapes (including rectangles and circles) are represented in the segment memory as polygons, but vectors are permitted for the display of cursors, etc. In the case of polygons, each vertex is specified, and for each vertex the x-, y-, and z-coordinates, surface normal direction, shading, and transparency are specified. The segment memory provides data to the pipeline at a high speed, reducing the load on the host computer.

Viewing transformation. This operation transforms the vertex coordinates and the surface normals according to the current transformation matrix, applying translation, rotation, and scaling. After the lighting calculation, which computes the resultant shading for each vertex, a final perspective transformation is applied.

Triangulator. This device converts all objects to triangles: A rectangle is converted into two triangles, a two-dimensional circle is converted into a number of triangles with a common vertex at the center of the circle, a vector is converted into a triangle with one zero-length side, and an n-sided polygon is converted into $n-2$ triangles. Using triangles ensures that constant increments can be used in the Gouraud shading and transparency calculations. Even though all polygons could be required to be exactly planar in the x, y, and z dimensions, it is not possible to impose this restriction on polygons in the xyR, xyG, and xyB spaces (Figure 2). An additional advantage of dividing all polygons into triangles is that this algorithm does not require a sorted list of polygon edges, as other algorithms do.

Initializer. This device calculates the slopes of the triangle edges in order to initialize the edge-generating DDAs; it solves the plane equations in xyz, xyR, etc. to compute the increments of z, R, etc. for each pixel step in the x and y directions. The initializer also applies a correction to the initial values, a necessary function because the first pixel center does not exactly coincide with a vertex of the triangle. This correction process affects the initial x-positions of the edges on the first scan line for each edge and the values used in filling the triangle; thus, it makes possible the true subpixel addressability of the display.

Incrementing hardware. This hardware is capable of incrementing all applicable variables within the refresh memory write time. Emitter-coupled logic (ECL) devices

achieve this speed with the minimum amount of hardware.

Update port. This device performs the low-level tasks of (1) clipping (to suppress data outside the viewport), (2) comparing the z-value with the depth-buffer contents and cutting-plane value, (3) blending foreground and background intensities for antialiasing and transparency, and (4) updating the frame and depth buffers. These processes are controlled by mode signals, which specify whether the depth buffer is to be updated, whether the main frame buffer or the auxiliary frame buffer is to be updated, and the type of blending calculation to be performed. The use of a depth buffer for hidden surface removal eliminates any need for additional sorting.

Video refresh hardware. This hardware reads continually from the frame buffers, using a look-up table to convert the intensity values in the main RGB frame buffer to the levels required by the nonlinear characteristic of the CRT.

Optimized algorithm

The algorithm for our 3-D graphics system was initially implemented as a Fortran simulation on a Vax computer. This implementation was then modified in several stages

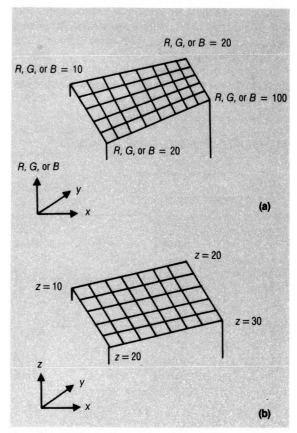

Figure 2. RGB shading components define nonplanar polygons in *xyR*, *xyG*, and *xyB* spaces (a), and planar polygons in *xyz* spaces (b).

into a final version suited to pipelined digital signal processors. The processors in the pipeline are Texas Instruments TMS 32010s, with a 200-ns instruction cycle, 16-bit word length, and built-in 16×16 parallel multiplier.

The high-speed divider is a separate piece of hardware that uses ROM to return the reciprocal $1/x$ of an operand x. This peripheral is shared by two of the 32010s to increase the speed of division operations. The polygon-rendering algorithm has been carefully calculated to minimize the number of division operations, resulting in very little contention between processors for the divider.

Fixed-point arithmetic is used throughout the algorithm. The interface subroutines in the host convert the user's floating-point values into fixed-point values of the required precision. (A fixed-point binary number is one in which a fixed number of binary digits precede the point, and a fixed number follow it. If, for example, four digits come after the point, the number can be thought of as an integer number of sixteenths.)

The viewing transformation consists of multiplications and additions, except for the perspective transformation, which requires division.

The triangulator uses an algorithm based on the areas of triangles. This involves multiplication and addition, but not division. The result is also passed on to the initializer, where it is used in calculating the increments.

The initializer performs in advance all the remaining multiplication and division operations needed to provide the initial values to the incrementing hardware.

The incrementing hardware itself performs only additions, subtractions, and compare operations. The update port performs additions, eight-bit multiplications, and compare operations.

Each stage of the pipeline receives only the data it requires, and passes on only the data required by the stage that follows.

Pipeline stages

Segment memory. The segment memory holds the display file and is divided into an object memory and a vertex memory. Both parts of the memory are directly addressable by the 68000 terminal controller, to which they appear as normal RAM.

The object memory is a "threaded" structure, containing commands and object descriptions which are processed sequentially to generate the image. (A threaded structure is so called by analogy to the use of a rosary as a mnemonic device.) The object descriptions contain pointers to the vertex data, which is stored in the vertex memory and includes x-, y-, and z-coordinates; R, G, and B shading values; and transparency coefficients for each vertex. Each vertex is generally referenced by several polygons, and the division of segment memory into two parts prevents the wasteful duplication of data.

The first 32010 in the pipeline accesses the segment memory by performing an input-data-from-port instruction. An external counter associated with the segment memory relieves the 32010 of the task of generating object memory addresses; a second counter is loaded with the vertex pointer and used to address the vertex memory. In this way, the entire segment memory appears to the 32010 as a single queue of commands (Figure 3).

Viewing transformation. The standard viewing transformation consists of translation, rotation, and scaling operations. It transforms the image into coordinates relative to the viewpoint and is applied only to vertices. Straight lines transform to straight lines, and planes to planes; thus, it is not necessary to calculate the transformation for intermediate points. Applying the composite transformation matrix involves nine multiplications and nine additions for each vertex (Figure 4).

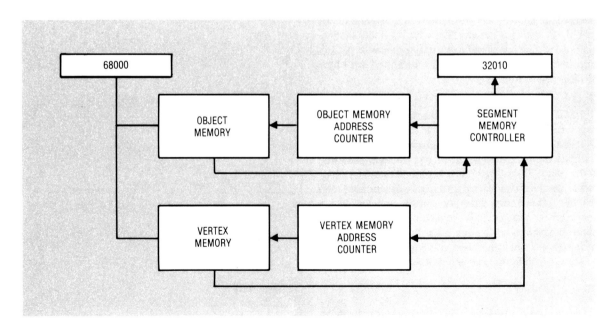

Figure 3. Two components of segment memory appear as separate areas of RAM to the 68000; they appear as a single command queue to the 32010.

Composite rotation is applied to the surface normals at each vertex, and Gouraud shading is used to give a smooth appearance to the surface. The surface normal stored in the segment memory is an average of the surface normals for all the polygons sharing a particular vertex. The rotated surface normal is used to calculate the effect of illumination at each vertex.

The standard perspective transformation[1] is then applied to the x-, y-, and z-coordinates of each vertex. It is necessary to transform z into z' because the transformation of x and y into x' and y' is nonlinear, involving a division by z. If z were not transformed, planes would transform into curved surfaces and the intersections of these surfaces would be curved rather than straight lines. The transformation of z to z' also ensures that the full range of depth values and the greatest possible depth precision are used for hidden surface removal (Figure 5).

Triangulator. The triangulator was designed to be very efficient in processing the most common types of polygons. Polygons with more than five sides are very rare, and, in practice, most polygons are convex. The triangulator first checks for a three-sided polygon, which is very common in some applications. If the polygon has more than three sides, the triangulator counts the number of reflex vertices (interior angle greater than 180 degrees). If there are two or more reflex vertices, the whole polygon is transferred back to the 68000, where a general triangulation algorithm is applied for closed polygons without holes. If the number of reflex vertices

is zero or one, conversion of the polygon into triangles follows immediately (Figure 6).

A quantity called the vertex product is stored for each vertex of a polygon (except for a three-sided polygon, in which case only one copy of the vertex product is stored). The vertex product is equal to twice the area of a triangle formed by bridging the vertex (Figure 7). This value is calculated with the signed values of the x and y spans of the two edges that meet at the vertex. If the vertices are given in counterclockwise order, the vertex product will be negative for a reflex vertex. If the order is reversed, the sign will be reversed. Thus, the vertex product can be used to detect reflex vertices. For the first and last triangles of each polygon, the vertex product is also passed to the initializer, which uses it to calculate increments.

The method of counting reflex vertices is to proceed through all vertices, checking the sign of the stored

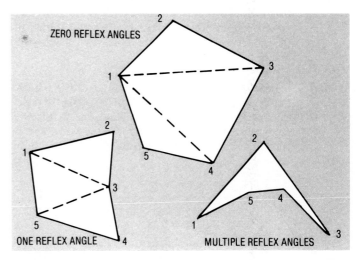

Figure 6. Triangulation is immediate, except in the case of multiple reflex angles.

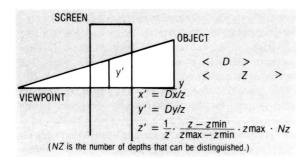

Figure 4. Application of the transformation matrix: the general form of composition transformation (a); evaluation, requiring nine multiplications and nine additions (b).

(a)

$$[x'\ y'\ z'\ 1] = [x\ y\ z\ 1] \begin{bmatrix} a & b & c & 0 \\ d & e & f & 0 \\ g & h & i & 0 \\ j & k & l & 1 \end{bmatrix}$$

(b)

$$x' = ax + dy + gz + j$$
$$y' = bx + ey + hz + k$$
$$z' = cx + fy + iz + l$$

SCREEN

OBJECT

$$x' = Dx/z$$
$$y' = Dy/z$$
$$z' = \frac{1}{z} \cdot \frac{z - z\min}{z\max - z\min} \cdot z\max \cdot Nz$$

(NZ is the number of depths that can be distinguished.)

Figure 5. Perspective transformation is a projection onto the screen along a line from object to viewpoint. The z-coordinate transformation ensures that polygons remain planar and optimizes the use of the depth buffer.

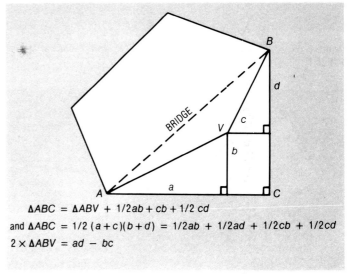

$$\Delta ABC = \Delta ABV + 1/2\,ab + cb + 1/2\,cd$$
and $\Delta ABC = 1/2\,(a+c)(b+d) = 1/2\,ab + 1/2\,ad + 1/2\,cb + 1/2\,cd$
$$2 \times \Delta ABV = ad - bc$$

Figure 7. The vertex product for vertex V is equal to twice the area of the triangle ABV formed by bridging the vertex.

vertex product, counting the number of negative values, and retaining one pointer to the last vertex with a negative value and a second pointer to the last vertex with a positive value. At the same time, the vertex with the lowest y-coordinate is identified. (Either extreme in the x or y direction can be used equally well.) This vertex cannot be reflex, and this fact is used to determine whether a negative value or a positive value identifies a reflex vertex.

The algorithm in the 68000 that triangulates complex polygons proceeds through all the vertices, bridging nonreflex vertices where it can form a triangle that does not enclose a vertex (Figure 8).

This algorithm is complicated by the fact that the polygon it is processing effectively changes as each triangle is generated, and the vertex product must be recalculated every time a particular vertex is examined. Testing to determine whether a particular vertex is enclosed by a triangle can require up to three calculations of the same type as the vertex product calculation. This part of the algorithm is implemented in the 68000 for greater ease in programming, since the architecture of the 68000 is considerably more regular and flexible than that of the TMS 32010.

Initializer. The initializer maintains an active triangle buffer, which stores a description of the current triangle, eliminating the need for the triangulator to transfer redundant information. For example, the x-, y-, and z-coordinates of each polygon vertex are transferred from

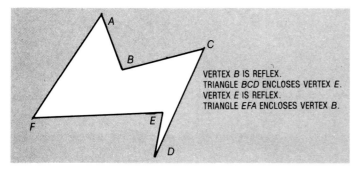

Figure 8. A complex polygon: vertices B, C, E, and F cannot be bridged.

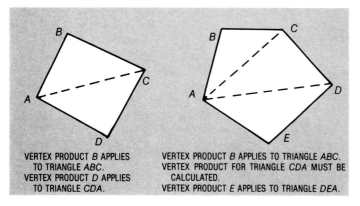

VERTEX PRODUCT B APPLIES TO TRIANGLE ABC.
VERTEX PRODUCT D APPLIES TO TRIANGLE CDA.

VERTEX PRODUCT B APPLIES TO TRIANGLE ABC.
VERTEX PRODUCT FOR TRIANGLE CDA MUST BE CALCULATED.
VERTEX PRODUCT E APPLIES TO TRIANGLE DEA.

Figure 9. The vertex product is calculated by the initializer for only $n-4$ triangles in an n-sided polygon, $n>4$.

the triangulator to the initializer only once, even though the vertex may be shared by two or more triangles. The slope of each edge is also calculated only once, even though the edge may be shared by two triangles. (External edges of the polygon may be shared by two polygons; in this case, the slope will be calculated twice.) The vertex product is calculated only when necessary (Figure 9).

The slope of each edge is calculated as a fixed-point quantity; to reduce the number of bits required, this value is always represented as a fraction. If the absolute value of the y-span is less than that of the x-span, the slope is considered *gentle*; otherwise it is considered *steep*. The slope of gentle edges is y-span/x-span; for steep edges it is x-span/y-span. The type of slope, stored as 0 or 1, is needed for initializing the edge generators (but it is not itself used directly in edge generation); it also plays an important part in antialiasing.

The increments of z, R, G, B, etc. per unit step in the x or y direction are calculated with the general plane equation $Ax + By + Cu + D = 0$, where u is equivalent to z for xyz space, u is equivalent to R for xyR space, and so on. By rearrangement and partial differentiation:

$$Cu = -Ax - By - D$$
$$\partial u/\partial x = -A/C$$
$$\partial u/\partial y = -B/C$$

The ratios A/C and B/C are found by substituting the known values of x, y, and u at each of the three vertices, with the result:

$$-A/C = \frac{(u2-u1)(u3-u1) - (u3-u1)(y2-y1)}{(x2-x1)(y3-y1) - (x3-x1)(y2-y1)}$$

$$-B/C = \frac{-(u2-u1)(x3-x1) + (u3-u1)(x2-x1)}{(x2-x1)(y3-y1) - (x3-x1)(y2-y1)}$$

The denominator of these fractions is independent of u and is, in fact, equal to the vertex product, which has already been calculated. The reciprocal of the vertex product is stored to minimize the number of division operations, and the division is replaced by multiplication. (If the vertex product is zero, then the apparent area of the triangle is zero and the reciprocal is not required, since the triangle is assumed to be "edge-on" and is not displayed.)

In the present design, all initialization is performed by one TMS 32010 processor. (We are still considering the possibility of adding another digital signal processor stage at this point in the pipeline.)

The next step is to sort the vertices of the triangle into ascending y-order and to distinguish between two possible orientations of the triangle. For a triangle with two left edges, it is necessary to initialize the left edge generator twice; for a triangle with two right edges, the right edge generator must be initialized twice (Figure 10).

The triangle is processed scan line by scan line, starting with the scan line below the lowest vertex and ending with the scan line above the highest vertex. The initial x-coordinate for each edge depends on where that edge intersects the scan line immediately below its lower vertex (Figure 11).

Once the lowest vertex and the starting pixel have been identified, the initial values of z, R, G, B, etc. are set, using the values for the lowest vertex but adjusting for

IEEE CG&A

the distance in x and y from the lowest vertex to the starting pixel center.

Edge generation also requires the initial distance from the edge, the change in edge distance per unit step in the x-direction, and the change in edge distance per unit step in the y-direction. In fact, the slope of the generated edge depends on the ratio of the latter two quantities. The values are

$$\partial s/\partial x = 1 \qquad \text{steep edge}$$
$$\partial s/\partial y = \text{slope} \quad (\text{slope} = dx/dy)$$
$$\partial s/\partial x = \text{slope} \quad \text{gentle edge}$$
$$\partial s/\partial y = 1 \qquad (\text{slope} = dy/dx)$$

Our antialiasing method must distinguish between upper edges and lower edges in the case of edges with gentle slope. To do this, the initializer determines the type of edge and transfers this information to the incrementing hardware. The initializer also specifies at which scan line the edge generator must be initialized and provides limits in the x-direction to prevent antialiasing from continuing beyond the endpoints of the edges.

Vectors are treated as a special case. The slopes of the left and right edges are set equal, and the edge generators are initialized only once for each edge. The starting x-coordinates of the two edges are not quite identical. The left edge is moved to the left and the right edge is moved to the right by approximately $0.17 \times$ slope. This straight-line formula is a fairly accurate approximation of the exact widening required, which is

$$\sqrt{(1+m^2)} - 1 \qquad \text{steep edge}$$
$$\left(\sqrt{(1+m^2)} - 1\right)/m \quad \text{gentle edge} \qquad \text{slope} = m$$

This prevents the apparent line thickness from being reduced in the case of oblique lines.

Incrementing hardware. The incrementing hardware performs two functions: an "outer loop" and an "inner loop." The outer loop performs edge generation and steps vertically (i.e., in the positive y-direction) from one scan line to the next. The inner loop updates the frame buffers and the depth buffer for the interior pixels on one scan line, between the left and right edges. These two functions are closely related, and both must be performed as quickly as possible. To process tall, narrow triangles as rapidly as low, wide triangles, the speed of the outer loop must be close to that of the inner loop. The processing time should be determined by the length of the edges and the total number of pixels—not by the orientation of the triangle. For these reasons, the incrementing hardware is designed as a single functional unit, not two distinct physical modules.

The edge generator, which is part of the outer-loop function, makes one step in the y-direction and updates the edge distance. If this exceeds one unit, the edge generator subtracts one and steps in the x-direction as many times as necessary for the distance from the true edge to the exterior pixel to exceed one unit. It then subtracts one unit from the edge distance in preparation for processing the next scan line. The edge distance is updated according to parameters provided by the initializer. This method depends on $\partial s/\partial x$ being one for

steep edges and $\partial s/\partial y$ being one for gentle edges.

As a by-product of edge generation, the pixel coordinates and distances from the true edge—required for antialiasing—are generated automatically; the edge generator thus controls the antialiasing process. Exterior pixels are brightened according to their proximity to the true edge. The edge distance is measured in the x-direction for steep edges and in the y-direction for gentle edges.[6] The shading and depth values (R, G, B, and z) for the exterior pixel are taken from the closest interior pixel, rather than extrapolating outside the true triangle (Figure 12). Taking the depth value from the interior pixel has an important effect on the hidden surface processing (depth buffer check).

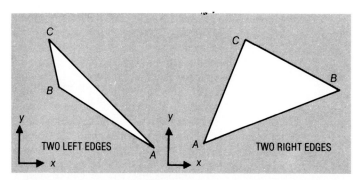

Figure 10. Two types of triangles are distinguished by the initializer, using the slopes of edges *AB* and *AC*.

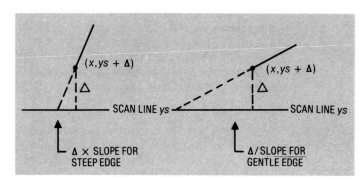

Figure 11. Calculating the initial *x*-coordinate for edge generation.

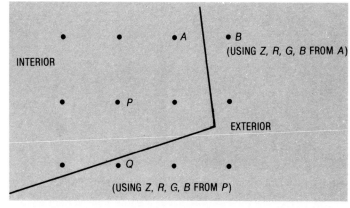

Figure 12. The values for depth and shading of pixels brightened by antialiasing are taken from the nearest interior pixel center.

June 1984

Pixels are treated as square areas with uniform shading, as calculated for the pixel center. When the pixel center is inside the polygon, pixel shading is not modified. This ensures that adjacent polygons on a surface will completely obscure the background. When the pixel center is outside the polygon, the shading is

$$(1 - s)f + sb$$

where s is the edge distance, f is the foreground shading, and b is the background shading. (The actual blending of foreground and background is performed by the update port.)

The "jaggies" eliminated by antialiasing are caused by displaying point samples of an image that contains information at spatial frequencies higher than the sampling frequency. These high-frequency components can be suppressed by treating an edge as a gradual transition in brightness, spread over a distance at least equal to the pixel width. In practice, the same effect can be achieved by integrating the image data over the area of each pixel, instead of sampling at the pixel center.

The antialiasing formula (which two of the authors published previously[6]) was derived using an adjustable Fourier window. It can also be justified by considering a square window of the same size as a pixel, with its edges parallel to the x and y axes and its center lying on the true edge of the triangle (Figure 13). An area equal to $1 - s$ receives the foreground shading, and an area equal to s retains the background shading (using the pixel size as the unit of length). Antialiasing during edge generation is superior to post-antialiasing because it can represent information that would otherwise be lost. For a polygon of subpixel dimensions, interior pixels cannot be displayed and post-antialiasing is impossible (Figure 16). This is a serious problem for post-antialiasing methods. All x and y screen coordinates are processed to an accuracy of one-sixteenth of a pixel. Antialiasing provides an effective resolution of less than one-eighth of a pixel.

The inner-loop processing fills the interior of the triangle, along the scan line from the starting interior pixel provided by the left-edge generator up to and including the ending interior pixel provided by the right-edge generator. Using fast ECL registers, it updates the depth

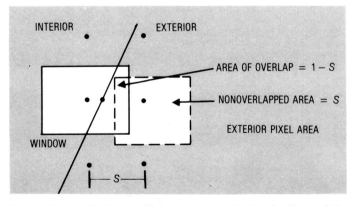

Figure 13. Antialiasing coefficients are equal to the fractions of the area of an exterior pixel which are covered and not covered, respectively, by a pixel-size window centered on the true edge (at the same x-coordinate as the exterior pixel for a gentle edge, and at the same y-coordinate for a steep edge).

and shading values incrementally for each pixel by adding the x-direction increments calculated by the initializer. The initial values in these registers for each scan line are set up by the left-edge generator; the final values for each scan line are used by the right-edge generator as the initial values for antialiasing.

This very fast hardware implementation is made possible only by the preceding stages of the pipeline, which ensure that the incrementing hardware need perform only simple operations.

Update port. The outer and inner loops of the incrementing hardware provide control signals and data to the update port, which buffers all signals for one pixel so that the incrementing hardware can proceed to the next pixel. Buffering more data would not improve performance because, at this stage in the pipeline, the data rate is nearly constant (during image generation).

For a normal interior pixel of an opaque polygon, the updating process is quite straightforward. The depth value z of the pixel is compared to the current depth value for the cutting plane, and the x- and y-coordinates are compared to the four edges of the viewport (which may be smaller than the complete screen). If the pixel is above the cutting plane or outside the viewport, it is not displayed. But if the pixel is below the cutting plane and inside the viewport, the depth buffer value for this pixel address is accessed. Also, if the pixel is below the depth buffer value, it is not displayed. If it is above the depth buffer value, it is displayed by writing the shading data into the frame buffer, and the contents of the depth buffer for this pixel address is replaced by z.

The process is the same for an interior pixel of a transparent polygon, except that the shading values are combined with the background shading using the current transparency value, and the depth buffer is checked but not updated. Because the depth buffer is not updated, an opaque object can be drawn after a transparent object, which would otherwise obscure it. However, in this case the shading would not be correct. A correctly shaded image is obtained by displaying all opaque objects in the segment memory before displaying any transparent objects.

The updating of the depth buffer is also suppressed when the object being drawn is the 3-D cursor. The cursor is drawn in the same way as other objects, except that the shading values are written to the auxiliary frame buffer and the depth buffer is not updated. The cursor shape is specified by the application software. It consists of a number of polygons or vectors, which may either lie in a plane or form a curved surface or solid object such as a sphere. It is possible to display two or more cursors simultaneously under software control. A plane 3-D cursor—either shaded or a wireframe grid—can be used interactively to specify and display the depth and orientation of the cutting plane. Contour-line generation is not performed in the same way as 3-D cursor display—it is performed by software in the 68000, which accesses the depth buffer directly.

The processing for an exterior pixel is similar to that for an interior pixel of a transparent polygon: the depth buffer is checked but not updated, and the foreground

IEEE CG&A

shading is blended with the background shading. As we have said, the shading and depth values are taken from the closest interior pixel. The depth value is also checked against the depth buffer value for the closest interior pixel. The update port uses control information provided by the incrementing hardware to address the correct location in the depth buffer. As a result, an exterior pixel is modified only if the closest interior pixel is visible.

When an exterior pixel of a transparent polygon is processed, it is necessary to read the background shading only once. The effects of transparency and antialiasing both contribute to the final shading of the pixel.

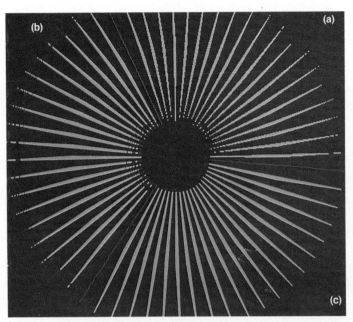

Figure 14. Narrow triangles with no antialiasing (a), post-antialiasing (b), and present method of antialiasing (c). Note that post-antialiasing produces smooth edges but fails to recover subpixel-size detail.

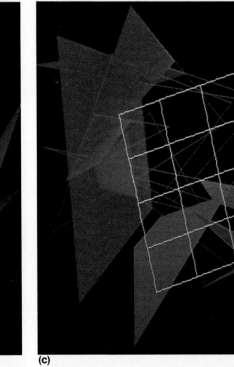

Figure 15. Intersecting triangles demonstrate depth buffer capabilities: with wireframe 3-D cursor (a); plane 3-D cursor (b); cutting plane and 3-D cursor (c). Red lines show original triangle outlines. Note that the present algorithm does not antialias intersection lines.

(a)

There is one situation in which the antialiasing is imperfect: if polygon A obscures part of polygon B, and polygon B is drawn after polygon A, then the antialiased edges of polygon A will not be antialiased correctly in the final displayed image.

The high speed of the update port—limited only by the access time of the frame-buffer memories—leads to

(b)

(c)

Figure 16. Transparent triangles with maximum transparency at the center of the picture and minimum transparency at the perimeter: approximated real transparency on a white background (a) and on a black background (b); also shown (c) is transparency simulated by the simple blending formula $(1 - w)f + wb$.

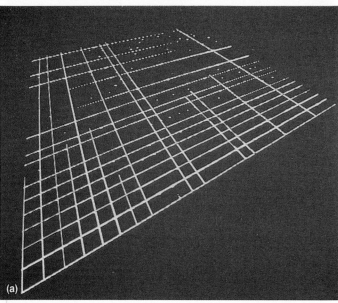

(a)

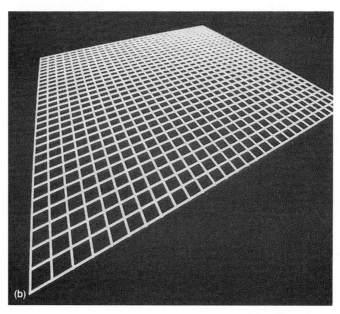

(b)

Figure 17. Antialiased perspective images of a square grid composed of narrow polygons: (a) was produced by the graphics package Movie.BYU; (b) was produced by the present algorithm, which can represent subpixel-level detail.

the requirement for comparably high speed in the incrementing hardware; this, in turn, demands high speed in the preceding pipeline stages.

Current status of the system

A simulation of this system—programmed in Fortran—is currently running on a Vax computer, with communication between pipeline stages simulated through a set of queue-handling subroutines. The order of processing depends on a random-number function invoked by these subroutines; this enables the simulation of asynchronous operation of the pipeline stages. Fixed-point arithmetic subroutines have also been developed to confirm the precision required for each of the various calculations.

The performance of the digital signal processors has been estimated by considering the instruction sequence required to perform the processing. The estimates will be revised when the Texas Instruments cross-development software is used to assemble the programs and simulate their execution.

The 68000 terminal controller is now operational, and the software to handle the transfer of segment data from host to terminal is under development. The frame buffers, look-up table, and video-refresh circuits are standard components or options in Graphica's earlier display terminals, and the depth buffer will be implemented by adding extra boards of the type used in the main frame buffer. Up to eight bits are provided for each RGB component, and up to 16 additional bits will be used for the depth buffer.

Experimental results

The photographs in Figures 14-19 were made with a Graphica M-508 terminal driven by the Fortran simulation (except for the comparison photographs from a widely used graphics software package). The M-508 was used for development purposes because it has a relatively low resolution (512×512 pixels), and the effects of aliasing are quite noticeable.

The quality of the antialiased triangles can be seen in the photograph comparing three methods of displaying long, narrow triangles (Figure 14). The difference demonstrates the superiority of our present method over previous methods of post-antialiasing, especially where subpixel-level detail is involved. In fact, the results of antialiasing are indistinguishable from those obtained by algorithms using sophisticated filtering functions.

In Figure 15, the three photographs of intersecting triangles illustrate the high resolution of the depth buffer, the two types of 3-D cursors, and the effect of the cutting plane.

The photographs of many overlapping transparent triangles demonstrate the combination of antialiasing with transparency (Figure 16).

Figure 18. A smooth-shaded object defined by 84 polygons, displayed with random colors at the vertices to demonstrate antialiasing.

June 1984

We expect the performance of the system to be determined by the rate at which the digital signal processors can process polygons—not by the access time of the segment memory or the frame buffer. Present estimates predict a performance in excess of 10,000 polygons per second (or 100 microseconds per polygon). This will allow users either to generate moving images of several hundred polygons or to generate very detailed images in a few seconds.

Applications

The Graphica system is a general-purpose graphics display designed for interactive applications that require a fast response time. The system's special advantage is its ability to generate high-quality images rapidly.

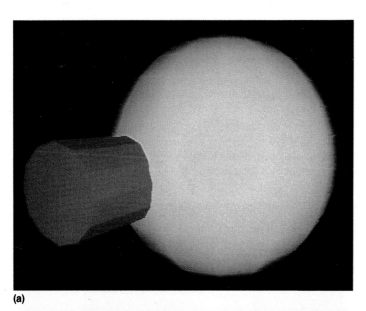

(a)

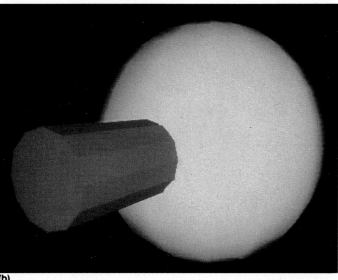

(b)

Figure 19. Intersecting surfaces with smooth (Gouraud) shading and highlighting: (a) generated by a package that does not perform the perspective z-transformation of Figure 5; (b) generated by the present algorithm. Note the improvement in the intersection line in (b).

The 3-D cursor, the cutting plane, and the contouring and transparency capabilities are expected to be very useful CAD tools. In many applications, the ability to rotate an image of several hundred polygons in real time will help scientists and engineers show and understand three-dimensional structures. The ability to update an image in real time may also permit the use of the display system as a training simulator.

Another use of the system's ability to display very detailed images in a few seconds could be the production of animated sequences for film or videotape. If a 50,000-polygon image can be generated in five seconds, it should be possible to produce a ten-second animated sequence of such images in less than thirty minutes. The transparency feature could be used in the representation of motion blur, to prevent temporal aliasing effects.

The Graphica display will also be interfaced with solid modeling packages, such as Euclid and Movie.BYU.

Future development and research

Future developments will center on improving the quality of the image, increasing the speed, adding new capabilities, and reducing the cost. The first planned development is a texture-mapping capability. When this is implemented, the terminal will be capable of supporting all features of the Core graphics standard, including raster extensions.

One subject for research is the problem of antialiasing when the background is drawn after the foreground. If these edges can be detected, it should be possible to correct them by post-antialiasing (that is, by modifying the pixel-shading after the whole image has been drawn).[7] The same method may be applicable to the intersection lines of intersecting polygons.

The system's speed could be increased by (1) adding stages to the pipeline, (2) using more than one pipeline in parallel, or (3) using faster processors in the pipeline. Its cost could be cut by reducing the size of the depth buffer or by using fewer stages in the pipeline. The hardware divider could be replaced by a slower software routine as another way to reduce production costs. It is probable that more than one model of the system will eventually be marketed.

Conclusion

The methods described in this article* make possible the construction of a high-performance, general-purpose interactive terminal for 3-D graphics applications. This terminal will be able to display at least 10,000 Gouraud-shaded, antialiased polygons per second, for high-speed rendering of smooth surfaces. While generating the display, the terminal will simultaneously apply viewing transformations and perform hidden surface removal, using a depth-buffer algorithm. Additional features include a 3-D cursor, cutting plane, contouring, and

*Some of the devices and processes described in this article may be the subject of patent applications.

transparency. We expect the terminal to find successful applications in a number of areas, including CAD, training simulators, and animation. ■

References

1. William M. Newman and Robert F. Sproull, *Principles of Interactive Computer Graphics,* 2nd ed. ("Perspective Depth," and "The Depth Buffer Algorithm," chapters 23 and 24), McGraw-Hill, New York, 1979.

2. Burkard Wördenweber, "Surface Triangulation for Picture Production," *IEEE Computer Graphics and Applications,* Vol. 3, No. 8, Nov. 1983, pp. 45-51.

3. Henri Gouraud, "Continuous Shading of Curved Surfaces," *IEEE Trans. Computers,* Vol. C-20, No. 6, June 1971, pp. 623-629.

4. Franklin C. Crow, "The Use of Grayscale for Improved Raster Display of Vectors and Characters," *Computer Graphics* (Proc. Siggraph 78), Vol. 12, No. 3, Aug. 1978, pp. 1-5.

5. Peter R. Atherton, "A Method of Interactive Visualization of CAD Surface Models on a Color Video Display," *Computer Graphics* (Proc. Siggraph 81), Vol. 15, No. 3, Aug. 1981, pp. 279-287.

6. Akira Fujimoto and Kansei Iwata, "Jag-Free Images on Raster Displays," *IEEE Computer Graphics and Applications,* Vol. 3, No. 9, Dec. 1983, pp. 26-34.

7. Jules Bloomenthal, "Edge Inference with Applications to Antialiasing," *Computer Graphics* (Proc. Siggraph 83), Vol. 17, No. 3, July 1983, pp. 157-162.

Additional reading

Catmull, Edwin E., "Computer Display of Curved Surfaces," *Proc. Conf. Computer Graphics, Pattern Recognition and Data Structure,* May 1975, pp. 11-17; reprinted in *Tutorial and Selected Readings in Interactive Computer Graphics,* Herbert Freeman, ed., IEEE Computer Society, 1980, pp. 309-315.

Crow, F. C., and M. W. Howard, "A Frame Buffer System with Enhanced Functionality," *Computer Graphics* (Proc. Siggraph 81), Vol. 15, No. 3, Aug. 1981, pp. 63-69.

Foley, J. D., and A. van Dam, *Fundamentals of Interactive Computer Graphics,* Addison-Wesley, Reading, Mass., 1982, p. 438.

Gupta, Satish, and Robert F. Sproull, "Filtering Edges for Gray-Scale Displays," *Computer Graphics* (Proc. Siggraph 81), Vol. 15, No. 3, Aug. 1981, pp. 1-5.

Newell, M. E., R. G. Newell, and T. L. Sancha, "A New Approach to the Shaded Picture Problem," *Proc. ACM Nat'l Conf.,* Vol. I, Aug. 1972, pp. 443-450.

Sabella, Paolo, and Michael J. Wozny, "Toward Fast Color-Shaded Images of CAD/CAM Geometry," *IEEE Computer Graphics and Applications,* Vol. 3, No. 8, Nov. 1983, pp. 60-71.

Akira Fujimoto, formerly Wieslaw Romanowski, is a chief engineer with the Software Research Division of the Graphica Computer Corporation, a company that produces computer graphics and image processing systems. His research interests include computer graphics for raster-scan devices, applications of computer graphics in scientific and engineering analysis, and CAD.

Fujimoto received an ME in mechanical engineering from the Technical University Szczecin (Poland) and from the University of Tokyo, where he subsequently obtained his PhD. He is a member of the Society of Naval Architects of Japan, the Computer Graphics Society (GCS), and the GKS Japan Committee of GCS.

Christopher G. Perrott is a software engineer with the Software Research Division of Graphica Computer Corporation. Previously, he has worked on airline reservations software, radar systems, and process control in Europe and North America. His present interests include software and hardware for computer graphics systems.

Perrott received a BA and an MA in physics from Oxford University.

Kansei Iwata is president of Graphica Computer Corporation, which he founded in 1975. From 1970 to 1975, he was employed by Iwatsu Electronic Company, Ltd., where he was the chief of the Electronic Circuit Research Laboratory at the Technical Institute in 1974 and 1975. His research interests are related to pulse transmission and electronic circuit design.

Iwata received his BA and PhD in electrical engineering from Tohoku University in Sendai, Japan. He is a member of the IEEE and the ACM.

The authors' address is Graphica Computer Corporation, 6-21-6 Nagayama Tama-shi, Tokyo 206, Japan.

June 1984

Chapter 2: Graphics Processors and Special Function Units

Basically, a (general) raster-scan graphics generation system consists of an image creation system (ICS), an image storage system (ISS) (*bit-map* or *frame buffer*), and an image display system (IDS). The architecture of such a system is depicted in Figure 2.1. When compared with the functional model in Figure 1.1, the ICS corresponds to the sub-pipeline from the application model (AM) to the display processing unit (DPU), ISS to the linear display file (LDF), and the IDS to the display controller (DC) and display screen. This organization reflects the major transitions of the scene from the object space representation, as is input to the ICS, to the image space representation of the ISS, then to the final image displayed by the IDS.

The contents and format of the AM are entirely dependent on the type of application and the types of access needed to the various parts of the object. Therefore, there must be a flexible way for the construction and manipulation of the AM. This requires general purpose processing. Obviously, the host is an appropriate environment for the AM and the display file compiler.

As the scene is rendered along the various steps of the pipeline shown in the functional model, representations of the scene become more and more application independent, which implies that it is more cost effective to have hardware support at later stages of the image generation pipeline.

In this chapter, some hardware enhancements found in the ICS (especially the DPU) will be discussed.

2.1: Dedicated Graphics Processors

There are two fundamental processes carried out in the ICS. Graphics object are first geometrically transformed and then rendered into the pixel array representation of its visual representation. This image *rasterization* process usually employs a scan-conversion algorithm to generate the corresponding bit-map image of the scene. Visual cues are added, if required, to indicate the object's true physical characteristics, such as texture, shininess, or color, in a given illuminated environment (see Figure 2.2).

However, there is a fundamental mismatch between the two-dimensional array of pixel values used to represent the display image and the graphics primitives. To turn these descriptions into the raster image, each pixel has to be calculated separately. As a result, a tremendous amount of computation is needed to render a picture. In addition, the higher the resolution of the display, the longer it will take to render an image. The duration can easily be tens of minutes or even hours, which can be prohibitively high for the user to do productive graphics work like mechanical design or architectural layout.

Unfortunately, both the vertex transformation and the rasterization processes are very computation intensive.

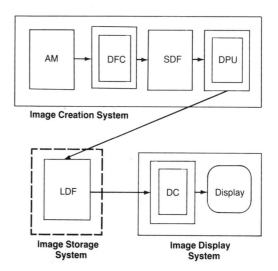

Figure 2.1: A typical raster-scan display system.

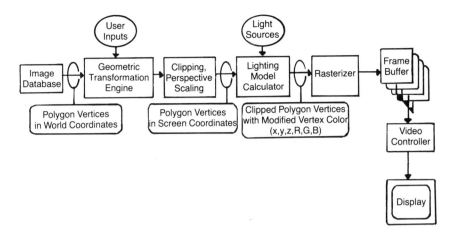

Figure 2.2: Processing sequence of an image.

Therefore, it would be a waste of the host computer's resources to require its processor to perform all of the highly repetitive tasks associated with transformation and scan-conversion processes. This is a major motivation for using dedicated graphics processors or special graphics function units to offload some of the work that otherwise must be performed by the host computer. Moreover, since both vertex transformation and pixel evaluation are fairly straightforward and need to be executed a large number of times per each frame of image, they are a good candidate for the hardware, especially VLSI, solution.

There are three major types of graphics processors. The first type consists of those processors dedicated to simple raster graphics operations [KISN84, MAEJ84]. These processors manipulate the frame buffer and perform such activities as rendering simple geometric objects, filling bounded areas with solid color, or moving blocks of pixels around. Some graphics controllers also include a *video controller*, which administrates the sending out of pixels for video refresh.

The second type of graphics processors includes those committed to geometric transformations, clipping, windowing, etc. [CLAR80, CLAR82, STRO84]. These graphics processors are also known as *geometry processors*. In some applications, an image frame may include thousands of graphics primitives. The host computer's central processor can get tied up if all the activities illustrated in Figure 2.2 must be performed by the host. Moreover, executing geometric transformations by the host's general-purpose processor is inefficient. Therefore, a geometry processor is essential for interactive generation of complex images.

The third type of graphics processors are those especially designed and built for the purpose of scan-converting

graphics objects into corresponding bit-map patterns (see Chapters 4, 5, and 6). Owing to the complexity of image rasterization, parallel-processing architectures are usually employed for this type of graphics processors.

2.2: Special Function Units

When vectorgraphics was still dominating the computer-generated graphics, various image-rendering functions had already been converted into electronic circuitries for improving the throughput of the picture generation process. With the advent of raster graphics, this trend has found new momentum.

If the sequence of processes by which images are generated is examined, the following four processes are found, each of which is a candidate for implementation in hardware.

Modeling Hardware

The generation of displayed images from a computer model involves traversing the model representation. (One such representation is the CGS-tree representation of a solid used in CSG graphics systems (see Chapter 6 for more details).) This process should ideally be carried out very rapidly so that the effect of changing the model is quickly reflected on the screen.

The degree to which hardware can be used to speed up the modeling operations depends on their complexity and on the extent to which they change from one application to the next.

Transformation Hardware

The most common way to accomplish the modeling and

viewing transformations is with 4×4 matrix multiplications. However, matrix multiplication requires many intermediate multiplication steps. Thus, the transformation of object coordinates can be one of the most time-consuming processes in the entire graphics output sequence.

From the early days of computer graphics, a great deal of effort has been put into the design of transformation hardware. Early designs were either very limited in their range of transformations or were complex and expensive; only with the use of homogeneous matrix techniques has it become possible to produce satisfactory transformation processors.

The forerunner of modern transformation hardware was the matrix multiplier, designed and built in 1968 by Seitz and Sutherland. It used a bank of four parallel multipliers that could multiply a four-element vector by a 4×4 matrix in four steps, taking 20 microseconds in all. The matrix multiplier was designed to work in conjunction with the clipping divider (see below), feeding its output to the input registers of the clipping divider in a pipeline fashion. Recent matrix multipliers have used much simpler designs based on general-purpose microprogrammed processors.

Clipping Hardware

The first hardware clipping device was built in 1968, using the midpoint variant of the Cohen-Sutherland clipping algorithm. It was designed to clip both two- and three-dimensional images and was called the *clipping divider* because it included hardware to perform the division required for perspective projection. More recent designs for clipping hardware, many of them based on the clipping divider, have tended to use a general-purpose microprogrammed processor to simplify the control of the device and to reduce its cost.

Rasterization Hardware

In raster-scan graphics, image rasterization is usually the most computation-intensive process in the entire image-generation pipeline. Therefore, hardware implementation of DDA (digital differential analyzer) has been used for the generation of lines, circles, or curves. Other hardware enhancements have also been constructed to provide a richer set of graphics primitives. An example is the hardware generation of alphanumeric patterns, which has already become an essential part of any picture display system.

2.3: Article Overview

The "Geometry Engine" proposed in the first paper, "The Geometry Engine: A VLSI Geometry System for Graphics" by Clark, is a powerful graphics processor. The "Geometry System" (composed of three subsystems, each of which is composed of Geometry Engines) is designed for high-performance, low cost, floating-joint geometric computation in computer graphics applications.

In the next three papers, three new special purpose graphics processors are introduced. They are the Texas Instruments' 34010, National's advanced graphics chip set (which includes the RGP, the DP8510 BPU, the DP8512 VCG and the DP8515/16 VSR), and Intel's 82786 graphics coprocessor.

The paper by Guttag et al. [GUTT86] discusses design requirements for a graphics processor. The authors point out that a graphics controller is too restricted in terms of flexibility because of its "hardwired" command set and recommend that a graphics processor should be specialized in performing graphics tasks while maintaining its programmability like a general purpose processor.

The 34010 is a graphics microprocessor whose instruction set contains a combination of general purpose and graphics specific instructions and is described in "The Texas Instruments 34010 Graphics System Processor" by Asal et al. Basic graphics activities such as drawing vectors, filling areas, windowing, pixel block transfers, and simple image processing tasks can easily be done with the 34010.

National's RGP (Raster Graphics Processor), described in "National's Advanced Graphics Chip Set for High-Performance Graphics" by Carinalli and Blain, is the main graphics processor with a RISC-like architecture. The DP8510 BPU is a bitblt (bit block transfer) processing unit. It can be used as a slave data manipulator to offload the host in doing the time consuming bitblt operations. When supplemented with the DP8512 video clock generator and the DP8515/16 video shift register, a high speed frame buffered raster graphics display can be built.

The Intel's 82786, described in "A New VLSI Graphics Coprocessor: The Intel 82786" by Shires, has integrated on a single chip a high-performance graphics coprocessor along with an advanced windowing display processor. In addition to its rich set of graphics specific instructions, Intel's 82786 is also especially designed to work in the microcomputer environment. Unlike TI's 34010, which can be used as a standalone CPU, Intel's 82786 is designed to work along with a general purpose CPU such as Intel's 80286 or 80386.

References

[CLAR80]   Clark, J.H., "A VLSI Geometry Processor for Graphics," *Computer,* Vol. 13, No. 7, July 1980, pp. 59–68.

[CLAR82]   Clark, J.H., "The Geometry Engine: A VLSI Geometry System for Graphics," *Computer Graphics,* Vol. 16, No. 3, July 1982, pp. 127–133.

[GUTT86]   Guttag, K., J. Van Aken, and M. Asal, "Requirements for a VLSI Graphics Processor," *IEEE Computer Graphics and Applications,* Vol. 6, No. 1, Jan. 1986, pp. 32–47.

[KISN84]   Kisner, M. and J. Ladd, "A New-Generation Video Processor Boosts Resolution," *Electronics,* Jan. 28, 1984, pp. 121–124.

[MAEJ84]   Maejima, T., K. Katsura, K. Minorikawa, and H. Yonezawa, "VLSI for Performance Graphics Control Which Utilizes Multi-Processor Architecture," *Proceedings of 1984 IEEE Intl. Conf. on Computer Design,* Computer Society, Washington, D.C., 1984, pp. 586–591.

[STRO84]   Stroll, Z.Z., E. Swartzlander, Jr., J. Eldon, and J.L. Ashurn, "Image Rotation Controller Chip," *Proc. of 1984 IEEE Int. Conf. on Computer Design,* Computer Society, Washington, D.C., 1984, pp. 274–279.

The Geometry Engine:
A VLSI Geometry System for Graphics

by

James H. Clark

Computer Systems Laboratory
Stanford University
and
Silicon Graphics, Inc.
Palo Alto, California

Abstract

The *Geometry Engine* [1] is a special-purpose VLSI processor for computer graphics. It is a four-component vector, floating-point processor for accomplishing three basic operations in computer graphics: matrix transformations, clipping and mapping to output device coordinates. This paper desribes the Geometry Engine and the Geometric Graphics System it composes. It presents the instruction set of the system, its design motivations and the Geometry System architecture.

Keywords: VLSI, Geometric processing, real-time graphics, arithmetic processing

CR Categories: 3.3, 3.4, 3.7

Geometry System Overview

The *Geometry System* is a floating-point, geometric computing system for computer graphics constructed from a basic building block, the *Geometry Engine*. Twelve copies of the Geometry Engine arranged in a pipeline compose the complete system in its most general form. In its present form, the Geometry Engine occupies a single, 40-pin IC package.

The notable characteristics of the system are:

- **General Instruction Set** - It executes a very general 2D and 3D instruction set of utility in all engineering graphics applications. This instruction set includes operations for matrix transformations, windowing (clipping), perspective and orthographic projections, stereo pair production and arbitrary output device coordinate scaling.

- **Curve Generation** - The system will generate quadratic and cubic curves and all of the conic sections, i.e. circles, parabolas, hyperbolas, etc.

- **Device Independent** - The system is independent of the output device used and works equally well in either vector-based or raster-based systems. It allows color or black and white polygons, lines and characters.

- **Flexible Input Format** - The system accepts input coordinates in either integer or floating point format.

"The Geometry Engine: A VLSI Geometry System for Graphics" by J.H. Clark, which appeared in *Proceedings of SIGGRAPH 82*, 1982, pages 127-133. Copyright© 1982, Association for Computing Machinery, Inc., reprinted by permission.

- **High Performance Floating Point** - Its effective computation rate is equivalent to 5 million floating-point operations per second, corresponding to a fully transformed, clipped, scaled coordinate each 15 microseconds.

- **Reconfigurable** - Each Geometry Engine is "softly" configured; that is, one device with a single configuration register serves in twelve different capacities.

- **Selection/Hit-Testing Mechanism** - The Geometry Engine has a "hit-testing" mechanism to assist in "pointing" functions, such as are required for a fast, interactive graphics system with a tablet, mouse or other input devices.

- **Scales to a Single Chip** - The system can be put in a smaller number of IC packages as soon as the technology for fabrication reduces the size of the Geometry Engine design. Ultimately, the entire 12 Engine system will fit on in one IC package, be a factor of 4 faster and be correspondingly reduced in cost.

The Geometry Engine is a four-component vector function unit whose architecture is best illustrated by the chip photograph shown in Figures 1 and 2. Each of the four function units along the bottom two-thirds of the photo consists of two copies of a computing unit, a mantissa and characteristic. The chip also has an internal clock generator, at the top left corner, and a microprogram counter with push-down subroutine stack, shown at the top right. The upper third of the chip is the control store, which holds the equivalent of 40k bits of control store. This control store contains all of the microcode that implements the instructions and floating-point computations described below.

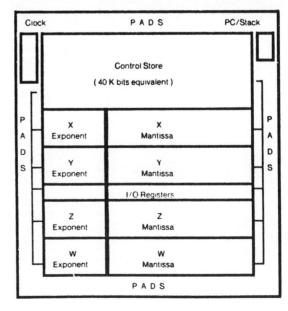

Figure 1: A Block Diagram of the Geometry Engine corresponding to the photo in Figure 2.

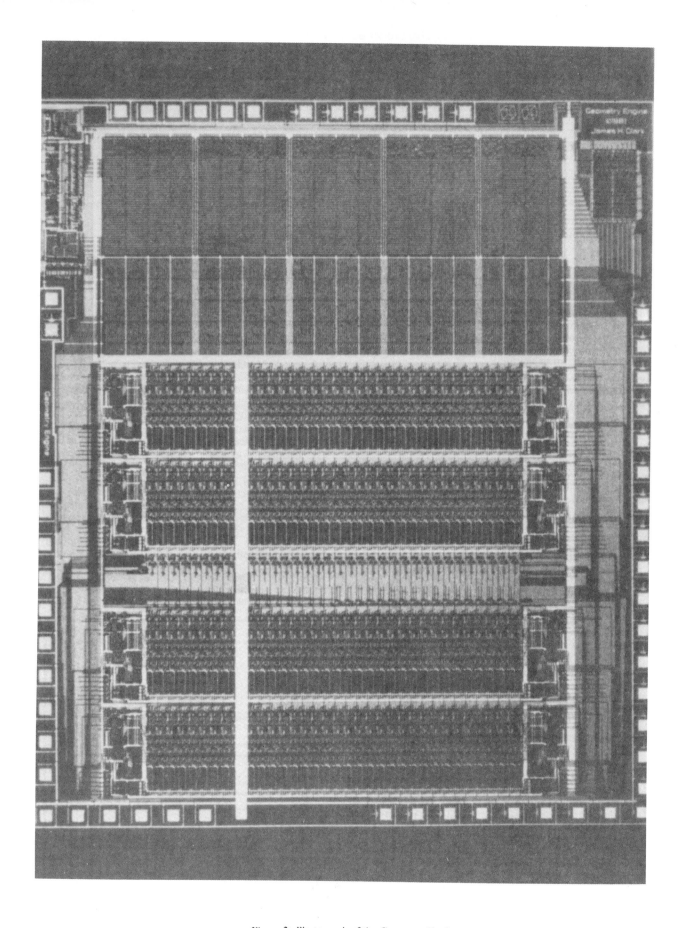

Figure 2: Photograph of the Geometry Engine.

Geometry System Functions

The Geometry System [2] is designed for high-performance, low-cost, floating-point geometric computation in computer graphics applications. It is composed of three subsystems, each of which is composed of Geometry Engines. These subsystems are illustrated in Figure 3. The particular position of a Geometry Engine in the pipeline determines its particuar function in the whole system. Each Engine has a configuration register that is loaded when the system is powered on, after a Reset command is issued. Until the system is reset again, the Engine behaves according to the configuration code.

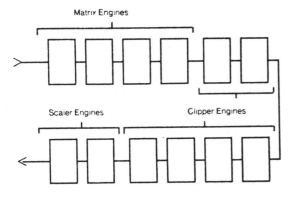

Figure 3: Geometry System; each block is a Geometry Engine.

The subsystems are:

- **Matrix Subsystem** - A stack of 4x4 floating-point matrices for completely general, 2D or 3D floating-point coordinate transformation of graphical data.

- **Clipping Subsystem** - A windowing, or clipping, capability for clipping 2D or 3D graphical data to a window into the user's virtual drawing space. In 3D, this window is a volume of the user's virtual, floating-point space, corresponding to a truncated viewing pyramid with "near" and "far" clipping.

- **Scaling Subsystem** Scaling of 2D and 3D coordinates to the coordinate system of the particular output device of the user. In 3D, this scaling phase also includes either orthographic or perspective projection onto the viewer's virtual window. Stereo coordinates are computed and optionally supplied as the output of the system.

The characteristics of each of these subsystems follows.

Matrix Subsystem

The matrix subsystem provides arbitrary 2D and 3D transformation ability, including object rotations, translations, scaling, perspective and orthographic projection. Using this matrix, it is possible to define a completely arbitrary 2D or 3D viewing window and accomplish all affine transformations.

The matrix transformation subsystem is the first four Geometry Engines in the pipeline. Distributed over these Engines is a 4x4 matrix and an eight-deep, 4x4 matrix stack to accommodate picture subroutine structure. The top element of the stack is the *current* matrix that is used to multiply all incoming coordinates. Full, floating-point transformation of all incoming coordinates is done by this subsystem in 15 microseconds. Transformed points are supplied by this subsystem to the clipping subsystem.

The matrix stack allows the use of picture subroutines. All incoming matrix multiplication commands cause the *current* matrix (top-of-stack) to be multiplied by the incoming matrix. This allows a graphic object to be attached to a "parent" graphic object, thereby providing for a hierarchical drawing. This is done in the same way that a push-down stack is used in a general-purpose computer for storing arguments to subroutines. The **LoadMM** command causes a new matrix to be loaded onto the top of the stack, while a **MultMM** command causes the current top of the stack to be multiplied by the supplied matrix.

The matrix stack can be manipulated by user instructions. In addition to the normal **Push** and **Pop** commands, there is also a **StoreMM** command to provide for overflow handling of the stack if picture structure depth exceeds the eight levels allowed by the depth of the stack.

This subsystem also generates cubic and rational cubic curves [3]. An incremental difference matrix for forward difference curves can be loaded onto the top of the stack, and a special **Iterate** command causes the forward differences of this matrix to be computed, with the result that a new coordinate on the curve is output to the clipping subsystem. Conic curves are generated using rational cubics. New points on the curve are generated in 10 microseconds.

Clipping Subsystem

The four to six Geometry Engines following the Matrix Subsystem comprise the Clipping Subsystem. Each Geometry Engine in the clipping subsystem clips the objects to a single boundary (plane) of the viewing window. Thus, if there is no need or desire to clip objects to the *near* or *far* clipping boundaries, either or both of the corresponding Engines may be eliminated, with no undesired side effects. This might be done to decrease the cost of the system.

The clipping subsystem gets all input data after it has passed through the matrix subsystem, so that only transformed coordinates are supplied to it. It has no explicit registers that the user may manipulate. It always clips transformed coordinates to specific boundaries. The boundaries are made to correspond to particular boundaries of the user's drawing space by altering the transformation matrix so that the desired portion of the environment to be within the window is scaled to be within the standard clipping boundaries.

As an assistance in testing objects for intersection with the viewer's window, a special *hit-testing* mode is included in the clipping subsystem. This mode disables output of certain data from the Geometry System. For example, to *select* an object on the screen that is being pointed to by the input device *cursor, hit-testing* is enabled and a special hit-testing matrix is loaded into the *current* matrix. This matrix is computed from the screen coordinates of the cursor; it might correspond to a tiny window centered at the pointing device's screen coordinates. If anything comes out of the geometry system in this mode, it signifies that an object has passed within the tiny window near the cursor position. Of course, the hit-testing window may be of any size, so that this feature can be useful in area-select functions, as well.

To provide further information useful in identifying *how* objects pass through the *hit-window*, each drawing instruction gets from one to six bits set in it to signify which of the one to six clipping boundaries were intersected by the line-segment drawn. To assist in identifying the object, a special object naming convention is used, thereby providing a completely general selection and hit-testing mechanism.

Scaling Subsystem

The last two Geometry Engines in the pipeline are the Scaling Subsystem. This subsystem converts output from the Clipping Subsystem to the coordinate system of the output device. This process causes the *window* on the user's drawing space, which is specified by loading the appropriate matrix into the Matrix Subsystem, to be mapped onto a *viewport* of the output device, which is specified by loading the scaling subsystem's *viewport* registers. The viewport registers allow up to 24-bit integer values, depending upon the coordinate system of the output device; they are the only device-dependent part of the system. In 3D, the mapping process includes an orthographic or perspective projection and stereo pair production.

Because the Geometry System is a homogeneous system that treats all three coordinates (x,y,z) the same, the Scaling Subsystem also maps the z coordinate. Thus, by loading the z viewport registers with appropriate values, either perspective depth values or intensity depth-cue values will be supplied by the Geometry System, according to the manner in which the output device interprets the z values. Of course, if no depth values are needed in the particular application, they may be discarded.

Either two or four integer values are output by the Scaling Subsystem for each coordinate point that comes out of the system. When two values come out, they are X and Y, in screen coordinates. If the Scaler Engines are configured properly, these four values are:

- X right - the x screen coordinate for the right eye.
- X left - the x screen coordinate for the left eye.
- Y - the y screen coordinate for both eyes.
- Z - the perspective depth value for both eyes.

Geometry System Computations

The matrix system does the computation:

$$[x' \; y' \; z' \; w'] = [x \; y \; z \; w] \, M,$$

where M is the top of the matrix stack and $[x \; y \; z \; w]$ is the input vector to be transformed. The coordinates $[x' \; y' \; z' \; w']$ are supplied to the clipping subsystem, which clips them so that they satisfy

$$-w' < x' < w',$$
$$-w' < y' < w',$$
$$\text{and } -w' < z' < w'.$$

Note that these clipping boundaries are somewhat different from those used in most homogeneous clipping systems [4], in that the z coordinate is treated identically to the x and y coordinates. This simplifies the system, and is equivalent to all other homogeneous clipping systems if the correct matrix is used and the proper viewport scale factors are used.

After clipping, since all points coming out of the clipper satisfy these inequalities, the scaler does the final mapping to output device coordinates with the following computations:

$$D = (z'/w')*Ss + Cs,$$
$$Z = (z'/w')*Sz + Cz,$$
$$X = (x'/w')*Sx + Cx,$$
$$\text{and } Y = (y'/w')*Sy + Cy.$$

The coefficients Sx and Cx are the X half-size and X center of the viewport in the coordinate system of the output device. Similarly for the Y and Z values. The Ss and Cs values are explained in the next section.

Stereo Computation

The Geometry Engine can be used to obtain stereo pair pictures at no extra computational cost. Consider first the ordinary monographic case.

Monographic Case

In a system where the origin is the perspective projection point, the ordinary projection for 3 dimensional scenes [4] is to divide both x and y by z. That is, the screen coordinates of the point are given by

$$X = (x/z)*Sx + Cx$$
$$\text{and } Y = (y/z)*Sy + Cy,$$

where (Cx,Cy) is the center of the "viewport" and (Sx,Sy) is its half-size.

If homogeneous coordinates are used, these equations are modified to compute perspective depth. The transformation on [x,y,z] is modified to compute homogeneous coordinates as follows:

$$[x' \; y' \; z' \; w'] = [x \; y \; z \; 1] \, M.$$

M is chosen to yield

$$[x', \; y', \; z', \; w'] = [x, \; y, \; az+b, \; z],$$
$$\text{where } a = (1+N/F)/(1-N/F)$$
$$\text{and } b = -2N/(1-N/F).$$

N and F are the respective distances of the Near and Far clipping planes from the projection point. With these definitions, the projected coordinates are computed from

$$X = (x'/w')*Sx + Cx, \quad (1)$$
$$Y = (x'/w')*Sy + Cy,$$
$$\text{and } Z = (z'/w')*Sz + Cz = (a+b/z)*Sz + Cz,$$

where we have substituted the values of $z' = az+b$ and $w' = z$, from above.

This yields the same values for X and Y as before. In addition, however, it computes perspective depth, which can be useful in hidden-surface computations. With this computation, points at the Near clipping plane will be mapped into Cz-Sz and points at the Far clipping plane will be mapped into Cz+Sz.

Stereographic Case

For proper stereo, we wish to compute two different views, one for the left eye and one for the right eye. In other words, there are two different projection points that differ in a displacement in the x direction only:

$$Xright = ((x'+dx)/w')*Sx + Cx.right,$$
$$\text{and } Xleft = ((y'-dx)/w')*Sx + Cx.left,$$

where dx is half the distance between the two projection points (distance from the center of the head to each of the eyes), Cx.left is the center of the left projection viewport and Cx.right is the center of the right projection viewport. The Y and Z coordinates are unaffected.

Defining Cx.offset to be the offset of the right and left viewports from a "center" viewport, Cx, we have

$$Cx.left = Cx - Cx.offset$$

and Cx.right = Cx + Cx.offset.

The foregoing equations then become

Xright = (x'/w')*Sx + Cx + { (dx/w')*Sx + Cx.offset }
and Xleft = (x'/w')*Sx + Cx - { (dx/w')*Sx + Cx.offset },

or

Xleft = X + D,
and Xright = X · D,

where X is the "normal" X computation in Equation 1 and D is the quantity in brackets.

Note that D is a computation like that of X,Y and Z in Equation 1. In other words, it involves a division, a multiplication and an add. Inspection of the third of Equation 1 suggests that we define "stereo viewport" parameters as follows:

Ss = dx*Sx/b,
and Cs = Cx.offset - a*(dx*Sx/b).

Then the quantity D is computed to be

D = (z'/w')*Ss + Cs,

giving the required result for D when these substitutions are made.

The Geometry Engine has four floating-point function units; two are required to accomplish one computation of the sort

A = (B/C) * E + F.

Therefore, one Engine will perform two of these computations, for example for the X and Y coordinates. Since another Engine is required to compute Z, it has two free units that can be computing D as well, using the Ss and Cs values defined above. If the Engine computing D and Z is put in the pipeline before the X and Y Engine, the X-Y Engine's microcode can compute X+D and X-D, outputing the four values [X+D,X-D,Y,Z]. Of course, if no stereo is desired, but Z is still needed, the coefficients Ss and Cs can be zero. The Geometry Engine implements this stereo computation, and when properly configured, will output these four quantities.

Programming the Geometry System

The Geometry System is a slave processor. It has no instruction fetch unit; it must be given every instruction and data value by a controlling processor. Likewise, the display controller must take each value that comes out of the Geometry System.

The instruction/data stream supplied to the system is a high-level graphics instruction set mixed with coordinate data. Instructions and data are supplied to the system via its input port, which is the set of input pins of the first Matrix Subsystem Engine, and output data and instructions are taken from its output port, which is the set of output pins of the last Scaling Engine. A convenient view of the system is as a hardware subroutine: in fact, this is precisely the first way it will be used, as a hardware subroutine to the IRIS processor/memory system, which is based on the Motorola 68000 and IEEE Multi-bus.

Input data must always be in user's virtual-drawing (integer or floating-point) coordinate system, and except in special non-display circumstances such as hit-testing, output data is always in the coordinate system of the user's output device.

Instruction Set Summary

The instruction set for the geometry engine partitions into three types:

- **Register Manipulation** - These instructions alter the matrix, matrix stack, or viewport registers. They are used to set the *window* for a particular view of the virtual drawing, load the *viewport* registers, change the matrix or matrix stack to draw a different object, orient a particular object (rotate, translate, etc.) or save the state of the matrix stack for later restoration. Instructions in this category are:

    o **LoadMM** - Load the following 16 floating-point data values onto the top of the stack, destroying the current matrix. The 16 floating-point numbers are the 4x4 matrix.

    o **MultMM** - Multiply the *current* matrix on the top of the stack with the following 4x4 matrix.

    o **PushMM** - Push all matrices on the stack down one position, leaving the current top of stack unaltered. (After this operation the second stack position is a copy of the top of the stack.)

    o **PopMM** - Pop all matrices in the stack up one position.

    o **StoreMM** - Store the top of the matrix stack. This instruction input to the geometry system causes the StoreMM instruction, followed by the 4x4 matrix (16 floating-point numbers) to come out of the Geometry System at its output port. It can be used to save the complete state of the matrix stack.

    o **LoadVP** - Load the viewport registers. Following this instruction, eight 32-bit numbers describing the viewport parameters must be supplied.

- **Drawing Instructions** - These instructions actually cause graphic objects to be drawn. All drawing instructions are followed by four 32-bit floating-point numbers, representing the (x,y,z,w) coordinates of the point being supplied to the Matrix Subsystem for transformation. Each drawing command assumes that there is a current point in the drawing, for example the current pen position in a virtual-space plotter. Certain instructions update that position, while others cause things to be drawn from that point. We refer to this position as the Current Point. Assuming clipping does not eliminate them, each of the following instructions except **Curve** comes out of the Geometry System at its output port, followed by the device coordinates.

    o **Move** - Move the Current Point to the position specified by the floating-point vector that follows.

    o **MoveI** - Same as **Move**, but integer data is supplied.

    o **Draw** - Draw from the Current Point to the position specified by the following data. Update the Current Point with this value after drawing the line segment.

    o **DrawI** - Same as **Draw**, except that integer data is supplied.

    o **Point and PointI** - Cause a dot to appear at the point specified in the following data. Update the Current Point with this value after drawing the point.

    o **Curve** - Iterate the forward differences of the matrix on the top of the matrix stack; issue from the Matrix Subsystem to the Clipping Subsystem a **Draw** command followed by the computed coordinates of the point on the curve. The Current Point is updated just as with the **Draw** command. This command should *not* be followed by data as with the other drawing commands.

    o **MovePoly and MovePolyI** - In Polygon mode, move

the Current Point to the position supplied by the following data. This command must be used rather than Move if a closed polygon is to be drawn.

- o DrawPoly and DrawPolyl - In polygon mode, same as Draw command.

- o ClosePoly - Close the currently open polygon, flushing the polygon from the clipping subsystem.

- **Miscellaneous Commands**

  - o SetHit - Set Hit Mode. This causes the state of the Clipping Subsystem to change so that only commands, and not data, are output. Refer to the **"Selection and Hit-testing"** section for a complete description.

  - o ClearHit - Clear Hit Mode. This restores the state of the Clipping Subsystem to normal. Refer to the **"Selection and Hit-testing"** section for a complete description.

  - o PassThru - This instruction allows the passing of a variable number of 16-bit words through the geometry system unaltered and uninterpreted. It is useful for passing instructions and data that are unique to the display controller and that have no meaning to the Geometry System. The number of words to be passed through is specified by a 7-bit field in the instruction.

Selecting and Hit-testing

In an interactive computer graphics environment it is frequently necessary to select certain objects that appear in the display for special attention. This is usually done with the aid of some type of input device, such as a light-pen, mouse, tablet or joy-stick.

If the input device being used is a light-pen, the common selection mechanism varies, but involves detecting in hardware when the "beam" of the CRT is under the field of view of the light-pen. This approach is good for pointing at objects on the screen but poor for entering new objects into the drawing, because a tracking mechanism must be drawing some type of tracking object that the light-pen must be sensing. Because of the extra expense of the light-pen tracking mechanism and because many people no longer believe it necessary to actually point to objects directly on the screen, the light-pen is not feasible in low-cost systems.

The alternatives to the light-pen, the tablet and mouse (we chose to ignore the joy-stick), are useful for entering new data into drawings, but without an extra mechanism, they are poor for pointing at existing objects in a drawing. The hit-testing mechanism in the Geometry System solves this problem.

The common software mechanism for doing this selection task is to check each object to see if it is in the selection area. This selection area might be an area specified by identifying some portion of the drawing space to check objects against or it might be a small neighborhood around the cursor, which is tracking the position of the mouse or tablet. Intelligent operations can be done to reduce the amount of time spent in checking. For example, the bounding box around an object can be tested to see if any portion of the object is in the selection area; if it is not, then none of the object is in the selection area and therefore need not be further tested. This selection task is basically a clipping task, and the Geometry System has a special mode for handling it.

The Hit-testing mode disables all data from coming out of the Geometry System. However, specific drawing instructions still come out of the system, missing their corresponding data. Thus, in hit-testing mode, if anything comes out of the output port of the system, this means that there was a "hit." In other words, something was in the selection area established by loading the

selection matrix into the Matrix Subsystem.

For a completely general selection mechanism, one might not only like to know whether an object passes through the selection window, but also which boundaries it intersects, or whether it is completely contained within the selection area, or perhaps completely surrounds the area. To accommodate these needs, the Geometry System provides information in the form of "hit-bits" that tell which of the six clipping boundaries are intersected by each drawing command. In this way, the device that is receiving Geometry System output may assemble the necessary information by "integrating" the various "hit-bits" from successive drawing commands used in drawing the object.

Hit-testing is useful only when combined with a naming mechanism for identifying the objects being drawn. This can be done by loading a *name* register in the display controller before drawing each object that is to be identified with a hit. This can be done using the **PassThru** instruction.

Character Handling

Characters provide a special problem for any geometric transformation subsystem. Of course, characters may be defined as strokes, or vectors, and supplied just as all other data to the Geometry System, but since the number of strokes to make up a character might be quite large, we ordinarily do not wish to draw characters in this way. On the other hand, any other approach will not provide for complete, general rotations, etc. of 3D characters. As a result, most systems must make a compromise and provide characters as a special case.

The usual problem with characters is that if they are a special case, then clipping them is a special case. The Geometry System clips characters only if they are defined as strokes, just like all other data. However, since it must make possible the clipping of special-case characters and character generation in the display controller, the LoadVP instruction and corresponding data is always passed on to the output port of the system. The reason for this is that this data defines the boundaries of the *character* clipping window in the display controller.

Mixing special-case characters and graphics presents another problem. There are two cases:

- Putting characters in a drawing - this is handled by combining special sentinels to the display controller via the **PassThru** command with the **Point** command. The **Point** command is used to position the beginning of the character string. The Raster Subsystem, which is designed as a companion to the Geometry Subsystem, does the actual character clipping. Completely general character clipping is accomplished by proper use of these subsystems together.

- Putting a drawing with characters - This case is straightforwardly handled by properly modifying the transformation matrix to reflect the character clipping window position. Then drawing can proceed as usual. The particular modifications for each case are handled by the software package mentioned above.

The IRIS Graphics System

The Geometry System is being implemented on the a system called the Integrated Raster Imaging System, IRIS, which consists of the following components:

- A processor/memory board with the Motorola 68000 and 256k bytes of RAM: the memory can be expanded to 2M bytes. The 68000 microprocessor executes instructions in the on-board memory at 8 MHz. This memory is fully mapped and segmented for 16 processes. Additional memory is accessed over the Multibus at normal Multibus rates.

- A Geometry Subsystem, with a multibus interface, FIFO's at the input and output of the Geometry System and from ten to twelve copies of the Geometry Engine.
- A custom 1024x1024 Color Raster Subsystem, with high-performance hardware for polygon fill, vector drawing and arbitrary, variable-pitch characters. The hardware and firmware provide for color and textured lines and polygons, character clipping, color mapping of up to 256 colors and selectable double or single-buffered image planes.
- A 10 Megabit EtherNet interface board.

Summary

The Geometry System is a powerful computing system for graphics applications. It combines a number of useful geometric computing primitives in a custom VLSI system that has a future because of its scalable nature. It is quite likely that within 5 years the system will be implemented on one, 1/2-million transistor, integrated-circuit chip, with a correspondingly reduced cost and increased speed.

Acknowledgements

Many people provided advice and suggestions during the two years over which this project has been done. Marc Hannah's masterful ability with VLSI Design Tools and UNIX and his graphics understanding were indispensible. Professor John Hennessy provided an indispensible microcode development tool in SLIM, and his willingness to help us when in need is appreciated. Lynn Conway of Xerox PARC made resources available during the formative stages of the project, and without them, it probably would not have been carried out; we are indebted to her for this. Forest Baskett of Stanford made it possible by supporting us in the early stages. Dick Lyon was an important first advisor on IC design. Martin Haeberli was very helpful in the testing phase. Valuable conversations were had with Chuck Thacker, Bob Sproull, Alan Bell, Martin Newell, Ed Chang, Danny Cohen, Doug Fairbairn, John Warnock, Chuck Seitz, Carver Mead, and Lance Williams. Hewlett-Packard Corporation fabricated the first copy of the first part of the data-path, and Bob Spencer and Bill Meuli of Xerox PARC's Integrated Circuits Laboratory fabricated the first fully functional copy of the entire chip.

We are especially grateful for the enthusiasm and support of Xerox Corporation's Palo Alto Research Center; this project could not have been done without the support of the insightful people there.

The research was supported by the Advanced Research Projects Agency of the Department of Defense, DARPA, under contract number MDA 903-79-C-0680.

References

1. Clark, J.H. "A VLSI Geometry Processor for Graphics." *Computer 13*, 7 (July 1980), 59-68.

2. Clark, J. H. Graphic Display Processing System and Processor. Patent Pending.

3. Clark, J. H. Parametric Curves, Surfaces and Volumes in Computer Graphics and Computer-Aided Geometric Design. Tech. Rept. 221, Computer Systems Laboratory, Stanford University, November, 1981.

4. Newman, W. and Sproull, R. F.. *Principles of Interactive Computer Graphics.* Addison-Weseley, Reading, Mass., 1980.

The Texas Instruments 34010 Graphics System Processor

Mike Asal, Graham Short, Tom Preston,
Richard Simpson, Derek Roskell, and Karl Guttag

Texas Instruments

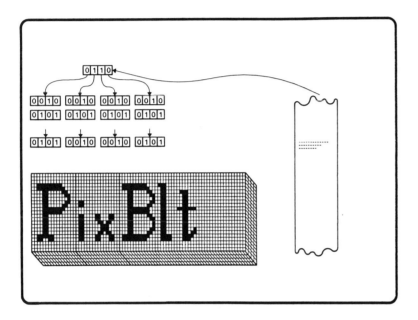

The 34010 Graphics System Processor is a 32-bit graphics microprocessor capable of executing high-level languages. It combines a full general-purpose instruction set with a powerful set of graphics instructions that includes arithmetic as well as Boolean pixblts (pixel block transfers). Because it is completely programmable, the 34010 can be used in many different graphics and nongraphics applications. It was designed to support a wide range of display resolutions and pixel sizes, as well as applications such as page (laser) printers, ink jet printers, data compression, and facsimile transmission.

The 34010 includes such system features as an onboard instruction cache, full interrupt capability, wait and hold functions, and display timing control, as well as test and emulation support. Unique among today's microprocessors, the 34010 addresses all memory down to the bit level with variably sized fields rather than the common byte or word addressing. For example, the 34010 can push a 5-bit quantity onto a stack. This field-processing capability is an integral part of the basic architecture.

The developments leading to the 34010 began at Texas Instruments four years ago. Bitmapped graphics was just starting to find wide use in high-end systems where color was important, and the dominance of vector stroke/scanned high-end graphics systems was diminishing. Terminal and personal computer text displays were almost exclusively handled by hardwired text controllers that generated blocked text typically of 80 columns by 25 rows.

Groups such as those at Xerox PARC[1] were demonstrating that bitmapped graphics could provide better human interfaces and text capabilities as well as more advanced graphics. The improved capability and falling cost of dynamic RAMs indicated that bitmapped graphics would soon be widely used in almost all display systems.

During this period the first VLSI devices aimed at bitmapped graphics were introduced[2] These chips provided hardwired implementations of a few graphics primitives such as one-pixel-wide line and

Reprinted from *IEEE Computer Graphics and Applications*, Volume 6, Number 10, October 1986, pages 24-39. Copyright © 1986 by The Institute of Electrical and Electronics Engineers, Inc.

circle drawings, but text was generated by a hard-wired block text display mode that was not compatible with the display of bitmapped graphics.

In defining the 34010, Texas Instruments decided that to simply extend the number of hardwired algorithms would be a fundamental mistake for several reasons:

1. The number of functions would be fixed. Not only would hardwiring support relatively few algorithms, but new or different algorithms could not be supported.
2. Even the most basic functions could require many attributes such as line style, width, color, and endpoint shape. Hardwiring would mean selecting the attributes to be supported and those to be left out.
3. Customers' experience in quality graphics absolutely required very fine control over the algorithms. Conceptually, drawing to a bitmap means selecting the nearest "integer" pixel, and thus some rounding error shows up as "jaggies" or aliasing. A quality graphics package might need access over any error terms or other parameters.
4. The format of display lists or commands varies according to user requirements. For example, simple block text might require a simple format, while variably sized text requires more complex display lists. The only way to support any format is to have a programmable processor interpret the commands.

The 34010 designers wanted to remove all arbitrary barriers imposed by hardwired controllers on both text and graphics. With the 34010, graphics algorithms could be added as required by a particular application or graphics standard. General-purpose instructions would be used to interpret display lists, with special graphics instructions used for fast pixel manipulations. A complete general-purpose instruction set that could support high-level-language programming (such as C) was blended with very powerful graphics instructions such as the pixblts.[3]

The 34010 was designed to give this flexibility without sacrificing speed in comparison with the hardwired controllers. Hardware such as an instruction cache, a large register file, a barrel shifter, a field mask and merge, and an independent memory controller was intended for the efficient implementation of any function.

The need for a video RAM

While the increased density and falling cost of dynamic RAM have triggered the change to bitmapped text and graphics, the increasing depth of the RAMs creates a fundamental problem. Most display devices must be constantly refreshed, which requires the entire displayable contents of memory to be read out at a periodic rate. Competing with these display refresh reads, a processor must access the memory to update the display's contents. The denser RAM devices, even with faster access modes, were making it impractical or even impossible to read their contents fast enough to support display refresh, let alone allow a processor accesses for updating.

At the beginning of the 34010 program, the designers recognized this problem and worked with the memory group within Texas Instruments to help define the industry's first multiport video RAM. The video RAM[4,5] incorporates a memory array with a large parallel-load and serial-output shift register function. The memory array can transfer a large number of bits (256 in the original version) from the memory array to the shift register in a single memory cycle time. The shift register supports the display refresh function while leaving the random access array free (except for an occasional memory-to-shift-register transfer) for updating.

The 34010 execution model

The 34010 has a 32-bit internal architecture. The CPU is made up of a 256-byte instruction cache; control ROM (CROM) and control logic; and the data path, which includes two 32-bit ALUs, barrel shifter, mask-merge logic, 31 32-bit user registers, left-most-one detection hardware, and window comparators. In addition to the CPU, the 34010 has CRT control, DRAM interface, a separate host processor interface, and an independent memory processor that pipelines accesses to the memory while arbitrating between the various sources generating requests—all integrated on a single chip.

The 34010 combines some of the best attributes of the so-called RISC (reduced instruction set computer) and CISC (complex instruction set computer) approaches into a single architecture. Each approach has its merits,[1] and the design goal with the 34010 was to properly blend these merits. Consistent with the Berkeley RISC[6] concepts, the 34010 has a large register file, simple direct-instruction decoding, low instruction pipelining for fast jumps, move-to-register instructions that zero-extend or (optionally) sign-extend external operands of different sizes to the full register size of 32-bits, and fast register-to-register operations. However, unlike the Berkeley RISC machine and similar to CISC machines, the 34010 allows for multiple-cycle instructions such as multiplies, divides, and the very complex pixblt instructions; pipelined writing to

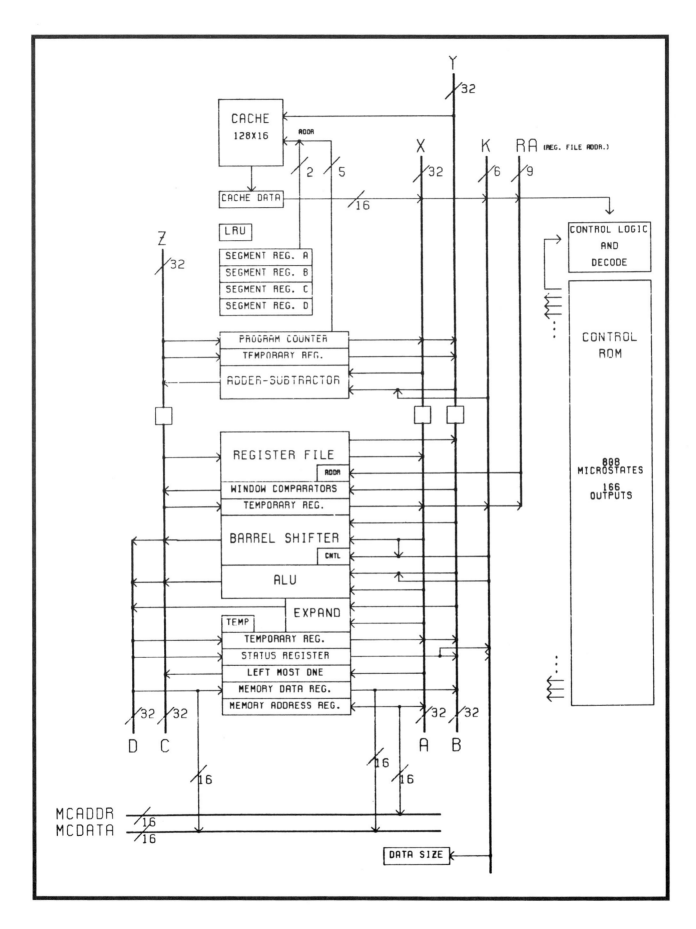

Figure 1. Block diagram of the CPU.

memory; memory-to-memory move instructions; and a wider selection of addressing modes. Additionally, the 34010's instruction cache boosts performance without requiring very fast external memory.

Every memory-to-register, register-to-memory, or memory-to-memory operation is in effect a field extract or field insert. For example, a memory-to-register move operation involves reading a field at a given bit address in memory and either sign-extends or zero-extends the number to 32 bits before it goes into a register. Memory-to-memory move instructions involve reading (extracting) a field at one bit address and storing (inserting) the field at a second bit address. These operations can involve reading, barrel shifting, merging data, and performing read-modify-write operations.

The 31 registers in the register file are organized as two register files, the A and B files, which share the stack pointer. Effectively, the stack pointer can be thought of as both A15 and B15. All of the registers can be used as address or data registers. Of these, only the stack-pointer register is fully dedicated in that it is assumed to point to the stack on which context information is saved in the event of interrupts or subroutine calls. The more complicated graphics functions use some or all of the B file registers as default parameters. When these graphics functions are not being used, these registers can serve any purpose. The A file registers have no predefined function in any instruction and are therefore totally at the user's disposal.

The single-register operand instructions can use any of the 31 registers. With two-register operand instructions, all 31 registers are available as the source operand register, but the destination register must be from the same register file (either A or B) as the source. The move register to register is an exception in that it can be used to move an A file register to a B file register or vice versa. Also, as mentioned earlier, the stack pointer is in both files, so that data from either file can be moved to or from the stack.

In typical applications the large register file can greatly improve performance, as all frequently used variables can be kept in the file for fast access and manipulation. An advantage with the 34010's register file is the ability to support the mixture of high-level-language control and assembly-coded, time-critical functions in separate register files and thus accelerate context switches. The first C compiler used only 13 of the A file registers (more than some other 32-bit CPUs *have*), leaving the B file totally free for assembly code. These registers will often be used by graphics instructions, which can involve many parameters. For example, the complex pixblt uses 15 registers to specify all the possible parame-

ters and to store intermediate variables in the case of an interrupt.

A block diagram of the CPU and its major buses is shown in Figure 1. Three buses run the length of the data path; each can be split into two buses, allowing the data path to operate simultaneously as two independent units. For example, the A-X bus can be split into the A bus and the X bus.

Much of the 34010's power comes from the microcode contained in the CROM, which controls all of the hardware in the CPU. There are 808 microstates and 166 outputs, and nearly half of this very large CROM is devoted to the implementation of the pixblt instructions.

The 256 bytes in the instruction cache are organized as four segments of 32 16-bit words each. Each segment has a corresponding register which contains the base address of the section of memory from which the segment can be loaded. Thus the 34010 can execute code from the cache, which is located in four completely separate areas of memory. The four segments of memory can also be contiguous, allowing fairly lengthy loops to reside entirely in cache. If execution begins in a new area of memory, the new segment replaces the least recently used segment.

These replacements are controlled by the LRU register, which retains a record of the segment least recently used. Segments are further divided into eight subsegments, each with an associated "present flag" to indicate whether the subsegment has actually been loaded. Segments are loaded one subsegment at a time. Thus a segment would be brought into a cache by loading and executing four words, bringing in the next four, and so on.

In general, registers are read out onto buses (A,B,K) at the start of a machine cycle. These buses provide the inputs to the functional units such as the ALU or barrel shifter. Evaluation takes place during mid-cycle. Finally the results of the various operations are loaded onto output buses (C,D), which are then loaded into the appropriate registers.

The next microstate to be executed is determined in parallel with the activity in the data path. With a single-cycle instruction, the CROM address of the next microstate is obtained from the opcode word, which is always read from the cache. If the word indicated by the PC is not currently in cache, then that word, along with the other three words in the subsegment, is loaded. In the case of a multiple-cycle instruction, the next CROM address is contained within the control word of the present microstate. This address is a base address which can be conditioned to allow microbranching to one of several microstates.

To illustrate the internal workings of the CPU, we will take the instruction MOVE RS,·RD+,0 as an

TMS34010 INSTRUCTION SET SUMMARY
(SYNTAX ONLY)

GRAPHICS INSTRUCTIONS[1]

ADDXY	RS,RD
CMPXY	RD,RD
CPW	RS,RD
CVXYL	RS,RD
DRAV	RS,RD
FILL	L
FILL	XY
LINE	Z
MOVX	RS,RD
MOVY	RS,RD
PIXBLT	B,L
PIXBLT	B,XY
PIXBLT	L,L
PIXBLT	L,XY
PIXBLT	XY,L
PIXBLT	XY,XY
PIXT	RS,*RD
PIXT	RS,*RD.XY
PIXT	*RS,RD
PIXT	*RS,*RD
PIXT	*RS.XY,RD
PIXT	*RS.XY,*RD.XY
SUBXY	RS,RD

MOVE INSTRUCTIONS

MOVB	RS,*RD
MOVB	*RS,RD
MOVB	*RS,*RD
MOVB	*RS,*RD(Disp)
MOVB	*RS(Disp),RD
MOVB	*RS(Disp),*RD(Disp)
MOVB	RS,@DAddress
MOVB	@SAddress,RD
MOVB	@SAddress,@DAddress
MOVE	RS,RD
MOVE	RS,*RD,F
MOVE	RS,−*RD,F
MOVE	RS,*RD+,F
MOVE	*RS,RD,F
MOVE	−*RS,RD,F
MOVE	*RS+,RD,F
MOVE	*RS,*RD,F
MOVE	−*RS,−*RD,F
MOVE	*RS+,*RD+,F
MOVE	RS,*RD(Disp),F

MOVE	*RS(Disp),RD,F
MOVE	*RS(Disp),*RD+,F
MOVE	*RS(Disp),*RD(Disp),F
MOVE	RS,@DAddress,F
MOVE	@SAddress,RD,F
MOVE	@SAddress,*RD+,F
MOVE	@SAddress,@DAddress,F

GENERAL INSTRUCTIONS

ABS	RD
ADD	RS,RD
ADDC	RS,RD
ADDI	IW,RD
ADDI	IL,RD
ADDK	K,RD
AND	RS,RD
ANDI	L,RD
ANDN	RS,RD
ANDNI	L,RD
BTST	K,RD
BTST	RS,RD
CLR	RD
CLRC	
CMP	RS,RD
CMPI	IW,RD
CMPI	IL,RD
DINT	
DIVS	RS,RD
DIVU	RS,RD
EINT	
EXGF	RD,F
LMO	RS,RD
MMFM	RS,List
MMTM	RS,List
MODS	RS,RD
MODU	RS,RD
MOVI	IW,RD
MOVI	IL,RD
MOVK	K,RD
MPYS	RS,RD
MPYU	RS,RD
NEG	RD
NEGB	RD
NOP	
NOT	RD
OR	RS,RD

ORI	L,RD
RL	K,RD
RL	RS,RD
SETC	
SETF	FS,FE,F
SEXT	RD,F
SLA	K,RD
SLA	RS,RD
SLL	K,RD
SLL	RS,RD
SRA	K,RD
SRA	RS,RD
SRL	K,RD
SRL	RS,RD
SUB	RS,RD
SUBB	RS,RD
SUBI	IW,RD
SUBI	IL,RD
SUBK	K,RD
XOR	RS,RD
XORI	L,RD
ZEXT	RD,F

PROGRAM CONTROL INSTRUCTIONS

CALL	RS
CALLA	Address
CALLR	Address
DSJ	RD,Address
DSJEQ	RD,Address
DSJNE	RD,Address
DSJS	RD,Address
EMU	
EXGPC	RD
GETPC	RD
GETST	RD
JAcc	Address
JRcc	Address
JRcc	Address
JUMP	RS
POPST	
PUSHST	
PUTST	RS
RETI	
RETS	[N]
TRAP	N

Figure 2. TMS34010 instruction set summary.

example. The syntax for the instruction is as follows: The field to be moved is in the source register from the register file, which is RS. The destination register, RD, is used as a pointer to a memory location and is incremented by the field size after being loaded into the memory address register. The field size is given by either the field size 0 or field size 1 quantity, both of which are contained in the status register. In this case the trailing 0 indicates that field size 0 is to be used. Assuming the instruction is in the cache, only one machine cycle is required for the execution of this instruction. The CPU can execute further instructions from the cache while the memory controller completes the write to memory.

The address in RD is gated onto the A bus, which

is then gated to the memory controller address (MCADDR) bus, if the memory controller is free to start the memory cycle immediately. The A bus is simultaneously loaded into the MA register, which will otherwise provide the address when the memory controller becomes available in a subsequent cycle. Field size 0 is gated from the ST register to the K bus. This value is loaded into the data size register (DS) used by the memory controller to determine the number of bits to be inserted into memory. The A and K buses also provide the inputs to the ALU, which performs an add operation to increment the pointer by the field size.

While these operations are taking place, the data in RS is gated onto the B bus, which is input to the barrel shifter. The four LS bits of the memory address on the A bus determine the alignment of the data within a 16-bit memory word, and hence are used by the barrel shifter as the rotate amount.

At the end of the evaluation phase, the output of the adder-subtractor is gated onto the Z bus, which then loads the PC. The ALU output goes onto the C bus, which is written into RD. Lastly, the BS output gates onto the D bus. Like the address on the A bus, the data on the D bus can be used immediately if the memory cycle has been initiated in that same machine cycle. The MD register is loaded from the D bus and provides the memory controller access to the data in subsequent cycles.

General-purpose instructions

The general-purpose instructions of the 34010 are designed to support a complete programming environment, including the use of high-level languages. The instructions available with the 34010 are listed in Figure 2.

As mentioned earlier, the 34010 supports bit addressing and fields rather than the more common byte addressing. Consequently, all memory operations involve field extraction and/or insertion. The data quantities moved are specified by one of two field sizes, which are programmable and contained in the status register. The field size can be from 1 to 32 bits in length and can begin on arbitrary bit boundaries within a memory word.

When data moves from memory into a register, the field is right justified and either sign- or zero-extended to 32 bits. Register-to-register Boolean, arithmetic, and shift instructions then use the 32-bit data paths to perform 32-bit operations in a single CPU cycle.

The addressing modes for the MOVE instructions reflect the register-based nature of the machine. Register-to-memory, memory-to-register, and memory-to-memory moves are supported for the five types of addressing modes. These are register

indirect, register indirect predecrement (by the field size), register indirect postincrement (also by the field size), register indirect with displacement, and absolute addressing. The 34010's large register file and fast register-to-register instructions make it easy to synthesize more complicated addressing modes.

The integer arithmetic instructions include addition, subtraction, add with carry, subtract with borrow, and signed and unsigned multiplication and division. Most simple integer operations and all eight Boolean operations execute at six million per second out of the instruction cache. The signed and unsigned multiplications use 2-bits-at-a-time hardware to give a 64-bit product in roughly 3 microseconds.

The barrel shifter and sign control logic are used to perform rotate left/right, shift left logical, shift right arithmetic, and shift right logical by any amount (specified either in a register or as a constant) from 1 to 32 bits in a single CPU cycle.

The program flow control instructions give the user conditional jumps, subroutine calls and returns, decrement-skip-jump instructions for looping, program counter and register exchange, and 32 software traps. The 34010 is designed to execute conditional jumps quickly, requiring only one cycle if the jump is not taken and two if the jump is taken.

Instructions are also included for status register modification, including interrupt enabling/disabling and setting of the field size and field extension control.

Graphics instructions

In addition to the conventional linear addressing, the 34010 supports an optional *x-y* addressing function for graphics instructions. Most of these instructions provide a choice between *x-y* or linear addressing. For example, the pixblt instruction allows the source and destination array pointers to be in either format. Consequently there are four different versions of the instruction.

x-y addressing

With *x-y* addressing, a single 32-bit value is treated as separate 16-bit *x* and *y* halves. The two 16-bit values are converted automatically—within the instructions that use *x-y* addressing—to a linear address needed by memories. The generation of the linear address is a function of the *x* and *y* values, the *x-y* array's "pitch" (the linear address difference between two vertically adjacent pixels), and a 32-bit offset that allows the *x-y* address to be relative to any point in memory. The conversion process is shown in Figure 3. The clipping of figures and

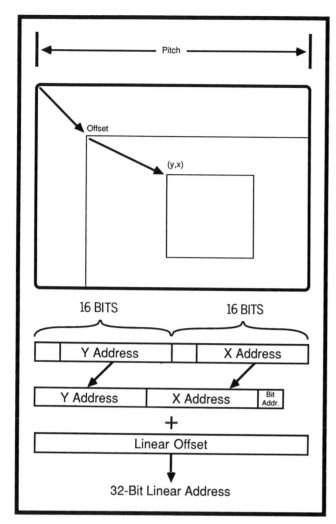

Figure 3. Conversion from _x-y_ address to linear address.

The basic pixblt instruction combines the pixels in the source array with those in the specified destination array. The relative word alignments of the source and destination arrays can be totally arbitrary. Edge conditions are taken care of, and pixels are moved a memory word at a time except at the edges, where read-modify-writes may have to be performed. An added complication for the two-array transfer is the bit alignment of the source and destination arrays, which may be aligned differently with respect to memory word boundaries. Thus the source data must be shifted to align to the destination location before it can be written. This instruction aligns the source and destination arrays automatically and with very little, if any, decrease in performance.

An important feature supported in pixblts is the ability to have different values for the source and destination pitches. For example, an array only 16 bits wide can be stored off screen packed as 16-bit words. When transferred to the bitmap, the source pitch is 16 bits, while the destination pitch is the number of bits in one line of display memory.

Window clipping

A window is specified as a rectangular region that is optionally protected from being overwritten. Probably the most common use is the implementation of a viewport concept. Only the pixels that lie within the window are written to the bitmap.

Four different window clipping options are supported. The "no clipping" option ignores windowing boundaries and does not protect any pixels. The "clip-to-fit" option prohibits pixels outside the window from being written. The "interrupt on window violation" immediately aborts the operation if any point in an operation will lie outside the window. The window violation interrupt is then set and will be taken immediately if it is enabled. The "pick" option determines whether any pixel lies within the window. With the pick option, all pixel drawing is inhibited and the window violation interrupt is issued whenever a pixel would be drawn within the pick region.

For the pixblt instructions with the clip-to-fit option, the destination array is preclipped to the window before any data is transferred. This preclipping avoids the potential waste of large amounts of time computing addresses for pixel transfers that will end up being clipped. Adjustment of the source array is based on adjustment of the destination array.

Pixel processing

Every pixel transferred with the graphics instructions of the 34010 can use pixel processing operations, which combine each source pixel with

arrays to fit within a rectangular region is also supported by _x-y_ addressing.

Other instructions for _x-y_ address manipulation perform _x-y_ addition, subtraction, and comparison. Moves between registers of _x_ or _y_ halves are also provided.

Pixblt

The pixel block transfer instructions give the user a powerful tool for manipulating two-dimensional arrays of pixels. Pixblt supports the combinations of two rectangular arrays of pixels using any of the 22 Boolean and arithmetic pixel processing operations, plus transparency, plane masking, and window clipping options. In addition to simple filling, the FILL instruction supports a single value operating on a rectangular array of pixels with any of the pixel processing options.

Table 1. The 22 pixel-processing options.

PP	Operation				Description
00000		S		→D	Replace destination with source
00001	S	AND	D	→D	AND source with destination
00010	S	AND	D-	→D	AND source with NOT destination
00011			O	→D	Replace destination with zeroes
00100	S	OR	D-	→D	OR source with NOT destination
00101	S	XNOR	D	→D	XNOR source with destination
00110			D-	→D	Negate destination
00111	S	NOR	D	→D	NOR source with destination
01000	S	OR	D	→D	OR source with destination
01001			D	→D	No change in destination*
01010	S	XOR	D	→D	XOR source with destination
01011	S-	AND	D	→D	AND NOT source with destination
01100			1	→D	Replace destination with ones
01101	S-	OR	D	→D	OR NOT source with destination
01110	S	NAND	D	→D	NAND source with destination
01111			S-	→D	Replace destination with NOT source

*Although the destination array is not changed by this operation, memory cycles still occur.

The following six pixel-processing codes perform arithmetic operations on pixels of size 4, 8, and 16 bits.

PP	Operation		Description
10000	D + S	→D	Add source to destination
10001	ADDS(D,S)	→D	Add S to D with saturation
10010	D – S	→D	Subtract source from destination
10011	SUBS(D,S)	→D	Subtract S from D with saturation
10100	MAX(D,S)	→D	Maximum of source and destination
10101	MIN(D,S)	→D	Minimum of source and destination

the corresponding destination pixel before overwriting the destination pixel with the result. Both logical and arithmetic processing are supported. The 16 standard Boolean operations are familiar from their use in bitblts.[7]

Less familiar but very important for pixblts are the arithmetic operations that operate on entire pixels rather than on the individual bits within pixels. For multiple-bits-per-pixel applications, these operations are not only desirable but necessary.[3] Six of these options are supported. The entire list of 22 pixel processing options is shown in Table 1.

Plane mask

The plane mask enables the user to inhibit writes to some or all of the bits within a pixel. For example, when a pixel contains information for a group of planes, the bits associated with a given plane or planes can be protected. Thus text can be modified in one plane while the graphics information in other planes remains unaffected. This mask is applied to pixel data as it is read into the chip as well as to the data to be written externally.

Transparency

Transparency detection can be selected to treat zero-value pixels as transparent. This detection is applied to the result of pixel processing and plane masking. With transparency enabled, a pixel of zero value does not overwrite the destination pixel, leaving the background unchanged. In this way, only the part of a rectangular array that makes up the desired shape (such as a text character) is actually written. The overlaying of text on graphics then becomes a very simple task.

Direction of pixblt

For the basic pixblt instruction, any of the four corners can be selected as the starting corner. This in turn determines the direction in which the transfer takes place. Thus the overlapping of source and destination arrays (which commonly occurs with scrolling) can be handled in a manner that prevents the overwriting of subsequent source data by writes to the current destination location.

Expand

The pixblt with expand option is very useful for transforming a 1-bit-per-pixel shape such as a text font to a color image in the bitmap. Each pixel is expanded from 1 bit to either a "one color" or "zero color," which can be 1, 2, 4, 8, or 16 bits in length. This process is illustrated in Figure 4. After expansion, any of the arithmetic and Boolean operations can be applied, as well as such options as transparency and plane masking.

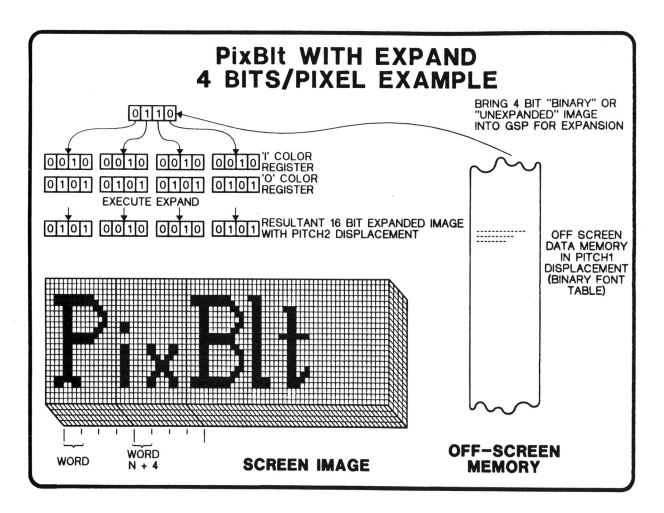

Figure 4. Expansion of the 1-bit-per-pixel representation to a color image.

Single-pixel instructions

There are several instructions for manipulating individual pixels. A set of single-pixel transfer (pixt) instructions supports both *x-y* and linear addressing for either the source or destination pointers. Windowing, pixel processing options, transparency, and plane masking are all supported for this instruction.

The Draw and Advance (DRAV) provides the basis for incrementally drawing figures such as lines and circles. This instruction combines a single-pixel draw (with pixel processing operations) with an addition to both the *x* and *y* halves of an *x-y* address pointer.

A simple assembly language implementation of the inner loop of Bresenham's line algorithm[8] using DRAV is shown in Figure 5. The code for the inner loop requires just seven 34010 instructions, but for any given pixel to be drawn, the conditional branching causes only four of the instructions to be executed.

To draw a line from $(y0, x0)$ to $(y1, x1)$, where $a =$ $x1 - x0$, $b = y1 - y0$, and $a \geq b$, the registers used are set up according to Figure 5. The microcoded LINE instruction replaces the code shown in the figure, nearly doubling the performance. This instruction still supports very flexible endpoint and jagged-line control by letting the programmer control the decision variable (or error term). The action taken when the decision variable is zero is also programmable. Windowing, pixel processing, transparency, and plane masking are all available, as with the other pixel transfer instructions.

Compare Point to Window

One additional instruction extremely useful in the software implementation of many graphics algorithms is Compare Point to Window (CPW). Executing in a single cycle, CPW compares the *x* and *y* values of a given point to the corresponding values of both the window start and window end registers, generating a 4-bit code. This code indicates in which of the nine regions relative to the window the point lies. This concept, illustrated in Figure 6, is best

```
A0 = Destination pointer    (y0,x0)
A1 = Increment1             (1,1)
A2 = Increment2             (0,1)
A3 = Pixel count            a - 1
A4 = Decision variable      d
A5 = Temporary1             2b - a
A6 = Temporary2             2b
B9 = Pixel color1


LOOP:
  JRN DNEG       ; Jump to DNEG if the decision
                 ;   variable d is negative
  DRAV A1,A0     ; Write pixel to location specified
                 ;   by A0 and add the increment
                 ;   value in A1
  ADD A5,A4      ; Add the temporary value in A5
                 ;   to d
  DSJS A3,LOOP   ; Decrement the count and loop
                 ;   until zero
  RETS           ; Finished

DNEG:
  DRAV A2,A0     ; Write pixel to location specified
                 ;   by A0 and add the increment
                 ;   value in A2
  ADD A6,A4      ; Add the temporary value in A6
                 ;   to d
  DSJS A3,LOOP   ; Decrement the count and loop
                 ;   until zero
  RETS           ; Finished
```

Figure 5. Implementation of Bresenham's line algorithm using DRAV.

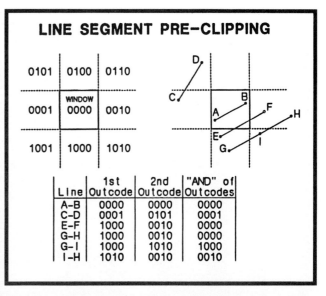

Line	1st Outcode	2nd Outcode	"AND" of Outcodes
A–B	0000	0000	0000
C–D	0001	0101	0001
E–F	1000	0010	0000
G–H	1000	0010	0000
G–I	1000	1010	1000
I–H	1010	0010	0010

Figure 6. The 4-bit code produced by the CPW instruction is very useful in clipping algorithms.

known for its use in the Cohen-Southerland line-clipping algorithm.[9]

The 34010 design architecture

The 34010 currently is driven by a 50-MHz input clock whose frequency is divided by 8 internally to give a machine state rate that allows execution of more than 6 million instructions per second from the cache. It uses 1.8-μm CMOS technology to integrate 200,000 transistors on the chip with a typical power dissipation of 0.5 watt. The 34010 is housed in a 68-pin plastic package. A die photo is shown in Figure 7.

Local memory control

The 34010 provides a comprehensive set of signals for external memory control. The high frequency of the input clock allows generation of signal timing with sufficient resolution to efficiently interface to DRAMs. Eight control signals and a 16-bit address/data bus allow most combinations of external memory devices to use minimal additional logic. Two signals, DEN and DDOUT, can be used to control bidirectional transceivers where buffering is required. LAL is provided to latch the multiplexed column address so that the triple-multiplexed bus is free to function as a data bus. RAS, CAS, and W are standard DRAM control signals which, together with the 16-bit multiplexed address/data bus, provide a direct DRAM interface. The TR/QE signal can be used as a simple output enable for RAMs as well as the shift register transfer control for video RAMs. A "ready" function is also provided on another pin to cater to slow memories.

The memory controller is a separate autonomous controller interfacing to "local" memory systems. Its main function is to service requests from the CPU, the host interface, and the display refresh and DRAM refresh mechanisms. The memory controllers must be fairly intelligent to handle the bit-addressable, variable-size field requests from the 34010's CPU. For example, in a register-to-memory transfer, the CPU will define the field size (1-32 bits) to be moved and the bit location where the first bit of the field is to be placed. The memory controller must translate the CPU request into one or more memory cycles. Since the memory controller is autonomous, on write cycles the CPU does not have to wait for the write cycle(s) to complete; instead the CPU can execute code while the memory controller writes to memory.

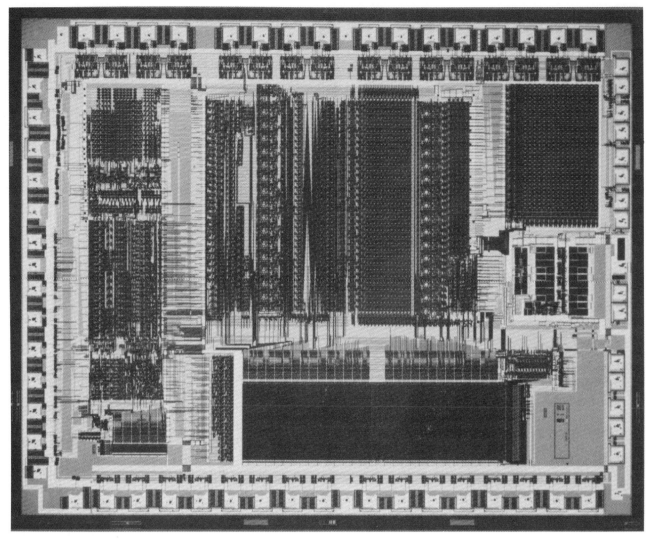

Figure 7. Die photo of the 34010 Graphics System Processor.

Video controller

The video control section of the 34010 provides the sync and blanking signals used in CRT control as well as direct support of video RAMS. The video clock input (VCLK) can be totally asynchronous with respect to the 34010's main CPU processor clock (INCLK), so that the processor and video timing can be independently optimized. Eight 16-bit timing control registers support generation of horizontal and vertical timing waveforms for essentially any display resolution. In internal sync mode the 34010 will generate the sync outputs from VCLK. In external mode the video controller will read either one or both of the sync signals as input(s) and synchronize screen refreshes accordingly. This permits graphics images created by the 34010 to be superimposed on images created externally.

In addition to sync and blank generation, the video controller performs the video-RAM-to-shift-register cycles needed to refresh the screen. Three I/O registers (DPYADR, DPYCTL, and DPYSTRT) allow screen refreshing to be configured to whatever memory configuration is adopted.

DRAM refresh

The 34010 has a separate counter that schedules DRAM refresh cycles. It can be configured to provide either RAS-only refresh with 8 bits of refresh address, or CAS-before-RAS refresh where no address is needed.

Host interface

The 34010 has been designed to maximize system performance and ease of use while minimizing system chip count. The external interface signals and their various groupings are shown in Figure 8.

The 34010 contains a host interface consisting of a 16-bit bidirectional data bus and nine control pins. The control pins are designed to support any of the commercially available microprocessor interfaces with little external logic, and the upper and lower bytes of the 16 data pins can be wired together to support 8-bit microprocessors. The interface can be configured to work either high-byte first or low-byte first (addressing the so-called Little Endian/Big Endian problem faced in processor-to-processor interfaces).

This interface supports a pipelined indirect pointer mechanism for having a host processor access the memory space of the 34010. It can support sequential reading or writing of up to 5M bytes per second. This is one of two ways that a host processor can access the 34010's memory. The other method uses a conventional hold interface, described below.

The host interface consists of a 32-bit address register and 16-bit data and control registers. The address pointer can point to external local memory or to the 28 memory-mapped I/O registers inside the 34010. The interface to the host can be totally asynchronous. The HRDY (host-ready) pin is used to signal a host in case overrunning the pipeline makes it necessary to stretch a cycle. The dedicated interrupt pin can be used by the 34010 to signal the host.

Also provided in the host interface are two 8-bit host control registers. The host control register enables the host to halt the 34010's CPU at the end of the current instruction. (The memory controller keeps running to give the host and refresh control access to the memory.) It also allows the host to generate a nonmaskable interrupt to grab control of the 34010 or generate a maskable interrupt with a 3-bit code for message passing.

Hold

A straightforward hold/hold-acknowledge system provides direct access to the 34010's local memory by another processor. Asserting hold will cause the local memory address/data and control pins to enter a high-impedance state so that external devices can access local RAM directly. The hold-acknowledge output tells the requesting processor that the bus is in a high-impedance state.

Emulation

The 34010 was designed to directly support hardware development systems by building emulation capability into the chip. The RUN/EMU pin, together with an emulation acknowledge output, controls the emulation mode. This allows a development system to dump and load the contents of

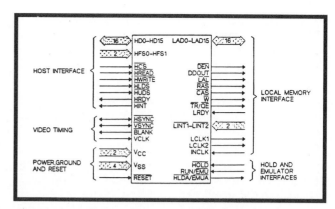

Figure 8. Pinout with interface groupings.

the 34010 under the control of a code placed on the three pins LINT1, LINT2, and HOLD.

Testability

The increasing demands for complex devices fuel an increasing demand for effective and thorough testing. A special effort was made to incorporate a comprehensive test mechanism. Testability strategies for VLSI circuits aim to increase the controllability and observability of internal storage nodes (or bits). The 34010 was designed so that on any CPU cycle the machine can be stopped, and then every storage node on the device can be dumped and/or loaded. This permits the necessary observation into the machine as well as control in setting up the state of the machine.

Power and interrupts

A total of four separate ground lines and two separate power lines provide for fast-switching outputs with low noise. The reset input performs a hardwired reset function, clearing various registers and performing a trap 0 on release. Two pins in this group are provided for external interrupts from either a host or coprocessor.

Applying the 34010

In defining the 34010, the designers learned about the breadth of graphics functions that should be supported in a complete graphics system. We will offer just a few examples of the types of functions a 34010 can be called on to perform and try to give a little insight into some of the 34010's features that are particularly useful in each application.

Text

Text has been and will remain the most important graphical element for most systems. Applications generally have different text display requirements. Text displays will vary from emulating the older block text to very sophisticated electronic publishing displays. The complexity of the display list structure that defines what will be displayed varies accordingly.

With bitmapped graphics, characters can be of essentially any size. Characters commonly have different widths so that they can be packed tightly together, with narrower letters requiring less storage space. To further save memory space, the fonts are generally not stored in memory with the same "pitch" as the display memory.

Geometric (or equation-defined) text descriptors give even further flexibility. Geometric text can be scaled or rotated to provide variations that would require an infinite amount of storage if different sizes and orientations for each character had to be stored individually. Theoretically, geometric text could be slow to compute the shape of each letter, but in most text applications the overhead can be very small. Typically the text will consist of only a few sizes, styles, and orientations, and thus once a letter has been translated from equation to a bitmapped image, it can be used repeatedly via block transferring. The 34010 could generate the fonts from the equations and, of course, block transfer the characters onto the screen memory.

The 34010's general-purpose instructions can be used to interpret any display list structure, be it simple or complex. The result of the display list interpretation will be a pointer to the font (or shape) of each letter and a pointer to where the character should appear on the display. A pixblt instruction (often the pixblt with color expand) will then be used to copy the font image onto the display memory.

The pixblt itself can be quite complicated. The binary-to-color expand option supports efficient storage of arbitrary-size fonts at 1 bit per pixel. Any of the Boolean or arithmetic operations can be called on for combining the text with the current image. Transparency detection can be used for handling overlapping color characters. The pixblts can automatically clip each character to fit within a rectangular window. The screen image might be x-y addressed with one memory pitch, while the character would be linearly addressed with a different memory pitch. Any plane or group of planes can be masked (or locked). And all of the above-mentioned operations can be performed by a single 34010 pixblt instruction.

Line, circle, ellipse, and general figure drawing

Most figure drawing with a 34010 will be performed using "incremental algorithms," which have been widely described.[10-12] The fast general-purpose

instructions and special instructions that allow independent addition/subtraction of the x and y halves of a 32-bit register are used to generate essentially any function.

Incremental algorithms generally have one or more decision variables. Among other things, these variables keep track of the error term(s) associated with rounding to an integer pixel grid and maintain the mathematical accuracy as a figure is drawn. To maintain full accuracy for common figures generated on typical display resolutions requires up to 32 bits of precision. For example, long and thin ellipses can roll over 16 bits of error term and have been known to cause rather undesirable effects.

The 34010's 32-bit-wide by 31-register file is large enough to hold all the decision variables for any of the common figure-drawing algorithms. If a figure to be drawn starts at a noninteger coordinate (as can easily happen when a figure is clipped or results from floating-point math), the decision variable must be initialized, a task the arithmetic instructions of the 34010 can perform.

Simple forms of antialiasing (gray-scale smoothing) can be performed relatively quickly by using the decision variable to control the intensity of what is being written.[13] As these antialiased figures are drawn on top of each other, operations other than replace or Boolean functions must be used to prevent the faint fringes of one figure from obliterating the solid part of a previously drawn figure.[14] The MAX and MIN operators can provide a reasonable mechanism for drawing and combining certain classes of antialiased objects.

Filled objects

Just drawing one-pixel-wide outlines of objects is not enough for most of today's graphics applications; filling is often required. The two basic ways to generate a filled object are by direct filling of the object from the equations defining it, or by seed (flood) filling a region enclosed by some boundary.

Seed filling is sometimes useful in artistic applications such as MacPaint, where it is intuitively easy to use; one simply draws a border (or outline) and floods the region with a color and/or pattern, analogous to children's coloring books.[15] Within the class of seed filling there are several variations. The algorithm can vary because of how the border is "connected."[16] The border can be defined by pixels that are equal to a certain value, not equal to a certain value, inside or outside a range of values, or by many other functions. Combinations of general-purpose instructions, fill (with pixel processing) instructions, and pixblts have been used to implement seed-filling algorithms on the 34010.

While seed filling is useful in some interactive applications, it cannot be used for many applications, and direct equation-controlled filling is necessary. Seed filling is slower than direct filling, as pixels must be read and checks for the border made. For a seed fill of a general figure not seeded by human intervention, it can be difficult to determine an "interior pixel" so that the drawing can begin. Seed filling cannot, for example, handle the drawing of one object on top of another because pixels in the object below might be interpreted as the border.

There are many different approaches to direct-equation filling, and often there are very important trade-offs between speed and the complexity of the object that the algorithm can render. The 34010 can, of course, be programmed to handle any degree of complexity.

Convex objects such as polygons (Figure 9a), circles, ellipses, and pie wedges lend themselves to faster fill algorithms. The procedure for performing convex polygon filling using the 34010 is outlined below (some special cases and details are left out for simplicity):

1. Sort the endpoints of all the figures to be drawn by their y (vertical) values. This task uses the 34010's x-y compares, and its conditional jumps and moves.
2. The filling starts with the two lines that share a common point with the lowest y value. With the exception of the special case of one of the two lines' being horizontal, there will be a left line and a right line. The 34010's fast arithmetic, conditional jumps, and special ADDXY instructions will be used to compute each line incrementally. Each line algorithm is run until it steps vertically. Once both have stepped vertically one pixel, a horizontal line is drawn between the two computed endpoints (using either a FILL or pixblt instruction). This step repeats until one of the two lines is done.
3. The endpoints of the next line segment from the y sorting (which should share an endpoint with the line just finished) are then used to start a line that replaces the one that has been completed. This process continues until all line segments are used up.

The convex polygon fill demonstrates how some of the features of the 34010 can be used. The 34010's register file is large enough to contain all the variables for both lines as well as the parameters for the FILL instruction. The instruction cache is large enough to hold both of the line-draw algorithms as well as algorithms for fetching new lines. Holding all the parameters and instructions on chip permits fast execution of the convex fill algorithm even though it can be programmed to the user's exact requirements.

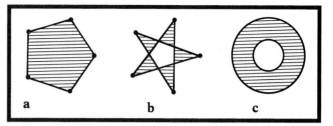

Figure 9. (a) Convex polygon; (b) self-intersecting polygon; (c) figure with a hole.

Filling more general figures (such as Figures 9b and 9c) may involve greater complexity. The five-pointed star of Figure 9b is a polygon that self-intersects. Figure 9c is a doughnut ring with a hole. In both cases, determining what is inside (filled) and what is outside (not filled) involves some ambiguity. Thus rules have to be adopted that define the inside and outside. With the parity rule, a pixel is defined to be inside the object if an odd number of boundary crossings is required to get to the given pixel. In the doughnut, for example, it takes two crossings to get to the hole, and thus the pixel is outside.

Perhaps the simplest way to implement arbitrary filled objects with the parity rule is to first draw the outlines defining the object at 1 bit per pixel into a scratchpad area. The scratchpad has a 1-bit-per-pixel mapping of the screen image[17] and is at least as large as the minimum enclosing rectangle of the image. When the outline is drawn, it is important to use the XOR operation; without it there is the possibility of "leaks" if the outline crosses. Once the outline is drawn, each horizontal line of the scratchpad space is scanned, counting the number of times a pixel defining the boundary is crossed. Between pixels where the number of crossings is odd, a fill (perhaps with a texture) is made to the corresponding part of the display memory at the full pixel depth.

With the 34010, the single CPU cycle left-most-one instruction can be very useful for scanning the horizontal line for the even or odd number of ones. The fact that the 34010 can flexibly handle different numbers of bits per pixel is useful in dealing with the 1-bit-per-pixel scratchpad and the screen's frame buffer, which has perhaps many bits per pixel. The ability to support different array pitches allows the 34010 to efficiently place the scratchpad area.

In dealing with filled objects (or almost any other graphics figure), there are many subtle and not-so-subtle variations that users may want to make; thus, the ability to use different algorithms is important. A classic problem is how to deal with the pixels on the edge of the polygon.[18] This problem is evident when dealing with two adjacent polygons that share a common edge. If neither polygon draws the pixels on the edge, then there will be a gap; but if both draw the edge, they may not generate the desired image. This is a problem particularly when a pixel-processing operation is involved, as it will be performed twice on the pixels along the edge.

Image compression/expansion

Graphics images can require extremely large amounts of memory. A single 640 × 480 × 8 medium-resolution image requires about 300K bytes of memory, roughly the entire capacity of a typical PC's floppy disk, if stored uncompressed. Even with significant advances in storage technology, images will clearly have to be compressed for both storage and transmission.

Image compression is based on identifying some way in which the image contains redundant information and then using fewer bits to describe the redundant parts. For some applications, such as encoding a television picture or photograph, the goal may be to save an image that will appear good enough to the naked eye while allowing some sacrifice of the "digital fidelity" of the original image to improve the compression. In other applications it will be necessary to maintain an exactly reproducible version of the original image. Practical trade-offs will also be made in the time required for compression versus the amount of compression an application may require.

Most algorithms assume a particular kind of redundancy that has been shown empirically to occur. Different images will compress better with different algorithms. More intelligent programs can adapt and select a compression algorithm that best compresses all, or given portions, of the image.

Take, for example, the CCITT group 3 and 4 compression standards,[19,20] which were defined to generate a reasonable compression for the type of images that commonly occur in facsimile transmission. The compression involves looking for alternating "runs" on each horizontal line of white and black ("0" and "1") dots and using variable-length codes. Shorter codes are used for run lengths that occur more frequently. Occasionally, the compression can be negative; that is, it may produce more bits than it saves. The standard has a provision to "adapt" and send a special code that indicates a string of uncompressed code.

In compressing a CCITT image, the 34010's single CPU cycle left-most-one (LMO) and shift instructions can be used to scan across bits, looking for the run lengths. (Using a NOT instruction before the LMO allows it to look for the leading "0.") Once the length of the run has been identified, a table lookup can be used to translate the run length into the variably sized code. Each table entry would have the bits corresponding to the code and the size of the code. The code size would be used as the field size for a 34010 MOVE instruction to move the code to the output stack. For decompression, a combination of table lookups and field moves can be used to extract and turn the codes into the number of bits to be drawn in a run. The run length is then used by the FILL instruction to determine how many bits are to be drawn.

Summary

The 34010 provides a unique combination of general programmability, graphics processing power, and system integration on a single integrated circuit. The design philosophy was to not restrict graphics to a few primitive functions, but rather to support whatever functions are required in any application. ■

References

1. D.H. Ingalls, "The Smalltalk Graphics Kernel," *Byte*, Vol. 6, No. 8, Aug. 1981, pp.128-194.

2. J.L. Wise and H. Szenjnwald, "Display Controller Simplifies Design of Sophisticated Graphics Terminals," *Electronics*, Vol. 54, No. 7, Apr. 7, 1981, pp.153-157.

3. K. Guttag, J. Vanaken, and M. Asal, "Requirements for a VLSI Graphics Processor," *IEEE CG&A*, Vol. 6, No. 1, Jan. 1986, pp.32-47.

4. Ray Pinkham, Mark Novak, and Karl Guttag, "Video RAM Excels at Fast Graphics," *Electronic Design*, Vol. 31, No. 17, Aug. 18, 1983, pp.161-182.

5. Mary C. Whitton, "Memory Design for Raster Graphics Displays," *IEEE CG&A*, Vol. 4, No. 3, Mar. 1984, pp.48-65.

6. Robert P. Colwell et al., "Computers, Complexity, and Controversy," *Computer*, Vol. 18, No. 9, Sept. 1985, pp.8-19.

7. D.A. Patterson and C.H. Sequin, "A VLSI RISC," *Computer*, Vol. 15, No. 9, Sept. 1982, pp.8-21.

8. J.E. Bresenham, "Algorithm for Computer Control of a Digital Plotter," *IBM Systems J.*, Vol. 4, No. 1, 1965, pp.25-30.

9. J. Foley and A. Van Dam, *Fundamentals of Interactive Computer Graphics*, Addison-Wesley, Reading, Mass., 1982, pp.144-148.

10. M.L.V. Pitteway, "Algorithm for Drawing Ellipses or Hyperbolae with a Digital Plotter," *Computer J.*, Vol. 10, No. 3, Nov. 1967, pp.282-289.

11. J.E. Bresenham, "A Linear Algorithm for Incremental Display of Digital Arcs," *Comm. ACM*, Vol. 20, No. 2, Feb. 1977, pp.100-106.

12. Jerry R. Van Aken, "An Efficient Ellipse-Drawing Algorithm," *IEEE CG&A*, Vol.4, No. 9, Sept. 1984, pp.24-35.

13. Akira Fujimoto and Kansei Iwata, "Jag-Free Images on Raster Displays," *IEEE CG&A*, Dec. 1983, pp.26-34.

14. A.R. Forrest, "Antialiasing in Practice," in *Fundamental Algorithms for Computer Graphics*, R.A. Earnshaw, ed., Springer-Verlag, New York, 1985, pp.113-134.

15. Henry Lieberman, "How To Color in a Coloring Book," *Computer Graphics* (Proc. SIGGRAPH 78), Vol. 12, No. 3, Aug. 1978, pp.111-116.

16. J. Foley and A. Van Dam, *Fundamentals of Interactive Computer Graphics*, Addison-Wesley, Reading, Mass., 1982, pp.446-451.

17. A.C. Gay, "Experience in Practical Implementations of Boundary-Defined Area Fill," in *Fundamental Algorithms for Computer Graphics*, R.A. Earnshaw, ed., Springer-Verlag, New York, 1985, pp.153-160.

18. Michael Dunlavey, "Efficient Polygon-Filling Algorithms for Raster Displays," *ACM Trans. Graphics*, Vol. 2, No. 4, Oct. 1983, pp.264-273.

19. "Standardization of Group 3 Facsimile Apparatus For Document Transmission," recommendation T.4, CCITT, 1984.

20. "Facsimile Coding Schemes and Coding Control Functions for Group 4 Facsimile Apparatus," recommendation T.6, CCITT, 1984.

Tom Preston is currently working for General Datacomm in Connecticut. Previously he spent almost 10 years with Texas Instruments in both the US and England. In his most recent assignment for TI, he was logic design manager on the TMS34010 from 1983 to 1986. Before that he worked on the TMS9995 and the development of VLSI memory components.

Preston received a BSc in physics from Birmingham University, England, and a master's degree from Southampton University, England. He was elected a senior member of the technical staff at TI in 1986. He holds several patents in the area of microprocessors, and he is a member of IEEE.

Richard Simpson is a group member of the technical staff at Texas Instruments' MMP Division's Bedford, England, design center. He was in charge of all circuit design for the TMS34010. Simpson joined the Bedford MOS Design Centre in August 1977 as a MOS design engineer and has worked on the design and testing of several VLSI MOS devices: the TMS9914 GPIB, the TMS9995 16-bit microprocessor, the TMS32010 digital signal processor, as well as the TMS34010. He is presently design manager for an upgraded version of the TMS34010.

Simpson received his BSc in electrical engineering from Imperial College, University of London, in 1977.

Derek Roskell is a design manager in Texas Instruments' Microprocessor and Microcomputer Products (MMP) Division's design center in Bedford, England. He was the design manager for the TMS34010. Roskell joined TI in 1965 and worked on semiconductor test equipment design until 1971. He transferred to the Bipolar Linear Department as a design engineer and worked on I2L design of teletext chips. In 1978 he joined what is now the Microprocessor and Microcomputer Products Division as a project manager on the TMS9995 16-bit microprocessor. In 1986 he became a senior member of the TI technical staff.

Roskell received his BSEE from Leicester College of Technology in 1963.

Mike Asal is a design engineer in the Microprocessor and Microcomputer Products (MMP) Division of Texas Instruments in Houston, Texas. He is currently working on the definition and design of the next generation graphics microprocessor. Since joining TI in 1982, he has worked on the specification, internal architecture, and design of the TMS34010. His specific design responsibilities were CPU logic and microcode. His research interests include microprocessor architecture and the use of VLSI technology in computer graphics.

Asal received a BSEE and an MSEE from Bradley University in 1981 and 1982, respectively. He is a member of the IEEE.

Karl M. Guttag is the graphics strategy manager for the Microprocessor and Microcontroller Division of Texas Instruments in Houston, Texas. Since 1982 he has been responsible for graphics products definition, including the TMS34010 graphics system processor and the early multiport video RAM definition. From 1979 to 1981 he was the IC architect of the TMS9995 and TMS99000 16-bit microprocessors. He started with TI in 1977 as a design engineer on the TMS9918 Video Display Processor. In 1982 he was made a senior member of the technical staff of Texas Instruments. He currently holds 15 patents in the areas of microprocessors and computer graphics.

Guttag received his BSEE from Bradley University in 1976 and his MSEE from the University of Michigan in 1977. He is a member of IEEE and ACM.

Graham Short is a design engineer with Texas Instruments' MMP Division's Bedford, England, design center. He joined TI in 1980 and has worked on logic entry, design verification, and, more recently, on silicon test, debug, and characterization of the TMS34010. He worked for two years with the Design Automation Department in Bedford developing software for microcomputer boards, including a graphics board based on the TMS9995. After a brief assignment on robot controllers, he moved to MOS design to work on the TMS34010.

Short graduated from Kent University with a degree in math and computer science. He recently received an MSEE from the University of London.

The authors can be contacted at Texas Instruments, PO Box 1443, MS 6407, Houston, TX 77001.

National's Advanced Graphics Chip Set for High-Performance Graphics

Charles Carinalli and John Blair
National Semiconductor

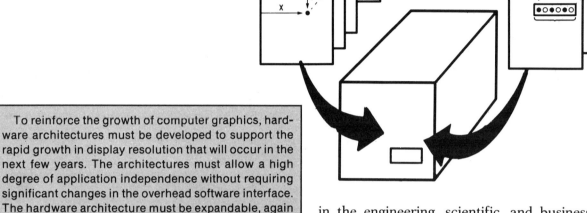

To reinforce the growth of computer graphics, hardware architectures must be developed to support the rapid growth in display resolution that will occur in the next few years. The architectures must allow a high degree of application independence without requiring significant changes in the overhead software interface. The hardware architecture must be expandable, again avoiding significant software changes. Finally, the architecture must be implemented in VLSI for reasons of cost and speed.

This article will describe a graphics hardware architecture that meets these criteria.

Computer graphics is one of today's fastest growing market segments. The fundamental reason for this dramatic growth is the productivity improvement that a graphic representation can bring to problem solving in engineering, scientific, business, and consumer applications. Nothing does more to simplify the human-to-computer interface for data presentation and interpretation than a graphics display and efficient application software.

The decreasing cost of high-quality CRT displays and significant reductions in the cost of dynamic RAM have enabled computer graphics to rapidly penetrate all market segments in the past few years. A number of graphics-oriented VLSI integrated circuits are now becoming commercially available and will further decrease the cost of high-performance graphics hardware.

Now that more people have become aware of the impact of computer graphics on job productivity, the demand for higher resolution, faster graphics, and greater affordability will increase significantly

Portions of this article were originally presented at Wescon/85.

in the engineering, scientific, and business communities. Attainment of these goals by developers of graphics hardware will expand both the use of computer graphics and its application areas.

Graphics architecture

This article will not discuss all the varied aspects of software and hardware computer graphics architectures. We will address the problems of hardware architectures in the area of list-driven display generation, manipulation, and screen refresh. Current monochrome graphics hardware architectures generally do not satisfy the current demands of high-performance computer graphics, which include display resolutions of 1000 × 1000 pixels or more, very high speed screen manipulations, and color.

Key performance issues

Figure 1 is a block representation of the logical hardware and software partitioning associated with a typical graphics system. The left block represents the application interface and image creation segments. Data must be translated from the database found on disk (or received via communications networks) to a format that will be meaningful in the CRT display. At the application level this may involve database interpretation and translation to and from graphics standards such as GKS and CORE. But it also involves the final translation from what is described as the "world space" representation to

Reprinted from *IEEE Computer Graphics and Applications*, Volume 6, Number 10, October 1986, pages 40-48. Copyright © 1986 by The Institute of Electrical and Electronics Engineers, Inc.

the "normalized" coordinate space associated with the hardware of the particular graphics system in use. This is done with the main CPU in software or through hardware acceleration made possible by a number of VLSI integrated circuits on the market.

Once this translation is completed, the transfer to the actual display coordinates is usually accomplished through an instruction list given to a graphics processor linked directly to the CRT frame buffer. The function of this graphics processor is to offload the main CPU in the creation and manipulation of the massive amounts of data in the actual bitmap in the frame buffer. Without this block, any large bitmap manipulation would cripple the main CPU in its principal application chores.

The final blocks of the figure represent the portion of the graphics system that handles the lower level image movements and manipulations as well as the screen refresh function. High-speed hardware implementation of these blocks with an architecture that links closely with the graphics processor is the only way performance can be maintained as display resolution increases along with the increasing number of memory planes for color.

We will focus on the performance issues of the last two major blocks of Figure 1 and factors that will influence

- list-driven display generation
- graphic data manipulation and movement
- screen refresh

The technical problems inherent in providing cost-effective architectural solutions with present hardware (given the current and future performance requirements) make these functions ideal candidates for VLSI integrated circuits.

The graphics frame buffer— screen refresh architecture

To focus on these performance issues requires a good understanding of the trade-offs associated with the graphics frame buffer. Figure 2 is a simplified diagram of a typical graphics workstation. The graphics controller is shown closely linked to the memory associated with the CRT screen display (called the CRT refresh memory or the frame buffer) and the main CPU with its associated graphics geometry-processing hardware and software. This figure shows the popular configuration in which a special processor is allocated to handle graphics functionality, thus relieving the main CPU of fundamental graphics operations. Those operations are list-driven on the basis of a lower level graphics software language. Later we will discuss

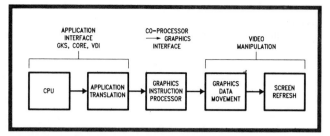

Figure 1. The logical hardware and software partitioning of a typical graphics system.

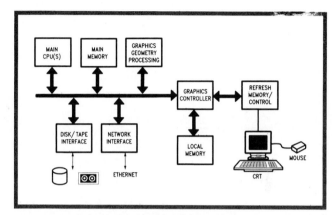

Figure 2. Typical graphics workstation.

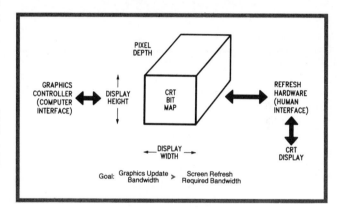

Figure 3. Graphics frame buffer.

the advantages of this arrangement and some specific implementations.

The image stored in the frame buffer is actually stored conceptually in three dimensions, as shown by the cube represented in Figure 3. Each pixel on the screen can be mapped to multiple bits (in the case of color) contained within this cube. Access to the data stored in the cube is necessary for screen refresh, update, and data manipulation. Ideally, the amount of time available for manipulation should greatly exceed the time required for screen refresh, thus enabling very quick display update and image movement.

The fundamental graphics trade-offs involve the

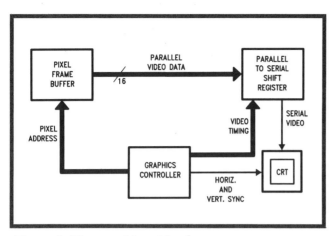

Figure 4. The graphics video loop.

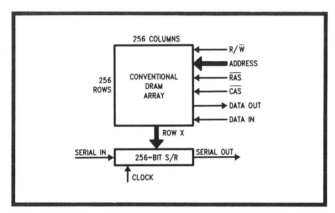

Figure 5. The video DRAM.

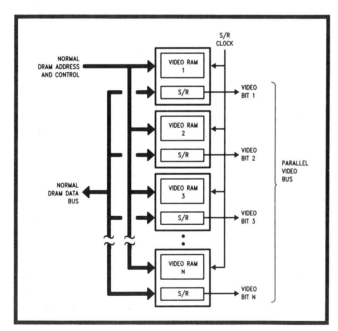

Figure 6. Multiple video DRAMs.

need to maximize CPU or graphics controller access to the frame buffer while maintaining regular (required) CRT refresh. As display resolution in-

creases and color becomes more important, these issues become significant in the design and cost of the graphics subsystem.

Current video rates for medium-resolution graphics systems easily exceed 50 MHz. High-resolution systems attain video rates on the order of 100 to 125 MHz, with clear trends to rates in excess of 125 MHz in the near future. Given these clock rates, screen refresh has become a significant problem in the design of the graphics subsystem.

The high video rates have necessitated a graphics memory organization for refresh like that shown in Figure 4. Since the frame buffer is large, cost and space considerations make the DRAM the desired memory component. However, the DRAM does not have access speeds suitable for current high-resolution displays. As a result, screen refresh is implemented through a parallel-to-serial conversion in the video loop. To refresh the screen, the graphics controller presents a word address to the frame buffer; the resulting data word (usually 16 pixels) is then converted into a serial video stream via an external (usually TTL to ECL) shift register under the timing and control of the graphics refresh hardware. Figure 4 shows the implementation for a single-plane system; multiple-plane systems would require the same number of 16-bit refresh pixel words and parallel-to-serial video shift registers as the number of planes.

If the video rate is 100 MHz, this parallel-to-serial buffering reduces the need for a parallel word from the frame buffer to a clock rate of 6.25 MHz if the word is 16 bits wide. This is still an access time of 160 ns. Thus it is clear that with conventional time-multiplexed DRAM design, the only time left for data manipulation and screen update will be during horizontal and vertical blanking when screen refresh is disabled. With the demands of current graphics end applications, this is clearly not enough.

A number of frame buffer architectures have been developed to get around this problem. These include double frame buffering, dual porting, and making maximum use of page-mode access. The most popular solution is the one provided by a new type of DRAM called the video DRAM, shown in Figure 5. The video DRAM is a conventional DRAM with a 256-bit shift register on board. This shift register is connected such that a complete row of memory cells can be loaded into the shift register at one time. The shift register has its own output, which can be controlled with separate input lines to the video DRAM.

When the video DRAM is configured as shown in Figure 6, it is apparent that a dual-ported memory has been implemented. The left side is configured as a typical DRAM interface. The right side is configured for screen refresh, with the parallel word being generated from the shift registers of the video DRAM. (This parallel configuration is still needed, since the video DRAM shift registers are not able to clock at the full video rate in high-performance systems.)

This configuration provides the advantage of nearly full-time access for screen update and manipulation, since only one load to the shift register is generally needed per scan line. While the preloaded video data is clocked out of the shift register, random access can occur in the frame buffer by either the graphics controller or the main CPU.

Many configurations of the video DRAM are becoming available, with multiple vendors committing to the architecture already in place. It will clearly become the standard component for building graphics frame buffers. Any new graphics hardware architecture must be designed to optimize the use of this type of memory component.

The graphics frame buffer— update/manipulation architecture

We have discussed the preferred frame buffer architecture with respect to screen refresh. Now we will evaluate the trade-offs associated with the update and manipulation side. The performance issues associated with the graphics processor or main CPU update or manipulation of the image in the frame buffer have a major influence on the data and address configuration of the frame buffer. There are generally three such configurations: pixel, plane, and mixed.

The pixel architecture, shown in Figure 7, is best described as one in which the frame buffer data is manipulated one pixel at a time. For multiple planes, the address to the frame buffer generates a data word that is composed of pixels at the same location across multiple planes—thus the term "pixel depth." This architecture is often found in image processing and solid modeling applications, where the value of each pixel is very computation intensive because of color value or shading variations. These applications typically require 16 to 32 memory planes.

In the plane architecture, Figure 8, the frame buffer data is manipulated one word (usually 16 bits) at a time within each plane. To change one bit, 15 others must be carried along. Also, because of the word boundary of the 16 bits, a barrel shifter is required if image placement and movement accuracy are needed down to the actual pixel level. Despite these disadvantages, the plane architecture is the most popular in engineering and business, since these applications require less intensive pixel computation but more intensive data creation and image movement computation. This architecture

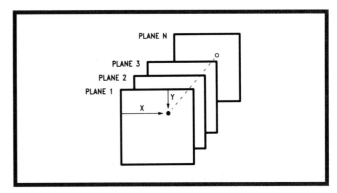

Figure 7. Pixel architecture.

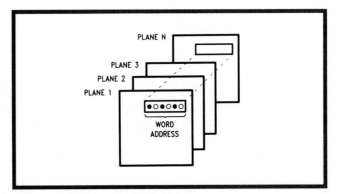

Figure 8. Plane architecture.

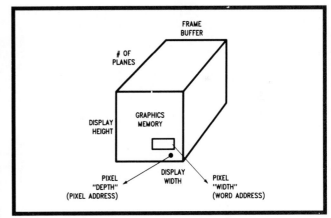

Figure 9. Plane and pixel architecture.

costs less and brings with it higher performance when large bitmaps must be manipulated.

Where the application needs both types of architectures, the mixed architecture shown in Figure 9 is implemented. Here, access to the frame buffer can be at either word width or pixel depth, thus providing the best of both architectures. In the past, this architecture has been implemented only in the more expensive workstations because of the overhead hardware costs. But the applications of workstations that need high-speed update along with

October 1986

93

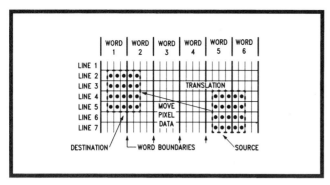

Figure 10. Plane-oriented translation (word-boundary aligned).

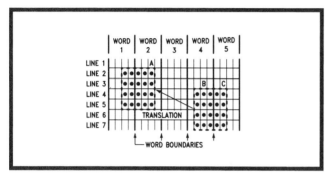

Figure 11. Plane-oriented translation (nonword-boundary aligned).

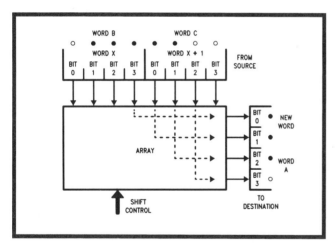

Figure 12. The barrel shifter.

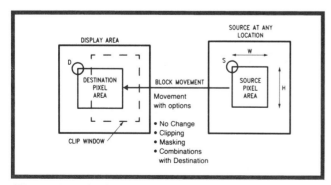

Figure 13. The bitblt operation.

computation-intensive displays are increasing. The time has come for a graphics hardware architecture that can efficiently merge these two architectures.

Word boundaries and the barrel shifter

In engineering and business, the plane architecture is the most popular frame buffer architecture. But as the quality of these displays has increased, restrictions associated with the plane architecture word-boundary constraints have limited the flexibility and performance of these systems. As a result, some of the designs have switched to the pixel architecture. With the "correct" architectural solution, this switch would not have been necessary.

Figure 10 demonstrates the word-boundary problem via a 4-bit-word example. This figure demonstrates a "word-boundary aligned" translation. The relative pixel locations of the 4-bit word are the same at the destination image as at the source image. Thus the pixels maintain the same alignment to the word boundary. This is a simple transfer where the pixel positions in the source word need not be manipulated to transfer it to the destination.

In Figure 11 the source-word pixel alignment does not agree with the desired pixel destination alignment. In this transfer the source pixel map is shifted one pixel to the right in the transfer. This type of control is not available if the frame buffer is addressed by words. If the frame buffer is addressed by pixel, then the price paid for overhead access to perform this simple manipulation is significant. A better solution is to employ an additional hardware function called a barrel shifter and maintain word-boundary addressing.

A simplified diagram of a barrel shifter is shown in Figure 12. To maintain consistency across word boundaries on a shift like that shown in Figure 11, two source words must be read to create a new shifted destination word. The barrel shifter resolves the fundamental restrictions of the plane architecture with respect to exact pixel manipulations. But if these manipulations occur within the main CPU, or for that matter in the main graphics processor, a new performance bottleneck may result in multiple-plane color systems. The ultimate performance of such a system is associated with the speed of the barrel shifter and its location. The ideal arrangement for maximum performance would be a barrel shifter for each plane.

Bitblt

The growth of display resolution and the resulting demand for movement of massive amounts of data, particularly in today's window-oriented software, has increased the need for a lower level graphics

IEEE CG&A

operator that well describes these data movements and manipulations. The most popular operator or function is bitblt (for bit boundary block transfer), originally developed at the Xerox Palo Alto Research Center. This function is also called raster-op (short for raster operator).

Basically, bitblt is a data transfer operation similar to the traditional "string-move" operation found in many general-purpose microprocessors. However, bitblt differs from a string move in three fundamental ways:

1. Bitblt moves "rectangular" regions of bitmaps, rather than being restricted to contiguous linear arrays.
2. Bitblt operates at any pixel boundary, rather than being restricted to byte or word boundaries.
3. Bitblt can mix the source and destination pixels with a Boolean logical operation such as XOR, rather than being restricted to a simple "replace destination with source" transfer.

Bitblt should thus be viewed as a lower level primitive operation for graphics bitmaps. Figure 13 shows how bitblt works. The block on the right is a source bitmap area which can be outside or within the view area of the frame buffer. On the left is the destination area, which is generally—though not necessarily—within the view area of the frame buffer. If the graphics hardware is implemented with bitblt in mind, a single simple setup from the main CPU (via an instruction list) can cause the graphics controller to move massive amounts of data. The only information needed is the size and location of the source, destination, and clip window.

The result of this single setup is that any size bitmap can be moved without intervention from the main CPU. Additionally, if a barrel shifter is integrated within this operation, the bitblt is not bounded by word-boundary constraints. Finally, if multiple bitblt processors and barrel shifters are used—for example, one set per plane—transfers within all planes can be done in parallel.

If interaction is desired between the source image and the destination area, logical operations such as AND, OR, and XOR can be implemented within the bitblt operation. To do this, the source data is first read and barrel shifted to align with the destination word. The destination word is then read and the desired operation is performed, creating a new destination word. This word is then transferred to the destination. This is described by the following equation:

$$\text{Source op destination} \rightarrow \text{destination}$$

where op can be a logical operator such as AND, OR, XOR, etc.

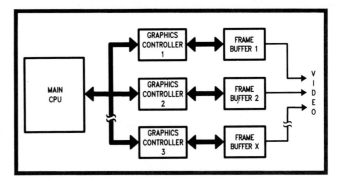

Figure 14. Current graphics chips' color application.

Bitblt is particularly well suited for applications with a heavy mix of graphics, text, and windowing. It provides accelerated solutions for pop-up menus, icons, accelerated filling, wide-line drawing, and high-speed text transfer.

Clearly, an architecture intended to facilitate high-resolution displays and fast screen update should not have the main CPU involved in the simplest of image movement chores. The main advantage of bitblt functionality comes from relieving the main CPU of the detailed bitmap operations and at the same time adding a powerful functional operator.

Previous solutions

Historically, graphics VLSI controllers have not satisfactorily addressed the high-resolution color applications of modern bitmapped graphics terminals. As a consequence, much of the graphics hardware was implemented with bipolar bit-slice processors and random logic, much of which was Schottky TTL or ECL. The result was a costly high-power solution, difficult to map into future high-resolution, multiple-plane applications.

A new generation of graphics VLSI integrated circuits is being introduced this year by a variety of semiconductor vendors. Many of these ICs have been developed to address the performance problems associated with high-performance bitmapped displays. In nearly all cases, to make these controllers effective, a graphics hardware architecture had to be selected. Usually this has restricted the performance and applicability of these devices across the spectrum of graphics applications.

Typically, most of these architectures suffer from inflexibility in the processor-to-memory-plane interface. Figure 14 exemplifies this problem. Some of these architectures are designed to directly support one, four, or eight planes of memory. Transition to more planes requires additional processors. The result is an associated cost increase in hardware,

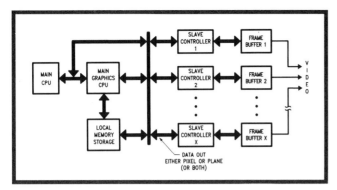

Figure 15. Optimum solution has parallel processing.

usually coupled with a degradation of performance because of synchronization problems between processors.

Although performance may be good within the fundamental bounds of a single processor, the rules significantly change with the transition to multiple processors. Nearly without exception, this new generation of VLSI components has the main controller or processor intimately involved with both frame buffer addressing and data manipulation. This is the main limitation: when memory-plane expansion occurs, the graphics processor again becomes the bottleneck that obstructs graphics system performance. It matters little whether this is a bitblt-based architecture with internal barrel shifters; the common data and address graphics function is the limitation to expansion and performance.

Optimum architecture

The only practical way to solve these problems and still adequately address all the performance issues we have discussed here is to implement an architecture like that shown in Figure 15.

In this diagram a single graphics processor assumes the responsibility of address and timing associated with the graphics frame buffer while maintaining the classical address and data interface with the main CPU and processing functionality with its local program storage memory.

Such a processor, based on a bitblt architecture, is responsible for frame buffer address operations, while actual data manipulation is the responsibility of the slave bitblt data manipulation functions.

The slave controller (data manipulator) is a data-handling chip which receives all control from the single main graphics processor. It is responsible for all masking, barrel shifting, and Boolean logical bitblt operations associated with its own memory plane.

A separate control bus from the graphics processor passes all control and setup information to the

slave manipulators in parallel with other control information via the data bus. Once this initial information is set up, the main graphics processor is no longer involved in graphics data manipulation while the graphics function is implemented. The slave manipulators can be configured via the control and data bus for the exact destination left and right masking, Boolean logical bitblt operation, and amount of barrel shift.

Additionally, operations can occur in parallel, with all slave manipulators working within their own plane. When plane-to-plane transfers are required, one slave manipulator acts as the source, and any number or combination of slave manipulators act as the destination. Here again, any bitblt operation, either within a plane or between planes, is fully set up via a single graphics processor independent of the number of planes used.

Most importantly, performance is independent of the number of planes. Operations for 32 planes of bitblt require only as much time as if one plane were used, since the architecture is the same. Plane-to-plane transfers take place at the same speed whether you are transferring the image to one plane or 16.

In summary, in this architecture the main graphics processor is concerned with graphics setup and addressing to the frame buffer during the graphics operation. With a bitblt architecture, large data movements, character/text transfer, and line drawing and filling all exhibit high performance. Since the processor function occurs only once in the system, the higher cost associated with such processors is a constant and remains independent of the number of planes.

The more cost-effective slave manipulators are concerned with the actual data manipulation via control from the main graphics processor. They are local to each memory-plane frame buffer and fully synchronized by the main controller for transfer operations within or between planes.

This architecture provides one consistent hardware interface independent of the number of memory planes used; it is the same for one plane or 32. Thus the architecture lends itself to a level of software consistency not found in any other graphics architecture.

Finally, the level of parallelism in this architecture creates a consistent growth path for performance. As the number of frame buffer memory planes increases, the performance does not degrade but remains equal to that of a single-plane architecture. In fact, with proper implementation in VLSI components, the true speed limitation of such an architecture is the speed of the DRAM used for the frame buffer.

IEEE CG&A

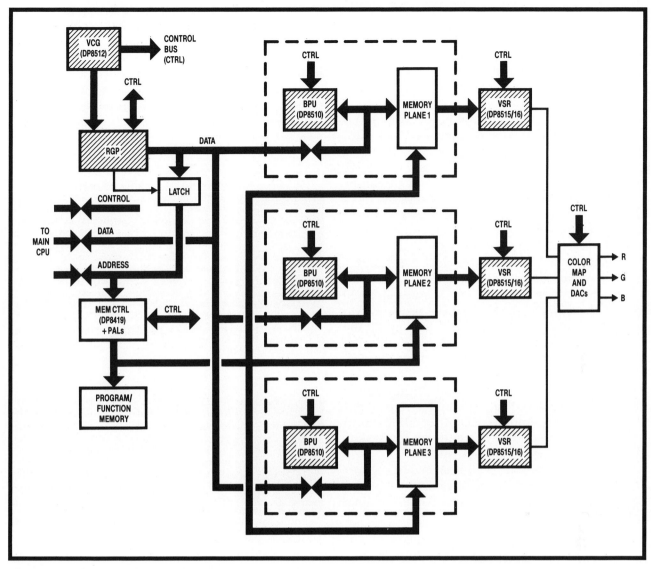

Figure 16. A typical three-plane design.

VLSI implementation

National Semiconductor's Advanced Graphics Chip Set has been designed to match this graphics architecture. The first four chips in this set will be available before the end of the year and are shown in Figure 16 as an example of a three-memory-plane system. The chip set is fully expandable to any number of memory planes.

By partitioning the functional support for this architecture into a family of chips, rather than pursuing a single-chip solution, National Semiconductor is able to address both the flexibility and performance requirements of the graphics designer today and in the future.

National's RGP (raster graphics processor) is the main graphics processor, a fully programmable 20-MHz RISC-like microprocessor tuned specifically for graphics applications. It contains dedicated circuitry to provide both solid- and patterned-line drawing speeds of 10 million pixels per second in any direction, and bitblt fill speeds of 160 million pixels per second. This performance is, of course, independent of the number of color planes.

The RGP also contains specialized instructions for operating on text strings, allowing the support of complex high-resolution fonts such as Chinese and Kanji. Fonts can be stored at 1 bit per pixel to minimize memory storage while being displayed in full foreground and background colors of the user's choice.

Besides the native graphics operations provided by the RGP, a programmer can use the RGP's instruction set to easily and efficiently code any special functions, such as proprietary graphics

October 1986

algorithms, directly in the language of the RGP. Using specialized circuitry, the RGP performs graphics clipping in parallel with the drawing operations. Thus this additional functionality is provided with no degradation in drawing performance.

National's DP8510 BPU (bitblt processing unit) is the slave data manipulator, operating at clock rates up to 20 MHz. It performs all of the masking, barrel shifting, data transfer, and Boolean logic necessary for bitblt operations. Any number of BPUs can be controlled by a single RGP, which allows the flexibility of using the same core architecture and software to design a family of products ranging from monochrome to 24 bits (or more) per pixel.

National's DP8512 VCG (video clock generator) is the timing and control generator for the graphics system. It provides system clocks at rates up to 20 MHz for the RGP and the BPUs. It also provides load clocks for controlling the parallel loading of the shift registers, as well as pixel clocks at rates up to 225 MHz for controlling shift-register serial output.

National's DP8515/16 VSR (video shift register) converts parallel data words from the frame buffer into a high-speed serial data stream for video input to the CRT at a maximum clock rate of 225 MHz. An on-board FIFO eases the system timing constraints encountered at these high clock rates.

The entire chip set has been designed to support all types of RAM components that might be used in the frame buffer, including static RAM, dynamic RAM, and video DRAM.

Summary

The National Semiconductor architecture is very well suited for plane-oriented architectures but can work equally well in pixel-oriented architectures. Additionally, it is the first chip set to provide a complete solution for mixed-mode applications. The flexibility and performance provided by the Advanced Graphics Chip Set ensure that it can be used for designing graphics hardware products well into the 1990's. ■

Charles Carinalli is director of new product development for interface circuits and advanced peripheral products at National Semiconductor. He has been involved in the definition, development, and application support of a wide variety of integrated circuits since 1970. Most recently, his focus has been on complex peripheral VLSI circuits providing complete system-level application solutions using both CMOS and bipolar technologies.

Carinalli has a BS in electrical engineering from the University of California, Berkeley, and an MS in electrical engineering from Santa Clara University.

John Blair is the strategic marketing manager for graphics at National Semiconductor. He has been involved with computer graphics since 1972, working in areas ranging from workstation CAD/CAM applications to microcomputer systems-level graphics. Since 1980 he has participated in ANSC X3H3, working on US and international graphics standards.

Blair has a BS in engineering from the California Institute of Technology and an MBA from Santa Clara University.

The authors can be contacted at National Semiconductor, 2900 Semiconductor Dr., PO Box 58090, MS 16-197, Santa Clara, CA 95052-8090.

A New VLSI Graphics Coprocessor— The Intel 82786

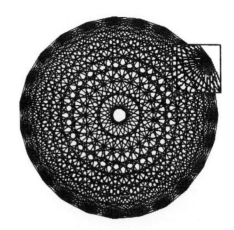

Glen Shires
Intel Corporation*

The hardware window capability of the Intel 82786 allows two views onto the same bitmap. Editing changes made in the magnified view are also made in the global view.

Most graphics systems available today suffer from low performance, minimal flexibility, or high cost and high component count. Intel carefully looked at these problems and designed the 82786 chip to address them. The 82786 combines into a single chip a high-performance graphics processor capable of supporting today's graphics standards and a powerful display processor that supports windowing in hardware.

Before designing a new graphics chip, Intel took a deep look at the features required by interactive graphics systems and determined that a better graphics chip would have the following:

Higher speed. Most personal computers and low-cost workstations simply take too long to create and display images. The problem is becoming more apparent as the new windowing programs come into popular use. Such programs and operating systems have great user interfaces, but nearly all seem "slow" when compared with their nongraphic counterparts. Many users still prefer fast text to slow graphics. A landmark study[1] has demonstrated that more performance in the interaction cycle correlates directly with dramatic improvements in end-user productivity. Better productivity becomes even more important with graphics-based user interfaces.

Greater flexibility. Some solutions attempt to increase speed by placing a graphics processor between the CPU and the graphics memory so that the processor can quickly draw images in the graphics memory, relieving the CPU from this tedious task. Unfortunately, the graphics processor is usually limited to a certain set of operations, for example, line drawing. If another type of operation, such as character drawing, is required, it can be quite difficult to emulate. Systems consisting only of display controllers, which require the CPU to do all the drawing into the graphics memory, are highly flexible—but too slow. Traditionally, there has been a trade-off between speed and flexibility. What is required is an architecture that accelerates the most frequently used functions, but still allows the CPU full access to the graphics memory.

A common mistake is to implement too much of the functionality directly in the silicon. This increases the cost of the silicon, without a corresponding improvement in performance for the user. Consistent with the current RISC approach, the most frequently used functions should be the first to be supported by silicon.

Lower component count. In a world where "multifunction" cards and small "half-cards" are common, why do most display controllers still require a full-size PC card? Only through space-saving mea-

*The author is now an independent consultant.

October 1986

EH0273-3/88/0000/0099$01.00 © 1986 IEEE

99

Reprinted from *IEEE Computer Graphics and Applications*, Volume 6, Number 10, October 1986, pages 49-55. Copyright © 1986 by The Institute of Electrical and Electronics Engineers, Inc.

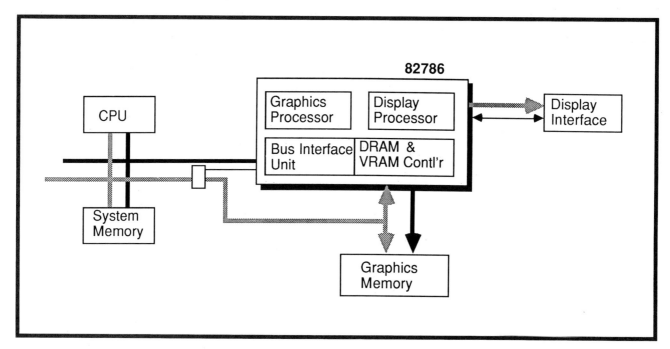

Figure 1. Block diagram of the 82786.

sures such as gate arrays or surface-mount packages are smaller cards constructed. Component cost is important; however, graphics architectures that lead to smaller numbers of components will ultimately lead to the lowest cost system. A good coprocessor design would help to lower the ultimate cost of a system without sacrificing interactive performance.

Intel's new 82786 graphics/display coprocessor[2] was designed to achieve each of these goals. It contains a fast graphics processor that performs a rich set of drawing operations and a display processor that performs video generation and windowing operations in hardware. The architecture does not lose any flexibility, because the graphics memory is still directly accessible by the CPU. The 82786 also integrates into the chip many of the functions that traditionally have required extra support chips, such as DRAM/VRAM control, and bus and video interface logic.

The chip will provide to desktop computers costing less than $5000 the graphics performance available in expensive engineering workstations. Thus, graphics-based user interfaces will be available for everyone's favorite applications software, resulting in productivity gains in offices, homes, and industry.

The 82786 is fabricated using a 1.5-micrometer, double-level metal CMOS VLSI process. Production will start late this year, and initially the chip will come in an 88-pin ceramic grid array package. Figure 1 gives the block diagram.

The graphics processor draws lines, arcs, and characters, as well as does bit block-level transfers (bitblt) into bitmaps in memory to create and modify text and graphics images, as shown at the top of Figure 2.[3] Several complete bitmaps can be contained in graphics memory, either created by the graphics processor or loaded into memory by the CPU. Multiple bitmaps can be constructed and maintained. The only limit to the number of bitmaps is the amount of memory installed. (The 82786 can directly access up to 4M bytes.) The chip has a 32-bit internal architecture to allow for future expansion, and contains an internal 32-bit bus that cycles at 100 ns.

The graphics processor has been optimized to perform the common primitives required by most graphics applications, including formal and de facto standards such as CGI, NAPLPS, Microsoft Windows, and Digital Research GEM. Common primitives such as bitblt operations, characters, and lines, combined with a rich set of attributes, implement the frequently used operations of the high-level structures in standardized software. Since the host CPU has full access into the graphics memory, host-based programs can implement important but infrequent operations easily.

The display processor (lower part of Figure 2) generates the scan-line video for the display device by accessing one or more bitmaps in memory, according to a tile description of the display surface. The display processor can organize the display into

IEEE CG&A

Table 1. 82786 graphics processor drawing speeds.	
Lines,PolyLine, Polygon	2.5 million pixels per second
Circles,Arcs	2 million pixels per second
Characters	25 thousand characters per second (for 16×16 pixel characters, faster for smaller characters)
Bitblt	24 million bits per second
Fills	30 million bits per second (using horizontal-line-fill command)

many different windows, with each window containing a view from a different bitmap. These windows might display bitmaps created by different applications, pop-up menus, or views into different areas of the same bitmap. The bitmaps can have different depths (numbers of bits per pixel).

Unlike traditional display controllers which display only a single bitmap from memory, the display processor generates the screen by scanning through the various bitmaps in real time. Because the video stream is assembled in real time, there is no need to copy images from various bitmaps into one viewable bitmap, normally called the frame buffer. Thus memory space is saved and required memory bandwidth reduced. Digital video for displays up to $640 \times 480 \times 8$ can be directly generated. Higher resolution displays are also supported with some external logic.

The real-time video generation technique for windowing also means that changes to the windows—updating, scrolling, or moving the entire window—can be displayed instantaneously: changes are visible by the next frame. Lexidata has shown the advantage of and provided a sophisticated daughter board for performing windowing in its Lex 90/35 hardware.[4] With the 82786 this function is part of a single chip.

The display processor is optimized to drive CRTs, but is flexible enough to drive other output devices such as LCDs and laser printers. Most of these devices are scanned in a way similar to a CRT. The display processor runs slowly enough for LCDs and can provide the addressability required by laser printers. The graphics and display processors are not only capable of providing very fast drawing and display generation; they also can execute these pixel-intensive functions autonomously, freeing up the CPU to perform other tasks and improving overall system throughput.

Graphics processor

The 82786 graphics processor is a high-performance drawing engine that in many cases is more than 10 times faster than other VLSI graphics chips and 20 to 50 times faster than popular microprocessors in software. Table 1 shows the continuous drawing rates of the graphics processor when the

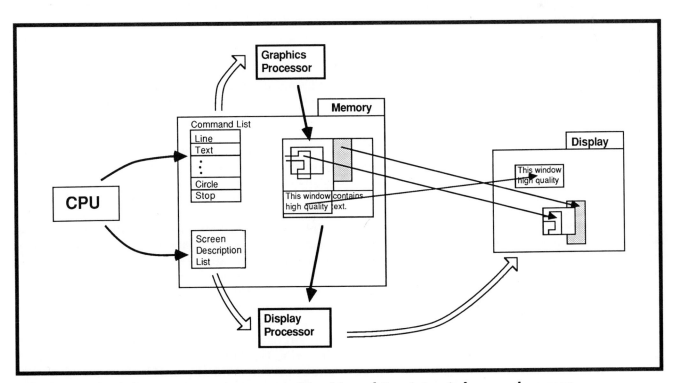

Figure 2. Multiple bitmaps in memory are combined in real time into windows on the screen.

October 1986

Table 2. 82786 graphics processor drawing attributes.	
Logical operations	All 16 possible binary functions between source and destination including AND, OR, XOR, SET, and REPLACE and all negations of each
Bit mask	Can specify which bits of each pixel are to be modified
Pattern	Can specify pattern for dotted/ dashed lines
Foreground, Background colors	Used to draw characters and textured lines
Opaque/ Transparent	Allows solid or transparent background color
Clipping rectangle	Optionally confines all drawing to a user-defined rectangle within the bitmap

display processor requires minimal memory bandwidth.

In addition to the standard line-drawing command are PolyLine and Polygon. They use a table of relative coordinates to draw multiple lines with a single command. The fact that they draw the endpoint of consecutive lines only once can be very important for some applications. If a polygon were drawn into a bitmap using an XOR function, the vertices of the polygon would disappear if they were drawn twice.

For over one million desktop computers with a windowing user interface, the most important graphics operation is the bit block-level transfer (bitblt), an operation copying any rectangular block of pixels from one area and moving it to another. It is often used as a primitive in graphics operations such as pattern fills, graphic arts character fonts, and software windowing. The 82786 graphics processor uses a two-operand bitblt command. Any rectangular block located at any pixel can be moved from one place to another within the same bitmap, or to a different bitmap, with 16 raster operations available.

Many of the graphics components that support bitblt have difficulty with overlapping regions. Most implementations demand that an overlapping bitblt be a clean copy of the source placed at the destination. However, if the bitblt operation is done in the wrong direction, a portion of the source may be replicated over and over at the destination when the source and destination overlap. The 82786 graphics processor will automatically bitblt overlapping source and destination regions within the same bitmap in the necessary order to ensure a clean copy of the source. In fact, a fast way to set or reset an area is to make the source and destination the same, while performing a set or reset raster operation.

While bitblt is normally used for character drawing, the setup time for bitblt causes significant overhead for small character areas (16 × 16 and smaller). For these cases, the 82786 has a hardware character-drawing accelerator which minimizes the setup time and optimizes the storage format.

The character-drawing command uses a user-defined font which can be either fixed or proportionally spaced. Characters can be defined so that the next character will be written on top of the current character, providing a simple mechanism for underlining or simultaneous superscripts/ subscripts. The space between characters can be set so that an entire line of characters can be justified.

Several fonts can be stored in the graphics memory, and a simple command switches fonts. The character strings can use 8-bit indexes to be compatible with ASCII and other standards, or 16-bit indexes to permit a large number of characters in the same font. Since characters are drawn into a bitmap and are displayed directly from the bitmap, there is no limit to the number of different fonts that can be displayed on a screen simultaneously. Characters can also be rotated and drawn in four different directions, facilitating, for example, placing labels on the sides of a graph.

The graphics processor also provides an efficient method for filling arbitrary polygons or flood-filling areas. The CPU must only create a table with the endpoints of the object to be filled, and then a single command will draw the series of horizontal lines required to perform the fill with a pattern. By hatching several horizontal patterns together, any two-dimensional fill pattern can be generated. The horizontal patterns used for fill are automatically aligned to the bitmap edge.

All the graphics operations can use any combination of attributes (see Table 2) and still execute at full speed. Most powerful perhaps is the set of logical operations that allows any of the 16 possible binary functions to be selected for any graphics operation. For example, a character string could be drawn on any background color using the XOR logical operation and it would always show up. Later the same string could be drawn at the same position, again using the XOR logical operation, and the string would be erased. Another example—the bitblt operation with the AND logical operation will combine two pixel images.

IEEE CG&A

A bit-mask attribute allows the programmer to define the bits within each pixel that should be modified by graphics operations. For example, he might want to draw a circle using only the green pixel bits and leave the rest of the bits untouched.

A 16-pixel pattern attribute is definable for all lines, arcs, and circles, permitting dotted, dashed, or other textured vectors. This feature can be combined with user-defined foreground and background colors to draw colored lines, arcs, and circles. An opaque/transparent attribute selects whether the textured lines, arcs, and circles should be drawn with two colors, or only as the foreground color with transparent spaces between the dashes.

The foreground/background colors and opaque/transparent attributes can also create characters in a foreground color on a solid background, or in a foreground color on top of an image that was already there.

A clipping rectangle may be specified to restrict all drawing to a specific area within any bitmap. If clipping is not required, the rectangle can be set around the entire bitmap to ensure that all drawing affects only one bitmap, and not any of the other items stored in the graphics memory. The graphics processor can be set to interrupt if any command draws beyond the clipping rectangle.

The clipping rectangle can also determine what item a user has pointed to, perhaps with a mouse or other pointing device. Placing the invisible rectangle at a position indicated by the cursor and executing in "pick" mode the graphics commands that drew the bitmap, the user will automatically locate the command that draws within the rectangle.

The graphics processor is programmed with sequences of commands, in a linked list format, located in memory much like a standard CPU. Instructions include all drawing commands and attribute selections, as well as other control instructions. Graphics register load and store commands are provided to make saving and restoring the state of the graphics processor easy, providing multitasking operating system support.

The command list format allows the 82786 to be easily programmed, since a separate development system is not needed. It also provides a very compact way to store images and is useful for the "pick" mode described earlier.

Macro call and return instructions compact command lists further. These instructions can include a series of graphics commands that create common images or symbols. For example, a floor diagram for an office building could be created by first describing macros containing the common objects (such as chairs and desks) and then building the image by repeated calls to these macros. Be-

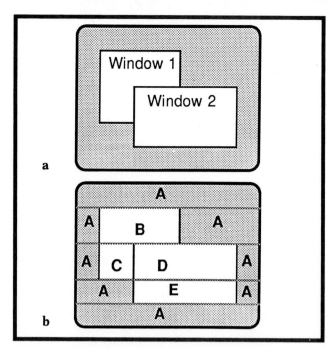

Figure 3. A screen with two windows: (a) as seen by the user; (b) the underlying tile description.

cause the macros use a stack in memory to save the return address, they may be deeply nested.

The ability to totally separate bitmap creation from bitmap display means that separate tasks can run concurrently and can update their bitmaps completely independently.

Display processor

The display processor takes the images that were written into the bitmaps and displays them on the screen. These bitmaps may have been generated by commands to the graphics processor, or may represent scanner data stored on disk and moved into the graphics memory for display.

An important capability of the newer, graphics-based user interfaces, originally developed at Xerox PARC, is the use of windows to organize information on the display. Probably the most unusual feature of the 82786 display processor is that the display can be split into multiple areas, called tiles, with the images for each tile being read directly from the various bitmaps. A tiled representation of a screen with two windows is shown in Figure 3.

In Figure 3, tiles A are the field area, and may be an arbitrary color. Data is not fetched from memory for these tiles, since the color value is stored on chip. The areas of tiles B and C are the visible portion of Window 1. The display processor fetches video data from the proper place in the bitmap for Window 1. Areas of tiles D and E are the visible portion of Window 2. For example, to compose the

Table 3. Display resolutions provided by a single 82786 at 60 Hz noninterlaced frame rate. Multiple 82786's can be used to generate greater resolutions and/or depths.

Maximum pixel depth	Dual-ported DRAMs	Static-column DRAMs	Standard DRAMs
256 colors	1024×1024	640×480	460×340
16 colors	2048×1024	870×650	640×480
4 colors	2048×2048	1144×860	870×650
Monochrome	4096×2048	1472×1104	1472×1104

top scan line in tile C, the display processor first generates the field, then fetches data from bitmap area C, then fetches data from bitmap area D, then generates the field. If the user puts Window 1 on top, then the display processor fetches more data from bitmap C, and less from bitmap D.

Many windows can be displayed on the screen in any arrangement, with the one restriction that at most 16 different tiles can be displayed across one scan line. For example, eight windows can be arbitrarily positioned. A linked list of descriptors defines the windows by splitting up the screen into as many horizontal strips as necessary, with each strip containing up to 16 rectangular tiles. The descriptors specify where the tiles are located on the screen and which part of what bitmap should be displayed in the tile, as well as other parameters describing the tile type such as the depth in bits per pixel.

Because the tiles are defined by a set of pointers, operations such as panning and scrolling bitmaps within the window—or even resizing and moving the window about the screen—can be performed simply by manipulating these pointers. And because the window images are read directly from the bitmaps, the changes are always visible on the next frame.

By correctly arranging these tiles, we can create overlapping, nonoverlapping, and nonrectangular windows. Most applications will probably use windows that have straight sides, but with a more complex linked list any shape—even circular windows—can be created.

Not only can several windows be simultaneously placed on the display, but the windows can also have different amounts of color (pixel depth). We might want to use an 8-bit-per-pixel window for an image using 256 different colors, and use a 1- or 2-bit-per-pixel window for a document displayed on the same screen. Thus both memory space and memory bandwidth are conserved where appropriate, but the amount of color used is not restricted. The principle is that the bitmap depth should be application software dependent, not hardware dependent.

The windows can be individually zoomed using pixel replication and can have a single-pixel border. The hardware cursor can be any shape up to 16 × 16 pixels, or it can be a full-screen cross hair.

The windows also can use special modes to display bitmaps compatible with the IBM Color Graphics Adapter and monochrome Hercules Graphics Controller. Since these are display controllers, software written for them uses the CPU to draw directly into the bitmap, and the 82786 can then display these images.

The screen timings generated by the display processor are completely programmable and able to generate a wide variety of display sizes and interface to virtually any CRT. The resolution provided by the 82786 is a function of the maximum pixel depth used and the frame rate. Table 3 shows typical resolutions.

Note that the important 640 × 480 × 8 design point is achievable with the new CMOS DRAM technology, expected to become the mainstream DRAM component at the 1-Mb level. This technology allows an interleaved memory to supply successively addressed data at a 50-ns-per-16-bit word rate.

Software design

The 82786 graphics processor uses high-level commands to simplify software development and to provide hardware acceleration for frequent operations. These commands have been optimized to make implementation of standards such as CGI, GKS, NAPLPS, Windows, and GEM small and fast.

The display processor is intended to work well with window manager systems. It allows the window manager software to concentrate on the organization of the display area, and not on the need for creating and updating the window contents. One of the more exciting prospects is the potential of the 82786 display-processor functions to become the silicon support for display managers in the same way that the graphics processor has become the silicon support for standardized graphics software.

Even though many fast and flexible graphics primitives are provided, applications always require some graphics operations that are not contained in the primitives. Some graphics engines do not allow the CPU to access the bitmap, and there is no effective way to handle such operations. It is better to have an open architecture, such as the one used by the 82786, where the CPU has free access to the bitmaps, just in case. A separate CPU allows the designer to select cost and performance trade-offs.

IEEE CG&A

Hardware design

The 82786 combines on a single chip much of the hardware required for a graphics subsystem. A complete DRAM controller is built in so no logic is needed between the 82786 and the DRAMs that form the graphics/display memory. The DRAM controller can take advantage of static-column or fast-page-mode DRAMs and of interleaved configurations to provide up to 40M-bytes-per-second memory bandwidth. Dual-ported (video) DRAMs can also be used to further increase the bandwidth available to the graphics processor or CPU for faster drawing.

The video logic is integrated so that no external logic is required to implement scrolling, panning, windowing, or displaying bitmaps with different numbers of bits per pixel. Two status bits per window allow a palette RAM to be easily utilized.

The system bus logic has a synchronous mode to optimize it for an 80286 or 80386 microprocessor and an asynchronous mode for any 8-, 16-, or 32-bit microprocessor.

Three different system configurations are common. A simple, low-cost system could use the 82786 not only as a graphics controller, but also as the DRAM controller for the single memory. A higher performance system could eliminate memory contention by using separate memory for the CPU and have the dedicated graphics controlled by the 82786. Finally, a very high resolution graphics system could use several 82786 chips working in tandem.

Summary

The 82786 has integrated on a single chip a high-performance graphics processor along with an advanced windowing display processor. The chip also includes most of the required system interface logic. Thus three major needs in graphics were met:

- Speed—The 82786 has a fast graphics processor to create bitmap images as well as a display processor to perform video generation and windowing functions in hardware.
- Flexibility—The host CPU has direct access to the graphics memory, allowing special and infrequent operations to be performed.

- Component count—Along with the graphics and display processors, the 82786 also contains a complete DRAM/VRAM controller, CPU interface, and much of the video interface, substantially reducing the number of support chips required.

The 82786 reduces the cost and complexity of interactive graphics while maintaining very flexible, high-performance drawing and windowing functions. ∎

October 1986

References

1. J. Brady, "A Theory of Productivity in the Creative Process," *IEEE CG&A*, Vol. 6, No. 5, May 1986, pp.25-34.
2. 82786 CHMOS Graphics Coprocessor, Data Sheet, Intel Corp., May 1986.
3. 82786 Architectural Overview, Application Note AP-259, Intel Corp., Nov. 1985.
4. B. Suydam, "Lexidata Does Instant Windows," *Computer Graphics World*, Vol. 9, No. 2, Feb. 1986, pp.57-58.

Glen Shires worked at Intel Corporation as an application engineer for the 82786, designing the hardware configurations around the chip and working on its feature definition. He also worked on the 80386 32-bit CPU in a similar capacity and has worked as a design engineer in Intel's IBM-PC add-on board division. He is now an independent consultant, primarily involved in designing similar graphics and microprocessor boards. He received his BS and MS in electrical engineering at the University of Wisconsin-Madison.

Shires can be contacted at Innovative Designs, 3166 Dallas Court, Santa Clara, CA 95051.

Chapter 3: Frame Buffer Design

Raster-scan refresh buffer displays offer the advantage of being capable of displaying complex flicker-free images and are becoming increasingly popular because of the decreasing cost of high-density random access memory. A raster-scan image is generated by plotting the intensity of each pixel (picture element) on a two-dimensional matrix of pixels. According to the functional model described in section 1.1, the display processing unit (DPU) generates a set of bit patterns. These bit patterns are generated according to the graphics primitives defined in the structured display file (SDF).

The device that buffers the bit-map image is called the frame buffer, or the image memory, which is usually implemented with a number of RAM chips. Each storage cell corresponds to a pixel that maps to a point on the display screen.

The image stored in the frame buffer is generated by the image rasterizer, a device that translates a scene' defined in high level graphics descriptions into a "pixel-wise" description. The data stored in the frame buffer are then used by the *video controller,* which systematically reads the frame buffer and repeatedly scans a CRT monitor on which the image is revealed (see Figure 2.2). To get a stable *flicker-free* image, the image must be scanned at least 30 times a second.

3.1: Image Display System

The job of the video controller is to cycle through the frame buffer row by row (hence, scan line by scan line), typically 30 or 60 times per second. Memory reference addresses are generated in synchronism with the raster scan, and the contents of the memory are used to control the CRT beam's intensity. The video controller has the general or-ganization shown in Figure 3.1. The raster-scan generator produces deflection signals that generate the raster scan. It also controls the X and Y address registers, which in turn define the location of image storage to be fetched next to control the CRT beam.

At the start of a refresh cycle, the X address register is set to zero and the Y register is set to $N - 1$ (the top scan line). As the first scan line is generated, the x address is incremented up through $M - 1$ (let the resolution be $N \times M$). Each pixel value is fetched and used to control the intensity of the CRT beam. After the first scan line, the x address is reset to zero, and the y address is decremented by one. The process continues until the last scan line ($y = 0$) is generated.

For the depicted image to be stable, or flicker-free, the video controller must supply the data that will be routed to the monitor rapidly. The *refresh rate* of a display is the number of complete images, or frames, drawn on the screen in 1 second. A typical refresh rate for CRT displays is 60Hz. As the electron beam sweeps from the left to the right, some finite amount of time is required to return from the right extreme back to the left. This activity is called *horizontal retrace,* and the time taken is termed as horizontal retrace time. Similarly, after a raster is completely scanned, the electron beam needs to return to the top margin. This activity is called *vertical retrace,* and the time required is the vertical retrace time. During retraces, the electron beam is turned off such that no new image data are displayed. The video signal is said to be blanked, and the respective times are called horizontal and vertical *blanking intervals.* When not blanked, the signal is said to be *active.* Figure 3.2 [WHIT84] shows how total frame time is composed of vertical retrace time, horizontal retrace time, and active time. From the expression shown in Figure 3.2, the pixel

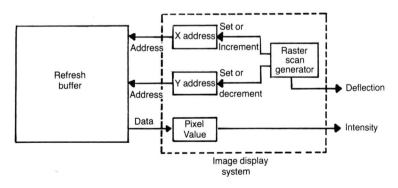

Image display system

3.1: Image Display System.

Table 3.1: Video timing for various display formats.

VISIBLE AREA PIXELS × LINES	REFRESH RATE IN HZ	INTER-LACED?	VERTICAL RETRACE TIME IN μS	HORIZONTAL RETRACE TIME IN μS	TOTAL LINE TIME IN μS	PIXEL TIME IN NS
512×485	30	YES	1271	10.9	63.56	102.8
640×485	30	YES	1271	10.9	63.56	82.3
512×512	30	YES	1203	10.9	60.4	96.7
1024×768	30	YES	1250 [a]	7 [a]	40.1	32.37
1024×1024	30	YES	1250	7	30.11	22.57
1280×960	30	YES	1250	7	32.12	19.62
1280×1024	30	YES	1250	7	30.11	18.06
512×485	60	NO	1250	7	31.79	48.41
640×485	60	NO	1250	7	31.79	38.73
512×512	60	NO	1250	7	30.11	45.14
1024×768	60	NO	600 [b]	4 [b]	20.92	16.52
1024×1024	60	NO	600	4	15.69	11.42
1280×960	60	NO	600	4	16.74	9.95
1280×1024	60	NO	600	4	15.69	9.13

(a) Nominal RS-343-A specifications.
(b) Typical high-performance monitor specifications.

times for several popular display formats are evaluated and tabulated in Table 3.1 [WHIT84].

3.2: Memory Contention Between Image Rasterizer and Video Controller

One measure of the performance of a raster graphics system is its level of *interactivity;* that is, how fast a new image can be generated in response to the user's input. Interactive use of a display requires the capability of updating the display frequently. This task is done by the image rasterizer. However, updating the image in a frame buffer often requires alteration of a large amount of memory cells even for conceptually simple operations. Therefore, not only the processing power of the image rasterizer affects the performance of the entire system but also of particular significance is the availability of the *frame buffer access bandwidth* to the image rasterizer for image updating. The frame buffer access bandwidth, or simply *frame buffer bandwidth,* can be defined as the rate that the frame buffer can be accessed.

From the expression in Figure 3. 2 and the values tabulated in Table 3.1, we know that there is a very tight timing requirement for video refreshing. To satisfy the video refresh requirements, the video controller must access the frame buffer regularly. As a result, the image rasterizer and the video controller contend for a finite number of available memory cycles.

Advances in technology further amplify the problem. Image rasterizer of higher processing speed is able to compute pixel data at a rate significantly faster than memory cycle times. Therefore, it will consume more memory cycles. Introduction of cheaper and larger semiconductor memories means that higher resolution frame buffers can be

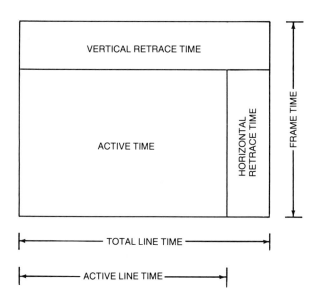

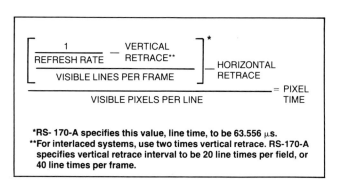

Figure 3.2: Timing partition of a video frame and the computation of pixel time.

Table 3.1 is reprinted from "Memory Design for Raster Graphics Displays" by M.C. Whitton from *IEEE Computer Graphics and Applications*, March 1984, page 52. Copyright © 1984 by The Institute of Electrical and Electronics Engineers, Inc.

built with fewer memory chips. This further reduces the already limited memory bandwidth. Monitor technology has so improved that higher refresh rates are possible, with the consequence that the video controller must read data from the frame buffer more frequently.

Now, the problem of memory contention between the image rasterizer and the video controller is obvious. For the finite frame buffer access bandwidth, a fixed amount of it must be allocated to the video controller for the vital video refreshing activity. The leftover can then be used by the image rasterizer for image updating. From the above discussion, it is clear that high frame buffer access bandwidth is essential for a high performance frame-buffer-based display. Several articles related to this issue have been published recently [GUPT81, FALL84, MATI84, OSTA84, PARK86, SPRO83, WHEL82, and WHIT84]. Although there is no clear cut boundary, the attempts proposed in these articles can be categorized into two classes: (1) efforts to increase the actual access bandwidth of the frame buffer by implementing it with a more effective RAM device and (2) endeavors to lessen the number of frame buffer accesses required for image updating.

3.2.1: Special RAM Architectures Boost the Frame Buffer Bandwidth

It is obvious that the access bandwidth of the frame buffer is directly affected by the speed of the RAM chips used to build the frame buffer. Therefore, a straightforward approach to increase the frame buffer access bandwidth is by making use of faster RAM devices. Unfortunately, high speed memory is expensive, and thus it is not economical to be used for frame buffer implementation where a large number of RAM chips are needed. Therefore, hardware designers get around the problem by customizing conventional RAM to suit some peculiarities of image updating and scan-out activities. In the following discussion, approaches of this kind will be studied. These approaches are mainly based on faster intra-row memory access and/or dual-ported memory techniques.

The memory accesses by the video controller are serial in nature. Dynamic RAM architectures that provide fast access to serial data streams can take advantage of this characteristic to help meet the raster-scanning requirement.

Random access memory chips usually store the bits in a large two-dimensional array of memory cells. For example, a 64K bit RAM will probably contain 256 rows of 256 columns each. Addresses for such a RAM are provided on eight multiplexed address lines. The row address selects which row is to be driven onto the bit lines. The subsequent column address is used to gate one sense amplifier to the data output. Figure 3.3 shows the floor plan of a typical n × 1 RAM.

Owing to this internal architecture, access to a new column address within the same row can be made somewhat faster by using new fabrication techniques and more static memory circuitry. If the data from the row of cells can be retained on the bit lines for a sufficiently long period, successive column addresses can be used to shift the bits out. This can be exemplified by the so-called *video RAM* [PINK83]. In this memory device, an access to the memory usually causes an entire row of RAM cells to be loaded into a shift register. This suggests that by arranging a scan line of raster pixels sequentially in a row of memory cells, the raster pixels can be read more rapidly. Bits can be read forward, backward, or even pseudorandomly without any degradation in access time as long as the bits are all within the same row.

In systems that use scan-line raster conversion algorithms, new pixel values are generated in an intra-row manner. This property again favors the mentioned intra-row memory access method. Since transfer of data between the image rasterizer and the frame buffer and between the frame buffer and the video controller can be done more rapidly, the throughput of the graphics system can be improved.

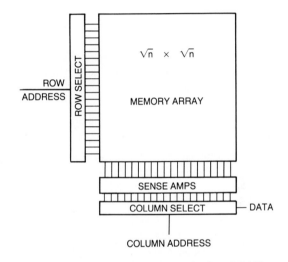

Figure 3.3: Floorplan of a typical *nx1* RAM.

Another straightforward way to boost the bandwidth of the frame buffer is to increase the parallelism in accessing the memory. *Double buffering* has been a well-known technique for this goal. In a double-buffered graphics system, the frame buffer is partitioned into two image memory areas, each of which is capable of storing an entire frame of image. Therefore, the image rasterizer and video controller can virtually work on the same memory area simultaneously without collision. This approach doubles the bandwidth but is expensive because it requires twice as many memory chips to implement the frame buffer as an ordinary system.

To improve on memory utilization, dual-ported memories can be considered. When *dual-ported memories* are used for the frame buffer, the image rasterizer and the video controller communicate with the frame buffer through different ports. This arrangement almost doubles the frame buffer bandwidth and can be adopted to decouple the accesses required for picture update from those for CRT video refresh. However, a true dual-ported memory is expensive and is unnecessary for the raster graphics application. Notice that the video controller needs only to read the frame buffer in a serial manner. Therefore, the ability of random read and write to the frame buffer by the video controller is not necessary. An optimal approach is to incorporate a second serial output port to an ordinary DRAM to accomplish the desired facilities for frame buffer implementation.

Recently, a special customized, *quasi-dual-ported RAM chip* has been developed [MATI84]. Figure 3.4 shows the schematic of the chip. It is quasi-dual-ported because its secondary port, which is linked to the video controller, is a serial output port. A quasi-second port is added to the conventional memory chip by providing along side the sense amplifiers a row of latches into which the outputs of the sense amplifiers can be gated. This set of latches is called the *row buffer* and can be viewed as a separate, largely independent static memory that can be connected to the main array through the sense amplifiers or totally isolated from the array by the isolator switches. It is only during the transfer of the data from the main array to the row buffer that there is any need for synchronism between the two memories. If the row buffer is configured as a serial shift register, with its output provided as an independent data output pin (secondary port), then successive bits on the row can be shifted out. This is exactly how the video controller would like to extract data from the frame buffer.

This (or the similar) idea of implementing the display memory can be found in Texas Instrument's TI4161 dynamic memory chip. Much like conventional 64K RAMs, the chip is organized as a 256×256 array of memory cells. The difference is that a 256-bit 40 nanosecond shift register is included. A command causes an entire row to be transferred to the shift register; the chip then acts as two inde-

pendent chips: the 256-bit shift register and a normal $64K \times 1$ DRAM. In this manner, the chip allows a low system parts count while not tying up memory for scan-out (one memory cycle accesses 256 pixels).

3.2.2: Effective Utilization of Memory Bandwidth by the Image Creation System

Owing to the limited access bandwidth of the frame buffer, an efficient way to draw a pattern to the frame buffer becomes crucial to the overall performance of a frame buffer-based image rasterization system. Because of the differences in their pixel-to-memory assignment geometry, unequal number of frame buffer accesses may be required to draw the same pattern for various mapping schemes [CHOR82, GUPT81, MATI84, PARK86, SPRO83].

Conventional frame buffer designs are usually constrained by the high memory bandwidth required to refresh the screen. As shown in Table 3.1, the actual pixel time is much shorter than a typical cycle time of a RAM chip. Therefore, to satisfy the high data rate required for refresh, the frame buffer memory is generally organized into words with each word containing more than one pixel (assume each pixel is 1 bit wide). With an appropriate memory-to-screen mapping scheme, or simply *mapping scheme,* the pixels in a word can be made to lie along a scan line. With this arrangement, the video controller can simply load the word into a shift register and shift the pixels out through a D/A converter as a video signal for the display device. The mapping of pixels in a word along a scan line is known as the *scan-line mapping scheme.* With this arrangement, each time the video controller accesses the frame buffer, several pixels can be read.

A mapping scheme not only influences the efficiency of the video scan-out but also the speed with which an image can be updated. Obviously, for the scan-line mapping scheme, horizontal lines can be "drawn" at a high speed to the frame buffer because of its particular pixel assignment strategy. However, when dealing with vertical lines, this scheme performs poorly. Therefore, a frame buffer designer prefers a scheme that has a good performance on various types of graphics objects (horizontal, vertical, symmetrical, etc.).

In the next few sections, several major mapping schemes will be studied. Concentration will be on the effect of these schemes on the performance of image rasterization systems and the costs involved in implementing them.

3.2.3: The Scan-Line Mapping Scheme

In the scan-line mapping scheme, memory cells from each chip with the same address are assigned to a string of adjacent pixels along a scan line (see Figure 3.5). As was mentioned, this scheme is motivated by the high output rate

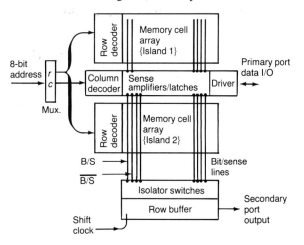

Figure 3.4: Schematic of quasi-dual -ported RAM.

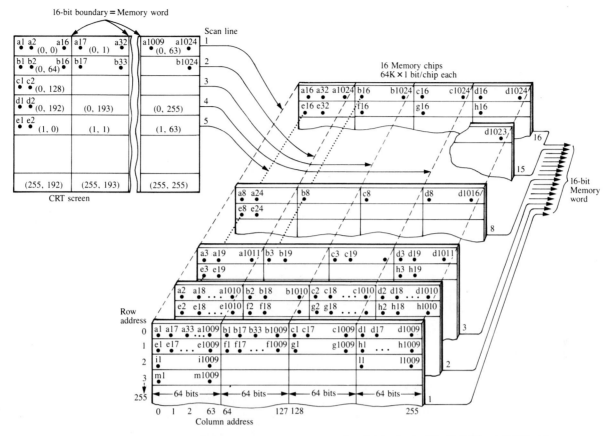

Figure 3.5: Scan-line mapping scheme for a system implemented with 16 64K × 1 RAM chips.

required by the video signal generator. Theoretically, the video refresh controller should have a new pixel value ready for every pixel cycle, which is a very short period. For example, the actual required pixel rate for a 1024 × 1024 60Hz non-interlaced display is approximately 1 pixel per 11.5ns. With a typical memory cycle of 150ns for single bit reads (e.g., the 4164 64K × 1 DRAM), more than 13 pixels must be read simultaneously in a single memory cycle to achieve the desired pixel rate. Scan-line mapping is particularly good for high output parallelism. In the example shown in Figure 3.5, an effective pixel rate of 1 pixel per 9.375ns, is potentially achievable.

Writing an *h*-x-*w rectangular pattern* onto the screen is done by updating an appropriate *h*-x-*w* grid of pixels in the frame buffer. A 1-x-*n* grid of pixels (n is the number of chips) in the frame buffer can be updated extremely fast in the scan-line mapping scheme provided that the grid is well matched with the *word boundary*. Assuming the pattern is already available in a buffer or a latch, which is called the *pattern buffer,* a single access with an appropriate word address to all the frame buffer chips is adequate. However, it

becomes more complicated when the 1-x-*n* grid spans a word boundary (see Figure 3.6). Addresses sent to chips that contain pixels on the right side of the word boundary must be adjusted. To be able to update a random 1-x-*n* grid in one memory cycle, address adjusting circuitry must be included in the frame buffer. Moreover, data alignment hardware is also required to match the data with the word boundary before it can be correctly written into the destination grid.

Figure 3.6 depicts the procedure to write a 1-x-16 pattern into an arbitrary 1-x-16 grid. The leftmost pixel of the pattern is to be written to the location (r', c') of chip 5. Similarly, the next 11 pixels are to be stored into the cells (r', c') of chips 6, 7, . . ., and 16 respectively. Starting from the thirteenth pixel, the remaining four pixel values are to be stored at location (r', c' + 1) for chips 1, 2, 3, and 4. The data in the pattern buffer must first be aligned with the word boundary. This can be done by shifting the pattern data around until the leftmost cell holds the pixel to be written into chip 1. The next step is to give appropriate addresses to all the chips. In the example, chips 1, 2, 3, and

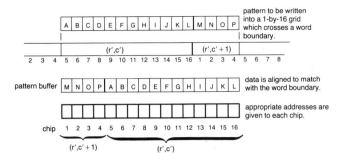

Figure 3.6: Address transformation and data alignment mechanism in the scan-line mapping scheme in a 16-chip system.

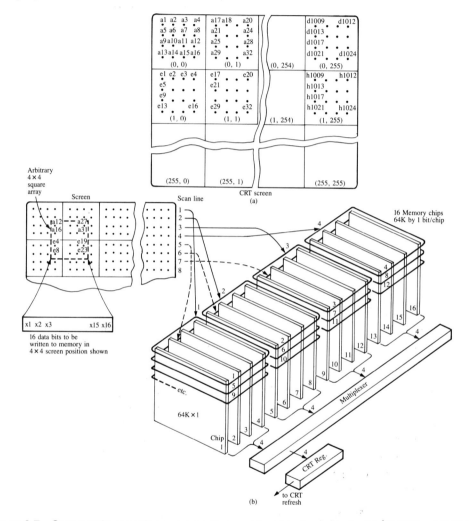

Figure 3.7   Symmetric mapping scheme for a system implemented with 16 64K × 1 RAM chips.

4 are given the address $(r', c'+1)$ and the others the address (r', c').

3.2.4: The Symmetric Mapping Scheme

The major drawback of the scan-line mapping scheme is its poor performance in dealing with *vertical objects,* such as a vertical vector. (In this chapter, a rectangular pattern where the width is larger than its height is classified as a *horizontal object,* otherwise it is a *vertical object.*) In the scan-line mapping scheme, all the pixels along a vertical vector are stored in the same chip [GUPT81, MATI84, SPRO83]. Therefore, pixels along the vector must be written sequentially.

Figure 3.7 is reprinted with permission from "All Points Addressable Raster Display Memory" by R. Matick, D.T. Ling, S. Gupta, and F. Dill, from *IBM Journal of Research and Development*, Volume 28, Number 4, July 1984, page 383. Copyright © 1984 by International Business Machines, Inc.

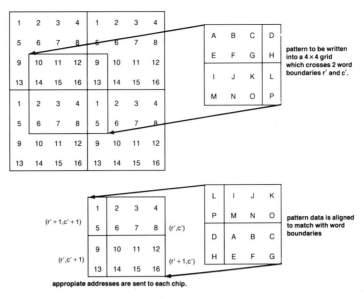

Figure 3.8: Address transformation and data alignment needed to update an arbitrary 4-by-4 grid in a 16-chip system.

In the symmetric mapping scheme, the pixels in a word of storage, which were lying along a scan line, are arranged in a square array on the screen (see Figure 3.7). Update complexity for the symmetric scheme is symmetric with respect to the x and y axes. Owing to this symmetry, it is expected that on the average few memory accesses are required to draw an image. Therefore, the limited bandwidth of the frame buffer can be used more effectively. However, the symmetric mapping scheme is more expensive to implement since it requires additional supporting circuitry to support the symmetric read/write activities of the bit-map.

An obvious drawback of symmetric mapping is a slower update rate for horizontal objects. For applications that generate more horizontal objects, the scan-line mapping scheme is definitely better than the symmetric mapping scheme. Another disadvantage is that the number of pixels that can be provided to the video controller in parallel is decreased considerably. If $n = k^2$ chips are used in the scan-line mapping scheme, the n pixels read from location (r', c') of all the chips lie along a scan line. A single read from the frame buffer by the video signal generator supplies n pixel values for the same scan line. In the symmetric mapping scheme, the n pixels are read as k rows of k pixels. Among them only one row of pixels belongs to the current scan line and is immediately needed by the video signal generator. The remaining $(k-1)$ rows of pixels are either discarded or saved up in a *refresh buffer* [SPRO83].

The refresh buffer must be capable of holding $2k$ complete scan-lines [SPRO83]. It is used as two k-line sections that alternately supply data to refresh the display and are replenished from the frame buffer. During the display of one set of k lines, information for the next set of k lines is transferred from the image memory to the refresh buffer. Shift registers or FIFO memories are commonly used to build the refresh buffer for their speed to shift out data.

With a refresh buffer, the average achievable pixel rate remains the same as that of the scan-line mapping scheme. But the extra cost involved to implement the buffer is considerable, since thousands of pixels have to be buffered in expensive high speed memories.

Furthermore, a k-x-k square pattern may now mismatch to a horizontal as well as a vertical word boundary. Hence, more complicated address transformation and data aligning mechanism must also be employed (see Figure 3.8). This adds even more to the cost of the system.

3.2.5: Mapping Schemes That Support Flexible Access Geometry

The scan-line and symmetric mapping schemes can only support a single access geometry; namely a horizontal grid for scan-line mapping and a square grid for symmetric mapping. However, many image processing operations require that an image, or partial image, be stored in a memory system that permits access to an arbitrary rectangular grid. A number of authors [BUDN71, COLE67, WHEL82, LAWR75, PARK86, WEIN67, VANV78] have described several methods that permit simultaneous access to elements in row, column, diagonal, and/or rectangular area of a memory system.

In particular, Van Voorhis and Morrin [VANV78] have essentially solved the problem of deciding how to assign image points to memory locations such that simultaneous access to row, column, and rectangular grids of pixels is possible. They discussed (1) six memory module assignment functions that distribute the image points among memory chips, (2) two address assignment functions that determine the addresses of the image points, and (3) circuitry that calculates the addresses within memory modules simultaneously. The address calculation circuitry was later improved by Park [PARK86].

Van Voorhis and Morrin [VANV78] demonstrate the possibility of having a mapping scheme that supports more than one access geometry. Since the mathematics involved in their approach is quite complicated, we will not discuss the issue any further. In addition, such a highly flexible mapping scheme is not necessary for many graphics applications. A simpler mapping scheme, described in [OSTA84], allows simultaneous access to horizontal and vertical lines.

3.3: Article Overview

The first paper, "Memory Design for Raster Graphics Displays" by Whitton, serves as a very good reference on various aspects of frame buffer design. Issues like basic frame buffer based architectures, video refresh requirements, double buffering, and memory-to-screen mapping schemes are discussed in this well-written article.

Whitton's discussions on frame buffer architectures is further supplemented by the paper "Frame Buffer Display Architectures," by Sproull, which provides a very thorough discussion of various frame buffer architectures and enhancements.

Pixel phasing, discussed in "Pixel Phasing Smooths Out Jagged Lines" by Oakley et al., virtually increases the resolution of a raster by four. This is extremely useful in combating the aliasing jaggies.

Finally, in the paper, "A Configurable Pixel Cache for Fast Image Generation" by Goris, Fredrickson, and Baeverstad, a new device called the *pixel cache* is proposed. The pixel cache essentially matches the bandwidth between a high-speed serial stream of pixels (from the image rasterizer) and a slow parallel stream of pixels (to the frame

buffer). With this technique, generating multiple pixels in parallel is no longer a necessity for high-speed image-rendering hardware.

References

[BUDN71]   Budnik, P. and D.J. Kuck, "The Organization and Use of Parallel Memories," *IEEE Transactions on Computers,* Vol. C-30, No. 9, Sept. 1971, pp. 691–699.

[CHOR82]   Chor, B., C.E. Leiserson, and R.L. Rivest, "An Application of Number Theory to the Organization of Raster-Graphics Memory," *VLSI Memo No. 82-106,* Massachusetts Institute of Technology, Cambridge, Mass., 1982.

[COLE67]   Coleman, C.D. and A. Weinberger, "Bank of Memories System for Multi-Word Access," *IBM Technical Disclosure Bulletin,* Vol. 9, Feb. 1967, pp. 1182–1183.

[FALL84]   Fallin, J., "CHMOS DRAMs in Graphics Applications," *Solutions,* Intel Corp., May/June 1984, pp. 20–27.

[GUPT81]   Gupta, S., R.F. Sproull, and I.E. Sutherland, "A VLSI Architecture for Updating Raster-Scan Displays," *Computer Graphics,* Vol. 15, No. 3, March 1981, pp. 333-340.

[LAWR75]   Lawrie, "Access and Alignment of Data in an Array Processor," *IEEE Transactions on Computers,* Vol. C-24, No. 12, Dec. 1975, pp. 1145–1155.

[MATI84]   Matick, R., D.T. Ling, S. Gupta, and F. Dill, "All Point Addressable Raster Display Memory," *IBM Journal of Research and Development,* Vol. 28, No. 4, July 1984, pp. 379–392.

[PARK86]   Parke, J.W., "An Efficient Memory System for Image Processing," *IEEE Transactions on Computers,* Vol. C-35, No. 7, July 1986, pp. 669–674.

[OSTA84]   Ostapko, D.L., "A Mapping and Memory Chip Hardware Which Provides Symmetric Reading/ Writing of Horizontal and Vertical Lines," *IBM Journal of Research and Development,* Vol. 28, No. 4, July 1984, pp. 393–398.

[PINK83]   Pinkham, R., M. Novak, and C. Guttag, "Video RAM Excels at Fast Graphics," *Electronic Design,* Vol. 31, No. 17, Aug. 1983, pp. 161–182.

[SPRO83]   Sproull, R.F., I.E. Sutherland, A. Thompson, S. Gupta, and C. Minter, "The 8 by 8 Display," *ACM Trans. on Graphics,* Vol. 2, No. 1, Jan. 1983, pp. 381–411.

[WEIN67]   Weinberger, A., "Multiword, Multidirectional Random Access Memory System," *IBM Technical Disclosure Bulletin,* Vol. 10, Dec. 1967, pp. 997–998.

[WHEL82]   Whelan, D.S., "A Rectangular Area Filling Display System Architecture," *Computer Graphics,* Vol. 16, No. 3, July 1982, pp. 356–362.

[WHIT84]   Whitton, M.C., "Memory Design for Raster Graphics Displays," *IEEE Computer Graphics & Applications,* Vol. 4, No. 3, March 1984, pp. 48–65.

[VANV78]   Van Voorhis, D.C. and T.H. Morrin, "Memory Systems for Image Processing," *IEEE Transactions on Computers,* Vol. C-27, No. 2, Feb. 1978, pp. 113–125.

This tutorial examines the origin and nature of the problem of contention for memory cycles—a problem that impacts the image update performance of every raster graphics system.

Reprinted from *IEEE Computer Graphics and Applications,* Volume 4, Number 3, March 1984, pages 48-65. Copyright © 1984 by The Institute of Electrical and Electronics Engineers, Inc.

Memory Design
for Raster Graphics Displays

Mary C. Whitton

Whitland Associates

One measure of the performance of a raster graphics system is its level of interactivity, that is, how fast a new image can be generated in response to user input. The entire system architecture affects this figure of merit, but of particular significance is the architecture of the image memory. Even though display processor access to the image memory for image update is a major factor in the design of memory systems, the architecture is significantly constrained by strict video timing standards as well as by the realities of semiconductor memory devices. This article is not intended to be a "how to" guide to frame buffer design but is rather a discussion of factors that affect image update rate and an examination of typical image memory architectures for readers without an extensive background in hardware design.

The memory in which an image is stored on a pixel-by-pixel basis is central to any raster graphics system. This memory is accessed by the display processor, which writes data into the memory, and by the video refresh controller, which reads from the memory and routes the pixel data to the video output circuitry and display monitor. The display processor changes the viewed image by writing new data into the memories. Dynamic, interactive, or real-time graphics requires that hundreds of thousands of pixels be written every frame time, a requirement that demands that the display processor have access to many memory cycles. For the viewed image to be stable, the video refresh controller must supply the data that will be routed to the monitor according to strict timing requirements. To meet this required data rate, the video refresh controller must have adequate access to the memories. As a result, the display processor and the video refresh controller contend for a finite number of available memory cycles.

Advances in technology have aggravated the problem of contention for memory cycles between display processor and video controller. Processing speeds have increased with the result that pixel data is computed at rates significantly faster than memory cycle times. Cheaper, larger semiconductor memories mean that higher resolution image memories can be built with fewer chips but that each chip must be accessed more often. Monitor technology has improved so that higher refresh rates are possible, again with the result that each memory chip must be accessed more often.

The problem of contention for memory cycles impacts the image update performance of every raster graphics system and is a significant factor in the architecture of a display system that includes a memory system, a display processor, and a video refresh controller. In this article, I will examine the origin and nature of the contention problem by focusing on the basic concepts of raster graphics systems, video timing, and semiconductor memories and by discussing typical architectures that use either available or announced parts.

Basic concepts

Today's raster graphics systems typically include display processor hardware in addition to the image memory and video output circuitry, the interaction of which significantly affects update performance. For this article, I have categorized these raster systems as having an interface(s) to other devices and the user (host, workstation computer, interactive devices); display processor hardware; an image memory; a video refresh controller; video output circuitry, which can include color lookup tables; and a monitor.

Raster display systems definitions and terminology. The *display processor,* sometimes called the display generator, graphics processor, or image creation system, generates and manipulates graphics data or performs image processing functions. It can write to and read from the image memories. An image memory port can be dedicated to the display processor, as shown in Figure 1, in which case all data written to the image memories must pass through the display processor. Alternatively, the image memories have a port on the system bus that is shared by the display processor and other devices on the bus, as shown in Figure 2. In such a case, the host processor can directly load a stored image into the image memories without going through the display processor.

The display processor must be able to compute and efficiently write to memory several classes of figures, including curved and straight lines, polygons and other filled areas, and characters or other symbols. The system must also efficiently execute the Raster Op function, which copies from one area of memory to another. The data written by Raster Op can be a logical combination of source data, destination data, and a constant.

The *video refresh controller,* called the refresh controller, display controller, or frame buffer controller, reads the contents of the image memory in the proper format and with the proper timing to feed the video output portion of the system. Video output hardware converts data values to intensity levels or colors and passes them to the monitor. The video refresh controller generates addresses for the image memories and controls functions such as pan, scroll, and window, which involve manipulation of these addresses.

When the video refresh controller accesses the image memories, it fetches and stores multiple pixels in the *video buffer.* A major function of the controller is to convert the data stream from parallel pixels to serial pixels. If the video buffer is a shift register, this serialization can occur without additional hardware. However, additional hardware is needed if the video buffer is, for instance, a FIFO memory. The term *shift register* is used here as a functional name for this additional hardware even though the implementation may not use shift-register devices. (Refer to Figure 7.)

The *image memory,* called the frame buffer memory, display memory, or bit map, holds an array of values that represent an image. The size of the array, often 512×512

or 1024×1024, is the *resolution* of the memory, with each element of the array being one picture element, or *pixel.* A memory array holding one bit per pixel contains one *bit plane.* A frame buffer memory may have multiple bits of storage per pixel, hence multiple bit planes. The term *image plane* is commonly used in image processing to mean a set of eight bit planes, i.e., one image with eight bits per pixel. The number of bits per pixel is called

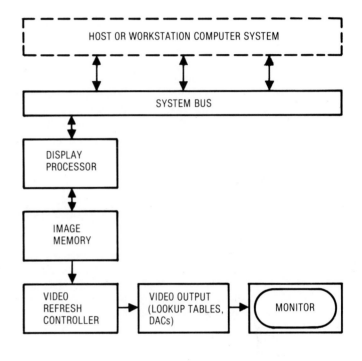

Figure 1. Raster graphics system block diagram showing the image memory ported to the video refresh controller and the display processor.

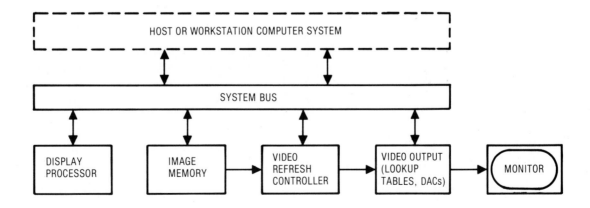

Figure 2. Raster graphics system block diagram showing image memory ported to the video refresh controller and the system bus.

the *pixel depth* or *color resolution* of the image memory. A *full-color* system has 24 bit planes, eight bits each for red, green, and blue.

Image memories are often *dual-ported* or *multiported* devices. The memories are not dual ported in the sense that the same memory can be accessed by two devices simultaneously. The phrase is more commonly used to indicate that the memories have two or more data paths on their input/output and that the memory is timeshared between them. Figure 3 shows a dual-ported image memory with one port used by the display processor and one port used by the video refresh controller.

Some frame buffer systems contain enough memory to store two complete images of the resolution and pixel depth desired. In such a system, it is possible for the video refresh controller to access and display from Memory 0 while the display processor writes a new image into Memory 1. When the new image is completed, the video refresh controller begins to access and display from Memory 1, and the processor begins writing into Memory 0. This technique is called *double-buffering,* or *ping-pong,* operation and is discussed further in the section on double-buffer systems.

Video terminology. Since the video refresh controller must access the image memory in such a way as to meet the timing requirements imposed by the display device, it is important that system designers have an understanding of video timing and terminology. The dominant display device in computer graphics is the cathode ray tube or CRT monitor, a technology well developed in the television industry before its application in raster graphics.

The pattern that the electron beam in the CRT sweeps out as it *scans* or draws the image in each frame is a series of horizontal lines moving from the top to the bottom of an image and from left to right on each line as displayed in Figure 4. The pattern is called a *raster,* and each line drawn is called a *scan line,* or *raster line.* The *refresh rate*

of a display is the number of complete images, or frames, drawn on the screen in a second and is measured in frames per second. The duration of each frame, or the *frame time,* is the reciprocal of the refresh rate.

Some finite amount of time is required for the electron beam to return to the left side of the screen from the right and to the top of the screen from the bottom as the image is displayed. The returning beam *retraces,* and the time it takes is called the horizontal or vertical retrace time, during which the beam is turned off and no new data is displayed. The video signal is said to be *blanked,* and the times are alternately called the horizontal and vertical blanking intervals. When not blanked, the signal is said to be *active.*

In the early days of television, engineers devised a system in which the display of odd lines of an image (*odd field*) alternated with the display of even lines (*even field*) of the image, a type of display called *interlaced.* The two fields, odd and even, are required to make a frame. In a *noninterlaced* display, all lines are drawn in order from top to bottom. A common specification for displays is 60 Hz, noninterlaced: The entire image is drawn on the screen 60 times each second in top-to-bottom scan-line order. A 30-Hz refresh rate almost universally implies an interlaced format, while a 60-Hz refresh rate implies one that is noninterlaced.

Objects in an image, particularly horizontal lines, that are drawn on the screen only 30 times a second appear to flash on and off, or *flicker.* Flicker is not a problem in 60-Hz refresh displays. Refresh rates between 30 Hz and 60 Hz are sometimes used to reduce apparent flicker without incurring the additional costs of a 60-Hz refresh display.

Two standards developed by the Electronic Industries Association define the timing of video signals. EIA standard RS-170-A defines the signal for color and black-and-white broadcast television and applies to systems that display 525-line images at 30 frames per second, interlaced. The second standard, RS-343-A, applies to

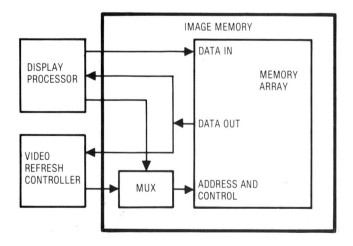

Figure 3. Dual-ported image memory: Data, address, and control lines to chips are timeshared between the display processor and video refresh controller.

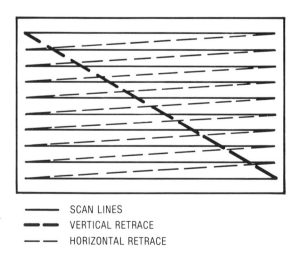

SCAN LINES
VERTICAL RETRACE
HORIZONTAL RETRACE

Figure 4. Noninterlaced raster pattern.

IEEE CG&A

high-resolution television systems, such as 1024×1024 images at 30 frames/sec, interlaced, and 512×512 images displayed at 60 frames/sec, noninterlaced. RS-343-A gives specific timing for a limited number of display formats and functions as a guideline for others. The standard specifies the nominal vertical blanking interval at 1250 microseconds and the nominal horizontal blanking interval at 7 μs. Of course, vertical blanking must be an integer multiple of the total line time.

Images recorded on videotape from raster graphics systems for use in broadcast television must exactly meet the requirements in the RS-170-A standard. Odgers[1] describes the problems and pitfalls of recording for broadcast.

The 512×512, 60-Hz, noninterlaced and the 1024×1024, 30-Hz, interlaced display formats are very much alike: For the 512×512 image the same 512 lines are displayed in both odd and even fields, and each pixel is displayed twice as long as those in the 1024×1024 image.

Although monitor technology has advanced to the point that 1280×1024, 60-Hz refresh display formats are possible, a timing standard has not yet been developed. In the absence of a standard, manufacturers design to the nominal horizontal and vertical retrace time specifications given for the monitors designated to be driven by their graphics systems. Sample values are vertical retrace at 600 μs and horizontal retrace at 4 μs.

It is essential to know how often a new pixel must be supplied to the video output hardware in order to determine how fast the image memory must be accessed to support display refresh. Pixel time can be derived from the refresh time, vertical blanking interval, horizontal blanking interval, number of lines displayed per frame, and number of pixels displayed per line.

Figure 5 shows how total frame time is composed of vertical retrace time, horizontal retrace time, and active time. Total line time is the quantity frame time (one/ refresh rate) minus vertical retrace time divided by the number of visible lines per frame. This line time includes both active and blanked times. Active line time is figured by subtracting the horizontal retrace time from the total line time. Pixel time is the active line time divided by the number of visible pixels per line. Figure 6 shows this information in formula form.

Table 1 gives the values used to derive pixel times for several popular display formats. Although pixel times vary from system to system depending on the number of visible lines and the number of pixels per scan line, the following numbers are typical and accurate enough (and round enough for easy computing) for this discussion: 512×512, 30 Hz—100 nanoseconds; 1024×1024, 30 Hz —25 ns; 512×512, 60 Hz—45 ns; and 1024×1024, 60 Hz —10 ns.

Standard television images have a 4:3 width-to-height aspect ratio. If a 512×512 image is displayed as a full screen with a 4:3 image aspect ratio, the pixels become rectangular. However, square pixels are desirable so that images sampled on a square grid can be faithfully reproduced and computationally derived figures such as circles have the expected and desired shapes.

Several methods can produce square pixels. A decrease in the horizontal deflection of the beam within the CRT

can alter the raster pattern to provide a 1:1 aspect ratio. This is called horizontal *underscanning*. Some frame buffer memories provide 640×480 or 1280×960 displayable memories, which preserve a 1:1 aspect ratio for the pixels and give a 4:3 aspect ratio for the image. Other frame buffer manufacturers display a 512×512 image in such a way that the pixel aspect ratio and the picture aspect ratio are both 1:1. In this case, the 512 pixels along a scan line are displayed faster, and the active portion of the line is decreased. Pixel time becomes equal to that of a system that displays 640 pixels/line.

Memory terminology. Display system image memories are built with semiconductor memory devices. (For an excellent history of early frame buffer devices, see Baecker.[2]) Static or dynamic random access memories are available. Cost considerations make the dynamic RAM, or DRAM, the most commonly used part. Dynamic RAMs store data by placing a small charge on each memory cell. The charge leaks off the cell and must be refreshed on a regular basis for the data to remain valid. This memory *chip refresh* process is entirely dif-

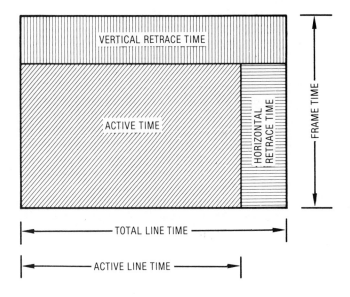

Figure 5. Timing components of a video frame.

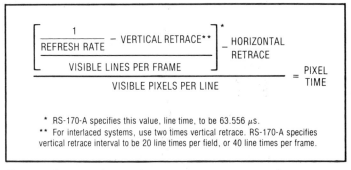

Figure 6. Computation of pixel time.

ferent from *video refresh*. Chip refresh is accomplished by accessing the memory locations for a normal read/write cycle or by carrying out special refresh cycles. Because of the internal architecture of the chip, multiple locations are refreshed on each cycle.

A typical 64K × 1 DRAM requires 256 cycles of chip refresh every four milliseconds. Systems that access every memory location for display can meet this chip refresh requirement with no additional circuitry. Systems that allow display of only a portion of the memory, as with a zoom function, must make provision for chip refresh of memories that are not fully addressed. Memory designers implement chip refresh so that it is transparent to users and impacts system performance as little as possible. Compared with the demands made on the memories by the video refresh controller and the display processor, the chip refresh function takes very little time.

Once data is stored in a static RAM, it remains valid until power to the chip is turned off. No chip refresh is required. Static RAMs are faster, more expensive, and smaller (fewer bits per device) than dynamic RAMs and are used for image memories only in applications such as flight simulators where performance is the most important consideration. Although static RAMs are used in the high-end version of the new Ramtek 2020, widespread use of the devices in graphics systems for the mass market is probably some years away.

Two basic timing figures characterize memory chip performance: access time and cycle time. *Access time* is the minimum time required for data to become valid at the output of the chip after the chip is addressed. *Cycle time* is the minimum time between successive accesses to the same chip.

To keep down the number of pins per chip, large semiconductor memories, 16K and larger, multiplex the incoming addresses. Since the internal structure of the memory is an array, the two parts of the address are called the row address and the column address. One memory cell is uniquely addressed where the row and column cross. The row address is first presented to the chip and is strobed, or latched, onto the chip by the signal RAS—row address strobe. The column address is then presented on the same pins and strobed by CAS, the column address strobe.

In addition to address, data in, data out, and RAS and CAS lines, each memory chip has a *write enable* control line, which allows an additional level of chip decoding. For instance, if multiple chips are accessed by the same address, e.g., eight chips representing eight bits of depth for one pixel, a write function to a single bit of the pixel, a single bit plane, can be accomplished by controlling the write enable lines to the eight devices.

The desire for high data rates has led manufacturers to develop 64K × 1 DRAMs with special features. In addition to operation as standard 64K × 1 chips with single-bit access, chips with a page mode, nibble mode, or ripple mode capability allow multiple bits of data to be read or written within an extended cycle.

Page mode accesses occur when one RAS cycle is followed by multiple CAS cycles. A row or page of data is enabled by the decoding of the address latched with RAS. Any memory cell on that row can then be accessed by supplying the appropriate column address and CAS signal. Sequential accesses need not come from sequential locations. Up to 256 bits of data, one page of memory, can be accessed in this manner. Page mode CAS cycle times, an additional important timing specification for these chips, are as low as 125 ns. Page mode operations are limited by the amount of time that can elapse before the row address must be refreshed. If this time is less than active line time, the design of the memory is complicated by having to allow for the additional RAS time during the active portion of the line. *Extended page mode,* available from some manufacturers, solves this problem by lengthening the maximum time between RAS cycles to 75 μs, well beyond the active line time for 512 × 512, 30-Hz displays.

Nibble mode allows four bits of data to be accessed for each RAS cycle. Although still organized externally as if it were a 64K × 1 chip, the internal structure of a chip with nibble mode is 16K × 4. Each eight-bit row address and the upper six bits of column address are used to ac-

Table 1.
Video timing for various display formats.

VISIBLE AREA PIXELS × LINES	REFRESH RATE IN HZ	INTER-LACED?	VERTICAL RETRACE TIME IN μS	HORIZONTAL RETRACE TIME IN μS	TOTAL LINE TIME IN μS	PIXEL TIME IN NS
512×485	30	YES	1271	10.9	63.56	102.8
640×485	30	YES	1271	10.9	63.56	82.3
512×512	30	YES	1203	10.9	60.4	96.7
1024×768	30	YES	1250[a]	7[a]	40.1	32.37
1024×1024	30	YES	1250	7	30.11	22.57
1280×960	30	YES	1250	7	32.12	19.62
1280×1024	30	YES	1250	7	30.11	18.06
512×485	60	NO	1250	7	31.79	48.41
640×485	60	NO	1250	7	31.79	38.73
512×512	60	NO	1250	7	30.11	45.14
1024×768	60	NO	600[b]	4[b]	20.92	16.52
1024×1024	60	NO	600	4	15.69	11.42
1280×960	60	NO	600	4	16.74	9.95
1280×1024	60	NO	600	4	15.69	9.13

(a) Nominal RS-343-A specifications.
(b) Typical high-performance monitor specifications.

cess four bits of data, which are placed in an on-chip latch. The lowest two bits of column address enable one of the four bits from the latch to the chip output. By strobing the CAS line, with no additional addresses supplied to the chip, the other three bits of data are enabled to the output sequentially. Sustained data rates of 80 ns/bit are possible with nibble mode chips.

Ripple mode access operates very much like extended page mode but with significantly faster cycle times, 40 ns versus 125 ns. The improved performance is due in part to look-ahead circuitry on the column adddress buffer.

The rapid data access provided by chips having page mode, nibble mode, or ripple mode features is well suited to the operation of the video refresh controller, which must provide data to the video output in scan-line order. Display system designs using chips with extended page mode,[3] with nibble mode,[4] and with ripple mode[5] appear in the literature. In addition to a full description of ripple mode, the third article includes a concise discussion of image memory architectures.

The problem

In the following discussion of architectures, all numbers are based on a single bit plane, a one-bit frame buffer. For increased intensity or color resolution, the design is simply replicated. The designs also assume that the minimum number of memory chips are used and that all memory chips in the system are accessed simultaneously. An additional simplifying assumption is that data are stored in horizontal scan-line order; that is, the data left to right along the scan line are stored at sequential memory addresses. Although memories are available with cycle times of less than 400 ns, that figure is used for all memories to simplify the explanation. Exceptions to these assumptions are discussed where significant.

Refresh requirements. Since a stable display is generally the foremost requirement of a graphics system, the first consideration when beginning the design of a frame buffer system is how the video refresh controller is going to supply data to the video output hardware when the pixel time is less than memory cycle time. When the nature of the solution to this problem is known, the question of access to the memories by the display processor can be addressed and trade-offs made as needed.

Consider a design common a few years ago: a 512 × 512 × 1 frame buffer with a 30-Hz refresh rate that is built with 16K × 1 DRAMs. Sixteen chips with a typical cycle time of 400 ns are needed to store the entire image. Since memory cycle time is longer than pixel time, multiple chips must be accessed simultaneously. The video refresh controller addresses and reads all the chips simultaneously. The resulting data for 16 pixels is latched in parallel into a shift register and is then serially read out to the video output hardware at the required video rate of 100 ns/pixel. This typical frame buffer architecture is shown in Figure 7.

One 400-ns memory cycle supplies sufficient pixel data for 1600 ns of display. During active line time, the frame buffer memories are unused for 1200 ns of each 1600 ns.

The display processor can use three cycles between each video refresh cycle. In addition, the memories are unused by the video refresh controller during the horizontal and vertical blanking intervals. During this free time, the memories can be accessed by the display processor, or chip refresh can occur. Figure 8 shows the allocation of memory cycles across the scan line to the video refresh controller and display processor.

As chips become larger but retain their one-bit-wide design, × 1, the percentage of memory cycles used by the refresh controller dramatically decreases. Table 2 shows that the problem is even worse for 60-Hz refresh and 1024 × 1024 systems.

For 16K × 1 memories, 16 chips are required for a 512 × 512 display, and 25 percent of the memory cycles available during the active line time are required for display refresh. For 64K × 1 DRAMs, four chips are required, and 100 percent of the memory cycles during the active line time are required for display refresh. A single 256K × 1 DRAM can hold an entire 512 × 512 × 1 image, but it cannot be used for that purpose because the data cannot be accessed at the required video rate. Larger memory chips in × 1 organization make the memory access problem worse.

Although the pixel time for a 640 × 485 image is shorter than that for a full-screen 512 × 512 image, the required memory speed is not higher. A 512 × 512 display requires four 64K × 1 DRAMs. A 640 × 485 display requires five 64K × 1 DRAMs. Table 1 gives a displayed pixel time of 96.7 ns for a 512 × 512 display and 82.3 ns for a 640 × 485 display. In the 512 system, four pixels representing 388 ns of display time are fetched in each cycle, allowing the video data rate to be met. (Cycles of 400 ns were chosen for computational convenience; typically, 64K × 1 RAMs have cycles under 300 ns.) In the 640 system, five pixels, representing 412.4 ns of display time, are read in each cycle, also meeting the required video

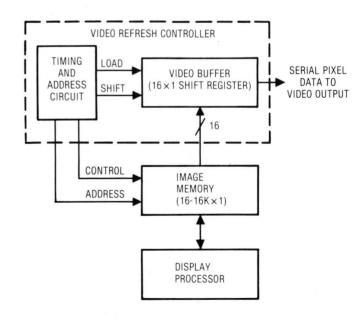

Figure 7. A 512 × 512 image memory built with 16K × 1 DRAMs.

data rate. Neither additional memory cycles nor faster parts are required. The same type of analysis can be applied to a 1280×960 system. The fact that additional memory chips are needed to store the additional image data means that more pixels are accessed per refresh read cycle and a very similar overall access rate is máintained.

Advances in processing. While the number of image memory cycles available to the display processor has decreased with improvements in memory technology, concurrent improvements in processor technology have increased the speed at which new pixel data values can be calculated. The faster new data is available, the more often the display processor needs to reference the image memories and the greater the problem of contention for the available cycles.

Processor design and access to memory are both influenced by the operations the processor is to perform. If the processor is to perform scan-line algorithms, sequential access to the memories is desirable. If area-oriented algorithms are to be performed, area access is preferred. If video rate input to the memories is required simultaneously with video output, as in many image processing systems, an input write data path similar to the video refresh controller read data path is required.

No image generation functions were embedded in the earliest display systems. The systems were "dumb frame buffers" and simply displayed data written from the host CPU. Built with 4K×1 DRAMs, the systems were nearly always available for the host to transfer data into the memories.

Many early frame buffers were used for image processing. The first computations that moved into the display systems were special hardwired imaging operations such as image filtering and operations on two images. Because the results of the computations were fed back into the frame buffer memory (feedback loop processing), the

Table 2.
Video refresh controller (VRC) memory cycle requirements during active line time.
Assume 400-ns memory cycles and no use of page, ripple, or nibble modes.

(a) 512 × 512 display

CHIP SIZE	NO. CHIPS	PIXELS PER ACCESS	30 HZ: 100-NS PIXEL		60 HZ: 45-NS PIXEL	
			TIME BETWEEN VRC ACCESSES	% CYCLES FOR VRC	TIME BETWEEN VRC ACCESSES	% CYCLES FOR VRC
4K×1	64	64	6400	12.5	2280	14
16K×1	16	16	1600	25	675	64
64K×1	4	4	400	100	180	*
256K×1	1	1	100	*	45	*

(b) 1024 × 1024 display

CHIP SIZE	NO. CHIPS	PIXELS PER ACCESS	30 HZ: 25-NS PIXEL		60 HZ: 10-NS PIXEL	
			TIME BETWEEN VRC ACCESSES	% CYCLES FOR VRC	TIME BETWEEN VRC ACCESSES	% CYCLES FOR VRC
4K×1	256	256	6400	6	2560	16
16K×1	64	64	1600	25	640	63
64K×1	16	16	400	100	160	*
256K×1	4	4	100	*	40	*

* Display cannot be supported with the given assumptions.

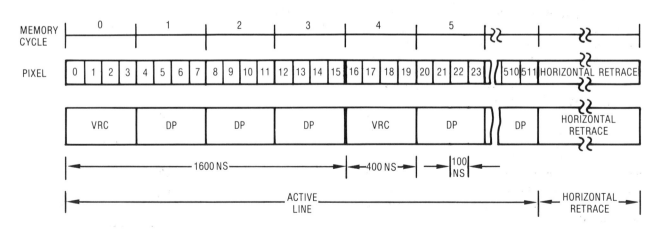

Figure 8. Allocation of active line time memory cycles to video refresh controller (VRC) and display processor (DP); 512 × 512, 30 Hz, 16 16K × 1 DRAMs.

memories needed the capability to be read from and written to at video rates.

The first graphics functions to move into the display system were vector and character generation. These functions were hardwired, with the host computer sending the required data and control signals to the hardware. Only adds and shifts were required to generate the pixels along a vector using a digital differential analyzer. The hardware implementation of a DDA was straightforward. With DDA hardware, vectors could be generated at approximately 800 ns/pixel or 1.25M pixels/second. Memory technology at the time offered $4K \times 1$ or $16K \times 1$ chips, so adequate cycles were available to write the new data into the memories. Figures 9 and 10 show the architecture and the allocation of memory cycles to video input, video output, and the processing hardware.

Later systems employed a microprocessor front-end interface to the vector- and character-generation hardware. The host could then transfer a file, which included both data and instructions for the display processor, and the display device would generate the new pixel data without further host intervention.

The next major change in functionality of display processors came with the introduction of bit-slice processors. Vector-drawing and other more general display algorithms could now be executed outside of the host computer. Bit-slice machines are capable of vector-drawing rates of approximately 400 to 500 ns/pixel, including setup time. This rate would have one pixel available per memory cycle—if the memory cycles were available.

Bit-slice processors and $16K \times 1$ memories became available at approximately the same time. An early design is described by England.[6] Since only 75 percent of the memory cycles are available to the processor and 100 percent can be used, this is the first case in which the machine was limited in drawing new images by the lack of memory cycles. Many manufacturers did not incorporate bit-slice processors into their designs until they began to use $64K \times 1$ DRAMs for the frame buffer memory; consequently, the access problem became even worse.

The current generation of display devices often incorporates both a bit-slice processor and special-purpose hardware. In systems designed for the CAD/CAM market, the bit-slice processor can be used to set up data for the fast vector-drawing hardware. Vector-drawing rates of 40 to 50 ns/pixel are advertised. The problem of memory access grows as computation speeds increase.

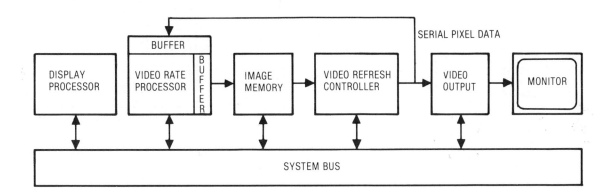

Figure 9. Block diagram of system supporting video rate processing, video refresh, and display processor; 512 × 512, 30 Hz, 16 16K × 1 DRAMs.

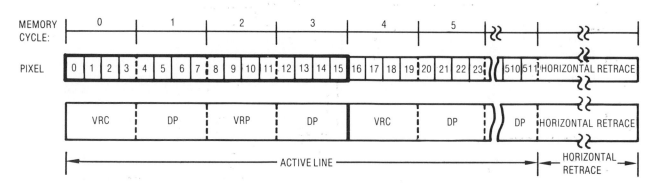

Figure 10. Allocation of 400-ns memory cycles to video rate processor (VRP), video refresh controller (VRC), and display processor (DP). Pixel time is 100 ns; 512 × 512, 30 Hz, 16 16K × 1 DRAMs.

Architectures with 64K RAMs

The prevalence of $64K \times 1$ memories in raster graphics systems has led to the development of several designs that improve display processor access to the image memories.

Double-buffer systems. The simplest way to solve the problem of access to the image memories is to use a double-buffer scheme in which one memory area is accessed by the display processor as it draws in a new image and the other memory area is accessed by the refresh controller to feed data to the video output. Double buffering is expensive in that it requires twice as much memory; however, it is essential to ensure a smooth transition between successive images in applications in which an entirely new screen of data cannot be computed and/or written into the memories in the vertical retrace interval. Even if a new image can be written to the memories in one frame time, the display must be erased between frames, and this causes flicker. Displays of moving, smooth-shaded solids and complex vector objects almost always require double buffering.

Double buffering can be implemented in two ways: either by splitting the available memory in pixel depth and using two buffers with reduced color resolution or by splitting the X-Y resolution of the memory and retaining full pixel depth. When the two buffers use entirely separate sets of memory chips, the display processor and the video refresh processor have complete access to their respective memories. If the buffers must share memory chips, little or no access improvement results, but image transition is smoothed.

Depth splitting. A $512 \times 512 \times 32$-bit frame buffer can be treated as two $512 \times 512 \times 16$ buffers. The two banks of memory may or may not be separately addressable. If not, write protect and write enable must be possible on the bit planes. The video output circuitry must be able to handle 16-bit data. Some sophisticated systems allow further effective division of the pixel depth by hardware in the video output chain.[7]

The advantage of the pixel-depth splitting approach is that the system can be used as a single-buffer system for full-color applications, such as image processing or realistic computer-generated imagery, and as a double-buffered system with reduced color resolution for

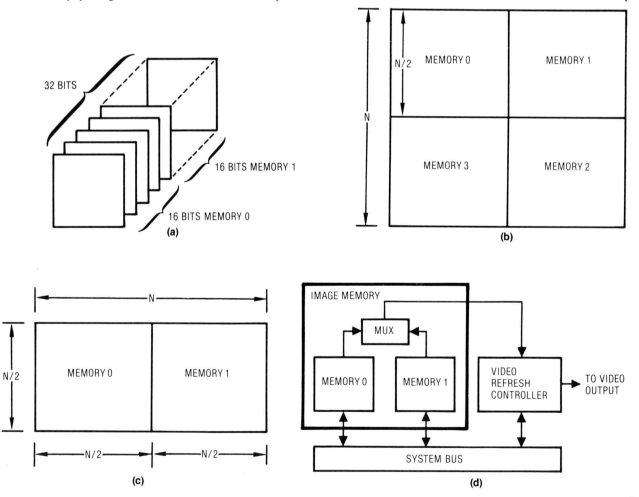

Figure 11. Double-buffering techniques: depth splitting (a); X-Y splitting (b), (c), (d).

IEEE CG&A

dynamic applications that may not need full-color capability, such as CAD and instrumentation simulation.

X-Y *splitting*. In systems with at least twice as much memory resolution as the desired output resolution, double buffering is accomplished by treating the memory as if it were two or more distinct buffers of the desired size. In some systems X-Y memory storage resolution is larger than the maximum displayable resolution, i.e., a 1024×1024 storage memory in which only 512×512 can be displayed at any time. The window function can be used to display any 512×512 area within the larger memory space. Correctly designed addressing and window circuitry allow the use of different quadrants of the memory as multiple buffers. (In a system that does not have a separate Z memory, an additional advantage is realized: One quadrant of the memory that is not displayed can be used to store Z values for a Z-buffer hidden-surface algorithm.)

In other systems the second buffer is adjacent to the first in address space, making a rectangular memory array, i.e., 1024×512. Again, windowing can be used to switch between the two buffers (or to pan through the memory). In the third case, the two banks of memory are entirely separate. See Figure 11.

In systems incorporating window and zoom features, it is possible to treat a 512×512 buffer as four 256×256 buffers with full pixel depth maintained. There is less improvement in access, and the images have lower resolution than in full double buffering. Zoom is set to a factor of two, and the video refresh controller changes the window to switch buffers. In an image memory built with four $64K \times 1$ DRAMs, each chip holds every fourth pixel along the scan line of 512 pixels. Because of this, reads for display and writes of new data use the same chips. Memory cycles during the active portion of the line time become available to the display processor because the effect of the zoom is to make the pixel time twice as long. Half as many memory accesses are required to support display refresh, and, consequently, the display processor has increased opportunity to access the memory. Refer to Figure 12.

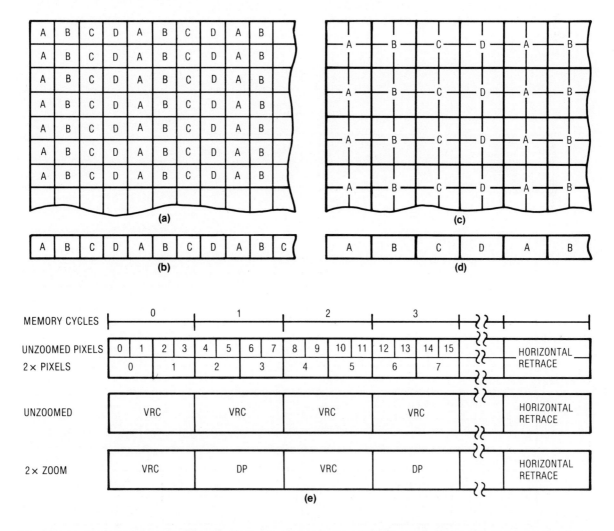

Figure 12. Timing for a 512 × 512, 30-Hz display built with four 64K × 1 DRAMs with and without two times zoom. Chip-to-pixel mapping with no zoom (a); single-scan line with no zoom (b); chip-to-pixel mapping with two times zoom (c); single-scan line with two times zoom (d); pixel timing and allocation of memory cycles to VRC and DP for unzoomed and two times zoomed display. DP has access to memory cycles during horizontal and vertical retrace times (e).

Variable resolution memories. Some systems, for example Adage 3000, offer users the ability to trade pixel depth for X-Y resolution. For instance, a $1024 \times 1024 \times 8$ memory can be alternately addressed as a $512 \times 512 \times 32$ memory. Double buffering can be implemented in these systems by using the higher resolution format and the X-Y splitting technique.

Variable resolution is accomplished by manipulation of the video buffer. A buffer that can support one bit/pixel at 10 ns/pixel can also support four bits at 40 ns/pixel and eight bits at 80 ns/pixel. The video refresh controller formats the video buffer bits into pixels of a specified depth and passes them on to the video output circuitry at the rate required by the specified display resolution and refresh rate.

Writes during blanking. The most economical way to build an image memory of $64K \times 1$ DRAMs is to accept the fact that the display processor can write into the memories only during blanking times and make little or no special provision to increase this access. Righter[3] mentions several techniques for decreasing processor wait time in this type of architecture. With the timing figures for 512×512, 60-Hz display, blanking periods account for 4.83 ms of each 16.67-ms frame time, permitting over 12,000 400-ns cycles to be performed during the available time. If this rate can be maintained, a new frame of data can be written in 22 frame times. However, to meet the maximum figure, data must be available from the display processor for every cycle.

To illustrate the problems in using a general-purpose microprocessor in such a system, consider a design with an 8080 processor running a 2-MHz clock (500-ns cycle) as the display processor. It will not be able to supply data at the rate desired. In an 8080 processor, an add function takes four clock cycles; a conditional jump, 10; and a move from memory to register, seven. The time required to do any useful function easily can exceed the entire horizontal retrace interval of 7 μs. In the worst case, a processor, executing an algorithm such as a Z-buffer that requires read/modify/write operations, would read a value from the frame buffer at the beginning of the horizontal blanking interval, perform computations that require longer than 7 μs to complete, and wait the entire next line time before being able to write the new data value out to the memory. While one pixel per scan line (15,750 pixels/second, 16.6 seconds/full frame) is not an acceptable data rate for interactive applications, it may be acceptable for others.

Adding a FIFO memory to the display processor decreases display processor wait time and increases the writing rate into the memories. The FIFO buffers data

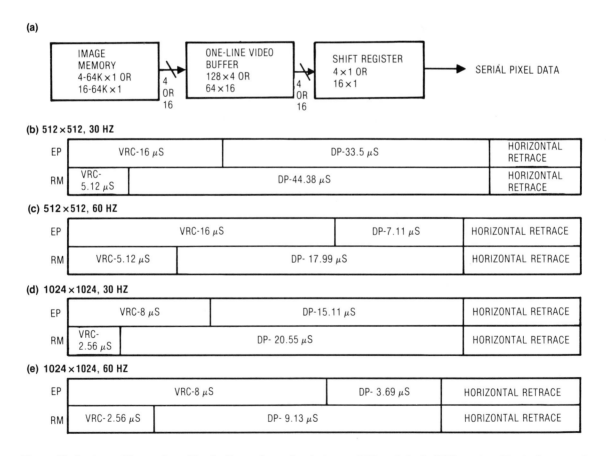

Figure 13. System with one line video buffer, using extended page (EP) and ripple (RM) modes. Block diagram of a 512 × 512 or 1024 × 1024 system (a); allocation of line time for memory cycles by the VRC and DP (b through e). DP also has access to cycles during horizontal and vertical refresh times.

IEEE CG&A

and addresses to be used to write to the image memory when the cycles are available. If data is placed in the FIFO so that it is in scan-line order, one of the faster writing methods, such as page, nibble, or ripple mode, can be used to gain additional speed.

The use of FIFO memory for data to be written does not improve the situation for algorithms, which require reads from the frame buffer memory. In addition to the more elaborate uses of read/modify/ write for Z-buffer, antialiasing to background color, and transparency, these operations are needed to perform flood-fill algorithms, which are available on even the simplest graphics devices. An interesting way to see the difference that read cycles have on performance is to compare the time it takes to draw a rectangle filled by single-pixel writes with the time required to flood fill a previously drawn rectangle of the same size.

If the processor is executing a scan-line algorithm that requires reads, performance can be improved by reading and buffering an entire scan line before line processing begins. Page, nibble, and ripple mode can speed this process.

Larger video buffers. Additional cycles become available for the display processor when the number of reads performed by the video refresh controller is decreased. Adding larger video buffers accomplishes this.

Consider a system with four $64K \times 1$ DRAMs and a 512-pixel video buffer. The video buffer is a 128×4 FIFO memory. A 4×1 shift register is used for the final parallel-to-serial conversion. An entire line of data can be read using 128 extended page mode reads. Page mode cycle times are as low as 125 ns, and a little over 16 μs is required to read an entire 512-pixel scan line. This design incurs the cost of a large video buffer but frees 75 percent of active line time for 30-Hz displays and 30 percent of active line time for 60-Hz displays. Using ripple mode, the line can be read in less than 6 μs, freeing proportionately more of the image memory cycles during the active line time for display processor accesses. Figure 13 shows a block diagram of a system with a line buffer and the allocation of line time to refresh controller and display processor memory cycles.

Nibble mode DRAMs are available in speeds that make it possible to access all four data bits within a 500-ns nibble mode cycle. In a system with four $64K \times 1$ DRAMs, 16 pixels can be accessed in one 500-ns cycle. Even slow chips with nibble mode have 230-ns random access cycle times. Figure 14 shows an implementation with a 4×4 video buffer and a 4×1 shift register. For 30-Hz display, 80 percent of the cycles are available for

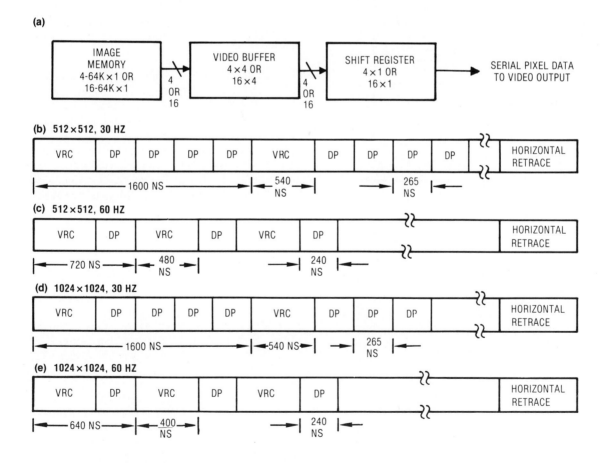

Figure 14. Nibble mode block diagram with 4 × 4 video buffer (a); allocation of memory cycle for VRC and DP (b). DP also has access to cycles during horizontal and vertical retrace.

the display processor. By using a slightly faster part, a 60-Hz display can be supported with alternating cycles for the video refresh controller and the display processor. External circuitry for the nibble mode design is somewhat less complex than that for page mode because in addition to using a significantly smaller video buffer (16 pixels versus 512), column addresses do not have to be supplied to the memory chip in order to access the additional data bits.

Table 3 summarizes the video refresh controller memory cycle requirements for page, ripple, and nibble modes with 64K × 1 DRAMs.

Cache solutions. An obvious way to speed up the overall writing rate is to write to all chips during a cycle just as all chips are read at one time during a video refresh read cycle. Data for the parallel write is computed and stored in a *cache* buffer. Typically, the number of cache locations matches the number of memory chips in the system; i.e., a 1280 × 1024 system built with 20 64K DRAMs has a 20-pixel cache.

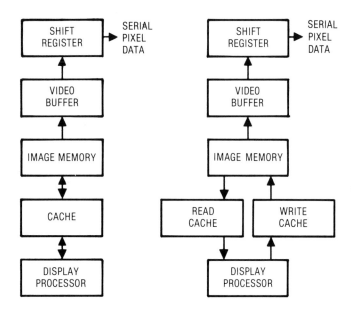

Figure 15. Cache memory for parallel operations on memory.

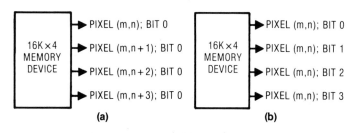

Figure 16. Wide-word DRAM used for width (a) and depth (b).

The cache is built with high-speed parts so that it can accept data at the maximum rate of the display processor. Since all access to the image memory from the display processor is through the cache, the cache has a read-write port to both the display memory and the display processor. An alternative solution is to have separate read and write caches. Such an architecture facilitates Raster-Op and other functions that require read/modify/write operations.[8] See Figure 15.

State-of-the-art memories

Ever-larger memory chips with a ×1 design are not useful for raster display systems. New memory devices with wide-word capabilities and devices designed specifically for graphics systems are opening up new image memory design possibilities.

Wide-word memory devices. The first memory chips with wide-word capability and the size and speed needed to make them useful for raster graphics display systems are the 16K × 4 chips with a total storage of 64K bits. Vendors have announced plans for devices with various organizations, such as 8K × 8, 64K × 4, and 32K × 8, reflecting the influence of the small-systems market on new products. Frame buffer manufacturers have been the secondary beneficiaries of these new parts. Wide-word memories can be used in one of two ways in an image memory: They can be arranged as multiple pixels per chip (width) or as multiple bits per pixel per chip (depth). See Figure 16.

Wide-word memories—multiple pixels. When the data bits of a wide-word memory are used to represent multiple pixels and all memories are still accessed simultaneously, more pixels can be fetched during each memory read cycle. The frequency of video refresh controller cycles decreases and the display processor access to the memories increases. This is true for memories that have a total storage of 64K bits. Designs that use chips storing 256K bits organized in 64K × 4 arrangements encounter the same problems that designs using parts with 64K × 1 organization do: Every cycle is needed by the video refresh controller.

A 1024 × 1024 bit plane requires the same number of 16K × 4 and 64K × 1 chips—16. Chip count is not reduced. The advantage is that a single cycle can access 64 pixels rather than just 16. The video buffer must be correspondingly larger. For a 30-Hz refresh display, less than 20 percent of the memory cycles are required for display refresh. A 60-Hz refresh system, not easily implemented with 64K × 1 chips, requires every cycle for refresh unless a method such as page mode operation is used.

At least two vendors have announced 256K chips organized as 64K × 4. While allowing a fourfold reduction in parts count and the attendant savings in power, reliability, and cost, these solutions do not improve access to the memories. A single chip is needed to build a 512 × 512 memory plane and four chips to build a 1024 × 1024 plane. For a 30-Hz display, an access for display must occur every 400 ns; for a 1024 × 1024, 60-Hz display, an access must occur every 160 ns.

One announced 32K × 8 part provides somewhat better performance. Since the word is twice as wide, the memories must be accessed half as often. At 30 Hz, memory cycles can alternate between video refresh controller and display processor. Assuming that cycles times will be under 320 ns, a 1024 × 1024, 60-Hz display can be supported with all cycles used by the video refresh controller.

The major disadvantage of using wide-word memories with multiple pixels in the word is the inability to address a single pixel in the memory system. Writing a single pixel requires that a read/modify/write cycle be executed. The problem is less of a handicap if the system is built with cache memory.

Wide-word memory—multiple bits per pixel. In the previous discussion, pixel depth was assumed to be achieved by replicating the single-bit-plane design. The use of a wide-word memory for pixel depth is a departure from this method. While still not reducing chip count from a 64K × 1 design, an architecture using 16K × 4 devices does increase display processor access to the memories.

Sixty-four 64K RAMs are required to build four bit planes at 1024 × 1024. In a system built with 64K × 1 chips, a fetch from memory retrieves 16 pixels, each of which is four bits deep. In a system of 16K × 4 chips, 64 four-bit-deep pixels are fetched simultaneously. The timing analysis becomes similar to that of a system designed with 16K × 1 RAMs, with the advantage of getting four bits of depth from one chip. Noninterlaced, 60-Hz designs must still include provision for increasing processor access.

Table 4 gives the percentage of image memory cycles during active line time that is required to support video refresh for wide-word chips used in width and depth. The same number of pixels are fetched per memory access regardless of whether the chip is used for width or depth.

Timing for 64K × 4 DRAMs used in depth is like that for 64K × 1 designs, and the same methods can be used to improve access. Designs using × 8 memories show significant increases in display processor access to the memories.

The penalty paid for the increased access is the size of the required video buffer. The buffer size can be reduced by *interleaving* the operation of the memories, that is, dividing the memory into several groups and staggering the starting time of cycles for each group. The smaller video buffer is then reloaded as data becomes available from each group of memories in turn. Interleaving also lowers peak power requirements for the memory system.

A major drawback of wide-word chips as depth is the inability to write to a single bit plane. Such a write requires a read/modify/write cycle. The loss of single-plane addressing can be a significant handicap in an application that uses many single-plane images or overlays.

Special graphics memory devices. The needs of raster display designers were the primary concern of Texas Instruments in their development of the 64K-RAM TMS4161 device. Recognizing the data-rate problem and its usual solution with an exernal shift register, TI designed the TMS4161 with an internal 256-bit shift register with full external shift register controls.

The device is a dual-ported RAM; one port operates as a standard 64K × 1 memory and the other as a 256 × 1 shift register. (Refer to Figure 17.) The chip can be ac-

Table 3.
Video refresh controller memory cycle requirements during active line time for page, ripple, and nibble modes with a full-line video buffer and nibble mode with an N x 4 video buffer.

(a) 512 × 512 display—64K × 1-DRAM memory array

CHIP TYPE	NO. CHIPS	PIXELS/ ACCESS	30 HZ: 100-NS PIXEL			60 HZ: 45-NS PIXEL		
			TIME BETWEEN VRC ACCESSES	VRC CYCLE TIME	% ACTIVE LINE FOR VRC	TIME BETWEEN VRC ACCESSES	VRC CYCLE TIME	% ACTIVE LINE FOR VRC
STANDARD	4	4	400 NS	400 NS	100	180 NS	400 NS	*
EXTENDED PAGE	4	512	60.4 μS (1 LINE)	16 μS	32	30.11 μS	16 μS	69
RIPPLE	4	512	60.4 μS	5.1 μS	10	30.11 μS	5.1 μS	22
NIBBLE	4	4	1600 NS	540 NS	34	720 NS	480 NS	67

(b) 1024 × 1024 display—64K × 1-DRAM memory array

CHIP TYPE	NO. CHIPS	PIXELS/ ACCESS	30 HZ: 25-NS PIXEL			60 HZ:10-NS PIXEL		
			TIME BETWEEN VRC ACCESSES	VRC CYCLE TIME	% ACTIVE LINE FOR VRC	TIME BETWEEN VRC ACCESSES	VRC CYCLE TIME	% ACTIVE LINE FOR VRC
STANDARD	16	16	400 NS	400 NS	100	160 NS	400 NS	*
EXTENDED PAGE	16	1024	30.11 μS	8 μS	35	15.69 μS	8 μS	68
RIPPLE	16	1024	30.11 μS	2.6 μS	11	15.69 μS	2.6 μS	22
NIBBLE	16	64	1444 NS	480 NS	33	640 NS	400 NS	63

*Display cannot be supported with the given assumptions.

Table 4.
Video refresh controller memory cycle requirements during active line time for wide-word memories.
Assume 400-ns memory cycles and no use of page, ripple, or nibble modes.

(a) 512 × 512 display

CHIP SIZE	NO. CHIPS DEPTH	NO. CHIPS WIDTH	PIXELS/ ACCESS	30 HZ: 100-NS PIXEL		60 HZ: 45-NS PIXEL	
				TIME BETWEEN VRC ACCESSES	% CYCLES FOR VRC	TIME BETWEEN VRC ACCESSES	% CYCLES FOR VRC
16K ×4	16	4	16	1600	25	720	56
8K ×8	32	4	32	3200	12.5	1440	28
32K ×8	8	1	8	800	50	360	100**
64K ×4	4	1	4	400	100	180	*

(b) 1024 × 1024 display

CHIP SIZE	NO. CHIPS DEPTH	NO. CHIPS WIDTH	PIXELS/ ACCESS	30 HZ: 25-NS PIXEL		60 HZ: 10-NS PIXEL	
				TIME BETWEEN VRC ACCESSES	% CYCLES FOR VRC	TIME BETWEEN VIDEO ACCESSES	% CYCLES FOR VRC
16K ×4	64	16	64	1600	25	640	63
8K ×8	128	16	128	3200	12.5	1280	31
32K ×8	32	4	32	800	50	320	100**
64K ×4	16	4	16	400	100	160	*

* Display cannot be supported with the given assumptions..
** Display cannot be supported with 400-ns devices, but there is a high probability that the port will be faster when it becomes available.

cessed simultaneously from the standard port, including page mode accesses, and from the shift register port. The memory cannot be accessed externally from either port during a move of data between the memory and the shift register.

Detailed descriptions of the device and a display memory design using the device are provided by Pinkham.[9] The internal shift register functions as a large video buffer. The parts count is reduced by eliminating the external video buffer, and display processor memory access is improved because of the buffer size.

The maximum speed of the shift clock in the TMS-4161 is 25 MHz, or 40 ns. To achieve the data rate necessary for a 1024 × 1024, 60-Hz system using 16 chips, a 16-bit external shift register is used. This shift register is loaded from the 4161 every 16 pixel times (every 160 ns). The serial port output enable line offers the possibility of further reducing the size of the shift register and time-multiplexing data to it.

For each 1024-pixel scan line, only 64 shift operations of the 4161 are required; thus, data must be transferred from memory to shift register only once every four scan lines. This operation can occur during horizontal retrace times. The shift starting position within the 256 bits of the internal shift register is designated on 64-bit boundaries by setting the upper two-column address bits during the memory-to-shift-register transfer. This feature allows the visible display to begin other than at the beginning of a stored line of the image (pan) and the display of interlaced and noninterlaced formats.

The TMS4161 will be most useful in single-buffer systems and systems that double buffer in a manner that shares memory chips. In a full double-buffered system, the saving occurs in the size of the shift register, since the display processor already has total access to one memory while the video refresh controller has total access to the other.

An internal shift register will be essential for using 256K RAMs in raster display systems. A 1024 × 1024, 60-Hz system built with four 256K RAMs could meet a 10-ns pixel rate if the chip were to have an internal shift register of at least 256 bits and a shift clock of at least 25

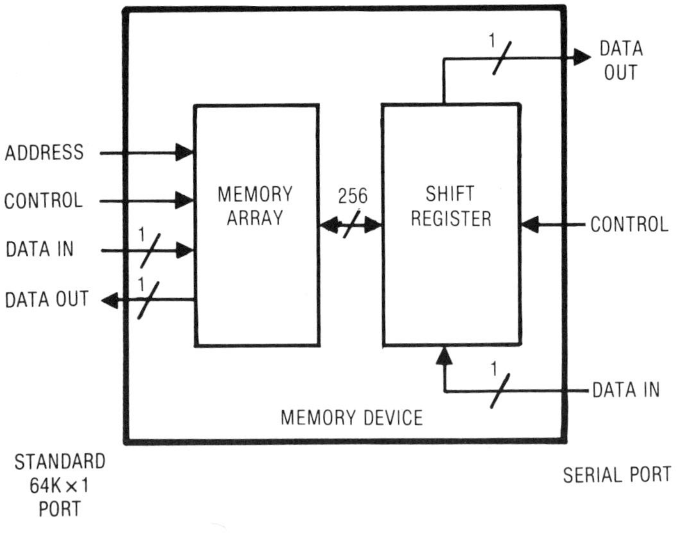

Figure 17. Block diagram of DRAM with internal shift register.

IEEE CG&A

MHz. Such a device appears to be a reasonable extension of currently announced memory products.

Data to be written to the TMS4161 memories can be shifted into the internal shift register and then moved to the memory in one operation. Because data used in this way must be generated not only in scan-line order but also in pixel order (a complicated procedure) or buffered in a scan-line buffer (an expensive procedure), this feature does not appear promising as a method for increasing write speed.

Although the internal shift register significantly simplifies frame buffer design and improves processor access to the memory, it does not help with the problem of writing to the memories significantly faster than the random access rate, or at best the page mode rate. These rates, inadequate in the light of improvements in display processor hardware, require that other ways of organizing a memory be investigated.

Other memory organizations

Display update performance suffers when a new pixel value can be computed faster than it can be written into the image memory. The solution appears to be found in writing multiple pixels into the memory in parallel, just as pixels are read out in parallel for display. Systems using a cache memory take advantage of parallel writes to image memory.

Mask mode, offered by some display manufacturers, is another example of a parallel write. A mask word with one bit for each memory device is generated, with the bits in the mask word serving as write enable for the chips. A data value (often shade) is prestored and used as data to all chips. When the write cycle occurs, the prestored value is written into each chip enabled by the mask word. Fill rates as fast as 12.5 ns/pixel can be achieved with mask mode in some applications.

The same scan-line-order mapping of pixels to chips that helps performance in video refresh reads of the memories can work against high performance in writing new data. Vector drawing and polygon shading are good examples. It is the exception that a vector is horizontal and can be written into the memory with parallel writes along the scan line. More typically, sequential pixels of a vector occur on different scan lines. While polygons usually have multiple pixels along a line, the entire figure covers multiple lines. Both of these cases suggest the use of memory so that a single operation accesses an array of pixels rather than a linear group.

Array organization. If a figure covers a small area (pixel array) such as a character or a small polygon, or passes through an area, such as a vector, a processor that generates data in arrays and a memory that can accept data organized in arrays in a single write cycle will give performance improvements. If the array is sufficiently large, say 8×8, and can be located on arbitrary pixel boundaries, at some level of image complexity it is reasonable to assume that entire polygons and other display primitives will fall within a single array and can be written to image memory in a single cycle.

The memory. Figure 18 shows a pixel-to-chip mapping for 16 64K $\times$ 1 chips for a 1024 $\times$ 1024 display. Sequential cells of the 16 chips along the scan line are alike; the cells have a symmetric organization, and only four chips appear in any one scan line. An array used in this manner has lost the advantage of parallel reads by the video refresh controller and cannot support displays at either 30 Hz or 60 Hz. If more, smaller chips are used and video buffer size is increased significantly, such a design is feasible. A system using 64 16K DRAMs in an 8×8-array configuration with a dual eight-scan-line video buffer is described by Sproull et al.[10]

Figure 19 shows an array in which the groups of four chips are offset one row in each cell, that is staggered.

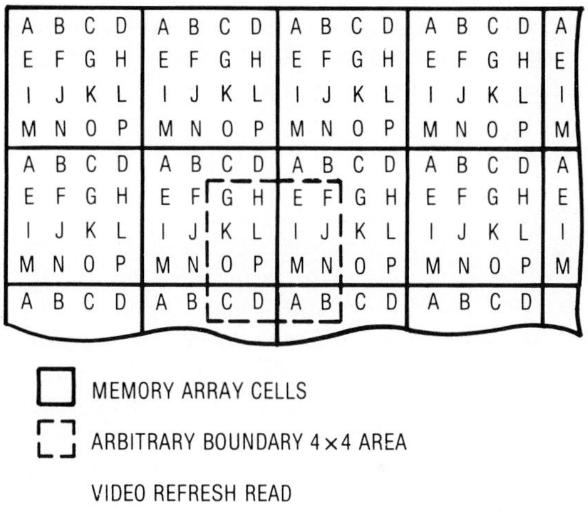

☐ MEMORY ARRAY CELLS

⌐⌐ ARBITRARY BOUNDARY 4 × 4 AREA

VIDEO REFRESH READ

Figure 18. Chip-(A through P)-to-pixel mapping for symmetric array organization.

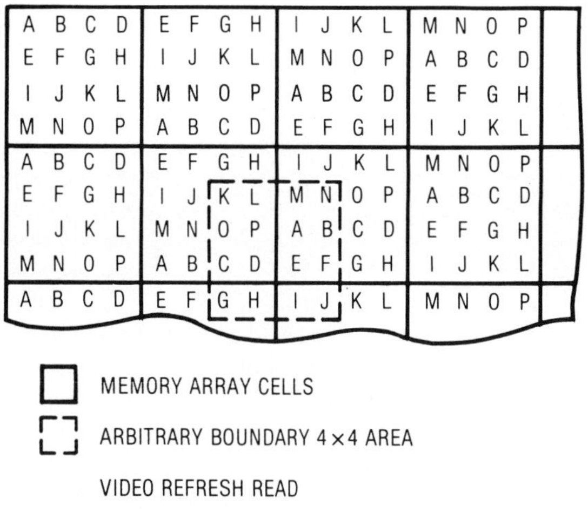

☐ MEMORY ARRAY CELLS

⌐⌐ ARBITRARY BOUNDARY 4 × 4 AREA

VIDEO REFRESH READ

Figure 19. Chip-(A through P)-to-pixel mapping for staggered array organization.

Each chip appears only once in each series of 16 sequential pixels on any scan line, and display can be supported. Since the 16 pixels are in four different cells, the video refresh controller must send the four groups of four chips different addresses to access the pixels along the scan line.

The video refresh controller reads an array-organized memory on regular cell boundaries. Performance is better if the display processor can read and write arrays on arbitrary pixel boundaries. In either staggered or symmetric array organizations, each chip contains only one pixel of any arbitrary 4×4-pixel area of the screen. Through the appropriate address manipulation, array writes on arbitrary boundaries can occur. The required address mapping is well defined but messy to implement. Gate arrays or programmable logic arrays (PLAs) make this type of memory organization more feasible.

Processors for generating array data. To take advantage of an array write into display memory, the display processor must generate data in an array format. Pixel data can be generated in serial fashion, and the results can be stored in an array cache or mask memory until written. This method works only if the display processor is so fast that the memory access is the limiting factor in the system. A system that includes special-purpose, 40 to 50-ns/pixel vector-generating hardware is an example.

A second method involves computing the mask directly. For characters and symbols, this is an easy task: The desired masks are stored in ROM or other nonviewable memory and need only be read, perhaps with a shift operation, into the mask registers. Raster-Op functions are likewise easily executed. Parallel generation of the mask for vectors or polygons is much more difficult but is aided by gate arrays, PLAs, or custom VLSI circuitry.

Page mode used to imitate array organization. In a 1024×1024 system built of $64K \times 1$ DRAMs, one 256-word page can represent four scan lines. By reorganizing the mapping of memory addresses to scan lines, one page of memory can be made to map to a 64-pixel by 64-line area. The video refresh controller must supply a new RAS address for every fourth cycle as the scan line is traversed. When writing, the entire 64×64 area can be accessed with only page mode CAS cycles.

This solution is particularly attractive for a double-buffered system in which the display processor has exclusive access to the memories. For instance, a vector-drawing routine must perform a RAS cycle, supplying a new row address, only when the vector crosses a 64-line or 64-pixel boundary. Within the 64×64 area, the memory can accept new data at full page mode rate.

In a single-buffered system, some buffering of both data and address should be provided to best take advantage of available memory cycles and to allow the processor to run continuously.

The fewer full RAS memory cycles required, the faster the overall data rate will be. Algorithms for antialiased vectors and polygons, with their higher number of pixels to be written, will benefit from this organization even more than vectors will.

Processor-per-pixel systems. The trend in display system architectures is to put more functionality into the display processor and to have higher resolution and faster refresh displays. A parallel movement involves putting more functionality into silicon. Two notable efforts involve multiple processors and very tight coupling of processors and memory.

Clark and Hannah[11] describe a memory system organized as an 8×8 array with a processor for each of the eight columns and one for each row of each column. The column processors pass data to the row processors, which perform the final rendering computations. The row processors also contain a memory interface processor, which controls image memory operations—that is, both reads and writes for the processors and reads requested by the video refresh controller. A preprocessor supplies data in the proper format to the processor/interface chips.

Fuchs and Poulton[12] propose a smart memory system using "pixel planes." The chip includes memory cells for both display and Z-buffer, and a fine-grained tree processor, which evaluates arithmetic expressions for hidden-surface removal and shading. A preprocessor prepares data in the format appropriate for the pixel-plane chips.

The performance specifications proposed for systems built with these two experimental chips are impressive. The fact that one system includes the memory as an integral part of the chip and the other includes memory control as part of the chip reemphasizes the point that the relationship of processor and memory is crucial to performance in a raster graphics system. ■

Acknowledgment

I would like to acknowledge the assistance given me by Nick England of Adage, Inc., in the preparation of this article.

References

1. Christopher R. Odgers, "An Introduction to Video Signal Terminology, Concepts, and Standards, and Their Influence on Frame Buffer Design," Siggraph '82 2-D Animation tutorial notes, 1982.

2. Ronald Baecker, "Digital Video Display Systems and Dynamic Graphics," *Computer Graphics* (Proc. Siggraph '79), Vol. 13, No. 2, Aug. 1979, pp. 48-56.

3. William H. Righter, "Using 64K DRAMs in Graphics Applications," *Electronic Imaging*, Vol. 2, No. 10, Nov. 1983, pp. 62-71.

4. Dennis Galloway, Brad Hartman, and David Wooten, "64-K Dynamic RAM Speeds Well Beyond the Pack," *Electronic Design,* Vol. 29, No. 6, Mar. 19, 1981, pp. 221-225.

5. Douglas L. Finke, "Dynamic RAM Architectures for Graphics Applications," *AFIPS Conf. Proc.,* 1983 NCC, pp. 479-485.

6. J. N. England, "A System for Interactive Modeling of Physical Curved Surface Objects," *Computer Graphics* (Proc. Siggraph '78), Vol. 12, No. 3, Aug. 1978, pp. 336-340.

7. K. S. Booth and S. A. MacKay, "Techniques for Frame Buffer Animation," *Proc. Graphics Interface '82,* pp. 213-220.

8. Robert A. Bruce, "Custom Processor Eases Display Design," *Digital Design,* Vol. 12, No. 13, 1982, pp. 62-64.

9. Ray Pinkham, Mark Novak, and Carl Guttag, "Video RAM Excels at Fast Graphics," *Electronic Design,* Vol. 31, No. 17, Aug. 18, 1983, pp. 161-182.

10. Robert F. Sproull, Ivan E. Sutherland, Alistair Thompson, and Charles Minter, "The 8 by 8 Display," *ACM Trans. Graphics,* Vol. 2, No. 1, Jan. 1983, pp. 32-56.

11. James H. Clark and Marc Hannah, "Distributed Processing in a High-Performance Smart Image Memory," *Lambda,* Vol. 1, No. 3, fourth quarter 1980, pp. 40-45.

12. Henry Fuchs and John Poulton, "Pixel Planes: A VLSI-Oriented Design for a Raster Graphics Engine," *VLSI Design,* Vol. 2, No. 3, third quarter 1981, pp. 20-28.

Mary C. Whitton is a consultant in computer graphics with Whitland Associates in Raleigh, North Carolina. She was co-founder and vice president of Ikonas Graphics Systems from 1978 until the acquisition of Ikonas by Adage, Inc., in 1982. At Adage, 1982-1983, she served as product manager for the Adage 3000 (formerly Ikonas RDS-3000) during its integration into the Adage product line. Her research interests include high-performance hardware, free-form surface display, and animation.

Whitton received a BA from Duke University and an MS from North Carolina State University in humanities and expects to receive an MSEE from North Carolina State University during 1984. She is an affiliate member of the IEEE Computer Society and a member of ACM and SWE (Society of Women Engineers).

Ann. Rev. Comput. Sci. 1986. 1:19–46

FRAME-BUFFER DISPLAY ARCHITECTURES[1]

Robert F. Sproull

Sutherland, Sproull, and Associates, Inc., 4516 Henry Street, Pittsburgh, Pennsylvania, 15213

INTRODUCTION

The frame-buffer display is now the most popular computer output device, as a result of the rapid decline in the cost of high speed semiconductor memories and the low cost of raster-scan displays. Frame buffers are incorporated in a wide range of equipment, from home computers to engineering workstations to flight simulators. All frame buffers have the same principal role—for every picture element on the screen, to record its intensity or color and to refresh the display image continuously. However, the size, structure, and performance of frame buffers differ markedly for different applications.

A frame-buffer display has strengths and weaknesses. Its principal strength is that it can show an arbitrary image, subject only to the limits of spatial and intensity resolution provided by the display. Because the memory holds a separate digital value for each picture element, or pixel, on the screen, arbitrary images can be displayed. A potential weakness of the frame buffer is that a great many bits must be changed in order to make major changes to the picture. Thus, a key concern in the design of frame-buffer displays is to provide high-speed access to the memory for display updates.

In many applications, the frame buffer serves a second role, in addition to refreshing the display: It records an image data structure that is used by the application program. For example, an image-processing application may retrieve pixel values from the frame buffer, apply a filtering or convolution computation to them, and return the results to the frame buffer.

This review of frame-buffer architectures begins by describing a conventional architecture, a simple design that introduces most of the features of frame-buffer displays. We then describe how applications influence frame-buffer design and exhibit some common design problems. Following is a synopsis of architectural variations in video generation, memory structure, and processor design. The review concludes with a discussion of the state of the art and some open problems. Readers unfamiliar with frame-buffer displays are encouraged to consult Conrac (1985), Newman & Sproull (1979), Foley & van Dam (1982), Baecker (1979), or Whitton (1984) for basic information.

---

[1] Notation: h = width of display, in pixels; v = height of display, in scan lines; p = number of bits recorded per pixel; d = number of bits of precision in analog intensity signal; r = display refresh rate, Hz; t_h = horizontal retrace time; t_v = vertical retrace time; n = number of rows or columns in a RAM chip; t = time to fill a memory chip; f = fraction of frame-buffer bandwidth used for refresh.

CONVENTIONAL ARCHITECTURES

The essential form of a frame buffer is a two-ported memory in which one port is used to read memory values at high speed for display and the other port is used by an update processor to change the display image by changing the memory contents. This memory is called a buffer because of the potentially different speeds of the accesses on the two ports. The *display port* reads the memory at very high speed in a regular pattern, synchronized to the sweep of the display's electron beam across the screen. By contrast, the *update port* makes irregular accesses and both reads and writes in the process of computing and storing the proper pixel values in the memory. Although the speed of these accesses governs the rate at which the update processor may change the image, the display will continue to function correctly even if the update rate is severely limited.

Figure 1 shows the basic frame-buffer structure. To the update processor, the frame-buffer memory behaves just like all other memory in the system. It responds to each request to read or write a byte, a word, or multiple words, as required. The display port is controlled by a *video generator,* which reads from the memory the pixel values that correspond to the raster scanning pattern used on the display. Typically, the scan starts at the upper left corner of the display, proceeds to the right along a horizontal line, and then proceeds downward, painting a series of horizontal scan lines. Each pixel value fetched from the frame-buffer memory is used to index a *video lookup table* (VLT) to obtain a digital value that is converted to an analog signal to control the intensity of the electron beam. The VLT establishes a correspondence between values stored in the frame buffer and colors on the screen.

The size and speed of the frame buffer must be chosen to match the properties of the display. If the display can show v lines, each of which is h pixels across, and each pixel can display 2^p different colors or intensities, then

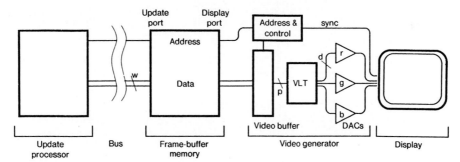

Figure 1 A conventional frame-buffer architecture consists of a dual-ported memory and a video generator. Pixel data is read through the display port, passed through a video lookup table (VLT) and digital-to-analog-converters (DAC) for red, green, and blue subchannels, and presented to the display. For monochromatic displays, only a single DAC is used. For binary displays, which show only two colors, the VLT and DAC are omitted.

the memory must contain at least vhp bits. The horizontal and vertical resolutions are influenced by the choice of display, while the number of bits stored for each pixel is partly determined by the display and partly by the application. Table 1 shows examples of typical choices.

The display port must be able to access the frame-buffer memory fast enough to refresh the display. Since cathode-ray tube displays require continual refreshing of the entire screen at rates from 30 to 70 times per second, very high memory bandwidths may be required. Table 1 shows the refresh rate, *r,* the number of times per second the display is scanned, and the resulting pixel time, the time available in which to display an individual pixel. The calculation of the pixel time, t_p, must allow time for the display beam's *horizontal retrace and vertical retrace,* during which no pixels are displayed. The fourth example in the table assumes a vertical retrace time $t_v = 600$ μs, incurred once for each refresh, and a horizontal retrace time $t_h = 4$ μs incurred once for each scan line. Thus the pixel time is $((1/r - t_v)/v - t_h)/h$, or 10 ns for the example. If each pixel is represented in the frame buffer with eight bits, the display port must be capable of reading at 800 Mbits/s.

Meeting the bandwidth requirements of the display port is the first objective of a frame-buffer design. This usually requires that each memory cycle read

Table 1 Characteristics of typical raster-scan displays

Application	h	v	p	hvp	r	Pixel time
Personal computer	320	200	2	0.13×10^6	30	166 ns
Image store, full color	640	480	24	7.4×10^6	30	83 ns
Workstation, black-and-white	1152	900	1	1.0×10^6	66	11 ns
Workstation for CAD, color	1280	960	8	9.8×10^6	60	10 ns

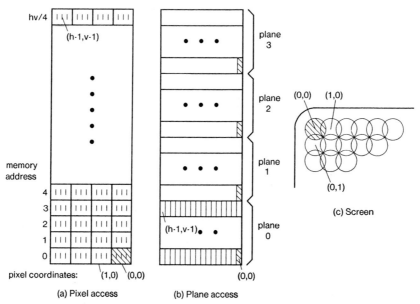

Figure 2 The two common methods by which the update processor addresses pixels in the frame buffer are (a) *pixel access* and (b) *plane access*. The bits in the frame buffer that represent the pixel at coordinates (0,0) are hatched.

values for more than one pixel, since pixel times are shorter than memory cycle times. Data read from the memory in parallel is placed briefly in a high-speed *video buffer,* from which individual pixel values are extracted as needed.

Some means must be provided to allow both ports access to the memory without undue interference. Meeting the bandwidth requirements of the display port is essential to ensure that the displayed image remains correct; the update port is usually given lower priority. To guarantee display access, the memory may be operated on a fixed schedule so that a fixed fraction of memory accesses are allocated to the display port, e.g. 1 in 2 or 2 in 3, with the remaining cycles allocated to the update port. A more restrictive method is to allow update accesses only during horizontal and vertical retrace periods, when pixels are not being displayed and the display port is idle.

How pixel values are mapped into the update processor's address space has a substantial impact on the speed with which the processor can alter the memory. The processor commonly accesses a word of memory, which contains information for more than one pixel (Figure 2). If the update port uses a *pixel organization,* one or more pixel values are packed into each word, as in Figure 2a. If p bits are recorded for each pixel, this is a packed two-dimensional array of p-bit values, indexed by the pixel coordinates *(x, y).* The update processor locates a pixel value by computing from its coordinates its word address in the array, reading the word, masking off the unwanted pixel values, and shifting the p bits to the right to obtain a p-bit integer. An alternative organization, the *plane organization,* is shown in Figure 2b. The memory may be viewed as storing p separate *bit-planes,* each of which is a packed array of single-bit values, one for each pixel. Hybrid organizations are also possible. For example, a memory with 24 bits per pixel may be organized as three *image planes,* each of which stores eight bits per pixel, organized for pixel access.

REQUIREMENTS

The design of frame buffers is determined in large measure by the requirements of the application. While the size and speed of the memory must clearly match the needs of the display monitor, the update port must be designed to have sufficient memory bandwidth to change the image rapidly enough to meet the interactive performance requirements of the application. Moreover, the kinds of memory accesses permitted by the update port can have a large impact on update performance.

The kinds of images presented on the display vary among applications, and the organization of the update port varies as a consequence. The four most important categories of imagery for interactive applications are as follows:

1. Geometric graphics. Patterns of pixels representing geometric shapes such as lines, circles, polygons, and curves are written into the frame buffer. Typical applications are computer-aided design, business graphics, drafting, and technical illustration.
2. Text and window-management. Text is written onto the screen in multiple fonts, often involving special symbols. The screen is sectioned into *windows* that appear to be separate writing surfaces, often overlapping. Moving, clearing, panning, and scrolling windows are important update functions. Typical applications are workstations for engineering, document production, programming, or education.
3. Continuous-tone images. The screen is used to show continuous-tone images, either synthesized by an algorithm or sampled from a television camera or scanner. Typical applications are in graphic arts prepress, "painting" with a computer, animation, cartography, and image analysis.
4. Feedback imagery. An interactive application will often present cursors, menus, and lines on the screen as temporary feedback to assist the user's interaction with an application. These images must be displayed and removed quickly, so as not to impede interaction speed. Moreover, when a feedback image is removed, the original image must be restored.

Many applications require mixtures of all four kinds of imagery. An engineering workstation, for example, may support all four but may emphasize geometric graphics and feedback imagery, which dominate drafting and other computer-aided design applications.

Auxiliary Data

In addition to serving as a refresh buffer, frame-buffer memories may serve as an image data structure for an application program. The best example is image-processing applications, where pixel intensities are used as input to sampling, filtering, or convolution algorithms. Likewise, most window-management software moves and scrolls windows by copying pixel values from one place on the screen to another (Pike 1983). In these cases, the update port must be able to read and write pixel values equally easily.

Some applications record more data for each pixel than just its intensity or color. This data is part of a data structure that is used by an algorithm to build or manipulate the image (Fournier & Fussell 1986). Examples are as follows:

1. Depth values, which are used in hidden-surface algorithms to find, for each pixel, the object closest to the viewer. As a new object is written into the frame buffer, it is visible at a pixel only if the depth of the new object is less than the depth of the object previously displayed at the pixel.
2. Occupancy bit. Hidden-surface algorithms based on a priority calculation can arrange to write objects into the frame buffer in depth order, with closest objects first. The occupancy bit indicates that the pixel has already been written by an object, so that any subsequent object that lies over the pixel will not affect the pixel's intensity.
3. Alpha. A scalar value, alpha, ranging between zero and one is recorded with each pixel to indicate the fraction of the pixel that an object covers. This value is used to combine images without introducing aliasing and sampling defects (Porter & Duff 1984; Duff 1985).
4. Sub-pixel mask. High-quality renderings of geometric objects require filtering, or antialiasing, in order to avoid a jagged appearance of high-contrast edges. Some algorithms compute pixel-coverage information at a higher resolution than that of the display, and record in a sub-pixel mask the parts of the pixel that are covered by an object (Carpenter 1984; Schumacker 1980).

While none of this auxiliary data is required to refresh the display, it associates data values with each pixel on the screen. As a consequence, storage for this data is often provided in the frame buffer memory itself, so that the addressing and accessing methods of the update port are available for accessing auxiliary data as well as pixel values.

Update Strategy

There are two techniques that an application may use to create each image in the frame buffer: It may make a global update to the image by erasing the buffer and drawing the image in its entirety, or it may make incremental updates to an existing image by changing only those pixel values required to make the new image. The choice of update strategy can influence how the frame-buffer memory is designed.

The incremental update strategy is used for most interactive applications, because only a portion of the image changes in response to a user's input actions. In a drafting application, for example, a typical update would be to write a line into the frame buffer or to erase an existing line. The rest of the image need not be changed, and redrawing the entire image would be slow.

By contrast, some applications create each image only once, or make extensive changes to an image, and so use the global update strategy. For example, flight simulators use the global update strategy because they generate a different image for each refresh of the screen in order to show motion.

Architectural Consequences

Some themes in the design of frame buffers apply to all applications, although their implications for each application may differ. The principal themes are as follows:

1. Organize the memory to provide sufficient bandwidth for both the display

and update ports. While it is tempting to skimp on update port bandwidth, this will lead to poor performance because the image cannot be changed fast. If the bandwidths of the two ports are equal, then the entire image can, in principle, be changed in one frame time.

2. Organize the update port to access the pixel data that is needed. If, for example, an application often alters only a single plane of the memory at a time, a pixel access architecture is inefficient because each memory access yields all bits of a pixel rather than only the plane that needs to be changed.

3. Organize the memory so that the spatial organization of the update port accesses those pixels that often need to be changed. The conventional organization, which alters a horizontal group of pixels in one access, is inefficient for writing thin vertical lines in the frame buffer.

4. Design the update port in concert with the processor that will use it. It may be necessary to build into the update port functions missing from the processor, or to design a special-purpose processor to compute updates at acceptably high speeds.

Specific frame-buffer requirements differ by application and the kinds of imagery used:

1. Access by pixel and/or by plane. Displaying continuous-tone images usually requires pixel access. Geometric graphics may use either form. When an application needs to use all 2^p colors to denote different kinds of information, as in business-graphics applications, pixel access is desirable. By contrast, certain computer-aided design applications find plane access preferable, because they draw different kinds of information in separate bit-planes, e.g. wiring paths in one plane and plumbing paths in another.

2. *Plane masking*, when pixel access is provided. Masking permits the update processor to modify certain planes while leaving the contents of other planes unchanged.

3. Fast operations on rectangular regions of the screen. These operations include clearing a region to a constant color, copying pixel data from one region to another, and modifying existing pixel data. The BitBlt (or RasterOp) primitive is often used for these applications (Ingalls 1981; Newman & Sproull 1979).

4. Fast changes to the VLT to allow limited dynamics and animation (Shoup 1979).

5. A VLT structure that allows feedback images to override other imagery in the frame buffer.

6. Methods to transfer large blocks of image data from the processor's main memory to the frame buffer. These are useful when transferring continuous-tone images between a disk file and the frame buffer.

7. Double buffering for dynamic displays. To achieve a smooth transition from one frame to the next, two frame buffers are used. While one buffer is used to refresh a single frame on the display, the other is erased and filled with an image. When the refreshing and refilling processes are completed, the roles of the two buffers are switched.

8. A frame buffer larger than the screen. It is often desirable to see on the screen only a portion of a larger image stored in the frame buffer.

VIDEO GENERATION

The job of the video generator is to fetch pixel values from the display port, convert them to analog voltages, and pass the results to the display monitor, where they will control the intensity of one or more electron beams (Figure 1).

The video generator also creates synchronization signals used by the display monitor to coordinate the beam's sweep across the screen with the arrival of pixel data.

The high speeds required in the video generator usually lead to a pipelined structure. Several pixel values are read from the display port in a single cycle and placed in a video buffer. While the controller is sequencing through the pixel values in the video buffer, the next read cycle on the display port may be started. Pipelining is also used in the rest of the path that the pixel data follows: looking up values in the VLT and presenting them to digital-to-analog converters.

In some designs, the video buffer is a first-in first-out queue (FIFO) large enough to contain one or more scan lines of pixel data. This design reduces the peak bandwidth required of the display port because pixels can be fetched during the entire scan-line time, even during horizontal retrace, rather than only when pixels are actively displayed. This reduces the display port bandwidth required between 17 and 25%, depending on the details of the raster-scan timing.

Video Lookup Tables

The video lookup table is a versatile device that is provided on nearly all frame-buffer displays. The table provides two principal features. First, it allows greater precision in intensity or color values than can be represented in the frame buffer directly ($d>p$ in Figure 1). Second, it allows certain kinds of dynamic displays because the table can be changed more rapidly than the contents of the entire frame buffer.

The principal uses of the VLT are summarized below:

1. The application can display 2^p arbitrary colors, because the VLT allows each of the 2^p pixel values recorded in the frame buffer to be mapped to an arbitrary color. It is common in computer-aided design applications to draw different kinds of data in separate bit planes and use the VLT to establish appropriate colors.

2. Pseudo-color can be achieved by using the VLT to produce a color coding of a scalar value recorded in pixel values. For example, if a pixel value represents temperature, the VLT can provide a mapping that shows low temperatures in blue and high temperatures in red, with appropriate colors in between.

3. Short bursts of animation can be achieved by using the VLT to select, for each frame, a subset of planes or pixel values to make visible. After each frame is refreshed, the VLT is changed to select visible pixel values for the next frame (Shoup 1979).

4. Feedback images can be presented with the help of the VLT. The feedback objects are drawn in a single plane, and the VLT is configured to show a specific feedback color whenever data is present in the feedback plane, and otherwise to show the color specified by the remaining planes. Thus the feedback image can be changed without altering the underlying picture, stored in the remaining planes.

5. The VLT can be used to select between two or more separate images stored in the frame buffer, simply by making visible only those pixel values corresponding to each image.

6. The table allows the digital values in the frame buffer to depart from a linear relationship to the voltages presented to the display. If pixel values measure intensity, then the VLT can apply *gamma correction,* which is required because the intensity of a pixel is not a linear function of the voltage delivered to the display. Alternatively, pixel values may record the logarithm of the intensity, so as to more closely model the sensitivity of

the human eye; the VLT can convert these values into voltages that produce the desired intensities (Catmull 1979).

The detailed design of VLT hardware varies a great deal. One variant uses a large enough VLT to contain several different color maps. The address for the video lookup table is the concatenation of the pixel value (p bits) and q bits obtained from an auxiliary register. This register in effect selects one of 2^q color maps very quickly, so that the color map can be changed without having to change individual VLT entries.

Equipment must be provided to store values into the VLT; this is not shown in Figure 1. To avoid transient errors on the screen, the VLT is changed between frames, during vertical retrace. This interval, which varies between 600 and 1200 μs, must be sufficient for all VLT entries to be changed, since animation may require that two successive frames use completely different lookup tables.

The configuration shown in Figure 1 rapidly becomes impractical as the number of bits per pixel, p, grows. The problem is that the VLT gets so large that memories become too costly or too slow. In this case, it is common to split the video generator into separate sub-channels, one for red, one for green, and one for blue, as in Figure 3. This arrangement has less flexibility in assigning colors to pixel values than that of Figure 1. Sometimes a fourth sub-channel is added to restore some flexibility. For example, feedback images may be stored in the fourth sub-channel and may cause a single color to be displayed wherever the feedback image is present. The fourth sub-channel can be used for monochromatic images that must be changed quickly for interaction, and it can coexist with color information that does not change as rapidly, perhaps displayed in another window on the screen. An alternative sometimes used is to design the digital-to-analog converters to have an *overlay* input driven by the fourth sub-channel that forces the analog voltage to its maximum, thus displaying white on the screen.

Image Transformations

Rather than displaying the entire contents of a frame buffer on the screen, the video generator can easily select a rectangular portion of the frame buffer and

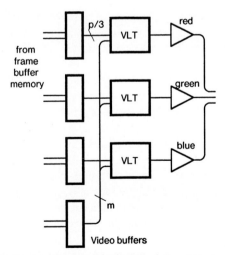

Figure 3   Three separate lookup tables are used in video generators that have more than about 12 bits per pixel. A fourth sub-channel is used for feedback imagery.

display it in a rectangular section of the screen (Kajiya et al 1975; Fischer 1973). The position of the rectangle within the frame buffer and the image on the screen can be determined independently. To implement this feature, the video generator waits until the scanning of the beam reaches a point within the screen rectangle, and then fetches from the frame buffer the corresponding pixel.

Flexible video generation of this sort permits two kinds of dynamically changing images. First, by moving only the rectangle within the frame buffer, the display appears to roam over a large image. Second, by moving only the rectangle on the screen, a fixed image appears to move on the screen, or perhaps to be dragged around in response to a user's commands. Changing the position of either rectangle can be accomplished easily between frames, since it is a matter of changing a few numbers that the video generator uses to count frame-buffer addresses and screen positions.

Normally, the sizes of the rectangle in the frame buffer and of the rectangle on the screen are identical. However, if the screen rectangle is allowed to be an integral multiple of the size of the frame-buffer rectangle, the image appears to be enlarged by the given integer (Fischer 1973). This allows the viewer to zoom in to see image detail. Zooming is usually implemented by repeating pixels within a scan line and repeating scan lines.

Crow & Howard (1981) show how rapid panning and zooming can be used to preview relatively long animation sequences. The frame buffer is divided into, say, a 4 × 4 array of rectangles, each one with 1/4 the dimensions of the entire screen. Sixteen successive frames are drawn in these rectangles. To display them in sequence, the display pans to successive rectangles on successive frames, enlarging each by a factor of four.

More sophisticated image transformations are also possible. An image may be rotated as it is read from the frame buffer (Catmull & Smith 1980). A high-resolution image may be filtered as it is read from the frame buffer and may be displayed at a reduced size or lower resolution. The filtering removes "jaggies" and other aliasing effects.

Combining Images

The video generator can combine several independent images into a single video signal to be displayed (Fischer 1973; Entwisle 1977; Commodore 1986). Similar in concept to mixing several analog video signals, combination within the video generator is done digitally, usually on the pixel values themselves. Two or more images are read from one or more frame buffers, or are obtained by digitizing the video signal obtained from a camera or other video source, which results in several channels of pixel values. The video generator uses some rule to switch between the channels, so as to determine which image will be visible at each pixel. Alternatively, the channels can be mixed rather than switched, so that one image can fade into another, or one channel can control the mixing of two other channels.

In the simplest arrangement, the independent channels have a fixed priority, so that any image present in a high-priority channel will override images in lower priority channels. If a particular pixel is *transparent* in a high-priority channel, then the pixel will take on the color of a lower priority channel. A particular pixel value can be reserved to indicate transparency, or an entire bit-plane in the channel can be used to indicate transparency. If an image does not fill the entire screen, the region outside the image is considered transparent.

The most common use for combining separate image channels is to provide a cursor, whose position can be controlled easily and which does not require a full bit-plane in the frame buffer. A small frame buffer, perhaps 32 × 32 pixels, stores pixel values for a cursor (Thacker et al 1981).

The ability to combine images as the screen is refreshed, together with the panning functions discussed above, provides a range of highly dynamic effects, used frequently in video games. Typically a relatively static background image, stored in a frame buffer, is combined with a dozen or more *sprites*, small high-priority images whose positions on the screen can be controlled individually. The pixel values for these images are stored in a memory, but they are so small that not much storage is required. Wherever a sprite is transparent, lower-priority sprites or the background image is visible. Sprites can be moved very rapidly, since the position of each is controlled by horizontal and vertical positions, which are updated between frames. In order to make video games inexpensive, sprites are supported by single-chip video generators such as the Texas Instruments TMS 9918 (see also Commodore 1986).

Applications that show overlapping windows of information on the screen can do so by combining the images of each window, using suitable priority rules. Most windowing systems combine the images into a single image using update algorithms (Pike 1983). Alternatively, the video generator may perform this function and allow windows to pan, scroll, and move around the screen rapidly (Wilkes et al 1984).

Video Input

Some frame buffers allow video input as well as video output. An analog video signal is passed through a high-speed analog-to-digital converter, and the results are written into the frame buffer. Of course, the memory must be designed to provide sufficient bandwidth. In some cases, video output is disabled while video input is being done, in order to avoid building a memory with a total bandwidth that is double the video bandwidth.

Some frame buffers allow transformed images to be rewritten into the frame buffer as they are displayed (Beg 1985). The simplest implementation returns to memory the results of the lookup performed by the VLT. This *feedback loop* is sometimes used in image-processing applications, in which the image transformation is used to compute a new image as a function of the previous one, e.g. a thresholded image.

Variations

Variations on the themes described above abound in video generators. A small amount of customization can yield enormous speed improvements for particular applications, especially when dynamic effects are required. Most of the variations are in the way image channels and sub-channels are combined and multiplexed and in the addressing used for the VLT.

MEMORY CHIP ARCHITECTURES

Because memory is the principal ingredient in a frame-buffer display, advances in frame-buffer architecture have been paced by memory chip advances in economics, performance, and structure. The decline in memory chip cost is largely responsible for the widespread use of frame buffers today. Display system designers have pressed the limits of memory chip performance in order to meet refresh and update bandwidth requirements. A recent change to the structure of memory chips, the addition of a shift register to form a "video RAM," has led to much higher bandwidths per chip. With memory chip capacities of 256K bits and larger, the video RAM structure is essential for frame-buffer design.

Dynamic Random-Access Memory Chips

Although early frame-buffers were built using rotating disk memory, core

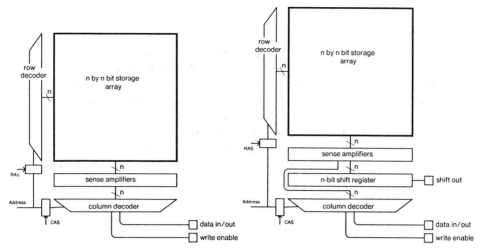

Figure 4 The internal structure of dynamic random-access memory (DRAM) chips that hold n^2 bits. (*a*) A conventional DRAM. (*b*) A video RAM, with an internal shift register.

memory, and semiconductor shift registers, it is the dynamic random-access memory (DRAM) that has made frame buffers practical. The characteristics of these parts are so critical to frame-buffer designs that we describe them briefly here.

Figure 4a shows the functional and physical structure of the simplest form of DRAM chip. The n^2 bits are stored in a square array of capacitors, with dimensions $n \times n$. A bit is read in two steps: First, an entire row of the memory is selected and connected to n sense amplifiers, and then a column decoder selects one of the sense amplifier outputs to transmit off the chip. Writing occurs by first connecting a row to the sense amplifiers and then using the column decoder to change a single sense bit, which is changed both in the sense amplifiers and in the row of capacitors. The two separate steps in accessing a bit are reflected in the way the chip is controlled. First, a *row address* is presented to the chip (RAS), and a row is connected to the sense amplifiers. Then a *column address* is presented (CAS), and a single sense bit is selected for reading or writing. A DRAM chip of this design reads only one bit in each memory cycle.

Although the structure shown in Figure 4a arose because of constraints on memory chip design, it provided display designers with an important feature called *page mode*. If several bits are to be read from the same row in succession, the row-selection step can be omitted from each memory cycle except the first. Once the sense amplifiers are connected to a given row, the column decoder can be used to read out any bits in the row. Since the row and column parts of a full memory cycle require about equal time, using page mode can almost double the bandwidth of a chip. In frame buffers, page mode is often used for display port accesses, provided the memory organization places adjacent pixels along a scan line in the same memory row.

Accessing Bits in Parallel

As the storage on a single memory chip has grown, maintaining sufficient read/write bandwidth has been problematic because the speed of the chips has not increased as much as their capacity. This effect is best demonstrated by computing the *time to fill, t,* the time required to write every bit in a memory chip using ordinary memory accesses. Table 2 shows these times for a number of DRAMs, assuming a memory cycle time of 400 ns. If the capacity of a memory chip is to be fully used, its entire contents must be read out in the time it takes to refresh a frame, i.e. the time to fill must be less than the refresh time $1/r$ (33 ms for 30-Hz displays and 17 ms for 60-Hz displays). The table shows that a 64K × 1 DRAM cannot be used efficiently with a 60-Hz display, since 26.2 ms is required to read the chip's contents, while the refresh must be completed in 17 ms. If we apportion only a fraction f of the memory's bandwidth for refresh, retaining the fraction $(1 - f)$ for update access, then the effective time to fill becomes t/f, which must be less than the frame refresh time.

By widening the data path for large DRAMs, the time to fill them is reduced. Table 2 shows that a 16K × 4 chip, which reads and writes four bits in a single cycle, provides four times the bandwidth of the 64K × 1 chip of equal capacity. The 16K × 4 chip has figured prominently in frame-buffer design, since it can support 60 Hz displays and still leave considerable bandwidth for update ($f=0.5$). However, as chip capacities grow still larger, this technique becomes impractical: to achieve performance equivalent to the

Table 2 Time to fill for different memory chip configurations

DRAM organization	Time to fill, t(ms)	t/f for $f=0.5$
4K×1	1.6	3.3
16K×1	6.6	13.1
64K×1	26.2	52.4
256K×1	105	210
16K×4	6.6	13.1
64K×4	26.2	52.4

16K × 4 chip, a chip with 256K-bit capacity would require a 16-bit data path, which requires too many pins to be economical.

Video Memory Chips

A recent innovation in memory chip design is the video memory, or VRAM, which greatly simplifies frame-buffer design and increases the memory bandwidth available (Matick et al 1984). These memories contain a shift register n bits long that can be loaded in parallel from the n sense amplifiers and subsequently shifted off the chip independently of the row and column access path (Figure 4b). In effect, this is a dual-ported memory chip, in which the normal row/column access constitutes one port, and the shift register the other. The ports are linked only in that a row access must be used to load the shift register. The Texas Instruments TMS4161 was the first commercial video RAM; several manufacturers now offer similar 64K chips and they plan 256K and larger capacities.

The shift register in the VRAM is used for refreshing the display; in effect, it forms a large video shift register. The addressing of the memory is arranged so that a row of the memory chip contains bits that describe adjacent pixels on a scan line. The shift register is loaded at the beginning of the scan line, and then shifted to obtain the values of subsequent pixels. Since the shift register can operate at only about 30 MHz, several chips are usually operated in parallel, and a final high-speed video buffer produces values at pixel rates. If necessary, the VRAM shift register can be loaded again during a scan line to accommodate long scan lines.

The shift register in a VRAM increases the bandwidth available relative to a typical RAM chip by a factor of 6–8 in a way that directly benefits frame-buffer display designs. For display refresh, n bits are obtained with a single row access cycle, so almost 100% of the normal row/column accesses can be devoted to the update port. Only infrequently must update accesses be suspended so that a row access can reload the shift register.

Some video RAMs can use the shift register for input as well as for output. A video input port can be easily provided by such a memory simply by shifting pixel data into the shift register. This feature can also be used to clear the memory fast, by filling the shift register with zeroes and writing a row of zeroes at a time. One way to fill the shift register with zeroes is to read a row of the memory that was previously set to zero.

MEMORY ORGANIZATION

Frame-buffer memories can be organized in a variety of ways, all subject to the constraint that they provide sufficient bandwidth to refresh the display. The organizations differ principally in the way the update port is given access to pixel values. There are three important issues:

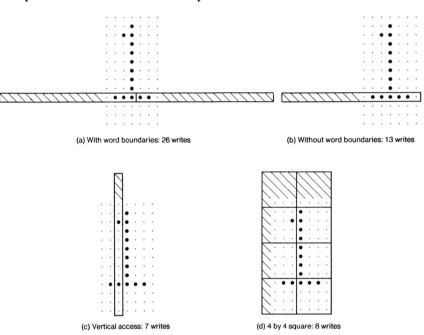

(a) With word boundaries: 26 writes   (b) Without word boundaries: 13 writes

(c) Vertical access: 7 writes   (d) 4 by 4 square: 8 writes

Figure 5   A 7 × 13 character matrix written using different frame-buffer memory organizations. (*a*) Conventional memory, with 16-pixel words aligned with horizontal scan lines. (*b*) Memory with word boundaries eliminated, or "pixel addressing." (*c*) Access to 16-pixel vertical strips. (*d*) Access to arbitrary squares, 4 × 4 pixels.

1. What pixels can be accessed in a single memory cycle?
2. What operations can be performed on the pixel values by the memory?
3. What is the correspondence between addresses supplied to the update port and pixel positions on the screen?

In order to compare different memory organizations, we shall show how a single character may be written into the frame buffer using each approach (Figure 5).

Masking

If the update port can access more than one pixel value in a single cycle, the memory may provide the ability to *mask* a write cycle, i.e. to alter some of the pixel values while leaving the remaining pixels unchanged. In this case, the processor provides data values as well as a mask to indicate which bits should be written. The mask may allow only certain bit planes to be written or may allow only certain pixels to be written, or both. In Figure 5, hatching indicates those pixels in each memory access that are masked off, i.e. that are left unchanged in the frame buffer.

A common implementation technique supplies the *write enable* signal to each memory chip (Figure 4) from the mask, while supplying the data to the chip's data pin. Only those chips that are enabled will write new data.

Read-Modify-Write Access

Many algorithms for updating the frame buffer read a group of pixels, compute new values, and write the pixels back into the frame buffer. For example, an incremental update that highlights a region of the screen using "video reverse" on a black-and-white display reads each pixel in the region, flips black pixels to white and white pixels to black, and writes the new pixel values back into the memory. Often the update port is designed to permit read-modify-write access because memory chips can perform a single read-modify-write cycle faster than two separate read and write cycles.

Eliminating Word Boundaries

The processor often wishes to access a group of adjacent pixels starting at an arbitrary position along a scan line, and not be confined to accessing entire words of the frame buffer. An arbitrary access can always be broken down into a series of accesses to separate words, as shown in Figure 5*a*. However, by providing suitable addresses to each memory chip, it is possible to allow a single-word access by the update port to cross word boundaries in the memory and thus to access an arbitrary group of adjacent pixels, as shown in Figure 5*b*.

Figure 6 shows how a collection of pixels can be accessed in a single cycle because each pixel is stored in a different memory chip. The figure illustrates a frame buffer with $w=16$ bits in a word, representing 16 pixels along a scan line ($p=1$), being used to write 16 adjacent pixels starting at $x=13$. Note that each of the 16 pixels being written lies in a different memory chip, because the frame buffer uses 16 chips to write a 16-bit parallel word. Thus the write could potentially be done in a single cycle, provided each chip is given the proper address. In the example, the three high-order chips receive address 0, and the thirteen remaining chips receive address 1. These are the same addresses as would have been used in two separate writes to words 0 and 1.

To endow the update port with pixel addressing, it is necessary not only to provide proper chip addressing but also to rotate the pixel data presented by the update port in order to align it with the word structure of the memory. In the example shown in Figure 6, if the 16 bits of pixel data are presented by the update port in a word, they must be rotated 3 positions to the right so as to align the data with the appropriate chips.

This scheme can be implemented in several ways. The obvious technique is to outfit each memory chip with a multiplexor that selects between two addresses. Alternatively, both an address and its successor can be sent to all chips in two steps, but by issuing the *row address strobe* (RAS) or *column address strobe* (CAS) signals selectively, the proper address can be steered to each chip (Sproull et al 1983). Or each memory chip can include an internal address incrementer invoked by an external signal, which is controlled so that selected chips will use an address one greater than the address transmitted (Gupta 1981). Bechtolsheim & Baskett (1980) describe a scheme in which the frame buffer uses a word width that is twice the update port width, so that all chips in each half-word can use the same address: a single multiplexor suffices to implement this arrangement.

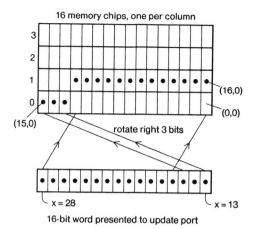

16-bit word presented to update port

Figure 6 Chip addressing to cross word boundaries. All 16 pixels from $x=13$ to $x=28$ can be written into the frame buffer in a single cycle, because each pixel is stored in a different memory chip. Note that different chips must receive different addresses. A word presented to the update port, with the first pixel in the low-order bit, must be rotated before it can be written into the memory.

Horizontal and Vertical Access

The frame buffer can be organized to allow access to horizontal and vertical lines of pixels in a single cycle (Ostapko 1984). The display port uses horizontal access to read pixel data along scan lines while the update port may offer both horizontal or vertical access, which the update processor can invoke when appropriate (Figure 5*d*). A suitable arrangement of memory chips and addressing will permit access across word boundaries (Figure 7). One advantage of this organization is its ability to rotate an image by 90° or to transpose it as it is written into the frame buffer. More elaborate arrangements allow access to horizontal lines, vertical lines, squares, and other rectangular regions (Gupta 1981; Chor et al 1982).

Square Organizations

The efficiency of the update port can be improved if the memory is organized to access a square of pixels rather than a row aligned with a scan line (Figure 5*c*). The reason for the improvement lies in the spatial extent of the objects

A	B	C	D	E	F	G	H	A	B	C	D	E
H	A	B	C	D	E	F	G	H	A	B	C	D
G	H	A	B	C	D	E	F	G	H	A	B	C
F	G	H	A	B	C	D	E	F	G	H	A	B
E	F	G	H	A	B	C	D	E	F	G	H	A
D	E	F	G	H	A	B	C	D	E	F	G	H
C	D	E	F	G	H	A	B	C	D	E	F	G
B	C	D	E	F	G	H	A	B	C	D	E	F
A	B	C	D	E	F	G	H	A	B	C	D	E
H	A	B	C	D	E	F	G	H	A	B	C	D
G	H	A	B	C	D	E	F	G	H	A	B	C
F	G	H	A	B	C	D	E	F	G	H	A	B
E	F	G	H	A	B	C	D	E	F	G	H	A

Figure 7 Screen layout for horizontal and vertical access to eight chips (labeled A to H). All pixels labeled A are stored in chip A. The heavy rectangles show that arbitrary horizontal and vertical access can be performed in a single memory cycle because each of the eight pixels accessed is stored in a different chip.

being written into the frame buffer: Graphical objects are no more likely to be short and wide than tall and thin, and a symmetric organization will favor all objects equally. Writing vectors of arbitrary orientation, characters, and filled objects such as polygons all benefit from the square organization. Several frame buffers based on this organization have been built (Sproull et al 1983; Walsby 1980; Page 1983; Clark & Hannah 1980).

To illustrate the performance of a square organization, consider a vector-generator that drives an 8 × 8 square array. Suppose that the update port is able to use page mode access to obtain 150 ns access to 8 × 8 squares. This will allow vectors to be drawn with 8 pixels per memory access, or about 20 ns per pixel. If lines are several pixels wide, as when antialiasing is applied, the efficiency rises even further because more than 8 pixels will be modified in a single memory access.

The square organization can be designed to allow access to an arbitrary square (Figure 8) using the techniques for eliminating word boundaries described above (Sproull et al 1983). For an 8 × 8 organization, this means that a 7 × 13 character can be written at an arbitrary position in two memory cycles. As with the horizontal and vertical organization, images may be written rotated by 90° or transposed.

A video generator for an *m* × *m* organization must be designed to accommodate the square access pattern. One technique is to read a row of squares into a video buffer that holds *m* scan lines and then read from the buffer the individual pixels in appropriate scan order. Two video buffers are needed, so that one can be refilled while the other is refreshing the display.

A	B	C	D	A	B	C	D	A	B	C	D	A
E	F	G	**H**	**E**	**F**	**G**	H	E	F	G	H	E
I	J	K	**L**	**I**	**J**	**K**	L	I	J	K	L	I
M	N	O	**P**	**M**	**N**	**O**	P	M	N	O	P	M
A	B	C	**D**	**A**	**B**	**C**	D	A	B	C	D	A
E	F	G	H	E	F	G	H	E	F	G	H	E
I	J	K	L	I	J	K	L	I	J	K	L	I
M	N	O	P	M	N	O	P	M	N	O	P	M
A	B	C	D	A	B	C	D	A	B	C	D	A

Figure 8 Screen layout using a 4 × 4 square memory organization. Sixteen memory chips, labeled A to P, store the pixels; all pixels labeled A are stored in chip A. The heavy square shows that an arbitrary 4 × 4 square can be accessed in a single memory cycle because each of the 16 pixels accessed is stored in a different chip.

With VRAMs, the shift registers in the memory chips serve as a video buffer that holds *m* scan lines.

UPDATE PROCESSORS

The architecture of a frame-buffer memory cannot be designed without considering the processor that is attached to the update port. In some cases, the processor and frame buffer are designed in concert to achieve high performance or low cost; in other cases, the processor is a general-purpose computer or microprocessor that accesses the frame buffer memory like all other system memory. There are also intermediate cases, such as a general-purpose processor augmented with a coprocessor designed to speed up graphics operations. In this section, we outline the different forms of processors and how they influence frame-buffer design.

General-Purpose Processors

For greatest flexibility, a general-purpose processor is often used to update a frame-buffer memory (Figure 9*a*). The flexibility is advantageous in several ways: Arbitrary algorithms can be used to update the frame buffer; the algorithms have access to necessary data structures in the application program; and the algorithms can build arbitrary data structures during their execution. This arrangement, though flexible, limits performance: General-purpose processors are not often suited to high-speed update algorithms, and their memory interfaces may preclude exotic frame-buffer organizations such as square arrays.

For a frame buffer to work with a general-purpose processor, its update port must provide the read and write accesses required by the processor: to words of a given width, to bytes, etc. In some cases, the frame buffer memory is an

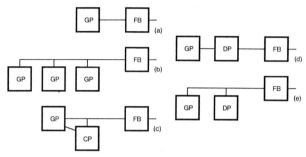

Figure 9 Alternative configurations for update processors. (*a*) A general-purpose processor (GP) directly addresses the frame buffer (FB). (*b*) Multiprocessor configuration. (*c*) A coprocessor (CP) handles graphics operations. (*d*) A display processor (DP) has exclusive access to the frame buffer. (*e*) Both general-purpose and display processors can update the frame buffer.

integral part of the system memory, which incorporates a display port (Thacker et al 1981).

One way to compensate for lack of facilities in a general-purpose processor is to build some processing into the update port. For example, the update port can help with addressing by allowing the processor to specify x and y addresses separately, and then providing read and write access to the addressed pixel. The update port can provide both plane and pixel access by mapping the frame buffer into the processor's address space twice, one mapping for pixel access and one for plane access. The update port can perform shifting and masking if the processor's corresponding instructions are slow (Bechtolsheim & Baskett 1980).

These measures may be less useful for high-performance processors. For example, although the MC68000 microprocessor is not particularly suited to graphics operations, the MC68020 represents a dramatic improvement. It has fast shift and rotate instructions, and its on-chip instruction cache will accommodate the inner loops of many graphics algorithms, allowing them to run dramatically faster. Shifting and masking functions in the update port thus become less valuable.

If the processor is outfitted with a data cache, special attention must be given to its interaction with the frame buffer. Data written by the processor must not be allowed to remain in the cache indefinitely, or it will not be written into the frame-buffer memory and participate in display refresh.

The principal disadvantage of using a general-purpose processor to update a frame-buffer display, its low performance, can be attacked by building multiprocessor systems. The most flexible multiprocessors use a collection of identical processors, all cooperating to solve a single problem. The frame buffer is part of the memory shared by all processors, each of which can assume all or part of the responsibility for updating the display (Figure 9*b*). A great many graphics algorithms decompose nicely into multiprocessing implementations suited for such hardware.

Coprocessors

A coprocessor can enhance the performance of a general-purpose processor by performing specialized graphics operations quickly. In these designs, the parent processor exercises absolute control over the actions of the coprocessor and retains its ability to access the frame buffer, so that algorithms not provided by the coprocessor can be programmed in the parent (Figure 9c).

A good example of a graphics coprocessor is a chip that contains 16-bit data paths to implement the shifting, masking, and functional combinations required to implement BitBlt (Bennett 1985). The parent processor executes a loop that generates the appropriate memory addresses, but the coprocessor is able to perform in a single read-modify-write memory cycle a set of operations that would otherwise require several instructions to implement on the general-purpose processor.

In most cases, a coprocessor uses the same memory interface as its parent processor, and the implications for update port organization are identical. However, one could build coprocessors designed for other update port organizations, such as the square array, precisely to act as an interface between a conventional processor and the update port format.

Display Processors

The job of updating a frame buffer is sometimes given to an independent *display processor,* which is connected to the update port of the frame buffer and is controlled by the host processor, which transmits drawing commands to the display processor (Figure 9d). Most display processors are designed to generate a range of geometric objects, such as lines, circles, text characters, polygons, and filled objects. Some may even include complex rendering algorithms that produce shaded images with hidden surfaces removed. Display processors were first attached to frame buffers by manufacturers to obtain products that could work with a variety of host computer systems. The host used a simple I/O channel to send commands and data to the display processor. Display processors are now being offered on single chips that include parts of the video generator and memory interface as well as graphic-generation logic.

The weakness of most display processors lies in their limited communication with the host processor and application program. Most have no access to the application program's data structures and so can neither fetch character fonts, symbol definitions, or display lists from application data structures nor write results into application data structures. Instead, the application must explicitly transmit data to and from the display processor. This weakness can be reduced somewhat by making the frame-buffer memory large enough to hold some of this additional data. Another problem arises because most display processors prevent the host processor from having fast access to the frame buffer. Update algorithms implemented in the host processor because they cannot be accommodated by the display processor will suffer poor performance. The remedy is to allow the host access to the frame buffer as well as to the display processor (Figure 9e).

Special Display Processors

Special applications and special frame-buffer organizations usually require special-purpose processors for updates. Very high update rates required for flight simulation imagery, movie animation, or raster-scan printing require special-purpose processors. These processors are often microcoded processors with data paths customized for the update algorithms required.

The square memory organizations described above all require special-purpose processors to generate graphical data at a sufficiently high rate to warrant the exotic memory organization. A line-drawing algorithm, for example, must generate square blocks of bits and may use multiple parallel processors to achieve the necessary speed (Sproull 1982; Gupta 1981).

To obtain the highest update rates, it is necessary to have more than one processor working on the same frame buffer. These processors are built into the frame buffer itself. The Chap processor, designed to combine images at high speed for animation applications, associates a separate processor with the red, green, and blue channels (Levinthal & Porter 1984). Some designs associate a processor with each memory chip in the frame buffer (Clark & Hannah 1980; Gupta et al 1981; Gupta 1981). To obtain even greater processing bandwidths, logic to update pixel values can be integrated into the memory chip so that it can be applied to an entire row of pixels at once (Demetrescu 1985). In the extreme, each pixel has an associated processor. The best example is the "pixel planes" display that provides each pixel with a small serial computer that can decide whether a pixel lies inside a polygon, whether the polygon is hidden because it lies behind another polygon visible in the pixel, and what its red, green, and blue shade should be (Fuchs & Poulton 1981; Poulton et al 1985).

In many of these designs, the distinction between the frame buffer and the update processor becomes blurred: Each processor controls some memory, parts of which behave like a frame buffer. Issues of addressing and data manipulation pertain to both the processors and their associated memory.

PERFORMANCE EVALUATION

Since frame buffers are often designed to meet certain performance requirements, it would be useful to compare the performance of different architectures. While it is relatively easy to specify the speed of each update access to a frame buffer, it is not always easy to relate this figure to overall performance. The problem lies in characterizing the kinds of updates that will be used in an application.

Part of the problem lies in the fact that each access may reference pixels that are not needed by the update. Let us define the *efficiency* of an access as the fraction of pixels accessed that are needed. When drawing a vertical line into a frame buffer that accesses 64 horizontally adjacent pixels in a single cycle, the efficiency is 1/64, or 1.6%. By contrast, when drawing a long horizontal line, the efficiency approaches 100%. In order to compare architectures, we need to know the distribution of updates that an application will require.

An example of the importance of knowing the precise character of updates comes from BitBlt. The BitBlt copy operation, when used with a conventional frame-buffer organization that accesses multiple pixels in a single cycle, requires the data to be shifted or rotated to align the source to the destination word boundaries. This would seem to suggest that a high-speed shifter is important. However, if most of the update port cycles used for BitBlt copying are for scrolling information vertically on the screen, the alignments of the source and destination data are identical, and no shifting is required. To complete the analysis, we need to know how much scrolling is done compared to other frame-buffer updates.

The little performance evaluation that has been done indicates an interesting phenomenon: While most of the graphics operations may involve short lines or small BitBlt copy operations, most of the frame-buffer memory traffic comes from long lines or large copies (Sproull et al 1983). Thus the update processor must ensure that each command is decoded and set up quickly, while the update port should cater for long lines and large copies. Note that for large copies, the spatial organization of the update port is irrelevant, since most accesses will be 100% efficient because all pixels referenced will be needed for the copy. By contrast, for line drawing, the spatial organization of the update port influences performance of lines of all lengths.

Performance evaluation would be aided if some "graphics instruction mixes," analogous to instruction mixes for general-purpose computers, were available for different applications. Mixes could be obtained by tracing graphical update commands in an application. Instruction mixes are needed to evaluate entire display systems, including software, operating-system drivers, and display processors, as well as the frame buffer.

STATE OF THE ART AND TRENDS

In early 1986, frame-buffer designs are characterized by (a) use of video RAM chips, (b) a variety of single-chip display processors available, and (c) integration of the video buffer, video lookup table, and digital-to-analog converter on a single chip. These products are designed for workstations used in office and computer-aided-design applications, which have up to 8 Mbit frame-buffer memories and require only modest update rates. Increasing integration of frame-buffer components onto single chips drives the cost of these displays down.

For frame buffers that require extremely high update rates, special-purpose processors are increasingly used, often in multiprocessor configurations. New memory chip designs with decreased cycle times also help, e.g. static column decode, "hierarchical memories." As image-processing techniques are increasingly integrated with geometric graphics algorithms, updates are computed by digital signal-processors, either singly, in pipelines, or in arrays. As processing power increases, more update functions become feasible, such as antialiasing, wide lines, and pixel resampling that allows image copying with arbitrary scaling and rotation.

A number of challenges remain for frame-buffer designers. Surprisingly, no one has yet built a very large frame buffer (e.g. 20,000 × 20,000 pixels) that can be used to roam around a large image. Such a display might prove valuable in VLSI design, mapping, image interpretation, and graphic arts applications.

An open problem is how best to implement window-management systems, using a combination of hardware and software. Ideally, each application in a multiprocess computing environment has access to a complete frame buffer or to a simulation of one. The mapping from what the application deems a frame buffer to possibly overlapping windows on one or more display screens is the job of the window-management system. Individual frame buffers combined by the video generator, as in Wilkes et al (1984), can handle only a limited number of windows. One can imagine a memory-mapping scheme that would give the appearance of a separate frame buffer in each application's memory space, but in reality would be mapped to a single frame buffer. Appropriate protection would be required to prevent one application from interfering with another, and some means must be provided to inform each application about the current size of its frame buffer (window), which might change as windows are moved.

Finally, the ability to combine the outputs of several frame buffers into a single video image suggests a modular architecture for frame-buffer systems. Imagine a structure consisting of one or more modules, each consisting of a frame buffer and its associated display processor(s), all feeding a common video generator that combines the channels. Different module designs could be specialized for different types of updates: text and graphics such as used on personal computers; dynamic three-dimensional images; image-processing functions, etc. The display system could then be easily configured to meet a wide variety of application needs.

CONCLUSION

This review has emphasized three aspects of frame-buffer design:

1. The organization of memory, both on chip and off, to support the bandwidth and access pattern required to refresh a raster display.
2. The organization of the update port to provide efficient access to the frame buffer and to couple to the update processor.
3. The ability of the video generator to combine images from various sources in various ways and to transform the images as they are displayed. These facilities are especially important for making dynamic images, since changes to the frame-buffer memory itself may be slow.

Although we have touched only briefly on the design of update processors, this topic is closely related to frame-buffer design. The trend to apply more specialized processing in displays, and to place the processing closer to the memory to reduce communication overhead, means that the processors and memories must increasingly be designed together.

In a paper written in 1968, two designers observed that display systems exhibit a "wheel of reincarnation," in which functions are gradually moved from the host processor to special processing in the display, culminating in the display acquiring a program counter and becoming a processor itself (Myer & Sutherland 1968). The wheel is evident in frame-buffer design as well, but it no longer poses much of a problem for designers. Adding one or more processors to a system is now very easy, thanks to single-chip microprocessors, bit-slice ALUs, buses that support multiple processors, and so on. Today, we cheerfully add processors to improve the performance of a display.

ACKNOWLEDGMENTS

Ron Baecker, Frank Crow, Satish Gupta, Ivan Sutherland, and Bert Sutherland helped me with this review.

Literature Cited

Baecker, R. M. 1979. Digital video display systems and dynamic graphics. *Comput. Graphics* 13(2):48–56

Bechtolsheim, A., Baskett, F. 1980. High-performance raster graphics for microcomputer systems. *Comput. Graphics* 14(3):43–47

Beg, R. 1985. Image-processing system serves a variety of uses. *Comput. Des.* 24(16):99–106

Bennett, J. 1985. Raster operations. *Byte* 10(12):187–203

Carpenter, L. 1984. The A-buffer, and anti-aliased hidden surface method. *Comput. Graphics* 18(3):103–8

Catmull, E. 1979. A tutorial on compensation tables. *Comput. Graphics* 13(2):1–7

Catmull, E., Smith, A. R. 1980. 3-D transformations of images in scanline order. *Comput. Graphics* 14(3):279–84

Chor, B., Leiserson, C. E., Rivest, R. L. 1982. An application of number theory to the organization of raster-graphics memory. *23rd IEEE Symp. Found. Comput. Sci.*

Clark, J. H., Hannah, M. R. 1980. Distributed processing in a high-performance smart image memory. *Lambda* 1980 (4th Quarter): 40–45

Commodore. 1986. *Amiga Reference Manual.* Reading, Mass: Addison-Wesley

Conrac Corp. 1985. *Raster Graphics Handbook.* New York: Van Nostrand Reinhold. 2nd ed.

Crow, F. C., Howard, M. W. 1981. A frame buffer system with enhanced functionality. *Comput. Graphics* 16(3):63–69

Demetrescu, S. 1985. High speed image rasterization using scan line access memories. See Fuchs 1985, pp. 221–43

Duff, T. 1985. Compositing 3-D rendered images. *Comput. Graphics* 19(3):41–44

Entwisle, J. 1977. An image-processing approach to computer graphics. *Computers and Graphics* 2(2):111–17

Fischer, M. 1973. MAPS—A generalized image processor. *Comput. Graphics* 7(3):1–9

Foley, J. D., van Dam, A. 1982. *Fundamentals of Interactive Computer Graphics.* Reading, Mass: Addison-Wesley

Fournier, A., Fussell, D. 1986. On the power of the frame buffer. *ACM Trans. Graphics.* Submitted for publication

Fuchs, H., ed. 1985. *1985 Chapel Hill Conference on Very Large Scale Integration.* Rockville, MD: Comput. Sci.

Fuchs, H., Poulton, J. 1981. Pixel-Planes: A VLSI-oriented design for a raster graphics engine. 1981 (3rd Quarter):20–28

Gupta, S. 1981. *Architectures and Algorithms for Parallel Updates of Raster Scan Displays.* CMU-CS-82-111, Comput. Sci. Dept., Carnegie-Mellon Univ., Pittsburgh, Pa.

Gupta, S., Sproull, R. F., Sutherland, I. E. 1981. A VLSI architecture for updating raster-scan displays. *Comput. Graphics* 15(3): 71–78

Ingalls, D. H. H. 1981. The Smalltalk graphics kernel. *Byte* 6(8):168–94

Kajiya, J. T., Sutherland, I. E., Cheadle, E. C. 1975. A random-access video frame buffer. *Proc. Computer Graphics, Pattern Recognition, and Data Structure, IEEE Comput. Soc., Los Angeles,* pp. 1–6

Levinthal, A., Porter, T. 1984. Chap—A SIMD graphics processor. *Comput. Graphics* 18(3):77–82

Matick, R., Ling, D. T., Gupta, S., Dill, F. H. 1984. All points addressable raster display memory. *IBM J. Res. Dev.* 28(4):379–92

Myer, T. H., Sutherland, I. E. 1968. On the design of display processors. *Commun. ACM* 11(6):410

Newman, W. M., Sproull, R. F. 1979. *Principles of Interactive Computer Graphics.* New York: McGraw-Hill. 2nd ed.

Ostapko, D. L. 1984. A mapping and memory chip hardware which provides symmetric reading/writing of horizontal and vertical lines. *IBM J. Res. Dev.* 28(4):393–98

Page, I. 1983. DisArray: A 16 × 16 RasterOp processor. *Eurographics 83,* ed. P. J. W. ten Hagen, pp. 367–77. Amsterdam: North-Holland

Pike, R. 1983. Graphics in overlapping bitmap layers. *ACM Trans. Graphics* 2(2):135–60

Porter, T., Duff, T. 1984. Compositing digital images. *Comput. Graphics* 18(3):253–59

Poulton, J., Fuchs, H., Austin, J. D., Eyles, J. G., Heinecke, J., et al. 1985. Pixelplanes: Building a VLSI-based graphic system. See Fuchs 1985, pp. 35–60

Schumacker, R. A. 1980. A new visual system architecture. *Proc. 2nd Interserv. Ind. Train. Equip. Conf., Salt Lake City,* pp. 1–8

Shoup, R. G. 1979. Color table animation. *Comput. Graphics* 13(2):8–13

Sproull, R. F. 1982. Using program transformations to derive line-drawing algorithms. *Trans. Graphics* 1(4):259–73

Sproull, R. F., Sutherland, I. E., Thompson, A., Gupta, S., Minter, C. 1983. The 8 by 8 display. *ACM Trans. Graphics* 2(1):32–56

Thacker, C. P., McCreight, E. M., Lampson, B. W., Sproull, R. F., Boggs, D. R. 1981. Alto: A personal computer. In *Computer Structures: Readings and Examples,* ed. D. P. Siewiorek, C. G. Bell, A. N. Newell, pp. 549–72. New York: McGraw-Hill. 2nd ed.

Walsby, A. M. 1980. Fast colour raster graphics using an array processor. *Eurographics 80,* ed. C. E. Vandoni, pp. 303–13. Amsterdam: North-Holland

Whitton, M. C. 1984. Memory design for raster graphics displays. *Comput. Graphics Appl.* 4(3):48–65

Wilkes, A. J., Singer, D. W., Gibbons, J. J., King, T. R., Robinson, P., Wiseman, N. E. 1984. The Rainbow workstation. *Comput. J.* 27(2):112–20

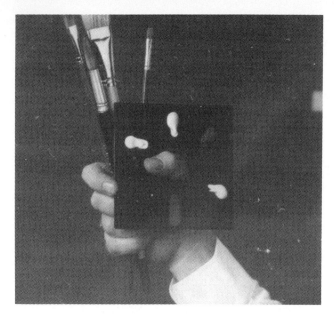

Pixel phasing smoothes out jagged lines

Anti-aliasing system for CRTs uses four extra bit planes

by David Oakley, Michael E. Jones, Don Parsons, and Greg Burke, *Megatek Corp., San Diego, Calif.*

□ One disadvantage of moderate-resolution raster-graphics imaging systems is a phenomenon known as aliasing, visible on cathode-ray-tube screens as jagged lines called jaggies. It is particularly apparent on lines and curves angled close to the horizontal and vertical axes. In personal computers, for example, users often see jagged circles when they attempt graphics on their low-to-moderate-resolution screens.

The cause of aliasing jaggies is the discrete nature of frame-buffer display memory. When data is written into the frame buffer, each pixel on a line or boundary is constrained to a discrete location on the screen, as represented by its address in the bit-plane memory or frame buffer. When the visual attributes of picture elements in a line are read from the frame buffer, they can be displayed only in these discrete locations—which may not be the optimum positions to represent a straight line or a smooth curve on the screen, thus causing the jaggies.

A patent-pending anti-aliasing technique called pixel phasing eliminates jaggies. This scheme uses four extra bit planes in the frame-buffer memory to store micropositioning information in order to move pixel screen positions by ¼-pixel increments, providing four times as many addressable points (3,072 by 2,304) on a standard 768-by-576-pixel monitor without requiring a 3,072-by-2,304-pixel bit map.

A magnetic diddle field, so called because it is a small augmentation to a larger field, deflects the CRT beam up- or downward from a bias position by small amounts to vertically displace pixels in lines that are within ±45° of the horizontal axis. A diddle digital-to-analog converter controls this displacement. Lines within ±45° of the vertical axis are corrected by displacing the left and right boundaries between pixels,

which is done through selecting the phase of the pixel clock that transfers data from the frame-buffer memory to the d-a converters.

A notable characteristic of this technology is that there is no apparant degradation in the sharpness of lines or polygon boundaries. Other anti-aliasing techniques currently on the market use a technique called spatial filtering to fill the intensities of adjacent pixels, but this causes the image to appear to be out of focus.

Sharpness retained

By contrast, instead of the apparent reduction in resolution associated with other anti-aliasing methods, pixel phasing brings a three- to fourfold increase in virtual screen addressability. In Megatek's new Merlin series of graphics-display products, 3,072 by 2,304 addressable points are displayed on the screen of a standard monitor.

The first, and most obvious, benefit of pixel phasing is that it eliminates jaggies. The second advantage is that the frame buffer's update rate is unaffected by the apparent increase in resolution. Third, memory is conserved, as the frame buffer does not need a 3,072-by-2,304-element bit map; rather, 768 by 576 bits are enough.

Without pixel phasing, the steps along a vector are large and widely spaced (Fig. 1a). With pixel phasing, the steps are smaller and closer, as well as more numerous (Fig. 1b). Consequently, the line appears continuous. In this example, there are four possible vertical positions of a pixel relative to where it would have been placed without micropositioning: −¼, 0, +¼, and +½.

Displacing the boundaries between pixels eliminates jaggies on near-vertical lines and boundaries. In a vector with a 4:1 gradient (Fig. 2a), for each large step, si-

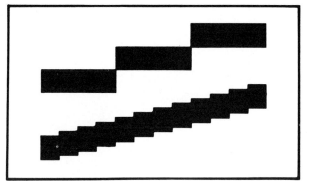

1. Vertical diddling. To get rid of jaggies on a vector that has a 1:4 gradient (a), pixel phasing diddles successive picture elements up or down by ¼-pixel increments in order to smooth out the line (b) without making it fatter.

2. Horizontal phasing. Pixel phasing can also remove jaggies from lines that are close to the vertical axis. In this case, the pixels can be shifted horizontally in ¼-pixel increments by changing the raster scan's phase for successive pixels.

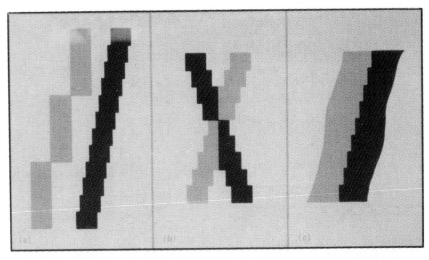

multaneously displacing the left and right pixel boundaries in ¼-pixel increments reduces the jaggies. Boundary displacement also works on intersecting lines (Fig. 2b) and between pixels of two solid areas (Fig 2c).

The output section of a conventional raster-graphics engine contains a digital vector generator, a frame-buffer memory, a color-lookup table, d-a converters, and control circuits. Pixel phasing is added by modifying the digital vector generator, including four extra bit planes per buffer within the frame-buffer memory, and generating a four-phase clock to enter data into the d-a converters. The four extra bit planes store subpixel addresses for both axes—2 bits for X-axis phasing and 2 bits for Y-axis diddling.

In the output-section architecture with pixel phasing in Figure 3, vector end points (X, Y, Z) from the display list are entered into the digital vector generator, which interpolates (X, Y) pixel addresses in a conventional manner. Subject to comparison with data from the Z-buffer, the pixels are written into a 12-plane read/write visual-attribute buffer. As the digital vector generator proceeds along the major axis, it creates an extra 2 bits of precision (the subpixel address) to indicate more accurately the location of pixels along the minor axis. These extra 2 bits are stored in the vertical or the horizontal subpixel address planes of the frame-buffer memory, depending upon whether the major axis is X or Y. For

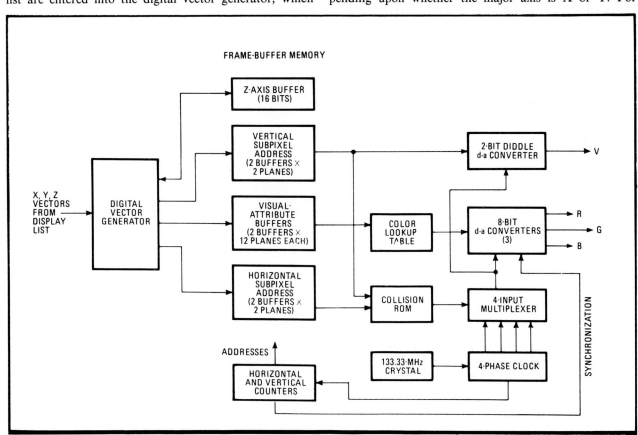

3. Sub-pixel addressing. The circuitry needed to do the subpixel addressing required for pixel phasing is little more than the typical output section of a graphics engine. Two planes of frame-buffer memory are added for each vertical subpixel and horizontal subpixel address. A collision read-only memory and a multiplexer are also needed.

VECTOR GENERATION BETWEEN TWO END POINTS			
Picture-element counter	X-axis position	Y-axis position	Subpixel address (x, y)
400	100.625	300.625	2, 2
399	101.625	300.875	2, 3
398	101.625	301.125	2, 0
.	.	.	.
.	.	.	.
.	.	.	.
1	499.625	400.375	2, 1
0	500.625	400.625	2, 2

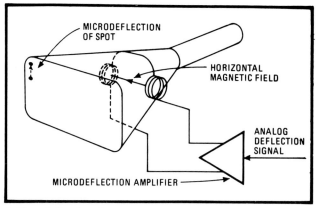

4. Microdeflection. The method for displacing pixels in the vertical direction—microdeflection—applies a small horizontal magnetic field between the coils at the side of the cathode-ray tube, which deflects the scanning electron beam up or down. The analog deflection signal controls the field.

example, in a vector written between (100.007,300,0) and (499.992,400.008,0), the origin is at the top left corner, X increases to the right, Y increases downward, and Z extends into the image. This vector has a 1 : 4 slope lying in a plane parallel to the image plane, and its end points are rounded off to the nearest integer. The digital vector generator adds the ½-pixel bias and an additional ¼-pixel rounding to the end points on each axis. It then sends out binary addresses shown in decimal format in the table.

Stored within the frame-buffer memory are the visual-attribute data at the XY address of each pixel and a subpixel address that describes each pixel's location to an extra 2 bits of precision. These 2 bits are a binary code, but the subpixel address is usually referred to in a decimal format. For example, (2,0) refers to binary (10,00), which is equivalent to a (½,0) correction of the pixel position because each value of the 2-bit subpixel address represents a move of ¼ pixel.

When all the data has been loaded into the frame-buffer memory's read/write buffer, it is copied into the read-only buffer. Both these buffers are part of the frame-buffer memory. Horizontal and vertical counters then scan the read buffer in a raster format. Visual-attribute data is entered into the color-lookup table, and the selected colors and intensities are transferred to the d-a converters. Vertical subpixel-address data is loaded into a diddle d-a converter that is synchronously clocked with the red-green-blue video outputs.

When pixels collide

Horizontal and vertical subpixel addresses are entered into a collision read-only memory, which compares pairs of contiguous subpixel addresses as the raster is horizontally scanned and sends the boundary displacement. Before writing data into the frame-buffer memory, the digital vector generator initializes the receiving buffer's subpixel planes with a (2,2) bias, to avoid errors greater than ¼ pixel. This moves the picture down and right by ½ pixel, thus allowing subpixel movement both ways in each direction—up or down as well as left or right.

Usually, the ROM produces the average of the horizontal subpixel addresses. For example, the boundary between (1,2) and (3,2) pixels is set at 2 (the average of 1 and 3). But if the previous or the current subpixel ad-

dresses, or both, are deemed to be background, determined by a subpixel address of (2,2), then the active pixel may override the background. For example, (2,2) followed by (0,2) has a boundary set at 0 because the 0 of the active pixel overides the 2 of the background pixel.

The boundary signal from the collision ROM controls a multiplexer that selects one phase of a four-phase clock. The clock period is 30 nanoseconds, so that the spacing between phases is 7.5 ns. Since with a raster scan the CRT spot moves from left to right, the horizontal position of the boundary between two pixels can be moved by clocking the video signal out of the d-a converter on a different phase. For example, selection of phase 0 for a 30-ns period on a line where all other pixels are clocked at phase 2 will advance the activation of one pixel by 15 ns and the pixel will be moved left by ½ pixel. On a 19-inch CRT, the width of a pixel is 0.5 millimeter, so this move equals a 0.25-mm shift to the left.

In the CRT, the beam is deflected upward by a right-to-left horizontal magnetic field (Fig. 4). The field's magnitude is a few thousand gauss and is applied across the rear section of the CRT funnel. Maximum vertical movement is about 0.5 mm.

The diddle field's deflection range covers ¾ of a pixel height. To minimize the size of blank areas where the beam deflects away from the normal horizontal scan-line location, the vertical spot position is biased at +¼ pixel, and the beam deflects to one of four positions: −¼, 0, +¼, and +½, relative to the bias point. Thus with no vertical correction, the complete picture shifts upward by ¼ pixel or about 0.1 mm.

A monitor with an in-line gun CRT must be used so that the three electron beams lie within the same plane. A quadrifilar deflection coil (four windows in parallel) and a quad-ported microdeflection amplifier keep deflection rise times below 10 ns. Thus the video and micro-deflection signals are synchronized. The coil is beneath the CRT deflection yoke to link the field through a low-reluctance magnetic return path and thus increase sensitivity. □

Electronics/June 28, 1984

A Configurable Pixel Cache for Fast Image Generation

Andy Goris, Bob Fredrickson, and
Harold L. Baeverstad, Jr.
Hewlett-Packard Co.

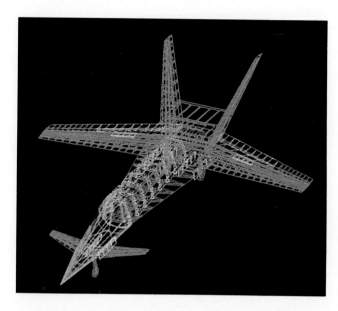

This article describes an approach to fast image generation that uses a high-speed serial scan converter, a somewhat slower frame buffer, and a pixel cache to match the bandwidth between the two. Cache hit rates are improved by configuring the cache to buffer either 4 × 4 or 16 × 1 tiles of frame buffer memory, depending on the type of operaton being performed. For line drawing, the implementation described can process 300,000 30-pixel vectors per second. For shaded polygons, the system can fill 16,000 900-pixel polygons per second. In addition to buffering pixel intensity data, the pixel cache also buffers z (depth) values, improving the performance of the z-buffer hidden-surface algorithm. By utilizing z-value caching, the system can process 5800 900-pixel shaded polygons per second with hidden surfaces removed.

The recent availability of fast arithmetic processors[1-3] has moved the bottleneck in the graphics pipeline to the input mechanism of the frame buffer. To achieve fast scan conversion, previous designs concentrated on the ability to calculate multiple pixels in parallel.[4-7]

Three considerations when designing a frame buffer include the input mechanism to the frame buffer, the actual RAM used to store the image, and the output mechanism used by the frame buffer to refresh the VDT.

Traditional frame buffers are designed so that sequential memory locations lie along a scan line. To refresh a raster scan display, the sequential pixels must be provided at a very high speed. In the past, display refresh required a significant percentage of the available RAM bandwidth. Recently, video RAMs[8] became available that separate frame buffer update from video refresh, allowing almost all of the RAM bandwidth to be used for image update.

Unlike video refresh, generation of images into the frame buffer is not necessarily dependent on scan lines. In fact, many display operations manipulate groups of pixels having two-dimensional locality. Gupta et al.[4,5] explored frame buffer memory organizations that allow the input mechanism of the frame buffer to update square *tiles*,* rather than scan lines. An organization using staggered tiles enables the frame buffer to be accessed as M×M tiles for vector generation, or as $M^2 \times 1$ tiles for scan line algorithms.

Demetrescu[6] and Fuchs et al.[7] developed logic-enhanced memory chips for use in frame buffer systems. Demetrescu's SLAM chip relies on the parallel update of 256 pixels along a scan line in any given memory chip. On-chip processing determines which of the 256 pixels are to be modified. Fuchs' pixel-planes design has on-chip processing to evaluate linear expressions for every pixel simultaneously.

Conventional computer systems use cache memory techniques to provide a memory with the speed and performance of an expensive system, while maintaining the lower cost of a large, slow memory.[9,10] The cache is usually a fast, small memory that sits between the processor and main memory. As the processor accesses instructions and data, they are read from the main mem-

---

*Gupta refers to two-dimensional arrays of pixels as *squares*, and scan lines as *spans*. In this article, arrays of pixels, in either one or two dimensions, are referred to as *tiles*.

Reprinted from *IEEE Computer Graphics and Applications*, Volume 7, Number 3, March 1987, pages 24-32. Copyright © 1987 by The Institute of Electrical and Electronics Engineers, Inc.

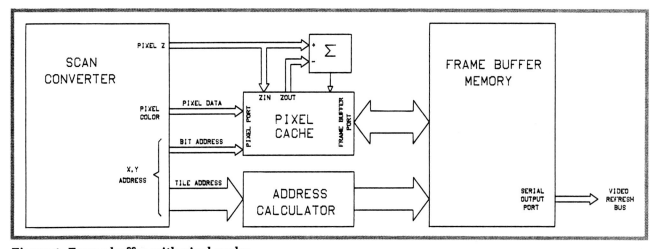

Figure 1. Frame buffer with pixel cache.

ory into the cache where they can be accessed quickly.

The cache-to-memory interface is usually constructed to transfer several words of data between the cache and memory at one time. Further, caches improve performance because of the *principle of locality*, which states that when a particular piece of data is fetched from memory, it is likely that the same or a nearby piece of data will also be needed. The scan-conversion process also exhibits the principle of locality, while the frame buffer resembles the main memory of a conventional computer system. This analogy is what led to the idea of a pixel cache.

Pixel-cache approach

Previous work on high-speed rendering hardware has concentrated on the ability to render multiple pixels in parallel.[4-7] This approach works well for simple shading algorithms, but requires extensive hardware as the complexity of the shading algorithm increases.

The pixel-cache approach uses a high-speed scan converter that calculates intensity values for only one pixel at a time, but at a much faster rate than the frame buffer access time. The scan converter writes the pixels serially into a pixel cache, which holds a rectangular array, or tile, of frame buffer pixels. An explanation of the scan convertor used in our implementation is offered by Swanson and Thayer.[11] Once the bounds of the tile are exceeded, its contents are transferred in parallel to the frame buffer and the process repeats itself. The pixel cache essentially matches the bandwidth between a high-speed serial stream of pixels (from the scan converter), and a slow parallel stream of pixels (to the frame buffer). A block diagram of this architecture is shown in Figure 1.

The frame buffer is accessed in tiles, or rectangular arrays of pixels. For the purposes of this article, tiles are perceived as non-overlapping and aligned on boundaries that are integer multiples of their height and width. This

allows an (x, y) address from the scan converter to be easily translated into a *tile address*, (derived from the x and y MSBs), and a *bit address*, (derived from the x and y LSBs). The tile address is used to access a tile of pixels in the frame buffer, whereas the bit address is used to access individual pixels within the pixel cache.

Pixel-cache operation

A block diagram of the pixel cache for one plane of frame buffer memory is shown in Figure 2.

The cache is implemented in a single 48-pin integrated circuit—building a frame buffer more than one bit deep requires one chip per plane. The main components of the cache are as follows:

• *Data cache*—In normal operation, pixel intensity data from the scan converter is stored in the data cache. As each pixel is received, four address lines direct it to the appropriate location in the cache. The pixel data port is bidirectional so that fast reads as well as fast writes may be performed.

• *Source register*—When the scan converter generates a pixel outside the current tile, the data cache is transferred to the source register and a frame buffer write cycle is started. The data cache is immediately cleared so that input of new pixels for the next tile can be overlapped with the writing of old pixels to the frame buffer.

• *Replacement rule register/logic*—This is used to perform Boolean operations on the frame buffer. Data from the scan converter can be ORed, ANDed, etc., with old frame buffer data before being written back to the frame buffer.

• *Destination register*—The destination register stores the existing contents of the frame buffer when they are needed by the replacement rule logic. For example, if scan converter pixels are to be XORed with old frame buffer data, a frame buffer read cycle is first performed into the destination register. This operation can be over-

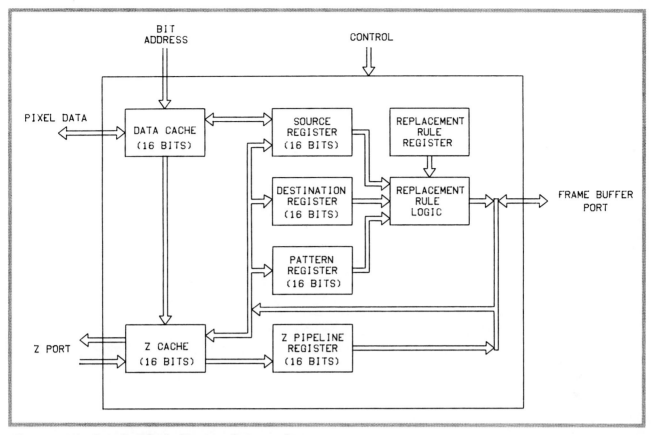

Figure 2. Pixel-cache block diagram for one plane.

lapped with the loading of pixels into the data cache and the transfer of the data cache to the source register. Once the source and destination registers have valid data, a frame buffer write cycle can proceed.

• *Pattern register*—Similar to the destination register, the pattern register is used to allow portions of the frame buffer other than the destination to be blended with scan converter data. This is useful for filling areas in the frame buffer with repeating patterns such as cross-hatching, which are stored elsewhere in frame buffer memory.

• *z cache & z pipeline register*—These registers perform the same function as the data cache and source register, except they are used to buffer depth (z) information rather than intensity information. This allows the same physical memory to be used for either z or intensity data, depending on the size of the frame buffer memory and the needs of the application.

An example vector

This example shows how data travels from the pixel port of the cache to the frame buffer during the drawing of a vector. A replacement rule that requires only the source register will be used. The z data paths will be ignored for now.

As shown in Figure 3, the scan converter is used to draw a vector from location (2, 2) to (10, 4). The upper left corner of the screen is (0, 0) and the pixel cache is configured to hold 4×4 pixels of frame buffer memory. The vector is nine pixels long, and the pixels have been labeled in the order they will be drawn, from A to I. Both tile addresses and bit addresses are shown on the frame buffer diagram.

Configurable tile organization

The pixel cache speeds pixel generation by allowing multiple pixel updates per memory cycle. It follows then, that the more pixels updated per cycle, the higher the pixel generation performance. The number of pixels updated per cycle is a function of tile size. A larger tile will give higher performance since it allows more pixel updates per frame buffer memory cycle. The choice of tile size is a price/performance trade-off. A larger tile size will give higher performance, but will also increase the size and cost of the pixel cache, since the data path and data registers in the cache must scale accordingly.

The number of pixels updated per tile is also a function of tile organization and type of operation being performed. For randomly oriented vectors, a square tile organization gives the highest average number of pixel updates per memory cycle.[4,12] For horizontal vectors that include polygon fill, a tile organized linearly in the

IEEE CG&A

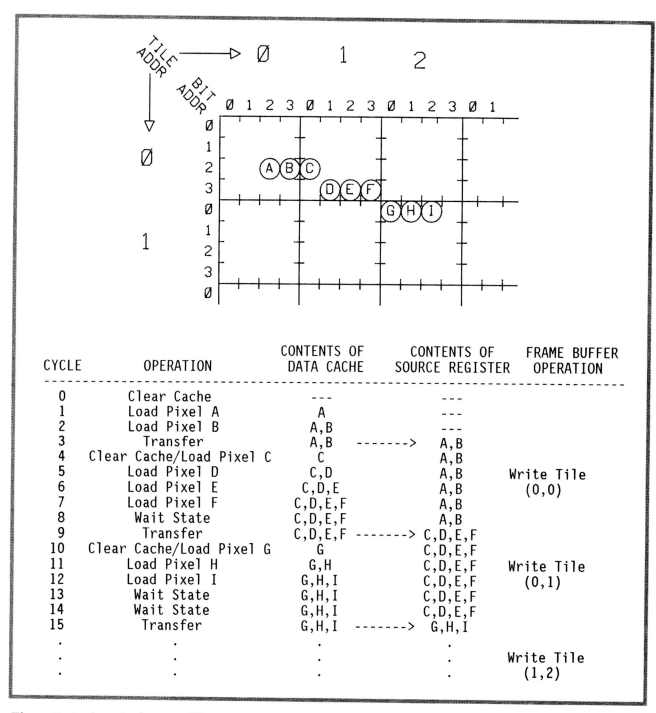

CYCLE	OPERATION	CONTENTS OF DATA CACHE		CONTENTS OF SOURCE REGISTER	FRAME BUFFER OPERATION
0	Clear Cache	---		---	
1	Load Pixel A	A		---	
2	Load Pixel B	A,B		---	
3	Transfer	A,B	------>	A,B	
4	Clear Cache/Load Pixel C	C		A,B	
5	Load Pixel D	C,D		A,B	Write Tile
6	Load Pixel E	C,D,E		A,B	(0,0)
7	Load Pixel F	C,D,E,F		A,B	
8	Wait State	C,D,E,F		A,B	
9	Transfer	C,D,E,F	------>	C,D,E,F	
10	Clear Cache/Load Pixel G	G		C,D,E,F	
11	Load Pixel H	G,H		C,D,E,F	Write Tile
12	Load Pixel I	G,H,I		C,D,E,F	(0,1)
13	Wait State	G,H,I		C,D,E,F	
14	Wait State	G,H,I		C,D,E,F	
15	Transfer	G,H,I	------>	G,H,I	
.	.	.		.	
.	.	.		.	Write Tile
.	.	.		.	(1,2)

Figure 3. A nine-pixel vector. The scan converter is used to draw a vector from location (2,2) to (10,4).

horizontal dimension gives the highest number of pixel updates per cycle. The effect of tile organization on cache hit rate for different cache sizes and some typical images is shown in Figures 4 and 5. (These images were rendered on a HP350SRX graphics workstation.)

The data in Figures 4b and 5b indicates there is no single tile organization that performs well in both cases. The wireframe image performs better with a square tile organization, whereas the shaded image performs bet-

ter with a horizontal tile organization. If the tile organization can change to match operations as they are performed, the overall pixel generation performance will be higher than that of a fixed tile organization.

Cost and performance goals of the system using the pixel cache dictated that its first implementation have a size of 16 bits and support both 4×4 and 16×1 tiles. To do this, three design constraints are required of the frame buffer:

March 1987

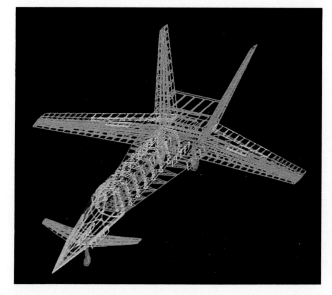

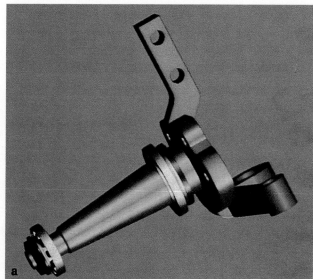

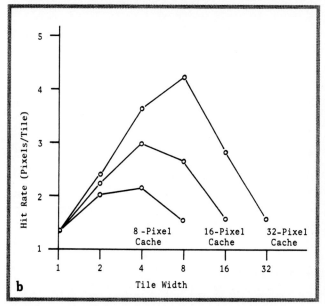

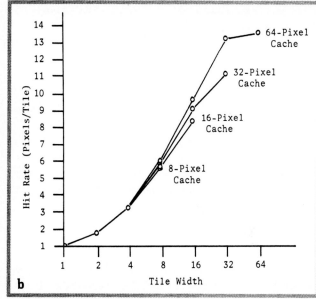

Figure 4. Wireframe jet (a), courtesy of Colin Cant-well, Crystal Chip, Inc., and cache hit rate (b).

Figure 5. Solid shaded spindle (a), courtesy of SDRC; and the cache hit rate (b).

• The number of RAM data lines must match the square tile organization. For example, a 4×4 tile requires 16 data lines.
• RAMs whose data lines map into a particular row of the square tile must be addressed independently of RAMs that map into the other rows of the tile.
• The display refresh circuitry must reorder the RAM outputs from line to line such that the display matches the tile organization.

An example of a one-plane frame buffer that supports 4×4 tiles and 16×1 tiles is shown in Figure 6. Figure 6a

shows a RAM array that has 16 data lines. Each of the four groups of data lines A, B, C, and D, may receive a different address. Figure 6b shows how the RAM data lines map into the display. Note in Figure 6b that for any 16 consecutive pixels in the horizontal dimension, each comes from a different RAM data line. Also, in any 4×4 group of pixels, each of the 16 comes from a different RAM data line. This allows a cache access of 16 pixels to originate from either a 16×1 or 4×4 tile, based on the addresses supplied to the different groups of RAMs.

We assume one row of the display is made up of M consecutive memory addresses or locations, and each loca-

IEEE CG&A

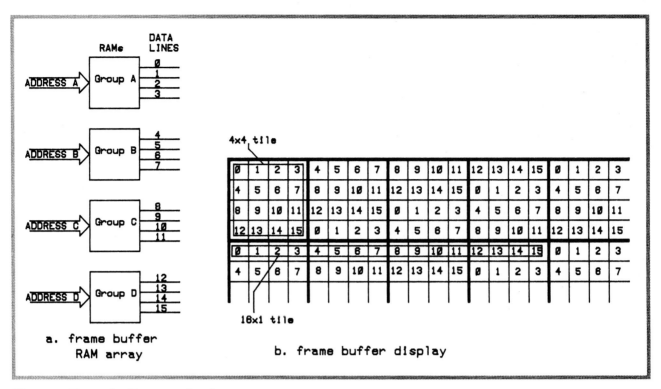

a. frame buffer RAM array

b. frame buffer display

Figure 6. Frame buffer organization.

tion contains 16 bits, one from each RAM data line. To access a 16×1 tile, all groups of RAMs receive the same address. To access a 4×4 tile, each group of RAMs receives a different address, namely ADDR, ADDR+M, ADDR+2M, and ADDR+3M. Which group of RAMs gets each of these addresses depends on the particular 4×4 tile being accessed. The fact that the four data lines within a group always have the same address fixes tiles on four bit boundaries.

z-buffer cache

Using a z-buffer for hidden-surface removal requires storage of the z value for each displayed pixel. During the rendering of an image, the existing z value for each pixel is read and compared against the z value for the new pixel to be drawn. Based on the comparison, both the pixel intensity and the z are updated to new values or both are left as they are. A significant performance improvement can be realized by reading several z values from memory in parallel, then overlapping the compare and update of new z values with writing of previously updated values to memory.

One way to implement the z-buffer is to use a separate z memory equipped with a z cache similar to the pixel cache just described. However, price/performance considerations led us to a different solution based on the following:

• The display resolution was 1280 wide by 1024 high (an industry standard), which, when implemented with 256K-bit video RAMs as shown in Figure 6, requires a 2048×1024 frame buffer. There are 768×1024 unused pixels: It would be nice if the extra memory could be used for the z-buffer.

• We wanted the frame buffer to be upgradable from eight to 32 planes in multiples of eight planes.

• It was desirable to allow z-buffering on all configurations from eight to 32 planes.

• The scan converter generates 16 bits of z data, so the z-buffer should also provide 16 bits of depth for each pixel. If off-screen frame buffer memory is used for the z-buffer, z resolution should not be dependent on frame buffer depth.

To meet these criteria, a z cache was added to the pixel cache as shown in Figure 2. To obtain 16 bits of z resolution from an eight-plane frame buffer, each plane must provide two bits of z. The 16-bit z cache in Figure 2 represents eight 2-bit quantities. When all eight planes are combined, this results in eight 16-bit z values. In other words, when z buffering is enabled, tile size is reduced to 8×1. The 16 bits of z for a given pixel always come from the same bank of eight planes, with each pixel-cache chip delivering two bits of the z word at a time. To cover the

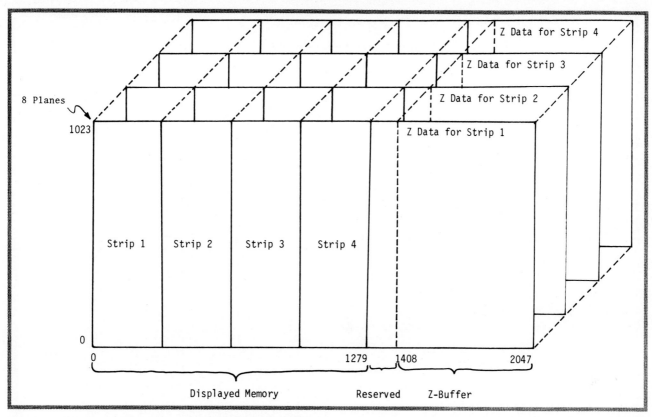

Figure 7. Memory usage for a 32-plane frame buffer.

entire screen, frame buffer memory is organized in strips as shown in Figure 7.

In systems with fewer than 32 planes, the image must be rendered in multiple passes, using the same z memory for each pass. On each pass, the z-buffer is cleared, the clip limits are set to the strip being rendered, and the display list is traversed. This allows a person with only eight planes to continue using the z-buffer hidden-surface algorithm with a loss of performance, but not functionality. This technique is referred to as "strip z-buffering."

Performance

The ultimate speed of the frame buffer is a function of three parameters: The rate at which pixels can be stored in the pixel cache, the cache hit rate, and the time it takes to write a tile to the frame buffer. The frame buffer constructed for use with the pixel cache has a cycle time of 360 ns, and the pixel cache has a cycle time of 60 ns. When z-buffering is enabled, the cycle time is extended to 120 ns to allow time for external circuitry to do the z-compare. When pixel port cycles and frame buffer write cycles are overlapped, the RAM cycle time becomes the dominating factor if fewer than six pixels within a tile are updated.

Line-drawing performance

When randomly oriented 30-pixel vectors were drawn to the frame buffer using 4×4 tiles, the average pixel-cache hit rate was measured at 3.25 pixels per tile. At 60 ns/pixel, this would normally yield a 16 Mpixels/sec. drawing rate. However, the RAM cycle time of 360 ns dominates, giving an average pixel write rate of nine Mpixels/sec. The effective throughput of the frame buffer system is 300,000 vectors/sec. The same frame buffer with no cache would have one-third the performance.

Polygon performance

When 30×30 squares at random positions and angles of orientation were filled using 16×1 tiles, the average pixel-cache hit rate was measured at 12 pixels per tile, giving a pixel drawing rate of 15 Mpixels/sec. This yields a performance of 16,000 polygons/sec. The same frame buffer with no cache would have one-fifth the performance.

Table 1. Summary of pixel-cache price/performance.

	PIXEL CACHE	FRAME BUFFER	PIXEL-CACHE + FRAME BUFFER
SIZE	16B	2MB	2MB
COST/BYTE	$6	.009¢	.01¢
ACCESS TIME/PIXEL 30-PIXEL VECTORS	60ns	360ns	111ns
ACCESS TIME/PIXEL 30X30 POLYGONS	60ns	360ns	69ns
ACCESS TIME/PIXEL POLYGONS WITH HIDDEN SURFACE REMOVAL	120ns	1080ns	192ns

Hidden-surface performance

To measure the performance of hidden-surface removal, 30×30 randomly oriented shaded polygons were rendered. Generating filled polygons with hidden surfaces removed requires two additional memory cycles in order to read and write the z data; z compares are overlapped with the extra frame buffer (z) write cycle, but not the extra frame buffer (z) read cycle. The average pixel-cache hit rate was measured at 7.2 pixels per tile. This corresponds to a pixel write rate of five Mpixels/sec., or 5800 polygons per second. This is a factor of five faster than the same frame buffer with no cache.

A summary of the price/performance characteristics of the pixel cache and frame buffer is shown in Table 1.

Summary

The method described uses a pixel cache to improve the performance of writing pixels to a frame buffer. The cache matches the bandwidth of a fast serial scan converter to slow frame buffer memory, giving the performance advantage of high-speed memory and the cost advantage of commercial dynamic RAM.

The pixel cache has been fabricated in a 1.6 micron CMOS process. It contains approximately 3700 gates and operates at 16.6 MHz. The frame buffer has been implemented using 256K-bit video RAMs and can be accessed by the cache chip as 4×4 or 16×1 tiles, to optimize cache hit rates for the operation being performed. One pixel-cache chip is used in each plane of the frame buffer. A high-speed scan converter was fabricated to generate pixel intensity and z values serially, and detect tile boundary crossings for use with the caching frame buffer. Analysis of the pixel-cache frame buffer system shows a substantial performance increase over traditional frame buffer designs, with a negligible increase in system cost.

There are a couple of areas to consider for future research. The cache described in this article requires that tiles be located on boundaries that are multiples of their size. However, the addressing scheme shown in Figure 6 allows 4×4 tiles to be aligned to any y boundary, and 16×1 tiles to be aligned to any (x MOD 4 = 0) boundary. Other possible schemes allow tiles to be located on any pixel boundary.[4,5,13] One area to study would be the effect of randomly aligned tiles on cache hit rate. Another would be caches that contain more than one tile of pixels. ∎

References

1. J.H. Clark, "The Geometry Engine: A VLSI Geometry System for Graphics," *Computer Graphics*, (Proc. SIGGRAPH 82), July 1982, pp. 127-133.

2. W.H. McAllister and J.R. Carlson, "Floating Point Chip Set Speeds Real-Time Computer Operation," *Hewlett-Packard J.*, Feb. 1984, pp. 17-23.

3. *Designing with the WTL 1032/1033*, Weitek Corp., Santa Clara, Calif., 1983.

4. S. Gupta, *Architectures and Algorithms for Parallel Updates of Raster Scan Displays*, doctoral dissertation, Carnegie Mellon Univ., Pittsburgh, Dec. 1981.

5. R.G. Sproull et al., "The 8 by 8 Display," tech. report, Computer Science Dept., Carnegie Mellon Univ., Pittsburgh, 1981.

6. S. Demetrescu, *Scan Line Access Memory (SLAM)—A New Highly Parallel VLSI Processor and Memory System for Cost Effective High Performance Graphics*, Computer Systems Lab., Stanford Univ., Stanford, Calif., Aug. 1984.

7. H. Fuchs et al.,"Fast Spheres, Shadows, Textures, Transparencies, and Image Enhancements in Pixel-Planes," *Computer Graphics*, (Proc. SIGGRAPH 85), July 1985, pp. 111-120.

8. S. Forman, "Dynamic Video RAM Snaps the Bond Between Memory and Screen Refresh," *Electronic Design*, May 1985, pp. 117-125.

9. K.R. Kaplan and R.O. Winder, "Cache Based Computer Systems," IEEE Computer Soc. Repository Paper R72-215, 1972.

10. A.V. Pohm and T.A. Smay, "Computer Memory Systems," *Computer*, Oct. 1981, pp. 93-110.

11. R.W. Swanson and L.J. Thayer, "A Fast Shaded Polygon Renderer, *Computer Graphics*, (Proc. SIGGRAPH 86), Aug. 1986, pp. 95-101.

12. M. Morgenthaler, *Performance Analysis of a Spectrum Based Simple Graphics System*, internal report, Hewlett-Packard Advanced Systems Lab., Computer Research Center, internal report, Jan. 1984.

13. T. Whitted, "Anti-Aliased Line Drawing Using Brush Extrusion," *Computer Graphics*, (Proc.SIGGRAPH 83), July 83, pp. 151-156.

Andy Goris is an electrical engineer in the R&D lab of the Technical Workstation Operation at Hewlett-Packard in Fort Collins, Colorado. Most recently, he was the hardware system architect of the 350SRX Graphics Workstation, which employs the pixel cache described in this article. His interests include image processing, advanced rendering algorithms, and hardware architectures for implementing these algorithms. He has worked on a number of hardware and software projects since joining HP in 1979.

Goris received his BS in 1977 and MS in 1979, both in electrical engineering from Texas A&M University. He is a member of ACM and SIGGRAPH.

Harold L. Baeverstad, Jr. is a project manager in the R&D Lab of the Technical Workstation Operation at Hewlett-Packard in Fort Collins, Colorado. His research interests include computer graphics architecture and graphics performance benchmarking. Baeverstad supervised the hardware development of the 350SRX Solids Rendering Workstation, and worked on a variety of computer graphics products since joining HP in 1977.

He received both BS and MS degrees in electrical engineering from the University of Kentucky. He is a member of ACM and SIGGRAPH.

Bob Fredrickson is an R&D project manager for Hewlett-Packard's Technical Workstation Operation in Fort Collins, Colorado. He is currently working on VLSI designs for graphics applications. A 1978 graduate of the University of Utah, Fredrickson has worked with HP on various graphics-related projects including software, hardware, and VLSI designs. He is a member of ACM.

The authors can be reached at Hewlett-Packard Co., 3404 E. Harmony Rd., Ft. Collins, CO 80525.

IEEE CG&A

Chapter 4: Smart Image-Memory

In the processing sequence displayed in Figure 1.1 (see Chapter 1), as the application model is progressively transformed into an image, the quantity of data for representing the scene increases also. Consequently, the computation required to render a scene becomes more and more intensive along the processing pipeline. Usually, image rasterization is the most time consuming step in the image-generation pipeline. Fortunately, the same algorithm is applicable to the evaluation of all of the pixels. In addition, the evaluation of a pixel is independent of the other pixels. This is particularly useful for applying parallel processing to the image rasterization process.

4.1: Integration of Processing and Buffering

An obvious approach in applying parallel processing to the image rasterization process is to divide the frame buffer into a number of subsets. Then each subset can be assigned to a dedicated processor that carries out the pixel evaluation process for its associated subset of pixels [FUCH79, CLAR80]. However, the memory access bandwidth of the frame buffer still imposes a certain burden to the performance of such a rasterization system.

Although by using parallel processing techniques the rasterizer can render a geometric object at a very high speed, the rate that the frame buffer can accept data is highly dependent on its memory bandwidth. Although many approaches have been suggested to relieve the bandwidth problem (see Chapter 3), conventional architectures for frame buffers can be still too slow for some real-time applications. Thus, although parallel processing can be employed for image rasterization, throughput of the image generation pipeline is still bounded by the frame buffer access bandwidth.

One of the major causes of the "bottleneck" of conventional frame buffers is its "narrow" I/O channel inherent in the structure of the RAM chips used to construct the frame buffer. Usually, the number of bits of data that can be accepted by the frame buffer in one access is nw, where n is the number of RAM chips used in implementing the frame buffer and w is the number of bits in a word of RAM storage. In most cases, nw is only a small value. Therefore, even if the rasterizer is able to generate pixels at a high speed, data will be jammed on the path to the frame buffer.

One possible way to solve the problem is by integrating the image rasterization circuits into the image memory.

With this approach, pixel data are generated and buffered within the same chip. Such special devices are called *smart image memories*.

4.1.1: Rectangular Area Filling Display System

The idea of incorporating local intelligence in image-memory can be noticed in many systems; for example, the *rectangular area filling display system* proposed by Whelan [WHEL82]. In his system, the primitive operation on the image memory is filling a rectangular area of pixels instead of writing a single pixel. This is achieved by modifying a conventional RAM.

A conventional static RAM contains a rectangular array of memory cells each similar to the one depicted in Figure 4.1. A single cell is selected by a two-step operation: (1) first selecting a row of memory array and then (2) selecting a bit within that row. Both selections are made by the binary decoders labeled *row select* and *column select,* as shown in Figure 4.2.

Once a cell is selected, the read or write operation can be performed on it. To reduce this two-step "select" into a single step operation, two-dimensional addressability must be provided to the rectangular area filling RAM. Notice that the static RAM of Figure 4.1 has only a single row select signal line running across the array. To achieve two-dimensional addressability, the rectangular area filling RAM will

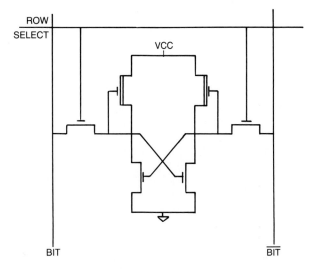

Figure 4.1: A six transistor static memory cell.

EH0273-3/88/0000/0169$01.00 © 1988 IEEE   169

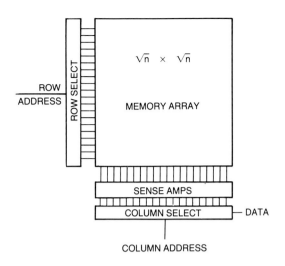

Figure 4.2: Floorplan of a typical *nx1* RAM.

Figure 4.4 demonstrates the complete architecture of the rectangular area filling RAM [WHEL82]. The memory array is surrounded on two sides by the row and column *banded decoders,* which define the band of rows and columns when the upper and lower x and y coordinates are given.

The rectangular area filling RAM is easy to build since it requires only a slight modification of the conventional RAM. However, it has some weaknesses that limit its usefulness. Although it can fill a rectangular area extremely fast, it is not faster at filling shaded rectangles since shading usually implies that neighboring pixels have slightly different values. For the same reason, the architecture does not help in the rendition of anti-aliased lines. Nevertheless, both shading and anti-aliasing can be performed by this system, since the size of the rectangle can be set to 1 × 1, causing the system to behave like an ordinary frame buffer.

Whelan's rectangular area filling system can be classified as a "processor per pixel" system since each RAM cell can be considered as a processor that sets its state bit if both its column and row selects are present (a simple decision making process). In general, the rectangular area filling RAM is weak in handling three-dimensional scenes because it does not facilitate hidden surface removal. Moreover, Whelan's system will degenerate to a pixel-wise (serial processing) system when shading is required.

4.1.2: Pixel-Planes

A three-dimensional scene is commonly represented by a number of planar convex polygons, such as polygon meshes [NEWM79]. Therefore, the performance of a graphics system is directly affected by its speed to process polygons. The

need column select signal lines running across the memory array as well. This involves the addition of two pass transistors as illustrated in Figure 4.3.

The operation of an array of such memory cells is as follows:

A memory cell is selected if its column and row select lines are both 1. When selected, the memory cell behaves as it did before. Notice, however, that if a band of column select lines and a band of row select lines are all set to 1, a rectangular area of memory cells are simultaneously picked. These cells may be written in the same way that a memory cell is written in a conventional RAM. Since there is only a single data line running down each column, only a single cell from each column can be read per memory cycle. For this reason, only a single row of cells can be read simultaneously in this RAM.

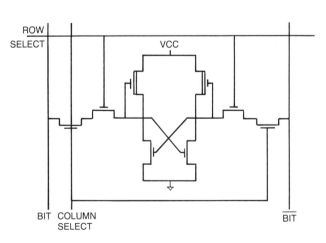

Figure 4.3: Static memory cell with row and column select capability.

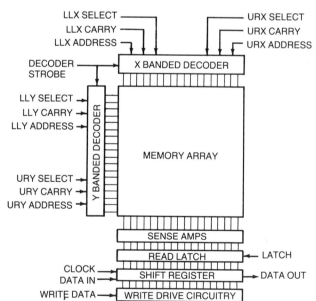

Figure 4.4: Rectangular area filling RAM architecture.

next smart memory system that we now consider can render three-dimensional planar convex polygons at a remarkable rate. It is the "pixel-planes" system proposed by Fuchs and his colleagues [FUCH81, FUCH82, FUCH85].

A pixel-plane is a smart memory chip especially designed for raster-scan graphics. The chip includes memory cells for both the pixel values and the z buffer, and two identical multiplier trees, one for the x dimension and one for the y, which evaluate arithmetic expressions for hidden-surface removal and shading. The fundamental operation of Fuchs' system is based on the calculation, simultaneously at each pixel, of the function $F\{x,y\} = A \cdot x + B \cdot y + C$, where x and y are the coordinates of the pixel in the display space.

Being able to evaluate $F(x,y)$ efficiently is extremely useful in three-dimensional image synthesis. First, each edge of a polygon can be expressed by an equation $E\{x,y\} = A \cdot x + B \cdot y + C = 0$. The $E\{x,y\}$ equations of the edges can be defined in such a way that the pixel (x', y') is inside the polygon if and only if all the $E\{x',y'\}$ are positive. Second, the depth value of the point (x',y') on the plane $P\{x,y\} = A \cdot x + B \cdot y + C$ can be determined easily by evaluating $Z\{x',y'\} = P(x',y')$. Finally, if Gouraud's smooth shading strategy is used to paint the polygon, the RGB value of (x,y) can be expressed by $R\{x,y\} = A_r \cdot x + B_r \cdot y + C_r$, $G\{x,y\} = A_g \cdot x + B_g \cdot y + C_g$, and $B\{x,y\} = A_b \cdot x + B_b \cdot y + C_b$.

Therefore, a polygon can be described as a set of $F\{x,y\}$ that defines its edges, depth, and shade functions. Since these $F\{x,y\}$ can be evaluated rapidly, a polygon can certainly be processed quickly. Consider the following recursive relations:

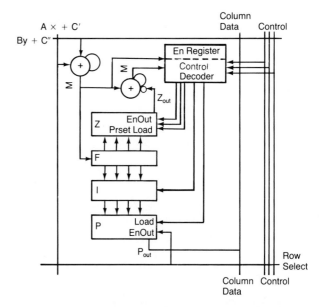

Figure 4.6: Evaluation of F {x,y} by a pixel-plane.

$$F\{x+1,y\} = F\{x,y\} + A$$
$$F\{x,y+1\} = F\{x,y\} + B$$

In general,

$$F\{x+i,y\} = F\{x,y\} + i \cdot A$$
$$F\{x,y+i\} = F\{x,y\} + i \cdot B$$

Given the F value of the pixel (x,y), the F value of its neighboring pixels can be evaluated readily by adding an appropriate constant to the value $F\{x,y\}$. It is this characteristic of the $F\{x,y\}$ that makes the evaluation of $F\{x,y\}$ by the pixel-planes so fast.

Before a polygon is processed, its descriptions are transformed into the corresponding set of planar equations $F\{x,y\}$, if necessary. Each planar equation is expressed as $F\{x,y\} = A \cdot x + C' + B \cdot y + C''$, where $C' + C'' = C$ (which is a constant term). The x multiplier tree and the y multiplier tree will calculate concurrently, for all x and y values, the functions $A \cdot x + C'$ and $B \cdot y + C''$, respectively. The structure and operation of the x multiplier tree is depicted in Figure 4.5; the y multiplier tree is identical to the x multiplier tree. In Figure 4.5, the leaves of the x multiplier tree generate the (serial) output $A \cdot x + C'$ for $x = 1,2, \ldots,7$. Similarly, the (serial) outputs $B \cdot y + C''$ for various y's are generated by the y multiplier tree. These $A \cdot x + C'$ and $B \cdot y + C''$ values are sent down the column and across the row of the image memory cells concurrently, as depicted in Figure 4.6. Each memory cell has an adder that calculates the sum of its associated functions $A \cdot x + C'$ and $B \cdot y + C''$ to generate the value of $F\{x,y\}$. The ultimate speed in evaluating the function $F\{x,y\}$ is achieved by simultaneous calculation of $F\{x,y\}$ at each memory cell for all x's and y's.

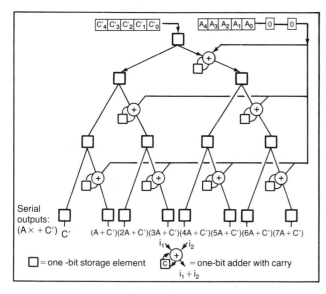

Figure 4.5: Structure and operation of the x-multiplier tree.

4.2: Article Overview

The smart image-memory proposed in the paper by Demetrescu, in "High Speed Image Rasterization Using Scan Line Access Memories," is called the *scan line access memory*. With this memory, an entire scan line can be updated with a single memory access. The architecture of this memory is rather simple. It is designed to deal with monochromatic images only. However, it clearly shows the concept of smart image-memory.

In the second paper, "A Parallel Processor System for Three-Dimensional Color Graphics" by Niimi et al., a two-level multiprocessor system is proposed. The system is composed of serveral scan-line processors (SLPs) each of which in turn controls several slave pixel processors (PXPs). The SLP prepares the specific data structure relevant to each scan-line, while the PXP manipulates every pixel data in its own territory. A similar system is described in the paper by Clark and Hannah [CLAR80]. This system utilizes a number of IMPs (image memory processors) that work in parallel to rasterize a scene.

The pixel-planes system is undoubtedly the most well known smart image-memory. In the three papers by Fuchs and his colleagues, "Pixel Plane: Building a VLSI-Based Graphics System," "Fast Spheres, Shadows, Textures, Transparencies, and Image Enhancements in Pixel-Planes," and "Quadratic Surface Rendering on a Logic-Enhanced Frame-Buffer Memory," the concept, structure, and potential of the pixel-planes system are discussed.

References

[CLAR80] Clark, J.H. and M.R. Hannah, "Distributed Processing in a High-Performance Smart Image Memory," *LAMBDA,* 4th Quarter 1980, pp. 40–45.

[FUCH79] Fuchs, H. and B.W. Johnson, "An Expandable Multiprocessor Architecture for Video Graphics (Preliminary Report)," *Proc. of the 6th Ann. Symp. on Computer Architecture,* Computer Society, Washington, D.C., 1979, pp. 58–67.

[FUCH81] Fuchs, H. and J. Poulton, "Pixel-Planes: A VLSI-Oriented Design for a Raster Graphics Engine," *VLSI Design,* Vol. 2, No. 3, 3rd Quarter 1981, pp. 20–28.

[FUCH82] Fuchs, H., J. Poulton, A. Paeth, and A. Bell, "Developing Pixel-Planes: A Smart Memory-Based Raster Graphics System," *Proceedings of 1982 Conf. on Advanced Research in VLSI,* Massachusetts Institute of Technology, Cambridge, Mass., 1982, pp. 137–146.

[FUCH85] Fuchs, H., J. Goldfeather, J. Hultquist, S. Spach, J. Austin, F. Brooks, Jr., J. Eyles, and J. Poulton, "Fast Sphere, Shadows, Textures, Transparencies, and Image Enhancements in Pixel-Planes," *ACM SIGGRAPH,* ACM, Inc., New York, Vol. 19, No. 3, 1985, pp. 111–120.

[NEWM79] Newman, W.M. and R.F. Sproull, *Principles of Interactive Computer Graphics,* 2nd ed., McGraw-Hill, New York, 1979.

[WHEL82] Whelan, D.S., "A Rectangular Area Filling Display System Architecture," *Computer Graphics,* Vol. 16, No. 3, July 1982, pp. 356–362.

High Speed Image Rasterization Using Scan Line Access Memories

Stefan Demetrescu

Vice President
Lasergraphics, Inc.
17671 Cowan Ave.
Irvine, CA 92714

Abstract

A Scan Line Access Memory (SLAM) consists of a dense semiconductor memory augmented with highly parallel but simple on-chip processors designed specifically for fast rasterization. A SLAM chip has been designed, fabricated and is now undergoing testing. An image frame buffer consisting of SLAM smart memory chips can fill an arbitrary horizontal pixel line segment in one memory access. When rasterizing polygons of 100 by 100 pixels, SLAMs increase the bandwidth to the frame buffer by factors of 100x to 1600x, thus allowing very fast polygon rasterization speeds. Unlike many other proposed rasterization architectures, SLAMs can also rasterize vectors and bit-mapped characters effectively. The SLAM system is compared with previously suggested architectures for rasterization. Due to its highly parallel architecture, this versatile system is shown to be capable of achieving performance comparable to the "processor per pixel" graphics processor architectures while avoiding the tremendous circuit density (and hence cost) penalty incurred by such approaches. Consequently, it is practical to build a SLAM based high performance real-time graphics system for costs comparable to that of a conventional frame buffer.

1 Introduction

Computer graphics output has moved away from calligraphic displays (e.g., randomly scanned vector CRTs, pen plotters) and toward raster displays (e.g., television displays, raster page printers). This conversion is due to many reasons: (i) raster displays cost significantly less than other display methods, (ii) most raster displays rely on a frame buffer and the cost of semiconductor memory has recently declined sharply, (iii) raster displays can fill areas with solid colors (and shading) whereas calligraphic displays can only draw outlines (efficiently), and (iv) raster displays can display characters in many font styles more naturally and efficiently than calligraphic displays.

This work has been sponsored by NASA contract NAGW—419, the Defense Advanced Research Projects Agency under contracts MDA903—83—C—0335, MDA903—79—C—0680 and N00039—83—K—0431, and by the Fannie and John Hertz Foundation.

The views and conclusions are those of the author and should not be interpreted as representing the official policies, either expressed or implied, of the Defense Advanced Research Projects Agency, of NASA, or of the U.S. Government.

Unfortunately, the move from calligraphic to raster displays has brought new problems. In a raster system, it is necessary not only to compute the positions of the graphical primitives but also to fill all of the pixels in the interior of the primitives with the desired values. Currently, the speed with which polygons can be filled is typically much slower than the speed with which the position of the polygons can be calculated. As a result, the use of raster displays for real time images has been limited and expensive.

In order to bring real-time raster based graphics into wide spread use, a low cost and yet highly parallel rasterization architecture must be employed. A fully custom VLSI chip called a Scan Line Access Memory (SLAM) (Figure 1) has been developed to meet these criteria.

The SLAM chip itself is first described, followed by a description of a typical rasterization system using SLAM chips. Lastly, the SLAM system is compared with other proposed parallel rasterization architectures for computer graphics. It is shown that the SLAM system performs much better than practical existing rasterization systems (expensive or not) and that it compares favorably with massively parallel and very expensive proposed rasterization architectures.

2 The Scan Line Access Memory Rasterization System

A graphical display system using a raster display is shown in Figure 2. Such a system is given high level descriptions of a two or three dimensional image in world coordinates (i.e. the coordinates which most naturally describe the image). This image is transformed and clipped (using well known graphical methods [NS 79]) into a two dimensional representation in terms of graphical primitives described in screen coordinates (these transformations have recently been incorporated into a VLSI

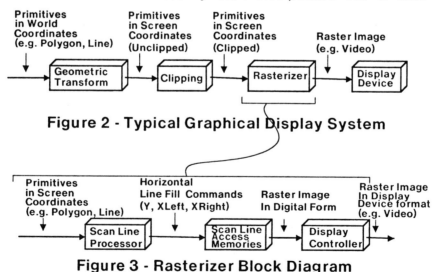

Figure 2 - Typical Graphical Display System

Figure 3 - Rasterizer Block Diagram

design [CI 82]). The rasterizer adds these primitives to the partially completed rasterized image and also displays it.

The rasterization process can be separated into three parts (Figure 3). Figure 4 shows an example of a system of 1024 by 1024 one bit pixels using SLAMs. The graphical primitives to be imaged are sent to the Scan Line Processors on a common bus.

Figure 1   Scan Line Access Memory

Each Scan Line Processor is responsible for 64 horizontal pixel lines (scan lines). The Scan Line Processors convert each graphical primitive into horizontal pixel subsequences to be filled (also known as *run length encoding*). The section titled **Scan Line Processor Operations** discusses this transformation further. These horizontal line fill commands are transmitted to the SLAMs through a common 19 bit bus. The Display Controller extracts the rasterized image from the SLAMs and displays it.

3 The Scan Line Access Memory (SLAM) Chip

Each SLAM contains and controls 64 lines of 256 pixels. Each of the 16 rows in Figure 4 represents 64 lines of 1024 pixels and can operate independently of the others. The SLAM chips maintain and modify the raster image in response to horizontal line fill commands sent by the Scan Line Processors. Figure 5

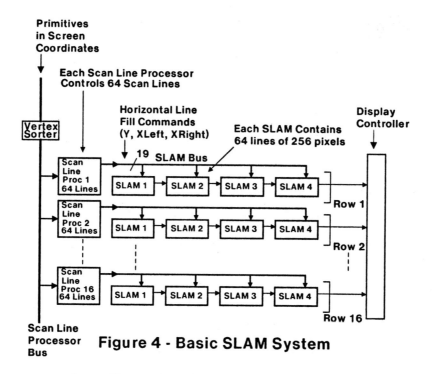

Figure 4 - Basic SLAM System

Primitives in Screen Coordinates

Each Scan Line Processor Controls 64 Scan Lines

Horizontal Line Fill Commands (Y, XLeft, XRight)

Each SLAM Contains 64 lines of 256 pixels

Display Controller

Vertex Sorter

19 SLAM Bus

Scan Line Proc 1 64 Lines

SLAM 1 | SLAM 2 | SLAM 3 | SLAM 4 — Row 1

Scan Line Proc 2 64 Lines

SLAM 1 | SLAM 2 | SLAM 3 | SLAM 4 — Row 2

Scan Line Proc 16 64 Lines

SLAM 1 | SLAM 2 | SLAM 3 | SLAM 4 — Row 16

Scan Line Processor Bus

summarizes the external interconnections and commands accepted by the experimental SLAM chip shown in Figure 1.

This architecture achieves the very desirable goal of communicating short commands (low bandwidth) to the SLAM chips through few pins (28 pins per SLAM chip) which can have the effect of modifying hundreds to thousands of pixels simultaneously (high bandwidth results). Thus, the wide bandwidth is confined to the interior of the SLAMs where is is inexpensive, rather than being exposed directly though many interface pins.

Because many SLAMs are used in each system, they have been kept as simple as possible so that only the highly parallel operations which must be next to the memory array are placed on the chip. All operations that can be performed externally without a loss of parallelism or an increase in the communication bandwidth have been left out. As a result, the task of transforming graphical primitives into sequences of line fill operations is performed in the Scan line Processor, not in the SLAM.

3.1 SLAM Operations

The SLAM chip executes commands which it receives over a 19 bit bus. Three bits indicate the desired function, and 16 bits represent function specific data (see Figure 5). The horizontal line fill operation is accomplished through the use of four of these commands (Figure 6). The first command specifies the scan line (i.e. the Y coordinate) on which the operation is to take place. Then, a 16 bit pattern is sent which is to be used to fill the selected part of the scan line. This pattern can be used either for halftoning the interior of polygons or for imaging rasterized characters. This is followed by the command to read the scan line from the memory. This command also specifies the rightmost X position to be affected. The next command specifies the leftmost X position to be affected and writes the modified scan line back into the memory array.

However, it is not necessary to always send all 4 commands for each horizontal fill operation. If the halftone pattern does not change it is not necessary to send it each cycle. In addition, each time a scan line is written the Y coordinate is automatically incremented by one. As a result, when filling a polygon it is necessary to specify the Y coordinate only for the first horizontal fill command.

Performance simulations indicate that each SLAM can execute 10 million commands per second. Thus, during a polygon fill operation a new scan line can be modified every two command times (i.e. 5 million scan line accesses per second).

Each SLAM can be programmed to respond to only a specified range of X and Y coordinates so that many SLAMs can be connected together on the same bus. Furthermore, many SLAMs can be connected in parallel to store more than one bit per pixel.

A scan line is displayed by loading it into a 256 bit shift register which is shifted out independently of other operations of the SLAM.

3.2 SLAM Design

The architecture of a conventional high density semiconductor RAM (16K for example) is highly parallel. Each time one bit of memory is accessed, a whole word consisting of 256 bits is recalled. One of the bits is selected and the rest are ignored.

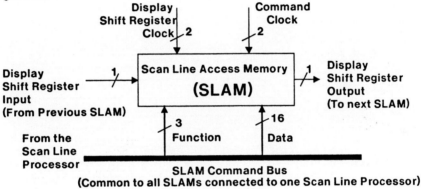

Principal SLAM Commands	
Function (3 bits)	Data (16 bits)
Load Y	Y value
Load Pattern	16 bit pattern
Load X right and read line	X right value
Load X left and write line	X left value

Other SLAM Commands	
Function (3 bits)	Data (16 bits)
Load Intensity 1	16 bit intensity
Load Intensity 2	16 bit intensity
Load X left and write line and load Display SR	X left value
Load ALU Operation	ALU Operation

Figure 5 - SLAM Chip Interconnect and Commands

Each row of such a RAM can be made to represent a scan line and each bit to represent a pixel. Thus the RAM becomes a frame buffer of 64 lines of 256 one bit pixels. Many such chips must be used to tile an image of typical size with many bits per pixel.

A Scan Line Access Memory (Figure 7) is simply a RAM array with a special purpose processor placed above it which can operate on some or all of a scan line every memory cycle.

The SLAM is composed of 6 main sections (see Figures 1 and 7):

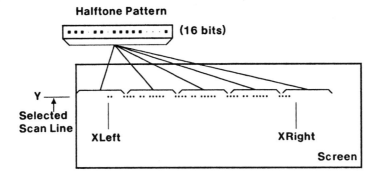

Figure 6 - Effect of Horizontal Line Fill Operation

(i) The main memory array with required circuitry. It is a standard dynamic or static RAM design. It is desirable to have an array much wider than it is long in order to achieve the largest amount of parallelism possible. The prototype SLAM shown is a 16K-bit RAM organized as 64 words (i.e. rows) of 256 bits (i.e. columns) each. Much bigger SLAMs can be made using more specialized state-of-the-art Dynamic RAM fabrication techniques.

(ii) the Halftone ALU intercepts the incoming 16 bit halftone pattern and performs one of four boolean operations on it. Its use is discussed in the **System Design Issues** section.

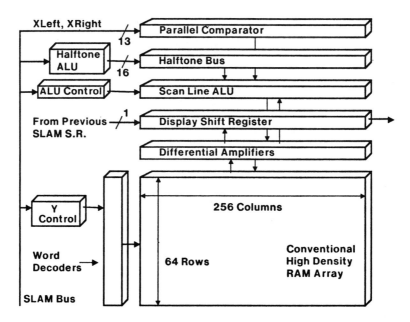

Figure 7 - Scan Line Access Memory Block Diagram

(iii) the Parallel Comparator accepts an X coordinate and generates a 256 bit mask which is true for all bit positions less than X and false for all bit positions greater than or equal to X. These limits are used by the Scan Line ALU to select the left and right limits of the pixels to be affected during an operation.

(iv) the Scan Line ALU (Figure 8) determines what value is to be stored back into the memory array given the input values from the Parallel Comparator, the Halftone ALU (through the halftone bus) and the memory array.

178

(v) the Display Shift Register latches a scan line so that it can be displayed. Once loaded, it can be shifted independently of the rest of the SLAM operation.

(vi) the Y Control and Word Decoder receives the Y coordinate and then selects the proper memory row (if any). It also auto-increments the Y coordinate each time a scan line is modified so that successive Y scan lines can be modified without explicitly setting the Y coordinate each time.

In order to distribute the repeating halftone pattern bits to the corresponding bits of the memory words, each of the 16 bits from the Halftone ALU is delivered to every 16th X position by running a 16 bit bus horizontally above the memory array. If it is desired to place patterns which are aligned with respect to the starting X coordinate (e.g. for rasterizing characters), it is necessary to rotate the pattern by X mod 16. This rotation can be performed by the Scan Line Processor without any increase in bandwidth.

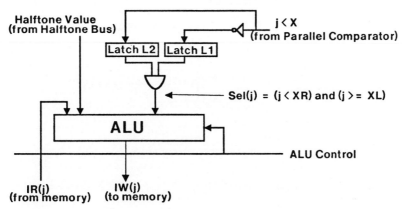

Figure 8 - Scan Line ALU for Pixel Position j

The following is a description of a typical cycle of the SLAM:

First, the (exclusive) right coordinate (XR) of the X extent is presented to the Parallel Comparator and its output is latched into L2 (see Figure 8). Thus, L2 is true for all locations along the scan line which are less than XR.

Second, the (inclusive) left coordinate (XL) of the X extent to be affected is presented to the Parallel Comparator and the inverse of its output is latched into L1. Thus, L1 is true for all locations along the scan line which are greater than or equal to XL. Consequently, SEL(j) is true for all X in the range [XL, XR).

By this time, the RAM array has retrieved the current values of the pixels (labeled IR(j)) in the currently selected scan line. The Scan Line ALU operates on the selected bits as desired and generates the pixels IW(j) to be written back into memory.

In order to keep the Scan Line ALU as simple as possible, only the following minimal set of operations has been implemented: (i) no operation, make IW(j) = IR(j), (ii) Replace the halftone pixels at all selected pixel locations, (iii) OR the halftone pixels with all selected pixels. Other functions are possible, at the expense of making the ALU larger.

4 Scan Line Processor

The Scan Line Processor transforms high level graphical primitives (i.e. polygons, lines, text), into sequences of commands to fill a specified section of a specified pixel scan line with a specified halftone pattern. This processor is an interface between the SLAMs and the rest of the system. Most of the power of this rasterization system stems from the parallelism achieved within the SLAMs. Hence, the Scan Line Processor will be described only in general terms. Such a processor is being built (from TTL components) by the author in order to test the performance of the SLAM chips. However, given the resources, one could easily integrate this function on one VLSI chip.

A simplified block diagram of a Scan Line Processor is shown in Figure 9. All commands are first buffered in a First-In-First-Out (FIFO) memory. This memory is needed in order to equalize the work load if multiple Scan Line Processors are operating in parallel. The commands are then interpreted by the command decoder which dispatches the commands to the appropriate sub-processor. These commands fall into two general categories: (i) Polygon fill, and (ii) Character imaging.

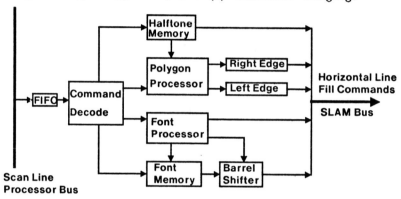

Figure 9 - Scan Line Processor Block Diagram

The Polygon Processor rasterizes polygons which are monotone in Y (i.e. any horizontal line intersects the boundary of the polygon at most twice). Convex polygons are a special case of monotone polygons. The polygon vertices are presented to the processor in descending Y order. Each vertex is also labeled as to whether it is part of the left or the right edge of the polygon. The two Edge Processors simultaneously calculate the beginning and ending X coordinates for each scan line to be rasterized. The processor also contains a 16 by 16 bit halftone memory which can be loaded with the desired halftone pattern to be used while filling the polygon. Lines are rasterized as thin polygons.

The Font Processor accepts commands to draw characters. It maintains an external Font Memory (or a character cache, which contains the most frequently used characters). This memory contains bit patterns of the characters to be drawn. A character is imaged by sending the Font Processor its Font Memory address and its XY location.

Characters are drawn one at a time. Each is treated as one or more small squares (16 by 16 pixels) each of which is filled with the halftone pattern (from the Font Memory) representing the appropriate part of the character.

5 System Design Alternatives

For the system shown in Figure 4, it is necessary to have 16 rows of SLAMs in order to get 1024 scan lines. Each row of SLAMs is shown having its own Scan Line Processor operating in parallel with the others. The first row contains the first 64 scan lines, the second row contains lines the second 64 lines, and so on. Because of the FIFO in the Scan Line Processors, all processors are typically busy, thus benefiting from the 16 way parallelism.

In order to lower cost, one can use fewer Scan Line Processors at the expense of some parallelism (Figure 10).

Double buffering is essential for real time graphics. In Figure 11 one set of SLAMs is displayed while the other set is controlled by the Scan Line Processors which are generating the next frame. This allows the Scan Line Processors to be fully utilized.

Systems with multiple bits per pixel can be designed as shown in Figure 12. Since all SLAM chips execute the horizontal fill commands in parallel, the performance of the system is completely independent on the number of bits per pixel being used. At system initialization each SLAM chip is assigned a different bit of the intensity value (up to 16 bits per pixel). Thus, all SLAM chips of all the bit planes can share the same 19 bit control bus.

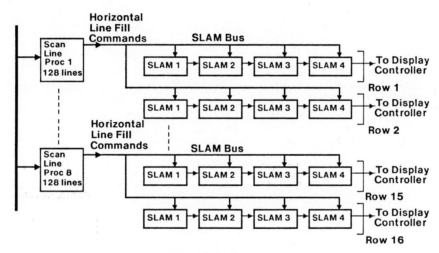

Figure 10
**Less Expensive and Less Parallel System
Where One Scan Line Processsor
Controls Two Rows of SLAMs**

In a multiple bits per pixel system, one can use the SLAM halftone ALU to interpret the incoming halftone pattern in one of four ways: (i) it is used as is, (ii) it is inverted before it is used, (iii) it is ignored and all 1s are used instead, (iv) it is ignored and all 0s are used instead. This allows for multiple value halftoning while imaging polygons. For example, in Figure 12 each pixel can have one of 8 levels of gray. It is possible to halftone by using a mixture of two of the 8 gray scale values. For example, to achieve an intensity of 5.5, a polygon can be filled with an alternating pattern of gray value 5 and 6. This effect can be achieved by issuing pixel fill commands to the SLAMs while commanding that the most significant bit plane use a halftone pattern of all 1s, the middle plane use the halftone pattern as given, and the least significant plane use the pattern inverted. This places a 6 in all locations where the halftone pattern is 1 and 5 elsewhere.

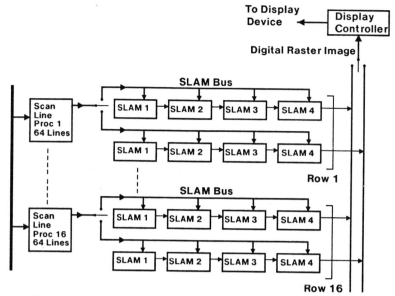

Figure 11 - Double Buffered SLAM System

One set of SLAMs is being displayed
while the other set is being filled by the scan line processors

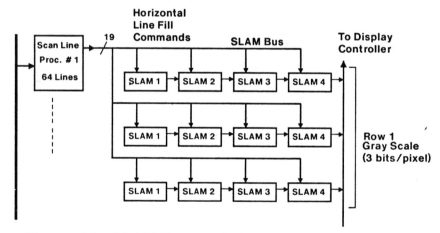

Figure 12 - SLAM System With Three Bits Per Pixel

Bus width and rasterization speed is same as for one bit/pixel

6 Windowing and Partial Updating

Multiple overlapping active windows for graphics and/or text are easily implemented in a SLAM system. The implementation is made simple by the high performance of the SLAM system.

In a real-time double buffered display the whole screen image is re-drawn from scratch each frame time (i.e. not incrementally updated). Windows are implemented by drawing the rear-most window first (while setting the appropriate clipping region), and so on to the top-most window. It is not necessary to make special provisions for overlapping and partially visible windows, since each window is redrawn each frame. For the same reason, all windows can be active simultaneously without any penalty or complication due to overlap.

In some applications most of the windows remain unchanged from one frame to the next, so it may be desirable to redraw only some of the windows each frame time. This can be accomplished as long as the windows to be modified often are not partially obscured. In that case, the unchanging image containing the static windows is stored in both buffers (if a double buffered system), and the real-time windows are erased and redrawn each frame time, on top of the static background image.

At times, the slow changing windows need to be updated. At such times, those windows can be erased and redrawn (along with all windows which partially obscure them).

7. Comparison With Existing Architectures

It is instructive to compare the maximum attainable performance of this new architecture (as shown in Figure 4) with that of other architectures which have been designed to perform similar functions. Any such comparison can not be "fair" because many of the architectures have functionality not available in the others. The author has picked one dimension shared by all designs and compared them along that dimension, while keeping in mind that other aspects of the architectures are being ignored.

Only the time required to rasterize polygons, lines and text is addressed. The size of the raster is taken to be 1024 by 1024 one bit pixels. Consequently, only the features relevant to this computation will be discussed. This comparison is not meant to establish which architecture is best, because that is highly dependent on the application to which the architecture is being put, and the relative importance of the features.

It is impractical to compare performance by measuring the "real" time needed to perform the various rasterization operations because many of the designs have a speed potential which has not been realized in hardware but which could easily be accomplished without any conceptual breakthroughs. Thus, the designs are compared on the basis of a standard of minimum achievable "memory cycle time", that is, the number of accesses to the image memory which are necessary to place the rasterized representation of the image in the memory. This assumes that the bottleneck is always the memory access time and bandwidth and that the processing takes comparatively little time. The author believes that this is a realistic assumption which provides a good measure of fundamental performance limitations.

The Table compares the performance of the SLAM system against that of five other architectures which rasterize graphical primitives. These architectures are briefly discussed below.

The conventional approach to raster displays has been to implement a frame buffer (henceforth known as FB). This is a part of the main computer memory of a conventional Von Neumann computer where each pixel is assigned a unique address. If special microcode or special co-processors are used, one memory cycle time is required for each pixel access. This is the most widely used architecture, principally because of its low cost.

To take advantage of the fact that many displays do not require more than one bit per pixel, some architectures have grouped these pixels into "words" (of 16 bits each typically) of memory (henceforth known as 16FB). This allows 16 pixels to be accessed simultaneously. This scheme has typically been augmented by special hardware capable of filling the memory at

Table

Comparison of the Number of Memory Cycles Required by Six Rasterization Architectures to Image Various Shapes

Shape	FB	16FB	8by8	PperP	RECT	SLAM
Horizontal Line Length = 1024	1024	64	128	60	1	1
Horizontal Line Length = 128	128	8	16	60	1	1
Vertical Line Length = 1024	1024	1024	128	60	1	64
Vertical Line Length = 128	128	128	16	60	1	8
45 deg. Line Length = 1024	724	724	91	60	724	46
45 deg. Line Length = 128	91	91	12	60	91	6
Axis Aligned Square 1024 x 1024	1048576	65536	16384	80	1	64
Axis Aligned Square 128 x 128	16384	1024	256	80	1	8
45 degree Square 128 x 128	~16384	~1024	~256	80	182	12
45 degree Square 16 x 16	~256	~16	~4	80	24	2
128 edge Circle Approx. R = 64	~12868	~804	~202	2560	128	8
Equilateral Triangle Edge Length = 128	~7095	~443	~110	60	111	7
Character 16 x 8	128	8-16	2	?	~16	1
Character 32 x 16	512	32-48	8	?	~32	2
Character 32 x 64	2048	128-256	32	?	~64	8

NOTE: The PperP is the only processor which does not use bulk memory. Hence, the number of "memory cycles" is actually the number of cycles required by the serial pixel processors to image the given shape.

the full memory bandwidth either by stealing main processor memory cycles [TM 82] or by employing a separate bulk memory which is maintained by a simple processor capable of accessing any arbitrary 16 contiguous horizontal pixels in one cycle [BB 80]. This approach is up to 16 times faster than the FB when large areas are to be filled. However, the edges of primitives (e.g. polygons) typically do not fall on 16 pixel boundaries, hence memory accesses sometimes occur which do not alter all 16 bits. In fact, one pixel wide lines often require that only one pixel be modified for each 16 pixel block which the line intersects. In such cases, the 16FB is no faster than the FB.

In recognition of this bottleneck, some suggestions have been made to make the process of rasterization more parallel. Two approaches ([GS 81], [CH 80]) use an array of 8 by 8 conventional processors each connected to some bulk memory (henceforth known as 8by8). Each processor is responsible for every 64th pixel of the image and is connected to the memory representing those pixels. These processors are capable of executing special purpose instructions for filling their part of the memory. During each memory cycle, the 8by8 approach can access at most 64 pixels. As with the 16FB however, primitives which do not set large blocks of contiguous memory simultaneously (such as thin lines) do not achieve the full parallelism.

In order to decrease the rasterization time even more, architectures have been suggested which contain some significant amount of computation at each pixel (e.g. [FP 81]). These methods are commonly referred to as the "processor-per-pixel" approach (henceforth known as PperP). In principle, this architecture is clearly the fastest since any raster operation (e.g. filling polygons, drawing lines, placing fonts) can be accomplished in one cycle time if the processors are sufficiently complex. However, because a typical image of 1024 by 1024 pixels has more than one million pixels (and consequently one million processors), the processors and their interconnections have to be kept rather simple.

The architecture described in [FP 81] uses a simple serial processor at each pixel capable of isolating the pixels which fall within a convex polygon in 20 cycles for each edge of the polygon (independent of the total area of the polygon). Nevertheless, this requires much more circuitry per pixel than the FB, 16FB or the 8by8 because the latter methods take advantage of high density dynamic RAM to store the raster and because the processing elements are shared among many pixels.

In an effort to minimize the size of the per-pixel circuitry, [Wh 82] has suggested building a two dimensional array of memory elements. Any rectangular subset of these memory cells can be set or cleared in one cycle time by specifying the starting and ending X and Y values (referred to as the RECT architecture). Thus, the per-pixel circuitry is reduced to a memory cell with two select lines (one for X and one for Y). Nevertheless, this cell is significantly bigger than a conventional RAM bit cell. This architecture can image any rectangular area which is aligned with the axes in one cycle time. However, if it is expected that the polygons and lines will seldom be aligned on the axes (as is the case for arbitrarily rotated images, for example), the analysis in [Wh 82] indicates that this method is on the average only twice as fast as the traditional FB method for drawing lines, and the fastest method to rasterize arbitrary polygons using this architecture is to rasterize them one scan line at a time. Thus, the number of memory cycles required to rasterize any polygon is on the average equal to the number of scan lines which the polygon occupies. Furthermore, characters must be imaged by specifying a list of all rectangular areas needed to image that character. For a typical character, this will be equal to twice the number of scan lines which the character occupies (i.e. there are 2 black pixel runs per scan line in a typical character).

As the Table indicates, no architecture is clearly superior to the others for all of the graphical primitives listed. Of the previously known architectures, the PperP exhibits the best performance except for: (i) axis aligned rectangular areas (in that case, the RECT architecture is superior), and (ii) objects with many edges or with small areas (due to the fact that the PperP incurs a large fixed cost per edge).

The SLAM system exhibits performance comparable or superior to the best previously known architecture (the PperP) without having to abandon the area cost advantages of a bulk memory architecture. In fact, it is expected that the cost of a SLAM system will be close to that of the low cost FB architecture. Even though the total number of processors is much greater in the PperP, much of the potential parallelism is lost due to the serial nature of each of its processors and because most polygons cover less than 1% to 10% of the total number of pixels. Furthermore, the SLAM architecture is well suited for rasterizing all of the broad range of shapes in the Table, whereas the performance of the others degrades significantly for some shapes.

8 Adding Gouraud Shading Capability

At the expense of complicating the SLAM architecture somewhat, it is possible to add Gouraud [Go 71] smooth shading capability (Figure 13). Each pixel is stored as a K-bit intensity value "vertically" along a column of the memory array as shown. The proper X pixel subrange can be computed by the parallel comparator as before. But, because the pixels are stored vertically, at least K memory cycles are required to store intensities into the selected pixels.

In order to smooth shade a polygon it is necessary to place linearly interpolated intensity values at each pixel along a scan line. Fortunately, it is easy to generate a bit serial linear interpolation by using a binary tree similar to a serial multiplier [Li 76] [FP 81]. Each node of the tree (shown in Figure 14) is either a simple serial adder or a unit delay. As the coefficient A and the

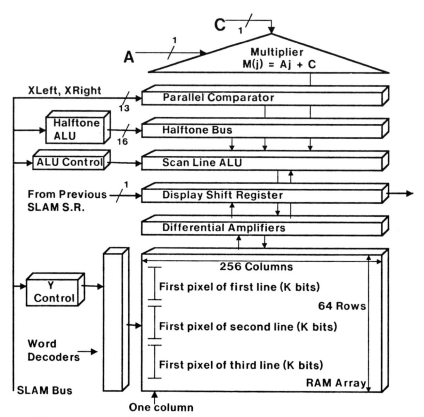

Figure 13 - SLAM With Smooth Shading

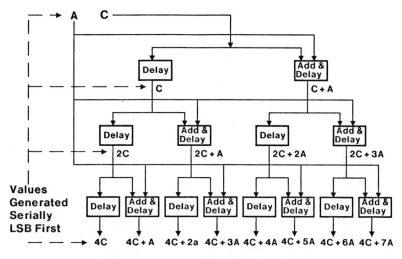

Figure 14 - Multiplier Tree

constant C are serially inserted into the tree (by the Scan Line Processor), each leaf node of the tree begins to generate one bit of the value Ax + constant, where x represents the physical position of the leaf in the tree as shown. If the intensities are to be accurate to within one intensity value, A must be represented as a fixed point number with a fractional part of size equal to the total number of bits required to represent the maximum X coordinate (called N) (e.g. if an 8 bit intensity is desired for a 1024 pixel wide screen, A must have 8 integer and 10 fractional bits).

As a result, each scan line of a smooth shaded polygon requires N + K processor cycles, of which only the last K store bits into the selected pixels. However, in order to represent a full K bits per pixel, one must now make a system with K times more processors (than for a one bit per pixel system) to hold the extra bits. These can all operate in parallel so the effective decrease in performance (with respect to a one bit per pixel system) is only (N + K) / K, which is about 2 if N and K are approximately equal. Thus, it only takes twice as long to fill a smooth shaded polygon as it does to fill a constant intensity polygon.

9 Effects of Increasing VLSI Density

The SLAM architecture is not only desirable for the present density achievable in VLSI but can be scaled up "gracefully" as VLSI densities increase. Furthermore, increasing the density of the design does not force degradation of performance due to communication constraints.

In fact, the design can be scaled in different ways depending on whether cost or performance optimization is desired: (i) the size of the memory array can be increased in both width and height (high density, low cost), (ii) the size of the memory array can be increased in width only (high parallelism, high speed), or (iii) the Scan Line Processor can be incorporated into the chip along with all the SLAMs which it controls (low chip count, low cost).

As memory sizes increase, larger and larger SLAM chips can be designed for little cost since the SLAM uses a conventional DRAM design with a small amount of special circuitry. Thus, SLAM chips of the future can benefit from the enormous amount of research aimed at increasing DRAM densities. Furthermore, SLAM chips can be manufactured using the same facilities as conventional DRAMs.

10 Continuing and Future Work

The SLAM chip shown in Figure 1 has been fabricated and tested successfully. Work is underway presently to incorporate the SLAM chips into a working graphics system to demonstrate the speed potential of the SLAM concept and to get experimental confirmation of the performance which has been projected for the design.

Future research related to the SLAM-based architecture will focus on methods of improving the design to include other desirable graphics features such as antialiasing, and hidden surface elimination. In principle any of the many well known curved and straight line scan line algorithms can be implemented in the Scan Line Processors. However, the challenge is to design these processors to generate a new scan line section every memory cycle time in order to take advantage of the parallelism made possible by the SLAM chips.

11 Conclusion

Low cost, high performance raster graphics requires the development of inexpensive yet highly parallel rasterization architectures. The Scan Line Access Memory (SLAM) architecture achieves these goals by placing the parallelism inside the image memory chips where it is inexpensive. Its high performance makes possible simple implementations of complex graphics functions such as multiple real-time overlapping windows. A prototype VLSI implementation has been fabricated and a complete system is being built. The SLAM architecture is capable of rasterizing many kinds of graphical primitives (both text and graphics) with uniformly good performance comparable to that of the fastest proposed architectures (i.e. the processor-per-pixel approaches) which cost many times more. Due to the high density storage of the image, the new architecture is much less expensive in integrated circuit area than other processors which exhibit similar performance. As a result, SLAM chips can replace conventional DRAMs in high performance yet inexpensive graphics systems of the future.

12 Acknowledgments

The author thanks Dr. Stephen Lundstrom, Dr. Manolis Katevenis, Dr. David Cheriton, Dr. Forest Baskett, Dr. James Clark and Mike Spreitzer for their suggestions and discussions regarding this work.

References

[BB 80]   Bechtolsheim, A.; Baskett, F.
High performance Raster Graphics for Microcomputer Systems.
In: *SIGGRAPH Conference Proceedings*, Seattle, July 1980.

[CH 80]   Clark, J. H.; Hannah, M. R.
Distributed Processing in a High-Performance Smart Image Memory.
In: *Lambda*, Vol I, No. 4, 1980, pages 40-45.

[CI 82]   Clark, James H.
The Geometry Engine: A VLSI Geometry System for Graphics.
In: *SIGGRAPH Conference Proceedings*, Boston, July 1982, pages 127-133.

[FP 81]   Fuchs, Henry; Poulton, John
           PIXEL-PLANES: A VLSI-Oriented Design for a Raster Graphics
           Engine.
           In: *Lambda*, Vol. II, No. 3, 1981, pages 20-28.

[Go 71]   Gouraud, H.
           Computer Display of Curved Surfaces.
           In: *University of Utah UTEC-CSc-71-113*, 1971.

[GS 81]   Gupta, Satish; Sproull, Robert F.; Sutherland, Ivan E.
           A VLSI Architecture for Updating Raster-Scan Displays.
           In: *SIGGRAPH Conference Proceedings*, Dallas, August 1981,
           pages 71-78.

[KL 80]   Kung, H. T.; Leiserson, Charles E.
           Algorithms for VLSI Processor Arrays.
           In: Mead, Carver; Conway, Lynn
           Introduction to VLSI Systems, Section 8.3.
           Addison-Wesley, 1980.

[Ly 76]   Lyon, Richard F.
           Two's Complement Pipeline Multipliers.
           In: IEEE Transactions on Communications, Vol. COM-24, April
           1976, pages 418-425.

[NS 79]   Newmann, W.; Sproull, R.F.
           Principles of Interactive Computer Graphics, second edition.
           McGraw Hill, 1979.

[TM 82]   Thacker, C. P.; McCreight, E. M.; Lampson, B. W.; Sproull, R. F.;
           Boggs, D. R.
           Alto: A Personal Computer.
           In: Siewiorek, D. P.; Bell, C. G.; Newell, A. eds
           Computer Structures: Principles and Examples, Chapter 33.
           McGraw Hill, 1982.

[Wh 82]   Whelan, Daniel S.
           A Rectangular Area Filling Display System Architecture.
           In: *SIGGRAPH Conference Proceedings*, Boston, July 1982, pages.
           147-153.

A Parallel Processor System for Three-Dimensional Color Graphics

Haruo Niimi
Dept. of Information Science
Kyoto University
Sakyo-ku, Kyoto, 606, Japan

Yoshirou Imai
Takuma Radio Technical College
Mitoyo-gun, Kagawa, 769-11, Japan

Masayoshi Murakami
Nippon Denshi Kagaku Co., Ltd.
Joyo-shi, Kyoto, 610-01, Japan

Shinji Tomita and *Hiroshi Hagiwara*
Dept. of Information Science
Kyoto University
Sakyo-ku, Kyoto, 606, Japan

Abstract

This paper describes the hardware architecture and the employed algorithm of a parallel processor system for three-dimensional color graphics. The design goal of the system is to generate realistic images of three-dimensional environments on a raster-scan video display in real-time. In order to achieve this goal, the system is constructed as a two-level hierarchical multi-processor system which is particularly suited to incorporate scan-line algorithm for hidden surface elimination. The system consists of several Scan-Line Processors (SLPs), each of which controls several slave PiXel Processors (PXPs). The SLP prepares the specific data structure relevant to each scan line, while the PXP manipulates every pixel data in its own territory. Internal hardware structures of the SLP and the PXP are quite different, being designed for their dedicated tasks.

This system architecture can easily execute scan-line algorithm in parallel by partitioning the entire image space and allotting one processor element to each partition. The specific partition scheme and some new data structures are introduced to exploit as much parallelism as possible. In addition, the scan-line algorithm is extended to include smooth-shading and anti-aliasing with the aim of rendering more realistic images. These two operations are performed on a per-scan-line basis so as to preserve scan-line and span coherence.

Performance estimation of the system shows that a typical system consisting of 8 SLPs and 8×8 PXPs can generate, in every 1/15th of a second, the shadowed image of a three-dimensional scene containing about 200 polygons.

CR Categories and Subject Descriptors: B.1.5 [Control Structures and Microprogramming]: Microcode Applications - Special-purpose; B.5.1 [Register-Transfer-Level Implementation]: Design - Data-path design; Memory design; C.1.2 [Processor Architectures]: Multiprocessors - Parallel processors; I.3.1 [Computer Graphics]: Hardware Architecture - Raster display devices; I.3.7 [Computer Graphics]: Three-Dimensional Graphics and Realism - Color, shading, and shadowing; Visible surface algorithm.

1. Introduction

Recent advances in LSI and video display technologies have brought remarkable changes in the computer graphics world. For instance, raster-scan graphic terminals have become widely used, with the display resolution growing higher and the graphical functions becoming richer and more powerful. At the same time, instead of the conventional wire-frame modeling, surface or solid modeling technique is more often adopted in various applications such as CAD/CAM or simulation of natural phenomena [8]. In these applications, especially in an interactive environment, rapid generation of a shaded image of the three-dimensional scene is essential for effective man-machine communication.

In order to make this feasible, it is necessary to reduce the time required for scan conversion. This speeding up can be attained by the use of a parallel and/or pipelined architecture as well as the proper adaptation of appropriate algorithm to the specific architecture.

Several multi-processor systems for high-speed image synthesis have been proposed [2][3][4][7]. Most of these proposals exploited parallelism offered by depth-buffer (z-buffer) algorithm. Since this algorithm is an integral collection of simple, granular processes performed on a per-pixel basis, it is fairly easy to adopt parallel processing. However, it is very difficult to embed in this algorithm, such calculations as anti-aliasing and shadowing, because these calculations require several values for pixels at a time and are history sensitive.

We are now designing an alternative to these systems: a high-speed parallel processor system for three-dimensional color graphics, called EXPERTS (an EXpandable Parallel processor Enhancing Real-Time Scan conversion). In the course of our design process, the following two major decisions were made.

First, scan-line algorithm is incorporated for the purpose of hidden surface removal, since
1) it is one of the most efficient hidden-surface algorithms over the domain of polyhedral models,
2) it can simply be extended to include techniques for achieving realism, such as smooth-shading or

@ SIGGRAPH'84

shadowing, and
3) it can be executed in parallel by partitioning the image space, so that the advantage of parallel processing can be exploited.

Second, the system is constructed as a two-level hierarchical multi-processor system. This is because scan-line algorithm can be divided into two distinct processing stages. The entire system is composed of several Scan-Line Processors (SLPs), each of which in turn controls several slave PiXel Processors (PXPs). The SLP prepares the specific data structure relevant to each scan-line, while the PXP manipulates every pixel data in its own territory. Internal hardware structures of the SLP and the PXP are quite different, being designed for their dedicated tasks. Hence, intra-level parallel processing as well as inter-level pipeline processing can be performed.

This system architecture is derived very naturally from deep investigation into scan-line algorithm and its parallel execution. The details of the system structure, the scan-line algorithm, and their relationship are described in chapter 2. Chapters 3 and 4 describe the processor architecture of the SLPs and the PXPs in detail, introducing their microinstruction formats and specific features.

The other hardware elements equipped to exploit parallelism are summarized in chapter 5. Chapter 6 suggests the strategy for dynamic load balancing among the processor elements, which is essential to make the best use of parallelism. System performance in the hypothetically typical cases is shown in chapter 7, using the number of relevant polygons and the depth complexity of the scene as parameters.

2. Scan-line Algorithm and the Processor Hierarchy of the EXPERTS

In generating images of three-dimensional environments, two kinds of processings must be executed:
(1) *Calculations executed prior to hidden-surface removal, e.g., coordinate transformations, polygon clipping, etc.* These processes take a substantial amount of time. However, since most of these operations are simple arithmetic loops, conventional hardware techniques such as pipelined array processors or matrix multipliers could work well. We have already developed a

dynamically microprogrammable computer with low-level parallelism, called QA-2[10]. Since the QA-2 employs four powerful ALUs which work in parallel, these geometrical calculations can be performed very efficiently.
(2) *Hidden-surface removal using scan-line algorithm (SLA).* This process requires sorting several list-structured data. Since sorting a list involves sequentially traversing the data-structure, it is hard to execute it in parallel. In addition, its computational complexity might grow according to a square-law. Thus, high-speed execution of SLA would require sophisticated techniques to make the best use of parallel and/or pipeline processing capability.

As a result of these considerations, we designed the EXPERTS to serve as a post-processor to the host machine. After geometrical computations, the host machine calculates a list of polygon data in the entire scene and transmits it to the EXPERTS. The EXPERTS receives the data and performs high-speed hidden-surface elimination (HSE) and some succeeding processes for enhancing realism.

In order to make the most use of parallel and pipeline processing capability of the hardware, we tried to divide the SLA into the following sub-tasks.

(I) Since SLA computes visible surfaces in a single scan line at a time and proceeds from the top scan line to the bottom, the entire image space can be divided into some bundles of scan lines where the algorithm is applicable independently of each other. This division means that, for each region, the display size is diminished in the vertical direction. Hence, no modification of the algorithm is required, and parallelism can be incorporated simply by allocating each bundle of scan lines to one of the processor elements.

(II) A process within one scan line can also be divided clearly into the following two successive processing stages, maintaining a data structure called Active Segment List (ASL) as the interfacing data between the two. The ASL is a linked list of active segments (intersections of polygons with a scan line – see Figure 1) which are sorted by the position of a segment's left edge.
[Stage-1]: This stage sets up an initial ASL for the first scan line at the top of the screen by reading a polygon list (PL) sent from the host machine. For each scan line in the rest of the display, this stage updates the previous ASL to make up the new ASL. Updating ASL involves deleting and appending segment data blocks from/to the list, calculating new positions of

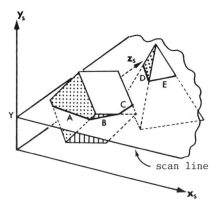

Figure 1(a). Polygons and a scan line in the screen coordinate system

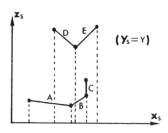

Figure 1(b). Active segments

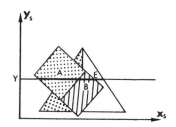

Figure 1(c). Segments: A, B, and E are visible.

191

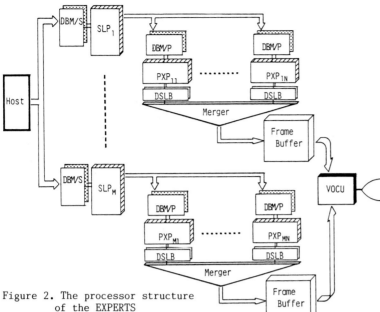

Figure 2. The processor structure
of the EXPERTS

DBM/S : Dual Buffer Memory for the SLP
DBM/P : Dual Buffer Memory for the PXP
DSLB : Dual Scan-Line Buffer
VOCU : Video Output Control Unit

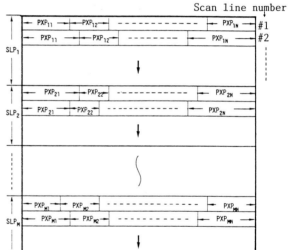

Figure 3.   Image space partitioning scheme

all segments in the list, and reordering the data blocks so as to keep the ASL correctly sorted. These computations may seem to be a serious burden. However, due to scan-line coherence [6], most of the computations are simple comparisons or additions using pre-computed edge slope values stored in each segment data block.

[Stage-2]: This stage, in turn, determines the set of visible segments in one scan line by exploring (or consuming) the ASL from the left to the right and identifying sample spans. Within each span, depth comparisons of segments are made to decide which segment is really visible, and then ultimate values of the pixels for the visible segments are calculated. If the identified visible segment is of a shadow polygon, it is treated as a transparent segment and the intensity of the next visible segment in the span is degraded. Techniques for rendering more realistic images such as smooth-shading or anti-aliasing are also applied to the calculation. To reduce these workloads, the algorithm also makes use of span coherence.

There is neither feed-back of data nor that of control from Stage-2 to Stage-1. Therefore, execution of Stage-2 might be completely overlapped in a pipelining manner with that of Stage-1, which is then processing the next scan line. Further, Stage-2 must be executed in parallel. This is because the computational amount involved in this stage is considerably larger than that in Stage-1. To keep a data stream in the pipeline smooth and regular, processing time taken by both stages must be balanced, or at least comparable.

These considerations are reflected in the processor structure of the EXPERTS, as shown in Figure 2; a multi-processor system having two levels of hierarchy. For convenience, the first (or higher) level processor element is called SLP (Scan Line Processor) and the second (or lower) level processor element is called PXP (PiXel Processor). The SLPs are prepared for Stage-1; performing initialization and updating of the

Active Segment List. The PXPs serve to execute hidden-surface elimination and anti-aliasing or smooth-shading in Stage-2. The resulting scheme of image space partitioning is depicted in Figure 3. The SLP and the PXP are designed to meet the requirements for high-speed processing of each dedicated task. The numbers of the SLPs ("M") and the PXPs ("N") need not be fixed, rather they can be so selected as to satisfy the performance requirement of the system. In our preliminary design, both are limited to 16 by hardware implementation constraints, but the value 16 is never crucial to the system design.

The Scan-Line Algorithm employed here is a novel one in that it introduces some new data structures to reduce the overhead which might appear in parallel processing. It should also be noted that the algorithm is extended to execute smooth-shading and anti-aliasing on a per-scan-line basis so as to preserve scan-line coherence and span coherence of the algorithm.

3. Processor Element: SLP (Scan Line Processor)

An SLP was particularly designed to enhance processing speed of ASL-initialization and ASL-updating processes, and transfers the results to its slave PXPs.

3.1 Hardware for ASL-initialization

ASL-initialization is only performed at the first of the scan lines allocated to the SLP. Suppose that a triangle *ABC* intersects the first scan line and will be registered in the ASL. Each vertex of the triangle is defined by a four-dimensional vector (three for screen coordinates and one for intensity), such that

$$A(X_a, Y_a, Z_a, I_a), B(X_b, Y_b, Z_b, I_b), \text{ and } C(X_c, Y_c, Z_c, I_c).$$

Using these vertex vectors, the ASL-initialization process calculates such coefficients as *dx/dy*, *dz/dy*, *dz/dx*, *di/dx*, etc. These coefficients will be maintained in the triangle *ABC*'s segment data block of the ASL and will be used in ASL-updating process as long as this triangle intersects the successive scan lines. A typical time-consuming computation appears in calculating *dz/dx*:

$$\frac{dz}{dx} = \frac{(Y_b-Y_c)(Z_a-Z_c)-(Y_a-Y_c)(Z_b-Z_c)}{(Y_b-Y_c)(X_a-X_c)-(Y_a-Y_c)(X_b-X_c)}.$$

Since every calculation is performed in the screen-coordinate system, 16-bit-wide data can offer sufficient precision. Only in division is floating-point arithmetic necessary to guarantee ample precision. To perform these computations at a high speed, the SLP employs a powerful functional unit (FU) as shown in Figure 4. It consists of
a) a 16-bit ALU (Arithmetic Logic Unit), using four AMD Am2903As,
b) a 16×16-bit multiplier, using an AMD Am29516,
c) a full adder attached to b) for calculating exponent parts of floating-point data,
d) an inverse approximation table for high-speed division,
e) data format converters between fixed-point and floating-point numbers, and
f) abundant register files.
In addition, interconnection buses among these components are designed to make their concurrent operations work efficiently.

3.2 Hardware for ASL-updating

ASL-updating is repeated until the allocated scan lines are exhausted. The total amount of computation will become large, but the inner computation is not so complicated as that of ASL-initialization. This is due to scan-line coherence. The problem here is rather how to access data blocks in an ASL efficiently and how to sort an ASL quickly.

Because access to a linked list is inherently sequential, the only way to speed up the process is to overlap the three operations: reading, modifying, and writing data. The SLP, therefore, is equipped with Scratch Pad Memory (SPM) for this purpose.

The SPM is composed of five logical banks of a high-speed, 32-word register file with autonomous memory access capability. As illustrated in Figure 4, the SPM is connected to five data buses; two memory buses (read and write buses) and three

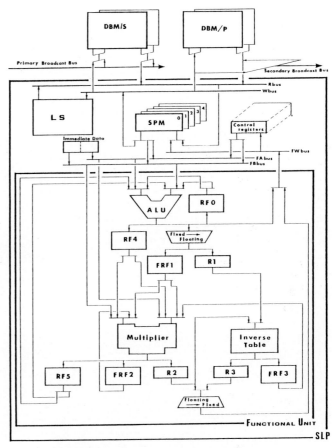

LS (Local Storage): 16bits × 64Kwords
SPM(Scratch Pad Memory): 16bits × 32words × 5
RF (Register File):
    RF0: 16bits × 16words
    RF4: 16bits × 16words
    RF5: 32bits × 16words
FRF(Floating point Register File):
    FRF1: 24bits × 16words
    FRF2: 24bits × 8words
    FRF3: 24bits × 8words
R-bus, W-bus: 16bits
FA-bus, FB-bus, FW-bus: 16bits

Figure 4. Hardware structure of the SLP

Functional-Unit buses (right source, left source and destination buses). All of the five banks can work simultaneously, and arbitrary one-to-one interconnection between banks and buses is possible. Data transfer between SPM and memory is carried out by hardware, so a program only signals its invocation specifying a transfer word count. The following operation, for instance, can be executed simultaneously:

    While a completed data block in the bank-0 SPM (SPM0) is being stored into the memory, calculation using operands fetched from the SPM1 and SPM2 can proceed with its result being written to the SPM3, and at the same time, the next data block is being loaded into the SPM4.

Each access to the SPM is to be done through its logical bank number. For the programmers' convenience, the correspondence between the logical bank numbers and the physical bank numbers can be instantly changed under program control.

193

Therefore, by successively exchanging the role of each bank of the SPM, sequential processing of list structured data, such as ASL-updating, can be executed effectively on the SLP. In fact, since memory accesses are performed autonomously by hardware and asynchronously with Functional-Unit operations, the time required for loading and storing data blocks can be thoroughly overlapped by the time for data modification process.

There are other facilities equipped for list processing: auxiliary MARs (Memory Address Registers) and a trap mechanism for illegal memory access. The auxiliary MAR is located at address 0 of each SPM bank (thus there are five, in total), and its contents are modified whenever the data is transferred from memory to that SPM bank. They are functionally equivalent to other ordinary MARs, but can be forced to hold a pointer value to the next data block in the list as long as data blocks are so designed. If a certain MAR contains "nil" and memory access using this MAR is signaled, the trap mechanism will be invoked. Through this hardware mechanism, successive traversal of a list structure can be initiated by a program without worrying about illegal memory access.

The SLP also contains various control registers, which are used for residual control, for saving system conditions or constants, and for other specific purposes. These include MARs and interrupt vector registers. The control registers are allocated in the address space of the SPM, hence they can be equally accessed from the Functional-Unit.

The SLP is designed as a microprogrammable computer. As shown in Figure 5, various hardware components are concurrently controlled by the different fields of a 101-bit wide microinstruction. The cycle time of the microinstruction is 200 nano seconds, using an AMD Am2910 for controlling the execution sequence of microinstructions.

4. Processor Element: PXP (PiXel Processor)

A PXP takes an Active Segment List (ASL) as input from its master SLP, and performs hidden-surface elimination (HSE). When a visible segment is identified, the span is determined in which pixels are filled with some values. Then the PXP calculates color and intensity value of each pixel in the span. Smooth-shading technique and anti-aliasing technique are applied to each pixel within the span and at the boundaries of the span, respectively. Finally the PXP transfers resulting color and intensity values to an image memory.

4.1 Hardware for Accessing List-structured Data

As in the case of SLP, the PXP needs to make frequent accesses to list-structured data. So, many features of the PXP hardware organization are the same as those of the SLP (see Figure 6). The SPM (Scratch Pad Memory) is analogous to that of the SLP, composed of high-speed, 32-word register files. But the number of logical banks is reduced to 4, as that is sufficient in this case. On the other hand, two words of auxiliary MARs are prepared in each bank of the SPM, because there is a substantial amount of processing performed over doubly-linked list structered data. The trap mechanism for nil-pointer access is also incorporated.

4.2 Hardware for Clipping

As already mentioned, each PXP is responsible for only a part of the entire scan line. As an ASL transferred from the SLP contains all active segments, the PXP must first perform clipping of the ASL. Notice here, that this clipping is done only at the left boundary of the allotted range of pixels. The end of the process can be recognized when the calculation of pixel values has reached the right most pixel, hence there is no need for a priori clipping for the right boundary. Since this clipping involves many multiplications, the PXP has a fixed-point hardware multiplier. The PXP does not support floating-point arithmetic, because every calculation is carried out in a screen coordinate system with at most 12-bits precision, and no division other than those by 2 is required.

4.3 Hardware for Smooth-shading

A smooth-shading technique employed here is based on the technique proposed by Gouraud [5]:

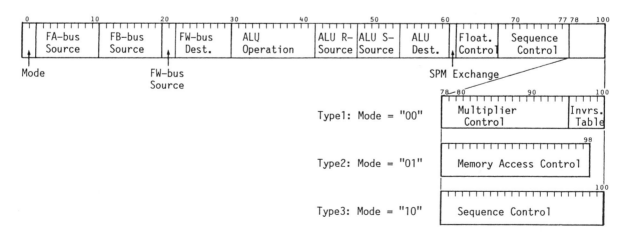

Figure 5. The microinstruction format of the SLP

linear interpolation of intensity values. Suppose that a segment *PQ* is identified as being visible, and, hence, the intensities at every pixel between the left edge *P* and the right edge *Q* must be computed. Let the intensity at *P* be *Ip* and the intensity at *Q* be *Iq*. Then intensity of every pixel between *P* and *Q* can be expressed by a linear combination of *Ip* and *Iq*, with the sum of their coefficients equal to 1. Notice that the differential coefficient of intensity, *di/dx*, has already been computed by the SLP, and is held in the segment block with the intensity *Ip*. Therefore, the calculation of smooth-shading is simplified to an incremental addition of the constant *di/dx*. Because this computation is trivial, it would be too wasteful for the ALU to be engaged in it.

As shown in Figure 6, S.S.Special is prepared for this computation. It is composed of a full-adder, a counter and some registers, and is able to operate concurrently with the ALU. Each of the registers plays a unique role in the course of computation. After values of the initial intensity "*Ip*", the constant "*di/dx*", and the length of the segment "*PQ*" are set to these registers and the counter, the S.S.Special can start calculating. The computation proceeds one pixel after another autonomously with the counter value being decremented. When the counter value gets equal to 0, the S.S.Special stops and a flag is set to indicate termination of smooth-shading.

4.4 Hardware for Anti-aliasing

An anti-aliasing technique employed here is unique among those proposed in many systems [1]. Since the PXP performs Hidden-Surface Elimination (HSE) scan-line by scan-line, computation for anti-aliasing must also be completed within the extent of one scan line. Aliases may occur only at the boundaries of polygons (i.e., at the edge), where visible segments are changing from the left to the right in the course of HSE. And if the pixel value at the boundary is determined from these values of left and right visible segments alternatively, alias will inevitably appear. Instead of selecting only one of the two pixel values of neighboring visible segments, a technique used here calculates a new value from the two by using the following formula;

Let *C1* and *Cr* be pixel-values of the left segment and the right segment respectively. Then the pixel value of the boundary pixel can be calculated as:

$$C = \alpha \cdot C1 + (1-\alpha) \cdot Cr,$$

where the coefficient α takes a value between 0 and 1.

Since both *C1* and *Cr* are calculated by the Scan-Line Algorithm and the succeeding smooth-shading process, the only problem is how to decide the value of α. Ideally, using the value of the area occupied by the left segment in the boundary pixel is supposed to be the most exact solution (see Figure 7a:"A"). However, it requires a considerable amount of computation. Our solution is to use the fractional part of a coordinate value of the boundary edge position, as illustrated in Figure 7b:"d". Note that, the calculation must be

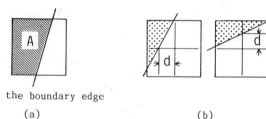

the boundary edge

(a)   (b)

Figure 7. Calculation of the anti-aliasing coefficient: α

Figure 6. Hardware structure of the PXP

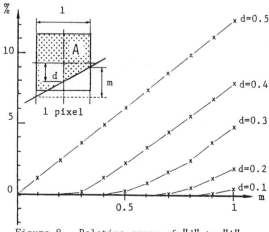

Figure 8. Relative error of "d" to "A"

altered according to whether the gradient of the boundary edge is larger than 45° or not.

This solution is fairly simple, because all of the necessary values have already been obtained in the segment data blocks and used by the Scan-Line Algorithm. Figure 8 shows that this is not a bad approximation. The problem is to minimize computational overhead in executing the above formula. Since each pixel value of $C1$ and Cr is expressed as a 4 dimensional vector (Red, Green, Blue, and Intensity), the calculation must be carried out four times.

A.A.Special in Figure 6 is specially designed for these computations. This component is in fact a set of look-up tables. Let's see the case of calculating a value for Red, for instance. After the values $C1:(R1,G1,B1,I1)$, $Cr:(Rr,Gr,Br,Ir)$, and α are all set to the specific registers, the A.A.Special concatenates $R1$, Rr, and α together (3, 3, 6 bits for each, and altogether 12 bits), and feeds it into the look-up table as an address. Then the result R will be put out from the table. The same process is also applied to the cases of Green and Blue. Only for the case of Intensity, is computation carried out through the ALU, because the number of bits assigned for the Intensity is too large (7 bits) to construct a look-up table (7, 7, 6 bits for each, hence altogether 20 bits!).

The PXP is also a microprogrammable processor controlled by a microinstruction of 88-bit wide. The cycle time for a microinstruction is 200 nsec. The microinstruction format of the PXP is presented in Figure 9.

5.   Hardware Facilities for Inter-processor Communication

As already mentioned, the EXPERTS employs a two-level hierarchical multi-processor architecture, incorporating pipeline processing and parallel processing. In order to make these processor elements co-operate smoothly, the following hardware components are installed around the processor elements (see Figure 2,4,6):

5.1 The Dual Buffer Memory for the SLP (DBM/S) and for the PXP (DBM/P).

The DBM/S is installed in each SLP and is used as a data buffer of the Polygon List (PL) transmitted from the host machine to the SLP. In

order to overlap the PL generation process of the host machine with the PL reading process of the SLP, the DBM/S is composed of two identical memory planes (we call these as plane-A and plane-B). While the host machine is putting out the PL to the plane-A(-B), the SLP can simultaneously make read-accesses to the plane-B(-A). Thus, the DBM/S is working as a FIFO queue of length 2. Although there are several DBM/Ss against a single host machine, all the DBM/Ss are allocated in the same position in the memory address space of the host machine. This is because the transmission of the PL is done in a broadcasting manner. From the SLP's view, in turn, the DBM/S is merely a local storage that can be freely read from or written to.

The DBM/P is identical to the DBM/S in its construction as well as in its function, except that the DBM/P is installed in each PXP and that it is used for the broadcasting of the Active Segment List (ASL) from the master SLP to the PXPs.

5.2 The Dual Scan-Line Buffer (DSLB) and the Merger.

Remember that several PXPs are connected to a single master SLP, and that they calculate pixel values in a certain scan-line simultaneously. Therefore, an access conflict problem of the image memory will arise among the PXPs. To solve this problem, the DSLB and the Merger were introduced.

The DSLB is a high-speed, pixel data cache for one scan-line which is equipped in each PXP, and is composed of two identical memories (the DSLB-A and the DSLB-B), one to be read from by the Merger and the other to be written to by the PXP.

The Merger is equipped in each SLP, and is directly connected to all the DSLBs of the slave PXPs.

Each PXP outputs the allotted extent of pixel values to its own DSLB. After all the PXPs finish their computations in a scan line, the roles of the DSLB-A and the DSLB-B are interchanged by the direction of the master SLP. Then, the Merger collects the latest output data scattered among the DSLBs, merges them correctly into an entire scan-line, and finally transfers them to the Frame Buffer.

The combination of the DSLBs and the Merger unit enables the PXP-level parallel processing to work more efficiently, since the memory access speed is enhanced through the high-speed memories in the DSLB and there will be no overhead caused due to memory contention.

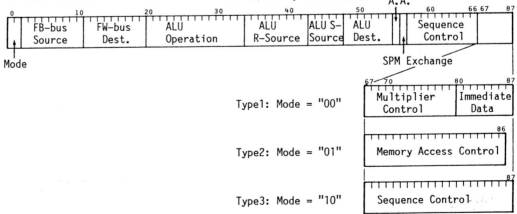

Figure 9. The microinstruction format of the PXP

5.3 Distributed Frame Buffers (FBs) and the Video Output Control Unit (VOCU).

As in the case of the PXP-level parallel processing, there will be an access conflict problem of the Frame Buffer among the SLPs, more precisely among the Mergers. However, note that the FB need not be constructed as a single, contiguous plane of memory, since only one scan-line of pixels should be prepared at a time for the raster-scan display. Here, we can bring in the remedy which is analogous to the DSLB and the Merger, i.e., distributed data placement and their regulated collection by hardware.

The entire screen of the FB is divided into some bundles of scan-lines and these bundles are distributed to each of the SLPs. At the same time, the autonomous hardware unit, the Video Output Control Unit (VOCU), is prepared for the data collection. Each distributed FB is a dual-plane memory, which enables the simultaneous operation of the Merger's data storing and the VOCU's data reading. Since each FB is accessed only by one SLP or by the VOCU, there will be no FB memory contention. Due to these hardware facilities, the SLP-level parallel processing is also enhanced.

6. Load Balancing Problem

In a parallel processing environment on a multi-processor system, it is ideal to distribute the total system workload equally among all the processor elements. However, in the case of the EXPERTS, it is very difficult or almost impossible to do such an ideal scheduling prior to the actual execution. This is because the total processing workload in the system does not simply depend on the number of input polygons, but deeply depends on the complexity of the geometrical relations between the polygons. Hence, some kind of feed-back control must be employed in controlling the load balance in order to tune the system activity and to attain higher performance.

Similarly, in a pipeline processing environment, the maximum pipeline processing effect is gained when every processing stage in the pipe completes its computation in an identical time. In the case of the EXPERTS, the processing time should be balanced among these three stages: i.e., the host machine, the SLPs, and the PXPs. However, if the number of the SLPs and the PXPs are not appropriately selected for the problem size of the application, this balancing cannot be controlled effectively by the processor elements themselves.

Therefore, it might be reasonable for the programs of the processor elements to assume that the system is appropriately configured for the given application.

Then, for example, if none of the slave PXPs has finished their computation when the master SLP terminates, any attempt of the SLP to balance the PXPs' workloads would have no effect upon the performance improvement of the entire system. On the contrary, if all the slave PXPs have finished their computations before their master SLP terminates its own computation, the SLP would not need to invoke the process to control the load balance among the PXPs.

Consequently, the following strategy for dynamic load balancing is planned to be applied to the EXPERTS. Here, we only present the case which

will be executed on the SLP in order to manage the workload distribution among its slave PXPs. The analogous procedure will be executed on the host machine in turn, to manage the SLPs.

Step-1) Until the SLP completes its own process, the SLP only receives the completion signals from the PXPs;

Step-2) When the SLP terminates, it counts the number of completed PXPs [Ncp];

Step-3) If the Ncp is less than $N/2$ (where N is the number of the PXPs connected to the master SLP) then the SLP waits idly until $N/2$ of the PXPs terminate;

Step-4) The SLP identifies the PXPs which have not yet terminated, and squeezes their allotted extent by a constant number of pixels, the sum of which, in turn, are distributed to the rest of the PXPs.

7. System Performance Estimation

The two types of processor elements of the EXPERTS: the Scan-Line Processor (SLP) and the PiXel Processor (PXP), are both microprogrammable processors, and all the programs are directly written in microcode.

Table 1 summarizes the size of the microprograms coded for various processing stages in the SLP and in the PXP. Due to the powerful hardware facilities and the optimal design of the microinstruction formats, the program sizes are small enough and the effective usage ratios of the various control fields of the microinstruction indicate high values.

The performance estimation of the EXPERTS has been carried out based on the results of the flow analysis applied to these microprograms. Each microprogram was analyzed into such components as straight paths, loops, and branches. Then, the number of microinstruction steps for every path and loop was calculated. And the success probabilities of the branch conditions were approximated. These data were collected and used in the calculation of the executed microinstruction steps.

We chose the parameters of performance estimation similar to those used in [9]; namely the number of relevant polygons:"Nr", the number of shadow polygons:"Ns", the depth complexity of polygons:"DCr", and the depth complexity of the shadow polygons:"DCs". For the accurate and precise definitions of these, see [9].

In addition, we assumed that the average number of the edges of a polygon is 4, and that the resolution of the display is 512×512.

As a result, we have obtained the following expressions which calculate necessary micro-steps executed. Note that they are the values obtained for the best case when the workload is completely balanced among all the processor elements.

1a) Initialization of the Active Segment List on the SLP:

$$(15+30 \cdot Nr+28 \cdot Ns) + (73 \cdot Nr+61 \cdot Ns)/M$$
$$\text{[micro-steps]},$$

where "M" is the number of the SLPs in the system.

1b) Updating the ASL on the SLP:

$$((1044 \cdot N+18065) \cdot S + 11.3 \cdot (Nr+Ns) + 22528)/M$$
$$\text{[micro-steps]},$$

where "N" is the number of the PXPs

Table 1. The size of the microprograms

(a) Initialization of the ASL on the SLP

	Size [micro-steps]				Type1: Field usage [micro-steps]				
	Type1	Type2	Type3	Total	ALU	MPY	INV	Fixed→Float	Float→Fixed
Initialization	11	4	0	15	11	0	0	0	0
Generation of Real Polygon Blocks	27	5	4	36	28	13	2	5	3
Generation of Real Edge Blocks	171	54	28	253	195	81	12	21	21
Generation of Shadow Polygon Blocks	14	5	2	21	16	5	1	2	1
Generation of Shadow Edge Blocks	52	8	16	76	60	26	4	6	6
Total	275 (68.5%)	76 (19.0%)	50 (12.5%)	401	310 (77.3%)	125 (45.5%)	19 (6.9%)	34 (12.4%)	31 (11.3%)

(b) Updating of the ASL on the SLP

	Size [micro-steps]				Type1: Field usage [micro-steps]				
	Type1	Type2	Type3	Total	ALU	MPY	INV	Fixed→Float	Float→Fixed
Deletion of Out-going Edges	1	3	5	9	4	0	0	0	0
Handling of In-coming Edges	44	40	40	124	89	0	0	0	0
Updating of Segment Lists	52	35	35	122	73	2	0	0	0
Dynamic Load Balancing	84	2	110	196	114	32	0	0	0
Total	181 (40.1%)	80 (17.7%)	190 (42.1%)	451	280 (62.1%)	34 (18.8%)	0 (0.0%)	0 (0.0%)	0 (0.0%)

(c) Calculation of pixel data on the PXP

	Size [micro-steps]				Type1: Field usage		
	Type1	Type2	Type3	Total	ALU	MPY	A.A.
Initial Clipping	42	26	27	95	59	0	0
Determination of Visible Segment	35	30	57	122	86	1	0
Handling of Penetrating Segments	75	42	70	187	136	3	0
Handling of Non-penetrating Segments	98	89	75	262	205	12	0
Anti-aliasing	41	2	18	61	51	8	2
Total	291 (40.1%)	189 (17.7%)	247 (42.1%)	727	537 (73.9%)	24 (8.2%)	2 (0.3%)

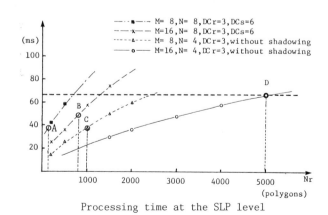

Processing time at the SLP level

Processing time at the PXP level

Figure 10. Estimated processing time

SIGGRAPH'84

connected to one SLP, and "S" is the number of relevant segments in a scan-line, such that

$$S = SQRT(DCr \cdot Nr) + SQRT(DCs \cdot Ns).$$

2) Typical case of the processing on the PXP:

$$(512/M) \cdot (80 + (2944 + S \cdot (100 + 21.6 \cdot DCt + \log_2(256/S) \cdot (6.5 + 6 \cdot DCt)))/N)$$
[micro-steps],

where "DCt" is the average number of the total depth complexity at the sample point, defined as

$$DCt = 2 \cdot (DCr + DCs).$$

The fraction coefficients appeared above are derived from the probability estimations attributed to the branch alternatives.

Using the expressions above, the system performance is estimated in various system configurations. Each graph in Figure 10 represents the respective cases when the relations between the parameters are varied or when some specific values of the parameters are used.

Figure 10 shows that, for example, the system configured with 8 SLPs and 8×8 PXPs will be able to generate the shadowed image of the three-dimensional scene which contains about 200 polygons, every 1/15th of a second (point "A" in the graph).

8. Concluding Remarks

We have described the design of a parallel processor system for three-dimensional color graphics, called EXPERTS. The EXPERTS employs a two-level hierarchical multi-processor architecture, which is suited to perform scan-line algorithm in high-speed. Two types of processor elements, called the SLP and the PXP, are newly designed. These processor elements are powerful, microprogrammable element equipped with many special facilities optimized to graphic applications, and supporting anti-aliasing and smooth-shading.

We are currently constructing a prototype of the EXPERTS, installing two SLPs and four PXPs, with two PXPs connected to one SLP. Although this is the minimum configuration capable of parallel and pipeline processing, every hardware function will be successfully tested on this prototype.

Each SLP is made of about 2,000 pieces of MSI and SSI ICs, and each PXP is made of about 1,100 pieces of MSI and SSI ICs.

The design of the EXPERTS enables 16 SLPs to be connected to each other and 16 PXPs to be connected to each SLP. So, the maximum configuration contains 16 SLPs plus 256 PXPs, in total 272 processor elements, constituting a huge multi-processor system.

Any intermediate scale of configuration is possible, that is, any SLP-PXP ratio will do. Hence, the system user will be able to choose the most cost-effective configuration. In addition, if any processor element gets out of order, the entire system can be restored to work well simply by disconnecting that processor element and with no serious influence on other components. So, the MTTR (Mean Time To Repair) of the EXPERTS is very short, and the system reliability as well as availability is greatly enhanced.

Acknowledgements

The authors wish to thank Yasuko Sakamoto for proposing the parallel scan-line algorithm employed in the EXPERTS, Takashi Fukunishi for writing microprograms of the SLP and the PXP, and Kouji Ohtani for designing the logic circuits of the SLP. We also thank Takayasu Obata, Kouichi Takeuchi and Yukihiro Kawaguchi for their enthusiastic cooperation to this project. Toshiyuki Nakata gave us a number of valuable comments on the earlier version of this paper.

This work is supported mainly by the Ministry of Education in Japan, Grant in Aid for Scientific Research (58850069), and in part by Wireless Research Laboratory of Matsushita Electric Industrial Co., Ltd.

References

[1] Crow, F.C.: "A Comparison of Anti-Aliasing Techniques," IEEE Computer Graphics and applications, Vol.1, No.1 (Jan. 1981), pp.40-48.

[2] Kaplan, M., and Greenberg, D.P.: "Parallel Processing Technique for Hidden Surface Removal," ACM Computer Graphics, Vol.13, No.2 (Aug. 1979), pp.300-307.

[3] Fiume, E., Fournier, A., and Rudolph, L.: "A Parallel Scan Conversion Algorithm with Anti-Aliasing for a General-Purpose Ultracomputer," ACM Computer Graphics, Vol.17, No.3 (Jul. 1983), pp.141-150.

[4] Fuchs, H., and Johnson, B.W.: "An Expandable Multiprocessor Architecture for Video Graphics(Preliminary Report)," IEEE 6th Conf. on Computer Architecture (1979), pp.58-67.

[5] Gouraud, H.: "Continuous Shading of Curved Surfaces," IEEE Trans. on Computers, Vol.C-20, No.6 (Jun. 1971), pp.623-629.

[6] Newmann, W.M., and Sproull, R.F.: "Principles of Interactive Computer Graphics," 2nd Ed. McGraw-Hill, 1979.

[7] Parke, F.I.: "Simulation and Expected Performance Analysis of Multiple Processor Z-Buffer Systems," ACM Computer Graphics (Jul. 1980), pp.48-56.

[8] Schachter, B.J. (Ed.): "Computer Image Generation," Wiley-Interscience, New York, 1983.

[9] Sutherland, I. E., Sproull, R. F., and Schumacker, R.A.: "A Characterization of Ten Hidden-Surface Algorithms," ACM Computing Surveys (Mar. 1974), pp.1-55.

[10] Tomita, S., Shibayama, K., Kitamura, T., Nakata, T., and Hagiwara, H.: "A User-microprogrammable, Local Host Computer with Low-level Parallelism," Proc. 10th Annu. Int'l Symp. on Computer Architecture (Jun. 1983), pp.151-157.

PIXEL-PLANES: Building a VLSI-Based Graphic System

John Poulton, Henry Fuchs, John D. Austin, John G. Eyles, Justin Heinecke, Cheng-Hong Hsieh, Jack Goldfeather, Jeff P. Hultquist, Susan Spach

Department of Computer Science
University of North Carolina at Chapel Hill

1. Introduction

Pixel-planes is a VLSI-based raster graphics machine that will support real-time interaction with three-dimensional shadowed, shaded, and colored images. The system's cost and complexity will be comparable to present-day line drawing systems, making it suitable for use with high-performance workstations. Potential applications include computer-aided design, medical display and imaging, molecular modeling, and simulators for flight and navigational training.

The fundamental ideas in this design have been previously published [Fuchs and Poulton, 1981; Fuchs *et al.*, 1982]. This paper reports recent progress toward building a full-scale working *Pixel-planes* system, development of a number of new graphics algorithms for the machine, and refinements in system architecture and design methods.

Much of current research in experimental graphics systems is aimed at improving the speed of image generation by dividing the display into small regions, each of which is handled by separate concurrent processors [Clark and Hannah, 1980; Gupta *et al.*, 1981; Demetrescu, 1985]. In *Pixel-planes*, this division is imbedded in a binary tree that performs the bulk of the system's computations and distributes the results to all pixels. Each pixel consists of an array of memory elements and a small processor that only performs operations local to the pixel. The heart of the system is a Smart Frame Buffer consisting of an array of identical custom chips that contain the binary tree, pixel memories and processors, and video

---

* This research supported in part by the Defense Advance Research Project Agency Contract number DAAG29-83-K-0148 (monitored by U.S. Army Research Office, Research Triangle Park, NC) and the National Science Foundation Grant number ECS-8300970.

** Department of Mathematics, Carleton College, Northfield, MN, on sabbatical at Department of Mathematics at the University of North Carolina.

scan-refresh circuitry. These enhanced memory chips employ a moderately dense, conventional dynamic RAM that takes up about 2/3 of the chip's silicon area; the processing circuitry takes up the remaining 1/3.

The fundamental operation of the *Pixel-planes* system is calculating linear expressions of the form $Ax + By + C$ where x and y are the coordinates of a pixel and A, B, and C are data inputs to the system. These expressions are calculated bit-serially in a binary tree multiplier/accumulator, simultaneously for all pixels. The system's hardware is not built to execute a specific set of graphics algorithms. Instead, many different algorithms can be recast into forms that evaluate linear expressions and/or require only pixel-local operations. We are continually surprised at the variety of algorithms that we and others are able to express in this form, and it is clear that the architecture is much more powerful and more general than we had first imagined.

2. Pixel-Planes Graphics System

2.1 System Overview

Figure 1 shows the relationship between the *Pixel-planes* graphics system hardware and a conventional color graphics system.

The 'front end' of the conventional graphics system is a pipeline of special processors that manipulates an image database. The database contains (typically) a list of polygons that tile the surfaces of the objects in a scene. Each polygon is described as a list of vertex coordinates (x, y, z in 'world' coordinates) and colors (values of *Red, Green, Blue* that specify the intrinsic color of the vertex). A transformation engine operates on the coordinates of the vertex list for each polygon, transforming the polygon to 'eye' coordinates in response to user input from joystick, trackball, or some similar device. Next, polygons (or portions of polygons) that are outside the viewing pyramid are clipped and perspective division is performed to transform 'eye' coordinates to 'screen' coordinates. Finally, a lighting model calculator modifies each vertex's intrinsic color according to the position and intensity of light sources. The output of the front-end pipeline is still a list of polygon vertices, but with vertex coordinates and colors transformed to the proper value for display.

In advanced color graphics systems, the rasterizer performs a series of steps needed to translate a list of polygon vertices into a smooth-shaded, rendered, digital image, with hidden surfaces properly removed, and perhaps anti-aliased to reduce pixelization artifacts. In general, these calculations must be performed for every pixel for every polygon processed, implying massive amounts of computation and very large memory bandwidth.

The *Pixel-planes* Graphics Engine replaces the rasterizer, frame buffer, and video controller of a conventional system. Its main component is a Smart Frame Buffer composed of custom VLSI enhanced memory chips. It addresses the computational problem with a highly parallel processor that mimics a processor per pixel. The memory bandwidth bottleneck is overcome by intimately connecting processing circuitry and memory.

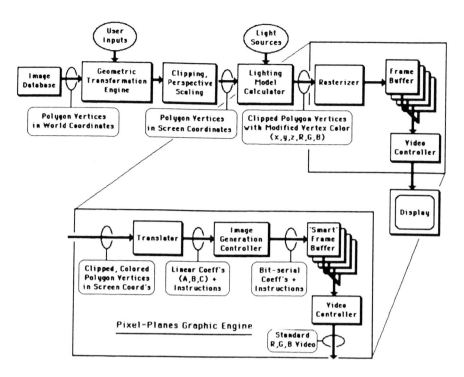

Figure 1: Pixel-Planes Graphics Engine replaces the rasterizer, frame buffer, and video controller in a conventional graphics system.

2.2 Pixel-Planes Graphics Engine

The components of the Engine are:

The Translator, a special purpose micro-programmable floating-point computer, converts the scene description from a polygon vertex list into the form of coefficients A, B, C of the linear expression $F(x,y) = Ax + By + C$. It also produces an encoded instruction for each step in processing polygons or other primitives (*e.g.*, edge, z-compare, circle, paint-Red). Translation will involve, for example, describing an edge of a polygon in the form $F(x,y) = 0$, or specifying the polygon's planar surface in the form $z = F(x,y)$. In the system now under construction, the Translator is a 5 MFlop micro-programmable engine based on the Weitek 1032/1033 floating-point chip set.

The Image Generation Controller (IGC) converts the word-parallel, floating-point A, B, C coefficients from the Translator to bit-serial, 2's complement data, decodes each instruction into a stream of control words, and outputs this data and control along with the clock for the Smart Frame Buffer. Currently, the IGC is implemented as a custom chip that serializes the coefficient data and a micro-programmable control sequencer built using standard TTL parts.

The Smart Frame Buffer is organized as a series of 'logical boards', each with an array of enhanced memory chips, as shown in Figure 2. This organization reduces the bandwidth (pin-count, operating speed) necessary at the memory chip's video-data output port. Each logical board contains a 32-bit-wide register for video data, and successive logical boards are daisy-chained together to form a high-speed shift-train. Every *L* cycles (where *L* is the number of logical boards), shifting is disabled and the shift-train is loaded from a parallel set of registers on each board. While shifting is enabled, these parallel registers are loaded, one byte at a time, from selected memory chips.

Data, control, and clocks both for image generation and video output are broadcast to the enhanced memory chips. No data or control need be returned from the memories to the IGC or Video Controller, so the busses can easily be pipelined for high-speed operation.

In addition to these two uni-directional busses, a single serial scan-path links all memory chips in the frame buffer. During system

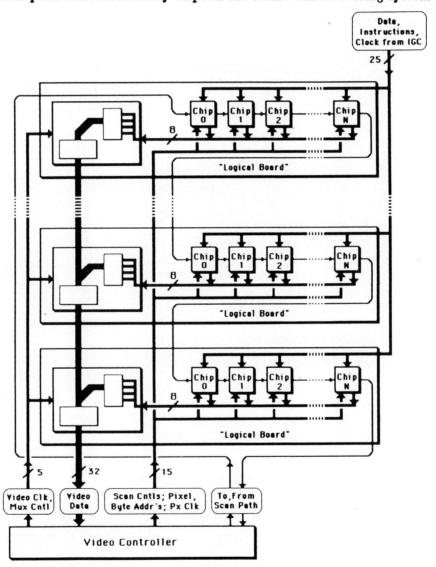

Figure 2: Pixel-Planes Smart Frame Buffer organisation.

operation, the scan-path takes the place of chip-address decoding, carrying a series of scan tokens that determine which set of memory chips is enabled for video output (only one chip on each logical board is enabled at one time). During system initialization, the scan-path is used to load various configuration registers, as discussed in Section 2.3.

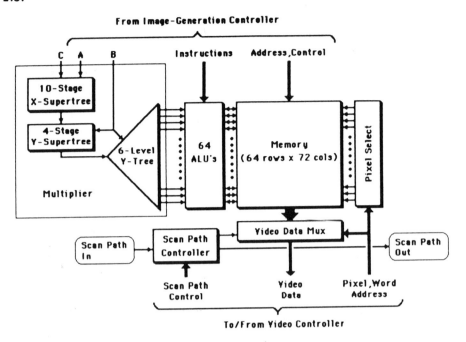

Figure 3: Block diagram of the Pixel-Planes memory chip.

The Video Controller is similar to those in conventional systems, with the exception of the token-passing method of addressing. The current version is capable of supporting a variety of display types (30 and 60 Hz, interlaced and non-interlaced, NTSC and non-standard) and any number of enhanced memory chips.

2.3 Enhanced Memory Chips

Figure 3 is a block diagram of the enhanced memory chip. It contains the Multiplier that implements the binary-tree linear-expression evaluator, an array of pixel ALU's, and a Memory system that stores data for each pixel and provides a video scan-out mechanism.

A conceptual model of a binary-tree multiplier/accumulator is shown in Figure 4. This structure is recognizable as a variation on the simple serial-parallel multiplier [Lyon, 1976], where both possible values of partial product are generated at each stage. If such a tree has N levels, and A contains K significant bits, A must be preceded by $(N-1)$ 0's; 2^N distinct values of $Ax + C$ will be generated $(0 <= x < 2^N)$, each value being $N + K + 1$ bits long.

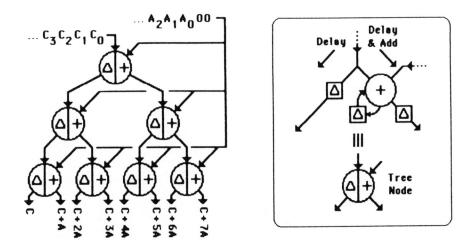

Figure 4: Conceptual model of binary-tree linear expression evaluator.

To generate the linear expression $Ax + By + C$, two binary-tree multiplier/accumulators are stacked one atop the other. For a system with 1024 x 1024 pixels, a 20-level tree is required. The top 10 levels of the tree calculate the 1024 values of $Ax + C$. The bottom 10 levels can be thought of as 1024 subtrees, each of which receives one value of $Ax + C$ as its root input, gets B as its side input, and generates 1024 values of $Ax + By + C$. For a system with N x N pixels, the binary tree requires $N^2 - 1$ multiply/accumulate stages. It performs the same function, at the same speed, as a full $2N$-stage multiplier at every pixel (requiring $2N^2 logN$ stages).

Only a small fraction of the pixels in a display can be put on a single chip, so it is necessary to break the binary tree into multiple chips. This is done by implementing a small sub-tree on each chip that covers only the pixels on the chip. A 'supertree' on each chip implements the tree levels above the sub-tree. It contains one multiply/accumulate stage for each level above the sub-tree. As shown in Figure 5, registers in the supertree are loaded at system initialization to map a path through the full tree to the local subtree. This defines the position of the chip's 64-pixel column in the full image.

It is possible, of course, to design a system without supertrees. If each chip were equipped with one extra tree node whose outputs go off-chip, the tree levels above each local subtree could be completed using inter-chip wiring. This external wiring would, however, reduce system speed and complicate board-level construction. The configurable supertree on our current chips has 14 levels, requiring only another 14 multiply/accumulate stages and 14 registers—a relatively modest penalty in silicon area. It also makes possible a module-redundancy scheme, described below, that supports fault tolerance in our system.

Figure 6 shows the block diagram of the ALU at each pixel. Logical operations in the ALU are performed by a one-bit adder with a multiplexer/complementer on each of its three inputs. All

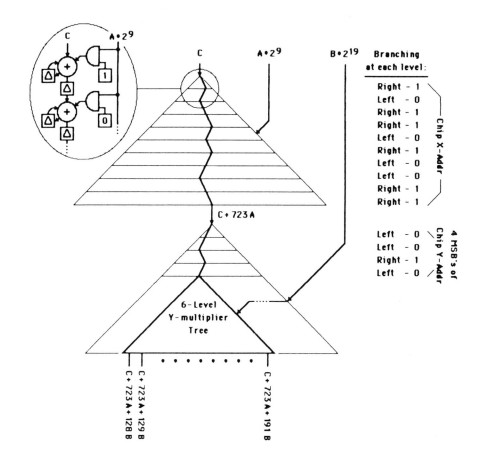

Figure 5: Supertree maps a path through full tree on each chip.

ALU's in the system receive function-select and register-load controls broadcast from the IGC, so the ensemble of memory chips has SIMD concurrency. The ALU contains an Enable register that con-

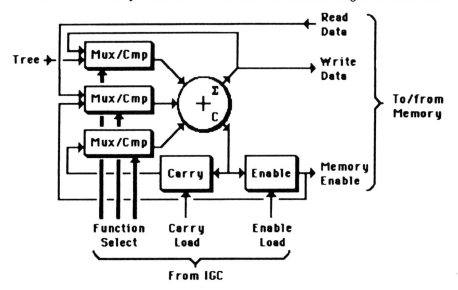

Figure 6: Block diagram of the pixel ALU.

trols memory write access, allowing each pixel to determine locally whether current memory contents can be overwritten.

The Memory system consists of a relatively dense dynamic RAM array. Each column of cells in the array contains corresponding bits in each pixel on the chip. Each row contains all of the bits in a pixel and is equipped with read/write circuitry; thus the 'word width' is extremely wide relative to a conventional memory. The memory also must provide a means for the Video Controller to access memory bits containing color-intensity information.

3. System Realizations

This section describes our experiences building several *Pixel-planes* display systems. Our first enhanced memory chip was intended as a first VLSI design exercise and not intended to become part of a working display. Two small prototype displays have been built with second- and third-generation enhanced memory chips (*Pxpl2* and *Pxpl3*), and they were sufficient to prove the basic concepts in the design. We believe, however, that it is extremely important to build a system large enough to support 'real' applications; only in this way will we convincingly demonstrate the utility of this approach to building high-performance graphics machines. We are therefore constructing a much more ambitious system using fourth-generation chips (*Pxpl4*) that will grow to a full-scale, full-speed working display within the next year.

3.1 Pxpl2

Our second memory chip design [Fuchs *et al.*, 1982] included the local subtree for 64 pixels, a memory array with 16 bits/pixel and a single read/write port, and a simplified ALU with only a Carry generator. It lacked circuitry for the remainder of the tree, and could therefore only be used to build a 'toy' system.

A chip tester was built using a microcomputer with a parallel I/O port, the 10 chips received from fabrication were tested, and four were found to be mostly functional. The tester then became the host for a small prototype display, with Translator and Image Generation Controller functions carried out by software running on the microcomputer. The *Pxpl2* prototype verified the basic concepts in the design, executing (very slowly!) a basic set of polygon-oriented operations (polygon area definition, hidden-surface calculations using a depth-buffer, Gouraud-like smooth shading).

This exercise immediately suggested a number of design improvements:

(1) Since the memory had only a single port, image-generation had to be halted to refresh the display. This required a complex control mechanism with an external scan-line buffer to allow both image generation and video data scan-out to access pixel memory. It was clearly essential to separate these functions and to allow them to be asynchronous.

(2) Working through the details of generating separate root inputs for the sub-trees on each chip led to constructive thinking about supertrees.

(3) Several interesting algorithms had been proposed for *Pixel-planes* that would require both a more complex ALU and more memory bits/pixel.

Neither chip testing nor system operation would have been easy (or perhaps possible) if we had not first written a functional simulator for the chip. This simulator modeled all of the circuitry in the chip at the gate level, was event driven, but did not model circuit delays. It essentially captured the functional specification for the chip in an executable form. This simulator was written in a standard programming language (Pascal), a practice that we have maintained through the current version of the design (current simulators are written in C).

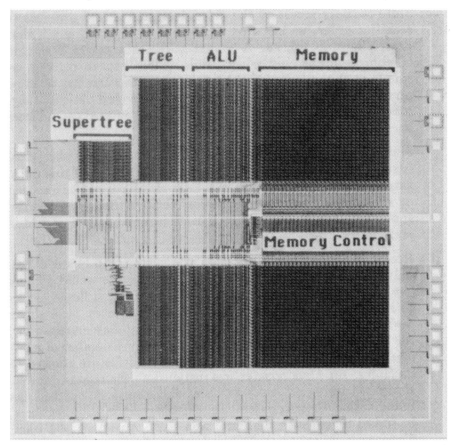

Figure 7: Photo of Pxpl3 memory chip showing major function blocks.

3.2 Pxpl3

Based on our experience with the first prototype, the next chip (Figure 7) contained many architectural improvements:

(1) A complete tree was included on each chip, implemented with the supertree notion described above.

(2) The ALU was modified to the form shown in Figure 6 to support a variety of new algorithms.

(3) Memory size was increased to 32 bits/pixel. We used a dual-ported memory cell to allow separate, asynchronous access to the pixel memory for scan refresh.

(4) Since memory access on the video-data port always proceeds in scan-line order, we installed a pixel-addressing mechanism that uses serial-shift tokens. A 'global' token that passes from chip to chip performs chip select, while a 'local' token register inside each chip manipulates the pointer to the currently selected pixel. The token-addressing scheme reduces chip pin-count significantly, and is a faster mechanism than conventional address decoders.

(5) Since a serial shift-path was already needed to support the global token mechanism, we elected to make multiple use of this path. During system initialization, this inter-chip path can be diverted on each chip into the 'configuration' register that programs the supertree, thus linking all configuration registers into one large scan-path.

(6) Reasonable yield from fabrication at 4 micron feature size allows only 64 pixels on a chip (1.5 micron feature size would allow a few hundred pixels per chip). Current fabrication limits led us to investigate other ways of getting more memory on a single packaged device. We saw that in future chip implementations, the 64-pixel chip might become merely one of a number of modules on a much larger chip, where some modules are allowed to be faulty. An Alive register was installed on the chip to provide a way of turning off faulty modules under software control. On initialization, these registers can, like the configuration registers, be linked together by the serial scan-path. A pattern of 1's and 0's scanned in corresponding to good and faulty modules. Modules (chips) with Alive set to 0 are disabled for video output, and their configuration registers are disconnected from the scan-path during supertree programming.

As in the *Pxpl2* prototype, a complete functional simulator was written for each of the image-generation functional blocks, the Translator, IGC, and Frame Buffer. This simulator could produce crude images to help check the correct operation of various algorithms. The simulators for the Translator and IGC, with slight modifications, became the driver programs for the actual hardware.

Chip testing was done essentially on the display system itself. Since the memory chips are intended to produce graphics images, we simply plugged a single chip into the prototype display, exercised its functions, and observed the results on a color monitor where groups of memory bits were interpreted as color intensities. This rather crude testing strategy was surprisingly effective, even in diagnosing design faults.

Testing revealed several problems with the design:

(1) Over-aggressive use of the newly-available buried contacts in the memory (design rules for burieds were still rather vague) was most likely responsible for rather poor yield (approximately 20%).

(2) The dual-ported memory cell design was flawed and failed to decouple the two ports fully. Image-generation and video scan clocks therefore had to be synchronized.

(3) Failure to carry through a rigorous timing analysis of the memory system and its video output circuitry led to a timing fault that drastically reduced scan-out speed (approximately 1 MHz), but still allowed the chip to function. Under this limitation, the prototype display could be populated only with eight chips per logical board.

The system works correctly under restrictions imposed by the design flaws. Its speed is limited not by hardware design problems, but by the software that emulates the Translator and IGC. Since this software runs about 1000 times slower than the on-chip processors, the system is fast enough to produce only very crude animation (about 2-3 updates per second on an image with 6 polygons).

The module-level fault tolerance scheme using the Alive register was successfully tested on the *Pxpl3* prototype. In fact, the entire serial-shift mechanism for Alive, supertree configuration, and global-token passing worked successfully on first silicon.

Building and testing the *Pxpl3* prototype brought forcefully to our attention the need to build hardware to execute the Translator and IGC functions. The experience also suggested three important design changes in the memory chip:

(1) The fabrication yield for the *Pxpl3* chips would have been greatly improved (better than 2x) with the addition of a redundant memory column and a redundant row.

(2) The dual-ported memory scheme did not appear to be a very effective way to support scan refresh, even had it been successfully implemented. It provides much higher bandwidth in the second port than is required by the scan-out process and requires a memory cell about twice the size of a conventional cell.

(3) Since the multiplier tree in *Pxpl3* is implemented essentially as shown in Figure 4, the tree must be flushed after the formation of each result, in order to clear the carry registers at each node.

A 30% speedup could be achieved if the multiplier were more fully pipelined.

3.3 Pxpl4

The improvements suggested by the *Pxpl3* prototype have been built into a new enhanced memory chip (*Pxpl4*), in fabrication at the time of writing. The chip contains 64 pixels, each with 72 bits of memory. In 4-micron nMOS, active circuitry (excluding pad frame and wiring) is 7.5 x 4.0 mm and contains about 33,000 transistors. Of this area, about 70% is devoted to memory, 20% to the binary-tree circuitry, and 10% to the pixel ALU. With MOSIS's 3-micron fabrication, two modules (128 pixels) can be built inside a MOSIS-standard pad frame.

The system built around this chip will be expandable to 512 x 512 pixels with 72 bits/pixel (or it can display 1024 x 1024 pixels with

18 bits/pixel). This system will be hosted by a high-performance workstation that will store and manipulate image data-bases, provide user interaction, and initially carry out part of the polygon transformation tasks in scene generation. (Later versions of the system will perform transformations using special hardware, such as the Geometry Engine in the Silicon Graphics IRIS [Clark, 1982]).

The following paragraphs detail various design enhancements in the current memory chip.

Multiplier Pipelining

Multiplier operations are fully overlapped by including a small amount of additional hardware for a pipeline register. Figure 8 shows the details of this scheme, which differs somewhat from that in conventional pipelined multipliers [Lyon, 1976]. The pipelining register is 'sticky': when it receives a logic-1 it is locked into this state until a global clear is generated. Thus, a stream of 1's marches down the multiplier just behind the formation of partial products contributing to the MSB of the result, and just ahead of the LSB of the new constant coefficient. When the stream of 1's reaches the last stage, a clear is generated that simultaneously re-enables multiplication at all stages.

Memory Design

Pxpl4 uses a 4-transistor dynamic memory cell that has the useful property of refreshing itself during a read operation. Since each memory row is connected only to its pixel ALU, no special sense amplifier is needed for read access; simulations show that the memory operates faster (about 20 MHz) without one.

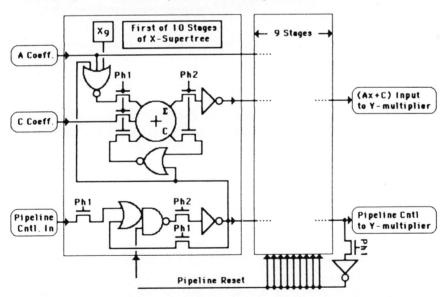

Figure 8: Circuitry for pipelining tree operations. The X-super-tree is shown, but the scheme is used in the Y-tree as well.

The video output port of the pixel memory is implemented as a single double-buffered register per chip, the Shadow Register, in which a copy of the currently selected pixel's memory is built up sequentially. The scheme is shown in Figure 9.

A pixel selector points at the pixel (memory row) needed for the next scan-line and puts a copy of the data from each bit onto a one-bit bus during each read or write cycle. Simultaneously, the memory address decoder output is delayed and used to load data from this bus into the element of the shadow register corresponding to the selected memory bit. Thus, as each bit of memory is 'visited' during image generation, it is copied into the master half of the Shadow Register. At the end of a scan-line, the Video Controller unloads the master into the slave of the Shadow Register, where the data is available for output. The Shadow Register mechanism is much more space-efficient than a full dual-ported memory. It requires some care, however, in design and in operation to avoid data corruption due to synchronization failure and to ensure that image-intensity bits are visited often enough to update the register once per scan-line. Neither of these problems is difficult to overcome in practice.

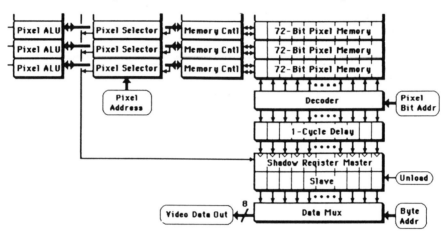

Figure 9: Video memory port implemented as a Shadow Register.

Redundant Modules and Circuits

Pxpl4 retains the Alive mechanism for module fault tolerance that was tested in *Pxpl3* and adds circuitry to support redundant memory elements to make each module more robust.

The chip contains one extra memory column. A redundant-column address register is added to the chip's configuration register, so that the address of the column to be replaced can be scanned in during system initialization.

Provision of a redundant row is somewhat more difficult, since one of the ALU-memory interfaces must be re-connected to the redundant memory row. Re-connection cannot be readily implemented without undue loss in system speed, so instead we provide an entire extra pixel with ALU and complete sub-tree path. The 6 nodes of local tree above the redundant pixel are realized simply by building a full 20 stages of supertree. The configuration (address) registers in these stages contain the address of the redundant pixel, and are loaded with the rest of the address at initialization. Redundant row and column enables are also provided to turn the entire mechanism off.

The redundant column circuitry requires only about 1.4% of the total active circuit area and the redundant row about 5.3%.

3.4 Buffered Pixel-Planes

One drawback of our present system is that the full parallelism cannot be utilized subsequent to scan-conversion. During visibility and painting calculations, all pixels outside the currently processed primitive are idle.

We are investigating an alternative system design, called 'Buffered Pixel-Planes', that improves parallelism. A modified Image Generation Controller with accept/reject circuitry and a FIFO is fully integrated onto a custom chip, and many copies are distributed across the system, each supervising a group of enhanced memory chips. The Translator sends bounding-box data for each primitive ahead of its coefficients and instructions. Each IGC accepts or rejects the current primitive based on the bounding box; if inside, coefficients and instructions are accepted and pushed into the FIFO for processing.

We have simulated the behavior of such a system processing images of moderate complexity (up to 1000 polygons), and we predict approximately 5-fold speedup with modest (10-polygon) FIFO size.

4. Design Methodology

4.1 Tools

For the nMOS realization of our current chips, we use mask-level layout, layout analysis, and circuit simulation design tools distributed by the University of California at Berkeley.

We have written in C the logic-gate-level simulators for the memory chip and for other system components. These simulators are used first to check the correctness of the logic design for the system, then to generate test vectors for switch-level simulation of the chip circuitry.

Most of the design of the custom chips was done by two designers working on a Digital Equipment VAX 11/750 minicomputer with two Lexidata 3700 color displays.

The lack of well-integrated design tools that go smoothly from silicon design to board design is a serious impediment to our work. Board-level logic design and analysis are still done using paper and pencil, with considerable assistance from standard UNIX program-development tools. Boards are layed out with a graphic chip-layout editor and fabricated using MOSIS's PC-board service.

For some time we have been working on a CMOS version of the enhanced memory chip. Mask-level design of CMOS projects is unattractive for two reasons: First, the additional complexity of CMOS technology makes an already-difficult layout task much more tedious. Second, the fabrication technology is developing rapidly, and it is not clear that scalable design rules for mask layout will be an effective way of tracking these advances. We have therefore been using (and assisting in the development of) the VIVID* symbolic-

---

* VIVID is a trademark of the Microelectronics Center of North Carolina

layout design system [Rosenberg *et al.*, 1985]. The system includes a hierarchical layout compactor that translates symbolic layout to mask with the help of a technology file that captures all relevant information about a particular fabrication process. In this way a given symbolic design can hope to survive considerable change in the target fabrication technology.

4.2 Design Style

Constructing a full-scale, full-speed system is a much more complex task than building a small prototype. The principal lesson learned from our early prototype construction was the need for complete documentation and precise interface specifications. We have therefore adopted for all system components a design style whose elements are:

(1) The system is decomposed into modules following a restricted hierarchy, in which only leaf-cells are allowed to contain circuit elements. The hierarchy is maintained in parallel in the physical domain (*e.g.*, chip layout) the logical domain (*e.g.*, logic schematics), and the behavioral domain (*e.g.*, simulators that model the logic). Composition cells may contain only interconnection information (abuttment, for example, within a chip layout) and other cells. Leaf cells may contain only circuit elements (logic gates in the logical description; transistors, wires, contact cuts in the physical description).

(2) Borrowing from strongly-typed programming languages, we impose a strong-typing scheme on all signals in the system. To ensure that modules are 'correctly connected' (*e.g.*, timing conventions and active-levels are observed), only a few signal types are allowed for connection between modules. The typing scheme is based on non-overlapping multi-phase clocks, and if applied carefully, avoids race conditions in sequential circuits. The signal types are encoded in a suffix attached to every signal name, providing a powerful documentation aid.

(3) Special hazards are involved where clocking convention (*e.g.* edge-triggered vs. level-sensitive latching) and implementation technology (TTL logic vs. custom MOS) changes, particularly at the chip I/O pads. To help assure that this interface will work properly, we define its timing conventions in a simple way, using two-sided timing constraints.

(4) Every major module in the design is modeled by a functional simulator. The simulated modules are tested separately, then plugged together to check the correctness of interfaces and overall operation of the simulated system. The simulators provide test vectors for chip simulation and testing.

The signal-typing/timing schemes are similar to [Noice *et al.*, 1982] and [Karplus, 1984]. Other elements of the style were influenced by [Lattin *et al.*, 1981; Stefik and Conway, 1982; Stefik *et al.*, 1982], among other sources.

4.3 Clocking Techniques

Our nMOS custom chips use a high-voltage clocking scheme ('hot clocks') suggested to us by [Seitz, 1982] and described in [Seitz *et al.*, 1985]. The main advantage of the technique is that n-enhancement transistors transmit a logic-HI without threshold drop and at much higher speed. In general, this clocking method produces layouts that are denser and much faster than conventional single-supply designs.

In a system with many custom chips, it is extremely inconvenient to generate these clock signals off-chip at a non-standard voltage. We have therefore built on-chip clock drivers that perform level translation and single-to-2-phase conversion. A separate input pin, biased typically at 8 volts, powers only these circuits. We have successfully built and tested a number of such high-voltage drivers, and our current design charges 100 pf to 7 volts in about 10 nsec.

The clock signals are produced in a single generator on the chip and distributed, so far as possible, continuously in metal wiring. For routing purposes, the clocks are second in importance only to Vdd and ground. For the inevitable cross-unders, we use 'low resistance wire', essentially an extended buried contact whose sheet resistance we have measured at about 7-8 ohms/square.

Level-sensitive register controls require qualified clocks that are generated in clocked, bootstrapped drivers [Joynson *et al.*, 1972]. The design of these compact drivers is not difficult, and they can be made to generate qualified clocks that follow the primary clock signal with nearly zero delay.

Polygon input data:
A_i, B_i, C_i for each edge i

For each edge i define:
$F(x,y) = A_i x + B_i y + C_i$

Pixel at (x,y) is inside polygon if and only if:
$F_i(x,y) > 0$ for all i

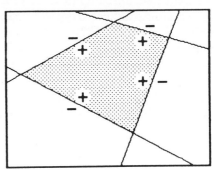

Figure 10: Scan-coverting polygons using linear expressions.

5. Pixel-Planes Algorithms

In this section we briefly describes how polygonal images are processed in *Pixel-planes*, and we outline several new algorithms, more fully described in [Fuchs *et al.*, 1985]. The timing estimates in this section assume that the *Pxpl4* chips are clocked at 10 MHz.

Rendering smooth-shaded polygons requires scan conversion, hidden surface elimination, and shading calculations:

Scan conversion is outlined in Figure 10. Processing begins by enabling all pixels in the display. Edges are encoded in linear equations of the form $F(x, y) = Ax + By + C = 0$, and the sign of F is tested at every pixel to determine visibility. Scan conversion leaves pixels outside the current polygon disabled; only those inside participate in further visibility and shading calculations.

Hidden surface elimination can be performed using a depth-buffer algorithm in which the z-coordinate of a pixel is encoded in a set of coefficients A, B, C by the linear expression $z = Ax + By + C$. Each pixel stores a value of z for the closest polygon so far processed and compares this value with the incoming z. If the new z is closer, the current polygon is visible at this pixel, and it remains enabled for shading, updating its z-buffer. If the stored z is closer than the new z, the pixel is disabled during shading.

Smooth shading is accomplished by computing a set of coefficients for each of R, G, and B, so that the color-intensity at each pixel is approximated by $F(x, y)$. Gouraud-like smooth shading can be carried out by painting each multi-sided polygon as a series of triangles (scan-conversion and hidden surface elimination, however, need only be done once for each polygon).

Polygon processing time depends on the number of edges and the number of bits needed to represent the function $F(x, y)$ for each operation. Approximately 30,000 4-sided polygons of arbitrary shape and orientation can be processed per second, using the steps outlined above.

Shadows are important depth cues in interactive systems, and we have developed a method, similar to [Brotman and Badler, 1984], for casting shadows from arbitrary light sources using using shadow volumes [Crow, 1977]. For each polygon in the image, the set of visible pixels that lie in the frustum of the polygon's cast shadow are determined, and the color intensity of these pixels is diminished by an appropriate factor. Shadows are post-processed after a non-shadowed polygon image has been generated. The shadows for approximately 78,000 polygons can be computed per second.

Filled circles can be rendered rapidly in *Pixel-planes* by treating a circle as a polygon with one edge. The method separates the equation of a circle into a linear part that differs for each circle size and position, and a quadratic part that is the same for all circles. The quadratic part is pre-computed and its distinct values are loaded into every pixel at system initialization. Circles are processed by encoding center-position and radius in coefficients A, B, C and adding the linear expression to the stored quadratic term at each pixel. This method can readily be extended to render the other conic sections, such as ellipses. Spheres can be approximated by a quadratic surface, depth-sorted using a Z-buffer, and highlighted from an arbitrary light source. Approximately 34,000 spheres can be processed per second.

Texture mapping can be performed by using the linear expression evaluator to compute a texture plane address at every pixel. The appropriate color value for a pixel is then looked up in a texture table, transmitted entry by entry to the Smart Frame Buffer.

Anti-aliasing may be accomplished by one of two methods. The first, similar to 'super-sampling', blends a newly computed image with a previously computed image in a series of steps that successively refine the image. To support rapid interaction, the image is only refined when stationary. A second approach uses a method similar to that used on the Evans and Sutherland CT-5 real-time image generation system [Schumacker, 1980]. This method assumes that a visibility ordering of the polygons has already taken place, and uses a sub-pixel coverage mask to compute the anti-aliased image.

Transparency effects can be produced using the sub-pixel coverage mask for successive refinement, or by disabling patterns of pixels (*e.g.* a checkerboard) during polygon processing.

Adaptive Histogram Equalization (AHE) [Pizer *et al.*, 1984] is a powerful image processing technique used for grey level assignment and contrast enhancement of Computed Tomographic (CT) images. A local histogram is computed for every pixel in the image, and then used to compute a new grey level assignment for that pixel. For a 512 x 512 image, this method requires about 5 minutes of computation on a VAX 11/780, and is therefore too inefficient for most uses. The parallel processing power of *Pixel-planes* can be used to compute simultaneously the grey level assignment for each pixel in the image, without the need for histogram calculation. A rank counter, maintained in a portion of each pixel's memory, can be incremented using the pixel ALU. The intensity of a given pixel is broadcast and compared, in parallel, to the intensity of all pixels that are within a local region. The rank counter is incremented at all pixels in the local region whose intensity is greater than the given pixel. After all pixels have been processed, the rank counter values are scaled and displayed. We estimate a 512 x 512 image will require approximately 4 seconds to compute on *Pixel-planes*.

6. Comparison with Other Architectures

We divide alternative VLSI-based architectures for graphics into two classes (as outlined in [Abram and Fuchs, 1984]): those that divide the image plane into sub-planes, with a processor for each subdivision, and those that divide the object database, assigning a processor to each subdivision. The *Pixel-planes* system is an example of the former, and we therefore compare it with two other systems of this type.

6.1 Architectures for Image-plane Subdivision

Several groups ([Fuchs and Johnson, 1979]; [Clark and Hannah, 1980]; [Gupta *et al.*, 1981]) have proposed systems that make more effective use of commercial RAM chips than conventional frame buffers; we refer to this as the *interlaced* approach. In [Clark and Hannah, 1980], the RAM's are interlaced so that on any 8 x 8 area of the screen, one pixel comes from each of the RAM's; each memory contains every eighth pixel in every eighth row. The scheme uses two layers of special processors organized in columns and rows, with a row-processor in charge of each RAM chip (or group of RAM chips when more than 1 bit/pixel). An entire 8 x 8 patch on the screen can be accessed with a single memory reference by the 64 row processors, so a polygon (or other primitive) roughly the size of a patch, or larger, can be processed with considerable parallelism.

A major advantage of the *interlaced* approach is that it uses high-density commercial RAMs and yet achieves performance greatly improved over conventional frame buffers with relatively few custom chips. This design is hampered, however, by the bandwidth limitations imposed by separating memories and processors onto separate chips.

Another recent approach, described in [Demetrescu, 1985], employs 'Scan-Line Addressable Memories' (SLAM's). A system with 1024 x 1024 one-bit pixels is organized in 16 rows, each with a Scan-Line Processor in charge of 4 SLAM chips. Each of these units contains and controls all of the pixels in 64 successive scan-lines. Each SLAM chip contains a conventional RAM array, organized as 64 rows of 256 one-bit pixels, augmented with an array of very simple processors that operate in parallel on all pixels in a row. In one cycle of operation, all pixels in 16 scan lines can be accessed. The Scan-Line Processors provide buffering of graphics primitives, so that very high parallelism can be achieved.

The system-level implementation of a SLAM-based display should be very clean. In contrast to the *interlaced* design, high-bandwidth memory-processor communication wiring is completely encapsulated in the SLAM chips. Commands and data are broadcast from each Scan-Line Processor to its SLAM's over a low-bandwidth bus. The SLAM design solves the display-refresh problem without interrupting image processing (by including a display shift register on the SLAM chip). These are the principal features common to the SLAM and *Pixel-planes* approaches.

6.2 Comparison with Pixel-planes

For today's high-performance workstations, where the display requires one or a few bit-planes and handles (mainly) multiple windows with text, lines, and flat-shaded polygons, the SLAM approach is extremely attractive. For such applications, it appears to be considerably faster than either the *interlaced* or *Pixel-planes* designs and is several orders of magnitude faster than conventional frame buffers. The cost of the approach, like ours, is the need to use custom-designed memory chips. The processors on the SLAM chip are extremely simple and appear to require very little area, however, perhaps as little as 1/10 that of our processors.

The *Pixel-planes* system is targeted at applications more demanding than the displays in current workstations, such as medical display and imaging, molecular modeling, mechanical design systems, and flight and navigational simulators. These applications require interaction with 3D images needing visibility determination, smooth shading, shadows, and textures; images with perhaps thousands of primitives and significant depth complexity must be updated at frame rates.

Methods for improving perceived image quality necessarily rely on storing additional information at each pixel. Clearly, the most effective means of improving performance is accessing and processing this data in parallel, closely associating a large amount of pixel memory with a pixel processor. The *Pixel-planes* design provides the power of a processor per pixel, at relatively modest cost in silicon area, and a very general method for computing images.

The *interlaced* approach cannot grow gracefully in the dimension of bits/pixel because of chip I/O limitations. In the SLAM design, one alternative for growth in this direction is multiple banks of SLAM, one for each bit plane. To expand such a system to the size accommodated by the current *Pixel-planes* chip would entail a copy of the processor for each of 72 bit-planes, an intolerable increase in silicon area. The other alternative is using a column in the SLAM to hold all bits of a pixel, then bit-serially processing data; this alternative is similar to our approach, but it fails to provide a very general image-computation method.

For applications that require accessing large amounts of memory per pixel, our system should be denser and faster than either of the other approaches. In effect, we have already paid the price of accessing many bits/pixel: bit-serial data access and a more general (and costly) method of display refresh.

7. Acknowledgements

We wish to thank Vernon Chi (Director), Mark Monger, and John Thomas, of the UNC Microelectronic Systems Laboratory, for design and technical assistance in building the *Pixel-planes* system. We also wish to thank Alan Paeth and Alan Bell of Xerox Palo Alto Research Center for collaborating in the design of *Pxpl2* and *Pxpl3*, Scott Hennes for assistance with the *Pxpl3* chip, Fred Brooks for the basic circle scan-conversion algorithm, and Turner Whitted for discussions about anti-aliasing and transparency algorithms.

8. References

Abram, G. D. and H. Fuchs. July, 1984. "VLSI Architectures for Computer Graphics," *Proceedings of the NATO Advanced Study Institute on Microelectronics of VLSI Computers*, Sogesta-Urbino, Italy.

Brotman, L. S. and N. I. Badler. October, 1984. "Generating Soft Shadows with a Depth Buffer Algorithm," *IEEE Computer Graphics and Applications*, 5-12.

Clark, J. H. and M. R. Hannah. 4th Quarter, 1980. "Distributed Processing in a High-Performance Smart Image Memory," *LAMBDA*, 40-45. (LAMBDA is now VLSI Design).

Clark, J. H. July, 1982. "The Geometry Engine: A VLSI Geometry System for Graphics," *Computer Graphics*, **16**(3), 127–133. (Proc. Siggraph '82).

Crow, F. C. July, 1977. "Shadow Algorithms for Computer Graphics," *Computer Graphics* , **11**(2), 242–248. (Proc. Siggraph '77).

Demetrescu, S. May, 1985. "High Speed Image Rasterization Using Scan Line Access Memories," *In these Proceedings*.

Fuchs, H. and B. Johnson. April, 1979. "An Expandable Multiprocessor Architecture for Video Graphics," *Proceedings of 6th ACM-IEEE Symposium on Computer Architecture*, 58–67.

Fuchs, H. and J. Poulton. 3rd Quarter, 1981. "Pixel-planes: A VLSI-Oriented Design for a Raster Graphics Engine," *VLSI Design*, **2**(3), 20–28.

Fuchs, H., J. Poulton, A. Paeth, and A. Bell. January, 1982. "Developing Pixel Planes, A Smart Memory-Based Raster Graphics System," *Proceedings of the 1982 MIT Conference on Advanced Research in VLSI*, Dedham, MA, Artech House, 137–146.

Fuchs, H., J. Goldfeather, J. P. Hultquist, S. Spach, J. D. Austin, J. G. Eyles, and J. Poulton. January, 1985. Fast Spheres, Shadows, Textures, Transparencies, and Image Enhancements in Pixel-Planes, Technical Report 85–002, Dept. of Computer Science, University of North Carolina at Chapel Hill.

Gupta, S., R. F. Sproull, and I. E. Sutherland. August, 1981. "A VLSI Architecture for Updating Raster Scan Displays," *Computer Graphics*, **15**(3), 71–78. (Proc. Siggraph '81).

Joynson, R. E., J. L. Mundy, J. F. Burgess, and C. Neugebauer. June, 1972. "Eliminating Threshold Losses in MOS Circuits by Bootstrapping Using Varactor Coupling," *IEEE Journal of Solid-State Circuits*, **SC-7**, 217–224.

Karplus, K. August, 1984. A Formal Model for MOS Clocking Disciplines, Technical Report 84-632, Dept. of Computer Science, Cornell University, Ithaca, NY.

Lattin, W. W., J. A. Bayliss, D. L. Budde, J. R. Rattner, and W. S. Richardson. 2nd Quarter, 1981. "A Methodology for VLSI Chip Design," *LAMBDA*, **2**(2), 34–44. (LAMBDA is now VLSI Design).

Lyon, R. F. April, 1976. "Two's Complement Pipeline Multipliers," *IEEE Transactions on Communications*, **COM-24**, 418–425.

Noice, D., R. Mathews, and J. Newkirk. 1982. "A Clocking Discipline for Two-Phase Digital Systems," *Proc., IEEE International Conference on Circuits and Computers*, 108–111.

Pizer, S. M., J. B. Zimmerman, and E. V. Staab. 1984. "Adaptive Grey Level Assignment in CT Scan Display," *Journal of Computer Assisted Tomography*, **8**(2), 300–305.

Rosenberg, J. B., C. D. Rogers, and S. Daniel. 1985. "An Overview of VIVID, MCNC's Vertically Integrated Symbolic Design System," *To appear in the Proceedings of the 1985 Design Automation Conference.*

Schumacker, R. A. November 1980. "A New Visual System Architecture," *Proceedings of the 2nd Annual IITEC*, Salt Lake City.

Seitz, C. 1982.Private Communication.

Seitz, C. L., A. H. Frey, S. Mattisson, S. D. Rabin, D. A. Speck, and J. L. A. Snepscheut. May, 1985. "Hot-Clock nMOS," *In these Proceedings.*

Stefik, M., D. Bobrow, A. Bell, H. Brown, L. Conway, and C. Tong. January, 1982. "The Partitioning of Concerns in Digital System Design," *Proceedings of the 1982 MIT Conference on Advanced Research in VLSI*, Dedham, MA, Artech House, 43–52.

Stefik, M. and L. Conway. April 28, 1982. Toward the Principled Engineering of Knowledge, KB-VLSI-82-18, Xerox, Palo Alto.

FAST SPHERES, SHADOWS, TEXTURES, TRANSPARENCIES,
and IMAGE ENHANCEMENTS IN PIXEL-PLANES *

Henry Fuchs, Jack Goldfeather† , Jeff P. Hultquist, Susan Spach‡
John D. Austin, Frederick P. Brooks, Jr., John G. Eyles, and John Poulton
Department of Computer Science
University of North Carolina at Chapel Hill
Chapel Hill, NC 27514

ABSTRACT: Pixel-planes is a logic-enhanced memory
system for raster graphics and imaging. Although each
pixel-memory is enhanced with a one-bit ALU, the system's real power comes from a tree of one-bit adders that
can evaluate linear expressions $Ax + By + C$ for every pixel
(x, y) simultaneously, as fast as the ALUs and the memory circuits can accept the results. We and others have
begun to develop a variety of algorithms that exploit this
fast linear expression evaluation capability. In this paper
we report some of those results. Illustrated in this paper
is a sample image from a small working prototype of the
Pixel-planes hardware and a variety of images from simulations of a full-scale system. Timing estimates indicate that
30,000 smooth shaded triangles can be generated per second, or 21,000 smooth-shaded and shadowed triangles can
be generated per second, or over 25,000 shaded spheres can
be generated per second. Image-enhancement by adaptive
histogram equalization can be performed within 4 seconds
on a 512×512 image.

* This research supported in part by the Defense Advance Research Project Agency, monitored by the U.S.
Army Research Office, Research Triangle Park, NC, under contract number DAAG29-83-K-0148 and the National
Science Foundation Grant number ECS-8300970.

† Department of Mathematics, Carleton College, Northfield, MN, on sabbatical at Department of Mathematics at
University of North Carolina at Chapel Hill

‡ Now at Hewlett-Packard Labs, Palo Alto, CA

1. INTRODUCTION

The Pixel-planes development grew out of earlier designs for speeding up raster image generation [Fuchs 1977;
Johnson 1979]. An enhanced design is described in [Clark
1980]. In these designs, the task of generating pixels is distributed between several dozen processors. Even when we
were designing these systems, we realized that the bottleneck in raster image generation was "pushing pixels," since
bottlenecks earlier in the image generation pipeline could
be eliminated by fast arithmetic hardware. Two present examples are the Weitek multiplier chips [Weitek] and a custom "geometry engine" chip [Clark 1982]. The limitation of
these earlier systems that we sought to overcome with Pixel-
planes was that once the number of processors increases to
one per memory chip, the bottleneck becomes data movement into the chip. Even if the processor were much faster
than the memory chip, in any one memory cycle, only one
address-data pair can be put into the chip. Pixel-planes
attempts to overcome this limitation by putting computation logic right onto the memory chip, with an entire tree of
processing circuits generating many pixels's worth of data
in each memory cycle.

Central to the design is an array of logic-enhanced
memory chips that form the frame buffer. These chips
not only store the scanned-out image but also perform the
pixel-level calculations of area-definition, visibility calculation and pixel painting. Recently, various individuals have
devised other algorithms for the Pixel-planes engine—for
computing shadows, sphere displays, and even image processing tasks. It is increasingly evident that the structure
of the machine has greater generality and applicability than
first imagined.

Although to many first-time observers Pixel-planes appears to be a variant of the parallel processor with a processor at every pixel, its power and speed come more from
the binary tree of one-bit adders that efficiently compute a
linear expression in x and y for every pixel in the entire
system. Given coefficients A, B, and C, the two multiplier trees and a one-bit adder at each pixel compute
$F(x, y) = Ax + By + C$ in bit-sequential order for each
(x, y) on the screen (see figure 1). If this expression had
to be calculated at each pixel with only the one-bit pixel
processor alone, the system would take 20 times as long to
complete the calculation!

For efficiency in the actual chip layout, the two multiplier trees have been merged into a single tree and that tree

compressed into a single column. Thus, the system contains a unified multiplier tree, a one-bit ALU at each pixel, a one-bit Enable register (controlling write operations of that pixel), and 32 bits of memory (72 bits in the Pxpl4 implementation now being built). Figure 2 illustrates the organization that is used on the actual memory chips.

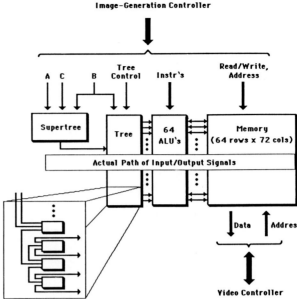

Fig. 2: **Floor plan** of Pixel-Planes 4 chip.

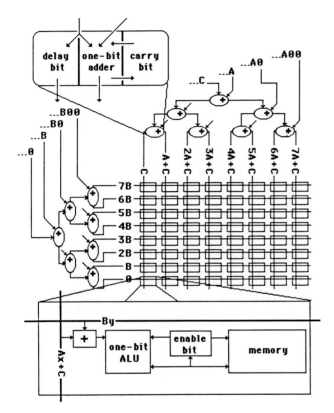

Fig. 1: **Conceptual design** of an 8×8 Pixel-Planes chip.

The system is driven by a transformation engine, which sends vertices of the database to the *translator*. This board converts this data to a series on linear equations which describe the location of each polygon in screen space. Each linear equation, together with an opcode, is passed to the *image generation controller*, which activates the control lines on the frame buffer chips (see figure 3). Figure 4 shows our latest small working prototype with the color image being generated by six Pxpl3 chips.

Details of the hardware design and the implementation are in [Paeth 1982] and in [Poulton 1985]. The latter of these papers outlines architectural enhancements that may increase the speed of the system by a factor of 5. In the future, we hope to integrate the Pixel-planes architecture with a silicon-based flat-screen display, so that the display itself will handle the display computations [Shiffman 1984; Vuillemier 1984].

2. ALGORITHMS IN PIXEL-PLANES

As explained above, the major feature of Pixel-planes is its ability to evaluate, in parallel, expressions of the form $Ax + By + C$, where (x, y) is the address of a pixel. The controller broadcasts A, B, and C, and the expression $Ax + By + C$ is evaluated and then compared and/or combined with information already stored in the memory in each pixel cell. The memory at each pixel can be allocated in any convenient way. A typical allocation might be:

1) buffers for storage of certain key values (e.g., a ZMIN buffer for depth storage, and RED, GREEN, and BLUE buffers for color intensity values)

2) several one-bit flags which are used to enable or disable pixels (via the Enable register) during various stages of processing.

The timing analyses apply to the Pxpl memories and scanout. They assume image generating pipeline modules before them—the geometric transformation unit, the translator, and the controller—operate fast enough to keep up with the Pxpl memories.

2.1 CONVEX POLYGONS

The display of objects made up of polygons is accomplished in three steps: scan conversion of the polygons, visibility relative to previously processed polygons, and shading.

2.1.1 Scan Conversion. The object of this step is to determine those pixels which lie inside a convex polygon. Initially, all Enable registers are set to 1. Each edge of the polygon is defined by two vertices, $v_1 = (x_1, y_1)$ and $v_2 = (x_2, y_2)$, which are ordered so that the polygon lies on the left of the directed edge $v_1 v_2$. Then the equation of the edge is $Ax + By + C = 0$, where $A = y_1 - y_2$, $B = x_2 - x_1$, and $C = x_1 y_2 - x_2 y_1$. Furthermore, $f(x, y) = Ax + By + C$ is positive if and only if (x, y) lies on the same side of the edge as the polygon. The translator computes A, B, and C, and these coefficients are then broadcast to Pixel-planes. A negative $f(x, y)$ causes the Enable register for (x, y) to be set to 0; otherwise the Enable register is unchanged. A pixel is inside the polygon if and only if its Enable register remains 1 after all edges have been broadcast.

2.1.2 Visibility. Once scan conversion has been performed, final visibility of each polygon is determined by a comparison of z values at each pixel. The translator first computes the plane equation, $z = Ax + By + C$, as follows:

Step 1: The plane equation in eye space has the form:

$$A'x_e + B'y_e + C'z_e + D' = 0. \quad (1)$$

The first 3 coefficients, which form the normal to the plane, are found by computing the cross product of the two vectors determined by the first three vertices of the polygon. Alternatively, an object space normal can be part of the polygon data structure and transformed appropriately to produce an eye space normal. Assuming that (x_0, y_0, z_0) is a vertex, the last coefficient is given by:

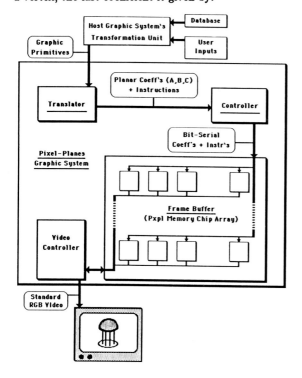

Fig. 3: Logical overview of a 3D graphics system using Pixel-Planes image buffer memory chips.

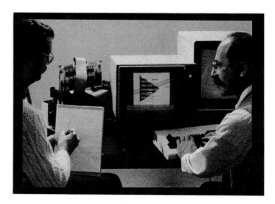

Fig. 4: Pixel-Planes 3 System. John Poulton (left) and Henry Fuchs and the working Pixel-Planes 3 prototype. (photo by Jerry Markatos)

$$D' = -A'x_o - B'y_o - C'z_o \quad (2)$$

Step 2: Using the transformation equations:

$$\begin{aligned} x_e &= (-x - k_1)/(z'r_1), \\ y_e &= (-y - k_2)/(z'r_2), \text{ and} \\ z_e &= -1/z' \end{aligned} \quad (3)$$

where r_1, r_2, k_1, k_2 are constants related to the screen resolution and the location of the screen origin, we can transform (1) to screen space and still retain the form:

$$z' = A'x + B'y + C' \quad (4)$$

Step 3: Given that n bits are reserved for the ZMIN buffer, and that the minimum and maximum z values z_1, z_2, for the object to be displayed are known, we can rescale the equation so that $0 \leq z \leq 2^n - 1$ by replacing z' by:

$$z = (2^n - 1)(z' - z_1)/(z_2 - z_1) \quad (5)$$

Combining this with (4) we can write z in the form $z = Ax + By + C$. The visible pixels are then determined by using the standard Z-buffer algorithm [Sutherland 1974] at each pixel simultaneously. The controller broadcasts the plane equation of the current polygon, $z = f(x, y) = Ax + By + C$. Each pixel whose Enable bit is still 1 compares its $f(x, y)$ to the value in its ZMIN buffer. The pixel is visible if and only if $f(x, y) < ZMIN$, so pixels with $f(x, y) \geq ZMIN$ set their Enable bits to 0. The controller rebroadcasts A, B, and C so that the still-enabled pixels can store their new ZMIN values.

2.1.3 Shading. To determine the proper color for each pixel, the controller broadcasts 3 sets of coefficients, one for each primary color component. For flat shading, $A = B = 0$ and $C = color$. A smooth shading effect similar to Gouraud shading [Gouraud 1971], created by linearly interpolating the colors at the vertices of the polygon, can also be achieved.

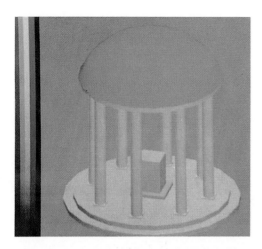

Fig. 5: The Chapel Hill "Old Well" rendered by a Pixel-Planes functional simulator with input of 357 polygons. Estimated image generation time (assuming a 10Mhz clock) is 9 msec.

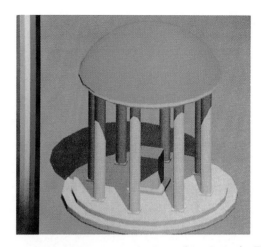

Fig. 6: "Old Well" with shadows (simulation). Estimated time: 13.8 msec.

For example, suppose the polygon has 3 vertices (x_1, y_1), (x_2, y_2), and (x_3, y_3) with red components R_1, R_2, R_3. Geometrically, one can visualize linear interpolation of the red component at (x, y) as selecting the third component of the point (x, y, R) that lies on the plane passing through (x_1, y_1, R_1), (x_2, y_2, R_2), and (x_3, y_3, R_3) in xyR-space. The translator computes the equation of this plane as follows:

Step 1: The vector equation

$$(x, y) = s(x_2 - x_1, y_2 - y_1) + t(x_3 - x_1, y_3 - y_1) + (x_1, y_1) \tag{6}$$

is solved for s and t which are written in the form:

$$\begin{aligned} s &= A_1 x + B_1 y + C_1 \\ t &= A_2 x + B_2 y + C_2 \end{aligned} \tag{7}$$

Step 2: The plane equation is written in the form $R = Ax + By + C$, where

$$\begin{aligned} A &= A_1(R_2 - R_1) + A_2(R_3 - R_1) \\ B &= B_1(R_2 - R_1) + B_2(R_3 - R_1) \\ C &= C_1(R_2 - R_1) + C_2(R_3 - R_1) + R_1 \end{aligned} \tag{8}$$

The controller broadcasts A, B, and C, and $Ax + By + C$ is stored in the RED color buffer for pixels that are still enabled after the scan conversion and visibility computations. If there are more than three vertices, the translator checks the colors $R_4, R_5, \ldots$ at the remaining vertices $v_4 = (x_4, y_4), v_5 = (x_5, y_5), \ldots$. Only in the case that for some i, $R_i \neq Ax_i + By_i + C$ is it necessary to subdivide the polygon by introducing new edges. Note that this subdivision is performed only during the shading stage and is not required during any other phase of processing.

Timing Analysis. The time it takes to process a polygon depends on the number of edges and the number of bits needed for the representation of $Ax + By + C$. Suppose we require an E bit representation for enabling pixels on one side of an edge, a D bit representation for the depth buffer, a C bit representation for each color component, and N bits for the representation of screen coordinates (usually 2 more than the log of the screen resolution), then scan conversion of an edge requires $E + N + 3$ clock cycles, and the visibility calculation of a polygon requires $2(D + N + 3)$ clock cycles. Once this is determined, shading of the polygon without subdivision requires $3(C + N + 3)$ additional clock cycles, while $3(C + N + 3) + (E + N + 3)$ additional cycles are needed for each subdivision. Hence, the total time to process a "worst case" n-sided polygon is:

$$\begin{aligned} &n(E + N + 3) + 2(D + N + 3) \\ &\quad + (n - 3)(E + N + 3) \\ &\quad + 3(n - 2)(C + N + 3) \end{aligned}$$

clock cycles. If we assume that $E = 12$, $D = 20$, $C = 8$, $N = 11$, $n = 4$, and a clock period is 100 nanoseconds, a 4-sided polygon can be processed in 33 microseconds. Hence, about 30,000 such polygons can be processed per second. This permits real-time display of quite complex objects (see figure 5).

2.2 SHADOWS

After the visible image has been constructed, shadows created by various light sources can be determined (see figure 6). Our approach determines shadow volumes [Crow 1977] defined as logical intersections of half-spaces. This is most similar to [Brotman 1984] except that explicit calculation of the shadow edge polygons is unnecessary in Pixelplanes. Briefly, the algorithm proceeds as follows:

Step 1: Flag initialization. For each pixel, a Shadow flag is allocated from pixel memory, and both the Enable register and Shadow flags are set to 0.

Step 2: Determination of pixels in shadow. For each polygon, the set of visible pixels that lie in the frustum of the polygon's cast shadow are determined and the Enable registers for these pixels is set to 1. The logical OR of Shadow and Enable is then stored in Shadow.

Step 3: Determination of color intensity of shadowed pixels. After all polygons have been processed, those pixels whose Shadow flag is 1 are in the shadow of one or more polygons. The color intensity of these pixels is diminished by an appropriate factor.

The implementation of this algorithm is based on the parallel linear evaluation capability of Pixel-planes, together with *ZMIN* value that is stored for each pixel. The idea is to disable those pixels which are on the "wrong" side of each face of the shadow frustum. We begin by choosing an edge of the current polygon, and finding the plane P determined by this edge and the light source. We want to disable those pixels which are not in the same half-space relative to P as the current polygon (see figure 7). The algorithm must handle two cases.

Case 1: P does not pass through the origin in eye space. In this case we observe that if the eye and the current polygon are in the same half-space relative to P, then it suffices to disable pixels that are farther away than P, and if the eye and the current polygon are in different half-spaces relative to P, then it suffices to disable pixels that are closer than P. In order to accomplish this we do the following:

a) The translator determines the equation of the plane P in the form $z = f(x,y) = Ax + By + C$, chooses a vertex (x_i, y_i) of the polygon not on P, and finds the sign of $f(x_i, y_i)$.

b) The coefficients A, B, and C are broadcast so that f can be evaluated simultaneously at all pixels.

c) If $f(x_i, y_i)$ is positive, all pixels whose *ZMIN* is less than $f(x,y)$ are disabled, and if $f(x_i, y_i)$ is negative, all pixels whose *ZMIN* is greater than $f(x,y)$ are disabled.

Case 2: P passes through the origin in eye space. This relatively rare case is easier to process than Case 1. We observe that P projected on the screen is an edge so it suffices to disable pixels which are not on the same side of this edge as the projected current polygon. We proceed as follows:

a) The translator determines the edge equation of the intersection of P with the plane of the screen in the form $Ax + By + C = 0$. In addition, the translator determines the sign of $f(x,y) = Ax + By + C$ at a vertex (x_i, y_i) not on P.

b) The coefficients A, B, and C are broadcast and those pixels whose $f(x,y)$ is not the same sign as $f(x_i, y_i)$ are disabled.

After each edge of the polygon has been processed in this manner, the pixels that are on the same side of the plane of the polygon as the light source must still be disabled. We let P be the plane of the polygon itself, and use

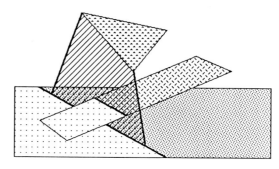

After shadow post-processing of first edge of triangle.

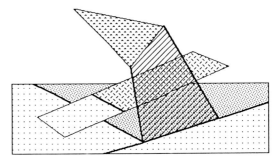

After shadow post-processing of second edge of triangle.

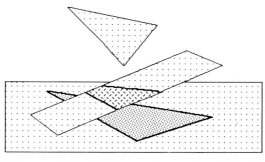

After completing shadow post-processing of triangle.

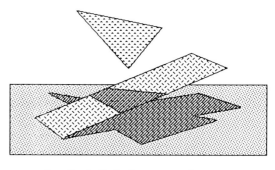

Result of all shadow processing.

Fig. 7: Shadowing Algorithm

either Case 1 or Case 2 above, with the one exception that we check the sign of f at the light source. Note that in the same half-space relative to P, we disable pixels for which $ZMIN = f(x,y)$, and if they are in different half-spaces we do not disable pixels for which $ZMIN = f(x,y)$. In this way, we can display either the lit or the unlit side of a polygon.

Timing Analysis. Step 1 requires 2 clock cycles for each polygon. In order to process each plane of the shadow frustum of a polygon, we need $(E + N + 3)$ cycles for the broadcast of $A,B,$ and C and 2 additional cycles for the resetting of the Shadow flag. After all polygons have been processed, $3C$ cycles are required to modify the color component. Hence, in order to process P polygons, we need $P\big((n + 1)(E + N + 3) + 2\big) + 3C + 2$ clock cycles. For example, if $E=12$, $N=11$, $n=4$, $C=8$, and a clock period is 100 nanoseconds, 78,000 polygons can be processed per second.

Fig. 9: **Trimethoprim** (simulation). Presorted data. Estimated time: 1.3 msec.

2.3 CLIPPING

Clipping of polygons by boundary planes, a procedure usually performed in the geometry pipeline, is not necessary when displaying an image in Pixel-planes. Time can be saved by performing only a bounding box type of trivial rejection/acceptance. Edges which lie wholly or partially off the screen will still disable the appropriate pixels during scan conversion. Even hither and yon clipping can be achieved by passing (at most) the two edges of the intersection of the polygon plane with the hither and yon planes, and disabling pixels which are on the appropriate side of these edges. The shadow volumes must be similarly clipped, by the addition of the shadow planes determined by the light source and the line of intersection of the plane of the polygon and each of the clipping planes (see figure 8).

2.4 SPHERES

Fred Brooks suggested to us a method for drawing filled circles in Pixel-planes. We have extended that method to spheres with Z-buffer and an arbitrary light source. Since Pixel-planes is essentially a linear machine, it might seem difficult to display objects rapidly which are defined via quadratic expressions. However, by using an algorithm that, in effect, treats a circle as a polygon with one edge, and by using some appropriate approximations, we can overcome these difficulties (see figures 9,10). Just as in polygon display, we proceed through a scan conversion, a visibility, and a shading phase [Max 1979; Pique 1983].

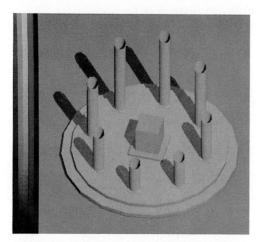

Fig. 8: **"Old Well" with shadows** cut by hither plane within the Pixel-Planes memories (simulation). 177 polygons after trivial rejection. Estimated time: 8.8 msec.

Fig. 10: **Trimethoprim with Z-buffer** (simulation). Unsorted data. Estimated time: 1.7 msec.

Step 1: Scan Conversion. Note that the equation of a circle with radius r and center (a, b) can be written in the form:

$$g(x, y) = Ax + By + C - Q = 0 \qquad (9)$$

where $A = 2a$, $B = 2b$, $C = r^2 - a^2 - b^2$, and $Q = x^2 + y^2$. A section of the memory at each pixel, called the Q-buffer, is allocated for the storage of $x^2 + y^2$, and is loaded with this value at system initialization time. The translator computes A, B, and C and $f(x, y) = Ax + By + C$ is evaluated at each pixel. The value in the Q-buffer is subtracted from $f(x, y)$ and those pixels for which $f(x, y) - Q$ is negative are disabled.

Step 2: Visibility. If the eye coordinate system is chosen so that the $z > 0$ half-space contains the sphere, then the visible hemisphere is the set of points (x, y, z) satisfying

$$z = c - \sqrt{r^2 - (x - a)^2 - (y - b)^2} \qquad (10)$$

where r is the radius and (a, b, c) is the center of the sphere. We can approximate this by

$$z = c - \left(r^2 - (x - a)^2 - (y - b)^2\right)/r \qquad (11)$$

which in effect approximates the hemisphere with a paraboloid. Using a method similar to that described in Step 1, the expression in (11) can be evaluated, compared with the existing contents of the ZMIN buffer, and then stored if necessary, in the ZMIN buffer. Visibility is then determined in the same way as it is for polygon display.

Step 3: Shading due to light sources at infinity. The unit outward normal at the visible point (x, y, z) on the sphere with center (a, b, c) and radius r is

$$
\begin{aligned}
\overline{N} &= (1/r)(x - a, y - b, z - c) \\
&= (1/r)\left(x - a, y - b, -\sqrt{r^2 - (x - a)^2 - (y - b)^2}\right)
\end{aligned}
\qquad (12)
$$

Let $\overline{L} = (l_1, l_2, l_3)$ be the unit direction of an arbitrary light source. Then the point of maximum highlight on the sphere is $(rl_1 + a, rl_2 + b, rl_3 + c)$. Denote by $CMIN$ the ambient color value and by $CMAX$ the maximum color value for a given color component. Then for diffuse shading of the sphere, the color value at (x, y) is

$$Color(x, y) = \qquad (13)$$

$$
\begin{cases}
CMIN + (CMAX - CMIN)(\overline{L} \cdot \overline{N}), & \text{if } \overline{L} \cdot \overline{N} \geq 0; \\
CMIN, & \text{if } \overline{L} \cdot \overline{N} < 0.
\end{cases}
$$

Using the parabolic approximation of the hemisphere as we did in Step 2, we can approximate $\overline{L} \cdot \overline{N}$ by:

$$
\begin{aligned}
\overline{L} \cdot \overline{N} \approx {}& (l_1(x - a) + l_2(y - b))/r \\
& - l_3(r^2 - (x - a)^2 - (y - b)^2)/r^2
\end{aligned}
\qquad (14)
$$

Then the color at a given pixel can be written in the form:

$$Color(x, y) = K(Ax + By + C - Q) + CMIN \qquad (15)$$

where

$$
\begin{aligned}
K &= -(CMAX - CMIN)l_3/r^2, \\
A &= -l_1 r/l_3 + 2a, \\
B &= -l_2 r/l_3 + 2b, \\
C &= l_1 ra/l_3 + l_2 rb/l_3 + r^2 - a^2 - b^2
\end{aligned}
\qquad (16)
$$

The translator computes A, B, C, and K. Multiplication by K is accomplished by first approximating K by the first n non-zero bits of its binary representation:

$$K \approx \sum_{i=1}^{n} 2^{j_i} \qquad (17)$$

Then for each j in the sum, the controller broadcasts $2^j A$, $2^j B$, $2^j C$. Q is shifted by j bits and subtracted from the linear expression determined by the three broadcast coefficients. The resultant value:

$$2^j(Ax + By + C - Q) \qquad (18)$$

is added to the contents of the appropriate color buffer, COLBUF. After all the terms in the sum have been processed, we set $COLBUF$ to 0 if $COLBUF < 0$. The constant value $CMIN$ is broadcast and added to $COLBUF$.

Timing Analysis. The initial loading of the Q-buffer requires $37(E + N + 3)$ clock cycles. Scan conversion and visibility are the same as in polygon processing and take $(E + N + 3)$ and $2(D + N + 3)$ cycles, respectively. Shading requires $4(C + N + 3)$ cycles for each term in the sum used to approximate K, and the broadcast of $CMIN$ requires 20 cycles. Hence, if k is the number of terms in the approximation of K, it takes

$$
\begin{aligned}
& 37(E + N + 3) \\
& \quad + S\big((E + N + 3) + 2(D + N + 3) \\
& \quad + 4k(C + N + 3) + 20\big)
\end{aligned}
$$

clock cycles to process S spheres. For example, if $k = 3$, $E = 20$, $N = 11$, $D = 20$, $C = 8$, then 34,000 spheres can be processed per second.

228

2.5 ADAPTIVE HISTOGRAM EQUALIZATION

In computed tomographic (CT) scan displays, CT numbers must be assigned (grey) intensity levels so that the viewer can perceive appropriate degrees of contrast and detail. Because the range of CT numbers is, in general, greater than the range of intensity levels, some compression has to take place. This makes it difficult to control the contrast in both light and dark areas. The standard method, selection of windows in the CT range, results in intensity discontinuities and loss of information. AHE [Pizer 1984] is an assignment scheme that makes use of regional frequency distributions of image intensities. The processed image has high contrast everywhere and the intensities vary smoothly (see figures 11,12). The method proceeds as follows. For each point (x, y) in the image:

Step 1: A "contextual" region centered at (x, y) is chosen, and the frequency histogram of CT numbers in this region is computed. Typically, this region is a circle, or a square with edges parallel to the screen boundaries.

Step 2: In this histogram, the percentile rank, r, of the CT number at (x, y) is determined.

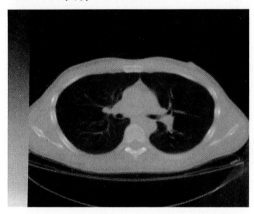

Fig. 11: Original CT scan image.

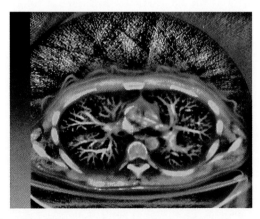

Fig. 12: CT scan image after AHE enhancement (simulation). Estimated time for this 256×256 pixel image: 1 second.

Step 3: This rank is used to compute an intensity level, i, in some grey scale ranging between , say, i_1 and i_2. Specifically, $i = i_1 + r(i_2 - i_1)$.

This method requires the computation of a CT distribution at every pixel in the image, and so it is far too inefficient for most uses, requiring approximately 5 minutes to compute on a 256×256 image on a VAX 11/780. A more efficient alternative, requiring about 30 seconds for a 256×256 image, is to compute the distribution only at a small set of sample points and use a linear interpolation scheme to approximate the intensity levels at the other points.

An efficient alternative, which finds the exact value at each pixel, can be implemented in Pixel planes. The idea is to make use of the parallel processing capability to construct the rank incrementally at each pixel simultaneously.

Step 1: The CT numbers are loaded into the pixel memories, and a counter at each pixel is initialized.

Step 2: For each pixel (x_0, y_0):

a) The coefficients necessary to disable those pixels that are outside the contextual region centered at (x_0, y_0) are broadcast. For example, if the region is a polygon or a circle, this is equivalent to the scan conversion step discussed earlier.

b) The CT number, $N(x_0, y_0)$, is broadcast and compared, in parallel, to the CT number, $N(x, y)$ which is stored at each enabled pixel (x, y). If $N(x, y) > N(x_0, y_0)$, the counter at (x, y) is incremented.

Step 3: After all pixels have been processed, the counter at each pixel contains the rank of the pixel CT number within its own contextual region. If both the number of pixels in the contextual region and the length of the grey scale are powers of 2, this rank can easily be scaled to an intensity by shifting bits.

Timing Analysis. It requires 25 cycles to load each pixel with its CT value and initialize its counter. It requires $2(E + N + 3)$ cycles to disable pixels outside each contextual region and 40 cycles to broadcast the CT numbers and increment the counters. On a 512×512 display with $N = 11$ and $E = 12$, we have estimated the time required to perform AHE is about 4 seconds.

3. ALGORITHMS UNDER DEVELOPMENT

This section describes algorithms still under development. Only functional simulations (rather than detailed behavioral ones) have been executed and the timing estimates are thus less precise. In particular, we are still exploring speedups for multiplication and division in the pixel processors. The timing estimates given in the figures are conservative (we hope), but still assume a 10MHz clock.

3.1 TEXTURE MAPPING

One way of producing a texture on a polygon is to compute a texture plane address (u, v) associated to each pixel (x, y) and then look up the appropriate color value in a texture table indexed by u and v. The Pixel planes linear evaluator can be used to determine, in parallel, this texture plane address.

To see how this is done, we proceed through some mathematical computations. In order to orient a texture on a polygon in eye space we first choose a point $P0$ on the polygon and 2 orthonormal vectors $\overline{S}$ and $\overline{T}$ in the plane of the polygon. Then the texture address (u, v) associated to the point X on the polygon is given by:

$$u = \overline{S} \cdot (X - P_0),$$
$$v = \overline{T} \cdot (X - P_0). \qquad (19)$$

If $\overline{S} = (s_1, s_2, s_3)$, $\overline{T} = (t_1, t_2, t_3)$, $P = (p_1, p_2, p_3)$, and $X = (x_e, y_e, z_e)$, equations (19) can be rewritten in coordinate form as:

$$u = s_1(x_e - p_1) + s_2(y_e - p_2) + s_3(z_e - p_3)$$
$$v = t_1(x_e - p_1) + t_2(y_e - p_2) + t_3(z_e - p_3). \qquad (20)$$

Substituting the equations (3), which relate screen space to eye space, into (20) and using the plane equation $Ax_e + By_e + Cz_e + D = 0$, we can write u and v in the form:

$$u = (A_1 x + B_1 y + C_1)/z$$
$$v = (A_2 x + B_2 y + C_2)/z \qquad (21)$$

The translator computes $A_1, B_1,$ and C_1, and the controller broadcasts them to Pixel-planes. The division of

$A_1 x + B_1 y + C_1$ by z (which is already stored in ZMIN) is done in parallel at the pixel level, and the result is stored in a U-buffer. The V-buffer value is found in a similiar manner. A texture table is then passed, entry by entry, to Pixel-planes, and each pixel selects a texture value corresponding to its stored (u, v) value. For periodic patterns (checkerboards, bricks, etc.) it is only necessary to transmit a small table defining the unit pattern (see figure 13).

Fig. 13: Bricked "Old Well" (simulation). 66 textured polygons out of a total of 357. Estimated time: 14.3 msec.

3.2 TRANSPARENCY

Transparency effects can be achieved by disabling patterns of pixels prior to polygon processing. For example, one could broadcast the coefficients 1, 1, 0 in order to evaluate $x + y$, and disable those pixels for which $x + y$ is even (see figure 14).

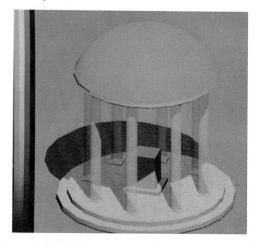

Fig. 14: "Old Well" with transparent columns (simulation). 64 transparent polygons out of a total of 357. Estimated time: 13.8 msec.

Transparency effects can also be produced with subpixel mask successive refinement, where transparent polygons are ignored on particular passes over the database. For example, transparent polygons can be ignored every other pass or every third pass, thereby yielding different degrees of transparency.

3.3 ANTI-ALIASING

We have been developing several anti-aliasing techniques for polygons. We have come to believe that the essential difference between various approaches is whether the visibility at the subpixel level is performed before or after the anti-aliasing computations. Our first approach, which aims at producing an image rapidly and "improving" the image with each screen refresh, makes no assumptions about visibility determination before the Pxpl memories. The second approach, which takes more time, but produces a high quality anti-aliased image initially, assumes visibility ordering has already been done.

Method 1: Successive Refinement. Each pixel (x, y), is subdivided into a grid of subpixels so that each subpixel has an address of the form $(x + xoffset, y + yoffset)$. We generate the image several times (16, perhaps), each time offsetting the image slightly by some $(xoffset, yoffset)$ in such a way that the sample points within a pixel's area form a reasonable distribution. (The shift is easily achieved by adding $A \cdot xoffset + B \cdot yoffset$ to the C coefficient of each broadcast triple.) Two sets of color buffers are maintained, one to store the color generated by the latest image generation offset and the other to store a running average as we move around the subpixel grid.

The extra cost of the algorithm over standard sub-pixel "super-sampling" is the color blending between each pass over the graphic database. This is less than 1000 clock cycles (100 microseconds) per pass. This particular super-sampling successive refinement technique, however, supports dynamically interactive applications. The initial images appear similar to common anti-aliased images, and significant refinement is produced within a few additional sampling passes.

Method 2: Subpixel Coverage Mask. The polygons are sorted from front to back, perhaps by first transforming the polygon list into a BSP tree [Fuchs 1983]. Each pixel is subdivided into a number of subpixels and one bit of the pixel memory is reserved for each such subpixel. During the scan conversion step of polygon processing, the coefficients defining each edge are normalized to yield the distance from the center of the pixel to the edge. The coverage mask and area contribution of an edge can be passed from a precomputed table [Carpenter 1984] in the controller indexed by this distance and A, the coefficient of x. (Note that only one row of the table needs to be passed for any edge.) The number of ones in the mask is used to compute a color contribution which is added to the color buffers. When the number of ones in the coverage mask stored at each pixel reaches the total number of subpixels, the pixel is disabled. Since polygons are processed in front to back order, "leakage" of color from hidden polygons is avoided. This approach is somewhat similar to the one used in the Evans and Sutherland CT-5 real-time image generation system often used for flight training [Schumacker 1980].

4. CONCLUSIONS

We have highlighted in this paper the aspects of Pixel-planes that give it computing power and efficiency—the parallel linear expression evaluator embodied in the tree of one-bit adders. We have illustrated this capability by describing a variety of algorithms (shadows, spheres, image enhancement) that appear to run efficiently in this machine. Pictures from the Pixel-planes simulators indicate that high-quality images can be generated rapidly enough for dynamic, often real-time, interaction. The images from the working small prototype (see figure 4) are simpler than the images from the simulators due to the small number of custom chips presently available. We expect Pixel-planes 4, with considerably increased speed and resolution, to start working by June 1985. We expect that a full-scale (500–1000 line) display system can be built with less than 500 Pxpl memory chips in currently available (1.5micron CMOS) technology. We also hope that the algorithm developments, especially those based on simplifying algorithms into linear form, will be useful for those developing graphics algorithms on other parallel machines.

5. ACKNOWLEDGEMENTS

We wish to thank Fred Brooks for the basic circle scan-conversion algorithm, Alan Paeth and Alan Bell of Xerox Palo Alto Research Center for years of assistance with the design and early implementations of Pixel-planes, Scott Hennes for assistance with the implementation of the Pxpl3 memory chip, Hsieh Cheng-Hong and Justin Heinecke for discussions about architecture and algorithm interactions, Turner Whitted for discussions about anti-aliasing and transparency algorithms, Eric Grant for 3D data of the Old Well, Steve Pizer, John Zimmerman, and North Carolina Memorial Hospital for CT chest data, Mike Pique, Doug Schiff, Dr. Michael Corey and Lee Kuyper (Corey and Kuyper from Burroughs Wellcome) for Trimethoprim drug molecule data, Trey Greer for TEX help, and Bobette Eckland for secretarial support. Special thanks go to Andrew Glassner, who supervised the layout and paste-up of this paper.

6. REFERENCES

Brotman, L.S. and N.I. Badler. October 1984. "Generating Soft Shadows with a Depth Buffer Algorithm," *IEEE Computer Graphics and Applications*, 5–12.

Carpenter, L. July 1984. "The A-buffer, an Antialiased Hidden Surface Method," *Computer Graphics*, 18(3), 103–109 (Proc. Siggraph '84).

Clark, J.H. July 1982. "The Geometry Engine: A VLSI Geometry System for Graphics," *Computer Graphics*, 16(3), 127–133 (Proc. Siggraph '82).

Clark, J.H. and M.R. Hannah. 4th Quarter, 1980. "Distributed Processing in a High-Performance Smart Image Memory," *Lambda*, 40–45 (*Lambda* is now VLSI Design).

Crow, F.C. July 1977. "Shadow Algorithms for Computer Graphics," *Computer Graphics*, 11(2), 242–248 (Proc. Siggraph '77).

Fuchs, H. 1977. "Distributing a Visible Surface Algorithm over Multiple Processors," *Proceedings of the ACM Annual Conference*, 449–451.

Fuchs, H. and B. Johnson. April, 1979. "An Expandable Multiprocessor Architecture for Video Graphics," *Proceedings of the 6th ACM-IEEE Symposium on Computer Architecture*, 58–67.

Fuchs, H., J. Poulton, A. Paeth, and A. Bell. January, 1982. "Developing Pixel-Planes, A Smart Memory-Based Raster Graphics System," *Proceedings of the 1982 MIT Conference on Advanced Research in VLSI*, 137–146.

Fuchs, H., G.D. Abram, and E.D.Grant. July 1983. "Near Real-Time Shaded Display of Rigid Objects," Computer Graphics, 17(3), 65–72 (Proc. Siggraph '83).

Gouraud, H. 1971. "Computer Display of Curved Surfaces," *IEEE Transcations on Computers*, 20(6), 623–629.

Max, N.L. July 1979. "ATOMILL: Atoms with Shading and Highlights," *Computer Graphics*, 13(3), 165–173 (Proc. Siggraph '79).

Pique, M.E. 1983. Fast 3D Display of Space-Filling Molecular Models, Technical Report 83-004, Department of Computer Science, UNC Chapel Hill.

Pizer, S.M., J.B. Zimmerman, and E.V.Staab. April 1984. "Adaptive Grey Level Assignment in CT Scan Display," *Journal of Computer Assisted Tomography*, 8(2), 300–305, Raven Press, NY.

Poulton, J., J.D. Austin, J.G. Eyles, J. Heinecke, C.H. Hsieh, and H. Fuchs. 1985. Pixel-Planes 4 Graphics Engine, Technical Report 1985, Department of Computer Science, UNC Chapel Hill (to appear).

Schumacker, R.A. November 1980. "A New Visual System Architecture," *Proceedings of the 2nd Annual IITEC*, Salt Lake City.

Shiffman, R.R. and R.H. Parker. 1984. "An Electrophoretic Image Display With Internal NMOS Address Logic and Display Drivers", *Proceedings of the Society for Information Display*, 25(2), 105–152.

Sutherland, I.E., R.F. Sproull, and R.A. Schumacker. 1974. "A Characterization of Ten Hidden-Surface Algorithms," *ACM Computing Surveys*, 6(1), 1–55.

Vuillemier, R., A. Perret, F. Porret, P. Weiss. July 1984. "Novel Electromechanical Microshutter Display Device," *Proceedings of the 1984 Eurodisplay Conference*.

Weitek. 1983. *Designing with the WTL 1032/1033*, Weitek Corporation, Santa Clara, CA (Weitek publication 83AN112.1M).

A custom VLSI-based system offers rapid rendering of elaborate, curved objects defined by constructive solid geometry, paving the way for real-time interaction.

Quadratic Surface Rendering on a Logic-Enhanced Frame-Buffer Memory

Jack Goldfeather   Carleton College

Henry Fuchs
University of North Carolina at Chapel Hill

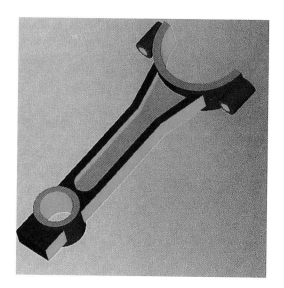

Reprinted from *IEEE Computer Graphics and Applications*, Volume 6, Number 1, January 1986, pages 48-65. Copyright © 1986 by The Institute of Electrical and Electronics Engineers, Inc.

A new system, Pixel-powers, has been designed for the rapid rendering of curved surfaces. This system is a generalization of the design of our logic-enhanced frame buffer memory system, Pixel-planes. Our new design can directly evaluate quadratic expressions of the form $Ax^2 + Bxy + Cy^2 + Dx + Ey + F$ for every pixel (x, y) in the image in parallel. Sample images generated by a high-level simulation of the new system are shown.

The Pixel-planes system was designed to generate 3D, smooth-shaded polygonal images rapidly enough to support real-time interaction.[1-3] The system design takes advantage of the fact that many of the calculations necessary to generate a polygonal raster graphic image (polygon scan conversion, z-buffer visibility testing, and Gourand shading) often are linear in the pixel coordinates. The design incorporates a tree of adders to compute expressions of the form $Ax + By + C$ simultaneously at each pixel (x, y).

In essence this tree, which we shall call the Linear Expression Evaluator (the "multiplier tree" in previous reports), receives the three bit streams A, B, and C as input, and distributes the calculations for the linear expression $Ax + By + C$ in terms of the binary representation of the pixel coordinates (x, y). With our colleagues, we have built

three generations of small prototypes of this system, and have developed image-generation algorithms for them.

This article reports a major enhancement to the Pixel-planes design, for directly handling second-order curved surfaces as well as planar ones. This enhanced system also appears to generalize to still higher order surfaces. We call the new system Pixel-powers.

Pixel-powers has a more elaborate tree structure than Pixel-planes, one that can directly evaluate expressions of the form $Ax^2 + Bxy + Cy^2 + Dx + Ey + F$ for every pixel (x, y) simultaneously, when the coefficients A, B, C, D, E, and F are input directly to the enhanced tree structure. We call this module the Quadratic Expression Evaluator. Briefly, the QEE is constructed by linking two LEE's together with some additional delays and adders.

With this capability, Pixel-powers should be able to generate elaborate, smooth-shaded, curved objects defined, for instance, by constructive solid geometry (CGS) in real time. The primitive objects (cylinders and spheres, for example) are calculated efficiently with the enhanced tree structure, and a one-bit ALU at each pixel calculates the logical combinations (union, intersection, difference) of these primitive objects.[4]

We estimate that Pixel-powers will have a 35 percent greater chip area than Pixel-planes, but should run at the same clock speed. We estimate that the presently running (10-MHz) Pixel-planes chips yield a system capable of generating approximately 30,000 smooth-shaded, full-color polygons per second, including *z*-buffer visibility computations.

We do not yet have a precise estimate of the speed of a 10-MHz Pixel-powers system, but our functional simulator generates images of an internal combustion engine connecting rod in 900 μs (simulated time) assuming the rest of the system can keep up (a difficult task).

It is important to note in passing that, although CSG representations are widely used,[4] there have been only a few custom VLSI-based designs for them.[5]

The Linear Expression Evaluator

A conceptual description of the LEE that is incorporated into the Pixel-planes system follows; a detailed description appears elsewhere.[2,3] The idea (similar to some serial multipliers[6]) is to construct a tree-structured, serial-parallel

multiplier which takes as input the three bit streams—*A, B*, and *C*—and produces as output the value of the expression $Ax + By + C$ simultaneously at every pixel (x, y) on the screen.

To illustrate how this tree is constructed, Figure 1 shows a three-level example which will evaluate $Ax + C$ for $x = 0$, 1, . . . , 7. The products Ax accumulate going down the tree as a series of partial products, with the appropriate multiple of A added at each level, as shown in Figure 1a. Figure 1b illustrates an efficient implementation of this idea. The three-level binary tree has at each node a one-bit adder/delay, a side bit-stream input, and a parent bit-stream input. The bit streams, least significant bit (LSB) first, are sent down the tree in the following way:

1. The left child is sent the parent stream delayed one time unit.
2. The right child is sent the sum of the parent stream and the side stream.

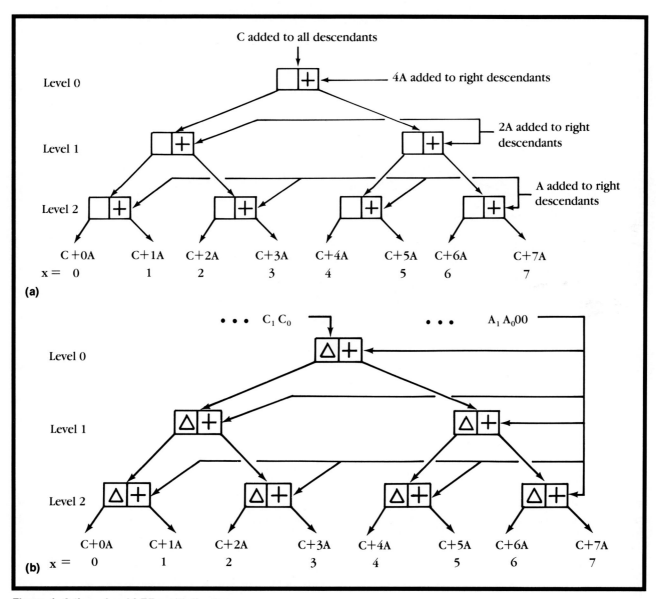

Figure 1. A three-level LEE multiplier tree.

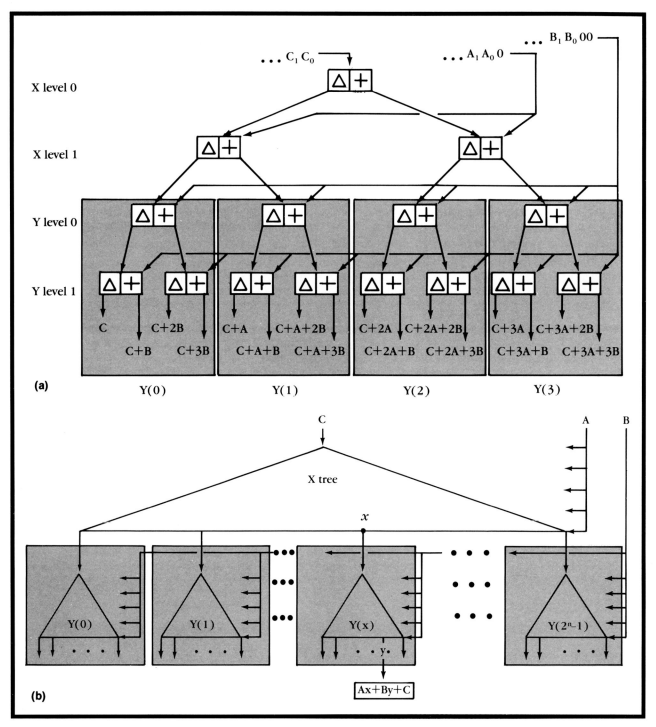

Figure 2. (a) Complete two-level XY-tree to compute Ax + By + C for x,y = 0, 1, 2, 3. (b) Schematic diagram of complete *n*-level XY-tree.

The delay to the left child is simply to keep the bit streams flowing down the left and right branches at the same rate. Note that the 0th bit of a level 0 side input reaches level 2 at the same time as the second bit from a level 2 side input. Hence, if A is the side input at level 0 (that is, the root node) it arrives at the leaf node as a $4A$, and if A is the side input at level 1, it arrives at the leaf node as a $2A$. In order to have something in the parent stream at level 2 when the LSB's of the side inputs arrive, we append two zeros in front of the LSB of each side input, and ignore the first two bits coming out of the leaf nodes.

If we want the eight bit streams emanating from the leaf nodes to be C, $C + A$, ..., $C + 7A$, then the root input must be C, and each side input must be A with two zeros put in front of them. For example, consider $6A + C$. The binary form of 6, $(110)_2$, defines a unique path through the tree: right branch at level 0, right branch at level 1, left branch at level 0. This translates to: add A shifted twice at level 2; add A shifted once at level 1. This, in turn, is equivalent to adding $4A + 2A + 0 = 6A$ at level 2. The root input C passes through the tree as a constant summand to each terminal bit stream.

The LEE is constructed by generalizing this design in the following way:

1. An n-level, binary adder/delay X-tree is constructed, each node of which has a parent-input bit stream and a side-input bit stream. Each node itself is a one-bit adder/delay that (a) delays the bit stream from the parent and sends this parent bit stream to the left child (the parent stream to the root node is C); and (b) adds the parent bit stream to the side bit stream $2^{n-1}A$ (that is, the bit stream with $n-1$ zeros preceding the LSB of A), and sends this sum of two bit streams to the right child.

   The purpose of the delay to the left child is simply to keep the bit streams flowing down the tree at the same rate, since the add operation delays the flow to the right child.

2. There are 2^{n-1} bit streams emanating from the leaf nodes of this n-level X-tree. By writing $Ax + By + C$ in the form $By + (Ax + C)$, we see that it suffices to construct, for each X-tree, another n-level binary adder/delay tree. This tree, called the Y(x)-tree, will receive root input $Ax + C$ from the xth bit stream of the X-tree, and side input B. Because the xth bit stream has already been delayed by $n-1$ as it passed through the X-tree, we must add $2n-2$ zeros in front of the LSB of B.

3. The bit stream emanating from the yth leaf node of the Y(x)-tree represents the value of $Ax + By + C$ for the pixel (x, y). Figure 2a illustrates a complete, small X-Y tree with two levels for X and two levels for Y. Such a LEE would suffice for a trivially small memory chip for a frame buffer with two scan lines and two pixels per scan line. Figure 2b is a schematic of the general X-Y tree.

Several observations about this construction will be useful in our discussion of the quadratic version of the LEE later in this article.

Leading zeros. The zeros that precede the LSB of each bit stream as a result of its multiplication by a power of two are necessary to "initialize" the computation. That is, the zeros are needed in every parent stream when the LSB of A in the X-tree (or B in the Y-tree) arrives from the side input. The appropriate number of "early arriving" bits to each pixel are discarded. For the rest of this article, unless otherwise indicated, we will omit mention of these leading zeros. For example, we will say the side inputs to the X-tree are A rather than $2^{n-1}A$.

Node labels. The effect of adding A at a node at level k ($k = 0 \ldots n-1$) in the X-tree is that of adding $2^{n-k-1}A$ to all pixels which are right descendants of that node. Suppose

each node at level k is labeled with the binary number $(b_0 b_1 \ldots b_{k-1} 1 0 0 \ldots 0)^2$ (b_0 is the most significant bit) where b_i is 1 if the node can be traced back to a right branch at level i, and is 0 otherwise. The root node ($k = 0$) receives the label $1 0 \ldots 0$. If $x = (b_0 b_1 \ldots b_{n-1})^2$, then the value that accumulates at location x in the X-tree is

Root Input $+$
$\sum_{k=0}^{n-1} 2^{n-k-1} b_k \cdot$ (Side Input at node $b_0 b_1 \ldots b_{k-1} 1 0 \ldots 0$)
$= C + \sum_{k=0}^{n-1} 2^{n-k-1} b_k A = Ax + C$

The xy term. Although not presently implemented in the Pixel-planes system, the outputs from the X-tree could be rerouted into the side inputs of the Y(x) trees, rather than into the root node. This modified LEE would produce Bxy when B is the side input into the X-tree.

Path design. Technology constraints make it impossible to put the entire tree on a single chip. A portion of the Y(x)-tree is put on the chip together with the path from the root node of the X-tree to this portion of the Y(x)-tree, as shown in Figure 3. The path is activated on each chip by using the binary code discussed above.

There are several possible schemes for the QEE, some of which may look simpler than others from the point of view of the global layout, but the one that we chose seems to be the most promising, considering the constraints mentioned above.

> *The key idea in the QEE design is to send a different side input to every node in the X- and Y (x)-trees.*

The Quadratic Expression Evaluator

We now illustrate the construction of an enhanced tree structure that accepts as input the six coefficients (A, B, C, D, E, F) and produces as output the expression $Ax^2 + Bxy + Cy^2 + Dx + Ey + F$ simultaneously for every pixel (x, y). The key idea in the design of the QEE is to send a different side input to every node in the X- and Y(x)-trees, rather than the same inputs as in the LEE. Recall that each node of the X-tree at level k can be labeled by the binary number $(b_0 b_1 \ldots b_{k-1} 1 0 \ldots 0)_2$ and that if

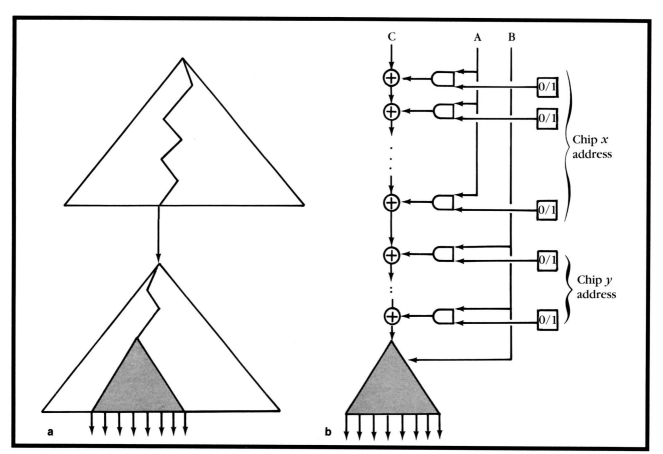

Figure 3. Path through X-tree and part of Y(x)-tree.

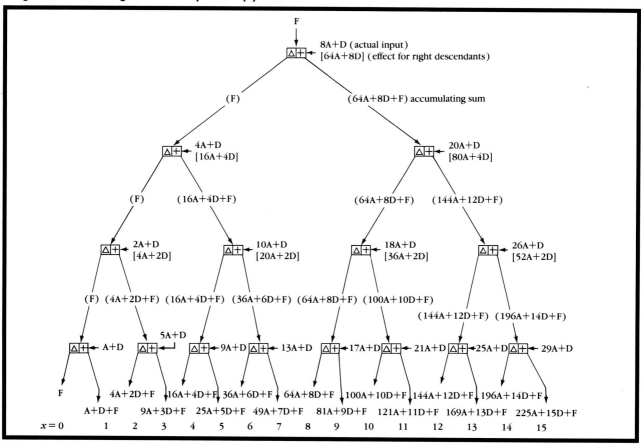

Figure 4. Side inputs for a four-level tree to produce $Ax^2 + Dx + F$ for $x = 0, 1, \ldots 15$.

$$x = (b_0 b_1 \ldots b_{n-1})_2 = \Sigma_{k=0}^{n-1} 2^{n-k-1} b_k$$

then the x bit stream is

Root Input +

$$\Sigma_{k=0}^{n-1} 2^{n-k-1} b_k \cdot (\text{Side Input at } b_0 b_1 \ldots b_{k-1} 10 \ldots 0)$$

We modify the side inputs to the X-tree to generate the expression $Ax^2 + Dx + F$. Since we already know how to evaluate $Dx + F$ (using side input D and root input F), we will concentrate for the moment on the Ax^2 part of the expression. Suppose we write x in the binary expansion form

$$x = \Sigma_{k=0}^{n-1} 2^{n-k-1} b_k$$

Then

$$x^2 = (\Sigma_{k=0}^{n-1} 2^{n-k-1} b_k)^2 =$$
$$\Sigma_{k=0}^{n-1} b_k^2 2^{2(n-k-1)} + 2 \Sigma_{k=0}^{n-1} \Sigma_{j=0}^{k-1} b_k b_j 2^{n-k-1} 2^{n-j-1}$$

If we observe that $b_k^2 = b_k$ (since $b_k = 0$ or 1) and use the convention that if $k = 0$ then $\Sigma_{j=0}^{k-1} (anything) = 0$, then we can write Ax^2 as

$$\Sigma_{k=0}^{n-1} 2^{n-k-1} b_k (2^{n-k-1} (A + \Sigma_{j=0}^{k-1} 2^{k-j} b_j (2A)))$$

Hence if we let the root input be F, and the side input to node $(b_0 b_1 \ldots b_{k-1} 10 \ldots 0)_2$ be

$$D + 2^{n-k-1} (A + \Sigma_{j=0}^{k-1} 2^{k-j} b_j (2A))$$

then the x bit stream is

Root input $= \Sigma_{k=0}^{n-1} 2^{n-k-1} b_k$ (Side input at
$b_0 b_1 \ldots b_{k-1} 10 \ldots 0)$
$$= F + \Sigma_{k=0}^{n-1} 2^{n-k-1} b_k (D + 2^{n-k-1} (A + \Sigma_{j=0}^{k-1} 2^{k-j} b_j (2A)))$$

$$= F + D \Sigma_{k=0}^{n-1} 2^{n-k-1} b_k +$$
$$\Sigma_{k=0}^{n-1} 2^{n-k-1} b_k (2^{n-k-1} (A + \Sigma_{j=0}^{k-1} 2^{k-j} b_j (2A)))$$
$$= F + Dx + Ax^2$$

See Figure 4 for a four-level example.

The problem of generating $Ax^2 + Dx + F$ has now been reduced to computing these side inputs to the X-tree. The key observation is that the summand

$$\Sigma_{j=0}^{k-1} 2^{k-j} b_j (2A)$$

can be evaluated by "siphoning off" the left child output of the corresponding node of another n-level tree with root input 0 and a constant side input $2A$.

Putting this all together, the side inputs into the X-tree that are necessary to evaluate the expression $Ax^2 + Dx + F$ at location x can be generated as follows:

1. A new "PX-tree" of adders identical to the X-tree is sent a root input of 0, and a constant side input of $2A$.
2. The left child output of a node at level k in the PX-tree, in addition to being sent down the PX-tree in the usual way, is (a) added to A, delayed $(n-1-k)$ time units, added to D; and (b) becomes the side input to the corresponding node of the X-tree.

Figure 4 shows an example of a four-level tree to evaluate $Ax^2 + Dx + F$, and Figure 5a illustrates the calculation that generates side inputs for the top two levels of the tree. Figure 5b is a schematic of the general node-to-node linking, referred to as a *Quadratic Linked X-tree* with inputs (A, D, F).

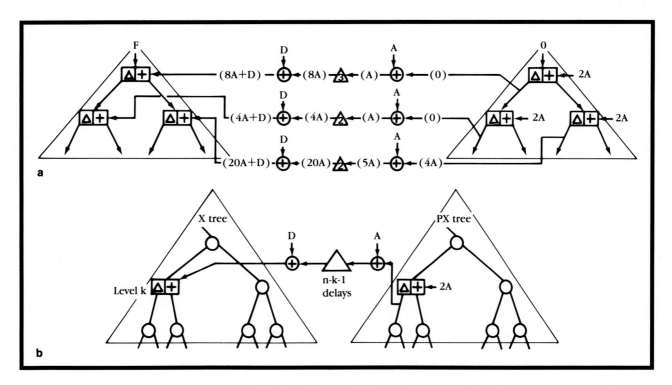

Figure 5. (a) Creating inputs for the top two levels of the tree in Figure 4. (b) PX-to-X node connection at level k.

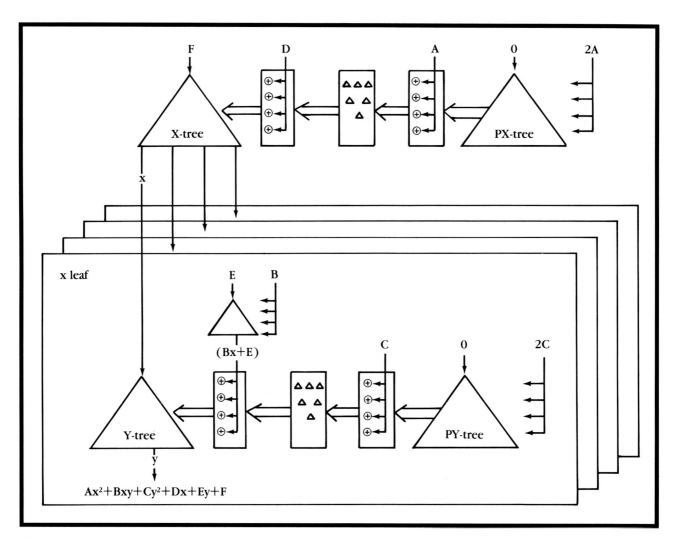

Figure 6. Schematic layout of the QEE.

The quadratic expression in two variables is an extension of this scheme. Suppose we write the expression $Q(x, y) = Ax^2 + Bxy + Cy^2 + Dx + Ey + F$ in the form $Cy^2 + (Bx + E) y + (Ax^2 + Dx + F)$. Then, to evaluate $Q(x, y)$ it suffices to construct a Quadratic Linked Y(x)-tree with inputs $(C, Bx + E, Ax^2 + Dx + F)$. The last two inputs are generated via a Linear X-tree and a Quadratic Linked X-tree, respectively. Figure 6 shows the complete schematic of the QEE.

Since the entire QEE for all pixels on the screen cannot be contained on a single chip, we proceed in a manner analogous to the path-to-subtree scheme of the LEE. On each chip, we put as much of the linked PY(x)- and Y(x)-trees as are needed for the pixels on this chip. Three

identical, complete X paths and two identical, partial Y paths are constructed, and linked appropriately to replicate that portion of the complete QEE relevant to the pixels on this chip. An illustration of this is given in Figure 7. Figure 8 illustrates the PY(x)- and Y(x)-subtrees that would be implemented on a small 16-pixel chip.

Implementing a system with a QEE

We have just begun to plan the implementation of Pixelpowers. It appears so far to be a straightforward expansion of the Pixel-planes implementation. A brief look at that implementation may help explain the one being planned.

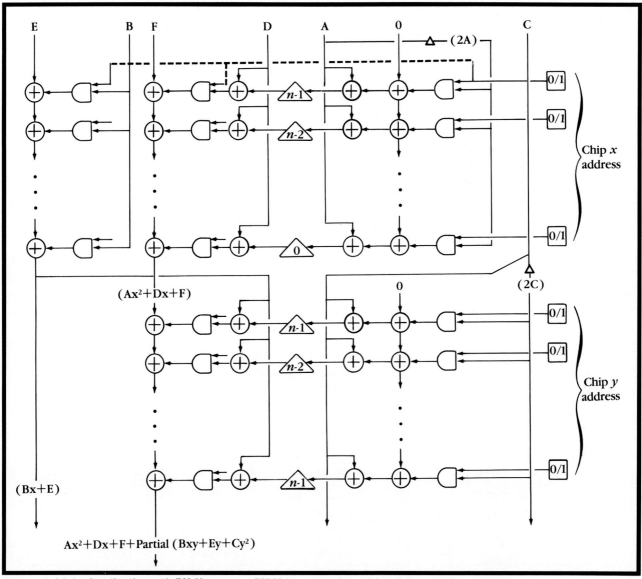

Figure 7. Linked paths through PX-X tree and PY-Y tree together with extra x path for xy term.

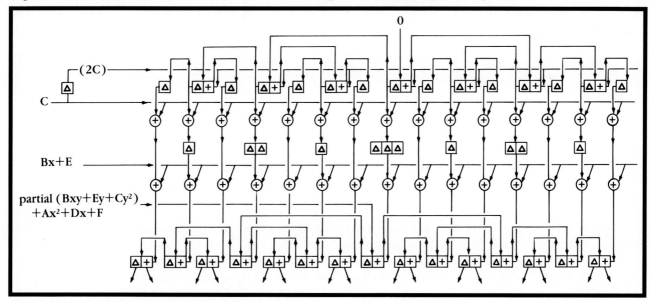

Figure 8. Chip organization of linked subtrees.

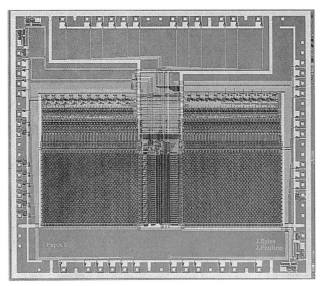

Figure 9. Micrograph of Pixel-planes4.0 memory chip (Melgar Photographers).

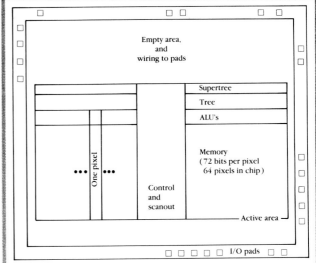

Figure 10. Pixel-planes4.0 general floor plan.

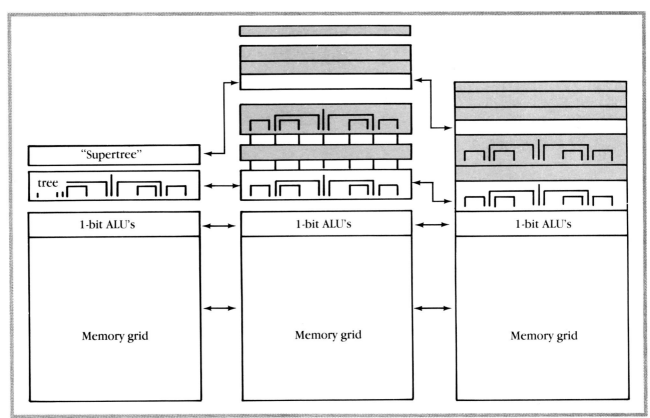

Figure 11. Pixel-planes to Pixel-powers organization (common central wiring channel not shown).

Figure 9 is a micrograph of our fourth-generation Pixel-planes4.0 memory chip, and Figure 10 is a general floor plan of this chip. (We actually have a newer, larger chip that is now working, Pixel-planes4.1, but since that chip is fundamentally two Pixel-planes4.0 chips, it is just as valid, but simpler, to use Pixel-planes4.0 as the basis of com-

parison.) To implement a QEE within such a system, we put a QEE in place of the LEE.

The LEE on a chip consists of two modules: the portion of the complete binary "multiplier tree" for the pixels on this chip, and the extra tree path ("supertree") to the root of the global tree. Figure 11 illustrates the transformation

IEEE CG&A

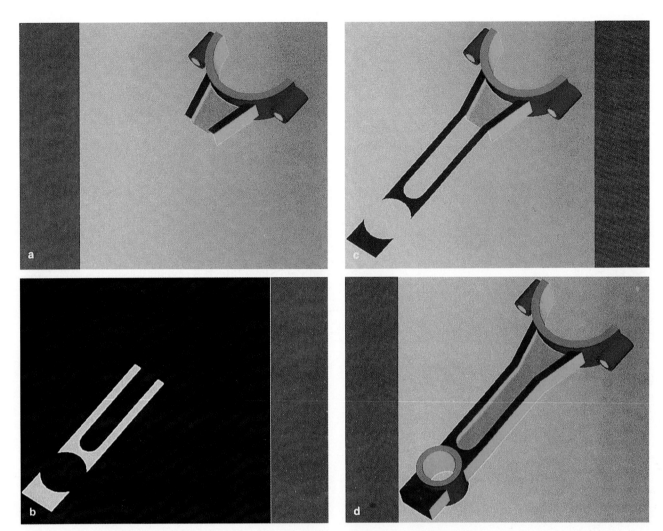

Figure 12. All images are produced by a functional simulator. (a) partial image after processing of 190 opcodes with 144 coefficient sets (46 opcodes do not need coefficient); (b) 28 opcodes specify the area and depth of the next face and disable pixels that are subtracted by other volumes; (c) enabled pixels are copied into the z-buffer and those still visible are shaded—total of opcodes is now 222; (d) completed simulation with a final total of 342 opcodes with 260 coefficient sets. Time to generate this image in a 10-MHz chip is estimated to be 900 microseconds.

of a Pixel-planes organization into a Pixel-powers one. Figure 11a shows the major parts of a Pixel-planes chip; Figure 11b shows the major parts of a Pixel-powers one. (Figures 7 and 8 show these parts in more detail.) The arrows between the Pixel-planes chip in 11a and the Pixel-powers chip in 11b indicate corresponding parts in the two designs. Figure 11c shows the Pixel-powers plan after compaction.

The areas for the various modules are estimated from the areas for the associated modules on the Pixel-planes 4.0 memory chip, shown in Figure 9. From this we estimate that Pixel-powers chips will be about 35 percent larger in area than corresponding Pixel-planes ones.

The clock speeds of the Pixel-powers chips should be close to that of the current Pixel-planes4 chips. Indeed, we see no reason why the basic clock cycle (10 MHz) should be different. For executing various algorithms, additional bits of precision are likely to be needed with Pixel-powers, so the time to process a primitive object may be somewhat longer than in Pixel-planes. On the other hand, the number of primitive objects typically would be much fewer in a Pixel-powers image than in a Pixel-planes one.

We have developed a high-level simulator to facilitate algorithm development for Pixel-powers. Using that simulator, Figure 12 illustrates the construction of a simple

CSG-defined object in Pixel-powers—a connecting rod of an internal combustion engine. The object has 17 primitives, of which 14 are evident in this image. Seventy coefficient sets (A, B, C, D, E, F) were required to generate the image. We estimate that the object could be generated by Pixel-powers memory chips in less than 900 μs. The image-generation process itself is described in an upcoming report.

Conclusions

The generalization of the LEE tree to a QEE gives vastly increased power to our logic-enhanced memory chips. Since the number of primitives in a curved surface model of an object is typically much less than a polygonal model of it, the effect of the extra power in the memory chip is even more dramatic. The challenge now is to develop algorithms and systems to convert efficiently the geometrically transformed representation into a form suitable for a frame-buffer system composed of these chips. ∎

Acknowledgments

We thank Jeff Hultquist for developing the functional simulator that generated the images in Figure 12, and John Eyles for developing a detailed simulator of the QEE. We also thank both Hultquist and Eyles, and John Poulton for valuable discussions and suggestions. We thank Paul Deitz and Paul Stay of the U.S. Army Ballistic Research Laboratory for the CSG data of the connecting rod.

This research is supported in part by the Defense Advanced Research Projects Agency, monitored by the U.S. Army Research Office, Research Triangle Park, North Carolina, under contract number DAAG29-83-K-0148, and the National Science Foundation grant number ECS-8300970.

References

1. Henry Fuchs and John Poulton, "Pixel-planes: A VLSI-Oriented System for a Raster Graphics Engine," *VLSI Design* (formerly *Lambda*), Vol. 2, No. 3, 3rd quarter 1981, pp.20-28.

2. Henry Fuchs, Jack Goldfeather, Jeff P. Hultquist, Susan Spach, John D. Austin, Frederick P. Brooks, Jr., John G. Eyles, and John Poulton, "Fast Spheres, Shadows, Textures, Transparencies, and Image Enhancements in Pixel-Planes," *Computer Graphics*, Vol. 19, No. 3, July 1985 (*Proc. SIGGRAPH 85*).

3. John Poulton, Henry Fuchs, John D. Austin, John G. Eyles, Justin Heinecke, Cheng-Hong Hsieh, Jack Goldfeather, Jeff P. Hultquist, and Susan Spach, "Implemention of a Full Scale Pixel-planes System," in *Proc. 1985 Chapel Hill Conference on VLSI*, H. Fuchs, ed., Computer Science Press, Rockville, Md.

4. Gershon Kedem and John L. Ellis, "Computer Structures for Curve-Solid Classification in Geometric Modeling," technical report TR84-37, Microelectronic Center of North Carolina, Research Triangle Park, N.C., Sept. 1984.

5. A.A.G. Requicha, "Representation for Rigid Objects: Theory, Methods, and Systems," *ACM Computing Surveys*, Vol. 12, No. 4, Dec. 1980, pp.437-464.

6. Richard F. Lyon, "Two's Complement Pipeline Multipliers," *IEEE Trans. Communications,* Vol. COM-24, April 1976, pp.481-425.

Jack Goldfeather is an associate professor of mathematics at Carleton College in Northfield, Minnesota, where he teaches a variety of undergraduate mathematics and computer science courses. His primary research in mathematics is in the area of algebraic topology, especially the algebraic properties of mappings between infinite, dimensional topological spaces. During a 1984-1985 sabbatical at UNC at Chapel Hill, he was a mathematics consultant to the Pixel-planes research group.

Goldfeather received a BA in mathematics from Rutgers University in 1969, and an MS and PhD in mathematics from Purdue University in 1971 and 1975, respectively. He taught at the University of Wisconsin at Milwaukee from 1975 to 1977 before joining the Carleton faculty.

Henry Fuchs is a professor of computer science at the University of North Carolina at Chapel Hill, where he has been teaching graduate courses in computer graphics and VLSI design, and directs the research of PhD students and research associates in graphics algorithms and VLSI architectures.

Fuchs is the principal investigator of research projects funded by DARPA, NIH, and NSF. He consults for a variety of industrial organizations. He is an associate editor of *ACM Transactions on Graphics* and was chairman of the 1985 Chapel Hill Conference on VLSI. He received a BA from the University of California at Santa Cruz in 1970, and a PhD from the University of Utah in 1975.

Jack Goldfeather can be contacted at Carleton College, Mathematics Department, One N. College St., Northfield, MN 55057; Henry Fuchs can be contacted at the University of North Carolina, Department of Computer Science, New West Hall 035A, Chapel Hill, NC 27512.

Chapter 5: Real-Time Scan-Conversion Hardware

Beside the consideration of its limited bandwidth, which frequently causes a bottleneck on image updating, the bit-map is expensive to implement since it requires a large amount of memory. The inefficiency of the frame buffer becomes most noticeable when we use it to store simple line drawings. Although the image is very simple, storing it in the bit-map consumes considerable amounts of time and memory. Time is consumed in scan converting the lines and in making the necessary memory accesses to modify the bit-map's contents. Memory consumption is high because the frame buffer's design makes no attempt to capitalize on the simple geometry of the image. That is, the memory requirement for the frame buffer is independent of the complexity of the images that it stores.

A popular alternative to the conventional frame buffer systems is the real-time scan-conversion technique. As we saw in Chapter 3, frame buffers are always considered as storage for the bit-map of the image. In a real-time scan-conversion system, the image in a linear display file (LDF) is not stored as an array of intensity values but as higher level geometric descriptions. The entire scene is rendered once or more per refresh cycle to generate the video signal. Modification to the image can be easily incorporated by varying the higher level geometric descriptions and the resulting scene is instantly visible on the display.

With real-time scan conversion, the image generation speed is no longer limited by the bandwidth of the bit-map. Since pixels are generated on-the-fly, they must be computed at a reasonably rapid rate and must somehow be synchronized with the raster scan beam. This requirement is a nontrivial burden on the conventional scan-conversion hardware. For a 512×512 60 Hertz noninterlaced display, a new pixel value must be calculated every 45 nanoseconds. As we saw in Chapter 1, the value of a pixel is the result of a sequence of fairly complicated calculations. To achieve the expected speed, it is necessary to make use of massive parallelism of processing.

5.1: Parallel Processing Architectures for Image Rasterization

There are two major parallel-processing architectural structures for image rasterization systems. They are (1) partitioned object-space structure and (2) partitioned image-space structure. These two structures are closely related to two important domains of graphics representations, namely, the *object space* and the *image space*.

The object space of an image is the set of graphics primitives, such as lines, polygons, and spheres, which compose the scene to be depicted. The image space of a scene is the set of raster elements (pixels) of the display and contains a fixed number (m) of elements that equals the resolution of the display.

The two architectural structures define the two main approaches in distributing processing parallelism in the two distinct spaces of image representation.

5.1.1: Partitioned Object-Space Architecture

In a partitioned object space architecture, the graphics objects in the object space are divided into a number of *groups* such that the union of these groups forms the object space itself. In addition, these groups are not necessarily mutually exclusive. Objects from the same group are handled concurrently. In most cases, an individual processor is assigned to each of the objects. Different groups of objects share the same processors and hence must be processed sequentially.

Examples of partitioned object space systems include Fussell's [FUSS82], Locanthi's [LOCA79], and Weinberg's [WEIN81] systems. In their systems, the entire object space is treated as a single group. Each object in the object space is assigned to an individual object processor and rendered simultaneously. A sequence of pixel values is generated by each object processor to synthesize the image of its associated object. The pixel generation activities of the *object processors* are synchronized such that they are all working on the same raster pixel at any instance.

5.1.2: Partitioned Image-Space Architecture

In this type of architecture, the image space (raster) is divided into a number of *partitions* of pixels. Pixels from the same partition are independent of each other and, hence, can be processed simultaneously. However, different partitions are processed sequentially. In most cases there is only one partition that contains all of the pixels in the raster considered. This architecture can be exemplified by the pixel-

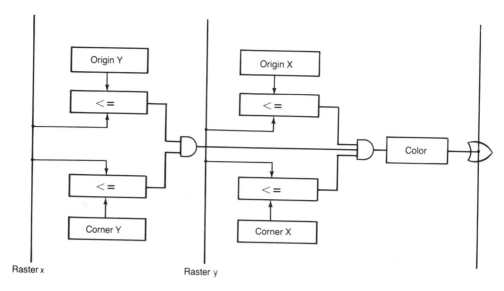

Figure 5.1: Rectangle cell.

planes system [FUCH81, FUCH82, POUL85]. Whelan's rectangle area filling system is also of this type [WHEL82].

In the pixel-planes system, the entire image space is grouped into a single partition. Since all pixels of the partition are to be processed simultaneously, there is an individual processor associated with each image memory cell that holds a pixel. In this way, all the pixels in the raster (image space) can be processed in parallel. The objects in the object space are rendered sequentially. According to the high-level descriptions of the geometric objects, each pixel processor executes a *pel-process* to determine the value of its corresponding pixel.

5.1.3: A Generalized Notation for Parallel-Processing Image Rasterizers

The two major parallel-processing techniques for image rasterization are the following:

Object-space partitioning scheme (OP-scheme) In a parallel processing architecture, the object space can be divided into a certain number of groups such that the objects in a subset can be processed in parallel. The object-space partitioning scheme defines the way graphics objects are grouped. An α-β-OP scheme is an object-space partitioning scheme that groups the graphics objects in the object space into α groups and the maximum cardinality of the α groups is β.

Image-space partitioning scheme (IP-scheme) The image-space partitioning scheme determines the way that the image of a display is partitioned. A γ-λ-IP scheme is an image-space partitioning scheme that divides the image space into γ partitions. The maximum cardinality of the partitions is λ. To rasterize a graphics object, the system will consider the γ partitions each having at most λ pixels.

In general, any image rasterizer can be identified by the way that its object space and image space are partitioned. For example, the pixel-planes system [POUL85] is constructed based on an n-1-OP scheme and a 1-m-IP scheme. In this system the object space that contains at most n graphics objects is partitioned into n subsets, each of which contains at most one object. However, the raster image of each object, which is made up of m pixels, is formed by a single image-space partition with exactly m pixels. Assume the total time required to execute a pel-process is T_{pel} units, then the pixel-planes system is able to obtain the entire raster image of an object in T_{pel} units of time. However, the objects in the object space must be processed sequentially.

At the other extreme, the Fussell's real-time scan conversion engine [FUSS82] uses a 1-n-OP scheme and an m-1-IP scheme. That means it is capable of handling all of the graphics objects simultaneously. However, only one pixel can be computed per T_{pel} units of time.

We call a system that employs an α-β-OP scheme and a γ-λ-IP scheme as an α-β-γ-λ *system*. Notice that the $\beta\lambda$ and $\alpha\gamma$ values can be regarded as indicators for the *hardware complexity* and *processing-time complexity* of an α-β-γ-λ-*system*, respectively.

5.2: Architectures for Real-Time Image Rasterization

There are two basic requirements for real-time image rasterization: (1) the entire image can be generated within a single refresh cycle and (2) generation of the raster pixels is sequenced in the same order as the raster is scanned and synchronized with the scan-out beam. For the first one, we need a system capable of generating the images reasonably fast. Either the partitioned image-space or the partitioned object-space type architectures is able to fulfill this requirement to a certain extent. However, the second requirement can only be satisfied with a partitioned object-space architecture.

5.2.1: Locanthi's System

The concept of achieving real-time image rasterization with partitioned object-space architecture can be demonstrated by Locanthi's system [LOCA79]. In this system, the processing for a bit-map raster is distributed over a centralized *display memory*. The display contains a collection of identical processing units, the *rectangle cells*. Figure 5.1 shows the layout of a rectangle cell.

A graphics object (rectangle) is described by its two diagonally opposing vertices, the bottom left and the top right vertices, namely, the *origin* and the *corner*. The color of the rectangle is defined by the parameter "color," which is an address to the system's color map. Colors are combined by ORing color map addresses.

Each rectangle in an image is processed by an individual rectangle cell. To render a rectangle, each pixel of the raster is tested for containment in the rectangle. As is shown in Figure 5.1, the origin and the corner of the rectangle are stored in the Origin X, Origin Y, Corner X, and Corner Y registers. The test for containment of the pixel $P(x,y)$ is performed by evaluating the logical function "contains$(P) = [origin \leq P$ AND $corner \geq P]$." More precisely, $P(x,y)$ is in the rectangle if the expression [(Origin $X \leq x$ AND $x \leq$ Corner X) AND (Origin $Y \leq y$ AND Corner $Y \geq y$)] is TRUE. When a pixel is found to be contained in the rectangle, it is assigned with the value stored in the register Color. Therefore, the result from a rectangle cell will be "0" if the pixel is not contained in the rectangle and the address of the rectangle's color in the color map if it is in the rectangle.

Since an image may consist of many rectangles, a test for containment must be performed on each pixel for every rectangle. These tests can be done in parallel because each graphics object is assigned an individual rectangle cell. To determine whether a pixel is in any of the rectangles, the results from all rectangle cells are ORed. It is much easier to understand how the "ORing" operation works if the rectangles are mutually exclusive. When overlapping of rectangles is allowed, a pixel may be contained by more than one rectangle. In this case, the ORing is assumed to give proper shading value for the overlaps of different rectangles.

The speed for computing a pixel's value is extremely fast. The shading value of a pixel can be obtained almost immediately after its (x,y) coordinates are fed into the *display memory*. Therefore, if the pixels $P(x,y)$ are given to the *display processor* in the same sequence as the raster is scanned and at a rate synchronized with the video timing, an image can be rendered at the same speed as the screen is refreshed.

Locanthi's system is a simple system that can only render rectilinear rectangles and is inadequate for most serious applications such as those requiring smooth shaded three-dimensional graphics. The Weinberg [WEIN81], Fussell [FUSS82], and Westmore [WEST87] systems have been proposed for three-dimensional smooth shaded graphics.

5.3: Article Overview

In the first paper, "A VLSI-Oriented Architecture for Real-Time Raster Display of Shaded Polygons," Fussell and Rathi describe a real-time scan-conversion engine. Similar to Locanthi's system, there is an individual object processor assigned to a geometric object in the scene. However, each object processor in Fussell's system is capable of handling a smooth shaded triangle in the three-dimensional space. In addition, Fussell's system is supplemented with special hardware to perform geometric transformations and clipping.

Westmore's paper, "Real-Time Shaded Color Polygon Generation System," is a continuation of Fussell's research and uses an object-processor based approach with one processor per triangle.

In Weinberg's paper [WEIN81], real-time scan conversion is further complemented with anti-aliasing capability. Unlike the former two systems, the output from the object processors is "pumped" through a serial comparator and a filter. In the serial comparator, the appropriate shade value of the current pixel is extracted. Then an additional adjustment on its shade is done in the filter to accomplish anti-aliasing.

Gharachorloo, in "Super Buffer: A Systolic VLSI Graphics Engine for Real-Time Raster Image Generation," takes a different approach in the pixel evaluation process. In the Super Buffer system the object processors are organized as a systolic array. Unlike the systems in the other reprints (in which an object processor is assigned to a particular graphics object throughout the frame time), processors in the systolic array are shared by various graphics objects. An object is rendered as it propagates through the array.

References

[FUCH81] Fuchs, H. and J. Poulton, "Pixel-Planes: A VLSI-Oriented Design for a Raster Graphics Engine," *VLSI Design,* Vol. 2, No. 3, 3rd Quarter 1981, pp. 20-28.

[FUCH82] Fuchs, H., J. Poulton, A. Paeth, and A. Bell, "Developing Pixel-Planes: A Smart Memory-Based Raster Graphics System," *Proc. of 1982 Conf. on Advanced Research in VLSI*, Massachusetts Institute of Technology, Cambridge, Mass., 1982, pp. 137-146.

[FUSS82] Fussell, D. and B.D. Rathi, "A VLSI-Oriented Architecture for Real-Time Raster Display of Shaded Polygons," *Proc. of Graphics Interface '82*, ACM, Inc., New York, 1982, pp. 373-380.

[LOCA79] Locanthi, B., "Object Oriented Raster Displays," *CALTECH Conference on VLSI*, California Institute of Technology, Pasadena, Calif., 1979, pp. 215-225.

[POUL85] Poulton, J., H. Fuchs, J. Austin, J. Eyles, J. Heinecke, C. Hsieh, J. Goldfeather, J. Hultquist, and S. Spach, "Pixel Plane: Building a VLSI-Based Graphics System," *Chapel Hill Conference on VLSI*, Computer Science Press, Rockville, Md., 1985, pp. 35-61.

[WEIN81] Weinberg, R., "Parallel Processing, Image Synthesis, and Anti-Aliasing," *Computer Graphics*, Vol. 15, No. 3, Aug. 1981, pp. 325-332.

[WEST87] Westmore, R.J., "Real-Time Shaded Colour Polygon Generation System," *IEE Proceedings*, Vol. 134, No. 1, Jan. 1987, pp. 31-38.

[WHEL82] Whelan, D.S., "A Rectangular Area Filling Display System Architecture," *Computer Graphics*, Vol. 16, No. 3, July 1982, pp. 356-362.

A VLSI-ORIENTED ARCHITECTURE FOR REAL-TIME RASTER DISPLAY OF
SHADED POLYGONS*

(Preliminary Report)

Donald Fussell
Bharat Deep Rathi
The University of Texas at Austin
Austin, Texas 78712

ABSTRACT

This paper describes the organization of a large-scale graphics hardware system which can produce color, shaded, anti-aliased, perspective images of complex three-dimensional scenes in real time. By complex scenes we mean those consisting of at least 25,000 polygons. In contrast, existing high-performance raster systems of this type can handle only 1000 to 4000 polygons. This level of complexity is attainable with reasonable cost and reliability only if large parts of the system can be implemented as custom VLSI chips. In particular, it is possible to replace a traditional frame buffer with a device which stores polygons rather than points and performs scanout, shading, and anti-aliasing on them. With the addition of other special-purpose chips which perform transformations, clipping, perspective projection, and lighting calculations, such a "polygon buffer" forms the core of a parallel, pipelined organization which achieves the desired level of performance.

KEYWORDS: Graphics hardware, raster display, real-time, VLSI

1.0 INTRODUCTION

Recent advances in the availability of design techniques and fabrication facilities for VLSI circuits have created new opportunities for designers to produce special-purpose architectures. Computer graphics is one of the application areas which has benefitted most from this situation to date. Using the custom VLSI design techniques introduced by Mead and Conway [11], a number of researchers in recent years have developed new hardware systems whose function is the high-speed implementation of algorithms essential to the production of high-quality images by computer [1] [2] [3] [7] [8] [14] [17]. These new approaches complement the work of designers of graphics hardware systems who did not have access to the technology of integrated circuit design and who therefore could not regard as feasible methods which may now may not only be possible, but in some cases even preferable.

The goal of this work is to design a hardware system which can produce color, shaded, anti-aliased, perspective images of complex three-dimensional scenes in real time. By complex scenes we mean those consisting of at least 25,000 polygons. In contrast, existing high-performance raster systems of this type can handle only 1000 to 4000 polygons in real time,

so our requirements include about an order of magnitude increase in the complexity of the scene. In order to achieve increased performance cost-effectively, it will be necessary to make use of massive parallelism of operations and of pipelining techniques, while carefully designing the system to consist of only a few basic module types and thus only a few chip types which can be used in large numbers to achieve the desired performance at a low cost. In this sense, the architecture we are proposing is a radical one in that it would have been impractical at the level of complexity we wish to obtain without the use of special-purpose chips.

The reduction of this complexity into a simple, regular structure suitable for VLSI implementation is a task which must proceed in a top-down fashion as the system design progresses. This paper is a preliminary report of an ongoing project, and thus only the higher levels of the design are described here.

---

*This work supported in part by NSF Grant MCS-8109489.

2.0 SYSTEM OVERVIEW

The functions which must be performed by a graphics system in order to produce a realistic image of a three-dimensional polygonal model are by now well understood. Figure 1 gives a pictorial representation of the operations which must be performed in transforming a database into an image on the screen. We may envision data as being pipelined through the various operations from the model data structure onto the display. The two ends of the pipeline represent the scene in object coordinates (the model) and image coordinates respectively. In the former case, the representation is more compact, due both to hierarchical encoding of the data and to the fact that at even the lowest levels of the hierarchy the geometric primitives used are polygons or higher-order parametric surfaces. The representation of the scene in image coordinates must ultimately be reduced to points, which are the lowest-level and least compact geometric primitives available for representation of complex scenes.

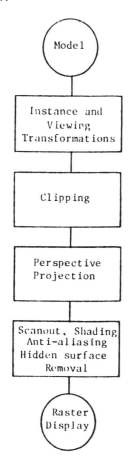

Figure 1

Image generation process

We can partition the operations being performed during the image synthesis process into two general classes. The first is a transformation from a model in object coordinate space to an image coordinate space description and the second is the reduction of a structured collection of high-level modeling primitives to a set of low-level output primitives, which for the case of raster displays are points. Instance transformations and viewing transformations are devoted primarily to the first task of coordinate system transformation (although instance transformations also serve to decode the structure of the model to form a simple collection of modeling primitives), while scanout, shading, and anti-aliasing are involved in the conversion from modeling to output primitives. Clipping may be considered to fit into the first category since it is peformed on high-level primitives as part of the transformation to an appropriate image-space representation. Hidden-surface removal can be considered an independent operation since it can be performed in conjunction with either process, although for the implementations we are interested in, it is intimately related to the primitive reduction process.

Hardware approaches to high-performance image generation have handled these two classes of operations independently, and the architecture we propose will follow this tradition. Both high-performance raster and vector display systems have long employed special-purpose array processing modules for doing the matrix-vector multiplications required for coordinate transformation as well as hardware clipping devices. The advent of VLSI technology has made possible the creation of special-purpose chips to perform the same operations at a lower hardware cost and with greater reliability. The Geometry Engine of Clark handles both of these functions with a set of 12 virtually identical MOS chips in current technology, which could be reduced to a single chip in the near future [1]. This system can currently process approximately 1000 polygons in real time, and with the projected reductions in size and concomitant increases in speed, this should increase to about 4000.

The second class of operations involving primitive reduction has been somewhat more difficult to handle at real-time rates and has therefore contributed more to the complexity and expense of real-time image generation systems. This is easily seen when the cost of a typical real-time vector display is compared with that of a raster display of comparable performance, since the primary distinction between the two in terms of hardware requirements arises as a result of the absence of most operations of this type. Most VLSI-oriented approaches to solving this portion of the image synthesis problem have begun with the idea of enhancing the capabilities of a frame buffer in order to allow it to tackle problems of this class [2] [7] [8] [17]. The work of Cohen [3] is a notable exception to this.

The architecture proposed here is based on the same idea, to take advantage of the opportunity to create custom chips in order to add processing capability to the previously passive memory function of the frame buffer. If we assume that each element of a frame buffer need not be merely a memory cell, that we have the freedom to make the unit more complex, endowing it with the capability to implement for itself some operations which must be done for image generation in parallel with all the other cells of the frame buffer, then the question arises as to whether it might not be better to make each unit a higher-level primitive than a mere point. This is the approach we take, which is distinct from those noted above, in which the primitives remain points but the points are provided with added processing power. In our system, the "frame buffer" consists of a collection of polygons rather than points. For simplicity and uniformity of implementation, the polygons are required to be triangles. The advantages of this requirement outweigh its limitations. Since any polygon can be easily triangulated, any scene described by a collection of polygons can be easily transformed into a description consisting only of triangles. In the process, any "non-planar polygons" which may have existed in the original scene description are removed. Moreover, procedures which are used for automatic generation of scene descriptions from real-world input data typically generate only triangles [5]. Finally, Gouraud shading, the most suitable smooth-shading technique for fast hardware implementation, produces no shading anomalies on triangles.

It makes sense to call this collection of triangle processing elements a frame buffer because it performs an analogous function in the graphics system to that of a traditional frame buffer in that it serves as a medium for storing the scene description after it has been transformed into image space. Of course, no reduction of high-level to low-level primitives has been performed before the image space scene description is stored, so this function must be performed by the frame buffer itself. From the point of view of the refresh controller for the raster display, the "triangle buffer" appears to be a frame buffer in that the controller outputs addresses to it on an address bus and receives in return a pixel's color value on a data bus. Each triangle processor performs a scanout of the triangle it contains, incrementally determining the color and Z coordinate value for each pixel.

These are fed through arbitration logic which determines which pixel is closest to the observer and returns the color of that pixel on the data bus. At the cost of added complexity, the arbitration logic can also be used to perform anti-aliasing, resulting in a filtered pixel color value being returned on the data bus. Thus the triangle buffer performs all operations involved in the reduction of high-level to low-level primitives.

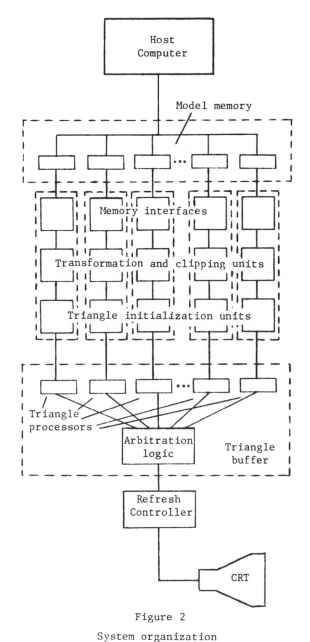

Figure 2

System organization

The remainder of the system implements the coordinate transformations, clipping, perspective division, and shading calculations for the vertices. It also contains a dual-ported memory for storing the object-space scene description.

3.0 SYSTEM ORGANIZATION

In this section we describe in more detail the organization of the major portions of the system. The overall organization is depicted in Figure 2. Our discussion will begin with a consideration of the triangle buffer, following which the modeling memory and transformation pipeline are described.

3.1 The Triangle Buffer

The triangle buffer consists of an array of triangle processing units, each of which performs scanout and smooth-shading of the triangle it contains. A triangle processor could be considered a smart, dual-ported memory "cell". It is connected on the one hand to a bus over which it receives information from a triangle initialization unit, and on the other hand to a comparator tree onto which it outputs color and Z coordinate values. It is also connected to an address bus through which the CRT refresh controller indicates the X-Y address of the current pixel. Since the data bus is write-only from the transformation and clipping unit into the triangle buffer, no corresponding address bus is required. When polygon data is output to the triangle buffer, it is simply accepted by the first free triangle processor available. The advantage of this scheme is that it simplifies the interface to the transformation and clipping units. The disadvantage is that it requires every polygon in the scene to be rebroadcast to the triangle buffer at every refresh cycle. The overall collection of triangle processors in the buffer is partitioned into a set of "slices", each containing the number of triangles which can be processed in real time by a single transformation, clipping, and triangle initialization pipeline. In our system this number is estimated to be about 1000.

3.1.1 The Triangle Processor -

Each triangle processor consists of 20 registers, with associated addition, comparison, and control logic, as shown in Figure 3. Each processor performs a simple scanout of the triangle, based on an identification of the

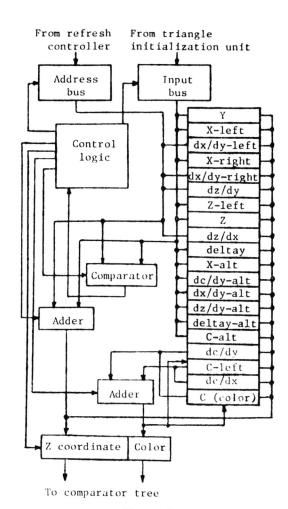

From refresh controller   From triangle initialization unit

Figure 3

Block diagram of triangle processor

initial left and right boundary edges and the third "alternate" edge by the triangle initialization module (see Figure 4). The processor monitors the address bus until a Y address equal to the value stored in the Y register is sent. If then monitors the X address until it reaches a value equal to X-left, at which time it outputs the initial color and Z coordinate. For each subsequent pixel, the color is incremented by dc/dx and the Z coordinate value by dz/dx and the new values are output. When the X address reaches X-right, the output is halted and the next scanline is prepared by adding dx/dy-left, dx/dy-right, dz/dy and dc/dy to X-left, X-right, Z-left, and C-left respectively. The values of Z and C are then set equal to Z-left and C-left and the value of deltay is decremented by 1. This process continues scanline by scanline until deltay

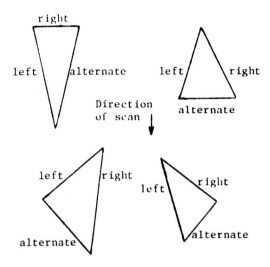

Figure 4

Assignments of triangle edges

reaches 0. At this point, X-alt is compared to X-left and X-right to determine whether the left left or right edge should be replaced by the alternate edge. The value of dx/dy-alt, is then copied into dx/dy-left or dx/dy-right as appropriate. In the former case, the values of dz/dy-alt and dc/dy-alt are copied into dz/dy and dc/dy respectively. deltay is set to the value of deltay-alt, and the processing continues until deltay once again reaches zero. At this point output is disabled, and the triangle processor enables itself for input of a new triangle. Note that this scanout procedure for triangles is similar to that of [12] and [15]. The use of trapezoids in which the top and bottom edges are horizontal, as done in [10] and [16], would allow a reduction of 5 registers and some simplification of the control. However, this would require the polygons in the scene model to be subdivided into such trapezoids each time they are transformed. By maintaining the scene model as a set of triangles, we totally avoid the need for polygon subdivision at each refresh cycle. All operations of the triangle processors are fixed-point. Operations on colors are assumed to be in RGB space, with the addition unit actually performing parallel operations on each of the three components. The use of separate, fast adder units for color and Z coordinate calculations assures that new values of each can be generated at the required bandwidth.

3.1.2 Arbitration Logic -

The triangle processors resemble the object processors proposed by Cohen [3] and Weinberg [16]. A significant difference in our approach is that we do not serialize the operation of these processors using a linear array of comparators. Instead, we use a binary tree of comparators, through which the depth and color values output by the triangle processors are pipelined. As a result, all triangle processors are equidistant from the endpoint of the pipeline and thus can operate on the same pixel simultaneously. This simplifies the synchronization and control of the system, and indeed allows the triangle buffer to resemble a frame buffer in its function. The complexity and number of comparators required is the same in both cases. Their operation is straightforward; they compare the two input Z values, and the closer of the two to the observer is output to the next pipeline stage along with its associated color. The root of the comparator tree outputs the color of the visible portion of the scene at the current pixel to the CRT refresh controller.

If anti-aliasing is desired, it is possible in principle to employ the method proposed by Weinberg [16], modified to work on a binary tree rather than a linear array of comparators. This method involves scanout of polygons at subpixel resolution so that the degree of coverage of the current pixel by each triangle can be determined. The comparators then maintain a list of partially visible polygon sections for the current pixel, sorted by Z. The last comparator outputs the list to a filter processor which calculates the appropriate color for the pixel. This algorithm requires that each comparator be able to merge two sorted input lists, which is no more complex as a pipelined algorithm for a binary tree than for a linear array. However, in addition to the added complexity of the comparator unit, this approach has the serious drawback that it builds a list which can grow as it passes through the comparator pipeline. Thus more values must be passed through later stages of the pipeline than through earlier ones, requiring that the bandwidth of the pipeline increase with proximity to the output end, or else that synchronous operation of the system be fatally disrupted. This drawback holds for a linear array of comparators as well as for a binary tree. As a result, we have chosen not to use this approach. For simplicity, the current system design does not include anti-aliasing, although we are investigating methods which can be used without unduly complicating the operation of the triangle buffer.

3.2 Modeling, Transformation, And Clipping

As mentioned in an earlier section, the object space representation of the scene is maintained in a separate, dual-ported memory. This memory contains a set of triangles, each of which consists of a color and a sequence of vertices described in world coordinates. In addition, each vertex is associated with a normal vector, which is the average of the normals to all polygons adjacent to the vertex, in order to perform smooth-shading. All coordinates are stored as floating-point numbers.

This memory is attached to the system bus of a host computer on the one hand, and to a set of transformation processors on the other. The host computer may be a general-purpose machine or a dedicated graphics processor. It is responsible for all manipulations of the scene database, for interacting with the user and for execution of all application software. If a hierarchically-structured model is used as a source database, this processor must decode the structure for use by the display system. It is also responsible for controlling the motion of the observer and of the objects in the scene. This involves specifying transformations to be performed on designated sets of polygons in the scene description. The transformations are encoded in the form of standard 4x4 homogeneous matrices. Only a single such transformation is performed by the transformation processing units on a triangle, so all concatenation of instance and viewing transformations must be done by the host processor.

The organization of the model memory and its interface to the transformation processors is shown in Figure 5. Each transformation unit communicates over a local bus with only as many polygons as it can process in real time, along with a set of transformation matrices which allow the set of polygons to be segmented into disjoint sets of objects. Each such matrix is associated with a pair of registers in which the identifiers of the first and last polygon in the corresponding object are stored. Thus an object is a contiguous sequence of polygons on the local bus. If a transformation pipeline can process 1000 triangles in real time, then about 23,000 words of memory will be accessible on each local bus if we allow 10 independent objects. In this way large numbers of triangles can be processed in parallel slices of 1000 triangles.

The transformation pipeline consists of an interface to a local model memory bus, a matrix-vector multiplier, a sequence of clipping units, and a triangle initialization unit, as depicted in Figure 5. The interface functions to access the object memory, load matrices into the

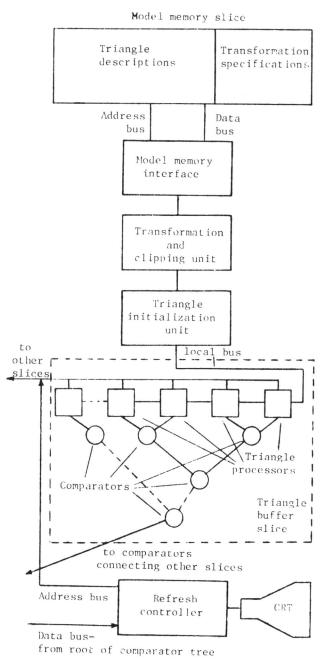

Figure 5

Detail of system slice

254

transformation processor, load clipping parameters into the clipping unit, and feed polygons into the pipeline. The transformation unit does matrix-vector multiplication, either as a systolic linear array [4] or as done by Clark [1]. The clipping pipeline consists of six identical units, each of which clips a polygon against a plane of the truncated viewing pyramid. The triangle initialization unit is primarily a division/subtraction engine which calculates the color for each vertex, performs perspective division, sorts polygon vertices by Y and then X, and then calculates the parameters of the triangle to be loaded into the triangle buffer. It also converts the floating-point values used by the transformation and clipping processors to fixed-point format for use by the triangle processors. Note that each triangle initialization unit communicates with only the triangle processors in a slice of the triangle buffer via a local bus analogous to that used to interface with the object memory.

4.0 VLSI IMPLEMENTATION

The system described here is a very large-scale project which requires the design of a number of special-purpose units. The dual-ported object memory is available commercially, but the other parts of the system must be custom designed. As stated before, the goal of the system is to allow real-time display of scenes consisting of at least 25,000 triangles. This implies 25,000 triangle processors and an equal number of comparators, and an estimated 25 transformation pipelines, along with approximately 575,000 words of object memory. To build such a system at a reasonable cost it will be necessary to make use of all the capabilities of today's VLSI design and fabrication technology. If we optimistically assume one micron feature sizes, we can reasonably estimate that two chips will suffice for each transformation pipeline and that perhaps 32 triangle processors and an equal number of comparators will fit on a large chip. With these assumptions, implementing a 32,000 triangle system will require 1000 triangle processor chips, 1000 simple comparator chips, 64 transformation pipeline chips, and 736,000 words of dual-ported memory. At a cost of $100 per chip, we obtain $264,000 for special-purpose chips, so we can generously estimate a $500,000 cost of goods for the system and thus a selling price in the neighborhood of $1 million. This is comparable to the cost of existing systems which provide an order of magnitude less performance.

The design of this type of system is certainly a non-trivial task, particularly in a university environment. We view this overall organization as a rich source of design projects which can be implemented and tested independently, with the object of consolidating them into a small-scale working prototype. The comparator unit, the simplest independent subsystem, has been designed and is currently being prepared for fabrication. The design of the triangle processor is currently underway, and the various parts of the transformation pipeline will be undertaken subsequently.

5.0 CONCLUSION

We have described a high-performance hardware organization suitable for real-time display of complex three-dimensional scenes. It is primarily intended to provide an order of magnitude increase in the capability of high-performance systems used for such applications as flight simulation. These goals are distinct from those of most other researchers who have applied the opportunities afforded by the availability of custom-designed integrated circuits to the design of graphics display hardware. The complexity of the system makes it more ambitious and its realization a more distant prospect than these other design efforts. Nonetheless, it illustrates at yet another level the exciting prospects made available to the field of computer graphics by recent advances in VLSI technology.

Acknowledgements

The authors would like to thank Sanjay Deshpande for his contributions to the development of this organization.

References

[1] Clark, J.H., A VLSI Geometry Processor for Graphics, Computer, July, 1980.

[2] Clark, J.H. and M.R. Hannah, Distributed Processing in a High-Performance Smart Image Memory, LAMBDA, vol.1, no.3, 1980.

[3] Cohen, D. and S. Demetrescu, A VLSI Approach to Computer-Generated Imagery, Technical Report, USC, 1979.

[4] Foster, M.J. and H.T. Kung, The Design of Special-Purpose VLSI Chips, Computer, January 1980.

[5] Fuchs, H., Z.M. Kedem, and S.P. Uselton, Optimal Surface Reconstruction from Planar Contours, _Communications of the ACM_, vol. 20, no. 10, October 1977, 693-702.

[6] Fuchs, H. and B. Johnson, An Expandable Multiprocessor Architecture for Video Graphics, _Proceedings of the Sixth Annual ACM-IEEE Symposium on Computer Architecture_, April 1979.

[7] Fuchs, H., J. Poulton, A. Paeth, and A. Bell, Developing Pixel-Planes, a Smart Memory-Based Raster Graphics System, _Proceedings, Conference on Advanced Research in VLSI_, Massachusetts Institute of Technology, January 1982, 137-146.

[8] Gupta, S., R. Sproull, and I. Sutherland, A VLSI Architecture for Updating Raster-Scan Displays, _Computer Graphics_, vol. 15, no. 3, August 1981, 71-78.

[9] Kaplan, M. and D.P. Greenberg, Parallel Processing Techniques for Hidden Surface Algorithms, _Computer Graphics_, vol. 13, no.2, August 1979, 300-307.

[10] Jackson, J.H., Dynamic Scan-Converted Images with a Frame Buffer Display Device, _Computer Graphics_, vol. 14, no. 3, July 1980, 163-169.

[11] Mead, C. and L. Conway, _Introduction to VLSI Systems_, Reading, Addison-Wesley, 1980.

[12] Myers, A.J., An Efficient Visible Surface Algorithm, Technical Report, Computer Graphics Research Group, Ohio State University, July 1975.

[13] Parke, F.I., Simulation and Expected Performance of Multiple Processor Z-Buffer Systems, _Computer Graphics_, vol. 14, no. 3, July 1980, 48-56.

[14] Roman, G. and T. Kimura, A VLSI Architecture for Real-Time Color Display of Three-Dimensional Objects, _Proceedings of the Delaware Valley Microprocessor Conference_, April 1979, 113-118.

[15] Romney, G.W., Computer Assisted Assembly and Rendering of Solids, Technical Report 4-20, Department of Computer Science, The University of Utah, 1970.

[16] Weinberg, R., Parallel Processing Image Synthesis and Anti-Aliasing, _Computer Graphics_, vol. 15, no. 3, 55-62.

[17] Whitted, T., Hardware Enhanced 3-D Raster Display Systems, Canadian Man-Computer Communications Conference, June 1981.

Real-time shaded colour polygon generation system

R.J. Westmore

Reprinted with permission from *IEE Proceedings*, Part E, Volume 134, Number 1, January 1987, pages 31-38. Copyright © 1987 by The Institution of Electrical Engineers.

Indexing terms: Computer graphics, Very large scale integration

Abstract: The paper describes a hardware architecture for a graphics system which can generate shaded, colour, perspective 2-dimensional images of complex 3-dimensional scenes, in real time. The architecture is capable of operating at the high pixel rates required to produce scenes on rasterscan displays with high spatial resolution (1280 H by 1024 V), high colour resolution (24-bit), and high refresh rate (60 Hz non-interlaced). The architecture of the pixel rate section is described in detail. The architecture is suitable for implementation using custom VLSI techniques.

1 Introduction

The ability to generate realistic images of 3-dimensional objects and real-world scenes by computation is useful in a wide variety of fields. Applications include art, advertising, entertainment, computer animation, computer-aided design, training simulators etc. The ability to generate the images in real-time is a desirable goal in all cases [1] and is necessary in more demanding applications such as the visual systems installed in flight training simulators.

The generation of full colour, perspective, images of 3-dimensional scenes on high-resolution displays is computationally intensive. Special-purpose distributed architectures are required to meet the high throughput requirements. A number of complex architectures capable of generating simulated images of 3-dimensional scenes in real time on low-resolution displays have been developed commercially by manufacturers of visual systems for flight simulators [2]. These architectures all exploit one or more of the following techniques; pipelining of operations, subdivision of the problem in object space, or subdivision of the problem in image space [3].

Object space is the 3-dimensional co-ordinate system in which the scene is defined. Image space is the 3-dimensional co-ordinate system appropriate to the position and orientation of the viewer. The image plane is a 2-dimensional plane which includes the display screen. The display screen is considered to be a window on the image plane.

An earlier computer graphics system which utilises all of the above techniques has been implemented at the University of Sussex [4, 5]. This system performed real-time scan conversion of polygons. Scan conversion is the

Paper 5014E (C2), first received 10th September 1985 and in revised form 11th August 1986

The author was formerly with Sinclair Research, Cambridge. His current address is 1021 Harlan Drive, San José, CA 95129, USA

generation of a rasterscan from some other form of description. One processor per polygon is used to perform the final stage of image generation. Only convex polygons of uniform colour are permitted. The output resolution of this system is sufficient to drive a 512 line interlaced display at a rate of 25 frames per second. The pixel period required for a display of this resolution is 64 ns.

Gouraud-shaded polygons [6] produce significantly more realistic images of curved surfaces and large flat surfaces than polygons with constant colour.

Gouraud shading, also known as bilinear shading, is the shading of a polygon by linear interpolation of colour values along the edges between each vertex, and along each scanline segment contained between the edges of the polygon. The architecture described in this paper uses a processor per polygon approach to produce complex perspective 3-dimensional images composed of Gouraud-shaded colour polygons. The polygons are restricted to triangles in object space. The architecture is capable of performing real-time scan conversion of shaded polygons on high resolution non-interlaced rasterscan displays. It is expected that pixel periods of 10 ns or less can be achieved with this architecture using current semiconductor technology. This would be sufficient to drive 1024 line noninterlaced display at a rate of 60 frames per second.

A previously proposed architecture for the real-time display of shaded polygons based on a processor-per-triangle approach has been described by Fussell [7]. Unlike the system to be described, his system requires the address of each pixel to be broadcast to each shaded triangle processor; parallel arithmetic operations are performed to generate the colour value of each pixel and a comparator tree is then used to select the output pixel which is closest to the observer. If a graphics system capable of processing many thousands of polygons were to be implemented using this architecture, the maximum pixel rate would be severely limited, first, by the interconnect delay between components (caused by large fanouts and the physical length of the wiring required) and secondly, by the time taken to perform the parallel arithmetic operations required to calculate the shaded colour values.

2 System overview

The graphics system uses an object processor based approach with one processor per convex polygon (Fig. 1). A convex polygon is a polygon in which the internal angles at each vertex are less than or equal to 180 degrees. Each object is modelled by collections of shaded polygons which approximate to the surfaces of the objects in the scene. The convex polygons are restricted to triangles in object space because Gouraud shading of polygons with greater than three sides is not invariant

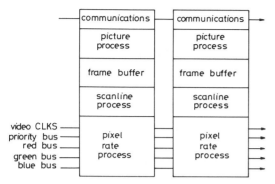

Fig. 1   *Object processors connected in a linear array*

under rotation. The picture process section of each object processor could contain two triangles provided that they could not both be observed simultaneously from any position or orientation in object space.

The architecture described is a real-time 3-dimensional graphics system based on a pipelined linear array of object processors (Fig. 1). The passage of the rasterscan through each object processor in turn allows the associated shaded triangle to add its contribution to the final image. The RGB colour values and the priority value of each pixel are modified each time they pass through an object processor. The stream of pixels which emerge from the last object processor form the rasterscan of the displayed image. The number of objects which can be generated in real time can be increased by adding additional processors. The linear array architecture allows this to be done without any increase in the maximum pixel rate. Latency will, however, increase linearly with the number of processors in the system. Each object processor increases the latency by one pixel period. Assuming that the maximum acceptable latency in the scan conversion section of the system is one frame time, the architectural limit placed on the number of processors which can be incorporated in a system of this type will be equal to the number of pixels on the display.

The real-time scan conversion performed by each object processor is synchronised to the display by vertical and horizontal synchronising pulses and by a pixel clock routed through each element. Each object processor is connected only to its adjacent neighbours. All signals routed through the real-time scan conversion section of the object processors are synchronised to the pixel clock. The scan conversion, hidden surface removal and colour shading of the polygons on the image plane is performed by the scanline and pixel rate sections of the object processor. The shading technique used is bilinear interpolation (Gouraud Shading).

A fixed priority scheme is used for hidden surface elimination. For a system with a fixed priority scheme to work it is necessary to impose two important restrictions on the system: the polygons cannot intersect and they must be single sided. A single-faced polygon is a polygon which is visible from the front only. These restrictions are acceptable because the cost of varying the priority value over the surface of the polygon using bilinear interpolation is disproportionately high. The high cost arises because priority resolution is performed in a bit-wise manner from the most-significant bit to the least-significant bit (see the Section on priority resolution), whereas the additions required to perform the interpolation are performed in a bit-wise manner from the

least-significant bit to the most-significant bit. If there are N bits in the priority word, then $N * (N - 1)$ delay elements would be required to align the output of a priority interpolator with the input to the priority resolver.

A block diagram of two object processors and the interconnection between the processors is shown in Fig. 1. Three distinct processes take place in each polygon processor: the picture process, the scanline process, and the pixel rate process.

The picture process is the set of calculations necessary to produce an image-plane description of the polygon from its object-space description. This process does not destroy the object-space description of the polygon. Object space is the 3-dimensional co-ordinate system in which all the polygons which together comprise the scene are defined. Each polygon is defined by its cusps. A cusp defines the position and colour of a point on the contour of a polygon. Each cusp in object space has six parameters: *x, y, z, red, green, blue*. The picture process first transforms the polygon from the 3-dimensional co-ordinate system of the object space to a 3-dimensional co-ordinate system called image space which is appropriate to the position and orientation of the viewer. The image-space description is then mapped on to a 2-dimensional image plane. The image plane description is then clipped to fit within a window on the image plane corresponding to the display screen. The worst case clipping of a triangle against the interior of a rectangular window produces a seven-sided convex polygon (Fig. 2).

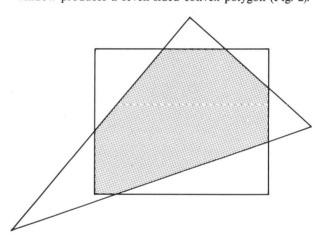

Fig. 2   *Clipping of a triangle to form a seven-sided polygon*

The clipping of the triangle is performed in such a way that the colour shading over the surface of the clipped triangle is consistent with that which would be produced over the surface if the clipping had not been performed. Algorithms to perform these transformations are well known [6] and will not be described here.

The resulting image plane description consists of a left-side cusp list, a right-side cusp list and a surface priority value. The cusps in each cusp list are sorted into the order in which they will be encountered during scan conversion (the '*y*' order). In a conventional horizontal rasterscan surfaces will be scanned from the left edge to the right edge. The cusps lists are organised in a similar manner. Left-side cusps contain starting information and right-side cusps contain ending information. After transformation to the image plane, the description of the clipped triangle is placed in the frame buffer (Fig. 1).

The object processor (Fig. 1) must have sufficient processing and storage capability to process a triangle in object space into a convex polygon with a maximum of seven sides on the image plane at a rate sufficient to create the illusion of movement. This is not necessarily the same as the rate at which the screen is refreshed, but should be related to it (e.g. a submultiple of the frame refresh rate). The rate of image generation required to give the illusion of movement depends upon the maximum degree of change in the image between successive frames and the required image quality. These factors will vary from application to application. Different image generation rates will therefore be required for different applications.

The image plane description of the shaded polygon stored in the frame buffer is scan converted in real time by the scanline and pixel rate processes. The scanline process reads the image-plane description from the frame buffer. Each cusp in the frame buffer is defined by nine parameters; the absolute values at the cusp: x, y, red, $green$, $blue$; and the gradients leaving the cusp: $d(x)/dy$, $d(red)/dy$, $d(green)/dy$, $d(blue)/dy$. This information is sufficient to allow correct interpolation towards the next cusp in the cusp list. In addition, Y_TOP and Y_BOTTOM define the range of scanlines which intersect the polygon. Y_TOP is the first scanline to intersect the polygon. Its value is the y-value of the first cusp in both the left and right cusp lists. Y_BOTTOM is the last scanline to intersect the polygon. Its value is the y-value of last cusp in the cusp lists. Algorithms for the scan conversion of convex polygons are well known. The part of the scan conversion process performed by the scanline process is listed in Appendix 8.1.

The scanline process passes nine parameters to the pixel rate process. Four parameters which define the first pixel on the scanline which forms part of the polygon: x_on, red, $green$, $blue$. Three parameters which define the colour gradients along the scanline from the initial position: $d(red)/dx$, $d(green)/dx$, $d(blue)/dx$. And two further parameters; x_extent, which defines the position of the last pixel along the scanline to form part of the polygon; and $priority$ which defines the visibility of the polygon relative to other polygons. The pixel rate process generates the required colour values for each pixel, and performs hidden surface removal on a pixel-by-pixel basis by comparing the priority value of the surface with the priority value already on the bus. The algorithm performed by the pixel rate process is listed in Appendix 8.2. Fig. 3 is a block diagram showing the major components of the pixel rate processor.

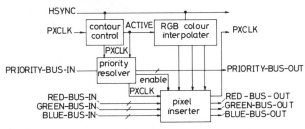

Fig. 3 *Overview of pixel-rate processor*

3.1 Pixel-rate process
The pixel-rate section of the shaded surface generator has four distinct parts; contour control, priority resolution, colour interpolation and pixel insertion (Fig. 3). The contour-control section is the top level of control. It activates the other sections of the shaded-surface generator when the pixel under consideration falls within the contour of the triangle served by its object processor.

When activated, the priority resolver compares the assigned priority value of the surface with the priority value of the pixel entering on the priority bus. If the comparison succeeds, the priority value of the surface is placed on the priority bus in place of the current priority value, and pixel insertion logic is enabled for pixel insertion. If the priority resolver is not activated, then the comparison fails, irrespective of the priority value of the triangle.

The pixel insertion logic either transmits the RGB colour data already on the colour bus unchanged or replaces it with the data output by the colour interpolators. The function of the pixel insertion units is controlled by the output of the priority resolver on a pixel-by-pixel basis.

The RGB colour interpolators perform linear colour interpolation along the scanline segments between the contours of the polygon. Linear interpolation is performed by adding a colour difference value to the previous colour value. Colour interpolation could be performed for each pixel along the scanline. However, in order to reduce power consumption, interpolation is performed once for each group of four pixels. The four-pixel groups are aligned with the intersection of the left-hand edge of the polygon and the current scanline. Simulated test images produced using this technique were of the same subjective image quality as simulated images produced with colour interpolation performed at every pixel position. The interpolators are activated by the output of the contour control section. The interpolation continues, irrespective of the result of the output of the priority resolver. This is because each processor deals with one triangle (or clipped triangle), producing the colour value of each pixel by incremental calculation. Therefore, if part of the object is hidden, the interpolation must still continue to ensure that the correct colour value is present when the surface emerges from hiding.

The priority resolver, the colour interpolation units and, consequently, the pixel insertion units are all composed of bit-level pipelined logic elements. The priority is resolved using a most significant-bit first technique in order that the comparison and substitution operations

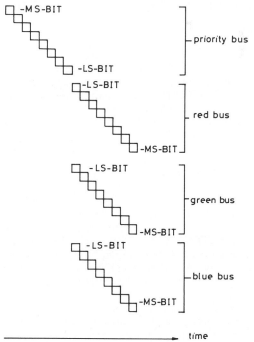

Fig. 4 *Relative time position of each bus-bit associated with a pixel*

required can be performed in a single pipelined operation. A diagram showing the relative time positions of each bit resulting from the pipelining is shown in Fig. 4.

The bit-level pipelining of simple logic elements allows a system with a high throughput to be constructed. The maximum pixel rate supported by this architecture will depend upon the implementation technology and the detail design trade offs. Pixel rates of 100 MHz can be readily achieved using current semiconductor technology. Pixel rates in excess of 200 MHz are achievable with high-speed bipolar semiconductor technologies. The maximum pixel rate attainable in a particular technology is constrained by the maximum switching speed of a transistor, and the ability to supply and dissipate sufficient power.

3.2 Contour control

The contour of the clipped triangle is passed to the contour controller (Fig. 5) of the pixel-rate processor by

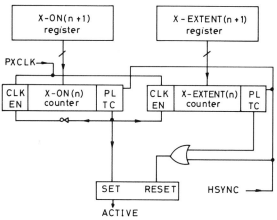

Fig. 5 *Contour control: block diagram*

EN = enable count down
PL = parallel load
TC = terminal count
HSYNC = horizontal synchronising signal

the scanline processor as two values, X_ON and X_EXTENT. The X_ON value specifies the position of the pixel which contains the left-most edge of the polygon. The X_EXTENT value specifies the width of the polygon on the scanline in pixels.

The X_ON and X_EXTENT values for the next scanline $(n + 1)$ are written into interface registers asynchronously during the current scanline (n). The values are transferred to count-down counters during horizontal flyback. The X_ON_COUNTER is then decremented once for each pixel clock cycle until it reaches its terminal value. An ACTIVE true signal is then output and the X_EXTENT_COUNTER enabled. This causes the other parts of the pixel rate processor to be set to an active state. The X_EXTENT_COUNTER is then decremented by one for each pixel clock cycle until it reaches its terminal value. The ACTIVE signal is then reset. This returns the pixel rate section of the object processor to an inactive state.

The X_EXTENT_COUNTER is also used to generate a local quarter-pixel-rate phase clock locked to the left-hand contour of the polygon being drawn. This clock is used by the colour interpolators.

3.3 Priority resolution

The priority value of the surface of the triangle is compared with the priority value on the priority bus. If the comparison succeeds, the priority value of the surface is placed on the priority bus and the pixel insertion logic is enabled for that pixel. If the comparison neither succeeds nor fails, then the comparison is deemed to have failed. This is done to ensure a consistent decision resulting in a consistent visual appearance.

Priority resolution is carried out in a pipelined bit-wise fashion using nearest-neighbour communication. The priority value on the priority bus is skewed in time to accommodate the bit-wise pipelining. The priority comparison starts at the most significant bit and proceeds bit wise to the least-significant bit (a technique previously used in open collector bus systems [8, 9]). The priority values are unsigned binary numbers. The priority of the surface is called SURFACE_Z and the priority on the bus is called Z_BUS. A block diagram showing the input and output connections of the basic element of the priority resolver is shown in Fig. 6. A block diagram

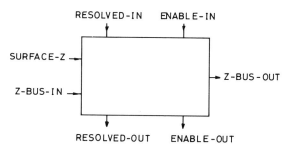

Fig. 6 *Priority resolution: basic element*

showing how the individual elements are connected to form a complete system is shown in Fig. 7. The ACTIVE signal originates in the contour control section. It allows

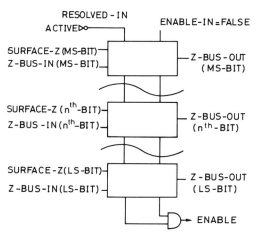

Fig. 7 *Priority resolution: block diagram*

the priority comparison to proceed normally when it is true and forces the result of the comparison to be false when it is false. The basic elements could be designed to perform the priority resolution on the basis of the maximum priority succeeding or on the basis of the minimum priority succeeding.

Assuming that the minimum priority succeeds, the algorithm performed by each basic function block is given in algorithm 1 (all variables are Boolean).

```
IF RESOLVED_IN = TRUE
  THEN
  BEGIN
    RESOLVED_OUT = RESOLVED_IN { or true }
    ENABLE_OUT = ENABLE_IN
    IF ENABLE_IN = TRUE
      THEN Z_BUS_OUT = SURFACE_Z
      ELSE Z_BUS_OUT = Z_BUS_IN
  END
  ELSE { RESOLVED_IN = FALSE }
  BEGIN
    IF Z_BUS_IN = SURFACE_Z
      THEN
      BEGIN
        RESOLVED_OUT = RESOLVED_IN
                            { or FALSE }
        ENABLE_OUT = DONT_CARE
        Z_BUS_OUT = Z_BUS_IN
                            { or SURFACE_Z }
      END
    IF Z_BUS_IN > SURFACE_Z
      THEN
      BEGIN
        RESOLVED_OUT = TRUE
        ENABLE_OUT = TRUE
        Z_BUS_OUT = SURFACE_Z
      END
    IF Z_BUS_IN < SURFACE_Z
      THEN
      BEGIN
        RESOLVED_OUT = TRUE
        ENABLE_OUT = FALSE
        Z_BUS_OUT = Z_BUS_IN
      END
  END
END
```

Algorithm 1 *Function of each one-bit priority element*

3.4 RGB colour interpolation

Each colour interpolator has as input an initial colour
value I and an incremental difference colour value D.
These values are stored in registers. The input values for
the next scanline $(n + 1)$ are written asynchronously to
buffer registers during the current scanline (n). The contents of the buffer registers are transferred to the active
registers during horizontal flyback. The accumulation
units are initialised when the contour control section sets
the ACTIVE signal. The colour interpolator clock cycle
time is four times the length of the pixel clock cycle time.
The required clock is derived from the X_EXTENT
counter of the contour control section.

RGB colour interpolation is performed by a bit-wise
pipeline of one-bit accumulation units (Fig. 8). These
accumulators have two functions; loading an initial value
and adding a difference value to their stored value. Both
the function and the data are pipelined through the accumulation units. The result produced is thus skewed in
time. The calculation proceeds in a bit-wise manner from
the least-significant bit to the most-significant bit. A
block diagram showing the inputs and outputs of a
one-bit accumulation unit and its relationship to the
input data registers is shown in Fig. 8. Each colour interpolator comprises a number of these units. The subset of
the interpolators output which represents the integer part
of the colour word is passed to the pixel inserters for conditional insertion on to the colour bus.

The algorithm performed by each accumulation unit

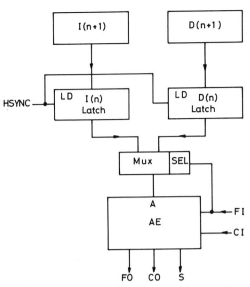

Fig. 8 *One-bit accumulation element and input registers: block diagram*

$I(n)$	= initial value for current scanline
$I(n + 1)$	= initial value for next scanline
$D(n)$	= difference value for current scanline
$D(n + 1)$	= difference value for next scanline
A	= data input of AE
AE	= accumulation element
FI	= function input
CI	= carry input
S	= sum output
CO	= carry output
FO	= function output
LD	= load control
SEL	= select input control

during each interpolation clock cycle is listed in Algorithm 2.

```
IF FI = INITIALISE
  THEN
  BEGIN
    FO: = FI
    CO: = FALSE
    S: = A
  END
IF FI = ADD
  THEN
  BEGIN
    FO: = FI
    CO: = (A AND S) OR (S AND CI) OR (A AND
                                            CI)
    S: = A XOR S XOR CI
  END
```

Algorithm 2 *Function of each one-bit accumulation
element*

A two's complement fixed point number representation is
used in the colour interpolators. The word size required
is made up of three components; sign, integer and fraction. The sign is a one-bit quantity, the integer is an
eight-bit quantity and the fraction is a quantity dependent upon the minimum colour gradient which must be
represented.

The result of the difference accumulation is always
positive. The sign bit may, therefore, be ignored. The difference value may be positive or negative. In two's complement arithmetic, the sign bit of the difference value
cannot influence the result at less significant bit positions.
Therefore, the sign bit need not have any physical representation within the colour interpolators.

The number of bits used to represent the fractional colour gradient is one more than that required to represent the minimum colour gradient. The extra bit is required to prevent an error in the least-significant bit position from propagating into the integer component of the colour word. The problem arises because an error in the least-significant bit position of the difference value will generate a successively larger accumulated error, in the result, with each successive accumulation. If the horizontal resolution is 1024 and the colour is interpolated at a quarter of the screen resolution, then the minimum colour gradient is 1 in 256. Eight fractional bits are required to represent this quantity. A 1-bit error will propagate 8-bit positions towards the most-significant bit after 256 successive accumulations. Therefore, nine fraction bits would be required for a system with a minimum horizontal colour gradient of 1 in 256.

If the number of fractional bits in the colour interpolator is equal to the number of bits in the priority word, then no delay elements will be required to align the ENABLE output of the priority resolver with output of the least-significant integer bit of the colour word.

3.5 Pixel insertion
The function of the pixel inserter is to conditionally substitute the output of the colour interpolators onto the colour busses. Both the control and data inputs of the pixel insertion multiplexers are pipelined to match the pipelining of the colour interpolators. A block diagram of the basic element of the pixel insertion logic is shown in Fig. 9. The way in which the individual elements are connected together to form a complete pixel insertion unit is shown in Fig. 10.

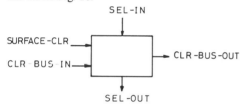

Fig. 9 *Pixel inserter: one-bit element*

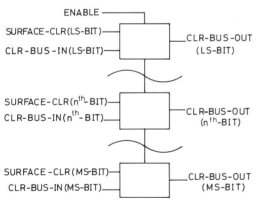

Fig. 10. *Pixel insertion: block diagram*

The algorithm performed by each pixel inserter element during each clock cycle is shown in algorithm 3. The source of the ENABLE signal is the output from the priority resolver.

```
IF SEL_IN = ENABLE
   THEN CLR_BUS_OUT: = SURFACE_CLR
   ELSE CLR_BUS_OUT: = CLR_BUS_IN
SEL_OUT: = SEL_IN
```

Algorithm 3 *Function of each one-bit pixel inserter*

4 Discussion

The use of uniformly coloured polygons to model curved surfaces results in images whose polyhedral natures are clearly visible. Gouraud shading of polygons provides a dramatic improvement in image quality by giving a smooth appearance to polyhedral approximations of curved surfaces. Gouraud shading can also improve the rendering of flat surfaces by allowing effects such as atmospheric absorption to be approximated over the surface.

Gouraud shading is an approximate technique and, as such, can give rise to defects in the image. The principal defect is the misrepresentation of colour due to the exaggeration of intensity change at any discontinuity in the magnitude, or rate of change of intensity. This phenomenon is called mach banding [6]. Highlights resulting from reflections may also be misrepresented. The effect of these defects on image quality is reduced by increasing the number of shaded triangles used to represent the scene.

A determining feature in the realism of images is the number of triangles used to represent the scene. The architecture presented is capable of generating images with as many triangles as there are pixels on the screen. In the case of a high-resolution 1000-line display, images containing up to a million shaded triangles can be generated.

Image quality can also be aided by the application of various antialiasing measures. Polygons which are too small to be rendered correctly on the display are excluded from consideration by the picture process. The visual impact of staircase edges along the edges of the polygons can be ameliorated on medium-resolution displays, 512 line, by generating a double-resolution raster and applying post processing to determine the colour value of the final pixel from its constituent subpixel values.

5 Future work

5.1 Depth interpolation
Depth interpolation would avoid the need to assign a fixed priority to each surface. It would also allow the use of intersecting polygons in the data base. A least-significant-bit first pipelined priority resolver would allow bilinear interpolation of the depth value over the surface of a polygon without the need for buffer elements. A most-significant-bit first difference accumulator would also allow this to be achieved.

5.2 Transparency
The effects of transparency could be achieved by positioning transparent surfaces last in the linear array of shaded-surface generators. They could then modify the existing colours if their priority comparison succeeded. The modification would be achieved by performing a conditional pipelined subtraction from the colour value on the bus. This approach would not allow reflections to be modelled.

5.3 Scanline algorithm
The scanline algorithm given in algorithm 1 interpolates colour at line resolution and recalculates the colour gradients on every scanline. The division operations required to calculate the colour gradients are expensive.

Reducing the number of additions which must be performed for each scanline by interpolating the colour at a quarter of the scanline resolution produces acceptable results. However, reducing the number of divisions performed by calculating the colour gradient once for each group of scanlines introduces cumulative inaccuracies which become strikingly obvious when they cause any of the colour interpolators to over or under flow.

The following *ad hoc* solution was used to produce acceptable simulated images: calculate the colour gradients every third scanline, or on any scanline which contains a cusp, interpolate the colours on every scanline and guard band the numerical colour range at each cusp. For example, if the full colour range available is from 0 to 255, use a minimum intensity cusp equal to 16 and a maximum intensity equal to 235.

5.4 Picture-rate processing

The picture-rate processing performed on each triangle is the same in each object processor. The picture rate process is, therefore, a good candidate for implementation using an SIMD-based parallel processor. The broadcast instructions can be pipelined between object processors to overcome fanout problems and ensure a high rate of instruction throughput.

6 Acknowledgments

This paper was written while the author was an employee of Sinclair Research Ltd. Their permission to publish this paper is acknowledged. The author wishes to thank his colleagues for their constructive comments and help in proof reading this paper.

7 References

1 DOHERTY, W.J., THADHANI, A.J.: 'The economic value of rapid response time'. IBM Research Report GE20-0752-0(11-82), White Plains, New York, USA
2 SCHACHTER, B.J.: 'Computer image generation' (Wiley-Interscience, 1983)
3 WEINBERG, R.: 'Parallel processing image synthesis and anti-aliasing', *Comput. Graphics*, 1981, **15**, (3), p. 55–62
4 GRIMSDALE, R.L., HADJIASLANIS, A.A., and WILLIS, P.J.: 'Zone management processor: a module for generating surfaces in raster-scan colour displays', *IEE J. Computers & Digital Tech.*, 1979, **2**, (1), pp. 21–25
5 GRIMSDALE, R.L., LOK, Y.C., PRICE, S.M., WESTMORE, R.J., and WOOLLONS, D.J.: 'Computer generation of images for flight simulators'. IEE International Conference on Simulators, Brighton, England, 1983, pp. 7–12
6 NEWMAN, W.M., and SPROULL, R.F.: 'Principles of interactive computer graphics', (McGraw-Hill, 1979, Second Edn)
7 FUSSELL, D., and RATHI, B.D.: 'A VLSI-oriented architecture for real-time raster display of shaded polygons (Preliminary Report)'. Proceedings of Graphics Interface 82, 1982, pp. 373–380
8 PRICE, S.M.: 'Priority resolution in bus orientated computer system'. UK Patent Application GB 2 143 349 A
9 LINDER, R.: 'Introduction to a simple but unconventional multiprocessor system and outline of an application'. NATO ASI on Computer Architectures for Spatially Distributed Data, Cetraro, Italy, June 1983

8 Appendix   Shaded surface generation algorithm

Version
Recalculate parameters on every scanline
Recalculate colour values for each group of pixels along scanline

8.1 Scanline algorithm
Inputs
From polygon frame buffer:
    LEFT, RIGHT : cusp lists
    Y_TOP, Y_BOTTOM : integer
    PRIORITY : positive integer
The following parameters are defined in each cusp in the cusp lists; X, Y, RED, GREEN, BLUE, d(x)/dy, d(RED)/dy, d(GREEN)/dy, d(BLUE)/dy.
Outputs
X_ON : integer;
X_EXTENT, PRIORITY : positive integer;
RED, GREEN, BLUE : positive integer;
d(RED)/dx, d(GREEN)/dx, d(BLUE)/dx : fixed point;
Scanline algorithm

Set the current left, and current right, cusps to the first left, and first right, cusps, respectively.

For each scanline in turn from the first scanline to the last scanline;
BEGIN
If scanline intersects the polygon
  (e.g. if scanline is between Y_TOP and Y_BOTTOM)
then
  BEGIN
    If a left cusp is on this scanline
      then
        BEGIN
        initialise X_LEFT, RED_LEFT, GREEN_LEFT, BLUE_LEFT with the values of the current left cusp;
        make the next cusp in the left cusp list the current cusp;
        END
      else
        BEGIN
        add the dy increments from the previous cusp to X_LEFT, RED_LEFT, GREEN_LEFT, and BLUE_LEFT;
        END;

    If a right cusp is on this scanline
      then
        BEGIN
        initialise X_RIGHT, RED_RIGHT, GREEN_RIGHT, BLUE_RIGHT with the values of the current right cusp;
        Make the next cusp in the right cusp list the current cusp;
        END

else
    BEGIN
    add the dy increments from the previous right cusp to X_LEFT, RED_LEFT, GREEN_LEFT, and BLUE_
    LEFT;
    END;

Calculate the extent, in pixels, of the intersection of the scanline and the polygon. Partially intersected pixels are included.

Calculate the extent, in pixel groups, of the intersection of the scanline and the polygon. Partially intersected pixel groups are included.

Calculate the red, green, and blue colour gradients, per pixel group.

Pass parameters to the pixel rate process.

END; { if scanline intersects polygon }
END; { for each scanline in turn }

8.2 Pixel-rate algorithm
Inputs
    From the Scanline Algorithm:
    X_ON : integer;
    X_EXTENT, PRIORITY : positive integer;
    RED, GREEN, BLUE : positive integer;
    d(RED)/dx, d(GREEN)/dx, d(BLUE)/dx : fixed point;

    From previous object processor:
    RED_BUS_IN, GREEN_BUS_IN, BLUE_BUS_IN : positive integer;
    PRIORITY_BUS_IN : positive integer;

Outputs
RED_BUS_OUT, GREEN_BUS_OUT, BLUE_BUS_OUT : positive integer;
PRIORITY_BUS_OUT : positive integer;

Algorithm
Initialise group counter.
    Set RED, GREEN, and BLUE to the input values.
    For each pixel in turn along the scanline from the first pixel to the last pixel.
    BEGIN
        If pixel is inside, or on the edge of the polygon
            (e.g. if pixel is between X_ON and (X_ON + X_EXTENT) inclusive)
        then
        BEGIN
        If priority is greater than PRIORITY_BUS_IN
            then
                Transfer the colour values RED, GREEN, BLUE to their respective output colour busses.
                Transfer the priority value to the priority output bus
            else
                Transfer the colour values on the input colour busses to the output colour busses.
                Transfer the priority value on the input priority bus to the output priority bus.
        END
        Increment group counter.
        If start of a pixel group
            then
                Add dx increments to the colour values RED, GREEN, and BLUE.
END

SUPER BUFFER: A Systolic VLSI Graphics Engine for Real Time Raster Image Generation

Nader Gharachorloo and Christopher Pottle

School of Electrical Engineering
Cornell University
Ithaca, New York

Abstract

Real time generation of raster images is of fundamental importance to computer graphics. Commercial and research efforts in the past have resulted in many interesting high performance architectures for real time raster graphics. No single system as yet stands out as the best solution.

This paper presents the Super Buffer family of systems for real time graphical processing of three dimensional, general purpose, interactive and dynamic color raster graphics applications. From the user's point of view, the simplest system in the family behaves as an extremely fast frame buffer. More advanced systems have the capability of real time hidden surface removal and polygon shading.

The Super Buffer is a virtual scanline system which is built around a single custom designed VLSI chip : the Systolic Raster Graphics Engine. The Engine is equipped with an array of identical specialized Pixel Processors which collaborate to break the real time computation barrier by performing several billion pixel operations per second in order to generate raster images in real time. The general purpose flexibility and high speed processing combined with the small size and economical cost of Super Buffers should satisfy a basic need for effective visual interaction with application problems via an inexpensive color graphics device.

1. Introduction: Frame Buffer and Super Buffer Systems for Raster Graphics

Although raster graphics have been used extensively in many applications for over a decade, the architecture of the "ultimate" raster graphics system remains a challenging problem in digital system design. About three orders of magnitude increase in performance and a similar reduction in size over conventional systems are required to make raster system architectures really fast, powerful and yet economical. It seems clear that fundamental advances in image generation algorithms and display processor architectures combined with high levels of circuit integration using custom VLSI technology will be required to bring about such dramatic changes.

It is the ultimate goal of any computer image generation system to display images for a user as if he were observing a real world environment. Of extreme importance in computer image generation systems is the architecture of the display processing unit that transforms computer generated commands and information into electrical voltages for controlling the position and intensity of the electron beam which traces and continuously refreshes the image on the screen. Because of the complexity of the human visual system, computer image generation systems have not been able to fully simulate a real world situation. The human observer can perceive a general class of images containing characters, vectors and filled polygons. The time behavior or the dynamics of the objects within the image are often as important to the user as the static contents of each frame. Furthermore the contents of future frames are not predetermined. Upon observing the contents of the past and present frames, the user may wish to interact in the image generation process at display time in order to influence the view, contents or dynamics of future frames. Finally, for presenting color images, refreshed raster displays are the ideal choice. Figure 1 lists several of the existing computer image generation systems and their partial capabilities in simulating a real world environment.

Several interactive dynamic vector graphics systems have already demonstrated the importance of real time image generation. High computation rates and large image memory bandwidths, however, have been major barriers to real time raster color image generation. The number of operations and memory references involved in generating real time raster images increases

	GENERAL PURPOSE	INTERACTIVE	DYNAMIC	RASTER COLOR
CHARACTER TERMINAL	NO	LIM	NO	NO
VIDEO GAMES	NO	YES	YES	YES
PREPROCESSED FILM	YES	NO	YES	YES
FRAME BUFFERS	YES	LIM	NO	YES
VECTOR SYSTEMS	YES	YES	YES	NO
SUPER BUFFERS	YES	YES	YES	YES

FIGURE 1: Listing of Computer Image Generation Systems

quadratically with the number of vertices in the frame, while the computational complexity for vector operations such as vertex transformation, clipping and vector drawing increases linearly. For example, drawing the perimeter vector points of a 100x100

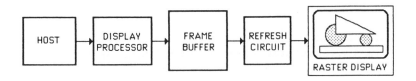

FIGURE 2a: A Frame Buffer Based System

for Raster Image Generation

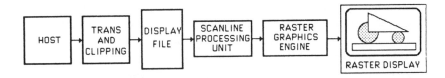

FIGURE 2b: A Super Buffer System for

Real Time Raster Image Generation

pixel square requires on the order of 400 operations while filling the raster area within the square needs about 10,000 operations. Since a typical image may contain a few thousand polygons and require at least 30 frames/sec refresh rates, real time raster image generation requires computation rates in the Gigahertz range, or about three orders of magnitude faster than sequential system throughput rates. In addition to the high computation rate, storing a 512x512 raster frame requires about one megabyte of frame buffer memory with an effective access time of 100 nanoseconds. For 1024x1024 display the size of the memory increases to four megabytes and the access rate drops to 25 nanoseconds, which is far beyond the reach of current high density MOS RAMs with 250 nsec access time.

The idea of storing an image in computer memory and repeatedly refreshing the raster display by scanning the stored image was originally introduced by Noll in 1971 [1]. Since then stored image or frame buffer based systems have dominated the field of raster graphics. As shown in figure 2a, the display processor receives high level polygon commands in screen coordinates and fills in the corresponding pixel locations in the frame buffer. The contents of the frame buffer are sequentially scanned at a fixed rate (about 10 MHz for 512x512 displays) in a raster fashion (left to right, top to bottom) by the refresh circuitry in order to refresh the raster display 30 times per second. The frame buffer is accessed in a dual mode: it is serially and periodically accessed for refreshing the screen and it is simultaneously accessed by the display processor for painting polygons at random locations in the frame. Using standard microprocessors, generating a new frame takes much longer than one frame refresh period. The complete frame must therefore be stored in a buffer. The same static frame is used repeatedly for refreshing the screen.

The problem with such a basic frame buffer system is that generating a typical frame containing a few thousand polygons will take several seconds which is much longer than one frame refresh period. Researchers have proposed several high performance frame buffer based system architectures for overcoming the high computation rates and/or the large image memory bandwidths. Unfortunately any attempt to increase the computation rate by multiprocessing is counterbalanced by small processor utilization and the large overhead involved in controlling the processors, distributing the task and communicating data between processors [2, 3, 4, 5, 6, 7]. Any attempt to improve the memory bandwidth by adding pixel processing logic to every pixel memory location in the frame is offset by a multifold increase in the overall size of the system, since the size of the processing logic is several times the area of the dynamic RAM cell [8, 9, 10, 11]. Generally, the overall result has been some increase in performance accompanied by a significant increase in system size and complexity.

Real time raster image generation requires that a new frame be generated for every screen refresh in order to give the illusion of motion and dynamic behavior. Given present circuit speeds, several processors working in parallel are required in order to generate a new frame during every refresh cycle. Assuming that the computations for generating a new frame can be performed in real time, one may then attempt to reduce the size of the frame buffer memory since it is no longer necessary to store a complete frame in order to refresh future frames. Because such real time images are generated and refreshed on-the-fly and in synchronization with the raster beam, polygons can no longer be painted at random positions in the frame, but have to be presorted according to the topmost line on which they become active.

In this paper we describe a novel real time raster system architecture based on a virtual scan line buffer. As the name implies, each frame is generated and refreshed on a line by line basis. This approach reduces the size of the image memory from a 512x512 frame buffer to a 512x1 scanline buffer. As shown in Figure 2b the Super Buffer system is composed of two main parts: a Scanline Processing Unit which buffers and transforms high level polygons into intermediate scan line instructions and a VLSI Raster Graphics Engine which simultaneously updates, buffers and refreshes one line of the raster image. Updating the image is performed by transforming each input scan line command into several low level pixel painting instructions. The image buffer is only one scan line and contains 512 pixel locations. The output of the engine is a raster stream of pixel intensities which is synchronized with the raster beam for direct refreshing of the screen. The details of the Scanline Processing Unit and the Raster Graphics Engine are discussed in the following sections.

In terms of image memory and processing tradeoff, the basic frame buffer system uses a single processor to paint a large image memory. In the opposite extreme, object oriented systems use a single pixel memory and several thousand processors to compute the intensity of each pixel directly from the object (or polygon) definition [12, 13]. An intermediate solution may be found by balancing the processing and memory requirements of the system. Compared to frame buffer based systems, a real time virtual scan line architecture tends to be highly processor intensive and requires much less image buffer memory. In the computer industry an increase in speed and performance is usually associated with an increase in size and cost. However, an optimal tradeoff between processing and memory results in the design of real time raster image generation systems which should be significantly faster but smaller and less expensive than existing frame buffer based designs.

2. The Scanline Processing Unit

The Scanline Processing Unit is the interface between the high-level graphics generator (host) and the Raster Graphics Engine. Its graphical function is to compute and generate scanline commands for all polygons intersecting the current scanline. Figure 3 shows the conceptual structure of the Scanline Processing Unit. The Painting Station is a special purpose hardware block which computes and generates a scanline command from the input polygon command. The Active Polygon Ring stores all polygons which are active on the current scanline. The polygon command which enters the Painting Station is either a newly activated polygon coming from the host or a previously activated polygon coming from the head of the Active Polygon Ring. When all polygons on the current scanline are processed, blank scanline commands are generated to preserve system timing. During the current scanline period, exactly one scanline command (blank or non-blank) is generated by the Scanline Processing Unit in every pixel clock cycle. The details of the Scanline Processing Unit will be discussed in this section.

2.1. Painting Station

The Painting Station computes the intersection of the input polygon command and the current scanline. It then generates the corresponding scanline command for the Raster Graphics Engine. Since the image is being generated in a raster fashion, computing the intersection of the current scanline and a polygon can be carried out incrementally using integer additions and requires no multiplication or division. Since one polygon will enter the

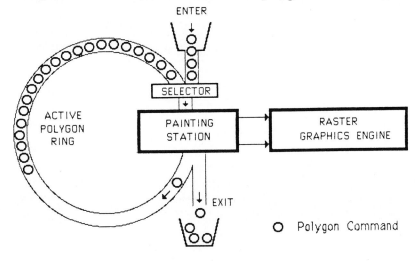

FIGURE 3: Conceptual Outline of the Scanline Processing Unit

Painting Station in every pixel clock cycle, all computations have to carried out in parallel and in hardware.

Figure 4 shows the format of a polygon command and a scanline command. A scanline command describes a horizontal line with the pixel position of its left and right endpoints and the color of the pixels on the line. A scanline command will paint a horizontal line which is one pixel high and may be as short as one pixel or as long as one raster line (512 pixels).

An active polygon command contains information about the current position of the left and right endpoints of the scanline, the slope of the two edges containing these endpoints, as well as information for changing the left and right slopes at polygon vertices. The additional fields contain the color of the polygon and the line on which it becomes deactivated.

Figure 4 also shows how a high level active polygon can be decomposed into several intermediate level horizontal scanline commands. Computing each row of the table from the previous row requires two integer additions for incrementing the left and right endpoints of the scanline and two compare and select operations for changing the left and right increments when the scanline intersects a vertex. All the above operations are

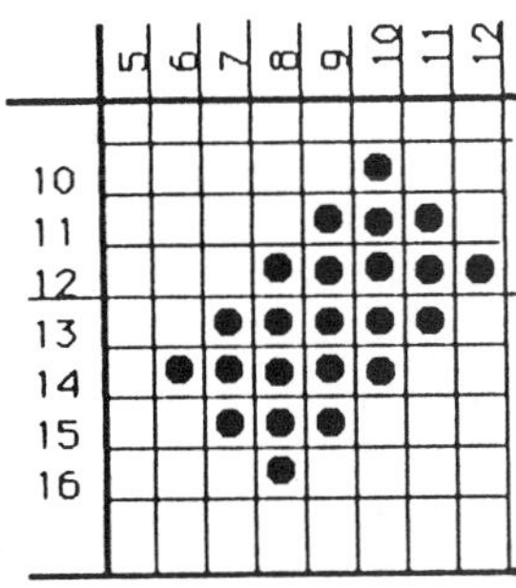

	ACTIVE POLYGON COMMAND										SCANLINE COMMAND		
	Y_cur_scan	X_left	ΔX_left	Y_left_mid	ΔX_left_mid	X_right	ΔX_right	Y_right_mid	ΔX_right_mid	Y_bottom	Color	X_left	X_right	Color
10	10	10	-1	14	+1	10	+1	12	-1	16	RED	10	10	RED
11	11	9	-1	14	+1	11	+1	12	-1	16	RED	9	11	RED
12	12	8	-1	14	+1	12	-1	12	-1	16	RED	8	12	RED
13	13	7	-1	14	+1	11	-1	12	-1	16	RED	7	11	RED
14	14	6	+1	14	+1	10	-1	12	-1	16	RED	6	10	RED
15	15	7	+1	14	+1	9	-1	12	-1	16	RED	7	9	RED
16	16	8	+1	14	+1	8	-1	12	-1	16	RED	8	8	RED

← REFRESH SCANLINE

FIGURE 4: Decomposition of an Active Polygon Command

into Horizontal Scanline Commands

independent and are computed in parallel by the Painting Station in a single clock cycle. Standard TTL parts can be used to perform these computations.

Note that the complete table does not have to be computed at once, but the next row can be dynamically computed from the contents of the current row whenever necessary. To represent an active polygon only one row of the table is stored in the Scanline Processing Unit. The expansion of the compact high level polygon command into scanlines and pixels is delayed as long as possible until the information is needed for refreshing the display. In frame buffer systems, polygons are immediately expanded into pixels which requires at least a megabytes of pixel memory. Assuming that each polygon can be represented with 20 bytes then storing the image in polygon format is more efficient than pixel format for images with less than 50,000 polygons per frame. For typical images with only a few thousand polygons, the advantages of storing the image in polygon format and rapidly expanding it into scanlines and pixels at display refresh rates are enormous.

2.2. Blank Scanline Commands and System Clocking

The number of active polygons intersecting a scanline varies dynamically from line to line, therefore active scanline commands are padded with blank scanline commands to give a total of 512 commands during each horizontal line cycle. One may define a static bit pattern as the blank command. Alternatively, a blank command may be dynamically defined as a command which does not change the state of the line buffer when it is fully painted. Hence the previous scanline command can always be used as a dynamic blank scanline command. This approach allows us to treat all commands equally without making any special exceptions for blank commands.

A pixel clock is used to synchronize the operation of the Super Buffer system with the raster beam. For a 512x512 display, a horizontal scanline period is composed of 512 clock ticks (about 100 nsec/cycle) for refreshing the pixels followed by several inactive clock cycles (about 110) corresponding to the horizontal blanking retrace. After 512 line cycles, the pixel clock remains inactive for several line cycles (about 23) for the vertical blanking retrace. A two phase non-overlapping clock can be easily derived from the pixel clock. Since the beam is blanked for about 20% of each line cycle, an optional pseudo-pixel clock which also ticks during the blanking period may be used to perform additional non-display-related computations during the retrace period.

2.3. Active Polygon Ring

The Scanline Processing Unit uses an Active Polygon Ring to store all polygons which are active on the current scanline. A polygon becomes vertically active when the current scanline intersects its topmost pixel. It remains active until the current scanline passes its lowest pixel. The polygon commands entering the Painting Station are selected from either a previously active polygon which is at the head of the Active Polygon Ring or a newly activated polygon which has just entered the unit. The active polygons will circulate around the Ring and through the Painting Station exactly once during each scanline period. Deactivated polygons are forced to exit the Active Polygon Ring.

Like the instruction cache in high speed computers, the Active Polygon Ring is a high speed memory for storing polygons which will be active during the next and possibly future lines of the frame. Assuming that each polygon is on the average active during 10% of the vertical screen resolution, then 98% of the scanline commands entering the Painting Station are derived from active polygons which are stored in the Ring.

Newly activated polygons should enter the Ring during the period when the current scanline is intersecting their topmost vertex. In order to ensure this condition, all the polygons in the frame have to be sorted into 512 buckets according to the vertical position of their topmost pixel. During each scanline period the corresponding bucket is emptied into the Ring. Unlike other sorting algorithms, bucket sorting with a limited range radix is an extremely simple and fast operation that requires O(1) operations per polygon. Instead of normally appending each polygon to the linear display file, it is simply inserted at the head of its corresponding bucket.

To resolve the visibility of overlapping polygons, frame buffer systems paint the image from a time priority ordered list of polygons. Polygons painted later in time may obscure all or portions of polygons already painted into the frame buffer. In Super Buffer systems the polygons should enter the Painting Station in increasing time priority order during each scanline period. This condition is guaranteed if merging the contents of the Ring with the contents of a bucket preserves the increasing time priority condition. As shown in Figure 5, to preserve the visibility information each polygon from the time priority list is time stamped with its position in the list before it is inserted into the proper bucket. Upon completion of the task, the polygons within each bucket are automatically arranged in increasing time priority order. If the Ring is originally empty then the polygons in the first bucket will enter the Painting Station in increasing time priority order. Later on, the time stamp of the command at the head of the Ring is compared to the time stamp at the head of the current bucket and the command with the smaller time stamp is selected for entering the Painting Station. Although the scanline commands generated by the Painting Station contain no time stamp information field, it is understood that the scanline commands generated later in the scanline period have a higher priority and may obscure all or portions of the previous scanline commands. The overhead involved in painting time priority ordered polygons includes the addition of the time stamp field to the polygon records and a simple integer compare and select for each polygon entering the Painting Station.

The Painting Station will generate a horizontal scanline command consisting of the left and right endpoints and the color of the line during each pixel clock cycle. Up to 512 horizontal scanline commands may be generated during each line cycle. The Active Polygon Ring should have the capacity to store up to 512 active polygon commands. The Ring can thus be implemented with about 512x20 bytes of high speed FIFO or dynamic RAM memory. Assuming that each polygon is on the average active during 10% of the vertical screen resolution, then a maximum of 5,120 polygons can be painted in each frame in real time. On the average each bucket may hold about 10 polygon commands. A small FIFO memory at the entrance to the scanline processing unit may be used to hold the contents of the next bucket in order to buffer any speed difference at the interface.

Consider now the result of painting the endpoints of the scanline commands leaving the Painting Station into a frame buffer. Observe that the resultant picture will be a vector drawing which outlines the perimeter of the polygons in the frame. The vectors are not drawn in a random manner, but emerge in a raster fashion from top to bottom. These intermediate scanline

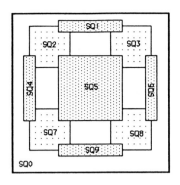

TIME PRIORITY LIST		BUCKET SORTED LIST		
1. SQ0	Buck_0	1. SQ0		
2. SQ2	•			
3. SQ3	Buck_1	6. SQ1		
4. SQ7	•			
5. SQ8	Buck_2	2. SQ2	3. SQ3	
6. SQ1	•			
7. SQ4	•			
8. SQ5	Buck_3	7. SQ4	8. SQ5	9. SQ6
9. SQ6	•			
10. SQ9	Buck_4	4. SQ7	5. SQ8	
	•			
	Buck_5	10. SQ9		

FIGURE 5: Bucket Sorting a Time Priority List

of Polygons

commands are actually passed along to the Graphics Engine which expands them into low level pixel painting instructions to fill all the pixels between the left and right endpoints of each scanline command. Assuming that we are dealing with an NxN square, then the high level square command is expanded into N intermediate scanline commands by the Scanline Processing Unit. Each intermediate scanline command is further expanded into N low level pixel painting instructions by the Graphics Engine, or a total of N**2 expansion from the original high level definition.

3. The Systolic VLSI Raster Graphics Engine

At the heart of the Super Buffer system is the Systolic Graphics Engine, a custom designed VLSI chip which is capable of real time image generation and screen refresh in synchronization with the raster beam. The image buffer memory for storage of pixel elements also resides on the same chip, eliminating the need for any external frame buffer memory. Problems associated with frame buffer based designs such as large memory size, fast image memory access rates, memory skewing and interleaving, and shared memory access contentions are also eliminated.

As shown in Figure 6, the Raster Graphics Engine is constructed by 512 replications of a basic Pixel Processor cell in a regular one dimensional array. The simple nearest-neighbor interconnection scheme provides efficient data communication between adjacent pixel processors and qualifies the Engine as a pure

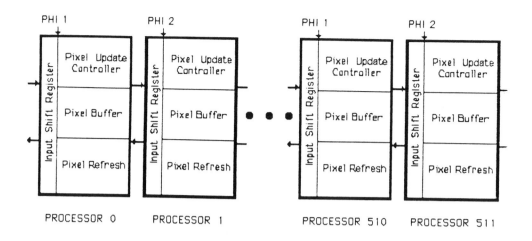

PHI 1   PHI 2   PHI 1   PHI 2

PROCESSOR 0   PROCESSOR 1   PROCESSOR 510   PROCESSOR 511

FIGURE 6: Block Structure of the

Raster Graphics Engine

systolic processor array [14]. Scanline commands and some control information flow to the right while the computational results (the raster video output stream) flows to the left. Only the first processor in the pipeline communicates with the outside world. Only the raster video output stream leaves the Engine; the scanline commands in the pipeline are discarded when they have been fully processed, thus reducing the number of external pins required for the chip. The similarity of pixel processors and the simple interconnection scheme allows optimization of the layout of a basic Pixel Processor to achieve high density and high speed with a minimum layout effort.

The Pixel Processors are synchronized by a two phase non-overlapping pixel clock. Even (odd) processors have valid input data during Phi1 (Phi2). Each Pixel Processor is made up of two vertical pieces; a dynamic shift register section followed by a block of logic and storage elements. Since the input to the odd processors is inverted, a Dual Pixel Processor is used where the even (odd) processor is implemented with positive (negative) logic. As will be shown, the simplicity and symmetry in the logic function (i.e.$A = B$ is symmetric to $\overline{A} = \overline{B}$) allows us to design the Dual Pixel Processor pair without doubling the layout effort. Although the function of each Pixel Processor is hard wired for faster operation, the overall Engine is flexible enough to paint any geometrical primitive which can be decomposed into horizontal scanlines. The logic and storage block of each Pixel Processor is divided into three horizontal pieces: Pixel Update Controller, Pixel Buffer Register, and Pixel Refresh Circuit.

A new scanline command will enter the Graphics Engine during every pixel clock cycle. Since one pixel intensity leaves the engine in every pixel clock cycle, up to 512 scanline commands may be painted on the current line before the next scanline is initiated. Scanline commands travel at the rate of two Pixel Processors per cycle. Scanline commands travel in the same order as they entered the engine. After 256 pixel clock cycles, the scanline command has visited all Pixel Processors and the painting process is completed. Upon exiting the last Pixel Processor, the scanline command is discarded.

3.1. Pixel Update Controller

Each Pixel Processor has a unique identification number (ID) corresponding to its position in the pipeline, and thus the pixel whose display it controls. The Pixel Update Controller will generate a write signal whenever the processor ID is between the left and right end points of a scanline command. More precisely:

IF Xleft $\leq$ ID $\leq$ Xright
  THEN Write := High
  ELSE Write := Low

With 512 processors, 9 bits are required to represent the scanline command variables Xleft and Xright. For a typical scanline command, the write signal will become active only for the processors between Xleft and Xright and will remain low for processors at the beginning and end of the line. Although this conditional write statement is equivalent to several machine instructions, each pixel processor is specialized to execute the above statement in one clock phase or 50 nanoseconds. 512 conditional statements from 256 scanline commands will be evaluated in parallel in every pixel clock cycle. This sums up to a total of 5,120 Million conditional write statements per second.

3.2. Pixel Buffer Register

As in sequential computers, frame buffer based systems are composed of an image memory block and a display processing block. In Super Buffer systems the image memory is distributed throughout the Pixel Processors. Each Pixel Processor can store the intensity of its pixel in its Pixel Buffer. Since the Pixel Buffer is local to the processor, no global address decoding is necessary. Unlike frame buffer memories, the Pixel Buffer is an extremely fast local register. Indeed the performance of the system is no longer limited by the image memory bandwidth but is determined by the processing delay. Furthermore, all Pixel Processors may be simultaneously accessing their own pixel buffer without causing any image memory access contentions.

The Graphics Engine contains 512 Pixel Buffers, one for each pixel in the scanline. Like any other memory unit, the Pixel Buffer is controlled by a write and a read signal. If the write signal is set by the Pixel Update Controller then the color information of the scanline command is written into the Pixel Buffer. If the read signal is set by the Pixel Refresh Circuit then the information in the Pixel Buffer is entered into the raster video output stream. Because the information stored in the Pixel Buffers is overwritten at least once during every horizontal line cycle, the Pixel Buffers may be implemented with dynamic memory cells without any need for external charge refreshing.

Color experiments have determined that the human eye can distinguish about 100,000 different colors on a raster display and that in general color images can be represented with 256 intensity levels of each of the three primary colors or a total of 24 bits/pixel. A color map (or color table lookup) is commonly used in frame buffer based systems to reduce the size of the image memory to 8 bits/pixel, limiting the image to 256 distinct colors. Upon screen refresh, the 8 bit pixel value is used as an address for selecting one of the 256 RGB triplets stored in the color map. The color map requires 256x3 additional bytes of memory but saves 512x512x2 bytes of frame buffer memory.

As in frame buffer systems, the Graphics Engine can use a color map and 8 bit Pixel Buffers for representing the pixel color and intensity. Operating three graphics engines in parallel, however, each with 8 bit Pixel Buffers, allows direct storage of the three primary colors using 24 bits/pixel. With the exception of the color information, the three Engines receive identical scanline commands. The advantages are clear; by using two extra Graphics Engine chips images may be represented in full color. The color map circuitry is totally eliminated from the system.

3.3. Pixel Refresh Circuit

At the beginning of each raster line, the Scanline Processing Unit generates a refresh token instead of a scanline command. A refresh token is a blank command with the refresh bit set. The refresh bit in standard scanline commands is not set. Upon entering the Engine, the refresh token travels across the pipeline along with all the other scanline commands. The processor containing the refresh token will set the read control line of the Pixel Buffer and the contents of the Pixel Buffer will enter the raster video output stream which flows to the left. Figure 7 demonstrates the journey of a refresh token across a pipeline with 4 Pixel Processors. After four pixel clock phases, the refresh token reaches the end of the pipeline. By that time half of the video information will have exited the pipeline while the remaining half is still within the pipe. In the following 4 clock phases the pipe operates without a refresh token and will accept scanline commands for the next line while the remaining video information is completely flushed out of the raster video output pipe. A new refresh token will be generated at the beginning of the next line.

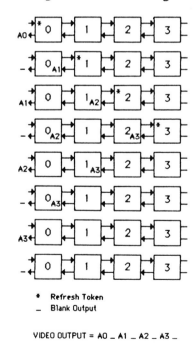

* Refresh Token
_ Blank Output

VIDEO OUTPUT = A0 _ A1 _ A2 _ A3 _

FIGURE 7: Refreshing a Scanline

The cycle repeats every four pixel clock cycles.

Exactly one pixel intensity leaves the pipe during every pixel clock cycle. Since the pipeline is synchronized and clocked at video rates, it is possible to refresh the raster screen directly from the output of the raster video stream. An additional video controller creates the analog composite video signal for connection to a color monitor. Observe that at any instant one processor may be refreshing the raster video stream while the remaining 511 processors are updating the contents of the virtual scanline buffer. If the refresh token is at the Ith Pixel Processor, then processors I+1 through the last processor are painting the remaining pixels in the current line while processor 0 through I-1 are simultaneously painting the next line of the image. Stated in different words, active and blank scanline commands for the current line will enter the Engine until refreshing of the current line begins at which point a refresh token is generated. Commands entering the pipe following the refresh token correspond to the next line of the image. Unlike conventional pipelines, the Engine operates continuously without any initial setup or final draining delays. Upon completion of the current line refresh and during the horizontal blanking period, the Engine will wait for the next refresh token. Using an optional pseudo-pixel clock, additional scanline commands (roughly 20% of 512) may be clocked into the Engine during the idle blanking period.

3.4. Implementation

A prototype Super Buffer system is currently under construction at Cornell University and is expected to become operational in the near future. The Scanline Processing Unit and the host interface are implemented with standard TTL parts and occupy a single prototype printed circuit board. The Graphics Engine chip also resides on the same board.

The entire Raster Graphics Engine prototype is integrated on a single chip using standard 4 micron NMOS technology. After several design iterations, our optimal pixel processor designs for the prototype 256x512 image (half frame) with 8 intensity levels contains about 150 transistors. The complete Engine containing 256 Pixel Processors and 36 input and output pads is implemented with less than 30,000 transistors and occupies a total silicon area of 5,000 microns by 7,000 micron (.5cm x .7cm). The system will be clocked at video rates (about 10 MHz) as if it were driving a full 512x512 display. Using a 2 micron NMOS technology, the Engine can be easily expanded to 512 Pixel Processors with 8 bit Pixel buffers and can be implemented with about 80,000 transistors on a similar silicon area. The conventional wisdom concerning a change to CMOS technology in order to lower the power consumption of a more compact implementation drastically is not as applicable to this design as to others since data is being constantly shifted across the Engine at full clock rate.

4. Enhancing the Basic Super Buffer System

The basic Super Buffer system presented in this paper has several limitations. With a 10 MHz pixel clock it can paint in real time a maximum of 512 active polygons on each scanline of a

512x512 raster color display. When compared to a frame buffer it is significantly faster and smaller, however simple variations of the basic architecture can greatly enhance the functionality and performance of the Super Buffer family of systems. The Scanline Processing Unit may be modified to handle geometric primitives other thanquadrilaterals. The functionality of the system can be enhanced by addition of hardware for real time removal of hidden surfaces and linear shading of three dimensional polygons. The performance of the system can be improved by using multiple Raster Graphics Engines to handle larger number of active polygons per scanline and/or larger display resolutions.

The Scanline Processing Unit may be modified to paint pixels, vectors, rectangles, trapezoids and even more complex primitives. Characters and other cell based objects can also be painted using table lookup. The tables contain the scanline commands for painting the cell. A character may have to be painted with more than one scanline command, i.e. E needs one, V needs two, and W needs three. When using multiple geometric primitives, each primitive is tagged with an object code which is decoded to identify the location of the data fields and the operations to be performed on each field.

Removal of hidden surfaces using the so-called Z-buffer approach requires incremental computations at every pixel location. If the image is to be generated in real time, then these computations must also be performed in hardware and in real time. The Scanline Processing Unit will store the depth of each polygon vertex and interpolate the depth along each edge to generate the depth of each endpoint of the scanline command. Since polygons are planar, the depth increment along the x-axis is constant for all horizontal lines in the polygon. Each Pixel Processor is enhanced with a Z-buffer, a comparator, and an adder. Whenever the Write signal is high, the input Z value is compared to the value stored in the Z-buffer. If the comparison is successful (i.e. input scanline closer to observer) then the input color is copied into the Pixel Buffer and the Z-buffer is simultaneously updated with the input Z value. In either case the input depth is incremented for the next Pixel Processor. The Z-buffers will be automatically initialized with the refresh token during every scanline.

Linear shading can be performed in a similar fashion by adding a color increment to the input color field in each active Pixel Processor.

Larger number of polygons per scanline can be painted using a number of techniques. One may attempt to paint two lines of the image simultaneously. This would double the effective scanline period and hence doubles the total number of polygons that can be painted on one scanline. This can be accomplished by connecting two Painting Stations in series and each polygon will go through both Stations in each circulation. Each Station is connected to its own Raster Graphics Engine. One of the Engines paints the even lines of the display and the other is responsible for the odd lines.

Similar techniques may be used to refresh higher resolution displays (i.e. 1024x1024). Because the resolution is doubled, an extra bit is needed for representing each of the polygon coordinates. In frame buffer systems this would quadruple the size of the image memory and increase the effective image memory access rate by a similar factor. Using two Painting Stations and connecting two Engines (512 Pixel Processors) to each will provide enough computation power for displaying 1024x1024 images in real time. It is usually the case that the number of polygons in each frame does not change drastically with an increase in screen resolution. As the circuit densities increase, we expect to design Raster Graphics Engines with 1024 Pixel Processors on a single chip.

5. Conclusions

Computer graphics has reflected the current state of hardware and software technology during its short history. LSI technology, MOS memories and single chip microprocessors gave birth to the early computer graphic systems. The advent of VLSI technology and special purpose chips have brought about further promising real time hardware solutions for many of the classical low level image generation operations. Geometric calculations such as vertex transformation, clipping and windowing can now be performed by the Geometry Engine [15], and image rasterization, polygon filling and even hidden surface removal and polygon shading may in the near future be performed by the Super Buffer family of systems. The overall system performance bottleneck will then no longer be in the graphics hardware, but rather in the application software's ability to generate and manipulate the high level polygons in the image. As a result of these advances, the visual joy of observing real time raster color images is no longer limited to the users of multi-million dollar flight simulation systems, but we anticipate that in the age of Modern Computer Graphics real time raster image generation systems, like minicomputers, will be mass produced for widespread use in various visual applications.

References

1. Michael Noll, "Scanned-Display Computer Graphics," *Communications of the ACM*, p. 143 (March 1971).

2. Satish Gupta, Robert F. Sproull, and Ivan E. Sutherland, "A VLSI Architecture for Updating Raster-Scan Displays," *Proceedings of SIGGRAPH 81*, pp. 71-78 (August 1981).

3. Robert F. Sproull, Ivan E. Sutherland, Alistair Thompson, Satish Gupta, and Charles Minter, "The 8 by 8 Display," *ACM Transactions on Graphics* 2(January 1983).

4. James Clark and Marc Hannah, "Distributed Processing in a High Performance Smart Image Memory," *LAMBDA*, p. 40 (October 1980).

5. A. Bechtolsheim and F. Baskett, "High Performance Raster Graphics for Microcomputer Systems," *Communications of the ACM*, p. 43 (1980).

6. Michael Kaplan and Don Greenberg, "Parallel Processing Techniques for Hidden Surface Removal," *Proceedings of SIGGRAPH 79*, p. 300 (1979).

7. Frederic I. Parke, "Simulation and Expected Performance Analysis of Multiple Processor Z-buffer Systems," *Proceedings of SIGGRAPH 80*, pp. 48-56 (1980).

8. H. Fuchs and J. Poulton, "Pixel Planes: A VLSI Oriented Design for a Raster Graphics Engine," *VLSI Design*, (Third Quarter 1981).

9. Henry Fuchs, John Poulton, Alan Paeth, and Alan Bell, "Developing Pixel-Planes, A Smart Memory-Based Raster Graphics System," *Conference on Advanced Research in VLSI*, pp. 137-146 (January 1982).

10. Daniel S. Whelan, "A Rectangular Area Filling Display System Architecture," *Proceedings of SIGGRAPH 82*, pp. 147-154 (July 1982).

11. Stefan Demetrescu, "High Speed Image Rasterization Using Highly Parallel Smart Bulk Memory," *Stanford University Tech Report 83-244*, (June 1983).

12. Bart Locanthi, "Object Oriented Raster Displays," *Proceedings of the Caltech Conference on VLSI*, pp. 215-225 (January 1979).

13. Donald Fussell and Bharat Deep Rathi, "A VLSI-Oriented Architecture for Real-Time Raster Display of Shaded Polygons," *Proceedings of Graphics Interface 82*, pp. 373-380 (1982).

14. H. T. Kung, "Why Systolic Architectures?," *IEEE Computer*, p. 37 (Jan 1982).

15. James Clark, "The Geometry Engine: A VLSI Geometry System for Graphics," *Proceedings of SIGGRAPH 82*, pp. 127-133 (1982).

Chapter 6: Image Generation Hardware for Constructive Solid Geometry and Ray Tracing

Two important image-rendering techniques are constructive solid geometry and ray tracing. In this chapter, we shall discuss some of the hardware aspects of these schemes.

6.1: Rasterization Hardware for the CSG Scheme

A simple method of defining three-dimensional objects is as a collection of lines representing the object's edges. These edges can then be viewed as a conventional wire frame image. However, one major disadvantage of this approach is that the internal definition of the object is extremely loose and often ambiguous, which prevents the extraction of features such as volume, intersection, center of gravity, and moments of inertia. However, such physical properties of the objects that are being modeled are important to many CAD/CAM environments, such as mechanical parts design, architectural design, piping design, medical diagnostic imaging, and molecular modeling.

Solid modeling techniques encompass procedures for defining three-dimensional objects. There are three broad approaches to solid modeling: boundary, sweeping, and constructive solid geometry (CSG) representation schemes. The boundary representation (B-rep) scheme employs surfaces to define an object's boundary; thus, a block would be defined as the enclosed volume from the intersection of six planes (a top, a bottom, and four side planes.) Sweeping technique incorporates the notion of a moving point creating a line, a moving line generating a surface, and a swept surface forming a volume. An object can be represented as a collection of areas swept along a trajectory or rotated about an axis.

Among the three approaches, CSG is the most popular. The CSG scheme defines an object from a set of geometric primitives such as cuboids, prisms, cylinders, and spheres. These primitives are linked by a data structure in the form of a binary tree, which also stores the relational operators binding the primitives. Such a binary tree-like data structure is called a *CSG* tree. The operators, often called *Boolean set operators,* include (1) union, which enables one object to be merged together with another object; (2) difference, which subtracts one volume from another; and (3) intersection, which defines the volume common to both objects.

The definition of an object (formation of CSG trees) is easy, but generating the images of CSG models is computation intensive.

6.1.1: Parallel Processing Architectures for CSG Graphics

The leaves of the CSG tree, which correspond to the components of the solid, are independent. Owing to this independence, they can be rasterized in parallel. This confirms the possibility of using a one-processor-per-leaf architecture for CSG graphics. Each *leaf processor* is referred to as an *L processor*. The output of these processors must then be combined by a number of logic operators, which means there should also be processing units to carry out the required "merging" tasks. Such merging processors are called *node processors,* or *N processors*. The outputs from two L processors are input to an N processor, which carries out the required operation on the two inputs. For a particular CSG

EH0273-3/88/0000/0281$01.00 © 1988 IEEE

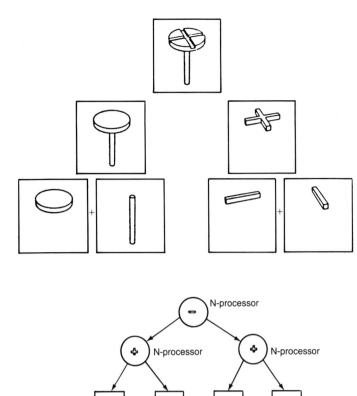

Figure 6.1: The processor network for a CSG tree.

tree, a number of L processors and N processor can be connected to form a tree network of processors that complies with the structure of the CSG tree. Figure 6.1 shows a CSG tree and its corresponding processor network.

Obviously, it is not feasible to have a customized processor network for every possible CSG tree. Therefore, one should be able to configure the L and N processor network to comply to any CSG tree. This requires the system to be topologically configurable [KEDE84, KEDE85, SATO85].

6.2: Hardware for Ray Tracing

In brief, ray tracing is a special technique to render a scene. Instead of recording the light rays emitted by the scene, a ray is assumed to be sent from the viewer through each pixel cell. Each ray is then intersected with each object in the scene to find the closest visible surface. At this intersection point, rays are spawned (1) toward each direct light source, (2) in the mirror reflection direction, and (3) in the refracted ray direction.

These spawned rays may again encounter another surface, and then the similar spawning activity is repeated. Thus, as a ray from the viewer through a pixel is traced, it may spawn many times before it leaves the scene or inter-

sects a nonreflecting surface. As a ray intersects with various surfaces, the contributions to the shading of the pixel is evaluated.

The ray-tracing technique is extremely computation-intensive because of the recursive ray-spawning algorithm. For each pixel an intersection tree is built that has at its root the pixel. Interior nodes are intersected surfaces, and leaves are direct light sources or nonreflective surfaces or the exterior of the scene. The branches of the intersection tree are the rays spawned during the tracing of the pixel. Since the computation of intersection trees are independent of each other, parallel processing is a good approach to implement ray-tracing algorithms.

6.2.1: Ray-Tracing Peripheral

As observed by Whitted and Rubin [RUBI80, WHIT80], most of the time in a ray tracing algorithm (70–90 percent) is spent in finding ray surface intersections. Therefore, if these intersection computations could be cast into hardware, one could significantly reduce the running time of the ray-tracing algorithm.

Ullner [ULLN83] proposed a ray-tracing processor that acts as a peripheral to a host computer. The host computer fires rays at the peripheral, which in turn returns the closest polygon intersected along with the intersection information. The ray-tracing peripheral has its own copy of the scene model which, besides reducing the load on the host's memory, also permits the model to be organized in a way that is suitable for intersection computation.

6.2.2: Ray-Tracing Pipeline

Ullner's ray-tracing peripheral (described above) is not very extensible and cannot be easily enhanced to accommodate more complex scenes. The ray-tracing peripheral has a single and fast intersection processor, but the intersection process has to be repeated for each polygon.

Consider the other extreme now. If there were a less complex and, therefore, a slower intersection processor, there could be many more of these processors working in parallel to achieve similar performance. The obvious advantage would be expandability. The greater the number of these intersection processing units, which could be implemented as custom VLSI processors, the shorter would be the time for rendering a more complex scene. Ideally, every object in the scene model could be assigned to one of these processors.

On the basis of the above observations, Ullner [ULLN83] also proposed the ray-tracing pipeline, which is composed of intersection processors strung together to form the pipeline. Each processor stores the description of a single polygon, and it passes the description of rays through its input and output ports. On receiving a ray description, the processor determines whether that ray intersects its stored polygon and, if so, locates the intersection point.

6.2.3: Ray-Tracing Array

In the ray-tracing array, a three-dimensional grid is superimposed on the modeling space to divide the volume into a collection of subvolumes. Each processor is then responsible for maintaining the surface models in its own subvolume as well as for computing the intersections of these surfaces with the rays passing through the subvolume. With such an arrangement, one would expect a three-dimensional lattice of processors, each connected to its six neighboring processors. However, the cumbersome nature of wiring entailed by such an organization acts as a major deterrent. Ullner overcame this problem by organizing the machine as a two-dimensional array of processors with the third dimension of the partitioning grid simulated within each processor in the array [ULLN83]. This structure allows each processor to communicate with its four neighboring processors. The processors have some special purpose intersection hardware to aid in intersection computation.

6.2.4: Dippé's Parallel Architecture

Load distributions are extremely difficult to calculate a priori and, hence, must be done dynamically during the actual execution of the ray-tracing process. A serious shortcoming of Ullner's ray-tracing array is that no attempt is made to address the issues of uniform load distribution over the subregions. Uneven object distribution among different subregions can lead to load disparities between processors, causing inefficient use of processing power. Dippé and Swensen [DIPP84] proposed a ray-tracing architecture quite similar to the ray-tracing array proposed by Ullner. The major difference between the two is that Dippé's parallel architecture allows the subdivision of the object space to be adaptively controlled.

6.2.5: LINKS-1 Multiprocessor System

LINKS-1 [NISH83] is an experimental machine that has been built and tested at Osaka University, Japan. The system consists of 64 unit computers, which are interconnected with a root computer such that a number of unit computers constitute a pipelined computer and such pipeline computers work in parallel, all controlled by the root computer. The number and length of each pipeline can be controlled dynamically. LINKS-1 organization is general enough to be used for many image-creation applications by means of sophisticated parallel processing schemes that use different numbers of pipelines, perhaps with different lengths. Intercomputer program/data transfer is greatly facilitated by the use of an intercomputer memory swapping unit (IMSU). Neighboring unit computers (and also each unit computer and the root computer) can exchange program/data by using IMSUs. There also exists a slow serial link between each unit computer and the root computer.

6.3: Article Overview

In "The Raycasting Machine," Kedem and Ellis propose a system for three-dimensional CSG graphics rendering using the ray-casting technique. In this system, a number of processors are arranged in a tree configuration that mirrors the CSG tree representation of the solid being processed.

CSG is not limited to three-dimensional solid modeling; it can also be employed to represent complex two-dimensional objects effectively. In the paper by Kedem and Hammond, "The Point Classifier: A VLSI Processor for Displaying Complex Two-Dimensional Objects," a VLSI system for two-dimensional CSG representation is proposed. This system displays complex two-dimensional objects in real time.

The multiprocessor system defined in the third paper, "Fast Image Generation of Constructive Solid Geometry Using a Cellular Array Processor" by Sato et al., is another machine built to tackle the rendering problem of CSG solids. The basic strategy for speeding up image generation in this system is to partition the image area into a number of subareas. Each subarea is processed by an individual cell of the array processor.

The paper by Dippé and Swensen, "An Adaptive Subdivision Algorithm and Parallel Architecture for Realistic Image Synthesis," describes a special architecture for ray tracing that employs an adaptive technique for object space division.

The next paper, "LINKS-1: A Parallel Pipelined Multimicrocomputer System for Image Creation" by Nishimura et al., describes a ray-tracing machine, the LINKS-1, built at Osaka University, Japan.

Usually, ray-tracing systems are restricted to objects described by polygons or quadratic surfaces. In the last paper, "The Feasibility of a VLSI Chip for Ray Tracing Bicubic Patches" by Pulleyblank and Kapenga, the possibility of a VLSI chip for ray-tracing bicubic patches in Bezier form is explored.

References

[DIPP84] Dippé, M. and J. Swensen, "An Adaptive Subdivision Algorithm and Parallel Architecture for Realistic Image Synthesis," *Computer Graphics,* Vol. 18, No. 3, July 1984, pp. 149–158.

[KEDE84] Kedem, G. and J.L. Ellis, "The Raycasting System," *Proc. of 1984 IEEE Int. Conf. on Computer Design,* Computer Society, Washington, D.C., 1984, pp. 533–538.

[KEDE85]   Kedem, G. and S.W. Hammond, "The Point Classifier: A VLSI Processor for Displaying Complex Two-Dimensional Objects," *Chapel Hill Conference on VLSI,* Computer Science Press, Rockville, Md., 1985, pp. 377–393.

[NISH83]   Nishimura, H., H. Ohno, T. Kawata, I. Shira-kawa, and K. Omura, "LINKS-1: A Parallel Pipelined Multimicrocomputer System for Image Creation," *Proc. of the 10th Symp. on Computer Architecture,* Computer Society, Washington, D.C., 1983, pp. 387–394.

[RUBI80]   Rubin, S.M. and T. Whitted, "A 3-Dimensional Representation for Fast Rendering of Complex Scenes," *ACM SIGGRAPH' 80,* ACM, Inc., New York, 1980, pp. 110–116.

[SATO85]   Sato, H., M. Ishii, K. Sato, M. Ikesaka, H. Ishihata, M. Kakimoto, K. Hirota, and K. Inoue, "Fast Image Generation of Constructive Solid Geometry Using a Cellular Array Processor," *ACM SIGGRAPH,* ACM, Inc., New York, Vol. 19, No. 3, July 1985, pp. 95–102.

[ULLN83]   Ullner, M.K., "Parallel Machines for Computer Graphics," *PhD Thesis,* California Institute of Technology, Pasadena, Calif., 1983.

[WHIT80]   Whitted, T., "An Improved Illumination Model for Shaded Display," *ACM Communications,* Vol. 23, No. 6, June 1980, pp. 343–349.

The Raycasting Machine

Gershon Kedem
Computer Science & Electrical Engineering
University of Rochester, Rochester, New York 14627

John L. Ellis
Computer Science & Computer Engineering
Rochester Institute of Technology, Rochester, New York 14623

Abstract

Geometric modeling is important in CAD/CAM, robotics, computer vision, and other fields. Ray-casting is a computational utility central to many applications of geometric modeling. Ray casting is used for calculating shaded displays and mass properties of solids. It could also be used for collision detection, null object or same object detection and so forth.

Ray casting algorithms are dependent on the means used to represent solids. In this work we focus on solids represented in Constructive Solid Geometry We developed a special computer structure that will allow ray casting to be done 10X - 1000X faster than in conventional computers. Two types of modules are needed: domain dependent line primitive classifiers, and domain independent classification combiners.

The ray casting machine described here is a parallel, pipelined bit serial machine that classifies a regular lattice of parallel lines. We describe the design of two-bit serial building clocks, the Classification Combine processor (CC) and the incremental, bit serial, pipelined Primitive Classifier (PC). These building blocks were designed from the outset for custom VLSI implementation. We describe how to use these building blocks to construct a highly parallel synchronous machine for ray casting. The building blocks are arranged in chips as machine slice units. By adding more slices, larger and larger machines can be built.

1. Introduction

CAD/CAM systems require means to store and manipulate computer representations of two and three dimensional objects. Moreover, there is a need to rapidly display these objects, compute their properties (such as volume and moments of inertia), compute if two objects interfere and so forth. One popular method for representing two and three dimensional objects is by means of constructive solid geometry (CSG).

To represent a solid one uses regularized set operations union intersection and difference on a set of primitive solids oriented in space. The primitive solids are simple objects like blocks, balls, cones, cylinders and tories. Internally, an object is represented as a binary tree. The leaves of the tree are the primitive objects and the internal nodes are the set operations. A more complete description of CSG solids representation could be found in [Requicha 1977 and Tilov & Requicha 1780].

One technique for generating shaded displays of 3D objects or computing the volume of 3D objects is to use ray casting. In ray casting one computes the intersection of a family of straight lines with the 3D object. Using the end points of the intersecting intervals one can compute the boundary of the object. Integrating along the intervals one could compute the volume and moments of inertia of the object. Ray Casting is a special case of Curve-Solid classification introduced by Tilove (see Tilove 1980). Following Tilove's notation we call the ray-casting computation line-solid classification.

Unfortunately, computing the intersection of a large family of lines with an object represented by a CSG representation is very computationally intensive and time consuming. In this paper we describe a special purpose computer that computes the intersection of lines with two and three dimensional solids represented as CSG trees. This special purpose machine computes these intersections in parallel at much higher speed than is possible with a general purpose computer.

In order to compute the intersection of a line with a composite CSG solid, first the intersection of the line with each primitive solid is computed. The line is represented as a one parameter family of points $P(t) = (x + at, y + bt, z + ct)$. Computing the line segments that are inside the primitive solid (called primitive classification), is equivalent to finding the interval segment of the parameter t for which the line is inside the solid. This give rise to a set of inequalities for the parameter t. Solving these equations yield the interval of intersection.

Once the intersection of the line with each primitive solid is known, one has to compute the set operations defined by the CSG tree on the line segments in order to compute the line intersections with the composite object (this step is called classification-combine). The results of the classification against primitive solids are propagated up the CSG tree. At each node of the tree the set operation on the results coming out of the two son nodes are computed.

2. The Ray Casting Machine

2.1. The main idea

The main idea behind the Ray Casting machine is to build a tree of processors that mirrors the CSG tree representing the solid being classified. The binary tree has two types of processors: Primitive Classifiers (PCs) at the leaves of the tree, and Classification Combine processors (CCs), at the internal nodes of the tree. (See figure 1).

The PCs task is to compute the intersection of the curve (line) with the primitive solids. Each PC compute the intersection of a curve with a given solid. The computation of each PC is independent from the computation at other PCs Therefor they all work in parallel. More details about the PCs are given in section 3.

The CCs compute the set operations (Union. Intersection or Difference) on stream of interval segment. The CCs are arranged as a binary tree. Each CC receives from it's son processors a stream of interval segments. It computes a set operation on the intervals, and sends a list of intervals to it's parent processor. The curve-solid classification results come out of the root processor. More details about the CC are given in section 4.

2.2. The Embedding of Binary Trees

When designing a ray casting machine, one is immediately confronted with the question of how to interconnect the combine processors. One needs to interconnect the combine processors in such a way that it would be possible to embed in the network of processors any binary tree of processors with N leaves. Since each combine processor is small and many of them could be integrated on a single chip, one

Reprinted from *The Proceedings of the 1984 International Conference on Computer Design*, 1984, pages 533-538. Copyright © 1984 by The Institute of Electrical and Electronics Engineers, Inc.

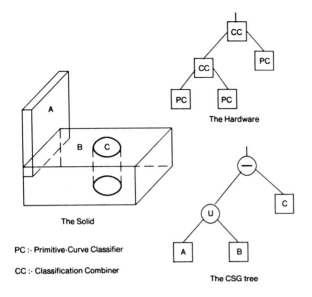

The Hardware

The Solid

PC :- Primitive-Curve Classifier

CC :- Classification Combiner

The CSG tree

Figure 1:   **CSG-Solids and Classification**

could afford to use more than N of them to embed a binary tree with N leaves. On the other hand, it is important to use all the primitive classifiers, since each of them is a large processor. Moreover, it is important to use a simple interconnection scheme so it would be possible to take advantage of VLSI technology.

Building a complete binary tree out of the processors is not very useful. Most CSG trees are not complete or even well balanced. Many of them tend to be highly unbalanced, almost linear. In the worst case, a complete tree with N leaves can only embed a linear tree (most unbalanced) of size $\log N$.

Unfortunately, it is impossible (in general) to balance CSG trees. This is due to the asymmetric nature of the difference operator. Therefore, what is needed is an interconnection scheme that will enable one to embed any given binary tree.

The problem of tree embedding in a grid has been studied before. A result due to Valiant [Valiant 1982] states that any binary tree with N leaves can be embedded in a rectangular grid with $O(N)$ processors in it. Valiant's result, however, is not very satisfactory since the leaves of the binary tree can be anywhere in the grid. If one requires all the leaves of the tree to be on the edge of the rectangular grid, $O(N)$ processors are not enough.

It was shown by Brent and Kung [Brent and Kung 1980] that if one insists that all the leaves of the binary tree will be on the boundary of the grid, it takes a grid of size $O(N\log N)$ to embed a binary tree with N leaves.

We have found that a $\log_2 N \times N$ grid can be used to embed any binary tree with N leaves. The $\log_2 N \times N$ solution is as follows:

First the tree is made right heavy; that is:

Definition:

A binary tree is right heavy if the number of nodes in each right subtree is greater or equal to the number of nodes of the corresponding left subtree.

Clearly each binary tree can be made to be right heavy by interchanging some of its left and right subtrees. In order to make a CSG tree right-heavy, one introduces two difference operators: The regular difference operator $-$ and the reversed difference operator $*-$. $A*-B$ is defined to be $B-A$. If the left and right subtrees of a difference operator $-$ are interchanged, the operator $-$ is changed to $*-$. With the other operators $\cup$ and $\cap$ there is no difficulty since they are symmetric.

A right-heavy binary tree with N leaves can be embedded into a $\log_2(N) \times N$ grid as follows:

The root is in the upper left corner. The leaves are at the bottom edge. Left links of the tree points downward on the grid and the right links point to the right. The tree is embedded by traversing the tree in preorder. If a leaf was encountered before the bottom of the grid was reached, the last link is extended to the bottom. Each right link is extended according to the following rule:

Let K be the number of leaves that are before the current node (in prefix order). The right link is extended so that the node is in Column $K+1$. (See Figure 2).

It is easy to see that the above procedure is a constructive embedding for any binary tree with N leaves in a $\log_2 N \times N$ grid.

The embedding is attractive for the following reasons:

1) All leaves are at the bottom.

2) All the processors are the same and therefore only one kind of chip has to be designed.

3) The interconnections to the outside grow slowly (like $\sqrt{N}$) as the number of internal processors grow. Only the processors that are on the perimeter of the grid have to be connected to the outside. Therefore, as technology advances, the number of processors that could be integrated on a single chip can grow with only moderate increases in the number of pins required.

4) It is easy to embed smaller trees. Moreover it is simple to embed more than one tree at a time if the total number of leaves does not exceed N.

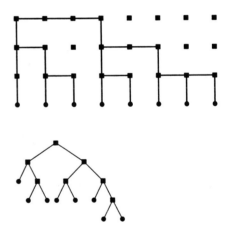

Figure 2:   **The imbedding of a binary tree in a grid**

2.3. The Ray Casting machine

The Ray Casting machine is made of an array of $(\log_2(N)+1) \times N$ processors. There are two kinds of processors: Primitive Classifiers (PCs), and Classification Combiners (CCs). The bottom row of the array is made of N PCs. Above it is $\log_2(N) \times N$ array of CCs. Each processor is a bit serial special purpose computer. The processors communicate bit serially via two bit wide connections. Section 3 describes the PC, section 4 describes the CC and section 5 describes the whole system.

3. The Primitive Classifier

3.1. Introduction

In order to compute Curve-Primitive classification one needs to solve polynomial equations. The curve is given by a parametric representation. The Primitives are given as a set of inequalities. For example a cylinder is given by:

$$X^2 + Y^2 \leq 1$$

$$Z \geq 0$$

$$Z \leq 1$$

One can simplify the computation by assuming that the primitives are linear or higher degree half spaces. In that case only a single inequality describes the primitive. Substituting the parametric representation of the line into the enequality result in an equation. The roots of this equation are the parametric values of the end points of the line intersecting the primitive.

In the mechanical CAD domain all the primitives are described by polynomial inequalities. With the exception of the torus, all the polynomial are of degree 2 and 1. Therefor the equations are either quadratic or linear (excluding the torus).

A serious problem is the fact that the amount of computation needed for classifying a "random" line is fairly large. First, one needs to transform the coordinates of the line to the primitive coordinate frame, then the polynomial equation has to be constructed and finally the roots of the polynomial have to be computed. All these computations require at best tens of multiplications and additions. Therefore, it is unlikely that the primitive classifiers could keep up with the combine array.

The computation could be done however at very high speed if it is done incrementally. The idea is not to compute the classification of one line but to classify an array of parallel lines. Most of the computation can be done once for the whole array as preprocessing step. The incremental amount of computation needed for each line is small (four additions, one subtraction, and one square root). The incremental algorithm is described in Section 3.2.

We designed a pipelined bit serial line classifier with relatively small amount of hardware to do incremental classification. The computation is done on a family of equally spaced parallel lines. The restriction is that the primitive objects are restricted to be only linear half spaces and quadratic half spaces, that is, balls, cones, cylinders, and so on. This does not mean that other primitives (say torus) could not be used. However, the classification of lines against more complicated objects will have to be precomputed by the general purpose host computer. This will result in reduced performance. Luckily, with the exception of the torus, the primitives used for CAD/CAM are all either linear or quadratic.

3.2. Incremental Algorithms for Classifying Parallel Lines

The main idea behind the incremental classification of a family of lines is as follows: One constructs a two-parameter family of straight lines $P(h,t)$. For each fixed value of h, say h_0, $P(h_0,t)$ is a straight line. By varying h one can construct a collection of lines.

If

$$P(h,t) = (a_0t + a_1h + x_0, \ b_0t + b_1h + y_0, \ c_0t + c_1h + z_0)$$

then we have a set of parallel lines. In order to classify the line against a primitive half space, say a unit cylinder: $x^2 + y^2 = 1$, one has to solve

$$(a_0t + a_1h + x_0)^2 + (b_0t + b_1h + y_0)^2 - 1 = 0$$

or

$$A(h)t^2 + B(h)t + C(h) = 0 \qquad \textbf{(1)}$$

where $A(h)$, $B(h)$, $C(h)$ are polynomials in the parameter h. It is not hard to show that for all quadratic half spaces (balls, cones, cylinders, and so on) the following is true:

1) $A(h)$ is independent of h; that is, $A(h) \equiv$ const.
2) $B(h)$ is a polynomial of degree one in h.
3) $C(h)$ is a polynomial of degree two in h.

The solutions of equation (1) are:

$$t_{1,2} = B/2A \pm \sqrt{(B/2A)^2 - C/A}$$

The discriminant $D = (B/2A)^2 - C/A$ is a second degree polynomial in h. To compute $t_{1,2}(h)$, one needs to compute the values of two polynomials $B(h)/2A$ and $D(h)$, for a given value of h. It is well known [Atkinson, Cohen] that if one needs to compute the value of an Nth degree polynomial over a set of equally spaced points one can use a difference table to compute the polynomial values using only N additions per value.

For example, Let $h_i = h_0 + i \times \delta h$ and let $P(h)$ be a second degree polynomial. Define: $P_i = P(h_i)$, $\Delta P_i = P_i - P_{i-1}$ and $\Delta^2 P_i = \Delta P_{i+1} - \Delta P_i$. Then

a) $\Delta^2 P_i$ is a constant independent of i. $\qquad$ (2.a)

b) $\Delta P_{i+1} = \Delta P_i + \Delta^2 P_i$ $\qquad$ (2.b)

c) $P_{i+1} = P_i + \Delta P_{i+1}$ $\qquad$ (2.c)

So if P_0, ΔP_0 and $\Delta^2 P_0$ are known, then P_i, $i = 1, 2, \cdots$ could be computed using the recurrence relations (2.b) and (2.c) with only two additions per point.

Therefore, $D(h_i)$ can be evaluated using two additions per point and $B(h_i)/2A$ can be computed using only one addition per point. Therefore, The set of parallel lines $P(h_i,t)$ $i = 0, 1, 2, \cdots$ can be classified against any quadratic half space using four additions, one subtraction and one square root operation per line.

The incremental algorithms for classifying parallel lines could be extended to work on a regular lattice of parallel lines, not only lines that lie in a single plane.

Let $P(s,h;t)$ be defined as:

$$P(s,h;t) = (x_0 + a_2s + a_1h + a_0t, \ y_0 + b_2s + b_1h + b_0t, \ z_0 + c_2s + c_1h + c_0t).$$

and

$$P_{i,j}(t) = P(s_i, h_j; t)$$

where $s_i = s_0 + i \times \delta s$, $i = 0, 1, 2, \cdots$ and $h_j = h_0 + j \times \delta h$, $j = 0, 1, 2, \cdots$

The collection of lines $P_{i,j}(t)$ form a regular lattice of parallel lines in space. For a fixed i, $P_{i,j}(t)$, $j = 0, \cdots N$, are classified by the incremental algorithm described above.

The problem is how to start the computation for the next index i. As it turns out, this computation can be done incrementally as well. The discriminant $D(h) = (B(h)/2A)^2 - C(h)/A$ is a second degree polynomial in h where the coefficients are functions of s. $d(h) = a(s)h^2 + b(s)h + c(s)$. As before, it is not hard to show that $a(s)$ is a constant, $b(s)$ is a polynomial of degree one in s, and $c(s)$ is a polynomial of degree two.

Now, in order to be able to compute the values of the polynomial $D(s_{i+1}; h_j)$, $j = 0, 1, 2, \cdots$, one needs the zero, first and second differences of the polynomial $D(s_{i+1}, h)$ at h_0. The second difference is constant since $a(s)$ is a constant. The first difference as

287

a function of s is a first degree polynomial and therefore can be computed incrementally from the previous first difference by one addition. The zero order difference, that is the value of $D(s,h)$, is a second degree polynomial in s. Therefore the value of $D(s_{i+1};h_0)$ can be computed from the difference table of $D(s_i,h_0)$ using only two additions. Therefore, in order to compute the coefficients of the difference table for $D(s_{i+1};h)$ at h_0 from the difference table of $D(s_i;h)$ at h_0 one needs three additions. Similarly, one addition will be necessary for computing the difference table for $b(s_{i+1};h)$ from the table for $b(s_i;h)$.

In conclusion, we have shown that four additions, one subtraction and one square root operation per line are needed for incrementally computing parallel line classification against quadratic half spaces. Four additions are needed to restart the incremental computation for lines in the next parallel plane.

3.3. Primitive Classifier Architecture

The primitive classifier is a bit serial pipelined processor, hard wired to incrementally compute line-primitive intersections. The PC can compute the intersections of lines with linear and quadratic half spaces. In addition the PC can receive data from the host computer and pass it to the CC it is connected to.

The PC is made of a pipelined bit serial data path, a main controller and an output section. The output section has an output buffer and an output controller. The data path is made of several units. A Quadratic polynomial Evaluation Unit (QEU), Linear polynomial Evaluation Unit (LEU), A bit serial square-root unit, a bit revers unit, a bit serial adder and a bit serial subtractor (See figure 3). The data flow from the QEU to the bit reverse unit, then to the SQRT unit. From the SQRT unit it flows to the adder and subtractor. The LEU work in parallel with the QEU. The output from the LEU is also feed into the adder and subtractor.

The QEU is made of two parts: The main unit is made of two bit serial adders adding two bits at a time and three registers. This unit is used to evaluate the quadratic polynomial D(h). The second unit of the QEU is the coefficient update unit. This unit is used to update the values of the registers of the main unit when going from one row of lines to the next. See section 3.2 for an explanation. The LEU is similar to the QEU, only simpler. It's bit serial adders add only one bit at a time.

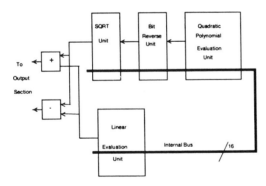

Figure 3: **Primitive Classifier Data Path**

The square root unit is made of a Controlled Adder Subtractor unit and two registers. It's design follows a well known algorithm for square root. See [Hwang 1979].

All the PC registers, including the output buffer and mode register are connected by a bus. Each register has a unique address and can be access from the outside by reading or writing into it's address. The programming of the PC is done by the host computer.

The host computer precomputes the divided differences and stores them in the PC registers. It also activates the PC by writing into a special address. The host also could send data directly to the CC array by loading it into the output buffer. This feature enables one to classify lines against primitives that PC cannot do (say a torus) and also enable one to classify lines with CSG solids that cannot fit at once into the Ray Casting machine. Larger solids could be broken down and classified using several passes. For testing purposes the register content could be read by the host computer.

4. The Classification-Combine processor

4.1. Introduction

Once the curves have been classified against the primitives, the next step is to combine the resultant line segment sets. Unlike curve-primitive classification, the combine steps are quite simple and domain independent. As was pointed out in Section 1 the line segments can be given in terms of the parameter, t, used to parameterize the curve. The combine steps are then set operations (union intersection or difference) on intervals of this independent parameter t.

The main idea behind the combine machine is to build a binary tree of combine processors. This binary tree will be exactly the same binary tree of operators describing the solid (See Figure 1). Each processor in the tree will correspond to a single set operator in the CSG tree. As inputs it will receive two streams of interval segments and it will compute the appropriate set operation on these segments. Each combine processor will accept streams of line segments from its sons and will send a stream of line segments to its parent processor. As indicated is Figure 2, links in the array of processors may need to be extended to the right or downward. Therefore each processor not only must do set operations on the incoming intervals but also must be able to pass the information, from the right or below, to its parent intact. In addition each processor can load a new instruction. (See section 5.3).

As was explained in section 2 the combine processors are arranged as a $\log_2(N)\times N$ array. Each bit serial combine processor receives its inputs from its neighbors at the right and from below. It passes its output to one of its neighbors above or to the left. The communication is bit serial, two bits at a time, a bit stream for each end-point of the line segments.

4.2. Classification Combine architecture

The classification combiner is a very simple bit serial pipelined processor. The CC must perform set operations on its input line segments. All of the necessary set operations can be performed in bit serial fashion using only minimum and maximum functions.

In our current design, each CC processor consists of six parts.(See Figure 4) There are three small finite state machines, two input-controllers, and one output-controller. There is also a larger main controller. In addition each CC has a combining section where the actual set operations are performed and two registers. One register is used to store the intermediate results and one is used to buffer the possible output line segment. The main controller keeps the global state of the machine, controlling the combining section and the input/output controllers. The input and output controllers communicate with their neighbors, transferring data and instructions. The communication is fully synchronous using a full hand shake protocol which will be described in section 5. The handshake protocol is necessary because inputs may be needed from below only, from the right only, or from both and because a set of inputs may result in 0, 1, or 2 output line segments.

The actual computation is done in the combine section by passing the data, in bit serial fashion, trough a network of three min-max function blocks. The computation is controlled by two multiplexors, one in front of the min-max network and one after it. The inputs to the input MUX come from the input controllers, the intermediate register and the output register. This MUX selects the two line segments to be input to the combined from among the three possible inputs. The output from the min-max network consists of the two input line segments, as well as the three minimum and maximum functions of their endpoints. These 10 bit streams then pass trough a second MUX. This MUX selects the four endpoints to be used for the inputs to the two register pairs, the intermediate and the output registers.

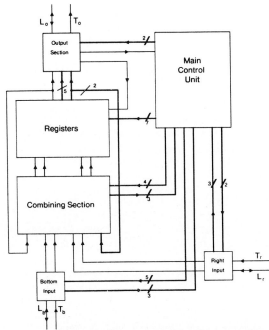

Figure 4:   **Combine Processor block diagram**

5. The Ray Casting system:

5.1. System Architecture

The curve solid classification system is made of a host computer and the Ray Casting machine. The Ray Casting machine is a $(\log_2(N)+1)\times N$ array of processors. The bottom row of the array is made of N Primitive Classifiers (PCs). Above it is a $\log_2(N)\times N$ array of Classification Combine processors (CCs). Each CC has two input ports and one output port. The input ports are connected to the bottom and right neighbors. The output port is connected to both the top and left neighbors. Each input and output connection is two bit wide.

Each Primitive Classifier (PC) has a two bit wide output port. That output port is connected to the bottom input port of the CC directly above it. In addition, each PC is connected to a local system bus. All the registers of the PC are accessible from the local bus. Each register is given a unique bus address. The local bus is connected via an interface unit to the host main system bus. The interface unit between the local Ray Casting bus and the system bus enable the host computer to write directly into each PC register. Thus the host computer can directly control the operation of each PC.

The output of the Ray Casting machine comes out of the output port of the top left most CC. The output from the Ray Casting machine is transferred to the host memory by a DMA interface unit. Figure 5 gives is a block diagram of the Ray Casting system.

The Ray Casting machine will be implemented with a machine "slice" chip. Each slice chip will hold between 4 and 8 columns of the Ray Casting machine. The machine is designed for maximum N of

512 so there are 9 rows of CCs. To build a Ray Casting machine, one only needs to connect the Ray Casting slice chips in a row.

5.2. System interface

The Ray Casting machine interface with the host computer via two bus interface devices:

5.2.1. Local bus interface

The first interface is an interface between the host bus and the local Ray Casting machine bus. The local bus (board level bus) has 16-bit data and 16-bit address lines.

Each PC is driven by the host computer via the local bus. The PC is programmed by writing onto it's registers. Each register is given a unique address and can be read and written to by the host computer. (reading the registers is only used for testing).

The DONE line is used to interrupt the host computer to signal that a PC has completed it's computation.

The interface unit will translate the multibus addresses into chip addresses and will drive the Ray Casting chips. It will also generate host interups that will tell the host which PC is idle. The host then will be able to inquire the status of the idle PC. For the most part the interface make the Ray Casting machine look like (slow?) memory to the host. The only exception is that interups are generated to notify the host when a PC is idle.

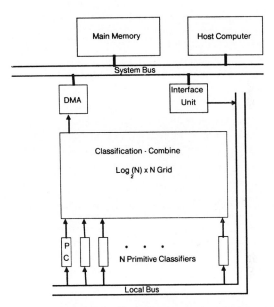

Figure 5: **The Curve-Solid Classification System**

5.2.2. DMA interface between the CC array and the Host Computer memory

The output from the Ray Casting machine comes out of the upper left corner of the CC array. The output is bit serial two bits at a time. The same handshake protocol that is used internally between the CC machines is used between the CC array and the DMA interface device (See Figure 5).

The DMA device task is to receive the data from the Ray Casting machine and store that data in the host memory. The DMA device receive from the host an address, buffer size, the number of lines to classify, and a start signal. It then proceed to transfer the output of the Ray Casting machine into the buffer. The DMA device interrupt the host when the buffer is full or if the transfer was complete. It then waits for a new address, buffer size and a start command to resume the transfer.

Each line classified against a solid can result in zero or more interval segments. Each interval segment is represented two 16-bit integers (fixed point numbers). The end of each line is represented by a 16 bit words with all the bits on.

In addition to the normal mode the DMA interface device will transfer only one 16-bit number per ray, corresponding to the first entry point of the ray to the solid.

5.3. Programming the Ray Casting machine

The Ray Casting machine is programmed by the host computer. The host stores the recurrence coefficients in the data path registers of each PC. There is also a mode register that tells the PC which output of the data path to take, the leading edge, the trailing edge or both. In addition the PC could be used to transfer data from the host to the CC array above intact. This is done by the host loading the output register of the PC and then loading the mode register by a transfer command.

The CC array is loaded with commands, bit serially. An instruction packet is passed to the CC array. The command packet has instructions for all the CCs in the column. Each CC strips three bits out of the front of the command packet and passes the rest to it's top neighbour. The command packet is loaded into the CC array from the PC, using the same protocol used to load data, only the header information differs.

5.4. Interprocessor communication

The Ray Casting machine is made of synchronous machines. All the machines, the PCs and the CCs work with the same master clock. To synchronize data transfer, all the machines follow a full hand shake protocol. The two wires that are used for data transfer between processors, are used for the hand shake protocol. As part of the protocol, two bits of header information are passed. The bits tell each CC if the comming data is an interval segment, a command packet or it is end-of-line signal (EOL). When EOL signal is passed no data is transferred.

Acknowledgment

The authors wish to thank H. B. Voelcker and A. A. G. Requicha for introducing them to this subject. This work would not have been possible without their help and encouragement. The authors thank I. Golan for his help with the tree embedding problem. This work has been supported in part by the National Science Foundation grant No. ECS-8306655

References

[1] Atkinson, K.E., *An Introduction to Numerical Analysis*, John Wiley Publishing Company, 1978.

[2] Boyse, J.W. and J.E. Gilchrist, "GMSolid: Interactive Modeling for Design and Analysis of Solids," *IEEE Computer Graphics and Applications*, 2, No. 2, March 1982, 27-40.

[3] Brent, R.P. and H.T. Kung, "On the Area of Binary Tree Layouts," *Information Processing Letters*, 11, 1980, 46-48.

[4] Brown, C.M., "PADL-2: A Technical Summary," *IEEE Computer Graphics and Applications*, 2, No. 2, March 1982, 69-84.

[5] Brown, C.M., "Special Purpose Computer Hardware for Mechanical Design Systems," *Proc. 1981 National Computer Graphics Assoc. Conf.*, Baltimore, Md., June 1981.

[6] Cohen, D., "Incremental Methods for Computer Graphics," Dept. of Eng. & Appl. Math., Harvard Univ., ESD-TR-69-193, April 1969.

[7] Goldstein, R. and L. Malin, "3-D Modeling with the Synthavision System," *Proc. First Ann. Conf. Computer Graphics, in CAD/CAM Systems*, April 1979, Cambridge, Mass., 244-247.

[8] Hwang, K.,*Computer Arithmetic: Principles, Architecture, and Design*, John Wiley 1979.

[9] Lee, Y.T. and A.A.G. Requicha, "Algorithms for Computing the Volume and Other Integral Properties of Solid Objects," *Comm. ACM*, 25, No. 9, 635-650, September 1982.

[10] Myers, W., "An Industrial Perspective on Solid Modeling," *IEEE Computer Graphics and Applications*, 2, No. 2, March 1982, 86-97.

[11] Requicha, A.A.G., "Representation for Rigid Solids: Theory, Methods, and Systems," *ACM Computing Surveys*, 12, No. 4, Dec. 1980, 437-464.

[12] Requicha, A.A.G. and H.B. Voelcker, "Solid Modeling: A Historical Summary and Contemporary Assessment," *IEEE Computer Graphics and Appl.*, 2, No. 2, March 1982, 9-24.

[13] Roth, S.D., "Ray Casting as a Method for Solid Modeling," Research Publication GMR-3466, Computer Science Dept., General Motors Research Laboratories, Warren, Mich., Oct. 1980.

[14] Tilove, R.B., "Null-object Algorithms for Use with CSG Representations," to appear, *Comm. ACM*, 1983.

[15] Tilove, R.B., "Set Membership Classification: A Unified Approach to Geometric Intersection Problems," *IEEE Trans. Computers*, Vol. C-29, No. 10, Oct. 1980, 874-883.

[16] Tilove, R.B. and A.A.G. Requicha, "Closure of Boolean Operations on Geometric Entities," *Computer Aided Design*, 12, No. 5, Sept. 1980, 219-220.

[17] Valiant, L.G., "Universality Considerations in VLSI Circuits," *IEEE Trans. on Comp.*, C-30, No. 2, February 1981.

[18] Voelcker, H.B. and W.A. Hunt, "The role of Solid Modelling in Machining-Process Modelling and NC Verification," *Proc. 1981 SAE Int'l Congress and Exposition*, Feb. 1981, Detroit, Mich., 1-8.

[19] Voelcker, H.B., A.A.G. Requicha, E.E. Hartquist, W.B. Fisher, J. Metzger, R.B. Tilove, N.K. Birrell, W.A. Hunt, G.T. Armstrong, T.F. Check, R. Moote, and J. McSweeney, "The PADL-1.0/2 System for Defining and Displaying Solid Objects," *Computer Graphics* (Proc. Siggraph '78), 12, No. 3, August 1978, 257-263.

[20] Wesley, M.A., "Construction and Use of Geometric Models," in *Computer Aided Design*, J. Encarnacao (Ed.), Springer-Verlag, New York, 1980, 79-136.

[21] Wesley, M.A., Lozlano-Perez, T., Lieberman, L.T., Lavin, M.A., and D.D. Grossman, "A Geometric Modelling System for Automated Mechanical Assembly," *IBM J. Res. Dev.* 24, 1, Jan. 1980, 64-74.

The Point Classifier: A VLSI Processor for Displaying Complex Two Dimensional Objects

Gershon Kedem

Microelectronics Center of North Carolina and Duke University, Durham

and

Steven W. Hammond

General Electric Company
Schenectady, New York

Abstract

We describe the Point Classification machine. The machine displays complex 2-D objects in real time. The machine implements in silicon the "Point classification algorithm" for generating the raster image of CSG objects. We start by defining 2-D CSG objects, then we describe the point classification algorithm. We give a description of an architecture that executes the Point Classification algorithm in parallel and at high speed. Detailed architecture and hardware realization of the building blocks are given.

1. Introduction

Recent advances in VLSI technology and circuit design have created new opportunity for system architects to design and build special purpose architectures. Computer graphics is one area that can benefit from VLSI technology. Real time response of raster graphics systems requires large computational bandwidth. On the other hand, many of the computational tasks in computer graphics are simple and repetitive, therefore amenable to parallel and pipelined computation. In the last few years several different approaches to "put into silicon" different computer graphic algorithms have been suggested. For examples see [Locanthi 79, Clark 80, Fuchs 81, Fussel 82], One of the systems [Clark 80] has reached the market place.

In this paper we describe a special purpose architecture for real time display of 2-D objects. The system generates, in real time, the raster images of general 2-D regions. Regions like polygons, rectangles, regions with holes, and regions with spline boundaries, can be displayed. Moreover, the machine can generate the image of either solid objects or ones with stipple patterns. A novel two dimensional array of functional blocks realizes a reconfigurable binary tree of processing units. Incremental computation greatly reduces the hardware needed.

We start by describing how one represents 2-D objects using "Constructive Solid Geometry" (CSG). The concept is borrowed from a representation describing three dimensional objects in the CAD/CAM area [Requicha 80]. Then we use point classification to compute the raster image of these 2-D objects. In section 4 we introduce the main ideas behind a Point Classification machine: a machine that can compute the raster image of complex 2-D objects at high speed. In section 5 we explain how to incrementally compute the values of bivariate polynomials and what kind of hardware one could use to do this computation at high speed. Section 6 gives a detailed description of the Point Classification system. Finally, section 7 describes our experimental implementation.

2. CSG representation of 2-D objects

Constructive Solid Geometry (CSG) is a popular method for representing 3-D solids [Requicha 80]. Loosely speaking, each CSG object is a set described by doing set operations on primitive solids. The primitive solids are objects like blocks, cylinders, balls, cones, etc. Each complex CSG solid is represented by a binary tree. The leaves of the tree are primitive solids oriented in space. The internal nodes of the tree are set operations (Union, Intersection, Difference).

Although CSG representation is used in CAD/CAM of mechanical parts, it need not be limited to that domain. CSG representation could effectively describe complex 2-D objects. To derive CSG representation for 2-D objects one specifies the set of primitive objects and the operations on the objects. In our representation, each primitive is described by single polynomial inequality. The set operations are all point-set operations.

General 2-D CSG solids can be described. For example all polygons, objects with holes, Pie charts, and objects with piecewise cubic boundaries (spline boundaries) could be represented. Figure 1 shows an example of a CGS object. The figure shows the image of a "NUT" a square with a hole. and the corresponding CSG tree representation of that object. The half spaces are represented by linear inequalities of the type: $ax + by + c < 0$ and the circle by $(x - x_0)^2 + (y - y_0)^2 - R < 0$.

3. Point classification of CSG objects

Representation of 2-D regions (objects) is not very useful unless one has effective ways to display the regions. The application we consider is computing the raster image of the 2-D region. Since the raster image of a 2-D object is a discrete set of points, we look at point classification.

Point classification is defined as follows: Given a point compute whether the point is inside or outside the region. To make the CSG representation mathematically consistent, one has to be careful. The set operations on CSG objects are not well defined unless one specifies what to do with the boundaries. For 3-D objects the problem is solved by using regularized set operations (see [Tilove 80]). We use enother approach. Since our application is raster graphics, we consider a discrete topology. We consider the plane to be a regular lattice of equally spaced points (If you wish you can think of them as the set of points with integer coordinates). Using discrete point topology, all the sets are both open and closed, therefore all the set operations are unambiguously defined.

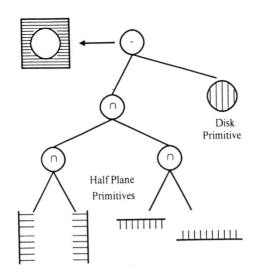

Figure 1: An object and its CSG representation

The point classification function takes a point and a CSG object as input and returns either 0 (if the point is outside the object) or 1 (if it is inside). The point classification function can be implemented by a simple recursive function. It computes the point classification of the left subtree, the point classification of the right subtree and then computes the boolean function at the root applied to the two results. The following is a point classification function written in C:

```
Boolean point_classify(X, Object)
Point X;
CSG_tree_Node *Object;
  {
  if (Object->type == PRIMITIVE) return (Object->Is_IN(X))
  else
  return(Object->Set_Function(point_classify(X,Object->left),
      point_classify(X,Object->Right)));
  }
```

Each CSG_tree_Node is a record with a type field. If the type is PRIMITIVE the record has a pointer to a function "Is_In" that returns whether a given point is inside the primitive. If the type is INTERNAL, then the record has a pointer to a boolean function "Set_Function" and two pointers to the left and right subtrees.

Since all the primitives are described by polynomial inequalities, one finds if a point is inside a primitive set by evaluating a polynomial and checking its sign. As we shall explain later, by choosing the proper primitives, one could also generate stipple patterns.

4. Point classification, machine Architecture

The hardware construction for point classification follows the main ideas developed for the "Ray-Casting" machine [Kedem &

Ellis]. We want a machine that will compute the raster image of complex 2-D CSG objects. The machine generates the image by classifying points on a lattice of equally spaced points.

The main idea is to construct a pipeline in the shape of the CSG tree that represents the object. The leaves of the tree are primitive classifiers that classify each point against a primitive. The internal processors (the Combine Blocks) compute the set operations that correspond to the set operations in the CSG tree. Each node in the tree is a stage in the pipeline. By starting each stage in the pipeline at the proper time, the pipeline could work with just a clock; no additional controls are necessary. To take advantage of the pipelining, the computation is done on a large regular lattice of points and not on a single point. Figure 2 shows a CSG object, its CSG tree representation and the hardware pipeline.

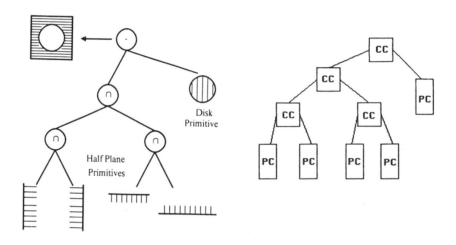

Figure 2: CSG object with the corresponding hardware pipeline

One problem one needs to solve is how to realize a binary tree of processors. Since the binary tree has to mirror the CSG tree it has to be general. Therefore, one needs a structure that will embed all possible binary trees with at most N leaves, N being the largest tree that could be accommodated. One needs a fixed way to interconnect the processors and, by programming them, embed all possible binary trees with N processors. Moreover, (for a reason that will become clear later), all the primitive classifiers have to be together in a linear array. We have found [Kedem & Ellis] that a $[(\log_2 N)+1] \times N$ array of processors could be used to embed any binary tree of processors with at most N leaves. This embedding is optimal in the sense that if one insists on embedding any binary tree with N leaves in a grid with all the leaves of the tree on the bottom row, then $O(N\log_2 N)$ processors are needed [Brent & Kung].

The embedding is done as follows: First each tree is made right heavy (that is each right subtree is at least as big as the left subtree), by possibly rotating some of the CSG subtrees. The root of the tree is in the upper left corner of the array. The leaves are at the bottom row. Left links in the tree point down on the grid, and right links point to the right. The tree is embedded by traversing it in preorder. If a leaf is encountered before the bottom of the grid is reached, the last link is extended to the bottom. Each right link is extended according to the following rule: *If the tree has K leaves before the current node (in prefix order), the right link is extended so that the node is in column $K + 1$.* See Figure 3.

The point classification machine is made of N primitive classifiers and $\log_2 N \times N$ array of combine blocks. Each Primitive classifier can compute values of polynomial of degree three or less. Each combine processor is a programmable universal function block. Each combine block is connected to its four neighbors. It gets its input from its right and bottom neighbors, and sends its output to both top and left neighbors. See Figure 4.

5. Incremental computation

Before we describe the primitive classifiers we describe an incremental method for computing the values of bivariate polynomials over an array of equally spaced points.

Each primitive classifier computes whether a given point is inside the primitive region. Since each primitive region is described by a single polynomial inequality, all one needs to do is to evaluate the polynomial at the point and check the sign of the result. We use strict inequalities so we don't have to check for zero.

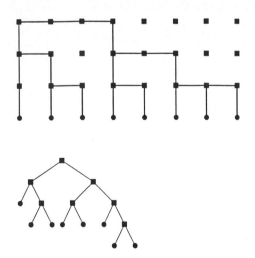

Figure 3: The embedding of a binary tree in a grid

If one had to evaluate the polynomial using multiplications, the operations would be slow and expensive. However, the computation can be done incrementally very fast and with only few additions. The idea is to compute the values of the polynomial

295

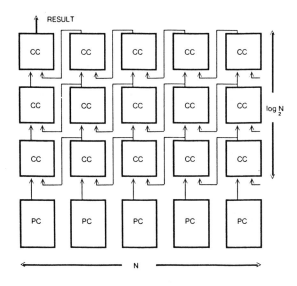

Figure 4: Block diagram of the Point Classification machine

on a two dimensional grid of equally spaced points. The computation is done in raster scan order.

Let $P(x,y)$ be a bivariate polynomial of degree M. For a fixed y_0, $P(x,y_0)$ is a polynomial of degree M in x. It is well known that any M^{th} degree univariate polynomial can be evaluated over a set of equally spaced points using a forward difference table [Conte 80]. Once the difference coefficients are computed, one can compute successive values of the polynomial using only M additions per point. Moreover, the computation can be pipelined. With pipelining, on every clock, one computes the value at a new point [Cohen 69].

For example; in order to compute the values of a third degree polynomial, one needs to compute $P(x_0)$, $\Delta P(x_0)$, $\Delta^2 P(x_0)$, and $\Delta^3 P(x_0)$. Once they are computed, the values of $P_i = P(x_0 + i \times h)$ can be computed using the following recurrence relations:

$$P_{i+1} = P_i + \Delta P_i$$

$$\Delta P_{i+1} = \Delta P_i + \Delta^2 P_i$$

$$\Delta^2 P_{i+1} = \Delta^2 P_i + \Delta^3 P$$

Figure 5 shows how to compute the above recurrence relations in a pipelined fashion.

So far we described how one can compute the value of the polynomial on a single scan line. We are however interested in evaluating the polynomial on many consecutive scan lines. In order to do that we construct a two dimensional difference table. Let Δ be the forward difference in the x direction and δ be the forward difference in the y direction. Let $P(x,y)$ be a polynomial of degree 3. $P(x,y)$ is a polynomial of degree 3 in x with coefficients that are polynomials in y. For a fixed x $P(x,y)$ is polynomial of degree 3 in y, ΔP is a polynomial of degree 2, $\Delta^2 P$ is a polynomial of degree one and $\Delta^3 P$ is a constant independent of y. Therefore, by computing P, ΔP, $\Delta^2 P$, $\Delta^3 P$, one can compute all the values of P on a single scan line and $\delta P, \delta^2 P$, $\delta^3 P$, can be used to compute the value of P on the beginning of the next scan line. Similarly,

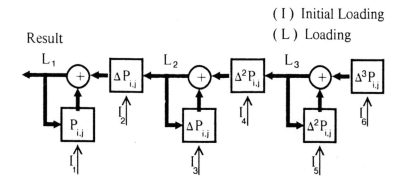

(I) Initial Loading

(L) Loading

Figure 5: The forward difference pipeline

ΔP, $\delta \Delta P$, $\delta^2 \Delta P$, can be used to compute ΔP on the next scan line and $\Delta^2 P$, $\delta \Delta^2 P$ can be used to compute $\Delta^2 P$.

The computation proceeds as follows: We first compute a two dimensional forward difference table for the polynomial P. Then the values of P, ΔP, $\Delta^2 P$, $\Delta^3 P$ are used to compute all the values of P on the scan line. At the end of the scan line these forward difference coefficients (in the x direction) are updated for the next scan line, then the next scan line is evaluated and so on.

6. Classification machine, Building blocks

In this section we describe the building blocks that make the point classification machine. The machine is made of two types of functional blocks: Primitive Classifiers (PC) and Combine Blocks. Each PC computes whether a given point is inside or outside a given polynomial region. The Combine Block (CB) computes a boolean function of its two inputs.

Point classification consists of evaluating polynomial inequalities at equally spaced points, using a forward difference scheme. We pipeline this operation with three additions per point (for polynomials of degree 3). Polynomials of degree two require two additions, and linear polynomials require one. The hardware required for these successive evaluations is shown in Figure 6. The unit is made of three adders. Each adder has two input registers. At each clock the adder adds the content of its registers and stores the result in the left hand register. In addition, under external control, the output of each adder can be passed to the right register of its left neighbor. By putting one, two, or, three adders in series, one can compute the values of first, second, and third degree polynomials.

We have limited the system to polynomials of degree three or less since we wanted to represent regions with piecewise cubic boundaries, and we saw no advantage in polynomials of degree higher then three.

Each primitive can be described by a polynomial of different degree (maximum degree 3), so in principle one would need to reserve three adders for each PC. However, in order to make the system more efficient, the chain of adders is not grouped into sets of three. By controlling the pass gates between the adders, it is possible to pack the PCs together. Each PC uses only as many adders as it needs. The next PC starts immediately to its left. The degree of polynomial that could be evaluated is only limited by the

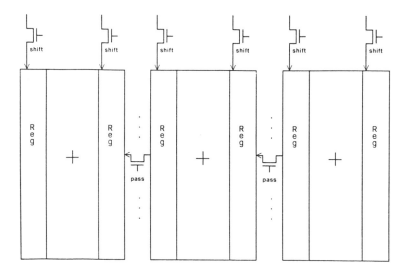

Figure 6: The primitive classification unit

size of the update unit (see next paragraph).

The PC registers are not only parallel load registers, but bit serial registers as well. When going from one scan line to the next, each left hand register is loaded, bit serially, with the output of the update unit below it. The update unit is made of four shift registers and three bit serial adders. Each update unit can compute (bit serially) values of polynomials of degree 3 or less. Figure 7 shows how the primitive classification unit and the update unit are interconnected.

The following operations compute the values of a polynomial on a $K \times J$ array of points. First, the difference coefficients are loaded into the classification unit and update unit registers. Then the classification unit is clocked for J clocks. That computes the values of the polynomial at a full scan line. Then the update unit is activated for a period equal to its register length. This has the effect of updating the difference coefficients for the next scan line. The above process repeats K times.

A simple modification to the Primitive classifier incorporates stipple patterns into the CSG representation. To get objects with a stipple pattern, define a primitive that is an infinite repetition of the stipple on the discrete grid. A simple stipple pattern generator is a circular shift register. Since each Primitive classifier already

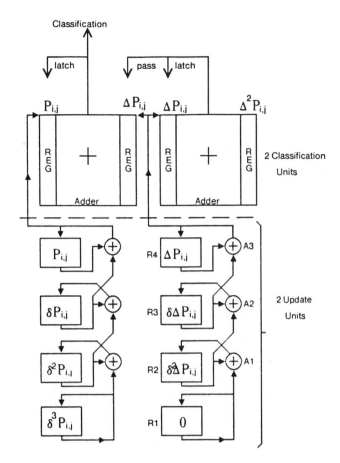

Figure 7: Primitive classifier with the update unit

has shift registers in it, it is easy to add a small amount of steering logic that will make the primitive classifier a stipple pattern generator as well. The circular shift register generates a repetitive pattern on a given line. The pattern is updated when going from one line to the next, by shifting a new pattern stored in the update unit.

The Combine Block is a "one of four" selector. The controls of the selector are the inputs to the Block. A four bit register is connected to the four inputs of the selector. By loading the appropriate bit pattern into the four-bit register, a given boolean function of two variables is computed. We use a register at the input of each Combine Block to pipeline the combine computation.

The Combine Blocks are arranged in a $\log_2 N \times N$ array. Each Combine block receives inputs from its right and bottom neighbor. The output of each combine block goes to both its top and left neighbor. Each combine blocks in the bottom row gets one input from the PC below and one input from their right neighbor. The PC output is the most significant bit (the sign bit) of the left hand register of the classifier unit.

The point classification machine is made of N columns of functional units. Each column has $\log_2 N$ combine blocks, an adder unit with two registers (the Primitive classifier unit), and three bit-serial adders with four registers (the update unit). In addition there is one bit controlling the pass gate between one adder unit and its next neighbor.

Controlling the array is a simple control unit. The control unit has two counters X_counter and Y_counter to control the number of points computed in the x and y directions, respectively. An additional small counter controls the update unit operation.

There is one additional point: For the pipeline to operate properly, the PC units (that is, the adder and its two registers) must be activated one at a time. Starting with the right most unit, each clock the next PC unit is activated. This effect is achieved by having a shift register that is cleared to zero. Then, by shifting 1s in, one triggers the PCs. Note that once the PCs are triggered, no additional synchronization is needed. The values out of the PCs will reach the combine blocks in the proper order and at the proper time.

7. Current Implementation

A small prototype chip, to test our ideas, was designed and laid out, using 4μ NMOS technology. The PCs were implemented with 8-bit ripple adders. The update units have 16-bit registers. The chip was designed with 6 PC units and a 3×6 array of combine blocks. We used a simple method to load the data into the machine. All bits in each column are connected into a large shift register. To program the machine, one has to shift the values in. We did not implement the stipple pattern generator. The chip was simulated but not fabricated.

Acknowledgements

The authors wish to thank Dr. A. Rosenberg and the reviewers for their critical reading of the manuscript and for their valuable suggestions. This work was done at the University of Rochester, Computer Science Department, in association with the Production Automation Project. This work was supported by a National Science Foundation grant, number ECS-8306655.

References

[Brent 80]
Brent, R.P. and H.T. Kung, "On the area of binary Tree Layouts", *Information Processing Letters*, 11, 1980, 46-48.

[Brown 82]
Brown, C.M., "PADL-2: A Technical Summary," *IEEE Computer Graphics and Applications*, 2, No. 2, March 1982, 69-84.

[Clark 80]
Clark, James H., "Structuring a VLSI System Architecture," *LAMBDA*, 2nd Quarter, 1980.

[Cohen 69]
Cohen, D., "Incremental Methods for Computer Graphics," Dept. of Eng. and Appl. Math., Harvard Univ., ESD-TR-69-193, April 1969.

[Conte 80]
Conte, Samuel D. and Carl de Boor, *Elementary Numerical Analysis*, 3rd ed., McGraw Hill, 1980.

[Fuchs 81]
Fuchs, Henry, John Poulton, Alan Paeth, and Alan Bell, "PIXEL-PLANES: A VLSI-Oriented Design for a Raster Graphics Engine," *VLSI Design*, Vol. 2, No. 3, 1981, pp. 20-28.

[Fussel 82]
Fussel, Donald, "A VLSI-Oriented Architecture for Real-Time Raster Display of Shaded Polygons," *Proceedings of Graphics Interface 82*, 1982, pp. 373-380.

[Hammond 84]
Hammond, Steven, W., "Digital Hardware for Point Classification," M.S. Thesis, Computer Science Dept. University of Rochester. August 1984.

[Kedem 84a]
Kedem, Gershon and John Ellis, "Computer Structures for Curve-solid Classification in Geometric Modeling," Tech. Report No. 137, Computer Science Dept., University of Rochester, 1984.

[Kedem 84b]
Kedem, Gershon and Ellis John, "The Ray-Casting Machine" *Proceedings ICCCD'84*, October 1984, 533-538.

[Locanthi 79]
Locanthi, Bart, "Object Oriented Raster Displays," *Caltech Conference on VLSI*, Jan. 1979, 215-225.

[Newman 79]
Newman, W.M. and R.F. Sproull, *Principles of Interactive Computer Graphics*, 2nd ed., McGraw-Hill, New York, 1979.

[Requicha 80]
Requicha, A.A.G., "Representation for Rigid Solids: Theory, Methods, and Systems," *ACM Computing Surveys*, 12, No. 4, Dec. 1980, 437-464.

[Requicha 82]
Requicha, A.A.G. and H.B. Voelcker, "Solid Modeling: A Historical Summary and Contemporary Assessment," *IEEE Computer Graphics and Appl.*, 2, No. 2, March 1982, 9-24.

[Tilove 80]
Tilove, R.B., "Set Membership Classification: A Unified Approach to Geometric Intersection Problems," *IEEE Trans. Computers*, Vol. C-29, No. 10, Oct. 1980, 874-883.

[Valiant 81]
Valiant, L.G., "Universality Considerations in VLSI Circuits," *IEEE Trans. on Comp.*, C-30, No. 2, February 1981.

[Whelan 82]
Whelan, Daniel S., "A Rectangular Area Filling Display System Architecture," *ACM Proceedings of SIGGRAPH 82*, 147-154.

Fast Image Generation of Constructive Solid Geometry
Using A Cellular Array Processor

Hiroyuki Sato   Mitsuo Ishii   Keiji Sato   Morio Ikesaka
Hiroaki Ishihata Masanori Kakimoto Katsuhiko Hirota Kouichi Inoue

Fujitsu Laboratories, LTD. Kawasaki
1015, Kamikodanaka, Nakahara-ku,
Kawasaki, 211, Japan

Abstract

A general purpose Cellular Array
Processor(CAP) with distributed frame buffers for
fast parallel subimage generation has been
developed. CAP consists of many processor elements
called cells. A cell has video memory for subimage
storage, a window controller to map each subimage
to an area on the monitor screen, and
communication devices, in addition to ordinary
microcomputer components such as MPU, RAM, and
ROM. Image data in a cell is directly displayed
via the video bus. The mapping pattern and the
position on the screen of subimages can be changed
dynamically. Various hidden surface algorithms
can be implemented in CAP using mapping patterns
appropriate for the algorithm.

Our goal is an efficient interactive visual
solid modeler. We adopted a general CSG hidden
surface algorithm that enables display of both
Boundary representation and Constructive Solid
Geometry. A technique for hidden surface removal
of general CSG models, requiring less memory space
for large models in many cases, has been proposed.
This technique subdivides the model into submodels
by dividing the CSG tree at union nodes. Images of
each submodel are generated by a CSG or a z-buffer
algorithm. If a submodel is just a primitive, it
is processed by the z-buffer algorithm, otherwise
by the CSG algorithm. Hidden surface removal
between submodels is done by comparing the z
values for each pixel which are saved in the z-
buffer.

CR Categories and Subject Descriptors: C.1.2.
[Processor Architectures]: Multiple Data Stream
Architectures(Multiprocessors) - Multiple -
instruction - stream, multiple - data - stream
processors(MIMD)

© 1985 ACM 0-89791-166-0/85/007/0095 $00.75

I.3.3. [Computer Graphics]: Picture/Image
Generation - display algorithms;
I.3.7. [Computer Graphics]: Three-Dimensional
Graphics and Realism - Visible Line/Surface
Algorithms;
Key Words and Phrases: computer graphics, hidden
surface removal, constructive solid geometry,
scan-line algorithms, z-buffer, solid modeling,
computer aided design

1. Introduction

Fast image generation of three-dimensional
objects has been one of the major topics in
computer graphics. Much work has been dedicated to
this area. Sutherland pointed out that hidden
surface removal is a sorting problem[11]. To
minimize sorting cost, many algorithms use
coherence properties of the scene to be
displayed[11,13,14]. Recently, the progress in
VLSI technology and the decreasing cost of
hardware have led us to consider other ways to
generate images quickly, using parallel
processing. Kaplan and Greenberg[1] tested two
algorithms, which divided the image area into
scan-line groups for scan-line algorithms and into
rectangular areas for area subdivision algorithms.
Since then, many parallel processing techniques
have been proposed[2,3,4,5,6,7,8]. Most of these
are based on the parallel subimage generation
techniques. Another parallel technique divides a
three-dimensional object space into subspaces[7].
In this case, whole sets of objects are divided
and processed in parallel. These systems
implement one of three major hidden surface
removal algorithms: the z-buffer algorithm[4,5],
the scan-line algorithm[2,8], or the ray-tracing
algorithm[6,7].

Our design goal is an efficient interactive
solid modeler. Fast image generation of solids is
the key for a good man-machine interface. We want
to be able to display both B-rep (Boundary
representation[10]) and CSG (Constructive Solid
Geometry[10]). We took two approaches:

(1) To develop a general purpose parallel
processor with distributed frame buffers for
subimage generation. Image generation algorithms
are implemented in software, rather than hardware.
This frees the processor for other problems that
can be processed in parallel. This is an advantage
for solid modelers, which require a lot of
calculation other than for image generation.

"Fast Image Generation of Constructive Solid Geometry Using a Cellular
Array Processor" by H. Sato, M. Ishii, K. Sato, M. Ikesaka, H. Ishihata, M.
Kakimoto, K. Hirota, and K. Inoue from Proceedings of ACM SIGGRAPH.
July 1985, pages 95-102. Copyright 1985, Association for Computing Ma-
chinery, Inc., reprinted by permission.

(2) To implement display algorithms that can be efficiently processed in parallel. Ray-tracing[12] and Ray-casting[15] are efficiently executed by parallel processors[6] and their implementations in CAP would be easy. But their speed would be still too slow for interactive use, if the number of processors is limited. We chosen a general CSG hidden surface removal algorithm[13] that can generate images of both B-rep and CSG models.

This paper focuses on the architecture of the Cellular Array Processor(CAP) and the CSG hidden surface algorithm we have been implementing. We also discuss experimental results.

2. Background

Solid modeling is an important technology for mechanical CAD/CAM, and many other fields in which three-dimensional data is handled. However, there are few systems that enable designers to model solids efficiently, because it is difficult to obtain quick responses from the system.

There are two main data representation schemes for solid modeling: B-rep[10] and CSG[10]. CSG represents solid models as combinations of primitive solids. Primitives are combined by boolean operators, such as union, intersection, and difference. The data is represented as a binary tree called a CSG tree. Constructing a CSG tree is easy, but generating images of CSG models requires a lot of calculation, because explicit surfaces are not saved in the data structure. One must determine the true surfaces of the solids beforehand, or perform boolean operations in the display algorithm. In the B-rep scheme, solid models are generally built from sequences of boolean operations of solids. Boolean operations take much time, increasing almost quadratically as the number of surfaces increases. However, once explicit surfaces are obtained, image generation is much easier than with CSG.

In addition to image generation of solids, there are many other time consuming tasks in solid modeling, such as interference checks and mass-property calculations. Therefore, many solid modelers are implemented on main-frame computers and used under time-sharing environments. For visualization of solid models, graphic display devices are connected to the host computer through communication lines.

For interactive use, engineering workstations provide a good man-machine interface. The performance of workstations so far is insufficient for interactive solid modeling. Thus we developed a dedicated processor for fast image generation and other tasks related to solid modeling, which can be attached to existing engineering workstations via a high-speed bus.

For the solid modeler, we adopted dual modeling scheme that separates the visual modeler from the exact analytical modeler[13]. We avoid unnecessary calculations for generating images while man-machine interactions are being done. Boolean operations are not done at the interaction phase, but the images of solids are generated by boolean operations within the display algorithms. Exact boolean operations would be done on a demand basis when it is necessary for certain applications.

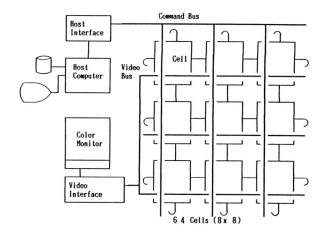

Fig.1 The System Hardware Configuration

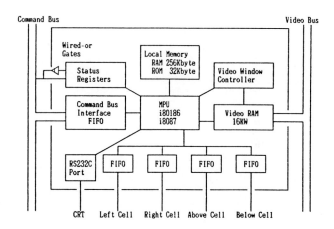

Fig.2 The Hardware Structure of a Cell

3. CAP Architecture

3.1 Overview

CAP is a general purpose oriented Cellular Array Processor with distributed frame buffers for real-time parallel subimage generations. Fig.1 shows the system hardware configuration and Fig.2 shows the hardware structure of a cell. Processor elements, called cells, are configured in a two dimensional array. This configuration is suited not only to parallel subimage generation but also to problems that can be mapped onto a two-dimensional cell array[9].

Command Bus: All cells are connected by a common bus called Command Bus. The Command Bus can be connected easily to existing workstations.

Video Bus: Each cell has a video memory which works as a partitioned frame buffer. Subimages are stored here and displayed on the screen automatically through the Video Bus.

Inter-cell communication: Each cell has parallel

communication interfaces to four neighboring cells (right, left, above, and below). Local communication is done using these lines.

3.2 Subimage generation

The basic strategy for speeding up image generation is to partition an image area into subareas, not necessarily continuous, and generate subimages in parallel, using many cells. Each cell has 16K words of video memory. A word is 24 bits long, 8 bits each for red, green, and blue. The window controller of each cell maps that cell's subimage data to a certain area of the screen.

A frame of image data, which is partitioned and distributed to many cells, is reconstructed as one complete image by window controllers in the cells. Window controllers read and send subimage data, once each refresh cycle (30 Hz interlaced), when the global pixel position counter's value is equal to one of the positions that cell is in charge of. Only 512 x 480 pixels can be displayed on the monitor screen at once. If there is an access conflict between the window controller and the MPU of the cell, the MPU waits.

The mapping pattern can be changed. Each cell has X and Y timing tables (XT(x) and YT(y)) in which x and y mapping information is stored. A window controller maps its subimage to the area for which logical AND of XT(x) and YT(y) is 1. By changing the bit pattern of XT and YT, various mapping are possible. Fig.3 shows some examples.

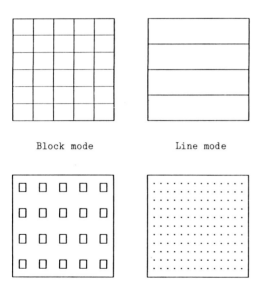

Block mode   Line mode

Dot mode   Discrete block mode

Block mode: A rectangular area for each cell
Line mode : Several equally spaced scan-lines
            for each cell
Dot mode : Dispersed pixels for each cell
Discrete block mode: Several rectangular
            areas for each cell

Fig.3 Examples of Subimage Mapping Patterns

This flexibility is very useful, because the best subimage mapping varies from one problem to another. For example, block mode is suited for area subdivision algorithms, whereas line mode is better for scan-line algorithms. Mappings of subimages to separate areas on the screen are often effective for evenly distributing calculation load between cells. The combination of a ray-tracing or a ray-casting algorithm and the dot mode is very effective, because these algorithms do not generally use coherence properties.

We developed a basic software package called Display Manager to do some standard mappings, and window clipping and zooming. The application programmer need only specify the mapping made such as line, dot, or block mode. Values of the X and Y timing tables for the selected mode are automatically calculated and set.

For subimage generation, all cells run with the same code. Only the contents of timing tables differ. This simplifies the programming efforts greatly.

3.3 Communication

Communication is an important part of parallel systems. In CAP, communication is done in two ways: Global communication using the Command Bus and Local communication using inter-cell communication lines.

Global communication: The host computer broadcasts programs and data to all cells via a common bus called the Command Bus. Any cell can also broadcast its data to other cells and to the host computer. Each cell receives the broadcast and saves only that information it needs. Unnecessary information is discarded. This method is effective when large amounts of data are sent to many cells.

Data is often distributed to many cells. After the distributed data has been processed, frequently it must be redistributed. Here, each cell requests to send its data to all other cells. The host computer continuously polls, granting the right to use the Command Bus to requesting cells. This polling continues until no requests are detected. This way, each cell can receive the all the new data. We call this global communication rebroadcast.

In addition to division of image areas, geometric data for the entire model is also divided and distributed to many cells and parallel calculations are done on the divided data. Then, the new data is rebroadcast for the next subimage parallel execution.

Local communication: Neighboring cells communicate with each other via inter-cell communication interfaces. A large amount of data exceeding the capacity of one cell is distributed to neighboring cells. This enables CAP to hold a lot more data, while the communication overhead does not increase by that much.

3.4 Multi-task Cell Monitor

In parallel processing, it is important to minimize the idle time of processors during execution. We implemented a multi-task real-time monitor in cells, to improve the efficiency of use of hardware resources such as the MPU, memory, and

I/O ports. Programs are divided into tasks, which are driven by messages received from other tasks or from the host computer. Messages are generally sent in packets except for direct communication in which large amounts of data are sent directly without packeting. Messages are passed by communication tasks. Application programs are often divided into several tasks. The CSG hidden surface removal program is divided into three tasks: A modeling task and two display tasks, one for the z-buffer algorithm, the other for the CSG hidden surface algorithm.

3.5 Synchronization

Wired-or status registers are used for synchronization. There are eight bit status registers, which can be read by the host computer or by any cell. Cells can set the status to indicate completion of a process. The host or any cell can read the logical OR (or AND) status of all cells to determine whether a process divided between many cells is completed. The number of wires can be minimized by hardware wired-or logic. Request signals for rebroadcast are also set in status registers.

4. CSG hidden surface algorithm for parallel subimage generation

4.1 General CSG hidden surface removal algorithm

CSG models are represented by Boolean combinations of primitive solids such as cubes, cones, and spheres. The boolean combinations are represented as a binary tree, each node representing a boolean operation (union, intersection, or difference). The leaves are primitive solids. Data structures of CSG models are more easily constructed than with the time-costly complex boolean operations of the B-rep modeler, which tests every possible crossing of faces of solids and reconstructs a new model. If CSG models can be displayed fast, CSG is favorable for an interactive visual solid modeler.

Peter Atherton proposed a scan-line hidden surface removal algorithm for CSG models that does boolean operations within itself[13]. The algorithm is an extension of a polygon scan-line hidden surface algorithm. He added one-dimensional boolean operations to detect surfaces that are logically true and nearest to the viewer. To process one segment span, this algorithm first does one-dimensional boolean operations for both ends of the span, then it checks the depth order of segments up to the visible points. If both depth orders are the same, the segment is visible within that span range. If not, there must be some crossing of segments, so it divides the span and does the same for each divided span (see Fig.4).

For purposes of visualization only, any kind of solid can be a primitive as long as it can be approximated by a polyhedron. Even a complex B-rep model can be a primitive.

We have been implementing this algorithm, with some changes for parallel subimage execution.

4.2 Partitioning of image area to separate scan-lines

This partitioning is effective for evenly distributing the calculation load between cells. However, it causes some loss of y-directional coherence. This increases the cost of calculation of segments and x-sorting of segment end points. We compensate for the increase of x-sorting cost by using x-bucket sorting of segments.

4.3 Boolean operation by status tree technique[17]

This technique differs from the ray classification method[15], which recursively descends from the top node of the CSG tree and obtains all in-out portions of the ray. We use a status tree to detect a ray hit against a logically true surface. The structures of status trees are almost identical to that of CSG trees except that each node keeps the current status of left and right children, and of the node itself. The node pointers are bottom-up.

Given a z-sorted list of segments, a ray proceeds along the z direction. If the ray hits any segment, that primitive's status is evaluated and its parent node status is evaluated. If the new status of the node is the same as the old status, the process stops immediately, otherwise the node status and the child status in the parent node are also updated. Then, the same process is performed for the parent node. This process continues while node statuses are being updated. If the root node's status becomes true for the first time, that point on the segment is a logically true surface point and nearest to the viewer. Rays behind visible points are not processed except when generating translucent images.

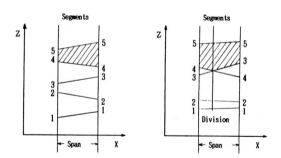

Fig.4 Division of a Segment Span

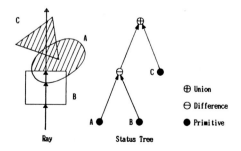

Fig.5 Boolean Operation by Status Tree Technique

This method is fast, because only surfaces up to the first logically true one are processed, but it requires a z-sorted list in advance.

The cost of sorting can be minimized by using span coherence, that is, by bubble sorting of the previous nearly sorted list.

4.4 Use of CSG combination coherence

Large models are often an assembly of parts, which are represented by union operators in CSG trees. That type of model can be displayed by using the scan-line algorithm for hidden surface removal of each part and the z-buffer algorithm for unions of parts. Fig.6 shows simple example. If the root node's boolean operator is a union, it is simply divided (Fig.6 A). On the other hand, if the root is not a union (in displaying cross-sections, a difference or intersection operator appears at the root), primitive 5 in the example (Fig.6 B) must be attached to divided submodels. We developed a recursive procedure to divide and take out submodels from a CSG tree. If the submodel is a primitive, it is displayed by the z-buffer algorithm.

This scheme reduces memory requirements of the CSG algorithm, if the model can be divided to smaller ones.

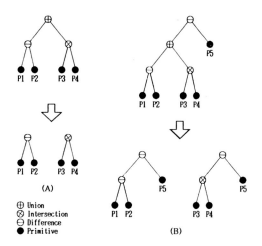

Fig.6 Division of CSG trees

5. Implementation

5.1 Program structure

The program is divided into three tasks: modeling, z-buffer, and CSG. The CSG modeler is in the host computer. The three tasks are resident in all cells. Modeling tasks contain geometric data on the model. When the modeling tasks receive a SHOOT command from the host, they send their data to the z-buffer tasks or to the CSG tasks.

5.2 Modeling task

Modeling tasks have following data items:

CSG tree: Each cell has the same entire CSG tree. This tree is constructed in the cell by commands from the host or is copied from the host.

Primitive data: Primitives are approximated with convex polygons and distributed to all cells, so the number of vertices is nearly the same for all cells, for purposes of averaging the calculation load and memory requirements. Modeling tasks take charge of coordinate transformations and intensity calculations of vertices of polygons. So far, polygonal approximation and coordinate transformations are done in the host computer because floating data processors (8087) have not yet been implemented.

When a modeling task receives a SHOOT command from the host, it does the following:

(1) It divides the entire CSG tree into subtrees if possible, by a division procedure.

(2) Performs transformation of vertex coordinates and normal vectors of polygons of the primitives in the subtree. Then calculates vertex colors or a surface color and depth increment values.

(3) Each cell sends data of the divided submodel to z-buffer tasks if the submodel is a primitive, or to CSG tasks if it is still a CSG model. The CSG tree of a submodel is sent to the CSG task in the same cell, while primitive data is rebroadcast so that the z-buffer or CSG task can receive all polygon data of the submodel. Only frontfacing polygons are sent to z-buffer tasks.

5.3 Z-buffer task

Z-buffer tasks generate an image of a primitive made up of polygons. A polygon has the following data items.

A. Primitive id.
B. Number of vertices
C. Number of colors
D. Vertex coordinates
E. Vertex colors or a surface color
F. Depth increment(dz/dx)

Each polygon is processed independently by the following procedure:

(1)   For each polygon received
(2)   For each scan-line the cell
           takes charge of
(3)   If polygon crosses the scan-line
               Then
(4)   Calculate segment data(start point
                   x, z, color, end point x, color,
                   and d(color)/dx)
(5)   For each pixel in the segment
                   Do ordinary z-buffer process
                   [16]

5.4 CSG task

CSG tasks generate an image of a CSG model from CSG tree data and the primitive's polygon data. The procedure is as follows:

(1) Receive a CSG tree

and construct a status tree
(2) For each polygon received
　　For each scan-line
　　　　If the polygon crosses the scan-line
　　　　Then
　　　　　　Calculate segment data(same as
　　　　　　z-buffer task)
　　　　　　Store segment in data structure(in
　　　　　　edge, segment, x-bucket tables)
(3) For each scan-line
　　For each span from left to right
(4)　　　Make left and right boundary
　　　　　segment list
　　　　　and sort in z-order.
(5)　　　Solve one-dimensional set operation
　　　　　by the status tree technique.
(6)　　　If the same z-order of the segments
　　　　　Then
　　　　　　Do the same as (4), (5) of
　　　　　　z-buffer task
　　　　　Else
　　　　　　Subdivide span and repeat
　　　　　　(4),(5) for each new span.

6. Experiments

First, we tested the communication speed of CAP. Table 1. shows the results. The size of a packet is 128 bytes, of which 18 bytes are header data. We have not obtained maximum communication speed so far because of some bugs in the FIFO LSIs. The speeds without bugs are in parentheses in Table 1.

Table 1. Communication Speed of CAP

Type of Communication		Time(ms)	Speed(Kbyte/s)
Global	Broadcast Packet	3.15*N (1.17*N)	35 (94)
	Rebroadcast Packet	2.06*N (1.17*N)	53 (94)
	Broadcast Direct	1.83*N (0.29*N)	60 (379)
Local(Packet)		1.62*N (1.62*N)	68 (68)

N: Number of Packets

Table 3. Test Models

Model	Number of primitives	Number of polygons	Number of vertices	Data size (Kbyte)
A	17	198	360	12.22
B	25	5320	5018	292.95
C	20	344	634	21.48
D	66	396	528	16.37

Table 4. Values of K1, K2, K3, and K4

Test	K1	K2	K3	K4
1	0.175	0.00036	0.108	80.3
2	2.937	0.00036	0.739	185.2
3	0.277	0.00036	0.714	209.9
4	0.444	0.00036	0.247	234.4
5	0.444	0.00036	1.019	280.3
6	0.277	0.00036	0.293	53.7

The CSG hidden surface program uses broadcast (packet) from host to cells and rebroadcast (packet) from each cell to all other cells. The broadcast speed is constant regardless of the number of cells, while rebroadcast increases the overhead as the number of cells increases, because polling interrupts tasks in cells. This overhead is 0.36*(number of cells) ms, for each polling cycle. We are designing a hardware mechanism for polling, to minimize overhead.

The host computer is Apollo Domain DN460[18]. All source code is written in C language, except time critical parts of the cell monitor, the communication tasks, and the Display Manager. All calculations in cells are done in integer arithmetics.

The models tested are in Table 3. The screen resolution was 512 x 384 for all tests.

We tested three cases:
(1) Performance of modeling and
　　z-buffer tasks (Test 1, Test 2, and 6).
(2) Performance of modeling
　　and CSG tasks (Test 3 and 4).
(3) Performance of the combined
　　method (modeling, z-buffer,
　　and CSG tasks) (Test 5).

The test results are shown in Table 2. The division number in the table is the number of cells to which primitive data is distributed.

7. Analysis of Results

Rebroadcast time is almost constant for each model, so the ratio of the overhead increases as the number of cell increases. The modeling task rebroadcast to the z-buffer tasks only frontfacing polygons, which is about half of that is sent to CSG tasks.

Suppose that the total execution time except idle time of a certain model is represented by Eq.1.

$$T = K1 + K2*Nc*Np + K3 + K4/Nc \quad (Eq.1)$$

T : Total execution time of a model
K1: Rebroadcast time
Nc: Number of cells used
Np: Number of polling cycles
K2*Nc*Np: Overhead for polling
K3: Overhead of a modeling task and
　　the hidden surface task
K4/Nc: Execution time inversely
　　proportional to Nc

The performance is:

$$P = 1/T$$
$$= 1 / (K1 + K2*Nc*Np + K3 + K4/Nc) \quad (Eq.2)$$

These parameters can be calculated from the experiments for each model and are shown in Table 4. Fig.7 shows the performance curves of the tests. Fig.8 shows the ratio of the performance to that with 16 cells. Plotted points in Fig.7 and 8 are expermental values. The improvement of the performance decreases as models become large.

The performance would be improved by optimizing the program code and replacing the FIFOs with bugless ones, but if the amount of polygon data becomes large, the overhead is still large.

Table 2. Test Results

Test (Model)	Algorithm	# Cell	Total Time(Idle Time) (s) Fast Cell	Average	Slow Cell	# Div.	Communication Average(s)	%	Other Time (s)	%
1(A)	ZB	16	5.31(0.04)	5.40(0.02)	5.47(0.00)	16	0.19	3.5	5.21	96.5
		32	2.78(0.04)	2.86(0.02)	2.94(0.00)	32	0.18	6.2	2.68	93.8
		48	1.92(0.06)	2.00(0.03)	2.06(0.00)	33	0.17	8.5	1.83	91.5
		64	1.54(0.06)	1.59(0.04)	1.64(0.00)	33	0.17	10.7	1.42	89.3
2(B)	ZB	24	12.50(2.11)	12.74(1.20)	13.15(0.31)	24	3.02	23.7	9.72	76.3
		32	10.62(2.18)	10.89(1.32)	11.17(0.30)	32	2.96	27.2	7.93	72.8
		48	8.64(2.36)	8.84(1.29)	9.08(0.40)	48	2.92	33.0	5.92	67.0
		64	7.87(2.53)	7.99(1.77)	8.23(0.70)	64	2.89	36.2	5.10	63.8
3(A')	CSG	40	6.33(0.18)	6.53(0.08)	6.69(0.00)	33	0.28	4.3	6.25	95.7
		48	5.35(0.19)	5.49(0.11)	5.68(0.00)	33	0.28	5.1	5.21	94.9
		64	4.26(0.08)	4.35(0.05)	4.49(0.00)	33	0.28	6.3	4.07	93.7
4(C)	CSG	32	7.99(0.12)	8.19(0.06)	8.41(0.00)	32	0.45	5.5	7.74	94.5
		48	5.38(0.15)	5.73(0.09)	6.05(0.00)	34	0.44	7.7	5.29	92.3
		64	4.30(0.15)	4.48(0.11)	4.68(0.00)	34	0.44	9.8	4.04	90.2
5(C)	ZB+CSG	32	9.75(0.17)	10.37(0.14)	11.32(0.00)	32	0.45	4.4	9.92	95.6
		48	7.49(0.17)	7.55(0.14)	8.28(0.00)	34	0.44	5.9	7.11	94.1
		64	4.86(0.20)	6.01(0.15)	7.16(0.00)	34	0.44	7.3	5.57	92.7
6(D)	ZB	16	4.04(0.00)	4.11(0.00)	4.12(0.00)	16	0.30	7.2	3.81	92.8
		32	2.28(0.00)	2.31(0.00)	2.36(0.00)	32	0.28	12.1	2.03	87.9
		48	1.65(0.00)	1.71(0.00)	1.76(0.00)	48	0.27	15.9	1.44	84.1
		64	1.42(0.00)	1.45(0.00)	1.48(0.00)	64	0.27	18.7	1.18	81.3

Model A:Union, Model A':Difference, ZB:z-buffer, #Cell:Number of cells used, #Div.:Number of cells to which primitive data is distributed.

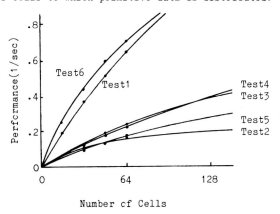

Fig.7 Performance curves of tested models

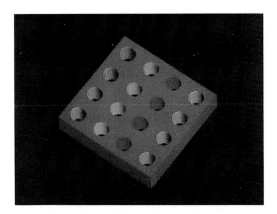

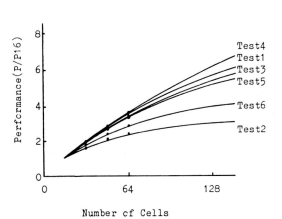

Fig.8 Improvement of Performance
by increasing the number of cells

7. Conclusions

The architecture of the Cellular Array Processor (CAP) and the implementation of the CSG hidden surface algorithm have been explained. Our conclusions are as follows:

(1) The changeability of subimage mappings enables various hidden surface algorithms to be easily implemented in CAP. Certain mapping patterns are often effective for evenly distributing calculation load.

(2) Distributing the calculation load by using line mode often compensates for the loss of coherence. Our preliminary experiments showed that the z-buffer algorithm with line mode was more than two times faster than that with block mode in many cases.

(3) The multi-task cell monitor is effective for decreasing the idle time of cells. The slowest cell's idle time was very small in the tests.

(4) Inter-cell communication ports can be used to access to data in neighboring cells. This enables amounts of data exceeding the capacity of one cell to be accommodated in CAP.

(5) If the communication time is relatively large, the system efficiency decreases. The polygonal approximation technique decreases the amount of calculation, but it increases the amount of communication and the amount of data. This worsens the performance of the algorithm. If much more cells are available, a more direct method without polygonal approximation such as ray-casting[15] would be faster.

(6) The status tree technique could be used by ray-casting and ray-tracing algorithms. It is faster than the ray-classification method[15], if the intersection points of the ray are sorted along the ray or the objects are sorted spacially.

(7) The combined CSG hidden surface algorithm is effective for decreasing memory requirements of the program. It is faster than the normal CSG algorithm if the divided submodels are primitives. But, sufficient experimentation has not been done for larger models.

We believe that CAP will be more powerful with upgraded hardware and software. However, there are still many problems remaining for further research.

Acknowledgements

The authors would like to thank Shigeru Sato, Yukihiko Minejima and Takao Uehara for promoting this research project, SIGGRAPH reviewers for suggesting improvements of the paper, and Kouichi Murakami for participating in our discussions and suggesting the idea of the status tree technique.

References

[1] Kaplan, M., and Greenberg, D.P.: "Parallel Processing Techniques for Hidden Surface Removal," ACM Computer Graphics, Vol.13, NO.2(Aug.1979), pp.300-307.

[2] Fiume, E., Fournier, A., and Rudolph, L.: "A Parallel Scan Conversion Algorithm With Anti-Aliasing for a General-Purpose Ultracomputer," ACM Computer Graphics, Vol.17, No.3(Jul.1983), pp.141-150.

[3] Fuchs, H., and Johnson, B.W.: "An Expandable Multiprocessor Architecture for Video Graphics(Preliminary Report)," IEEE 6th conf. on Computer Architecture(1979), pp.58-67.

[4] Parke, F.I.: "Simulation and Expected Performance Analysis of Multi Processor Z-Buffer System," ACM Computer Graphics(Jul.1980), pp.48-56.

[5] Fuchs, H., and Poulton, J.: "Pixel-Planes: A VLSI-Oriented Design for a Raster Graphics Engine," VLSI Design, No.3, 1981, pp.20-28.

[6] Nishimura, H., Ohno, H., Kawata, T., Shirakawa, I., and Omura, K.: "LINKS-1: A Parallel Pipelined Multimicrocomputer System for Image Creation," Proceedings of the 10th Symposium on Computer Architecture, SIGARCH(1983), pp.387-394.

[7] Dippé, M., and Swensen, J.: "An Adaptive Subdivision Algorithm and Parallel Architecture for Realistic Image Synthesis," ACM Computer Graphics, Vol.18, No.3(Jul.1984), pp.149-158.

[8] Niimi, H., Imai, Y., Murakami, M., Tomita, S., and Hagiwara, H.: "A Parallel Processor System for Three-Dimensional Color Graphics," ACM Computer Graphics, Vol.18, No.3(Jul.1984), pp.67-76.

[9] Hoshino, T., Shirakawa, T., Kamimura, T., Kageyama, T., Takenouchi, K., Sekiguchi, T., and Kawai, T.: "Highly Parallel Processor Array 'PAX' for Wide Scientific Applications," International Conference on Parallel Processing IEEE, pp.95-105,(Aug.1983).

[10] Requicha, A.A.G., Voelcker, H.B.: "Solid Modeling: A Historical Summary and Contemporary Assessment," IEEE Computer Graphics and Applications, Vol.2, No.2, Mar. 1982, pp.9-24.

[11] Sutherland, I.E., Sproull, R.F., and Schumacker, R.A.: "A Characterization of Ten Hidden-Surface Algorithms," ACM Computing Surveys, Vol.6, No.1(Mar. 1974), pp.1-55.

[12] Whitted, T.: "An Improved Illumination Model for Shaded Display," Comm., ACM, Vol.23, No.6, 1980, pp.343-349.

[13] Atherton, P.R.: "A Scan-line Hidden Surface Removal Procedure for Constructive Solid Geometry," ACM Computer Graphics, Vol.17, No.3(Jul.1983), pp.73-82.

[14] Crocker, G.A.: "Invisibility Coherence for Faster Scan-line Hidden Surface Algorithms," ACM Computer Graphics, Vol.18, No.3(Jul.1984),pp.95-102.

[15] Roth, S.D.: "Ray Casting for Modeling Solids," Computer Graphics and Image Processing, No.18, 1982, pp.109-144.

[16] Foley, J.D. and Van Dam, A., Fundamentals of Interactive Computer Graphics, Addison-Wesley, 1982.

[17] Murakami, K., Matsumoto, H.: "Ray tracing for CSG representation using status tree technique," 27th Information Processing Conference(Oct.1983), pp.1535-1537 (in Japanese)

[18] Nelson, D. ,L. and Leach, P.,J.: "The Architecture and Applications of the Apollo Domain," IEEE Computer Graphics and Applications, Vol.4, No.4(Apr.1984), pp.58-66

"An Adaptive Subdivision Algorithm and Parallel Architecture for Realistic
Image Synthesis" by M. Dippe and J. Swensen from *Computer Graphics*,
Volume 18, Number 3, July 1984, pages 149-158. Copyright 1984, Associa-
tion for Computing Machinery, Inc., reprinted by permission.

An Adaptive Subdivision Algorithm and Parallel Architecture
for Realistic Image Synthesis

Mark Dippé
Berkeley Computer Graphics Laboratory

John Swensen
Computer Science Division

Department of Electrical Engineering
and Computer Sciences
University of California
Berkeley, California 94720
U.S.A.

Abstract

An algorithm for computing ray traced pictures is
presented, which adaptively subdivides scenes into S
subregions, each with roughly uniform load. It can yield
speedups of $O(S^{2/3})$ over the standard algorithm.

This algorithm can be mapped onto a parallel architecture consisting of a three dimensional array of computers which operate autonomously. The algorithm and
architecture are well matched, so that communication
overhead is small with respect to the computation, for
sufficiently complex scenes. This allows close to linear
improvements in performance, even with thousands of
computers, in addition to the improvement due to subdivision.

The algorithm and architecture provide mechanisms
to gracefully degrade in response to excessive load. The
architecture also tolerates failures of computers without
errors in the computation.

CR Categories and Subject Descriptors: C.1.2 **[Pro-
cessor Architectures]**: Multiple Data Stream Architectures (Multiprocessors) - *Multiple-instruction-stream,
multiple-data-stream processors (MIMD)* I.3.3 **[Computer
Graphics]**: Picture/Image Generation - *display algorithms*; I.3.7 **[Computer Graphics]**: Three-dimensional
Graphics and Realism - *animation; color, shading, shadowing, and texture; visible line/surface algorithm;*

General Terms: Algorithms

Additional Key Words and Phrases: adaptive, parallel, ray tracing, subdivision

1. Introduction

Realistic three dimensional image synthesis is computationally very expensive. Rather than becoming less
expensive, the use of more realistic techniques with highly
complex scenes has increased the cost per image.[12] We
are interested in efficient realistic rendering of scenes that
change over time, using algorithmic and architectural
strategies.

The most viable rendering algorithm to date for
creating realistic images is ray tracing, because it models
the complex effects of light in an environment more
effectively than other existing synthesis techniques.

In the ray tracing model, rays are sent from the eye
through each pixel of the picture plane and traced as
they are reflected and transmitted by objects in space.
When a ray hits an object, new rays may be generated,
due to reflection, transmission, and/or relevant light
sources. These new rays are in turn traced. The ray tracing process thus forms a tree with the eye at the root and
rays as the branches. The initial branch is the ray pierc-
ing the picture plane. Internal nodes represent objects
intersecting the ray, and leaves represent light sources or
rays leaving the picture space. The reader is referred to
Turner Whitted's excellent introduction[22] for a more
detailed description of ray tracing.

Our approach is to adaptively subdivide the ray
tracing process, and to implement this subdivision on
parallel hardware.

The three dimensional space of a scene to be rendered is divided into several subregions. Initially the
space is divided to assign volume more or less uniformly,
and object descriptions are loaded into the appropriate
subregions. As computational loads are determined, the
space is redistributed among the subregions to maintain
uniformity of load.

The rendering process begins when the subregion
containing the eye or camera casts rays at the desired
image resolution. Associated with each ray is its home
pixel, so that the pixel can be appropriately colored after
the ray tracing operations are complete. When a ray
enters a subregion, it is intersected with the object
descriptions contained within the subregion. Rays that
exit a subregion are passed to the appropriate neighbor.

Each ray resulting from a ray-object interaction contains the fraction of the ray's contribution to its pixel. This fraction is the product of the fractional value of the impinging ray and the value resulting from the object intersection. Color information associated with the spectral properties of the ray/object interaction is also included.

When a ray terminates, becoming a leaf of the ray tracing tree, the rendered value is added to a frame buffer.

Subregion loads are monitored to determine the need for redistributions of space. When a subregion's load becomes too large relative to its neighbors' loads, a change in subregion definition is initiated.

A parallel architecture implementing this algorithm uses a three dimensional array of computers, each with its own independent memory. Each of the computers is assigned one or more subregions. Neighboring computers contain adjacent subregions, and communicate via a variety of messages. Messages not directed toward an immediate neighbor are passed on in the appropriate direction.

Image quality can be traded off with performance, and to this end, the algorithm and architecture provide various means of degrading to achieve a desired rate of image generation.

2. Adaptive Subdivision Algorithm

The synthesis problem is primarily concerned with the visibility of objects with respect to a viewpoint and with the interaction of light in the environment with these visible objects. Visibility is determined by a two dimensional projection of three dimensional space. Lighting interaction is much more complex in that its effect spans three dimensional space in a non-projective manner.

Previous synthesis techniques can be categorized by their generality of lighting model, and by their use of projective qualities of images.[18]

1) projective: z-buffer, painter, Watkins, priority, Warnock, Franklin[8]

These algorithms render and determine surface visibility primarily in image space, using projective transformations. They effectively model those aspects of the scene that are naturally projective with respect to the viewpoint. However, phenomena that are not directly projective with respect to viewpoint, such as shadows or inter-object reflections, introduce many complications.

2) quasi-projective: shadow polygons,[5] cluster planes, three dimensional cookie cutter[1]

These algorithms operate to a greater degree in three dimensional space. They do this by adding information that is non-projective, such as shadow polygons, and/or by attempting to sort three dimensional space, either by separating planes or by the faces of polygonal objects. However, complexity is increased when shadow polygons are incorporated in the rendering process. In addition, objects are often split, because three dimensional space cannot be easily sorted on the basis of visibility. These algorithms generally prepare the information for an efficient projective solution of the visibility problem.

3) non-projective: ray tracing, hierarchical bounding volumes,[17] wave based algorithms[14]

Algorithms in this group perform image synthesis in three dimensions. Modeling of a general class of lighting effects is facilitated. Hierarchical bounding volumes can be thought of as a modeling operation rather than a rendering one, but it is intimately related to rendering. It is a type of three dimensional subdivision which does not sort but uses containment information to aid in visibility determination. Ray tracing is the primary example of algorithms that inherently operate in three dimensional space, i.e. no projection with respect to viewpoint is necessary. The main disadvantage is that, in general, all of three dimensional space must be considered to arrive at a solution.

The complexity of ray tracing is associated with the testing of rays for intersection with the objects of the scene. The distribution of complexity in space is determined by the distribution of objects, and by the distribution or flow of rays among the objects. A region of space with many objects but with no rays has low complexity, as does a region with many rays but no objects. On the other hand, a region in which many rays are interacting with many objects has very high complexity.

Up to now, most algorithms have subdivided the two dimensional projection of three dimensional space when rendering. Our algorithm is completely non-projective in nature, and subdivides three dimensional space itself. The essential characteristics of the algorithm are:

1) Three dimensional space is divided into several subregions. Object and light source descriptions are distributed among the subregions according to their position. Each of the subregions is processed independently.

2) Rays are cast into three dimensional space and processed in the subregions along their paths. The rays within a particular subregion are tested for intersection with only those objects within that subregion. Rays that exit the subregion are passed to neighboring subregions. The rays are processed until they terminate and become leaves of the ray tracing tree.

3) The shapes of the subregions are adaptively controlled to maintain a roughly uniform distribution of load.

For any given ray, we only consider subregions along the path of the ray, and ignore all others. Thus, the problem is reduced from considering all objects, to considering only those objects along the one dimensional ray.

The three dimensional method for subdividing the ray tracing problem can be applied to the general image synthesis problem. The parameters can be thought of as:

1) objects, and

2) distribution of light through space.

The problem is to find the visual stimulus from such a world.

2.1. Subregions.

There are several issues concerning the shape of the subregions that subdivide space:

1) the complexity of subdividing the problem, e.g. intersecting objects or rays with the boundaries,

2) the ability to subdivide space without splitting objects, and

3) the uniformity of the distributed loads attainable with the shape.

The complexity of scenes is certainly not uniform, but varies according to the characteristics of the components of the scene. Our subregions do not divide space uniformly, but allow arbitrary subdivisions of space within the topological and geometrical constraints of the subregions. This provides us with a very powerful technique with which to subdivide the space to accommodate non-uniform complexity. The ability to dedicate processing power where complexity is concentrated and not waste it where it is unneeded is one of the fundamental aspects of the system.

Among the polyhedral shapes which could bound the subregions, the three most promising candidates are orthogonal parallelepipeds, "general cubes", and tetrahedra. More general shapes such as quadric surfaces are under investigation and may be useful in the future, but are not considered in this paper.

The most intuitively simple polyhedra are orthogonal parallelepipeds, which are constrained to have all boundaries parallel or perpendicular to the major axes. Figure 1a shows a two dimensional analog of orthogonal parallelepipeds. As subregions grow and shrink to redistribute the complexity of the scene, the boundaries remain orthogonal, and the subregions remain convex.

Boundary-intersection testing for orthogonal parallelepipeds is not a significant overhead. However, the orthogonality constraint does not allow local adjustments to a subregion to be made without affecting many other subregions, and in general, a scene's computational complexity will be less uniformly distributed than with more general boundaries. Unless either very few basic objects are contained in each subregion, or the scene has a uniform distribution of complexity over space, the low overhead of orthogonal parallelepipeds is unlikely to offset their greater non-uniformity of load.

General cubes resemble the familiar cube, except they have relaxed constraints on planarity of faces and on convexity. 2-D analogs of general cubes are shown in figure 1b.

With these relaxed constraints, the complexity of boundary testing is increased over that for the orthogonal polyhedra, and hence the overhead for each subregion is increased. However, general cubes allow much more local control of subregion shape, with the consequence that more uniform distributions of load can be achieved than with orthogonal subregions. Furthermore, the redistributions can be performed locally.

Tetrahedra are the simplest shapes, and are inherently convex. A space-filling collection of tetrahedra can be constructed with groups of six tetrahedra forming a cube, which are then arranged to fill space. The boundary of each subregion is defined by its four corners, and the interface with two neighboring subregions is defined by three of these corners. Figure 1c shows an analog of

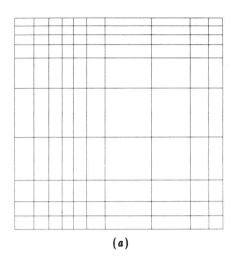

(a)

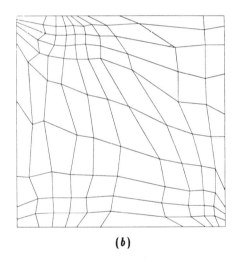

(b)

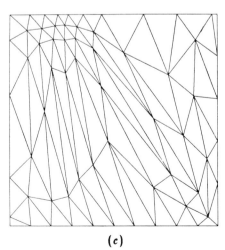

(c)

Figure 1. 2-D analogs of orthogonal parallelepipeds, general cubes, and tetrahedra, simulated with the same load.

tetrahedral subregions.

Tetrahedra have fewer boundaries than cubes, so the overhead of boundary testing is lower for them than for general cubes. They allow local control of subregion shape, but because vertices are shared among more subregions with tetrahedra than with general cubes, the control cannot be as local. Because tetrahedra have fewer vertices than cubes, they may not contain subregion-sized objects as well.

Simple, fixed connectivities have been assumed throughout the discussion. We have also considered arbitrary topologies for the subregions. However, fixed connectivities allow simpler calculations for the determination of how rays move among subregions, and the tradeoffs between more general topologies and shapes have yet to be fully determined. For these reasons, we only discuss arrays of general cubes for the remainder of the paper.

Given the basic scenario of how the subdivision algorithm operates and how space is subdivided, how do we carry out an actual subdivision to yield a uniform distribution of the problem? A direct optimal solution requires global knowledge, and is quite difficult. We would like to avoid these problems if possible.

Our solution is to allow neighboring subregions to share each others' load information, and to allow relatively more loaded subregions to adjust their boundaries to reduce load. This mechanism is a feedback scheme. It also provides a mechanism for adapting to the changing complexity of a scene in a distributed manner.

2.2. Adaptive Redistribution

It is difficult to calculate the distribution of load without actually simulating the ray tracing process. The algorithm redistributes the load among the subregions to adapt to changing conditions induced by the movement of objects, lights, the eye or camera, and other time varying behavior.

Load is redistributed by moving the points defining subregions and passing the object information as needed. The load of each subregion is compared to that of its neighbors. When a subregion's load is higher than its neighbors, some load should be transferred to them. More general relative load measures can also be used.

The load metric is determined primarily by the product of

1) number of objects and their complexity, and

2) number of rays.

Load is transferred by moving corners of a subregion. To simplify matters we only move one corner at a time. The corner's new position is chosen such that enough volume is transferred to equalize loads.

Once the new position for a corner of a subregion has been determined, object descriptions and other information are redistributed to reflect the new subdivision.

If the scene being rendered is too complex, then redistribution cannot entirely alleviate the problem. In such a case, degradation techniques must be applied. These techniques are discussed later.

This is a simplified scenario of the redistribution process, some of the more difficult points of which we discuss in the following section.

2.2.1. More Sophisticated Approaches

Subregions with elongated shapes, or those which are very concave, may cause rays to pass through more subregions than would be necessary with fatter, convex subregions. The load metric reflects the undesirability of elongated or concave subregions. When a subregion becomes too undesirable in shape, its load can be increased by a factor indicating its desire to become shapely. This more general framework will allow subregions to become unshapely when it is advantageous, while maintaining shapely subregions in general.

When selecting a corner of a subregion to move, we must take into account the difficulty involved in shifting the load; it may be easier to transfer load from one corner than another. We also wish to transfer the load differently to each of the affected neighbors, with more of the load going to those that are least loaded. Another important constraint on redistribution is to minimize the splitting of objects among neighboring subregions. This can be done relatively easily, because the overloaded subregion which is exporting objects can choose the new position of a corner to avoid splitting. In addition, by subdividing the subregions into smaller regions, within which statistics are kept about object distribution and ray flow, more precise decisions about object splitting and load movement can be made.

Our mechanisms for redistribution will not necessarily produce exactly uniform load distributions; this is tolerable, as long as the differences in load are small percentages of the average.

We would like to avoid oscillations in the redistribution process. Small oscillations can be damped by adding hysteresis so that load disparities of a certain size are required before a redistribution is allowed. Instability due to the shuffling of large objects across boundaries can also be detected and limited.

Global information about the distribution of loads is maintained, and is used to direct effective redistribution. When loads are highly disparate, large transfers of load are used. As the disparity decreases, smaller loads are transferred.

There are many subtle issues involved with the redistribution process, and further analyses and experiments must be performed to determine the best choices for this application. We hope to complete these studies in the near future.

3. Parallel Architecture

Our parallel implementation of the algorithm uses independent computers, each communicating with a few neighbors. Computers are responsible for one or more subregions and communicate with neighboring computers using messages. To simplify the discussion, we assume one subregion per computer.

Computers handle all rays and redistributions affecting their subregions. They have several other tasks as well. Messages may be sent to non-neighboring computers by passing them through intervening computers. Thus, computers must route messages.

Computers at the boundary of the array handle infinite extents of space. They also have fewer neighbors than those in the center, and so they are logical candidates to manage auxiliary storage devices and network interfaces. Computers in the center would access these devices via requests through messages. Because we do not want a direct connection to a frame buffer for each computer, the frame buffer will be connected to boundary computers and accessed via messages.

Besides the special role of disk and frame buffer connections for boundary computers, there are other special roles that certain other computers have:

1) The computer containing the eye or camera must cast the initial rays for each frame.

2) Interface and monitoring tasks, assigned to some computers, are used for dealing with user controlled system parameters as well as any other global tasks, such as initially distributing the image description or watching the system load as a whole and changing certain parameters automatically in response to load changes.

The parallelization of the image synthesis problem is based on subdivision of three dimensional space into adjacent polyhedral regions. The computers responsible for the subregions operate independently, adaptively redistributing the space as loads are determined, and gracefully degrading if their load is too large.

3.1. Architectural Perspective

A number of special purpose graphics engines and systems have been proposed and/or built. We briefly describe some of this work in the context of our architecture.

3.1.1. Multicomputers

The LINKS-1[15] multicomputer has been built to generate ray traced pictures. It consists of 64 unit computers, each of which is connected to two neighbor computers, a root computer, and a result collection computer. The root computer controls the system and facilitates non-neighbor communication among computers.

This topology allows work to be distributed by the root computer so that it can be performed independently in parallel, or pipelined from neighbor to neighbor, or some combination of both. Unfortunately, if scene descriptions are too complex to be duplicated in each computer's memory, then substantial communication among the computers is required, but this is hindered by the restricted connection topology. Furthermore, expansion of the system will be limited by the use of the global root and collection computers.

Recent work by other researchers[4, 20] has also addressed the application of parallelism to ray tracing. They consider geometrically uniform, orthogonal subdivisions of space. Both efforts favor two dimensional arrays of computers over three dimensional arrays.

However, they do not address the issues of achieving uniform load distribution over the subregions. The ability to adaptively redistribute over time is crucial to the success of this approach, not only because of temporal changes in the scene, but because load distributions are extremely difficult to calculate without actually simulating the ray tracing process.

3.1.2. Graphics Engines and Sub-processors

Clark uses twelve of his specialized VLSI processors, Geometry Engines,[11] to perform the floating point calculations necessary for geometric calculations prior to the rendering process. These types of operations are also useful for ray tracing operations, and similar hardware should be eventually be included in our system. However, we feel that because of the experimental nature of our system, hardware complexity should initially be applied to support general purpose processing, at the expense of special purpose operations.

Fiume and Fournier[7] describe a multiprocessor architecture which processes spans of scanlines using parallel processors, allowing some degree of anti-aliasing to be performed in each processor. The Pixel Planes system developed by Fuchs[9] uses a 1-bit processor per small number of pixels to perform scan-conversion and hidden-surface elimination on a per-polygon basis, using a z-buffer technique. In Pixel Planes, polygons are broadcast to the array of processors, one at a time, and are processed in parallel. The applicable algorithms for both of these architectures are by nature restricted to projected image space, and are not appropriate for our application.

A number of processor per polygon architectures have been proposed.[10, 21] These determine surface visibility at the pixel level using a number of depth comparators. As these have all worked in projected image space, they are also not appropriate for our approach.

3.2. The Nature of the Parallelization

A ray crossing the three-dimensional array of computers can pass over many computers, so global information about the system may be old. In particular, knowledge that all computers have completed their ray tracing operations may be out of date.

Rather than wait for messages to propagate, we adjust the computation so that all computers complete at approximately the same time. This has the consequence that new frames might be started before older frames have finished. This is not a problem, because minor variations can be absorbed by allowing computations on old frames to continue after newer frames begin. Ray tracing and frame buffer updating can overlap if several image frames are stored. In this way, late updates to frames can be made before displaying them.

3.3. Parallel Redistribution

Messages are used to initiate a redistribution. Each computer has 26 neighboring computers, even though it is only directly connected to 6, and each corner is shared among 8 computers. Thus, the load and redistribution messages must be routed through neighbors to allow complete determination of redistribution parameters for each computer (see figure 2). Load and redistribution messages will contain routing information to speed up the process.

In addition to object information and ray flow within a computer, other factors are related to load in the parallel architecture:

1) the number of messages dealt with,

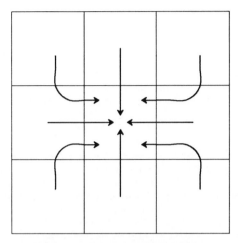

Figure 2. Load message routing.

2) the size of message queues (this measures how far behind a computer is, relative to its neighbors), and

3) idle time.

There other possible factors which are under investigation.

Once the computer has determined the new position for a corner, it sends out redistribution messages and begins passing objects and other information. To handle ties between two computers which decide to move the same corner at the same time, each computer is assigned a priority according to its position in the array.

If an overloaded computer's neighbors are also overloaded, so that no load transfers can take place, the computer must reduce its load using the degradation techniques discussed later.

To ensure that redistributions are carried out as quickly as possible, computers check their message queues periodically. If a redistribution message is found, it is acted upon immediately.

Note that the redistribution process is carried out in a local manner without a complex protocol.

3.4. Messages

We list some of the different messages and their fields:

1) ray: pixel, point of origin, direction, percentage of contribution to the pixel of this ray, color parameters of the ray

2) pixel: address, value

3) global parameter: name, value; for instance there is a message that tells the computer containing the eye or camera whether or not to send out the initial rays and perform rendering

4) object information: description; general objects such as splines,[2] fractals,[13] or blobby models[3] will be handled

5) disk i/o: request type, associated data

6) load value: computer ID, value, and possibly volume information for redistribution purposes; these messages are copied to a monitoring computer for global load statistics tracking

7) redistribution notification: corner to move, new location, routing information

By monitoring the messages being passed as well as examining load messages, the performance of the system can be easily measured. Thus, messages form a direct basis for evaluating the system.

4. Performance Degradation

If our algorithm/architecture is to be successful in an interactive environment, it must allow performance to degrade gracefully. Since any machine constructed must be finite, some problems will exceed its resources, and degradation will be unavoidable. If a computer is unable to reduce its load by moving boundaries, it can decrease its load by more drastic means.

One possible load-reducing action is to delete ray messages in a controlled manner, until a computer can keep up with the desired frame rate. This amounts to a local reduction in the height of the ray tracing tree. Messages significantly older than the youngest received message would be logical candidates for deletion. Some messages, such as disk requests, should not be deleted.

At a more global level, the image resolution or the depth of the ray tracing tree can be reduced, creating fewer rays, at the expense of less realistic simulation. In addition, the level of detail for rendering of objects can be reduced; for example, splines or fractals might be subdivided into fewer polygons.

Generally, the small errors in pixel intensity these degradation measures introduce will be visually tolerable. If they are not acceptable, the total workload must be decreased by reducing the rate of image generation.

By allowing a user to trade image quality for speed, an extremely effective tool for practical image synthesis is provided.

These adaptivity parameters may be controlled by the user, or by a computer which has been gathering statistics. They are used to tune the performance of the system.

5. Analysis

Symbol	Meaning
B	number of objects
C	number of parallel computers
D	depth of ray tracing tree
L	number of lights
N	number of rays from an object interaction
R	number of rays
S	number of subregions
β	boundary-intersection cost
κ	co-resident object overhead
ν	non-uniform distribution cost
π	ray passing overhead
σ	pixel energy summation cost
τ	subregion traversal overhead

We analyze the standard ray tracing algorithm, the adaptive subdivision algorithm, and the parallel architecture. Our coupled parallel implementation is also compared with a frame-parallel implementation.

The cycle counts for data transfers and floating point operations assume the computers are implemented using microprocessors augmented with floating point chips. Computers with faster floating point speeds will also tend to have wider data paths, so the relative speeds of arithmetic operations and data transfers will be similar.

5.1. Standard Algorithm

To perform ray tracing, rays are cast into a scene, and are tested for intersection with each object in the scene. As a result of an intersection, each ray may produce 0, 1, or more offspring, depending on the reflective and refractive properties of the objects, as well as the number of light sources. In a highly reflective environment, several levels of interaction testing - new ray generation must be performed for a realistic rendering.

We assume the ray tracing tree generated by recursive reflection/refraction rays is a complete tree of depth D. It has R_i nodes at each level, where $R_{i+1} = R_i N$ and N corresponds to the average number of rays produced by a ray-object interaction. The total number of arcs in this tree is given by

$$R_0 \sum_{i=0}^{D-1} N^i = R_0 (\frac{N^D - 1}{N - 1}),$$

where R_0 is the number of pixels, typically 512^2 to 1024^2. In addition to recursive rays, rays to light sources are cast at each node, so the total number of rays is

$$R \approx R_0 (\frac{N^D - 1}{N - 1})(1 + L),$$

where L is the number of light sources. We assume 10% of the intersections transmit rays, as well as reflect them. In addition, we consider two light sources and 500×500 pixels, and a ray tracing tree of depth 5 (a depth of 4 has been used to produce reasonable pictures). Thus, $N = 1.1$, $L = 2$, $R_0 = 250000$, and $D = 5$, so that the total number of rays is

$$R = 2.5 \times 10^5 \frac{(1.1^5 - 1)}{(1.1 - 1)}(1 + 2) \approx 4.6 \times 10^6.$$

The number of ray tracing operations for the standard algorithm is RB, for B objects, and if $B = 1000$, 4.6×10^9 ray tracing operations must be performed.

The cost of each ray tracing operation depends on the complexity of the objects; while a sphere is almost trivial to intersect with rays, a fractal object can be extremely costly. We assume a basic object which has roughly the same complexity as 250 triangles represented using a Rubin-Whitted[17] style model. This is a reasonable unit of object complexity, but is still simpler than many object models used today. When a ray is tested against one of our basic objects, we assume it will almost always be rejected after one bounding volume intersection test, at a cost of the equivalent of 25 floating point multiplications, which each require 100 cycles to execute. Thus a basic object requires about 2500 machine cycles to test for intersection with a ray, on the average.

5.2. Subdivision Algorithm

Testing each ray against each object can be avoided by adaptively subdividing the scene into a number of subregions, each with approximately the same load, and checking only the objects within the subregions along the ray's path. The algorithm for computing the image performs the ray tracing operations within the restricted domain of the subregions.

Subdividing space distributes load so that it is roughly uniform, but has accompanying overhead. We discuss the sources of the overhead before continuing with the analysis.

Breaking space up into subregions forces rays to pass through several subregions in order to cross the entire space; this traversal cost is τ. If the subregions are well-shaped, τ is bounded by $3S^{1/3}$. Each ray may be processed up to τ times, but this has no effect on the total number of rays.

Each ray must be tested for intersection not only with each object in the subregion, but with the boundaries as well, because a ray may intersect an object at a point outside the subregion, even though the object is partially inside the subregion. This adds a cost of β for each subregion, which is about the same as testing 4 basic objects.

Although our redistribution algorithm tries to avoid splitting objects across subregion boundaries, some splitting will be unavoidable, so some testing will be duplicated. If κ is the co-residency cost, this is as if there were κ times as many non-co-resident basic objects. For a scene consisting of a single sphere, κ could be S, but this type of scene is inappropriate for our algorithm. If instead we assume complex objects, such as spline surfaces, the amount of testing duplication may be small. Such object models are usually expanded into more primitive representations (e.g. triangles), and these expanded representations are distributed among the subregions. Determination of realistic values for κ require further investigation.

The number of ray tracing operations required to compute an image using the improved algorithm is the sum, over all subregions, of the traversal cost for each ray, times the number of rays in the subregion, times the sum of the objects in the subregions (including co-residency) and the boundary testing cost:

$$\sum_S \tau R_S (\kappa B_S + \beta).$$

If the distribution of load is uniform over all the subregions, then $R_S B_S$ is the same for all subregions. Using the arithmetic-geometric mean inequality,[16] it can be shown that

$$R_S B_S \leq RB/S^2.$$

Therefore, the number of ray tracing operations is bounded by

$$\sum_S \frac{\tau R (\kappa B + \beta S)}{S^2} = \frac{\tau R (\kappa B + \beta S)}{S}.$$

Assuming β is 4, τ is $S^{1/3}$, $S = 125$, and ignoring κ, we have

$$\frac{5 \times 4.6 \times 10^6 (10^3 + 4 \times 125)}{125} \approx 2.8 \times 10^8.$$

This is an order of magnitude improvement over the standard algorithm. As long as κ is less than 10, this algorithm is faster than the standard algorithm. Note that B must be greater than S if the speedup is to be large; otherwise the overhead of boundary testing will become significant.

Assuming complex scenes, boundary testing overhead is small relative to object intersection calculations. Under these conditions, the cost reduces to

$$\frac{\kappa \tau RB}{S} \approx \frac{\kappa S^{1/3} RB}{S} = \kappa RBS^{-2/3}.$$

Thus we obtain an $O(S^{2/3})$ speedup over the standard algorithm.

5.3. Parallel Architecture

In a parallel implementation of the algorithm, each computer is responsible for one or more subregions. We consider the limiting case of one subregion per computer.

Each ray may in the worst case be passed across a subregion boundary after each iteration. The cost, π, of passing a ray is less than 1/5 the cost of one basic object intersection, assuming a 100-byte ray message can be copied in 400 cycles or less.

When ray tracing is carried out in parallel, the pixel energies are distributed among all the computers, and must be collected before they can be sent to a frame buffer. In the worst case, one half of all rays will contribute to pixel intensities, and if the ten-byte energy messages are sent across at most $C^{1/3}$ computers, at a cost of 50 cycles per message per computer, the energy summation cost, σ, is $25RC^{1/3}$ cycles for all computers, or roughly $25RC^{-5/3}$ for each computer. The ratio of σ to the ray tracing cost per computer is less than 1%, and therefore σ can be ignored.

Unlike σ, the ray passing overhead must be included in the cost of a parallel implementation. The worst case number of ray tracing operations performed by each computer is bounded by

$$\max_C \{\tau R_C(\kappa B_C + \beta + \pi)\}.$$

If a uniform distribution of load can be achieved, then the worst case number of ray tracing operations per computer is

$$\frac{\tau R(\kappa B + \beta C + \pi C)}{C^2}.$$

When we substitute the same values as before (again ignoring κ), with $C = 125$ and $\pi = 1/5$, we get

$$\frac{5 \times 4.6 \times 10^6 (10^3 + 4 \times 125 + .2 \times 125)}{125^2} \approx 2.3 \times 10^6.$$

This is three orders of magnitude faster than the standard algorithm, due to both the $C^{2/3}$ factor from the subdivision, and the linear speedup from the C computers.

In general, loads will not be completely uniform. The cost, ν, of this non-uniformity is proportional to the ratio of the maximum load for any computer to the average load over all computers. This changes the number of ray tracing operations to

$$\frac{\nu \tau R(\kappa B + \beta C + \pi C)}{C^2}.$$

Accurate estimates of ν will require more extensive analysis, although preliminary studies indicate that values below 2 can be achieved for some scenes.

We have demonstrated speedups of $S^{2/3}$ due to subdivision, and C due to parallelism, with some loss due to ν, κ, β, and π. These improvements will increase with scene complexity.

5.4. Comparison of Coupled and Frame-Parallel Implementations

In justifying a specialized architecture, we must show that the performance of the coupled parallel architecture will exceed that of an equivalent number of independent computers assigned to the problem. In particular, when producing films of computer-generated images, an obvious exploitation of parallelism is to assign to each computer the task of generating a single frame, and let them compute independently, using a serial implementation of our new algorithm, or the standard algorithm. We compare this alternate parallel strategy to our parallelization.

5.4.1. Storage Requirements

The new algorithm implemented on the parallel architecture requires considerably more storage than a standard implementation. With the frame-parallel implementation, each pixel's tree of rays may be traced separately, and by traversing each tree of rays in depth-first order, very few rays need to be maintained in storage. With our parallel implementation, the entire ray tracing tree is traced concurrently, and is traversed in breadth-first order.

All objects must generally be maintained in local storage for a frame-parallel implementation, as each ray must be tested against all objects. When the new algorithm is implemented on our coupled parallel architecture, all objects must be held in some local memory, but they are distributed among all computers; each computer has on the order of B/C objects in its memory, on the average.

Each computer of the coupled parallel architecture need only be configured with on the order of $1/C$ times the data memory of a single computer, with consequent savings in addressing and decoding hardware, and memory management tables. However, if frame-parallelism is used, the C independent computers would each require separate image stores and access to a full memory complement, so that C times as much total memory could be required. Were a memory hierarchy using disk backing store used, the additional cost of many disk units, as well as the time penalty of remote access would be incurred.

Therefore, the coupled parallel architecture can use less total storage than as many frame-parallel computers running serial algorithms.

5.4.2. Storage Structures

For independent computers, it is assumed that memory is implemented in the standard hierarchy of paging disk / main memory / (possibly) cache memory. As always, performance will be severely degraded if the program's working sets do not fit in the appropriate memory.

A dense interconnection of the coupled parallel architecture does not allow convenient communication between computers and disk memory. Assuming only computers at the boundaries of the architecture are connected to backing-store devices, most disk accesses must pass through several other computers. This of course increases the cost of paging, and in order for coupled parallel computers to achieve memory performance similar to that of the independent parallel computers, a relatively higher ratio of local memory to problem size is necessary; sufficient local memory is crucial to this architecture.

6. System Considerations

An initial implementation of a parallel system would consist of eight computers, each managing one or more subregions. With so few computers, each would communicate with only three others, instead of six, as discussed earlier. One computer would communicate with a host computer, which would provide interactive control and access to disk storage. Another computer would communicate either with a frame buffer, or with a host connected to the frame buffer.

Each computer would consist of a commercial microprocessor with floating point support, 1/4 to 1/2 megabytes of RAM, and six unidirectional byte-parallel ports (possibly with DMA access to memory). Those computers communicating with a host or frame buffer would have additional ports. Each computer would run with its own clock, independent of the others.

After performing studies with the initial implementation to verify costs of communication, redistribution, etc., a larger system could be constructed. With larger systems, each computer would communicate with six neighbors or peripheral devices, and dedicated frame buffers and disks would be used.

An obvious physical topology for such a system would be an array of cubical modules, appropriately interconnected. However, this topology would not allow convenient access to central computers for debugging during operation.

An alternate topology resembles the layout of the CDC 6600,[19] with a number of panels fanning out from a central core. Each panel would house several subregion computers and their cooling. Inter-panel communication would be routed through the core, and because the topology is relatively compact, inter-computer communication times should be small. If panels were attached to the core with hinges, they could be spread apart to allow a technician to access all computers during operation.

As an alternative to many medium-speed computers, a few very fast computers could be used, such as the multiprocessor Cray X/MP. A two-processor version of the algorithm would have multiple subregions managed by each processor. Inter-processor communication would make use of the high speed inter-CPU data paths available on the Cray X/MP. The extreme speed of the CPUs would allow studies to be performed in a reasonable period of time, including efficient simulations of different topologies.

6.1. Hardware Issues

The parallel architecture for this algorithm allows high bandwidth, inexpensive communication among the computers, tolerance of computer failures, and great flexibility in the choice of CPU.

Messages are sent between neighboring computers via dedicated links, which allows each communication to be independent of all other computers. Because links are not shared, all communication can run in parallel, and very simple hardware and protocols can be used for them.

This lack of sharing also allows failed or uncooperating computers to be ignored by other computers, so

failures are localized at the computer, and do not propagate into the system. Furthermore, there are simple extensions to the adaptive subdivision algorithm which allow subregions lost to failed computers to be adopted by healthy neighbors.

The algorithms executed in each computer are general purpose, and require no special-purpose hardware. Consequently, any processor with a large address space and support for floating point computations can be used. This would allow development of a prototype using commercial microprocessors, while leaving the option of later upgrading to more sophisticated microprocessors, other CPUs, or special purpose ray tracing hardware, as appropriate, with virtually no impact on software.

7. Conclusions

We have presented an adaptive subdivision algorithm and a parallel architecture for the image synthesis problem. The algorithm provides a roughly uniform distribution of load among the computers. Degradation in response to overloading is also part of the system, ensuring that cost/quality tradeoffs in image generation can easily be made. The architecture has a fixed polyhedral connectivity, with communication between computers via messages. Failures of computers are tolerated by the system without loss of accuracy, and without severe degradation of performance.

The algorithm can yield performance improvements on the order of $S^{2/3}$, and the parallelization itself will provide linear gains in the number of computers used (i.e. C computers can reduce actual compute time by a factor of C). Since messages are directly correlated with load,

Figure 3. Image generated by a preliminary simulator.

simulation and performance analysis of the system is simplified. We are carrying out such simulations at the current time (figure 3).

The adaptive nature of the system is a very important property, and we are examining other techniques for adaptive control of the synthesis problem. In addition, the synchronic nature of the parallelization may provide additional improvements.

It is interesting to note that a two dimensional analog of our algorithm/architecture can be applied to the projective style of image synthesis. While subdivision of projective solutions has been studied to a great extent, the adaptability of our algorithm and the high degree of parallelism in the architecture will provide new performance gains.

There are many issues left to be resolved, but some, such as antialiasing of the subdivision algorithm,[6] have already been addressed. The algorithm is also applicable to the general image synthesis problem, and we are investigating new methods for increased realism within this framework.

Acknowledgments

We would like to thank the anonymous referees, as well as Brain Barsky, Rick Speer, Steve Upstill, Helena Winkler, and Princess Minnie for their careful readings and helpful criticisms and comments on this paper. A special thanks to E.B. for the *Lemma in E♭ minor*, and a host of others, for wagging the appropriate tails.

This work was supported in part by the National Science Foundation, under grant number ECS–8204381, the Semiconductor Research Corporation under grant number 82–11–00£, and Lawrence Livermore National Laboratories under grant number LLL–4695505.

References

1. Peter R. Atherton, Kevin J. Weiler, and Donald P. Greenberg, "Polygon Shadow Generation," pp. 275-281 in *SIGGRAPH '78 Conference Proceedings*, ACM,(August, 1978).

2. Richard H. Bartels, John C. Beatty, and Brian A. Barsky, *An Introduction to the Use of Splines in Computer Graphics*, Technical Report No. UCB/CSD 83/136, Computer Science Division, Electrical Engineering and Computer Sciences Department, University of California, Berkeley, California, USA. (August, 1983). Also Tech. Report No. CS-83-9, Department of Computer Science, University of Waterloo, Waterloo, Ontario, Canada.

3. James F. Blinn, "A Generalization of Algebraic Surface Drawing," *ACM Transactions on Graphics*, Vol. 1, No. 3, July, 1982, pp. 235-256. Also published in *SIGGRAPH '82 Conference Proceedings* (Vol. 16, No. 3),

4. John G. Cleary, Brian Wyvill, Graham M. Birtwistle, and Reddy Vatti, *Multiprocessor Ray Tracing*, Technical Report No. 83/128/17, Department of Computer Science, The University of Calgary (October, 1983).

5. Franklin C. Crow, "Shadow Algorithms for Computer Graphics," pp. 242-248 in *SIGGRAPH '77 Conference Proceedings*, ACM,(July, 1977).

6. Mark E. Dippé, *Spatiotemporal Functional Prefiltering*, Ph.D. Thesis, University of California, Berkeley, California (1984).

7. Eugene Fiume, Alain Fournier, and Larry Rudolph, "A Parallel Scan Conversion Algorithm with Anti-Aliasing for a General-Purpose Ultracomputer: Preliminary Report," pp. 11-21 in *Proceedings Graphics Interface '83*, (May, 1983).

8. W. Randolph Franklin, "A Linear Time Exact Hidden Surface Algorithm," pp. 117-123 in *SIGGRAPH '80 Conference Proceedings*, ACM,(July, 1980).

9. Fuchs, H. and Poulton, J., "Pixel-Planes: A VLSI-Oriented Design for a Raster Graphics Engine," *VLSI Design*. No. 3, 1981, pp. 20-28.

10. Fussell, D. and Rathi, B., "A VLSI-Oriented Architecture for Real-Time Display of Shaded Polygons," pp. 373-380 in *Graphics Interface '82*, (1982).

11. Clark, James H., "The Geometry Engine: A VLSI System for Graphics," pp. 127-133 in *SIGGRAPH '82 Conference Proceedings*, (July, 1982).

12. Roy A. Hall and Donald P. Greenberg, "A Testbed for Realistic Image Synthesis," *IEEE Computer Graphics and Applications*, Vol. 3, No. 8, November, 1983, pp. 10-19.

13. James T. Kajiya, "New Techniques for Raytracing Procedurally Defined Objects," *ACM Transactions on Graphics*, Vol. 2, No. 3, July, 1983, pp. 161-181.

14. Hans P. Moravec, "3D Graphics and the Wave Theory," pp. 289-296 in *SIGGRAPH '81 Conference Proceedings*, (August, 1981).

15. H. Nishimura, H. Ohno, T. Kawata, I. Shirakawa, and K. Omura, "LINKS-1: A Parallel Pipelined Multimicrocomputer System for Image Creation," pp. 387-394 in *Proceedings of the 10th Symposium on Computer Architecture*, SIGARCH,(1983).

16. George Pólya and Gabor Szegö, *Problems and Theorems in Analysis I*, Springer-Verlag, New York (1972).

17. Steven M. Rubin and J. Turner Whitted, "A 3-Dimensional Representation for Fast Rendering of Complex Scenes," pp. 110-116 in *SIGGRAPH '80 Conference Proceedings*, ACM,(July, 1980).

18. Ivan E. Sutherland, Robert F. Sproull, and Robert A. Schumacker, "A Characterization of Ten Hidden Surface Algorithms," *ACM Computing Surveys*, Vol. 6, No. 1, March, 1974, pp. 1-55.

19. J. E. Thornton, *Design of a Computer: The Control Data 6600*, Scott, Foresman and Company, Glenview, Illinois (1970).

20. Michael Ullner, *Parallel Machines for Computer Graphics*, Ph.D. Thesis, California Institute of Technology, Pasadena, California (1983).

21. Weinberg, Richard, "Parallel Processing Image Synthesis and Anti-Aliasing," pp. 55-62 in *SIGGRAPH '81 Conference Proceedings*, (August, 1981).

22. J. Turner Whitted, "An Improved Illumination Model for Shaded Display," *Communications of the ACM*, Vol. 23, No. 6, June, 1980, pp. 343-349.

LINKS-1: A PARALLEL PIPELINED
MULTIMICROCOMPUTER SYSTEM FOR IMAGE CREATION

Hitoshi NISHIMURA, Hiroshi OHNO,
Toru KAWATA, Isao SHIRAKAWA, and Koichi OMURA

Department of Electronic Engineeing,
Osaka University, Yamada-Oka 2-1,
Suita, Osaka, 565 Japan

ABSTRACT

A multimicrocomputer system is described, stressing mainly software and hardware architectures, which has been constructed mainly for image creation. This system is distinctive mainly in that (i) 64 unit computers are interconnected with a root computer, each of equal performance, such that a number of unit computers constitute a pipelined computer and such pipelined computers work in parallel, all controlled by the root computer, and (ii) an intercomputer memory swapping unit is introduced, which is to be linked with a pair of unit computers to transfer a great amount of data at a time from one to the other through the use of a bus exchange switch.

1. INTRODUCTION

Applications of computer technologies to image creation and processing have attracted a growing interest in a variety of areas, and a technological field of computer graphics has been given an assured status.

In this field, great efforts have been made to construct those software algorithms for creating various effects of images, which operate on conventional computer systems. Image creation algorithms consist mainly in computing the shading effects (intensity and color to display) of each pixel on a graphics screen associated with given objects, light sources, and a view-point in a three-dimensional space. It should be noted here that once necessary data are given, the shading effects of each pixel can be computed independently. Thus, image creation can be implemented typically through a variety of parallel processing schemes.

A great amount of computer concepts have been proposed and extensively developed for parallel processing. These are classified into the following three types [1].
   1° Computer Array (SOLOMON, ILLIAC IV, PEPE, STARAN, etc.),
   2° Pipelined Vector Computer (CDC STAR 100, CYBER 205, CRAY 1, etc.),
   3° Interconnection of Multicomputers (C.mmp, Cm*, etc.).

Computation for three-dimensional image creation consists primarily of vector and matrix calculus, in which the dimension is ordinarily very low. Hence, parallel computer systems of types 1° and 2° are not fit for such computation, since the CPU utilization ratio is not so high that the cost performance can be much expected. Thus, parallel computer systems of type 3° are most suitable for image creation. However, it should be pointed out that the interconnection scheme adopted such as in Cm* has some defects in that the packet communication through the use of a common bus, called the intercluster bus or map bus [2], can afford neither to transfer such a great amount of data as are necessary in image creation nor to pipeline the image creaing process, and hence it might result in a heavy overhead associated with bus conflict and data processing such as data partition and data distribution.

Motivated by this consideration, we have constructed a multimicrocomputer system for image creation, which is distinctive mainly in that
   (i) 64 unit computers are interconnected with a root computer such that a number of unit computers constitute a pipelined computer and such pipelined computers work in parallel, all controlled by the root computer, where the number of pipelines and the length of each pipiline are to be controlled dynamically by the root computer according to processing situations, and
   (ii) an intercomputer memory swapping unit is newly introduced, which is to be linked with a pair of microcomputers to transfer a great amount of data at a time from one to the other by means of a bus exchange switch.

In this paper, we first describe this multimicrocomputer system stressing mainly software and hardware architectures, and then analyzes the performance of image creation programs run on this computer system.

2. ARCHITECHTURAL CONSIDERATION

Parallel processing schemes may be successfully introduced into a multimicrocomputer system at the program level and function level, but those endeavored at lower levels might incur an excessive overhead especially with respect to communication. Thus, parallelism schemes are to be introduced by means of

"LINKS-1: A Parallel Pipelined Multicomputer System for Image Creation" by H. Nishimura, H. Ohno, T. Kawata, I. Shirakawa, and K. Omura from *Proceedings of the 10th Symposium on Computer Architecture*, 1983, pages 387-394. Copyright 1983, Association for Computing Machinery, Inc., reprinted by permission.

(a) partition of data such that each partitioned subset is to be processed independently of others, and

(b) pipelining a computation process such that a sequence of functional operations are to be implemented on a pipeline.

We first brief parallel processing schemes to be adopted according to (a) and (b) stated above.

[A] Parallel Processing

Fig. 1 shows a schematic model of parallel computation, where OM_1, OM_2,..., OM_n denote operation modules (or operators) working in parallel. The distribution module (or distributor) DM partitions programs/data and distributes them to operators, and then activates all operators OM_i and the collection module (or collector) CM by commands O_i and O_c, respectively, at a time. Each operator OM_i processes distributed data according to distributed programs, and sends signal a_i to the collector CM at the termination of processing. Once a_i is active, collector CM begins to collect output data of operators OM_i, where it should be noted that there may happen a case when collector CM collects output data from two or more operators OM_i, at the same time.

[B] Pipelining

When there are classes of data of the same structure, to which a procedure is to be applied repeatedly, we can decompose the procedure into a sequence of phases and construct a pipeline as illustrated in Fig. 2 such that each phase i can be implemented by an operator OM_i. In this pipeling scheme, if the processing time of each operator OM_i is estimated, activation by command O_i may be scheduled; however, if only the function of each OM_i is specified but the processing time varies according to given data, activation can not be scheduled, and hence each operator on the pipeline may have to be activated asynchronously.

Based on these considerations, we have constructed a parallel pipelined multimicrocomputer system of the structure schematically shown in Fig. 3, where operators OM_i work in parallel for vertical data flow, while they work sequentially for horizontal data flow to constitute a pipeline.

In the following, image creation process with the best use of these parallel processing schemes is to be described.

3. HARDWARE CONFIGURATION

An outline of the hardware configuration is shown in Fig. 4, where the root computer RC and node computers NC_i play the roles of distributor DM and operators OM_i, respectively, each constructed of a unit computer of the structure as illustrated in Fig. 5. Specifically, each unit computer is synthesized of a control processing unit (CU) with Z8001 (see Fig. 6), an arithmetic processing unit (APU) with i8086/8087 (see Fig. 7), a 1 MB memory unit (MU) (see Fig. 8), I/O unit (I/OU) (see Fig. 9), and an intercomputer memory swapping unit (IMSU) (see Fig. 10), each packaged on a two- or four-layer printed wiring board. A Zilog System 8000 computer in charge of I/O control of the whole system, is connected to the parallel port of RC by a parallel communication line, through which programs/data and computation results are transferred to and from RC, respectively.

We now touch on units CU, APU, I/OU, and IMSU of RC and NC_i in the following:

CU executes address calculation, data transfer, I/O data conversion, and commucication control, by means of Z8001.

APU conducts floating point calculation necessary for image creation by means of i8086/8087.

Theses two units communicate commands/data to each other through a common memory (APU memory) as shown in Fig. 7, where it should be added that Z8001 controls APU in the following way: It first loads programs/data for i8086/8087 onto the common memory, turns the bus switch to i8086/8087, and activates i8086 by a reset or an interrupt signal. Then, i8086/8087 initiates calculation, puts the result onto the common memory or Block Data port, sends a completion signal or an interrupt signal to Z8001, and then halts.

I/OU has an I/O port to be connected optionally to a peripheral, through the use of which monitoring and debugging for RC and NC is to be performed.

We now describe IMSU which has been newly devised and incorporated into our computer system for bus exchanging. IMSU is to exchange programs/data both between RC and each NC_i and between each adjacent pair of NC_i and NC_{i+1}, as shown in Fig. 4. Each IMSU has two memory areas which are connected to a pair of CU's through a bus exchange switch, as illustrated in Fig. 10. Let $IMSU_i$ be the one linked with CU's of RC and NC_i, and consider a case when data are to be transferred from RC to NC_i. In this case, RC first transfers data to the memory area connected to CU of RC. When NC_i becomes idle, it sends a bus exchange signal to $IMSU_i$. Then, $IMSU_i$ exchanges memory areas of RC and NC_i by turning over the bus exchange switch.

In a case when images to be created are so complex that image processing is to be implemented by a number of NC's in parallel, data associated with the corresponding part of objects have to be transferred to those NC's. To this end, IMSU is provided with the broadcasting function as illustrated in Fig. 11. As can be seen from Figs. 4 and 10, it may often happen that the capacity of memory connected to Z8001 of RC exeeds its addressing capability (i.e. 8 MB). To cope with this, as shown in Fig. 12, RC is linked with 64 IMSU's through a bus switch scheme of 8 banks, each of which is composed of memory of 8 IMSU's.

4. PARALLEL PIPELINED PROCESSING SCHEME OF IMAGE CREATION

Three-dimensional image creation process can be decomposed into two: hidden line surface elimination process f_1 and shading process f_2 [6], and the former in turn can be decomposed into sorting process f_{11} and ray tracing process f_{12}. These processes f_{11}, f_{12}, and f_2 are applied sequentially in this order, and hence these can be set up on a pipeline. Considering that image data for each frame can be partitioned into a number of classes such that each can be processed in parallel, we can see that image creating process is to be implemented through a variety of parallel pipeling mechanism.

To explain this in more detail, consider a simple example as follows: Given RC together with six NC's, construct two pipelines controlled by RC such that three NC's are set up on each pipeline with functions f_{11}, f_{12}, and f_2, as shown in Fig. 13(a), and let RC partition a set of the whole image data for each frame equally into two subsets such that each is to be processed on a distinct pipeline. Assume that a sequence D_1, D_2, D_3, and D_4 of image data, with each D_i for one frame, are given in this order and RC partitions each D_i into D_{i1} and D_{i2}. Then, this sequence of data are processed in this parallel pipelined scheme, step by step, as illustrated in Fig. 13, where DC and FM denote Data Collector and Frame Memory.

5. PERFORMANCE ANALYSIS

First, we analyzes the parallel processing performance of our multimicrocomputer system. Let m denote the number of node computers NC_i participating in the image creation process; and let t_d be the time of distributing image data from RC to all NC_i, t_p the maximum of all processing times of NC_i, and t_c the time of collecting the results from all NC_i to DC.

Assume that RC partitions image data without overlapping, and then distributes these partitioned data to NC_i. In this case, since there is no resource conflict and the overhead due to communication protocols is negligibly small, t_d is almost independent of m. Moreover, even if RC partitions image data for one frame with overlapping and then distributes them to NC_i, the overlapped part of data are to be distributed through the use of broadcasting facilities, and hence in this case, too, the increase in t_d may be supposed to be independent of m. On the other hand, it can be readily seen that t_c is also independent of m. Now, we consider the processing time of NC_i: Let T_p be the processing time of image creation for one frame when only one NC is used. Assume that the image creation process is partitioned equally into m such that each is to be implemented in parallel by a distinct NC, then the processing time t_{pi} of each NC_i is given by $t_{pi} = T_p/m$. Thus, $\bar{t}_p \triangleq T_p/m$ may be regarded as an estimated value for $t_p = \max t_{pi}$, and hence an estimated value for the total processing time $t \triangleq t_p + t_d + t_c$ may be given by $\bar{t} \triangleq T_p/m + t_d + t_c$.

To see how t approaches $\bar{t}$, we have conducted an experiment. Fig. 14(a) shows the output image used in the example, for which measured values for the total processing time t are plotted as shown in Fig. 14(b). It can be observed from the figure that the processing time t varies just in accordance with the expected value $\bar{t}$.

Next, we analyze the performance of the pipelining mechanism adopted in image creation. As stated in Section 4, the process of three-dimensional image creation can be decomposed into three stages, i.e. sorting f_{11}, ray tracing f_{12}, and shading f_2, which are to be executed in such a way as demonstrated in Fig. 13. Specifically, f_{11} is to search for all the objects supposed to be penetrated by a given collimation ray (see Fig. 15) and then to sort them; f_{12} is to seek the points at which a given collimation ray intersects those objects found in

f_{11}, to calculate distances from those points thus sought to the view point, and then to single out the one nearest to the view point; and f_2 is to compute the shading effects of the corresponding pixel on a graphics screen, based on image data of surface status concerning the nearest intersecting point determined in f_{12}.

We have prepared for the performance analysis of the pipelining mechanism the simplest type of a three-stage pipelined computer model in which only three unit computers are used, each in charge of fulfilling one of processing stages f_{11}, f_{12}, and f_2; and then applied to it two image data, DATA1 and DATA2, for which output images are obtained as depicted in Fig. 16. Table 1 shows processing times T_p and T_π run on one unit computer and the pipeline model, respectively. Now, assume

Table 1. Professing Times

proc. time	DATA1	DATA2
T_p	480 sec	624 sec
T_π	272 sec	368 sec

an n-stage pipelined computer in which n processing stages are to be implemented on a pipeline, and define a degree of parallelism of this computer by the following formula

$$\frac{T_p - T_\pi}{(n-1) \cdot T_p/n} \times 100 \ (\%).$$

Then, apply this formula to T_p and T_π of Table 1, and we have the degree of parallelism of 65% for DATA1 of Fig. 16(a) and that of 61% for DATA2 of Fig. 16(b). Furthermore, associated with DATA1, we have clocked waiting times between adjacent stages as shown in Table 2, and counted the program size of each stage as shown in Table 3. As may be seen from Tables 2 and 3, the processing

Table 2. Waiting Times

	f_{11}	f_{12}	f_2
waiting for input	——	1.7 s	27.5 s
waiting for output	92.6 s	10.1 s	——

Table 3. Program Size

f_{11}	f_{12}	f_2
3,164 B	4,232 B	3,560 B

load for f_{12} is dominant over the others. Thus, in order to improve the degree of parallelism for our pipelining scheme, the processing load for f_{11}, f_{12}, and f_2 should be more balanced. To this end, two approaches are to be considered: One is to arrange a set of objects intersecting complicatedly each other so that the nearest point hit by the collimation ray can be more easily computed, and the other is to provide a hardware facility designed dedicatedly to reduce the processing load for f_{12}. Thus, improvement is continuing more on sophisticated hardware and software facilities for the pipelined processing of image creation.

6. CONCLUDING REMARKS

We have described a parallel pipelined multimicrocomputer system intended mainly for image creation. As can be seen from the experiment, the processing time is much in accordance with the expected value in the parallel pipelined scheme, and this fact implies that the hardware is constructed in such a way that the overhead which may occur due to the introduction of parallelism can be retained considerably low. Finally, it can be much expected of this system that the performance is to be raised to cope with a variety of applications of image creation by means of more sophisticated parallel processing schemes associated with partitioning programs/data, controlling the number of pipelines and the length of each pipeline, etc.

ACKNOWLEDGEMENT: We wish to express our gratitude to our colleagues and students, Y. Egi, H. Deguchi, H. Yoshimura, M. Hirai, T. Nakayama, T. Kawai, T. Tatsumi, S. Yamashita, M. Nishida, T. Uchimura, T. Naito, S. Tanaka, N. Funato, M. Nasu, and T. Nakanishi, who have contributed instructive ideas, precious time, and unstinted energy toward the construction of this system. We are very grateful to Y. Fukushima, N. Yura, K. Ichihashi, T. Tsukada, M. Aizawa, and H. Kobayashi, Far East Laboratories, Ltd., S. Misaka, S. Yoshida, and Y. Kishimoto, Sharp Corp., T. Sagishima, A. Nishimura, and N. Hidaka, Matsushita Elec. Ind. Co., Ltd., and H. Takada, NTT, for providing us with guidance and support. Thanks are also due to M. Yamamoto, a motion picture producer, for providing us with inspiration and encouragement.

REFERENCES
[1] R.W. Hockney and C.R. Jessope, Parallel Computers, Adam Hilger, Bristol, 1981.
[2] M. Satyanarayanan, Multiprocessors: A Comarative Study, Prentice-Hall, 1980.
[3] J. Backus, "Can programming be liberated from the von Neumann style? A functional style and its algebra of programs," Comm. ACM, 21, pp. 613-641, 1978.
[4] T. Whitted, "An improved illumination model for shaded display," Comm. ACM, 23, pp. 343-349, 1980.
[5] H. Yoshimura, H. Nishimura, T. Kawata, I. Shirakawa, and K. Omura,"Image creation algorithms in LINKS-1 computer graphics system,"Mono. Inform. Proc. Soc. Japan, 24-5, 1982 (in Japanese).
[6] W.M. Newman and R.F. Sproll, Principles of Interactive Computer Graphics, 2nd ed., McGraw-Hill, New York, 1979.

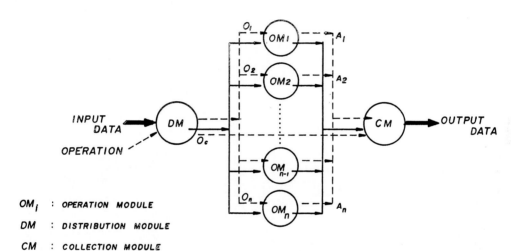

OM_i : OPERATION MODULE

DM : DISTRIBUTION MODULE

CM : COLLECTION MODULE

Fig. 1. Parallel Processing Structure by Means of Programs/Data Partition

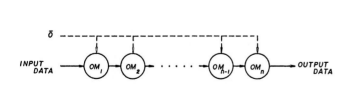

Fig. 2. Pipelined Processing Structure

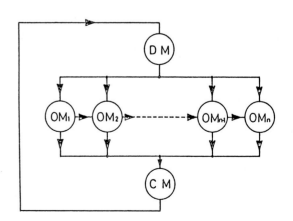

Fig. 3. Parallel Pipelined Processing Structure

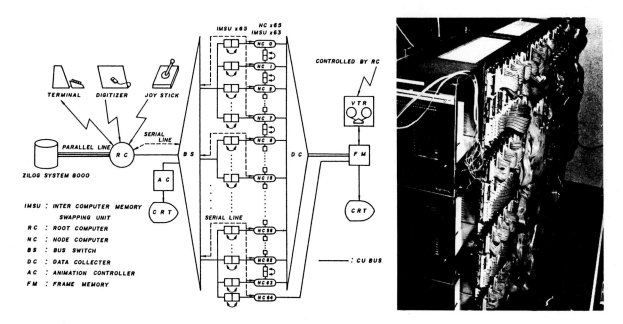

Fig. 4.   Hardware Configuration

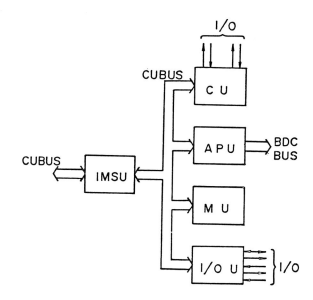

Fig. 5.   Block Diagram of Unit Computer

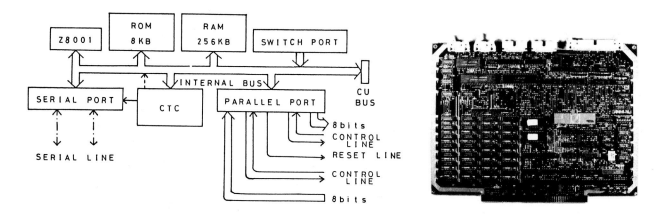

Fig. 6.   Functional Block Diagram of CU Board

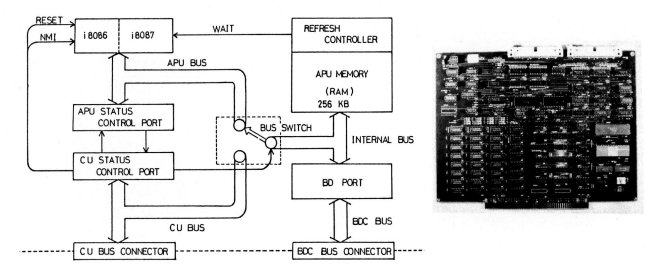

Fig. 7. Functional Block Diagram of APU Board

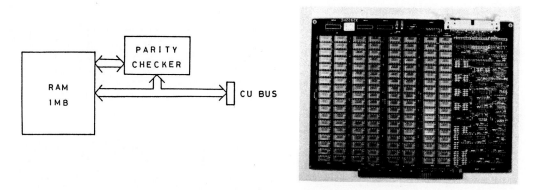

Fig. 8. Functional Block Diagram of MU Board

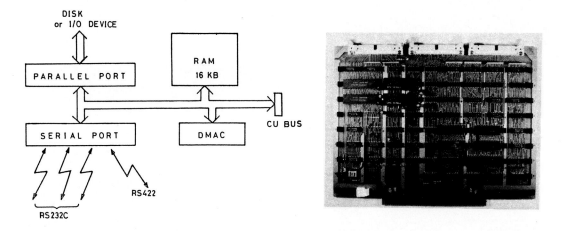

Fig. 9. Functional Block Diagram of I/OU Board

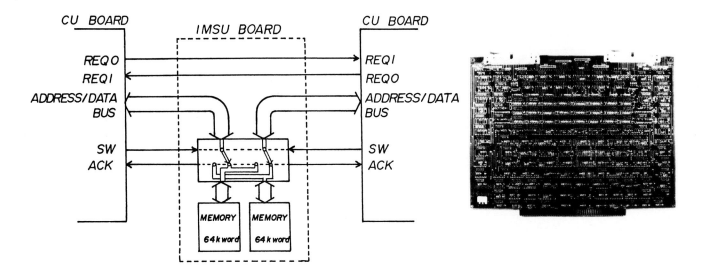

Fig. 10. Functional Block Diagram of IMSU Board

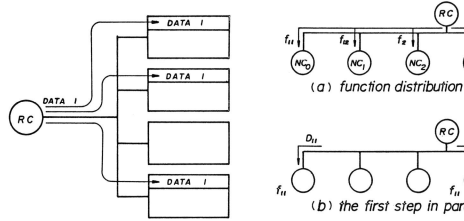

Fig. 11. Broadcasting

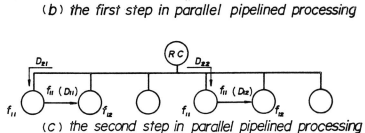

(a) function distribution

(b) the first step in parallel pipelined processing

(c) the second step in parallel pipelined processing

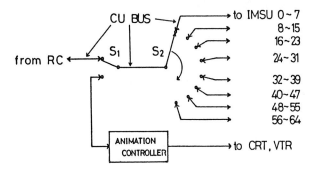

Fig. 12. Bus Switch

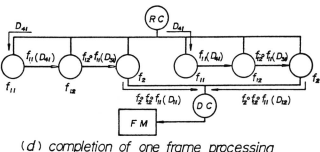

(d) completion of one frame processing

Fig. 13. Example of Parallel Pipelined Processing Scheme

(a) Output Image

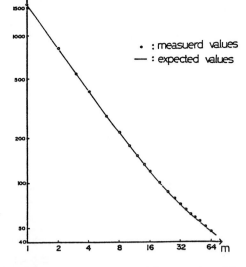

(b) Measured and Expected Processing Times

Fig. 14. Output Image and Processing Time

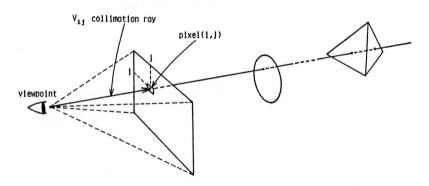

Fig. 15. Ray Tracing

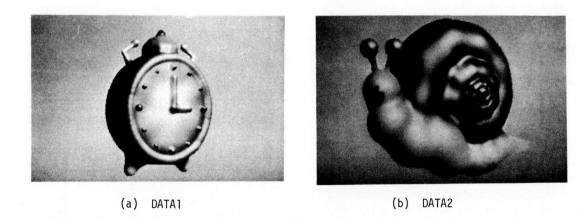

(a) DATA1   (b) DATA2

Fig. 16. Output Images

327

The Feasibility of a VLSI Chip for Ray Tracing Bicubic Patches

Ron Pulleyblank, HP Laboratories*

John Kapenga, Western Michigan University**

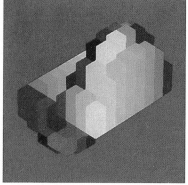

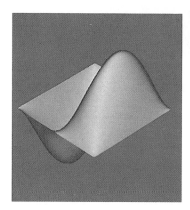

In this article we explore the possibility of a VLSI chip for ray tracing bicubic patches in Bezier form. The purpose of the chip is to calculate the intersection point of a ray with the bicubic patch to a specified level of accuracy, returning parameter values (u,v) specifying the location of the intersection on the patch, and a parameter value, t, which specifies the location of the intersection on the ray. The intersection is calculated by successively subdividing the patch and computing the intersection of the ray with a bounding box of each subpatch until the bounding volume meets the accuracy requirement. There are two operating modes: one in which only the nearest intersection is found, and another in which all intersections are found. This algorithm (and the chip) correctly handle the difficult cases of the ray tangentially intersecting a planar patch and intersections of the ray at a silhouette edge of the patch. Estimates indicate that such a chip could be implemented in 2-micron NMOS (N-type metal oxide semiconductor) and could compute patch-ray intersections at the rate of one every 15 microseconds for patches that are prescaled and specified to a 12-bit fixed point for each of the x, y, and z components. A version capable of handling 24-bit patches could compute patch/ray intersections at the rate of one every 140 microseconds. Calculations of the normal at the intersection point could be performed with the addition of nine scalar subtractions and six scalar multiplies. Images drawn using a software version of the algorithm are presented and discussed.

Ray tracing is the most powerful technique used to create very realistic images[1] and to compute properties of such solids as volume and moments in solid modeling systems.[2] Frequently these systems are restricted to objects described by polygons or quadratic surfaces and objects that are compositions of them. Curved surfaces can be described efficiently by bicubic patches,[3] which specify points on the surface with a function that is cubic in each of its two parameters, u and v. These patches are determined by a collection of 16 (three-dimensional) control points. Because these patches can be pieced together while maintaining second-order continuity at the boundaries, they are very useful for modeling smooth surfaces.

Bicubic patches are frequently displayed by decomposing them into polygons before further processing or by directly computing ray/patch intersections. Methods for computing these intersections based on root finding are complex, and most require great care in selecting starting points to avoid numerical stability problems.[4-7] This results in long computation times for typical images, which may require a hundred million ray/patch intersections. Subdivision techniques for bicubic patches have been used widely for display purposes[8-10] and for processing before beginning a search for roots.[5,7] Whit-

*This work has been supported in part by a grant from STW (The Netherlands) under the Megabit program.

**On leave to the Technical University of Delft, The Netherlands.

Reprinted fom *IEEE Computer Graphics and Applications*, Volume 7, Number 3, March 1987, pages 33-44. Copyright © 1987 by The Institute of Electrical and Electronics Engineers, Inc.

Finding Patch/Ray Intersections

Initialize Testpatch Stack
REPEAT
- Pop Testpatch from the Testpatch Stack
- Subdivide Testpatch into 4 Subpatches
- Compute Bounding Box for Each Subpatch
- Compute Intersections of Ray with Bounding Box Planes
- **IF** Ray Hits Subpatch's Bounding Box
    THEN
    - **IF** Termination Requirement Met
        THEN
        - Subpatch is an Intersection
        ELSE
        - Place Subpatch on Teststack
UNTIL Teststack is Empty

Figure 1. Finding patch/ray intersections.

ted [1] and Lane and Riesenfeld[11] have also used subdivision for direct calculation of ray/patch intersections in software.

So far the long delays due to the computational burden of the ray/object intersections have restricted the usefulness of both ray tracing and bicubic patches in computer graphics and solid modeling systems. Speedups of ray tracing have been achieved using hierarchical data structures and preprocessing to eliminate unnecessary intersection calculations.[12-16] Vector processors [17] have been used to speed up ray tracing, and thought has been given to how parallel processing,[18-20] and special-purpose VLSI[21] chips could be used to enhance ray tracing performance.

Subdivision of Bezier surfaces is well suited for VLSI implementation because it requires only additions and divisions by two, when restricted appropriately. Thus we have selected it to compute ray/patch intersections in what follows. The goal is to reduce the time required for ray/patch intersections to something that would make using patches in an interactive environment much more attractive. An additional goal is to accomplish this with relatively simple hardware. This approach to computing ray/patch intersections may also be attractive as a software technique when implemented in an integer arithmetic form.

Algorithm

The algorithm relies on the following few facts: Bezier curves are easily subdivided into halves,[10-11] requiring only additions and divisions by two of the control points, of which there are four in the cubic case. This basic oper-

ation is used repeatedly to subdivide a bicubic patch into quadrants.[11] The control points can be used to form a convex volume with polygonal sides, i.e., the convex hull of the control points, which completely contains the patch. A very simple but looser bounding volume can be found by taking the maximum and minimum of the x, y, and z components of the control points to form a rectangular bounding box that is aligned with the coordinate axes, and it is this method that is actually used in this algorithm. Six multiplications and 11 subtractions can be used to compute the intersection of a ray with each of these bounding planes and examine the results to determine if the ray intersects the bounding volume.

With these basic ideas in mind, the algorithm can be stated as follows:

To find the intersection of a patch with the ray, the patch is broken into four subpatches, each of whose bounding boxes are computed and tested for an intersection with the ray. If the ray hits the bounding box of a subpatch, and the termination conditions are not met— i.e., the patch is not smaller than a specified accuracy requirement and the maximum level of subdivision has not been reached—the subpatch is placed on a stack to be processed further. This process proceeds in a depth-first search for the subpatches whose bounding boxes intersect the ray and which meet the accuracy or maximum subdivision criteria. These "result" patches specify the intersection points. The (u,v) coordinates of the intersection point on the original patch and the parameter, t, which specifies the intersection point on the ray, are returned as results. Figure 1 provides a pseudocode statement of this algorithm.

Normally one bit of accuracy is obtained for each level of subdivision, and the computation is carried out with more bits than the maximum level of subdivision.

It is possible that more than one "result" patch is found for a single intersection. This is the case when the ray intersection is close to the boundary between subpatches or when the ray is parallel to and contained in a planar portion of the patch.

Two approaches may be taken to deal with this situation: The fastest and simplest approach is to report only the "result" patch nearest to the ray origin, i.e., the one with the smallest t as the answer. If more than one fits this criterion, an arbitrary patch may be selected, or all "result" patches that are "nearest" can be reported, leaving it to the host either to average these "results" or to compute the bounding box that contains all of the "results." Searching for the "nearest" intersection is well suited to displaying patches but forgoes the possibility of computing all the intersections of a ray and a patch as would be necessary when computing volumes or computing the portion of a ray "on" a surface.

A second approach is to report all "result" subpatches, leaving it to the host to group contiguous "results" together to form intersections, and to summarize the resulting intersections either by averaging the "results" or computing the bounding volume of the "results."

If only the nearest intersection is to be found, a faster operation would be to discard all subpatches that are hit by the ray beyond the bounding volume of the current nearest "result" patch, and sort, nearest to the origin first, those that remain before placing them on the test stack. The nearest "result" patch is updated when a closer one is found. The technique of sorting objects before placing them on a queue for further testing when searching for a closest result has been used previously, e.g., Kajiya.[22]

So that a restricted number of bits is used effectively, the patch control points are assumed to be presented to the chip in a coordinate system whose origin is at the minimum bounding box corner. This makes all control points positive numbers. They are also assumed to be scaled so that the largest control-point component is less than one and greater than or equal to one half. Effectively they are in "block" floating-point format with all bits used for the mantissa. The ray origin is also presented in this coordinate system, and it has been moved to where it intersects the bounding box of the original patch. The ray direction vector is normalized to one.

The Bezier form of the bicubic patch was chosen because these control points form a tighter bounding volume than do the corresponding B-spline (floating-end conditions) control points of the same patch. This is not a limitation, because patches can easily be converted between the Bezier, B-spline, and Hermite forms.[3]

Organization for VLSI implementation

The overall block diagram for the VLSI implementation of the chip is shown in Figure 2. The following considerations guided its organization: A bit serial implementation was chosen because of the large number of additions that are required. A parallel computation in x, y, and z was chosen because it operates three times as fast as a serial version, and there appears to be space enough on the chip to allow it.

The algorithm requires the saving of intermediate patches whose bounding boxes are hit by the ray and therefore require further subdivision. If the control points of these intermediate patches are to be saved, a very large control- point memory is required. It is possible, however, to regenerate these intermediate patches from the original while saving only the "path" to the subpatch from the original. This "path" is simply the (u,v) coordinates (binary fixed point) of the lower left corner of the subpatch on the original patch. As will become apparent as the discussion unfolds, a hybrid of these two approaches is most attractive.

A circuit that subdivides a patch and selects one of the resulting quadrants, or is bypassed completely, can be used in a chain to reproduce any intermediate patch. The resulting patch can then be fed to a subdivide circuit that produces the control points of all of its quadrants, which are, in turn, fed to four identical networks that test if the ray "hits" that subpatch. Each of these networks computes the bounding box of its input patch and the intersection points of the ray with the planes of the bounding box, checks the results for an intersection of the ray and the bounding box, and checks to see if the accuracy criteria are met. The ray "hit" and "accuracy met" information for each quadrant of the test patch is used to decide whether any of these subpatches should be saved for further testing. The "paths" to these patches that require further testing, together with the depth to which they have been divided, are pushed onto a stack for further testing.

If all test patches are produced directly from the original patch, then a subdivide chain that can divide to the maximum depth in a single pass is required. The maximum subdivision depth is approximately the number of bits of accuracy required, so the chain needs to be very long unless the accuracy required is small. This, of course, requires sizable chip area, but also time. The reason is that each subdivide and select circuit has a cascade of six additions, which may produce six carries, which when operating bit serially require six additional clock cycles for every subdivision stage in the chain. These clock cycles appear as buffer bits between successive patches to be subdivided.

The problem can be alleviated by not always generating a test patch directly from the original patch in one pass but saving the control points at selected intermediate points and then generating the test patch from the saved points. The control-point memory in this case is organized as a stack to allow for the storage of intermediate control-point arrays, and the length of the subdivide chain is $Ds = (D-1)/N+1$ where D is the maximum depth to which a patch must be subdivided and N is the number of subdivision stages. If a patch has been further subdivided Ds levels from the last set of stored control points, and it requires further testing, the control points of its immediate parent could be pushed onto the "control point" stack, and the path from these stored control points to it could also be saved. Further refinement would proceed by subdividing these intermediate control points.

With this organization, the time penalty is paid only for the additional levels of subdivision from the stored control points. Another benefit is that the test-stack memory required is smaller because only the path from the saved control points need be kept on the test stack. Additional patch memory is required for each stage, but there is a net savings in area for the proper choice of the number of stages.

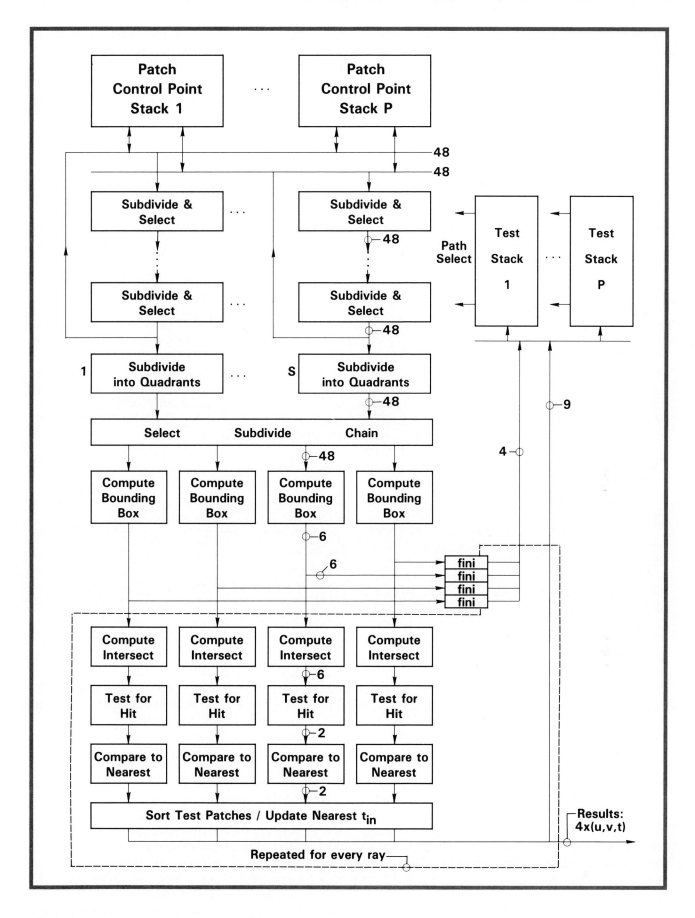

Figure 2. System block diagram.

IEEE CG&A

The time lost because of the need to provide buffer bits between successive patch subdivisions can be eliminated as far as the rest of the chip is concerned by duplicating the subdivide chain. Thus, when buffer bits are being clocked into one subdivide chain, a new computation can begin in a duplicate chain, and a steady stream of significant subdivided patch bits may be presented to the circuitry that computes bounding boxes.

The system can achieve high throughput by pipelining, but the depth-first search requires the result of a computation before a decision can be made on which way to proceed. Certainly the next subdivision can be started before the previous result is available, but by the time the last subdivision circuit is reached, the result must be there. Efficient use of the pipe can be maintained by having several patches on the chip and working on them in rotation. If the time to initiate a computation on each of the patches is greater than the delay, there will be no decrease in throughput. Additional memory for the control points and test stack for each of the patch intersection computations being carried out on the chip is required.

If the chip is seeking only "nearest" intersections, and if the current patch is a "result— i.e., if it is a "hit" that satisfies the accuracy or maximum subdivision criteria—then a comparison of the newest t value(s) for entering the bounding volume, t_in, is made with the t_in for the current "nearest result" patch. Also, the current "nearest" t_in is updated. Only hits that are closer than the "nearest result" are reported as "hits" in this mode of operation.

The chip, as described so far, carries out intersection calculations for a single ray against a patch, but it can also test the patch against a list of rays if the "compute intersection," "test for hit," and "compare to nearest" circuits are replicated for each ray. This is a useful addition for primary rays, which are highly coherent, and for multiple rays used to perform antialiasing.

This concludes the discussion of the overall block diagram shown in Figure 2. A discussion of each of the system blocks is provided in the Appendix.

Communication with the host

The I/O bandwidth requirements for this chip are very small. If L designates the number of bits used to represent each patch control point component, then it requires roughly L×L serial clock cycles to find an intersection and 48L bits to specify a new patch, 6L bits for a new ray, and 3L bits to report a result. If it is assumed that patches are kept "on board" and rays are fed in and intersections returned, and it is assumed that the I/O clock runs at one-half the serial clock rate, then 2 pins can handle the required bandwidth for L=12 and 1 pin is required for L=24. If a new patch is required in the same time, 8 additional pins are required to handle the bandwidth for L=12, and 4 additional pins are needed

for L=24. These numbers are very reasonable, so there is no cause for concern that lack of I/O bandwidth will reduce the effectiveness of the chip.

On this point, very little attention has been given to specifying exactly how the chip should communicate with its environment. The purpose so far has been to consider how one might compute patch/ray intersections with VLSI, and establish an idea of the performance and required complexity of the resulting chip. The next step is to use this information to design a system that could effectively use this chip, or better, many of these chips, to provide a powerful graphics and/or solid modeling workstation. With this clarified idea of how the chip is to be used, an intelligent choice of interface can be made.

Chip size and performance estimates

To get a feeling for how realistic it is to implement the circuit in VLSI and to get an idea of its performance, we estimated area and speed for implementation by a fast, highly integrated process, but one that is definitely out of the experimental stage. A 2-micron NMOS process was selected for the exercise. The following areas were assumed for the required circuits:

Circuit	Area (square microns)
full adder	900
half adder	450
dynamic shift register bit	300
static shift register bit	375
2:1 multiplexer	225

We used a serial clock rate of 20 megahertz and a whole chip was taken to be 36 square millimeters (0.056 square inch). No attempt was made to make a detailed estimate of the area required for data routing and control, although the serial data formula simplifies routing and the control is thought to be relatively simple. Instead we assumed that roughly half the chip would be required for routing, I/O, and control.

Rough estimates for the rate at which ray/patch intersections are calculated are provided by multiplying the average time to subdivide a patch once by the ratio of the total number of times the patch must be subdivided to the number of patch intersections found, an experimentally determined number. If delay time limits the intersection calculation rate, the average time to subdivide a patch is the delay time divided by the number of patch intersections simultaneously carried out on the chip.

However, if subdivide time is the limiting factor, the average time to subdivide a patch once is $\max((L+3\times Ds)/S, L+X)$ clock cycles for S subdivide chains where L is the number of bits per patch control-point component and X is the number of extra bits used to control round-off error.

Two examples are presented: one that corresponds to a level of accuracy relevant for display purposes, and the other a higher accuracy computation that might be required in a solid modeling context.

Example I		
Accuracy suitable for display purposes		
L	12	bits per control point component
X	0	extra bits to control truncation error
D	9	subdivisions maximum
N	2	stages of subdivision
Ds	5	subdivisions per stage maximum
S	3	subdivision chains
P	11	simultaneous patch/ray computations
R	4	rays tested against each patch

The average time required to compute a patch/ray intersection is estimated to be 15 microseconds, limited by the delay time required to subdivide the patch. In this example the chip is capable of simultaneously searching for the intersections of the patch with four different rays, which could possibly improve the intersection calculation rate to one every 3.7 microseconds.

System block	Area
patch memory	4.75
test stack memory	1.93
storage for ray parameters	0.11
storage for nearest t_in	0.20
storage for accuracy parameters	0.05
path selectors	0.07
patch selectors	0.18
subdivide chains	3.28
subdivide chain select	0.06
compute bounding box	2.20
compute intersection	1.49
test for hit	0.55
test for complete	0.02
sort t_in	0.19
compare to nearest hit	0.01
total area (sq mm)	15.
percentage of 36 sq mm chip	42.

Example II		
Higher accuracy		
L	24	bits per control point component
X	0	extra bits to control truncation error
D	21	subdivisions maximum
N	3	stages of subdivision
Ds	8	subdivisions per stage maximum
S	1	subdivision chains
P	6	simultaneous patch/ray computations
R	1	ray tested against each patch

The average time required to compute a patch/ray intersection is estimated to be 140 microseconds, limited by the time required to subdivide the patch.

System block	Area
patch memory	7.78
test stack memory	2.97
storage for ray parameters	0.05
storage for nearest t_in	0.05
storage for accuracy parameters	0.05
path selectors	0.01
patch selectors	0.03
subdivide chains	1.84
subdivide chain select	0.02
compute bounding box	4.10
compute intersection	0.72
test for hit	0.25
test for complete	0.01
sort t_in	0.08
compare to nearest hit	0.00
total area (sq mm)	18.
percentage of 36 sq mm chip	50.

Images

Identical perspective views of a single bicubic patch drawn with a software version of the algorithm described earlier are shown in Figures 3 to 8. The maximum subdivision level is varied as a parameter, and the accuracy requirement is set so that the maximum subdivision level terminates the subdivision process. The pixel intensity is a linear function of the dot product between the surface normal at the intersection point and the ray. An 8-bit color lookup table was used.

IEEE CG&A

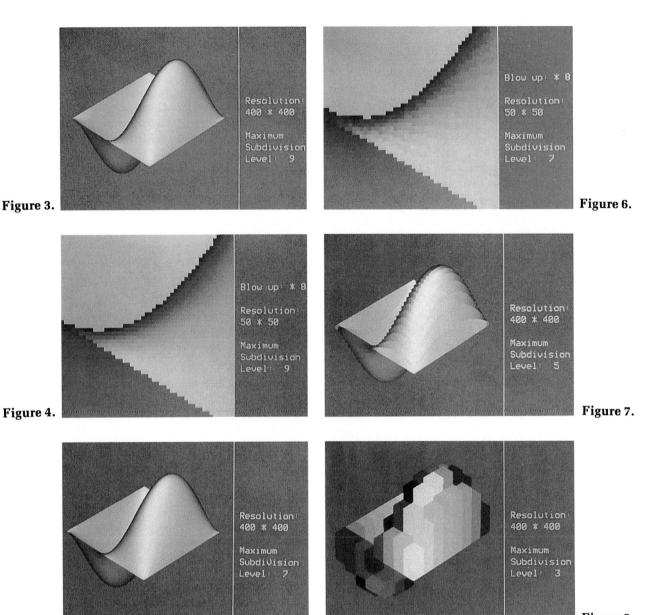

Figure 3.

Figure 6.

Figure 4.

Figure 7.

Figure 5.

Figure 8.

A 400-by-400 image was generated, which essentially spans the viewing window so that roughly 1/400 (2 to the power −8.5) of the patch projects to one pixel. This means that adjacent rays can be distinguished with roughly nine levels of subdivision. This is only approximately true, because the patch is subdivided uniformly in its parameter space, not in real space. The more uniformly spaced the Bezier control points, the better the approximation.

The impairments for images with nine or more levels of subdivision are imperceptible, even on the blowups, except for aliasing errors (jaggies), as can be seen in Figures 3 and 4. At seven levels of subdivision, small anomalies are visible in Figures 5 and 6, where a slight lighter, darker, lighter, darker, etc., pattern appears par-

allel to the silhouette edge, which is clearly not bicubic behavior but computational inaccuracy. Another impairment is that the color changes no longer appear continuous, causing the slightly noticeable "banded" appearance in Figure 5. This is due to the fact that the minimum size-bounding boxes, when projected onto the viewing plane, are significantly larger than individual pixels. An additional inaccuracy due to the same cause is that the straight line edge of the patch in the foreground appears discontinuous where the silhouette edge of the ridge meets the edge of the patch.

As the maximum subdivision level becomes smaller, the impairments become pronounced, as seen in Figure 7, until at three levels of subdivision the large bounding boxes shown in Figure 8 are very clearly distinguishable.

Extensions

The normal to the surface at the ray-intersection point is usually required in computer graphics applications for shading calculations. This information is easily obtained from the control points of the "result" patch calculated by the proposed chip, following from the fact that the four "corner" control points in the Bezier form are actually on the patch. The simplest way to extract a normal is to assume that "result" patches are approximately planar, subtract "corner" control points to form vectors in the plane, and take the cross product of the resulting vectors.

The control points of the "result" patch must be known to roughly twice the accuracy required for the intersection alone to calculate the normal to the same accuracy as the intersection. Because the VLSI implementation of the subdivide and select chain subdivides patches exactly, it can easily be adapted to produce the corner-point difference vectors to the required accuracy with a very modest increase in time. It might be possible to include the cross-product calculations on the chip. The trade-offs involved in doing this are the subject of a further investigation.

Comparisons are made at several points in the circuit to find minimum and maximum values. The circuits suggested for this are a series of simple bit-serial comparisons followed by a selection based on the result of the comparison. This approach is simple but results in a large delay. Many alternatives are available and are worth investigating in the context of this chip.

Conclusions

The subdivision approach to computing patch/ray intersections is suitable for VLSI implementation. It appears to fit comfortably on a single chip, its performance is not limited by the need for high I/O bandwidth, and estimates of its performance are attractive. A software version of the algorithm is being used to generate images to gain insights for the proper choice of the chip parameters. Further work is required to decide on the most effective way to use this chip to implement a powerful graphics or solid/surface modeling environment. This work will be carried forward with a focus on making as much use of these chips in a parallel configuration as possible.

Acknowledgments

We gratefully acknowledge the support for this work provided by a grant from STW (The Netherlands) under the Megabit program through the Network Theory Section of the Delft University of Technology. HP Labs support for a sabbatical leave for Pulleyblank is greatly appreciated, as are the many useful discussions with Ed Deprettere and Rein Nouta on VLSI implementation issues and the system described herein.

References

1. T. Whitted, "An Improved Illumination Model for Shaded Display," *Comm. of the ACM*, June, 1980, pp. 343-349.

2. S.D. Roth, "Ray Casting for Modeling Solids," *Computer Graphics and Image Processing*, 1982, pp. 109-144.

3. J.D. Foley and A. van Dam, *Fundamentals of Interactive Computer Graphics*, Addison-Wesley, Reading, Mass., 1982, pp. 514-536.

4. J.T. Kajiya, "Ray Tracing Parametric Patches," *Computer Graphics*, Proc. SIGGRAPH July 1982, pp. 245-254.

5. D.L. Toth, "On Ray Tracing Parametric Surfaces," *Computer Graphics*, July 1985, pp. 171-179.

6. K.I. Joy and M.N. Bhetanabhotla, "Ray Tracing Parametric Surface Patches Utilizing Numerical Techniques and Ray Coherence," *Computer Graphics*, (Proc. SIGGRAPH 86) Aug. 1986, pp. 279-285.

7. M.A.J. Sweeney and R.H. Bartels, "Ray Tracing Free-Form B-Spline Surfaces," *IEEE CG&A*, Feb. 1986, pp. 41-49.

8. E.E. Catmull, *A Subdivision Algorithm for Computer Display of Curved Surfaces*, doctoral dissertation, Univ. of Utah, Salt Lake City, 1974.

9. J.H. Clark, "A Fast Scanline Algorithm for Rendering Parametric Surfaces," *Supp. to Proc. SIGGRAPH 79* Aug. 1979, p. 74

10. J.M. Lane, L.C. Carpenter, T. Whitted, and J.F. Blinn, "Scan Line Methods for Displaying Parametrically Defined Surfaces," *Comm. of the ACM*, Jan. 1980, pp. 468-479.

11. J.M. Lane, and R.F. Risienfeld, "A Theoretical Development for the Computer Generation and Display of Piecewise Polynomial Surfaces," *IEEE Trans. on Pattern Analysis and Machine Intelligence*, Jan. 1980, pp. 35- 46.

12. A.S. Glassner, "Space Subdivision for Fast Ray Tracing," *IEEE CG&A*, Oct. 1984, pp. 15-22.

13. H. Weghorst, G. Hooper, and D.P. Greenberg, "Improved Computational Methods for Ray Tracing," *ACM Trans. on Graphics*, Jan. 1984, pp. 52-69.

14. M.R. Kaplan, "Space-Tracing, a Constant Time Ray-Tracer," *SIGGRAPH 85 Tutorial on the Uses of Spatial Coherence in Ray-Tracing*, ACM, New York, July 1985.

15. G.Wyvill, T.L. Kunii, and Y.Shirai, "Space Division for Ray Tracing in CSG," *IEEE CG&A*, Apr. 1986, pp. 28-34.

16. A. Fujimoto, T. Tanaka, and K. Iwata, "ARTS: Accelerated Ray-Tracing System," *IEEE CG&A*, Apr. 1986, pp. 16-26.

17. D.J. Plunkett and M.J. Bailey, "The Vectorization of a Ray-Tracing Algorithm for Improved Execution Speed," *IEEE CG&A*, Aug. 1985, pp. 52-60.

18. M.K. Ullner, *Parallel Machines for Computer Graphics*, doctoral thesis, Caltech, Pasadena, Calif., 1983.

19. J.G. Cleary, B. Wyvill, G.M. Birtwistle, and R. Vatti, "Multiprocessor Ray Tracing," Research Rpt. No. 83/128/17, Univ. of Calgary, Calgary, Canada, Oct. 1983.

20. M. Dippe and J. Swensen, "An Adaptive Subdivision Algorithm and Parallel Architecture for Realistic Image Synthesis," *Computer Graphics*, (Proc. SIGGRAPH 84), ACM, New York, July 1984, pp. 149-158.

21. G. Kedem and J.L. Ellis, "The Raycasting Machine," *Proc. IEEE Int'l Conf.on Computer Design*, 1984, pp. 533-538.

22. J.T. Kajiya, "New Techniques for Ray Tracing Procedurally Defined Objects," *Computer Graphics*, (Proc. SIGGRAPH 83), ACM, New York, July 1983, pp. 91- 102.

Appendix: Discussion of system blocks

A brief discussion of each of the system blocks follows, with block diagrams suggesting how some might be implemented with shift registers, full adders, etc. The purpose is to obtain an idea of chip size and performance for the task outlined above and not to present a polished design.

Patch memory

This memory—organized as a stack of static shift registers, which is read serially—is first required to store the control points of the original patch and the control points of any patches saved for further testing as they emerge from a complete stage of Ds-1 subdivisions. This memory must be provided for each of the P patch/ray computations and totals $48 \times L \times N$ bits for each P.

Test stack memory

This memory, organized as a stack of parallel (static) words, holds the path from the closest saved patch control points to it and the depth of subdivision from that saved patch. The memory contains $(3 \times Ds-2) \times N$ words, each of $(2 \times Ds + ceil(log2(Ds)))$ bits, and is repeated P times. If several rays are tested against each patch, a bit is required to record whether this patch is active for each ray.

Subdivide and select circuit

Each of these circuits bit serially subdivides the rows of the control-point array, selects one of the halves, subdivides the columns of that half, and selects one of its halves, thus producing the control points of a selected quadrant of the input patch. Provision is also made for bypassing the stage altogether. These circuits are cascaded to a depth of Ds-1, and repeated in parallel for the x, y, and z components of the patch control points. Each circuit requires 48 full adders, 48 2:1 multiplexers, and 96 dynamic shift register bits, and there is a total of $3 \times (Ds-1)$ circuits for each subdivide chain. A block diagram of the subdivide row or column circuit is shown in Figure 9, and that of a complete subdivide and select stage for one component is shown in Figure 10.

Subdivide into quadrants

This circuit, shown in Figure 11, differs from the previous in that it produces the control points for all four quadrants at its output. It requires 66 full adders and 132 dynamic shift register bits for each subdivide chain.

Compute bounding box

A series of bit serial comparisons is used to find the maximum and minimum values of the x, y, and z components in parallel. This operation is duplicated for each of the four quadrants of the patch under test. The circuitry required for one component of one patch is shown in Figure 12. It requires 22 half adders, 30 2:1 multiplexers $44 \times (L+X)$ dynamic shift register bits, and 22 static shift register bits. Twelve such circuits are required. The delay through this circuit is $4 \times (L+X)$ clock cycles.

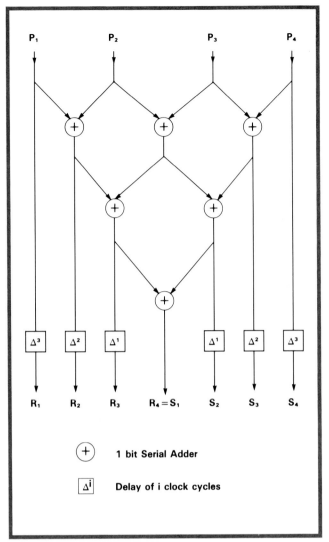

Figure 9. Bit serial circuit for subdivision of Bezier curve.

Test accuracy criteria

The minimum and maximum bounding box values for each component are subtracted to find the span of the bounding box in each dimension, which is in turn compared with the accuracy requirements to produce the signal labelled "fini." Three full adders and three half adders are required for each of these circuits shown in Figure 13.

Compute intersection

This circuit computes the intersection of the ray with the minimum and maximum bounding plane for that component. The resulting t values are sorted so that the smallest is output on one line and the largest on another. The smallest (largest) t value represents the point at which the ray enters (leaves) the "inside the bounding planes" region for that component. A block diagram is shown in Figure 14. The multiplier is a shift and add type

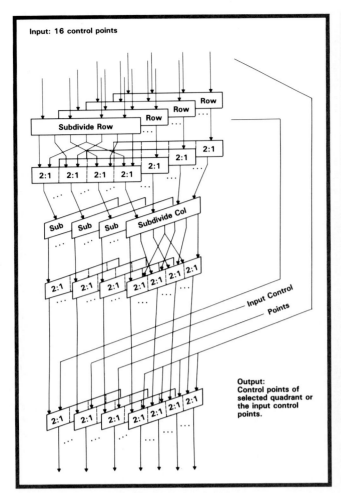

Figure 10. Subdivide and select block (one component).

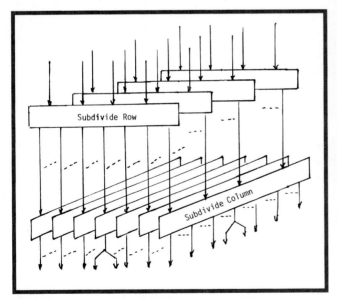

Figure 11. Subdivide patch into quadrants

and is pipelined so that it can work at the serial clock rate. The circuit for one component requires $2 \times (L+X+1)$ full adders, $2 \times (L+X)$ dynamic shift register bits and 2 2:1

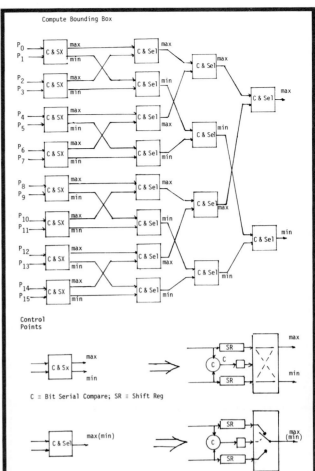

Figure 12. Compute bounding box.

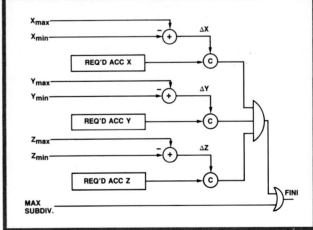

Figure 13. Test accuracy criteria.

multiplexers; it has a delay of $L+X$ clock cycles. In all, 12 components are required for each ray that is to be tested against the quadrants of the test patch.

Test for hit

A series of comparisons is used to find the minimum of the "largest" t values, those for leaving the bounding box, and the maximum of "smallest" t values, i.e., the t

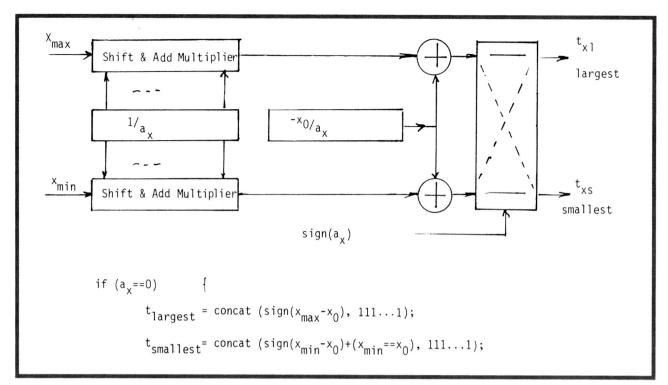

$$\text{if } (a_x == 0) \quad \{$$

$$t_{largest} = \text{concat } (\text{sign}(x_{max} - x_0), \ 111...1);$$

$$t_{smallest} = \text{concat } (\text{sign}(x_{min} - x_0) + (x_{min} == x_0), \ 111...1);$$

Figure 14. Compute intersection.

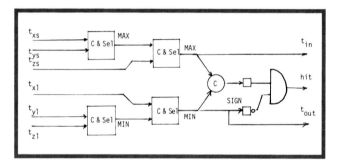

Figure 15. Test for hit.

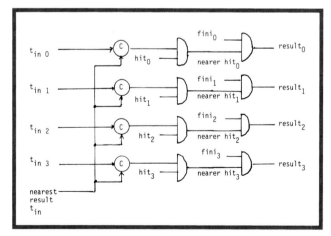

Figure 16. Compare with nearest result.

value for entering the bounding box. If the entering value is less than the leaving value, which must be positive, there was a hit. A possible realization for this circuit is

shown in Figure 15. It requires $8 \times (L+X)$ dynamic shift register bits, six static shift register bits, 5 half adders, and four 2:1 multiplexers for each ray tested against the subpatch. This circuit has a delay of $2 \times (L+X)$ clock cycles. Other circuits with much less delay are possible and should be investigated.

Sort new test patches and update nearest result

This circuit sorts the newly computed quadrants of the patch being tested so that those that need further testing can be placed on the test stack in such a way that those nearest to the ray origin will be tested first. When the first "result" patch is found, the corresponding (u,v) values and the t value for entering its bounding box are saved. When subsequent "hits" are found, their entering t values are compared with the stored value and the "hit" signals are disqualified if the new hits are beyond that stored for the nearest "result." If a new "hit" is also a "result," the stored (u,v) and t values are updated accordingly. It requires nine half adders, $10 \times (L+X)$ dynamic shift register bits and 33 multiplexers for each ray tested, and it has a delay of $2 \times (L+X)$ clock cycles. The block diagrams for the required circuits are shown in Figures 16 and 17.

Parameter storage

Static storage for $6 \times R$ words is required for ray parameters, P words for patch intersection accuracy requirements, and $R \times P$ words for storage of nearest t values where each word contains $L+X$ bits.

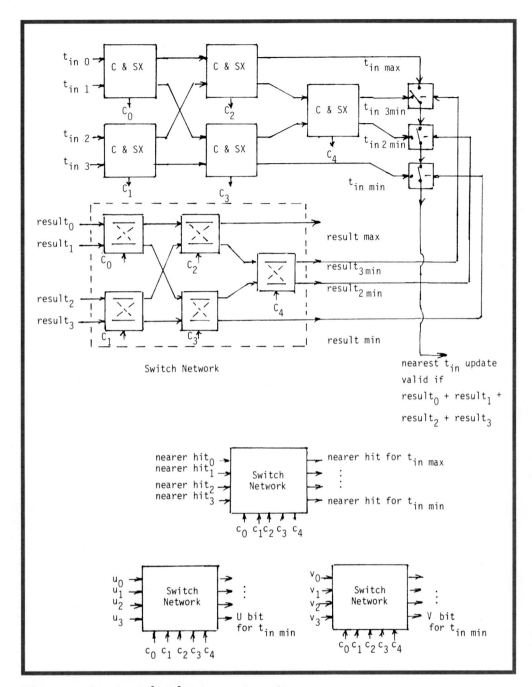

Figure 17. Sort t_{in} and update nearest result.

Ronald W. Pulleyblank is a member of the technical staff at Hewlett-Packard Laboratories in Palo Alto, California. He worked on digital transmission systems at Bell Labs in Holmdel, New Jersey, from 1969-1971. He taught electrical engineering at the University of Lagos in Nigeria (1971-1974) and at the University of the Pacific in Stockton, California (1974-1980). In 1980 he joined HP where he worked on communication system measurement problems and local area networks. He is currently interested in algorithms and hardware assists for graphics and solid modeling. Pulleyblank received his BS degrees in engineering physics and electrical engineering at the University of Michigan and his MS and PhD in electrical engineering from the University of Pennsylvania. He is a member of IEEE.

John A. Kapenga is an assistant professor with the Computer Science Department at Western Michigan University, Kalamazoo. He was supported in 1985-86 at the Delft University of Technology doing research in parallel processing. His research interests include graphics, parallel algorithms, and languages, as well as computations in robust stastics.

Kapenga received a PhD in mathematics from Western Michigan University. He is a member of ACM, IEEE, and SIAM.

The authors may be contacted at the Computer Science Department, Western Michigan University, Kalamazoo, MI 49008.

IEEE CG&A

Chapter 7: Image Processing Hardware

Processing of pictorial data by computer takes different forms in a variety of applications. It has been customary to classify such work into three general areas: graphics, pictorial pattern recognition, and image processing.

Graphics deals with the generation of images from non-pictorial information and covers diverse applications. On the other hand, pictorial pattern recognition deals with methods for producing either a description of the input picture or an assignment of the picture to a particular class. In a sense, pattern recognition is the inverse problem of computer graphics (see Figure 7.1). It starts with a picture and transforms it into an abstract description. An automatic mail sorter that examines the postal code written on an envelope and identifies the digits is a typical example.

Image processing deals with problems in which both input and output are pictures. Image transmission systems, where one is concerned with noise removal and data compaction, is an example. Overexposed, underexposed, or blurred pictures can be improved with contrast enhancement techniques. Sometimes it is desirable to apply more drastic transformations. An image with a wide range of illumination may be reduced into an image where one sees only two levels of illumination. The resulting silhouettes may be reduced further into stick-type figures. Other times a new image from a set of others may be created, such as constructing images of cross sections of the human body from lateral X-ray pictures.

7.1: Image Processing Applications

Although image processing and computer graphics share many similarities, their applications are very different in nature. Therefore, different algorithms and system architectures are required for each discipline.[1] Various common applications of image processing are introduced in this section. Notice that the complexities of these applications are so high that conventional computer systems are usually insufficient in terms of processing power and memory resources.

7.1.1: Enhancement and Restoration

The formation of an image, its conversion from one form into another, or its transmission from one place to another,

often involves some degradation of image "quality" with the result that the image then requires subsequent improvement, *enhancement,* or *restoration.* In practice, there are many different sources of image degradation. Image restoration has commonly been defined as the reconstruction or estimation of an image to correct for image degradation, and approximates an ideal degradation-free image as closely as possible. Image enhancement involves operations that improve the appearance of an image to a human viewer or operations that convert an image to a format better suited to machine processing.

7.1.2: Segmentation

Techniques such as restoration and enhancement involve an explicit transformation of the input image into an output image. Another group of techniques, including segmentation, is concerned with the situation where the output is a description of the content (or some part of it) of the input image. *Segmentation* is a generic term for those techniques that involve taking an image and extracting information relevant to specific picture "segments," such as lines, regions, and objects, and their interrelationship. It is basically a process of data compression by pixel classification in that an image is segmented into subsets by assigning individual pixels to particular classes. Obviously, this is an area of considerable practical concern.

Once an image has been segmented in some way, there is a need to establish a list of properties of the appropriate image subsets extracted by the segmentation algorithms. This list of properties should specify and interrelate the segmented regions in the context of a representation, implicitly or explicitly, appropriate to the task in hand. Represen-

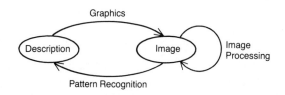

Figure 7.1: Diagram illustrating the relation between graphics, image processing, and pattern recognition.

---

[1] In our opinion, the subject of image processing hardware requires a separate treatment (in another book). This chapter is added only for completeness and comparison.

tations used in image processing typically involve relational structures such as directed graphs where the graph nodes represent "parts" and the graph edges represent "relations."

The representations used in practice must be judged in terms of their practical "adequacy." This must not be merely a mathematical adequacy. It must include enough elements of epistemological and heuristic (procedural and declarative) adequacy to enable all the requisite information to be available to the task in hand in such a way as to facilitate computation in a reasonable time.

7.1.3: Matching and Recognition

Image matching, particularly involving the use of correlation, has a long history. It has been used extensively for tasks such as the detection of change, character recognition, target recognition, aerial navigation, and stereo mapping. The requirement to match or *register* two images or *frames* in the context of real-time imagery can arise in a number of different situations.

Registration is a process fundamental to many matching tasks. Registration, in practice, is complicated by various geometric imaging distortions, such as "perspective," "barrel," and "pin cushion" distortion. Matching a pattern, or *template*, to its occurrences in an image is an important generic image processing task.

7.1.4: Understanding

Image understanding stands preeminent as the still essentially unachieved long-term goal of those researchers who work in the general area of computer-based image processing. It occupies a major niche within the subject of artificial intelligence (AI) and is often referred to by names such as image analysis and computer vision.

There is an enormous discrepancy between the tasks that can be performed by existing image understanding systems and the richness and sophistication of human visual process. It is rooted in some very fundamental shortcomings in our theoretical understanding of the computational paradigms underlying the visual process. It is in the area of image understanding that this fundamental lack of knowledge becomes most glaring.

7.2: Image Processing Systems

The performance of conventional computers in the rapidly expanding field of image processing (including image analysis) has been found to be quite inadequate for the majority of the applications that have been attempted or envisaged. An obvious goal for a robot vision system, for example, would be the analysis in real-time of television quality images. In such an application, even very modest image analysis tasks will often require billions of pixel operations per second.

Faced with these demands for impossibly high computation rates, the image-processing community has always been driven to explore ways and means for achieving a greatly improved performance from their computers. In general, it has been realized that either the processors must be more powerful in themselves or else the systems must be designed in which many processors can be assembled into a single and powerful composite structure. Fortunately, it has been found that an image-processing task can usually be decomposed into a set of subtasks distributed over the image.

Such decompositions point the way to simultaneous processing of different regions of the image (i.e., to parallel processing). Each region can be served by a relatively simple processor. In the limit, each pixel may be assigned its own processor, all executing the same broadcast sequence of instructions.

A completely different approach to parallelism is found in pipeline architectures. Whereas the first approach we have been discussing is spatially parallel across the image, the pipeline is temporally parallel. The image is passed through a chain of processors, each of which operates on the whole image. It is too early to say how useful this approach will be, but the prospects are encouraging.

A more "steam-hammer" method for introducing parallelism is exhibited by computer architectures in which a substantial number of processors (typically 16 or so) are connected via a high-speed bus to which are also attached several memory units. A master processor divides the task into blocks that can then be assigned to slave processors. In some systems, the slave processors will be identical, general-purpose computers; in others, the processors will be individually specialized for particular commonly occurring image processes (convolution, for example).

7.3: Article Overview

Owing to the volume of data that image processing applications deal with, high throughput systems are desired. As a consequence, specially designed parallel processing architectures are usually employed to achieve this purpose. The article by Danielsson and Levialdi [DANI81] is primarily concerned with architectures for image analysis, but it is also somewhat relevant to image databases and image coding.

SIMD processors are well suited to most low level algorithms and can also perform many simple feature extraction operations. Classification schemes, especially those involving syntactic methods, are very well suited to the MIMD structure. In the paper by Reeves [REEV84], the architectures that have been developed for low-level image processing are reviewed with emphasis on more recent designs. The features of proposed multiple SIMD (MSIMD) schemes for image processing applications are also discussed in that paper.

The domains of signal processing and image processing share the characteristic that the conputation is often regular and repetitive. The Warp machine, described by Annaratone, et al., of CMU, "Warp Architecture and Implementation," is a high-performance systolic array computer for these application domains. It has been used in areas such as low-level vision processing and image analysis.

The μPD7281 VLSI device [JEFF85] that exploits a data flow architecture is an example of the commercial image processing chips. The μPD7281 image-processor incorporates an internal circular pipeline architecture and has a powerful optimized image-processing oriented instruction set.

The MN8614 processor discussed by Kawakami and Shimazaki, in "A Special Purpose LSI Processor Using the DDA Algorithm for Image Transformation," is an LSI device that has been developed for high-speed binary image transformation. This device incorporates an extension of the conventional DDA (digital differential analyzer) to achieve the desired goal.

The last paper, "RAPAC: A High-Speed Image Processing System" by Elphinstone, et al., describes the design and operation of a real-time image processing system and outlines one of its application areas.

References

[DANI81] Danielsson, P. and S. Levialdi, "Computer Architecture for Pictorial Information Systems," *Computer,* Vol. 14, No. 11, Nov. 1981, pp. 53–67.

[JEFF85] Jeffrey, T., "The μPD7281 Processor," *Byte,* Nov. 1985, pp. 237–246.

[REEV84] Reeves, A.P., "Survey: Parallel Computer Architecture for Image Processing," *Computer Vision, Graphics, and Image Processing,* Vol. 25, No. 1, Jan. 1984, pp. 68–88.

Warp Architecture and Implementation

Marco Annaratone, Emmanuel Arnould, Thomas Gross, H. T. Kung, Monica S. Lam,
Onat Menzilcioglu, Ken Sarocky, and Jon A. Webb

Department of Computer Science
Carnegie Mellon University
Pittsburgh, Pennsylvania 15213

Abstract

A high-performance systolic array computer called *Warp* has been designed and constructed. The machine has a systolic array of 10 or more linearly connected cells, each of which is a programmable processor capable of performing 10 million floating-point operations per second (10 MFLOPS). A 10-cell machine therefore has a peak performance of 100 MFLOPS. Warp is integrated into a UNIX host system. Program development is supported by a compiler.

The first 10-cell machine became operational in 1986. Low-level vision processing for robot vehicles is one of the first applications of the machine.

This paper describes the architecture and implementation of the Warp machine, and justifies and evaluates some of the architectural features with system, software and application considerations.

1. Introduction

Warp is a high-performance systolic array computer designed to provide computation power for signal, image and low-level vision processing: the machine's first applications are vision-based control algorithms for robot vehicles, and image analysis for large image databases [3].

A full-scale Warp machine consists of a linear systolic array of 10 or more identical cells, each of which is a 10 MFLOPS programmable processor. The processor array is integrated in a powerful host system, which provides an adequate data bandwidth to sustain the array at full speed in the targeted applications, and a general purpose computing environment, specifically UNIX, for application programs.

As an example of performance, a 10-cell Warp can process 1024-point complex fast Fourier transforms at a rate of one FFT every 600 microseconds. This programmable machine can also perform many other primitive computations, such as two-dimensional convolution, and real or complex matrix multiplication, at a peak rate of 100 MFLOPS. Warp can be described as an array of conventional array processors; the machine can efficiently implement not only systolic algorithms where communication between adjacent cells is intensive, but also non-systolic algorithms where each cell operates on its own data independently.

While achieving a high computation throughput usually expected only from a special-purpose systolic array, Warp has a high degree of programmability. Each processor is a horizontal microengine; the user has complete control over the various functional units. To overcome the complexity in managing this fine-grain parallelism, we are developing an optimizing compiler to support a high-level programming language [2]. To the programmer, Warp is an array of simple sequential processors, communicating asynchronously. Initial results indicate that reasonable performance can be achieved with the compiler.

Carnegie Mellon designed, assembled and tested a 2-cell prototype machine (in use since Fall of 1985). Production of the full-scale machine is contracted to two industrial partners, General Electric and Honeywell. The first 10-cell machine was

delivered by General Electric in early 1986. It is used in vision research; for example, it performs the low-level vision processing for a robot vehicle built by Carnegie Mellon [8]. At least eight additional 10-cell Warp machines will be built in 1986 and 1987 for applications in areas such as robot vehicles and image analysis.

This paper describes the Warp architecture and implementation, justifies and evaluates the major architectural features with system, software and application considerations. We first present an overview of the architecture of the machine. We next discuss the architecture of the Warp processor array in more detail: the linear configuration of the array, our programming model of the array and its implications, and the architecture of the individual cells in the array. A description of the hardware implementation then follows. We then present the hardware and software architecture of the host system that controls the Warp machine. The last section includes some general discussions of the machine and concluding remarks.

2. Warp machine overview

The Warp machine has three components—the Warp processor array (*Warp array*), the interface unit (*IU*), and the *host*, as depicted in Figure 2-1. The Warp array performs the computation-intensive routines, for example, low-level vision routines. The IU handles the input/output between the array and the host, and generates addresses and control signals for the Warp array. The host executes the parts of the application programs that are not mapped onto the Warp array and supplies the data to and receives the results from the array.

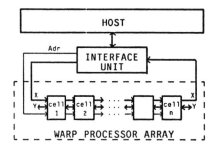

Figure 2-1: Warp machine overview

The Warp array is a programmable, one-dimensional systolic array with identical cells called Warp cells. Data flow through the array on two data paths (X and Y), while addresses and systolic control signals travel on the Adr path (as shown in Figure 2-1).

Each Warp cell is implemented as a programmable horizontal microengine, with its own program memory and microsequencer. A Warp cell has a 32-bit wide data path, as depicted in Figure 2-2. The data path consists of two 32-bit floating-point processing elements: one multiplier and one ALU, a 4K-word memory for resident and temporary data, a 128-word queue for each communication channel, and a 32-word register file to buffer data for each floating-point unit. All these components are interconnected through a crossbar switch as shown in Figure 2-2.

To reduce the inherent risk in prototyping a new architecture, the current implementation of the Warp machine uses conservative design principles and no custom-made parts. TTL-compatible parts are used throughout. Each Warp cell is implemented on a large board (dimensions 15" × 17"), and so is the IU. Figure 2-3 shows a photograph of a Warp cell.

The host consists of a VME-based workstation (currently a Sun 2/160), that serves as the master controller of the Warp machine, and an "external host", so named because it is *external* to the

The research was supported in part by Defense Advanced Research Projects Agency (DOD), monitored by the Air Force Avionics Laboratory under Contract F33615-81-K-1539, and Naval Electronic Systems Command under Contract N00039-85-C-0134, and in part by the Office of Naval Research under Contracts N00014-80-C-0236, NR 048-659, and N00014-85-K-0152, NR SDRJ-007. T. Gross is also supported by an IBM Faculty Development Award, H. T. Kung by a Shell Distinguished Chair in Computer Science.

Reprinted from *Proceedings of the 13th Annual International Symposium on Computer Architecture*, 1986, pages 346-356. Copyright © 1986 by The Institute of Electrical and Electronics Engineers, Inc.

workstation. The workstation provides a UNIX environment for running application programs and the external host provides a high data transfer rate for communicating with the Warp array.

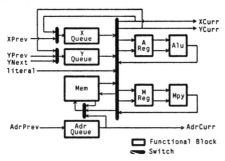

Figure 2-2: Warp cell data path

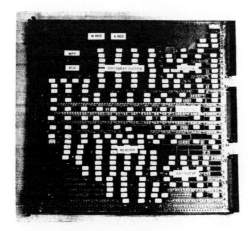

Figure 2-3: Warp cell layout

Figure 3-1 is a picture of the Warp machine. A single 19" rack hosts the IU, a Warp array of 10 cells, the external host, as well as associated power supplies and fans. The workstation is not visible in this picture.

The first 10-cell machine uses wire-wrap technology. Future Warp machines will be implemented with PC boards; the 19" rack will be able to host the IU and up to 24 Warp cells. For the PC board version, each cell will have increased local memory (at least 32K or 64K words) and enlarged queues.

3. Linear array of powerful cells

The Warp array is a linear array of identical cells with only neighboring cells communicating directly. The linear configuration was chosen for several reasons. First, it is easy to implement. Second, it is easy to extend the number of cells in the array. Third, a linear array has modest I/O requirements since only the two end-cells communicate with the outside world.

The advantages of the linear interconnection are outweighed, however, if the constraints of interconnection render the machine too difficult to use for programmers. The concern is whether or not we can efficiently map applications on the linear array of cells. While many algorithms have been designed specifically for linear arrays, computations designed for other interconnection topologies can often be efficiently simulated on the linear array mainly because the Warp cell, the building-block of the array, is itself a powerful engine. In particular, a single Warp cell can be time multiplexed to perform the function of a column of cells, and therefore the linear array can, for example, implement a two-dimensional systolic array effectively.

A feature that distinguishes the Warp cell from other processors of similar computation power is its high I/O bandwidth. Each Warp cell can transfer up to 20 million words (80 Mbytes) to and from its neighboring cells per second. (In addition, 10 million 16-bit addresses can flow from one cell to the next cell every second.) We have been able to implement this high bandwidth communication link with only modest engineering efforts because of the simplicity of the linear interconnection structure. This high

Figure 3-1: The Warp machine, serial number 1

inter-cell communication bandwidth makes it possible to transfer large volumes of intermediate data between neighboring cells and thus supports fine-grain problem decomposition.

For communicating with the outside world, the Warp array can sustain a 80 Mbytes/sec peak transfer rate. In the current setup, the IU can communicate with the Warp array at a rate of 40 Mbytes/sec. This assumes that the Warp array inputs and outputs a 32-bit word every (200 ns) instruction cycle. However the current host can only support up to 10 Mbytes/sec transfer rates. The smaller transfer rate supported by the host is not expected to affect the effective use of the Warp array for our applications for the following reasons: First, the Warp array typically performs one input and one output every two or more cycles. Second, for most signal and image processing applications, the host deals with 8-bit integers rather than 32-bit floating-point numbers, and therefore the I/O bandwidth for the host needs only be a quarter of that for the Warp array. This implies that 10 Mbytes/sec transfer rate for the host is sufficient. This I/O issue and the use of the IU for integer/float-point conversions will be discussed later in the paper.

Each cell has a large local data memory; this feature is seldom found in special-purpose, systolic array designs, and is another reason why Warp is powerful and flexible. It can be shown that by increasing the data memory size, higher computation bandwidth can be sustained without imposing increased demand on the I/O bandwidth [4]. The large memory size, together with the high I/O bandwidth, makes Warp capable of performing *global* operations in which each output depends on any or a large portion of the input [6]. Examples of global operations are FFT, component labeling, Hough transform, image warping, and matrix computations such as matrix multiplication. Systolic arrays are known to be effective for local operations such as a 3 × 3 convolution. The additional ability to perform global operations significantly broadens the applicability of the machine.

In summary, the simple linear processor array used in Warp is a powerful and flexible structure largely because the array is made of powerful, programmable processors with high I/O capabilities and large local memories.

4. Warp architecture

The domains of signal processing, image processing, and scientific computing share the characteristic that the computation is often regular and repetitive. That is, the control flow through a computation is independent from the input data; similar operations must be performed for all input sets. For these applications, a one-dimensional processor array can be used in two major modes:

- *Pipeline mode*: each processor constitutes a stage of the pipeline, and data are processed as they flow through the array; repetitive computation can often be decomposed into a number of identical pipeline stages.
- *Parallel mode*: the data are partitioned among the processors, and each processor performs the same function on data resident in its local memory.

In both the pipeline and parallel modes of operation, the cells execute identical programs. However, unlike the SIMD model of computation, where all the processing elements execute the same instruction in the same time step, the execution time of the cells may be skewed. That is, all cells perform the same computation; however, the computation of a cell is delayed with respect to that of the preceding cell by a constant amount of time. This delay gives valid data and results from preceding cells time to travel to the cell before the computation on the cell begins. We refer to this model, where all the cells execute the same function, but with a time delay between neighboring cells, as the *skewed model of computation*. Some of the optimizations and design decisions for Warp were based on our intended application domain and the model of how the machine would be used.

4.1. Local program control
Although the functions executed by the different cells of the array are identical, each cell has its own local program memory and sequencer. First, since the microinstruction words are very wide, it is not easy to broadcast them to all the cells, or to propagate them from cell to cell. Second, the skewed model of computation can easily be supported with local program control. Finally, the local sequencer supports conditional branching more efficiently. In machines where all cells execute the same sequence of instruction words, branching is achieved by masking. Therefore, the execution time is equivalent to the summation of the execution time of each branch. With local program control, different cells may follow different branches of a conditional statement depending on their individual data; the execution time is the maximum execution time of the different branches.

4.2. Computing addresses and loop controls in the IU
Since all the cells compute the same function, and the addresses used in the computation are often data independent, the cells typically have identical addressing patterns and control flow. For example, when multiplying two matrices, each cell computes some columns of the result. All cells access the same *local* memory location, which has been loaded with different columns of one of the argument matrices. This characteristic of the computation allows us to factor out address generation and loop termination signals from the individual cells; we migrate these functional blocks to the IU. Moreover, it is desirable that each Warp cell can make two memory references per cycle. To sustain this high local memory bandwidth, the cell demands powerful address generation capabilities, which were expensive to provide and therefore became a target for optimization. We can dedicate much more hardware resources to address generation if it is implemented only once in the IU, and not replicated on all Warp cells.

The IU has separate functional units for address generation and loop control. In each cycle, the IU can compute up to two array addresses, modify two registers, test for the end of a loop, and update a loop counter. In addition, to support complex addressing schemes for important algorithms such as FFT, the IU contains a table of pre-stored addresses; this table can be initialized when the microcode is loaded.

Data dependent addresses are sometimes necessary. They can be computed locally on the Warp cells, but at a significant cost since the address computation competes with other computations for use of the floating-point processing elements.

4.3. Compile-time flow control
In our application domains of signal and image processing, data independent control flow is typical; the same operation is performed on all input data. Hence, a bound on the timing of the input and output actions of each cell can be obtained at compile-time. Our decision is to let the compiler synchronize the actions of the communicating cells; that is, the compiler ensures that no data is fetched from, or stored into, the queues if they are empty,

or full, respectively. An alternative design is to provide the flow control at run-time by suspending a cell whenever it tries to read from an empty queue, or write to a full queue, until the status of the queue changes. Providing this capability would make the machine much more difficult to design, implement and debug.

While compile-time flow control is adequate in most of the cases in our application domain, run-time flow control is required in some occasions—for example, in three-dimensional graphics clipping algorithms, the number of points to be created or deleted is determined dynamically. Minimal support is provided to handle these cases: the status of the communication queues is accessible to the user. Therefore, the user can loop and continually test the status before each I/O action until the queue stops being empty or full. We note that although run-time flow control is possible, it is expensive since all the pipes in this heavily pipelined machine need to be emptied before each I/O operation.

4.4. Input control
The latching of data into a cell's queue is controlled by the cell that sends the data, rather than by the local microinstruction word. As a cell sends data to its neighbor, it tags the data with a control signal to instruct the receiving cell's queue to accept the data.

Our original design was that input data is latched under the microinstruction control of the receiving cell. This implies that intercell communication requires close cooperation between the sender and the receiver; the sender presents its data on the communication channel, and in the same clock cycle the receiver must latch in the input. This tight-coupling of cells appeared not to present any additional complexity to the compiler, since the compiler has full knowledge of the timing of all the I/O actions to ensure that no queue overflow or underflow results. We did not realize that such a design would cause an intolerable increase in code size.

To explain the increase in code size if the receiving cell were to provide the control to latch in the data, we first describe the compilation process. Consider a simple example where each cell receives a data item from its left neighbor and passes it to its right. The scheduling steps of the compiler are as follows:

1. Schedule the computation, disregarding the control to latch in the data. This sequence of instructions forms the computation process for a given cell. In the simple example, the computation consists of two steps: remove a data item from the X queue and output it on the X channel for the next cell. See Figure 4-1 (a).

2. Extract the output actions and construct the input counterpart of latching in the data. These input operations are executed by the next cell. As shown in Figure 4-1 (b), all output operations are simply turned into input operations. All the control constructs are retained; all other instructions are mapped into idle cycles (nops). This is the input process for the next cell.

3. Determine the minimum skew between neighboring cells such that no inputs are performed before the corresponding data are output from the preceding cell. (For simplicity, we assume that the queue is sufficiently large). Since the input process must execute in lockstep with the computation of the preceding cell, the computation process in the cell is delayed with respect to its own input process.

   In the example of passing a data item down the array, the queue cannot be dequeued until the data are output by the preceding cell. Therefore, the skew between cells in this case is 1. The result of merging the input and the delayed computation is shown in Figure 4-1 (c).

```
(a)              (b)         (c)

dequeue(X).      nop.        nop.
output(X).       input(X).   dequeue(X), input(X).
                             output(X).
```

Figure 4-1: Scheduling a cell program that passes data from cell to cell: (a) computation process, (b) input process, and (c) merged process

The problem of codesize increase shows up in the last step where the computation and the input processes are merged. The code length of the program that combines both the computation and input activities can be significantly greater than either of the original processes if they contain iterative statements. Merging two identical loops, with an offset between their initiation times, requires loop unrolling and can result in a three-fold increase in code length. Figure 4-2 illustrates this increase in code length when merging two identical loops of n iterations. Furthermore, if the offset is so large that two iterative statements of different lengths are overlapped, then the resulting code size can be of the order of the least common multiple of their lengths.

Having the sender control the latching of input data not only reduces the complexity of the compiler and avoids increasing the code size, but also allows us to handle conditional statements better. For example, if a data item is output to the next cell in each of the two branches of a conditional statement, the compiler needs only to ensure that the input action of the receiving cell is performed after the output actions of both branches. The data from each branch of the condition need not be sent out in the very same clock cycle.

4.5. Control path

The microcode for the Warp cell and the IU is completely horizontal. The user has full control over every component, and thus can tailor the schedule of the micro-operations according to the needs of specific applications. Each component is controlled by a dedicated field; this orthogonal organization of the microinstruction word makes scheduling easier since there is no interference in the schedule of different components caused by conflicts in the micro-instruction field assignment.

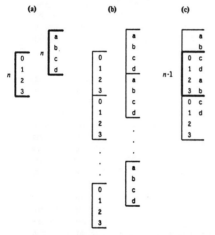

Figure 4-2: Merging two iterative processes (a) original programs (b) execution trace, and (c) merged programs

4.6. Data path

The data path of the Warp cell, shown in Figure 2-2, is carefully designed to ensure that the arithmetic units can be fully utilized. We now discuss each of the components in detail.

4.6.1. Arithmetic units

Each Warp cell has two floating-point processors, one multiplier and one ALU [9]. Floating-point capabilities are necessary for signal processing and scientific computation, and we believe that they will be important in vision as well. Until now most vision computation is done using fixed-point arithmetic, and this has meant careful analysis of algorithms to find upper bounds for the magnitude of intermediate results. If the intermediate results exceed the boundaries imposed by the word size available, the data must be scaled, or the algorithm must be modified. Using floating-point arithmetic, none of this analysis is necessary, so that the vision researcher can concentrate on the algorithmic aspects of the computation.

The convenience of using floating-point arithmetic does not imply a high cost in hardware implementation because high-performance floating-point arithmetic chips are commercially available. However at the time of design for the Warp machine, these floating-point chips depended on extensive pipelining to achieve high performance. Specifically, both of the ALU and the multiplier have 5-stage pipelines [9]. Deep pipelining has a devastating effect on the performance of general-purpose computation, where data-dependent branching is common. For-

tunately, our applications include few conditional branches and consist primarily of tight data-independent loops. Previous results have shown that pipelining is an effective optimization for systolic array algorithms [5]: while pipelining reduces the cycle time of a machine, the throughput rate of results per cycle can often be maintained.

4.6.2. Internal data bandwidth

Experience with the programmable systolic chip [1] showed that the internal data bandwidth is often the bottleneck of a systolic cell. In the Warp cell, the two functional units can consume up to four data items and generate two results per cycle. Several data storage blocks interconnected with a crossbar support this high data processing rate. There are six input and eight output ports connected to the crossbar switch; six data items can be transferred in a single cycle, and an output port can receive any data item. The use of the crossbar also makes compilation easier when compared to a bus-based system: conflicts on the use of one or more shared busses can complicate scheduling tremendously.

4.6.3. Data storage

The local memory hierarchy includes a local data memory and two register files, one for each functional unit. The local data memory can store 4K words of input data or intermediate results, and can be both read and written every (200 ns) cycle. The register files are 4-ported data buffers capable of accepting two data items and delivering two operands to the functional units every cycle.

4.6.4. Queues

Delay elements are often used in systolic algorithm designs to synchronize or delay a data stream with respect to another. In the original design of Warp, the queues were intended to serve simply as programmable delays; data were latched in every cycle and they emerged at the output port of the queue a constant number of cycles later. During the compiler development, the inadequacy of programmable delays was discovered. The Warp cell is a programmable processor with a relatively large local data storage; it is much more flexible than the typical inner-product nodes that appear in many systolic algorithms. Often, Warp programs do not produce one data item every cycle; a clocking discipline that reads/writes one item per cycle restricts the use of the machine. Furthermore, a constant delay through the queues means that the timing of the production of results must match exactly the timing of the consumption of data. Therefore, the architecture was modified to allow the user to conditionally enqueue or dequeue the data as they are produced or consumed.

The size of a queue is 128 words. This size was determined by the available RAM chips with sufficient speed to implement the queues. The queues are not large enough for vision algorithms that require buffering entire rows of images, which are at least 256 elements wide. The overflow data have to be stored in the local memory of a Warp cell in the current implementation.

The overflow problem for the address queue is much more severe than that for the data queue. First, while it is possible to use the memory as an extended storage for overflow data, this technique does not apply to addresses, as addresses are needed to access the memory. Second, the size of the address queue severely limits the grain size of parallelism in programs executable on Warp. In the pipeline mode of operation, a cell does not start executing until the preceding cell is finished with the first set of input data. The size of the data queue needs to be at least equal to that of the data set; the size of the address queue, however, needs to be at least equal to the number of addresses and control signals used in the computation of the data set. This problem would not exist if the Warp cells had the capability to generate addresses effectively.

Architectural revisions to deal with the above problems will be included in the PC board implementation of the Warp cell.

4.7. Compilation

While the parallelism potentially available in this machine is tremendous, the complexity of using it effectively is correspondingly overwhelming. To make the machine truly programmable, an optimizing compiler is developed [2]. The programmer simply thinks of the machine as a uni-directional array of sequential processors, communicating asynchronously. A sample program that implements the evaluation of a polynomial on an array of ten cells is included in the appendix. Since all cells perform the same function in our programming model, the user simply supplies the program for one cell. The programming language is Algol-like, with additional receive and send statements as communication primitives. The semantics of the communication protocol is that a cell is blocked when it tries to read from an empty queue or write to a full queue.

The compiler divides the operations in the cell program into three parts, one for each of the different components of the system: the host, the IU and the Warp cells. The input and output actions with the external environment are performed on the host and the IU. The data independent addresses and loop control are computed by the IU and are sent to the Warp cells via the address path. The rest of the operations are performed on the Warp cells.

The compiler currently accepts only programs where data flow uni-directionally through the array; flow control between cells is achieved by skewing the execution of the cells by the necessary amount to ensure that the input data is in the queue before it is used. Overflow of the queue is detected and reported, but not currently handled. The high degree of pipelining in the functional units of the Warp cell is another cause of concern for the compiler. Scheduling techniques based on software pipelining techniques are used [7]. The utilization obtained is reasonable; as an example, full utilization of the functional units is achieved for the sample program of polynomial evaluation in the appendix.

5. Implementation

5.1. Implementation of the Warp cell

The Warp architecture calls operates on 32-bit data. In the implementation, all data channels in the Warp array, including the internal data path of the cell (except for the floating-point processors), are implemented as 16-bit wide channels operating at 100 ns. There are two reasons for choosing a 16-bit time-multiplexed implementation. First, a 32-bit wide hardware path would not allow implementing one cell per 15" × 17" board. Second, the 200 ns cycle time dictated by the Weitek floating-point processors (at the time of design) allows the rest of the data path to be time multiplexed. This would not have been possible if the cycle time were under 160 ns.

High speed and parallel cell operations coupled with the tight synchronization of the Warp array presented a challenge to logic design. In particular, the design is required to address sensitive timing issues. Most of them were dealt with by adding pipeline stages to critical paths. Given that the floating-point units impose a multi-stage pipeline, the addition of yet another stage seems to be a good tradeoff when compared to added design complexity, increased chip count, and timing problems. To achieve high programmability without degrading performance, the timing of the control path must be balanced to the timing of the data path. Therefore, the microengine also operates at 100 ns and supports high and low cycle operations of the data path separately.

The cell is controlled by a pipelined microengine with a 112-bit wide microinstruction. Logically related micro-operations are typically grouped into the same microinstruction, although some data path elements require that control signals are presented at later cycles. For example, to initiate a multiplication, the microinstruction specifies the opcode and two source registers. First, the operands are retrieved from the register file; then, a cycle later, the opcode is fed to the multiplier unit. These delay adjustments are made in hardware using pipeline delays rather than in software to make code generation easier. However, the programmability of the microengine suffered from the limitations of the available microsequencer (Am2910A), especially in implementing nested loops.

A major portion of the internal cell hardware can be monitored and tested using built-in serial diagnostic chains. The serial chains access 36 registers of the Warp cell, covering almost all the registers outside the register files. This feature, along with the fully static operation of the cell, made testing easier and led to a fast debug time. In the best case, a wire-wrapped board was populated, debugged, and checked out in five days. The serial chains are also used to download the Warp cell programs. In-

itializing the Warp array with the same program for all the cells takes no more than 100 ms.

The Warp cell consists of five main blocks: input queues, crossbar, processing elements, data memory and microengine. Table 1 presents the contribution of these blocks to the implementation of the prototype with 4K-word data memory. The Warp cell contains 5422 pins in 6525 nets, and it consumes 94W (typ.) and 136W (max.).

Part	Chip count	Contribution (%)
Queues	63	25.1
Crossbar	32	12.7
Processing elements	8	3.1
Data memory (4K words)	30	11.9
Micro-engine	79	31.4
Other	40	15.8
Total for the Warp cell	252	100.0

Table 5-1: Metrics for Warp cell

5.2. Implementation of the IU

The IU handles data input/output between the host and the Warp array. The host-IU interface is streamlined by implementing a 32-bit wide interface, even though the Warp array has only 16-bit wide internal data paths. This arrangement reduces the number of transfers. Data transfer to and from the IU may be controlled by interrupts; in this case, the IU always behaves like a slave device. During data transfers, the IU can convert 8-bit or 16-bit integers from the host into 32-bit floating-point numbers for the Warp array, and vice versa.

The IU generates addresses and control signals for the Warp array. It supplies all the necessary signals to drive the cells of the Warp array, requiring little control and data bandwidth on the host side. For the address generation, the IU has an integer ALU capable of generating two addresses every 200 ns. All these operations are controlled by a 96-bit wide programmable microengine, which is similar to the Warp cell controller in programmability. The IU has several control registers that are mapped into the host memory space; the host can control the IU and hence the Warp array by setting these registers.

As each Warp cell, the IU is implemented on a single 15"×17" board. There are 5692 pins and 6170 nets on the board. The IU has a power consumption of 82W (typ.) and 123W (max.). Table 5-2 presents implementation metrics for the IU.

The IU generates the 20 MHz clock and plays a special role in system diagnostics; it generates the diagnostic signals for the Warp array. The host has total control of the clock generator and

Part	Chip count	Contribution (%)
Data-converter	52	18.9
Address generation	64	23.2
Clock and host interface	74	26.9
Micro-engine	44	16.1
Other	41	14.9
Total for the IU	275	100.0

Table 5-2: Metrics for the IU

can run the Warp array in step mode. After each step, most of the internal state of the array can be monitored using the built-in serial diagnostic chains. The IU can reach the serial chains of each Warp cell separately. This allows the debugging of each Warp cell in the array independently from any other cell.

6. Host system

Input and output are critical issues for any high-performance architecture. At its peak I/O rate, the Warp array can communicate with the outside world at the rate of 40 Mbytes/sec through the IU. This is a stringent requirement for a typical off-the-shelf, microcomputer-based system.

The system must also be able to execute those parts of an application that do not map well onto the Warp array, and to coordinate all the peripherals, which include the Warp array, digitizers, graphics displays, and similar devices. Moreover, for vision applications, the system must have a large memory to store images. These images are fed through the Warp array, and results must be stored in memory until used again. In addition, for vision research at Carnegie Mellon, it is crucial that the Warp machine exists within a UNIX environment.

These goals are achieved by integrating the Warp array with a host. This distinguishes Warp from other high-performance machines that define the interface close to the special-purpose hardware and leave the problem of system integration to the user.

6.1. Host architecture

Integrating Warp into a UNIX environment is accomplished by partitioning the host into a standard workstation supporting UNIX and an "external host." The workstation is also *master* and controls the external host. Figure 6-1 presents an overview of the Warp host.

The external host consists of two *cluster processors*, a sub-system called *support processor* and graphics devices. The external host is built around a VME bus. The two cluster processors and the support processor (all Motorola 68020 microprocessors) have dual-ported memories, with a private access on a local VMX32 bus and a shared access on the global VME bus. These three processors run stand-alone. Two *switch boards* allow the clusters to send and receive data to and from the Warp array, through the IU. Each switch has also a VME interface, used for debugging purposes and to start/stop/control the Warp array. The master (the workstation processor) is connected to the external host via a VME bus-coupler. All the boards with the exception of the switch are off-the-shelf components.

Application programs execute on the workstation and invoke functions for execution on the Warp array. The external host acts as intermediary in the interaction between workstation program and Warp array. Control of the external host is strictly centralized: the master issues commands to all external processors through message queues that are local to each external processor.

The support processor controls peripheral I/O devices and handles floating-point exception and other interrupt signals from the Warp array. These interrupts are serviced by the support processor, rather than by the master processor, to minimize interrupt response time. After servicing the interrupt, the support processor notifies the master processor. This organization does not conflict with the fundamental paradigm of centralized control inside the host.

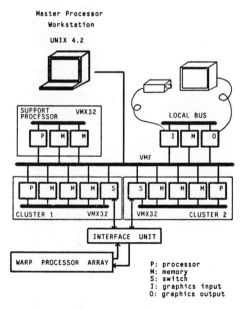

Figure 6-1: Host of the Warp machine

During computation, two clusters work in parallel, each handling a uni-directional flow of data to or from the Warp processor, through the IU. The two clusters can exchange their roles in sending or receiving data for different phases of a computation, in a ping-pong fashion. When the two clusters exchange their roles, there could be a danger that both clusters write to, or read from, the Warp array at the same time. To prevent this from happening, an arbitration mechanism transparent to the user has been implemented.

There are three memory banks inside each cluster processor to provide storage as well as efficiency. For example, the first memory bank may be receiving a new set of data from an I/O

device, while the second contains previous data to be transferred to the Warp array, and the third has the cluster program code. This arrangement allows overlapping the transfer of an image to the Warp array with the acquisition of the next image. Presently, the total memory in the external host is 8 Mbytes, and it can be upgraded to 16 Mbytes. In the current configuration, physical constraints limit the total storage to 36 Mbytes.

6.2. Host I/O bandwidth

To meet the stringent I/O bandwidth required by the Warp array, the host design exploits the fact that input/output data for signal, image and low-level vision processing are usually 8-bit or 16-bit integers. Because the data items in the host are either 8- or 16-bit integers, they can be *packed* into 32-bit words before being transferred to the IU. These 32-bit words are unpacked and expanded by the IU into four or two 32-bit floating-point numbers, before being shipped to the Warp array. The opposite process takes place with the floating-point outputs of the Warp array. Therefore, the data bandwidth requirement between the host and IU is reduced by a factor of 4 or 2, respectively. This I/O bandwidth reduction allows the Warp processor array to be fully utilized under the present microcomputer-based system, without having to rely on other custom-made hosts with higher I/O bandwidth capabilities. For example, if the input/output data are 8-bit pixels, then to support the peak Warp I/O bandwidth via the IU (40 Mbytes/sec) the host needs only to transfer 10 Mbytes/sec to and from Warp. This transfer rate can be sustained with two clusters each capable of handling a 5 Mbytes/sec transfer rate, which is within their current capabilities.

6.3. Host software

The Warp host features a run-time software library that allows the programmer to synchronize the support processor and two clusters and to perform the allocation of the memories in the external host. The run-time software handles also communication and interrupts between the master and the processors in the external host. The library of run-time routines includes utilities such as "copy", "move", windowing, and peripheral device drivers. The compiler generates program-specific input and output routines for the clusters so that a user needs not be concerned with programming at this level; these routines are linked at compile time to the two cluster processor libraries.

The application program usually runs on the master; however, it is possible to assign certain sub-tasks (e.g., finding the maximum in an output vector from the Warp array) to any of the external processors. This increases parallelism and boosts performance, since processing can now take place locally without transferring data from the external host to the master. Each transfer from the Warp array to the master processor memory passes through the VME bus repeater, which roughly doubles the transfer time (compared to direct VME access).

Memory allocation and processor synchronization inside the external host are handled by the application program through subroutine calls to the run-time software. Memory is allocated through the equivalent of a UNIX *malloc()* system call, the only difference being that the memory bank has to be explicitly indicated. This is necessary for reasons of efficiency. In fact, the programmer must be aware of the different memory banks, that can at any time be accessed simultaneously by different processors through different buses, thus achieving full parallelism.

Conditional execution of tasks inside each stand-alone processor is provided by *conditional requests* issued by the master processor. In other words, any task queued into the queue of each processor is always unconditionally executed; it is the issuing of the specific command that must satisfy a certain condition. A typical example is the execution of a certain task conditioned by the completion of a different task in a different processor: one call in the application code to the run-time software achieves this purpose.

7. Concluding remarks

Some of the Warp design decisions are influenced by the technology we use to implement the machine. These design choices must be re-evaluated if a different technology is used. For example, in the Warp architecture, the cells mostly rely on the IU to generate the addresses and loop controls. If the Warp cells are implemented in custom VLSI, however, the external data path for passing addresses through the cells is far more expensive than an on-chip address generation unit.

Direct hardware support for flow control should be considered. Currently, this functionality is provided in software; the compiler prevents a cell from reading from an empty queue, or writing into a full queue. Compile-time synchronization makes the hardware design easier; however, it complicates the compiler and limits the applicability of the machine.

The Warp project is not complete at this time, but our experiences so far support four conclusions. First, an early identification of the application area is important for experimental special-purpose machines with radically different architectures. Including the application users in the early phase of the project—the vision research group at Carnegie Mellon in our case—helped us focus on the architectural requirements and provided early feedback.

Second, software support tools are crucial for a programmable systolic machine. A compiler development effort contributes in two ways: it makes user programming easier and provides feedback on the architecture. To write efficient code for such a machine by hand is time-consuming, error-prone and requires a detailed understanding of the implementation. Only a compiler can free the user from the management of low-level details. Developing a compiler also benefits the architecture. Designing and implementing a compiler requires a thorough study of the functionality of the machine; this analysis uncovers the sources of real problems. Furthermore, a compiler enables the designer to get a larger set of test programs to validate architecture and implementation decisions. It is our conclusion that the compiler component is essential for architecture development.

Our third conclusion is that the integration of a special-purpose machine in an open and general purpose host environment is essential. The Warp host provides flexible I/O facilities as well as the UNIX programming environment, which are crucial to the usability of the machine. Moreover, early recognition of the importance of system integration allowed us to balance the I/O bandwidth of the host with the computation power of the Warp array.

Lastly, we conclude that the linear array configuration is suitable for most applications in signal processing, low-level vision, and scientific computation. A linear array with large local memory and powerful cells is efficient for global operations as well as for local operations. The Warp cell entails a high degree of pipelining and parallelism which needs to be managed explicitly. Our experience demonstrates that our compiler can produce effective code for the programs in our application domain.

Warp is a powerful and usable machine. Even with a conservative implementation, the current machine delivers a peak performance of 100 MFLOPS. The host system makes the Warp array accessible to users; it provides an environment for application development, and sustains the Warp cells with an adequate data rate. Program development for Warp is easy since the Warp compiler produces efficient code.

Acknowledgments

We appreciate the contributions to the Warp project by our colleagues at Carnegie Mellon: D. Adams, C. Bono, C. Chang, E. Clune, R. Cohn, P. Dew, J. Deutch, B. Enderton, P.K. Hsiung, K. Hughes, T. Kanade, G. Klinker, P. Lieu, R. Mosur, H. Ribas, J. Senko, Y. Shintani, B. Siegell, P. Steenkiste, Y-B Tsai, R. Wallace, and J-K Wang. We appreciate technical assistance and corporate support from General Electric and Honeywell, our industrial partners for the project. In particular, we thank A. Lock and C. Walrath of General Electric and L. Johnson and D. Kaylor of Honeywell, who spent four months at Carnegie Mellon working with us during the first half of 1985.

I. Sample program

In the sample program below, most statements have their obvious meaning. **Send** and **receive** transfer data between adjacent cells. The first parameter determines the direction of the transfer, and the second parameter selects the hardware channel to be used. The remaining two parameters bind the source (for send) or result (for receive) to local variables and formal parameters.

```
/*****************************************/
/*         Polynomial evaluation         */
/*   A polynomial with 10 coefficients is */
/*evaluated for 100 data points on 10 cells*/
/*****************************************/

module polynomial (data in, coeffs in,
                                    results out)
float data[100], coeffs[10];
float results[100];

cellprogram (cid : 0 : 9)
begin

    function poly
    begin
        float coeff, xin, yin, ans;
        int i;

/*Every cell saves the first coefficient that
reaches it, consumes the data and passes the
remaining coefficients. Every cell generates
an additional item at the end to conserve the
number of receives and sends.          */

        receive (L, X, coeff, coeffs[0]);
        for i := 1 to 9 do begin
            receive (L, X, temp, coeffs[i]);
            send (R, X, temp);
        end;
        send (R, X, 0.0);

/* Implementing Horner's rule, each cell
multiplies the accumulated result yin with
incoming data xin and add the next
coefficient                            */

        for i := 0 to 99 do begin
            receive (L, X, xin, data[i]);
            receive (L, Y, yin, 0.0);
            send (R, X, xin);
            ans := coeff + yin*xin;
            send (R, Y, ans, results[i]);
        end;
    end

    call poly;
end
```

References

1. Fisher, A.L., Kung, H.T., Monier, L.M. and Dohi, Y. "The Architecture of a Programmable Systolic Chip". *Journal of VLSI and Computer Systems 1*, 2 (1984), 153-169. An earlier version appears in *Conference Proceedings of the 10th Annual Symposium on Computer Architecture*, Stockholm, Sweden, June 1983, pp. 48-53.

2. Gross, T. and I am, M. Compilation for a High-performance Systolic Array. Proceedings of the SIGPLAN 86 Symposium on Compiler Construction, ACM SigPlan, June, 1986.

3. Gross, T., Kung, H.T., Lam, M. and Webb, J. Warp as a Machine for Low-level Vision. Proceedings of 1985 IEEE International Conference on Robotics and Automation, March, 1985, pp. 790-800.

4. Kung, H.T. "Memory Requirements for Balanced Computer Architectures". *Journal of Complexity 1*, 1 (1985), 147-157. (A revised version also appears in Conference Proceedings of the 13th Annual International Symposium on Computer Architecture, June 1986).

5. Kung, H.T. and Lam, M. "Wafer-Scale Integration and Two-Level Pipelined Implementations of Systolic Arrays ". *Journal of Parallel and Distributed Computing 1*, 1 (1984). A preliminary version appeared in *Proceedings of the Conference on Advanced Research in VLSI*, MIT, January 1984.

6. Kung, H.T. and Webb, J.A. Global Operations on the CMU Warp Machine. Proceedings of 1985 AIAA Computers in Aerospace V Conference. American Institute of Aeronautics and Astronautics, October, 1985, pp. 209-218.

7. Rau, B. R. and Glaeser, C. D. Some Scheduling Techniques and an Easily Schedulable Horizontal Architecture for High Performance Scientific Computing. Proc. 14th Annual Workshop on Microprogramming, Oct., 1981, pp. 183-198.

8. Wallace, R., Matsuzaki, K., Goto, Y., Crisman, J., Webb, J. and Kanade, T. Progress in Robot Road-Following. Proceedings of 1986 IEEE International Conference on Robotics and Automation, April, 1986.

9. Woo, B., Lin, L. and Ware, F. A High-Speed 32 Bit IEEE Floating-Point Chip Set for Digital Signal Processing. Proceedings of 1984 IEEE International Conference on Acoustics, Speech and Signal Processing, 1984, pp. 16.6.1-16.6.4.

A SPECIAL PURPOSE LSI PROCESSOR
USING THE DDA ALGORITHM FOR IMAGE TRANSFORMATION

Katsura Kawakami and Shigeo Shimazaki

Matsushita Research Institute Tokyo, Inc.
3-10-1 Higashimita, Tamaku, Kawasaki, Japan

Abstract

A new special purpose processor, named MN8614, has been developed for the high speed execution of binary image transformations. The processor carrys out the processing based on a new extension of the DDA algorithm to reduce the number of multiplications required for image processing. In addition, a machine instruction set has been developed which makes optimal use of the new method. The processor is fabricated on a single LSI chip with 16-bit data paths. Although the basic chip design is the same as that used in the construction of a general purpose microprocessor, the processing speed of MN8614 proves to be more than 30 times faster.

1. Introduction

The use of dedicated LSI image processors is expected to lower the cost of image processing systems. Nevertheless, a number of these systems have been implemented using bit-sliced microprocessors. Two factors contribute to this situation. Firstly, the size of the market for image processing systemss has not been large enough to make the development of a special purpose LSI processor viable. Secondly, since a large amount of information is required to represent an image (say 4 million elements for an A4 page of 8 elements/mm resolution), the processing time would be intolerably long if an interactive system was implemented using general purpose microprocessors.

However, the development of image processing systems has been accelerated by recent technological advances in the fabrication of major components of the systems at low costs and in small sizes, e.g., high-density RAMs for image memory, optical discs for filing devices and CCD scanners for input devices. It is also becoming increasingly common to provide image processing functions in office information systems, where there is a need to manipulate uncoded images such as maps, illustrations and photographs. These kinds of images cannot be represented by parameters such as the coordinates of the terminal points of a straight line or the radius of a circle. Hence, image transformation must be performed on all elements in the area of interest. Moreover, it is necessary to speed up processing so as not to irritate operators in an interactive environment. An image processor, the MN8614, has been developed

to respond to these requirements.

There are two problems which make it impractical to use general purpose microprocessors for such systems. Firstly, position calculation for each picture element is achieved by matrix-multiplications which take a long time for microprocessors. Secondly, the transformation of binary images requires many bit-manipulations. The overhead of instruction fetch would be significant in this kind of processing if it were programmed in byte- and/or word-oriented machine instructions. These problems are solved by extending the DDA algorithm which is an efficient method of line generation [1][2], and implementing it in microcode. The extension of the DDA (Digital Differential Analyser) and the architecture of the processor are presented in this paper.

2. Design Concepts

An image processor, the MN8614, has been developed to be used in office information systems. Accordingly, design effort was concentrated on strengthening the functions of image-transformation and generation of figures to achieve effective use of hardware. Other functions such as display/scanner control, image analysis and pattern recognition, are excluded. Similarly, the processor is dedicated to binary (black and white) image. Halftoned and/or chromatic images can be represented by plural planes of binary images.

Tow principle techniques have been adopted in the design of the processor to achieve high speed processing. These correspond to the two problems pointed out before. The first is the new algorithm based on the DDA for image transformation. The second is the microcode implementation of a dedicated instruction set for image processing.

2.1. Extension of the DDA algorithm

An extension of the DDA algorithm for image transformations, such as expansion, contraction and rotation, has been achieved. This eliminates a number of multiplications in the position calculations for transformed image elements. An improvement of one order of magnitude or more in performance has been achieved in comparison with the process in which the coordinate vectors are multiplied by an affine transform matrix for every picture element.

Reprinted from *Proceedings of the 11th Annual International Symposium on Computer Architecture*, 1984, pages 48-54. Copyright © 1984 by The Institute of Electrical and Electronics Engineers, Inc.

The MN8614 manipulates information stored in a bit-mapped memory in which one bit corresponds to an element, i.e., an image is composed of a 2-dimensional array of 1-bit elements. The transformation process is carried out by the transfer of a source element to the result element as shown in Fig.1. Hence, the transformation process does not depend on the contents of memory, i.e., the shape of existing figures in the bit map of the image.

The DDA algorithm is adopted on the assumption that in affine transformations adjacent elements on a source string are transformed to be adjacent on a result string. Source elements are projected onto the result string through a straight line by the new method. The gradient of the line is chosen to be equal to the ratio of expansion/contraction. The DDA algorithm is used to generate the line. The result of a projection may not correspond to a lattice point, and the lattice point nearest to the result is selected as the result element. Fig.2 illustrates the method of contraction as an example. A line of gradient 5/8 is used for the projection of a string of 8 elements to one of 5 elements.

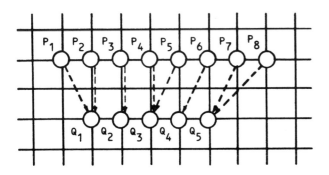

Fig.1 An example of data transfer in contraction

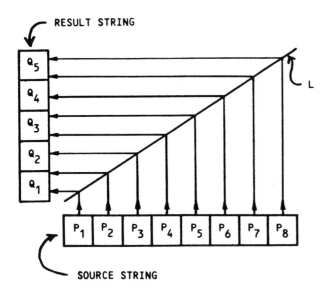

Fig.2 Projection method of contraction in MN8614

2.2. Microprogram control

It is well known that microprogramming is effective for the efficient implementation of complicated process [3], and it is obvious from practice that microinstructions are suitable for image processing because they are wider in bit-length, and can thus execute various kinds of operations in fewer steps. However, there is another factor that makes microprogramming suitable for image processing, especially in an LSI processor. Since the same computation process is frequently performed for a large number of picture elements, it is possible to design machine instructions which can be interpreted by repeated execution of microcode loops. The instructions of the MN8614 are designed to have parameters which designate the number of elements or the width of the area to be operated upon. Thus, the compaction of microprograms has been achieved so as to implement the control memory inside the chip. As a result, a number of instruction fetches have been eliminated, and the ratio of the number of instruction fetches to operand accesses has been improved significantly. This increases the throughput of LSI, which has been found to be a serious problem recently for single chip processors, from the viewpoint of pin/gate ratio [4][5].

Moreover, it is frequently required to perform operations on elements extracted from the same word. This kind of program would include much redundancy if programmed in byte- and/or word-oriented machine languages. Since such a machine instruction could be applied only for an element (1 bit) at a time, the same instruction has to be fetched 8 times in order to process a byte. The result is that the amount of information transfer due to instruction fetches becomes greater than the image data transfer to and from the processor, and the bus transfer capacity becomes a limit to the performance of the processor.

A simplified throughput model of the processor is shown in Fig.3. A and B represent the time required for processing a word inside the LSI chip, and the time to transfer a word through the LSI chip's pins, respectively. Assuming that C and T represent the number of cycles required to process a word, and the machine cycle time, respectively, then A is calculated to be

$$A = CT$$

B can be estimated from the transfer rate of an external bus connected to the processor. Usually it ranges from 200 to 1000 nsec per word. An increase in efficiency could be expected with greater complexity in the internal structure of the LSI chip, when A would be much greater than B. Using TTL technology for the external circuitry, however, the processing speed of a processor is limited by the speed of incoming information, since A is almost equal to B nowadays. For example, in the case of the MN1613, a 16-bit microprocessor marketed by Matsushita Electronic Corp., the cycle time is designed to be 300 nsec [6], and the mean value of C is evaluated to be 2.4 [7]. The time required to transfer a word between the processor and the main storage is designed to be 600 nsec. Then, A is calculated to be 720 nsec, very close to the value of B.

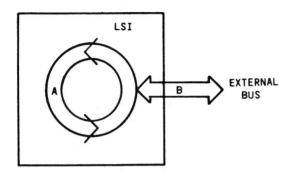

A : Processing time inside the LSI chip
B : Time for data transfer to and from the LSI processor

Fig.3 Throughput model of the LSI processor

On the other hand, the image processing instructons of the MN8614 are estimated to have the value of C greater than 100. This is because the number of machine cycles required to process a picture element ranges from 10 to 30, and, in a typical application, more than ten elements are processed. (The typical image display device and printer have about a million elements, for example.) The values of T and B of the MN8614 are the same as those of the MN1613. Hence, this value of C allowes us to expect that performance increases due to increasing semiconductor density will not be limited by the bandwidth of the external bus. Consequently we expect this architecture to retain its viability for some number of years.

3. Image Processing Algorithm

In the new metod of transformation, the relation between source and result elements of an image is determined by the projection through the line L, as shown in Fig.4. The basic sequence of operation in the processor is as follows:

a) Determine the point of intersection of the line L and a vertical line passing through the center of the source element P_i.

b) Determine the result element Q_j which covers the y-coordinate of this point of intersction.

c) Two cases exist:
if Q_j is a new element, then transfer the information from P_i to Q_j;
if P_{i-1} was mapped onto Q_j, then Q_j is not a new element, and the information from P_i is ORed with the existing Q_j to form a new value for Q_j.

This projection method makes the calculation process simple, because the coordinates of the marked points on the line L can be generated by the DDA algorithm. The y-coordinate of a new point on L can be calculated from that of the previous point by adding the constant value, $(N/M)\ell$ (the product of the gradient of the line L and the length of the lattice ℓ).

Assuming that $T_{y,i}$ is the y-coordinate of the i-th point, T_i, on L, and $Q_{y,j}$ is the coordinate of result point of the source element P_i, then,

$$T_{y,i} = Q_{y,j} + R_i : 0 \leq R_i < \ell , Q_{y,j} = k\ell$$

where k is an integer. The above equation can be rewritten as follows.

$$Q_{y,j} = \langle T_{y,i} \rangle , R_i = T_{y,i} - \langle T_{y,i} \rangle$$

where $\langle T \rangle$ represents $[T/\ell]\cdot\ell$, and $[x]$ represents the integer below x. The i+1-th points on the line L has the y-coordinate of

$$T_{y,i+1} = Q_{y,j} + R_i + (N/M)\ell$$

where N and M represent the numbers of elements in the result and source string, respectively. When $R_i + (N/M)\ell$ is greater than ℓ, then

$$Q_{y,j+1} = \langle T_{y,i+1} \rangle , \text{ and } R_{i+1} = R_i + (N/M)\ell - \ell$$

because there must be a boundary line of the lattice between T_i and T_{i+1}. Otherwise,

$$Q_{y,j} = \langle T_{y,i+1} \rangle , \text{ and } R_{i+1} = R_i + (N/M)\ell$$

In this case the result element is the same as the previous one. Thus, a corresponding result position is determined for each element of the source string, one after another. When the initial value of R_i is set to be 0 or 1/2, the lower element or the nearest element is selected as the result element, respectively. The relationship between i and j is expressed by the following equation.

$$j - 1/2 = [(N/M)(i-1/2)] + 1/2$$

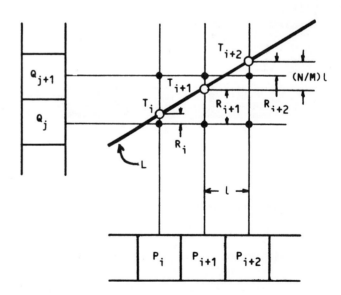

Fig.4 The projection method of transformation

353

The mechanism which implements the above calculation process is shown in Fig.5. Whenever a trigger T is generated, the value of the contraction ratio (N/M) is added to the remainder R_i, and simultaneously, the position assigned by the pointer of the source string is moved to the next position. When a carry is generated in the addition, the position designated by the result pointer is moved to the next one. Otherwise, the pointer remains unchanged. After each addition, the information belonging to the element designated by the source pointer is transfered to that of the result. The OR operation between the sources which correspond to one result prevents disappearance of fine lines by contraction. The mechanism for expansion is obtained by changing the direction of data transfer in Fig.5. Note that an image is exactly regenerated by contraction if it was previously expanded, in spite of the Moiré effect (although reverse is not true). Rotation of an image proceeds as follows: the processor sequentially processes elements along holizontal lines in the source image, and for each element, transforms its source coordinates to produce destination coordinates. The element at the destination coodinates is then set appropriately. The transformation is effected by the same mechanism as discussed above.

These mechanisms are implemented in microcode using the hardware of a general purpose microprocessor. The source and the result buffers, shown in Fig.5, achieve smooth processing between source and result elements, and efficient data

transfer to and from an external image memory. In addition, Bresenham's algorithm [2] is adopted in place of ratio-addition in order to avoid the division of N by M and the accumulation of errors. Two-dimensional transformation is realized by double processing of the one-dimensional transformation provided by the processor.

The degree of increase in performance due to this new method depends on the hardware of the processor. A new point is generated by 3 additions (to the Remainder and the pointers) and one conditional branch (on the Carry) instead of one multiplication in expansion/contraction. The improvement of processing speed is estimated to be more than one order of magnitude in the hardware environment of the processor. The number of programming steps in microcode is also reduced sinificantly.

4. Architecture of the processor

The MN8614 includes an emulator dedicated to processing image data in a bit-mapped memory connected to the external bus. In other words, the processor manipulates the information stored in ordinary memory, such as the main storage of a microprocessor, as a binary image. Therefore, the processor can be easily connected to "ready-made" systems without changing the structure of memory, and works as a co-processor. The hardware of the processor is also used in the construction of another 16-bit general purpose microprocessor, the MN1613, which contains 40,000 transistors [8]. The basic chip design of the two processor is the same. The only difference between MN8614 and MN1613 is in their microprograms, except for a part of the control circuit in the interface to the external memory.

A block diagram of the hardware of the processor is shown in Fig.6. The machine instructions enter from the bus lines and are routed to the Interpret Unit, through the Instruction Queue and the Instruction Register. The Interpret Unit, controlled by upper-level microcode, issues the start addresses of lower-level microroutines which are located in the Control Unit. The 16-bit ALU, General Registers and other units are controlled by the lower-level microprograms, except for the Input/Output interface which executes the instruction prefetch asynchronously. Five of the 16 general registers are designed to be explicitly referenced in machine instructions. The remaining eleven are used as working registers which include the buffers, the pointers and the registers holding the Ratio and the Remainder shown in Fig.5. WAR (Word Address Register) and BPR (Bit Position Register) designate one bit out of 4 megabits of image memory as the "current position" which is the key-point of the image area being transformed. The width of image space is defined by WDR (Width Defining Register). PR (Pattern Register) is used to hold painting-out patterns, as well as for the accumulator of ordinary operations, e.g., add, subtract and logical operations. The carry and overflow of operations are held in STR (STatus Register).

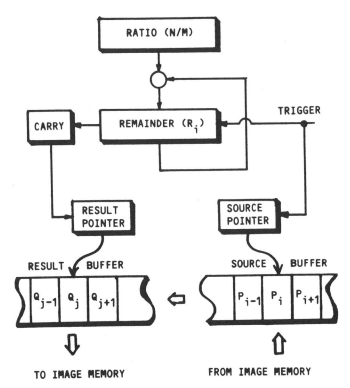

Fig.5 Mechanism of transformation in MN8614

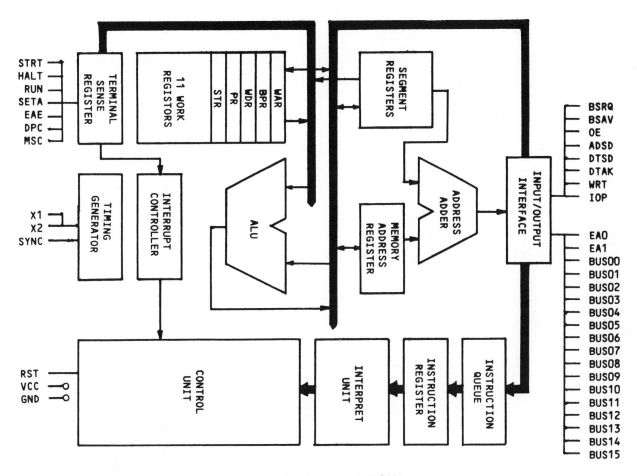

Fig.6 A block diagram of MN8614

18 address lines are provided to the processor in order to access the 256k words (4 megabits) of memory. This can just hold the information on a sheet of A4 at a resolution of 8 elements/mm. This capacity meets the international standard of group III facsimile [9]. Although an address adder and segment registers are implemented in hardware (used in MN1613) for storage segmentation, the programmer need not be aware of their existence. The space in control memory is primarily used for image processing rather than complicated storage management. The width of upper- and lower-level microinstructions are 20 and 27 bits, while their capacities are 72 and 720 words, respectively.

The machine instruction set of the MN8614 is devided into two categories. The first, consisting of 35 instructions, is for image processing. Most of the control memory is occupied by routines which interpret these instructions. The second, consisting of 43 instructions, is similar to that of general purpose processors. Instructions in this category are for program flow control and simple arithmetic operations such as subroutine branch, conditional branch and loop counting. These instructions are made as simple as possible because they are regarded as supplementary functions of the processor. As a result, 88% and 7% of the lower-level microprogram memory are used

to implement respective of categories machine instructions, as shown in Fig.7. In contrast, almost all of the space is used for the 97 instructions in the MN1613.

The chip is packaged in a 40-pin DIP. A microphotograph of the chip is shown in Fig.8. Fig.9 shows an output of an image editing system which has been developed using the MN8614.

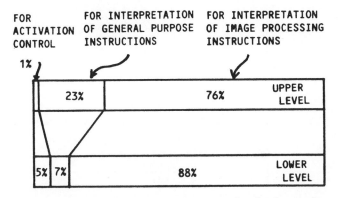

Fig.7 Space allocation in each level of microcode

355

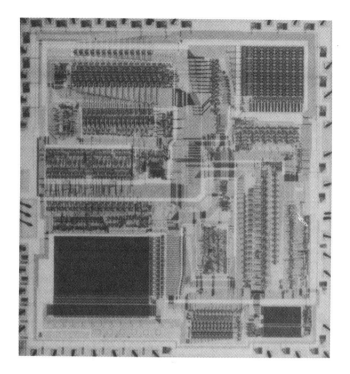

Fig.8 A microphotograph of the MN8614

Table 1 Comparison of execution times

Transformation	Execution time (us/element)		
	MN8614	MN1613	
Expansion	3.3	103	*1
Contraction	3.2	102	*1
Rotation (arbitrary angle)	7.8	800	*2
Rotation (90°)	6.4	88	*2
Painting-out (rectangle)	0.2	63	*2
Painting-out (arbitrary shape)	1.9	43	*2

*1 Element count is the total number of source and result elements
*2 Element count is the number of result elements

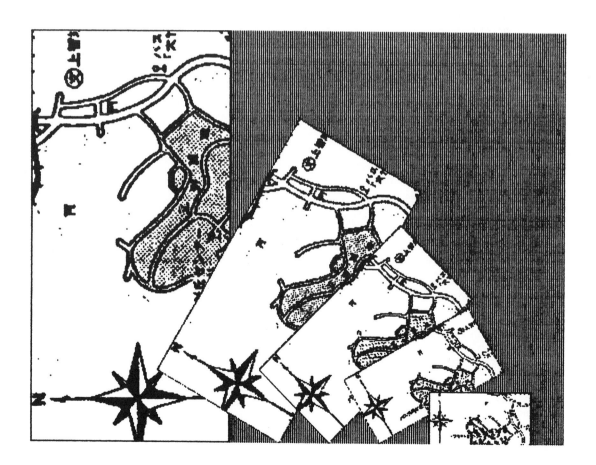

Fig.9 An example processed by the MN8614

5. Conclusion

The extended algorithm of the DDA for image transformation has been presented. This algorithm eliminates a number of multiplications in the affine transform of a continuous image stored in a bit-mapped memory, and has made it possible to implement an image processor which can be applied to interactive image editing systems. The image processing instructions are implemented inside the chip by compact microprograms. This has reduced the overhead of instruction fetches and has achieved high performance under the pin restriction of LSI packages. The execution times of the MN8614 for a variety of functions are compared to those of the MN1613 in Table 1. The execution time of the MN1613 is measured when it is programmed with the same algorithm as the MN8614. The performance of the MN8614 has proved to be 30 times faster than the MN1613 when performing expansion and contraction, although both have almost identical hardware.

Acknowledgement

The authors woud like to express their grateful appreciation to Mr. T. Tsumura of Panafacom Limited and Dr. I. Morishita of University of Tokyo for their suggestons and encouragements, and to Dr. T. Kawasaki of Matsushita Electronic Corp. for his promotion of the project. The autors also are grateful to Mr. K. Suzuki and Mr. H. Kotera for discussions from the view point of image processing, to Miss E. Hirokami for her microprogramming, to Mr. T. Sakuma for his help in the implementation, and to Dr. J. R. Gurd and Mr. M. V. Harmelen for their reading and comments on the draft manuscript.

References

1. W. M. Newman and R. F. Sproul, "Principle of Interactive Computer Graphics", McGraw-Hill, 2nd ed., 1981, pp 22-28.

2. J. E. Bresenham, "Algorithm for computer control of a digital plotter", IBM System Journal, Vol.4, No.1, 1965, pp 25-30.

3. W. T. Wilner, "Design of the Burroughs B1700", FJCC 1972, pp 489-497.

4. D. A. Patterson and C. H. Séquin, "Design Consideration for Single-Chip Computers of the Future", IEEE J. of SC, Vol. SC-15, No.1, Feb. 1980, pp 44-52.

5. I. Morishita, "Throughput Analysis for the Architecture Design of VLSI Microprocessors"- in Japanese, Internal Research Report IPTR 83-2, Dept. Math. Engineering and Instrumentation Physics, Univ. Tokyo, Tokyo, May 1983.

6. "MN1613 User's Manual" - in Japanese, Matsushita Electronic Corp., Kyoto, Japan, 1981.

7. K. Kawakami, S. Shimazaki and H. Nishikawa, "Two-level microprogramming for a 16-bit processor" - in Japanese, Proc. Ann. Symp. of Institute of Electronics and Communication Engineers of Japan, p6.40, No.1451, 1981.

8. H. Kadota, S. Ozawa, K. Kawakami and E. Ichinohe, "A New Register File Structure for the High-Speed Microprocessor", IEEE J. of SC, Vol. SC-17, No.5, Oct. 1982, pp 892-897.

9. CCITT Recommendation Standardization of Group III Facsimile Apparatus for document transmission", Vol.7, Fascicle VII.2, Rec. T.4.

RAPAC: a high-speed image-processing system

A.C. Elphinstone
A.P. Heron
Prof. G.S. Hobson
A. Houghton

M.K. Lau
A.R. Powell
L. Seed
R.C. Tozer

Indexing term: Image processing

Abstract: The paper describes the design and operation of a real-time image processing system and outlines one of its application areas. The system consists of a dedicated hardware processor called RAPAC (a reconfigurable attached processor architecture for convolution) and a host computer which is used for algorithm development and RAPAC control. RAPAC uses hardware processor units and multiple image memories, in a software controlled architecture, to process 5 MHz streams of pixel data. This processing rate allows it to process a 256×256 pixel image in 20 ms, one field time of a standard TV camera. The result is either a new 256×256 pixel image generated from the old image or a reduced data set which describes attributes of features in the image. These attributes are used by the host computer to calculate a decision output concerning the content of the image.

1 Introduction

In recent years there has been a continuous expansion of interest in image processing systems for a variety of applications. Much of the work performed to date has involved studies of image processing algorithms [1] using main-frame computers, and, as such, has been concerned more with algorithmic reliability and flexibility than with speed of execution. More recently the increasing availability of sophisticated hardware VLSI and high density memory chips has encouraged the development of effectively 'real-time' image processing systems [2–16]. The architectures of these systems are strongly influenced by the logical requirements of the processing and are made possible by the flexibility of the high density VLSI.

This paper describes the RAPAC (reconfigurable attached processor architecture for convolution) image processing system and its application to the collation of road traffic data. The system was designed to perform on-line industrial inspection tasks where the main requirement is to calculate a decision output such as a pass/fail decision, a measurement, grading or other classi-

fication in a period of time typically less than 1 s. Delayed or off-line processing cannot be used effectively for such tasks. The RAPAC system contains independent acquisition, display, framestore and processor units which exist in a reconfigurable architecture.

Each unit synchronously transfers a 256×256 frame of 8-bit pixel image data (raw or processed) through the hardware at TV frame rates (50 Hz). The system architecture, and operations performed by processor and framestore units, may be changed during each frame blanking period if necessary. Images are acquired using a standard TV (vidicon) camera, A/D converted at 5 MHz and held in framestores or processed with hardware processor units. Subsequent processors are used for feature extraction. The output is displayed on TV monitors, stored in framestores, or used by the host computer for decision making purposes.

RAPACs framestore/processor architecture is controlled by the host computer via a crosspoint data switching network. Consequently the complexity of the algorithms performed is primarily limited by the complexity of the hardware processing devices available. The advances being made in the fabrication of 'special-purpose' signal processing chips can easily be incorporated into the flexible architecture and 'plug-in processor' design of the system. Following an overview of design considerations on which the RAPAC system was based, there is a more detailed description of its building blocks.

2 RAPAC design considerations

The design of the RAPAC system was based on the experience gained in using its immediate predecessor, a system called MISISIPI [17], which used a microprocessor to perform all the image processing operations. The use of a microprocessor as the main processing element made the system very slow — it took of the order of 10 s to perform one operation on one frame of image data. This low processing rate presented two main problems. First, the time taken to provide a decision output was impractical for most realistic applications, and secondly, the data acquisition process was inconvenient because most readily available image acquisition units operated at a much higher data rate than the processor.

As a result of these considerations it was decided that RAPAC should be capable of processing a frame of data in 20 ms. This time scale was satisfactory from the point of view of the industrial applications which had been

Paper 5057E (E4) received 21st March 1986

The authors are with the Department of Electronic & Electrical Engineering, University of Sheffield, Mappin Street, Sheffield S1 3JD, United Kingdom examined with the MISISIPI system and was also compatible with the data rate from readily available low cost vidicon cameras. Constraining the system to work at TV frame rates was also considered to be highly desirable because of the wide range of other potentially useful equipment, such as video tape recorders and pyroelectric cameras, which would accept or provide data at such a rate.

It was clear from a brief survey of microprocessor execution times and the conclusions of other works [18, 19] that it would be necessary to provide a hardware processing system to operate on the image data at TV frame rates. At the same time it was recognised that a microprocessor-based system was convenient for algorithmic trials. Consequently the basic RAPAC structure had to be a hardware processing system attached to a host microcomputer. It was deemed desirable to design RAPAC in such a way that it could operate with any host computer. This would allow for updating of the host if more powerful machines became available and, perhaps more importantly, offered a degree of independence from any particular microprocessor manufacturer.

The geometric and grey level resolution of the framestore arrays for RAPAC was chosen as a 256 × 256 array of byte-wide pixels. Previous experience had indicated that 256 × 256 was a sufficient resolution for the majority of applications investigated. At the time RAPAC was being designed, 64K × 1 bit dynamic RAM chips which could operate at the speed required (5 MHz) were becoming available, a reality which made 256 × 256 a very convenient array size. The byte-wide format, although arguably excessive from a grey-level point of view, was used to allow the storage of intermediate results and to maintain compatibility with the basic word length of most available processors. It was considered sensible to construct a set of identical framestores so that neither the user nor the host computer would need to 'remember' where in the system architecture such different word length units were located.

The experience gained with the MISISIPI system made it very clear that the order in which operations needed to be performed varied from application to application. A fixed frame-store-processor architecture was unattractive from this point of view. The most appealing solution was to make the architecture of the system dynamically reconfigurable by using a crosspoint switching network. Physical size limited this network to eight byte-wide input ports and eight byte-wide output ports. The framestores and processors could then be permanently connected to this network and the architecture of the system reconfigured as required by the host computer. It was decided that, for maximum flexibility, the only crosspoint operation which should not be allowed was direct connection between input and output of the same unit (processor or framestore). Multiplexing of data inputs and data outputs in the crosspoint switch was avoided in order to prevent the possibility of data flow bottlenecks in the system.

The advantages of a dynamically reconfigurable architecture based on a large cross point switch are as follows:

(a) A processing path through the crosspoint switch consisting of processors joined in series can be set up. This is pipe-lining.

(b) Noncolliding processing paths through the crosspoint switch can run in parallel.

Both of these advantages lead to an increase in processing power due to the overlapping of operations. Fur-

thermore, the system architecture can be optimised for a given processing algorithm. These features are shown diagrammatically in Fig. 1.

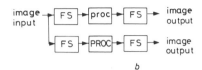

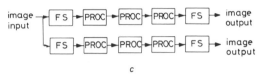

Fig. 1 *Optimising the system architecture for different algorithms*
→ image data flow
FS framestore unit
PROC processor unit
a Pipelined architecture
b 'Parallel' architecture
c 'Parallel pipelined' architecture

The overall structure of the system that emerged from the above considerations pointed towards a system which would have the following advantages:

(a) Only one refresh cycle generator was required for all the framestore units. This allowed a higher framestore density than would otherwise have been the case.

(b) The system would have to be synchronous with the frame rate of its vidicon acquisition system.

(c) There would be known time intervals in every frame when the updating of status registers in the processors, framestores and crosspoint switch could be performed.

It was recognised that rigid synchronism could cause some difficulties. In particular it would undermine the reliability of the last few pixels in an image for some of the longer processes. Solutions to this problem were considered, but it was decided that the extra hardware complexity involved was not justifiable for the sake of five to ten pixels at the bottom right-hand corner of the 64k pixel image.

3 RAPAC hardware description

3.1 Bus organisation

RAPAC is housed in its own 0.48 m (19 inch) Eurocard rack, and consists of a number of printed circuit boards which communicate with each other via two backplanes,

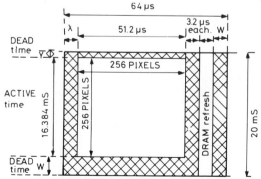

Fig. 2 *RAPAC system*

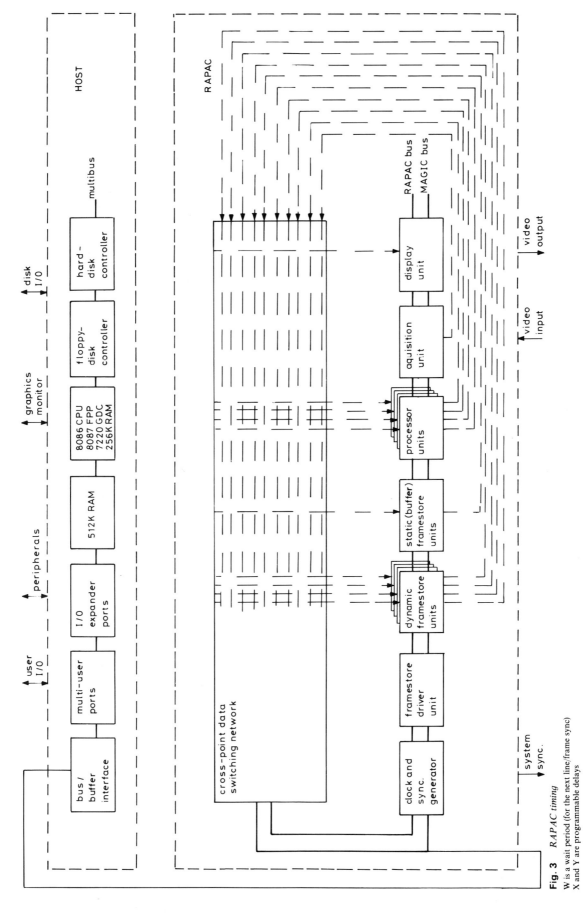

Fig. 3 *RAPAC timing*

W is a wait period (for the next line/frame sync)
X and Y are programmable delays

the RAPAC bus and the MAGIC (microprocessor and general purpose interface) bus (Fig. 2). These backplanes provide control signals to all of the units and determine the mode and timing of all image data transfers and processing in RAPAC. High-speed image data is not transferred on either backplane. These transfers take place via 16-way connectors on the front of each circuit board.

The RAPAC Bus, shown in Fig. 2, distributes all the high-speed (5 MHz) clocking signals used to control the pixel-by-pixel flow of a frame of image data through the system. These signals are only available during the active video region of a 20 ms TV frame, as shown diagrammatically in Fig. 3, and cause all high-speed data transfers.

The MAGIC bus allows the operation performed by each unit in RAPAC to be controlled by the host computer. It carries standard microprocessor backplane signals, hence allowing the interfacing of RAPAC to any host computer that can provide the standard address, data and control signals. The MAGIC bus is also used for the transfer of image data (for off-line image processing and archiving operations during the algorithm development stage) and the results of the data reduction/feature extraction operations, to and from the host computer.

3.2 Clock and sync generator
The system clock, line and frame sync signals are derived from a crystal oscillator and distributed to all the units in the system via the RAPAC bus. The line and frame sync signals are also made available for use by external devices such as TV cameras and display monitors.

3.3 Framestore driver
The framestore driver board uses the pixel clock and line and frame sync signals to generate all the clocking signals required by the framestores and processors. When a frame sync signal occurs, counters are used to gate 256 clock cycles (pixels) per line, and 256 lines per frame. This board also generates the signals required for the refreshing of the dynamic RAMS in the framestores. The timing of all the signals generated by the framestore driver board is shown diagrammatically in Fig. 3.

3.4 Acquisition board
The acquisition board uses a 7-bit analog-to-digital flash converter, running at 5 MHz to digitise the incoming video signal as shown in Fig. 4a. The output of the converter addresses a look-up table which allows several different pixel mapping functions to be realised. The loading and selection of a particular mapping function is controlled by the host computer. Such mapping functions including thresholding, histogram equalisation, quantisation or inversion. The image data from this look-up table is fed into the crosspoint switching network (described in Section 3.8) where it can be directed to the framestores and/or processors as required.

3.5 Display board
The display board contains four D/A channels, grouped together to give an RGB colour output and a monochrome output, as shown in Fig. 4b. Each channel contains a look-up table which is loaded by the host computer to produce false colour or monochrome output as required.

3.6 Framestores
The framestores contain 64 Kbytes of memory for a $256 \times 256 \times 8$-bit image, and have a read or write cycle

time of 200 ns. No read-modify-write cycles are used due to the longer cycle time they require. A block diagram of a framestore is shown in Fig. 5. The 16-bit address

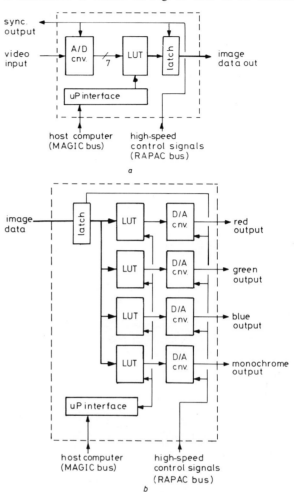

Fig. 4 *Acquisition and display units*
a Acquisition
b Display

counter consists of two 8-bit counters which are clocked by the 5 MHz pixel clock on the RAPAC bus. Both counters can be preloaded by the host computer to offset effectively the image in the X- and Y-directions. A 2 into 1 multiplexer provides the row and column addresses for the $64K \times 1$ dynamic RAMs.

There are two types of framestore in use in the RAPAC system. One uses static and the other uses

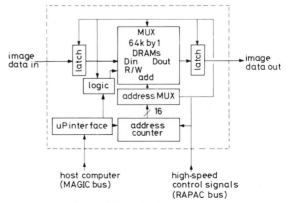

Fig. 5 *Dynamic RAM framestore design*

IEE PROCEEDINGS, Vol. 134, Pt. E, No. 1, JANUARY 1987

dynamic RAM. Both types operate identically in RAPAC. The majority of framestores use 64K dynamic RAMs due to their low cost, small physical size and the fact that their refresh requirements do not cause any contention problems with the read/write cycle timing as shown in the system timing diagram of Fig. 3.

Static RAMs are used in the buffer framestore unit. This is a dual ported framestore which in one mode is part of the attached processor and operates in exactly the same way as the dynamic framestores. In the other mode it exists as a directly addressable 64 Kbyte block of memory in the host computer's memory map. Using 64K static RAMs for this framestore greatly eased its design because no refresh or address multiplexing signals had to be generated for the memory mapped mode of operation. The purpose of this framestore is for transferring image data from the attached processor to the host computer (and vice versa) during algorithm development.

3.7 Processor units

3.7.1 Frame preprocessors: The frame preprocessors modify a frame of data. The units in use at present are an ALU processor, a 3 × 3 binary image convolver and a multiplier-adder combination. The ALU processor is shown in Fig. 6. It uses TTL logic to implement all the standard arithmetic and logical operations on two 8-bit data streams. These two data streams are either from the two input ports — A and B in Fig. 6 — or from port A and a one pixel delayed version of port A. This second

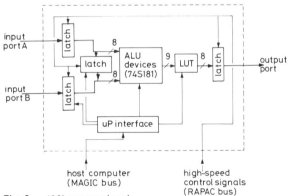

Fig. 6 *ALU processor board*

mode of operation is selected by the host computer and is used for performing edge detection along a line of data. The 9-bit output of the ALU feeds a look-up table for data rounding and mapping purposes.

The binary image convolver, shown in Fig. 7, is identical in concept to standard 3 × 3 operators which evaluate a pixel's new value from its old value and the values

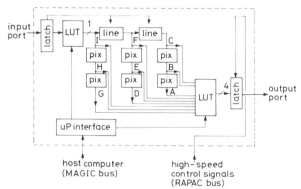

Fig. 7 *Binary image data convolver*

line   line delay element
pix   pixel delay element
ABC
DEF } 3 × 3 pixel neighbourhood
GHI

of its eight surrounding neighbours. For example, if A to I in Fig. 7 represent a 3 × 3 subarray in the 256 × 256 image, a new value for pixel E is calculated on the basis of the values of existing pixels, A to I. The nature of the operation performed depends upon the arithmetic or logic weightings ascribed to each pixel in the subarray. The 8-bit input data stream is thresholded by a look-up table whose single bit feeds a set of delay elements. The line delays are first in first out (FIFO) memories with 256 location, and the pixel delays are latches. The outputs of these delay elements constitute a 3 × 3 neighbourhood of pixels. On each clock cycle, the 3 × 3 neighbourhood advances one pixel. These (binary) pixels address another look-up table, whose output is the new value for the centre pixel E, and is fed to the data switching network. Both look-up tables are loaded by the host computer to provide a programmable set of threshold levels or windows and a variety of 3 × 3 operations such as

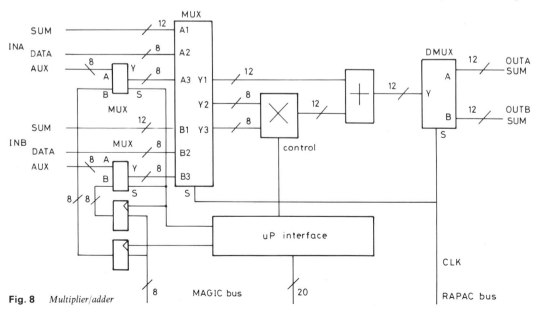

Fig. 8 *Multiplier/adder*

smoothing, edge detection (horizontal/vertical), and region shrinkage or growth.

The multiplier-adder, shown in Fig. 8, performs an 8-bit multiplication between a frame of data and either another frame of data or a selectable coefficient. The most significant 8 bits of the product are sign extended to 12 bits and fed to a 12-bit adder. The other input to the 12-bit adder is a frame of data. The adder, which can be configured as an accumulator, increases the versatility of this processor and makes it possible to perform operations such as arithmetic local neighbourhood operations as opposed to the logical operations described above.

The hardware multiplier and adder circuits employed in this processor operate sufficiently quickly to allow time multiplexing, and, as a consequence, two multiply-add functional units are available from one hardware system.

3.7.2 Feature extractor processors: After features in the acquired image(s) have been 'highlighted' by the operations performed by the frame preprocessors, the image data is routed through a 'feature extractor' processor. Its general form is shown in Fig. 9. The feature extractor

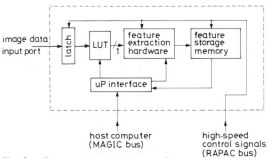

Fig. 9 *Feature-extractor processor unit*

initially thresholds the image data and then identifies and logs specific attributes of the white features in the thresholded image. For example, attributes such as the location and size of each white feature, the number of unconnected features or the weight of the image or parts of it are all attributes which can be extracted, stored in local memory and subsequently used by the host computer to assess the original content of the image.

The feature extractor in use at present uses an algorithm [20] which grows features down to their lower right-hand corner where the unique pixel arrangement of $\begin{smallmatrix}1&0\\0&0\end{smallmatrix}$ exists. On a second pass through this processor, coordinates of these pixel arrangements and the size of the features from which they were grown are extracted from the image. The reduced data set, therefore, contains a count of the number of unconnected features in the image, the position of each feature and its size. Unconnected objects in close proximity may be inadvertently merged during this process, hence making it unsuitable for some applications.

3.8 Crosspoint data switching network

The crosspoint data switching network consists of eight byte-wide input ports, eight byte-wide output ports and an array of byte-wide tristate gates (Fig. 10). The connections provided by the tristate gates are such that, under software control, each output port may derive its data from any of the input ports, except the one corresponding to its output, i.e. no processor or framestore can input data from its own output. This allows each data source (framestore or processor output) to feed one or more pro-

cessor or framestore inputs, so providing parallel or serial processing paths for a data stream. It is also possible to

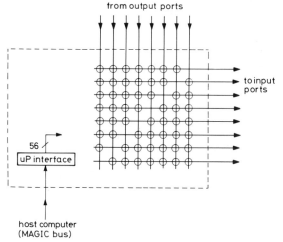

Fig. 10 *Crosspoint data switching network*
→ image data flow
⊕ crosspoint switch (tristate gates)

pipeline the processors and to obtain a parallel pipelined framestore and processor architecture, which may be required for some algorithms. The routing performed by the crosspoint switching network may be changed by the host computer for each frame of processing if required. This results in a flexible architecture which can fully utilise the processor units available and, if necessary, will provide multiuser facilities. The switching network may also be cascaded, although cascading would present a limitation on the connectivity which could only be overcome by building a larger matrix of crosspoints.

3.9 Bus buffer/interface board

This board is a bus extender which acts as an interface between the standard signals of the host computer and those used on the MAGIC bus. If a different host computer were to be used, then it would only require a different bus buffer/interface board to make its signals compatible with those required for the control of RAPAC.

4 Example of algorithm development

4.1 Algorithm development facilities

To provide image data for software algorithm development, the crosspoint data switching network sets up the RAPAC hardware as a simple frame grabber, using the buffer framestore (Section 3.6) and acquisition and display boards. The buffer framestore allows image data to be transferred between RAPAC and the host computer so that images can be acquired, grabbed, stored on hard disk, processed and displayed.

The software processing of images is either done from a library of basic imaging processing routines, or by the generation of new routines using the program development facilities which exist for more specialised algorithm development such as software simulations of a linear convolver. When an algorithm has been proven in software it is implemented in hardware as a processor unit, and forms part of the RAPAC system operating at the same speed as the rest of the hardware.

4.2 Application to traffic monitoring

A practical application of image processing which at present is receiving much attention is the analysis of moving traffic flow [21, 22]. A survey of the state of the art in this field is given in Reference 23. The RAPAC system has been used to count the number of vehicles travelling past and turning out of the T-junction shown in Fig. 11a. The algorithm which tracks the vehicles is

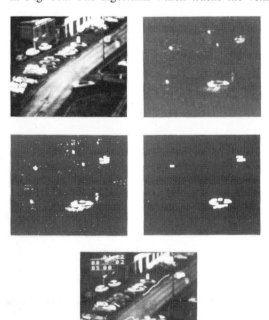

Fig. 11   *RAPAC system*

a Original image
b Difference image
c Thresholded difference image
d Extracted features
e Tracking information and extracted features superimposed on original image

executed by the host computer on the basis of data describing the frame by frame positions of vehicles. To extract this data the RAPAC system first uses the ALU processor described in Section 3.7 to subtract each incoming frame (Fig. 11a) from a previously stored vehicle-free background frame of the junction. The result is a difference image (Fig. 11b) which is thresholded at a low level (Fig. 11c) in order to preserve connectivity of features belonging to a single vehicle. The thresholded image contains residual pixel noise which is removed by performing a region shrink operation using the 3×3 convolver processor described in Section 3.7.1. This produces an image containing white vehicle features on a black background (Fig. 11d). The positions of these features are extracted by the feature extractor processor described in Section 3.7.2 and are used by the host computer to track the vehicles. A vehicle count occurs whenever a track enters a predetermined region of the image. A grey-level image of the T-junction is shown in Fig. 11e. It includes the positions of the three regions (top, side and bottom), vehicles overlayed by their grown binary features and the tracks caused by the movement of these features. The error rates in tracking the vehicles from one region to another are given in Table 1.

The counts for the top to bottom, bottom to top, side to top and side to bottom directions are encouraging when compared to the 10% error rate normally associated with manual counts. The bottom to side transition causes problems with the tracking algorithm because,

Table 1 : Error rates in tracking vehicles

Vehicle direction	Correct count	RAPAC count	% error
Top to bottom	87	72	−17%
Top to side	6	9	+50%
Bottom to top	72	64	−11%
Bottom to side	6	2	−66%
Side to top	8	8	0%
Side to bottom	6	6	0%

during the time that a vehicle is waiting to turn right, other vehicles overtake it on the left and 'steal' its track. As a result, the vehicle appears not to have a 'source' region and so cannot be counted.

The high count for the top to side direction is probably due to pedestrians, and present work includes efforts to eliminate them from the calculations. Work on improving the reliability of the tracking and counting algorithms and on generating high-speed vehicle identification algorithms is continuing using both visible and 10 μm infra-red wavelengths [24].

5   Conclusions

The RAPAC system is an attached processor unit designed specifically for the processing of packets of high-speed serial data, where identical operations need to be performed on each element of the data packet. It uses frame-by-frame acquisition of the data packets from a vidicon camera and has particular application in moving scene analysis which we have described as an application in road traffic monitoring.

The hardware of the system is highly flexible due to its software controlled architecture and plug-in-processor approach. The system's software has been designed to provide routines for both the software development of algorithms and the incorporation of new hardware processor units in RAPAC.

The existing system is a powerful processing machine for TV-frame rate images. The increasing availability of sophisticated signal processing chips and the possibilities offered by custom LSI are broadening the horizons of feasibility for economical RAPAC applications.

6   References

1 ROSENFELD, A.: 'SURVEY — picture processing: 1981', *Comput. Graph. & Image Process.*, 1982, **19**, pp. 35–75
2 SIEGEL, H.J., SIEGEL, L.J., KEMMERER, G.C., MUELLER, P.T., SMALLEY, H.E., and SMITH, S.D.: 'PASM: a partitionable SIMD/MIMD system for image processing and pattern recognition', *IEEE Trans.*, 1981, **C-30**, (12), pp. 934–946
3 ROESSER, R.P.: 'Two dimensional microprocessor pipelines for image processing', *ibid.*, 1978, **C-27**, (2), pp. 144–156
4 BRIGGS, F.A., FU, K.S., HWANG, K., and PATEL, J.H.: 'PM⁴ — a reconfigurable multiprocessor system for pattern recognition and image processing'. Proc. National Computer Conference, 1979, pp. 255–265
5 BATCHER, K.E.: 'Design of a massively parallel processor', *IEEE Trans.*, 1980, **C-29**, (9), pp. 836–840
6 RIEGER, C., BANE, J., and TRIGG, R.: 'ZMOB: a highly parallel multiprocessor'. Proc. Workshop on picture data description and management, August 1980, pp. 298–304
7 LAVIE, D., and TAYLOR, W.K.: 'A microprocessor controlled real-time image processor', *IEE Proc. E, Comput. & Digital Tech.*, 1983, **130**, (5), pp. 149–153
8 McILROY, C.D., LINGGARD, R., and MONTEITH, W.: 'Hardware for real-time image processing', *ibid.*, 1984, **131**, (6), pp. 223–229
9 SHERDELL, D.: 'A low architecture for a real-time computer vision system'. Proc. 5th International Conference Pattern Recognition, December 1980, **1**, pp. 290–295

10 WOODS, R.E., and GONZALEZ, R.C.: 'Real-time digital image enhancement', *IEEE Proc.*, 1981, **69**, (5), pp. 643–654

11 VAN DAELE, J., DE ROO, J., VANDERHEYDT, L., OOSTER-LINCK, A., and VAN DEN BERGHE, H.: 'Image computer configuration with video rate processing capabilities'. Proc. 1st Scandinavian Conference on Image Analysis, 1980, pp. 192–198

12 ARVIND, D.K., ROBINSON, I.N., and PARKER, I.N.: 'A VLSI chip for real-time image processing'. Proc. International Symposium on Circuits and Systems, May 1983, pp. 405–408

13 DUFF, M.J.B.: 'Review of the CLIP image processing system'. Proc. National Computer Conference, 1978, pp. 1055–1060

14 VAN DAELE, J., OOSTERLINCK, A., and VAN DEN BERGHE, H.: 'The Leuven automatic visual inspection machine (LAVIM)', *SPIE*, Imaging Applications for Automated Industrial Inspection and Assembly, 1979, **182**, pp. 58–64

15 FRANCHI, P., GONZALEZ, J., MANTEY, P., PAOLI, C., PAROLO, A., and SIMMONS, J.: 'Design issues and architecture of HACIENDA, an experimental image processing system', *IBM J. Res. & Dev.*, 1983, **27**, (2), pp. 116–126

16 FU, K.S.: 'Special computer architectures for pattern recognition and image processing — an overview'. Proc. National Computer Conference 1978, pp. 1003–1013

17 PRETTYJOHNS, K.N.: 'The application of image processing and microprocessor techniques to industrial inspection'. Ph.D Thesis, University of Sheffield, 1981

18 BROOK, R.A.: 'Development of techniques for automated industrial inspection in the U.K. in the age of microprocessors', *SPIE*, Imaging Applications for Automated Industrial Inspection and Assembly, 1979, **182**, pp. 79–82

19 ASADA, H., TABATA, M., KIDODE, M., and WATANABE, S.: 'New image processing hardware and their applications to industrial automation', *SPIE*, Imaging Applications for Automated Industrial Inspection and Assembly, 1979, **182**, pp. 14–21

20 FISHER, C.: 'Counting systems in image analysis employing line scanning techniques'. UK Patents 1 264 805 and 1 264 806 Feb. 1972 (also in, Ullman, J.: 'Video rate digital image analysis equipment', *Pattern Recognition*, 1981, **14**, (1–6), pp. 305–318)

21 NAGEL, H.H., HSU, Y.Z., and REKERS, G.: 'New likelihood test methods for change detection in image sequences', *Computer Vision, Graphics & Image Process.*, 1984, **26**, (1), pp. 73–106

22 SHAH, M.A., and JAIN, R.: 'Detecting time varying corners', *ibid.*, 1984, **28**, (3), pp. 345–355

23 INIGO, R.M.: 'Traffic monitoring and control using machine vision — a survey', *IEEE Trans.*, 1985, **IE-32**, (3), pp. 177–185

24 SEED, L., HOUGHTON, A., HERON, A., HOBSON, G.S., POWELL, A.R., and TOZER, R.C.: 'Real time processing of infrared images from road traffic', *Proc. SPIE*, 1985, **590**, pp. 233–240

Glossary

Aliasing: Aliasing has its origin in a branch of mathematics called "sampling theory," and describes a form of error introduced by systems that manipulate data in discrete units. In the area of computer graphics, visual aliasing occurs when display devices attempt to handle detail that exceeds the basic resolving power of the system. The effect is most obvious in pixel-based frame stores and manifests itself as jagged edges when edges almost vertical or almost horizontal are displayed.

Anti-aliasing: Anti-aliasing is a technique for disguising the aliasing errors introduced in discrete systems. Aliasing errors found in pixel-based frame stores manifest themselves as jagged edges, but these can be "softened" or anti-aliased, by filtering the shading intensities around the offending pixels to create a smoother transition of color changes.

Bicubic patch: An efficient description method for modeling smooth surfaces.

Bit-map: Frame buffer.

Calligraphic display: A display device developed in the mid-1960's still in use today. Also known as line drawing or vectorgraphic display.

Cartesian coordinates: The x,y (horizontal and vertical) coordinates that specify the position of a point on a plane, and the x,y,z (horizontal, vertical, and depth) coordinates that specify a point in a cube of spatial volume.

Clipping: A process through which any part of the object not in view inside the window is deleted.

Constructive solid geometry: CSG is a popular method for representing three-dimensional objects in CAD/CAM applications. Loosely speaking, each CSG object is a set described by doing set operations on primitive solids. The primitive solids are objects like blocks, cylinders, balls, and cones. Each complex CSG solid is represented by a binary tree. The leaves of the tree are primitive solids oriented in space. The internal nodes of the tree are set operations (union, intersection, difference).

CRT: Cathode ray tube. A "television" vacuum tube (and associated electronics) for converting voltages into a pattern of images on a phosphor-coated screen.

CSG: Constructive solid geometry. One of the chief methods of solid modeling, using solid primitives and Boolean set operators to construct complex solids.

D/A conversion: Digital-to-analog conversion. In computer graphics, images are stored digitally. A D/A converter must be employed to convert digital image data into analog (continuous) signal to drive the output device.

Dejagging: Smoothing out the jagged edges of raster–scan graphics (see also anti-aliasing).

Device coordinates: Coordinates that represent the area that can be displayed by a display device expressed in a coordinate system defining the digital limits of the device.

Device driver: The device-dependent part of a graphics system implementation intended to support a physical device.

Digital differential analyzer: DDA is a technique for generating line segments by using information about its end points.

Display pipeline: A functional model of computer graphics systems that consists of a pipeline of logical processors operating on representations of objects.

Display processor: Any display controller that can function entirely independently of the host CPU.

DRAM: Dynamic random access memory. This type of semiconductor storage device is commonly used for the implementation of frame buffers because of its low cost and high capacity. However, its memory cells must be refreshed periodically.

FIFO: First-in-first-out buffer. Information is read from a FIFO in the order that it is written into it.

Flicker: When a display device cannot refresh its screen at a rate compatible with the human eye's persistence, it appears to be on and off alternatively, or flickers.

Flight simulator: An extremely expensive and complex machine, which attempts to generate a realistic flying sensation for the user. It is used for pilot training.

Frame buffer: A solid-state memory in a computer graphics system that holds a matrix of digital values corresponding to the pixel pattern displayed (or about to be displayed) on the screen.

Frame time: The total amount of time available to sweep out a frame of raster image. Generally, it is determined by the required screen refresh rate of the display device. A typical frame time is $1/60$ second.

Geometric modeling: The creation of a computer model defined primarily by its shape and spatial layout.

Geometric transformation: Translation of the position, orientation, and size of objects in a drawing.

Geometry engine: Custom VLSI chips developed for implementing image transformations and clipping in hardware.

Hidden surface removal: A process in which obscured surfaces are removed and not displayed.

Host computer: The main computer that provides processing power for the terminals and peripherals connected to it.

Image: A particular view of one or more objects or parts of objects. It is the picture on a view surface.

Image memory: Frame buffer.

Image memory bandwidth: The frequency with which image memory can be accessed.

Image processing: The science of interpreting digital images by using computers and computer graphics techniques. Most image processing deals with data acquired by remote sensing devices aboard satellites or spacecraft. But the technique can be used in many branches of science, engineering, and the arts. It involves the processing of image data to enhance the image, perhaps to reconstitute damaged portion of the image or even to detect spatial information from the image.

Interactive graphics: A kind of computer graphics in which the user dynamically controls the picture's content, format, size, or color on a display surface with interaction devices like keyboard and joystick.

Interlaced display: A kind of raster display in which all odd-numbered lines are displayed for $1/60$ of a second, and all even-numbered ones in the next $1/60$, for an overall frame time of $1/30$ second.

Memory access time: The time delay between the receipt of stable address input to a memory device and the data output.

Memory cycle time: The required time delay between two consecutive accesses to a memory device.

Noninterlaced display: When a display is not of the interlaced type, it is called a noninterlaced display.

Normalized device coordinates: Device-dependent Cartesian coordinates in the range 0 to 1 used for specifying viewports, image transformations, and input obtained from a locator input device.

Object: The conceptual graphical unit in the application program.

Output devices: Devices that draw, print, photograph or otherwise display the images that have been created by the computer.

Output pipeline: A conceptualization of what happens when successive transformations are performed on an object description to produce an image of the object on a screen.

Pel: Picture element. A pel is also known as a pixel.

Picture: The collection of images on a view surface.

Pixel: In raster graphics, an image is made up of a two-dimensional array of dots each of which may be of different brightness. These smallest addressable points of the raster image are known as pixels.

Pixel cache: A fast and small memory that sits between the frame buffer memory and the scan converter. It takes advantage of the principle of locality exhibited by the scan conversion process to improve system performance.

Pixel phasing: An anti-aliasing technique to eliminate jaggies. Pixel phasing brings a three- to fourfold increase in virtual screen addressability.

Pixel-planes: A smart image-memory system developed at the University of North Carolina at Chapel Hill.

Quadratic surface: Quadratic surfaces are in general nonplanar and can be represented by a second order polynomial. Familiar objects composed of quadratic surfaces include the sphere (one surface), the ellipsoid (one surface), and the capped cylinder (three surfaces).

RAM: Random access memory.

Raster: The pattern of horizontal lines traced by the electron beam in an ordinary television or a raster graphics monitor.

Raster scan: The horizontal scanning pattern of a raster display.

Ray-casting: One technique for generating shaded displays of three-dimensional objects and for computing their properties (e.g., volume) is to use ray-casting. In ray-casting one computes the intersection of a family of straight lines with the three-dimensional object. Using the end points of the intersecting intervals one can compute the boundary of the object. Integrating along the intervals one could compute the volume and moments of inertia of the object. The ray-casting computation is also known as line-solid classification.

Ray tracing: A technique for creating realistic computer images by tracing rays from viewpoint to light source (i.e., the reverse path of light rays). It calculates both hidden surfaces and shading, but tends to be slow and very computation intensive.

Real-time image generation: In real-time image generation modifications to the geometry of the image are easily incorporated in the display file and are instantly visible on the display; hence the use of the term "real-time."

Refresh: The process of renewing the image on the display surface of a refresh tube (CRT), typically 30 to 60 times a second.

Resolution: A measure of the ability to discriminate between the smallest separate parts of an object or image. With raster graphics, screen resolution is determined by the number of available pixels in the display.

Scan conversion: The process of converting a stored definition of an image into a pixel array that approximates the original definition.

Screen coordinates: Device-dependent coordinates typically either in integer raster units or fractions between 0 and 1. Device drivers map normalized device coordinates to screen coordinates.

Segment: An ordered collection of output primitives defining an image that is part of the picture on a view surface.

Surface rendering: Generating elaborate, smooth shaded, curved objects defined, for instance, by constructive solid geometry.

Video RAM: A RAM that includes a high-speed shift register. When a particular command is issued, an entire row of memory cells in the video RAM is loaded into the shift register. Data in the register can be shifted out via a secondary serial port for raster scan-out.

Video refresh: Visual display units rely upon television technology to maintain a constant image on the screen, which entails rewriting or refreshing the image at a frequency to avoid flicker; typically, 30 cycles per second.

View surface: A two-dimensional logical output surface. Images on a view surface are drawn on the corresponding physical output surface in a device-dependent way by the device driver for that output device.

VLSI circuit: Very large-scale integrated circuit.

World coordinates: Device-independent three-dimensional Cartesian coordinates in which two-dimensional or three-dimensional objects are described to the graphics system.

Z-buffer: The Z-buffer image space algorithm (for hidden surface removal) requires not only a frame buffer but also a Z-buffer (also known as a depth buffer) in which Z-values can be stored for each pixel. Before scan-conversion, the Z-buffer is initialized to the largest representable Z-value, while the frame buffer (also known as the refresh buffer) is initialized to the background pixel value.

Bibliography

1. Graphics Processors and Special Function Units
2. Frame Buffer Design
3. Smart Image-Memory
4. Real-Time Scan-Conversion Hardware
5. Constructive Solid Geometry and Ray Tracing
6. Image Processing Hardware

1: Graphics Processors and Special Function Units

1. Bruce, R.A., "Custom Processor Eases Display Design," *Digital Design,* Vol. 12, No. 13, 1982, pp. 62–64.

2. Capowski, J.J., "Matrix Transform Processor for Evans and Sutherland LDS-2 Graphics System," *IEEE Trans on Computers,* Vol. C-27, No. 7, July 1976, pp. 703.

3. Chang, P. and R. Jain, "A Multi-Processor System for Hidden-Surface Removal," *Computer Graphics,* Vol. 15, No. 4, Dec. 1981, pp. 405–436.

4. Clark, J.H., "A VLSI Geometry Processor for Graphics," *Computer,* Vol. 13, No. 7, July 1980, pp. 59–68.

5. Clark, J.H., "The Geometry Engine: A VLSI Geometry System for Graphics," *Computer Graphics,* Vol. 16, No. 3, July 1982, pp. 127–133.

6. Danielsson, P.E., "Comments on a Circle Generator for Display Devices," *Computer Graphics and Image Processing,* Vol. 7, No. 2, April 1978, pp. 300–301.

7. Fujimoto, A., C.G. Perrott, and K. Iwata, "A 3-D Graphics Display System with Depth Buffer and Pipeline Processor," *IEEE Computer Graphics and Applications,* Vol. 4, No. 6, June 1984, pp. 11–23.

8. Guttag, K., J. Van Aken, and M. Asal, "Requirements for VLSI Graphics Processor," *IEEE Computer Graphics and Applications,* Vol. 6, No. 1, Jan. 1986, pp. 32–47.

9. Kisner, M. and J. Ladd, "A New-Generation Video Processor Boosts Resolution," *Electronics,* Jan. 28, 1984, pp. 121–124.

10. Mehl, M.E. and S.J. Noll, "A VLSI Support for GKS," *IEEE Computer Graphics and Applications,* Vol. 4, No. 8, Aug. 1984, pp. 52–55.

11. Myer, T.H. and I.E. Sutherland, "On the Design of Display Processors," *CACM,* Vol. 11, No. 6, June 1968, pp. 410–414.

12. Piper, T.S. and A. Fournier, "A Hardware Stochastic Interpolator for Raster Displays," *Computer Graphics,* Vol. 18, No. 3, July 1984, pp. 83–92.

13. Sproull, R.F. and I.E. Sutherland, "A Clipping Divider," *Proc. of Fall Joint Computer Conf.,* AFIPS Press, Reston, Va., 1968.

14. Stepoway, S.L., D.L. Wells, and G.R. Kane, "A Multiprocessor Architecture for Generating Fractial Surfaces," *IEEE Trans. on Computers,* Vol. C–33, No. 11, Nov. 1984, pp. 1041–1045.

15. Strothotte, T. and B. Funt, "Raster Display of a Rotating Object Using Parallel-Processing," *Computer Graphics Forum,* North-Holland, Amsterdam, The Netherlands, Vol. 2, 1983, pp. 209–217.

2: Frame Buffer Design

1. Chor, B., C.E. Leiserson, and R.L. Rivest, "An Application of Number Theory to the Organization of Raster-Graphics Memory," *M.I.T. VLSI Memo No. 82–106,* Massachusetts Institute of Technology, Cambridge, Mass., June 1982.

2. Cohen, C.L., "Full Wafer Memory for Color Displays Has 1.5 MB Capacity," *Electronics,* Jan. 26, 1984, pp. 77–78.

3. Crow, F.C. and M.W. Howard, "A Frame Buffer System with Enhanced Functionality," *Proc. SIGGRAPH '81,* ACM, Inc., New York, Aug. 1981, pp. 63–69.

4. Finke, D.L., "Dynamic RAM Architectures for Graphics Applications," *AFIPS National Computer Conf. Proc.,* AFIPS Press, Reston, Va., 1983, pp. 479–485.

5. Gupta, S., R.F. Sproull, and I.E. Sutherland, "A VLSI Architecture for Updating Raster-Scan Displays," *Computer Graphics,* ACM, Inc., New York, Vol. 15, No. 3, March 1981, pp. 333–340.

6. Jordan, B.W., Jr. and R.C. Barrett, "A Cell Organized Raster Display for Line Drawings," *ACM Communications,* Vol. 17, No. 2, Feb. 1974, pp. 70.

7. Matick, R., D.T. Ling, S. Gupta, and F. Dill, "All Point Addressable Raster Display Memory," *IBM Journal of Research and Development,* Vol. 28, No. 4, July 1984, pp. 379–393.

8. Oakley, D., M.E. Jones, D. Parsons, and G. Burke, "Pixel Phasing Smoothes Out Jagged Lines," *Electronics,* June 28, 1984, pp. 118–120.

9. Ostapko, D.L., "A Mapping and Memory Chip Hardware Which Provides Symmetric Reading/Writing of Horizontal and Vertical Lines," *IBM Journal of Research and Development,* Vol. 28, No. 4, July 1984, pp. 393–398.

10. Pinkham, R., M. Novak, and C. Guttag, "Video RAM Excels at Fast Graphics," *Electronic Design,* Vol. 31, No. 17, Aug. 1983, pp. 161–182.

11. Sproull, R.F., I.E. Sutherland, A. Thompson, S. Gupta, and C. Minter, "The 8 by 8 Display," *ACM Trans. on Graphics,* Vol. 2, No. 1, Jan. 1983, pp. 381–411.

12. Whitton, M.C., "Memory Design for Raster Graphics Displays," *IEEE Computer Graphics & Applications,* Vol. 4, No. 3, March 1984, pp. 48–65.

3: Smart Image-Memory

1. Clark, J.H. and M.R. Hannah, "Distributed Processing in a High-Performance Smart Image-Memory," *LAMBDA,* 4th Quarter 1980, pp. 40–45.

2. Demetrescu, S., "High Speed Image Rasterization Using Scan Line Access Memories," *Chapel Hill Conf. on VLSI,* Computer Science Press, Rockville, Md., 1985, pp. 95–102.

3. Demetrescu, S., "Moving Picture," *BYTE,* Nov. 1985, pp. 207–217.

4. Fuchs, H. and B.W. Johnson, "An Expandable Multiprocessor Architecture for Video Graphics (Preliminary Report)," *Proc. of the 6th Ann. ACM-IEEE Symp. on Computer Architecture,* Computer Society, Washington, D.C., 1979, pp. 58–67.

5. Fuchs, H. and J. Poulton, "Pixel-Planes: A VLSI-Oriented Design for a Raster Graphics Engine," *VLSI Design,* Vol. 2, No. 3, 3rd Quarter 1981, pp. 20–28.

6. Fuchs, H., J. Poulton, A. Paeth, and A. Bell, "Developing Pixel-Planes: A Smart Memory-Based Raster Graphics System," *Proc. of 1982 Conf. on Advanced Research in VLSI,* Massachusetts Institute of Technology, Cambridge, Mass., 1982, pp. 137–146.

7. Fuchs, H., J. Goldfeather, J. Hultquist, S. Spach, J. Austin, F. Brooks, Jr., J. Eyles, and J. Poulton, "Fast Sphere, Shadows, Textures, Transparencies, and Image Enhancements in Pixel-Planes," *ACM SIGGRAPH,* ACM, Inc., New York, Vol. 19, No. 3, 1985, pp. 111–120.

8. Goldfeather, J. and H. Fuchs, "Quadratic Surface Rendering on a Logic-Enhanced Frame-Buffer Memory," *IEEE Computer Graphics and Applications,* Vol. 6, No. 1, Jan. 1986, pp. 48–56.

9. Park, F.I., "Simulation and Expected Performance Analysis of Multiple Processor Z-Buffer Memory," *Computer Graphics,* Vol. 14, No. 3, July 1980, pp. 48–56.

10. Poulton, J., H. Fuchs, J. Austin, J. Eyles, J. Heinecke, C. Hsieh, J. Goldfeather, J. Hultquist, and S. Spach, "Pixel Plane: Building a VLSI-Based Graphics System," *Chapel Hill Conf. on VLSI,* Computer Science Press, Rockville, Md., 1985, pp. 35–61.

4: Real-Time Scan-Conversion Hardware

1. Fussell, D. and B.D. Rathi, "A VLSI-Oriented Architecture for Real-Time Raster Display of Shaded Polygons (Preliminary Report)," *Proc. of NRCC Graphics Interface '82,* ACM, Inc., New York, 1982, pp. 373–380.

2. Goldwasser, S.M. and R.A. Reynolds, "An Architecture for the Real-Time Display and Manipulation of the Three Dimensional Objects," *Proc. of the IEEE Intl. Conf. on Parallel Processing,* Computer Society, Washington, D.C., Aug. 1983.

3. Goldwasser, S.M., "A Generalized Object Display Processor Architecture," *IEEE Computer Graphics and Applications,* Vol. 4, No. 10, Oct. 1984, pp. 43–55.

4. Gharachorloo, N. and C. Pottle, "SUPER BUFFER: A Systolic VLSI Graphics Engine for Real-Time Raster Image Generation," *Chapel Hill Conf. on VLSI,* Computer Science Press, Rockville, Md., 1985, pp. 285–305.

5. Locanthi, B., "Object Oriented Raster Displays," *Caltech Conference on VLSI,* California Institute of Technology, Pasadena, Calif., Jan. 1979, pp. 215–225.

6. Piller, E., "Real-Time Raster Scan Unit with Improved Picture Quality," *Computer Graphics,* Vol. 14, No. 1, July 1980, pp. 35–38.

7. Schacter, B.J., "Computer Image Generation for Flight Simulation," *IEEE Computer Graphics & Applications,* Vol. 1, No. 10, Oct. 1981, pp. 22–68.

8. Weinberg, R., "Parallel Processing, Image Synthesis, and Anti-Aliasing," *Computer Graphics,* Vol. 15, No. 3, Aug. 1981, pp. 325–332.

9. Westmore, R.J., "Real-Time Shaded Colour Polygon Generation System," *IEE Proceedings,* Vol. 134, No. 1, Jan. 1987, pp. 31–38.

10. Whelan, D.S., "A Rectangular Area Filling Display System Architecture," *Computer Graphics,* Vol. 16, No. 3, July 1982, pp. 356–362.

5: Constructive Solid Geometry and Ray Tracing

1. Dippé, M. and J. Swensen, "An Adaptive Subdivision Algorithm and Parallel Architecture for Realistic Image Synthesis," *ACM Computer Graphics,* Vol. 18, No. 3, July 1984, pp. 149–158.

2. Kedem, G. and J.L. Ellis, "The Raycasting System," *Proc. of 1984 IEEE Int. Conf. on Computer Design,* Computer Society, Washington, D.C., Oct. 1984, pp. 533–538.

3. Kedem, G. and S.W. Hammond, "The Point Classifier: A VLSI Processor for Displaying Complex Two Dimensional Objects," *Chapel Hill Conf. on VLSI,* Computer Science Press, Rockville, Md., 1985, pp. 377–393.

4. Nishimura, H., H. Ohno, T. Kawata, I. Shirakawa, and K. Omura, "LINKS-1: A Parallel Pipelined Multimicrocomputer System for Image Creation," *Proc. of the 10th Symp. on Computer Architecture,* Computer Society, Washington, D.C., 1983, pp. 387–394.

5. Sato, H., M. Ishii, K. Sato, M. Ikesaka, H. Ishihata, M. Kakimoto, K. Hirota, and K. Inoue, "Fast Image Generation of Constructive Solid Geometry Using a Cellular Array Processor," *ACM SIGGRAPH,* ACM, Inc. New York, Vol. 19, No. 3, July 1985, pp. 95–102.

6. Ullner, M.K., "Parallel Machines for Computer Graphics," *Ph.D. Thesis,* California Institute of Technology, Pasadena, Calif., 1983.

6: Image Processing Hardware

1. Batcher, K.E., "Design of a Massively Parallel Processor," *IEEE Trans. on Computers,* Vol. C–29, No. 9, Sept. 1980, pp. 836–840.

2. Budnik, P. and D.J. Kuck, "The Organization and Use of Parallel Memories," *IEEE Trans. on Computers,* Vol C–30, No. 9, Sept. 1971, pp. 691–699.

3. Danielsson, P. and S. Levialdi, "Computer Architecture for Pictorial Information Systems," *Computer,* Vol. 14, No. 11, Nov. 1981, pp. 53–67.

4. Jeffery, T., "The µPD7281 Processor," *BYTE,* Nov. 1985, pp. 237–246.

5. Jong, W.P., "An Efficient Memory System for Image Processing," *IEEE Trans. on Computers,* Vol. C–35, No. 7, July 1986, pp. 669–674.

6. Kawakami, K. and S. Shimazaki, "A Special Purpose LSI Processor Using the DDA Algorithm for Image Transformation," *Proc. of the 11th Ann. Int. Symp. on Computer Architecture,* Computer Society, Washington, D.C., 1984, pp. 48–54.

7. Lawrie, "Access and Alignment of Data in an Array Processor," *IEEE Trans. on Computers,* Vol. C–24, No. 12, Dec. 1975, pp. 1145–1155.

8. Levinthal, A. and T. Porter, "CHAP—A SIMD Graphics Processor," *Computer Graphics,* Vol. 18, No. 3, July 1984, pp. 77–82.

9. Parke, J.W., "An Efficient Memory System for Image Processing," *IEEE Trans. on Computers,* Vol. C–35, No. 7, July 1986, pp. 669–674.

10. Reeves, A.P., "SURVEY: Parallel Computer Architecture for Image Processing," *Computer Vision, Graphics, and Image Processing,* Vol. 25, No. 1, Jan. 1984, pp. 68–88.

11. Rosenfeld, A. and A.C. Kak, *Digital Picture Processing,* Academic Press, Orlando, Fl., 1976.

12. Rosenfeld, A., "Parallel Image Processing Using Cellular Arrays," *Computer,* Vol. 16, No. 1, Jan. 1983, pp. 14–30.

13. Stroll, Z.Z., E. Swartzlander, Jr., J. Eldon, and J.L. Ashurn, "Image Rotation Controller Chip," *Proc. of 1984 IEEE Intl. Conf. on Computer Design,* Computer Society, Washington, D.C., Oct. 1984, pp. 274–279.

14. Van Voorhis, D.C. and T.H. Morrin, "Memory Systems for Image Processing," *IEEE Trans. on Computers,* Vol. C–27, No. 2, Feb. 1978, pp. 113–125.

Author Index

Subject Index